Gift to the

EVANSTON • PUBLIC
L I B R A R Y

from a friend

of the Libray

who wishes

to remain

anonymous

Gift Book Fund

HISTORY IN DISPUTE

ADVISORY BOARD

HISTORY IN DISPUTE

Volume **6**

**The Cold War:
Second Series**

Edited by **Dennis E. Showalter and Paul DuQuenoy**

A MANLY, INC. BOOK

ST. JAMES PRESS

AN IMPRINT OF THE GALE GROUP

DETROIT • SAN FRANCISCO • LONDON
BOSTON • WOODBRIDGE, CT

HISTORY IN DISPUTE

 ## Volume 6 ▪ The Cold War, Second Series

Matthew J. Bruccoli and Richard Layman, *Editorial directors.*

Karen L. Rood, *Senior editor.*

Anthony J. Scotti Jr., *Series editor.*

James F. Tidd Jr., *In-house editor.*

Philip B. Dematteis, *Production manager.*

Kathy Lawler Merlette, *Office manager.* Ann M. Cheschi, Dawnca T. Williams, Mary A. Womble, *Administrative support.* Amber L. Coker, Kathy Weston, *Accounting.*

Phyllis A. Avant, *Copyediting supervisor.* Thom Harman, *Senior copyeditor.* Brenda Carol Blanton, James Denton, Melissa D. Hinton, William Tobias Mathes, Jennifer S. Reid, Nancy E. Smith, *Copyediting staff.*

Zoe R. Cook, *Lead layout and graphics.* Janet E. Hill, *Layout and graphics supervisor.* Karla Corley Brown, *Layout and graphics.*

Charles Mims, Scott Nemzek, Paul Talbot, *Photography editors.* Jeff Miller, *Photo permissions.* Joseph M. Bruccoli, Zoe R. Cook, Abraham R. Layman, *Digital photographic copy work.*

Cory McNair, *SGML supervisor.* Linda Dalton Mullinax, Frank Graham, Jason Paddox, Alex Snead, *SGML staff.*

Marie L. Parker, *Systems manager.*

Kathleen M. Flanagan, *Typesetting supervisor.* Kimberly Kelly Brantley, Mark J. McEwan, Patricia Flanagan Salisbury, Alison Smith, *Typesetting staff.*

Walter W. Ross, *Library researcher.* Steven Gross, *Assistant library researcher.* Tucker Taylor, *Circulation department head, Thomas Cooper Library, University of South Carolina.* Virginia W. Weathers, *Reference department head.* Brette Barclay, Marilee Birchfield, Paul Cammarata, Gary Geer, Michael Macan, Tom Marcil, Sharon Verba, *Reference librarians.* John Brunswick, *Interlibrary-loan department head.*

Copyright ©2000
St. James Press
27500 Drake Road
Farmington Hills, MI 48331

ISBN 1-55862-412-0

St. James Press is an imprint of The Gale Group.

Printed in the United States of America

10 9 8 7 6 5 4 3 2 1

CONTENTS

CONTENTS

CONTENTS

CONTENTS

CONTENTS

ABOUT THE SERIES

History in Dispute is an ongoing series designed to present, in an informative and lively pro-con format, different perspectives on major historical events drawn from all time periods and from all parts of the globe. The series was developed in response to requests from librarians and educators for a history-reference source that will help students hone essential critical-thinking skills while serving as a valuable research tool for class assignments.

Individual volumes in the series concentrate on specific themes, eras, or subjects intended to correspond to the way history is studied at the academic level. For example, early volumes cover such topics as the Cold War, American Social and Political Movements, and World War II. Volume subtitles make it easy for users to identify contents at a glance and facilitate searching for specific subjects in library catalogues.

Each volume of *History in Dispute* includes up to fifty entries, centered on the overall theme of that volume and chosen by an advisory board of historians for their relevance to the curriculum. Entries are arranged alphabetically by the name of the event or issue in its most common form. (Thus, in Volume 1, the issue "Was detente

a success?" is presented under the chapter heading "Detente.")

Each entry begins with a brief statement of the opposing points of view on the topic, followed by a short essay summarizing the issue and outlining the controversy. At the heart of the entry, designed to engage students' interest while providing essential information, are the two or more lengthy essays, written specifically for this publication by experts in the field, each presenting one side of the dispute.

In addition to this substantial prose explication, entries also include excerpts from primary-source documents, other useful information typeset in easy-to-locate shaded boxes, detailed entry bibliographies, and photographs or illustrations appropriate to the issue.

Other features of *History in Dispute* volumes include: individual volume introductions by academic experts, tables of contents that identify both the issues and the controversies, chronologies of events, names and credentials of advisers, brief biographies of contributors, thorough volume bibliographies for more information on the topic, and a comprehensive subject index.

PREFACE

For fifty years from the end of World War II to the early 1990s the world was the stage for a conflict between two rival power systems and worldviews. Commonly known as the Cold War because of the absence of direct military engagement between the superpowers, it is better understood as a World War III, continuing—and arguably resolving—both a Western civil war that began in 1914 and the conflict between "the West and the rest" that goes back three centuries earlier. Anyone doubting the scale and seriousness of the stakes has only to juxtapose New York and Moscow as they stood on the morning of 25 December 1991. One wore the face of victory, the other the face of defeat—and there was no doubt anywhere on the globe which was which.

The Cold War's direct antecedents lay, as suggested above, in a European civil war between free states, societies, and economies and their managed counterparts. Even before 1914 the liberalism, individualism, and capitalism that had brought Western European and North American power and influence over the rest of the globe faced fundamental challenges on its home ground. The suffering and dislocation caused by industrialization produced increasing numbers of displaced and alienated groups and individuals. Foremost among their spokesmen were the Marxists, whose reaction to the brutalities of economic development on capitalist lines produced an ideological system that both explained capitalism's success and promised its destruction.

Marxism challenged an ethos of individualism and competition with one of cooperation and collectivism—both all the more powerful for being essentially untried. Marxism offered a system by which the oppressed could free themselves by raising their consciousness and acting on their new awareness, and it was enhanced by its strong appeal to an intelligentsia feeling underappreciated in a pragmatic, practical age. Marxism benefited as well from the heroic vital-ism that infused Europe at the turn of the twentieth century. The insistence of the philosophers Friedrich Nietzsche and Henri-Louis Bergson on the importance of will, while more generally identified with Fascism, informed left-wing parties as well during the next hundred years. Finally, Marxism offered a means of settling past scores for inequity and oppression.

Nonetheless, Marxism, specifically its Leninist variant, got its chance only after World War I had left Europe sufficiently exhausted to halt a revolutionary system taking control of the least Western of the great powers. Marxism was able to extend its influence into the West only because of the fear of Fascism. The Soviet Union of the 1920s and 1930s had little direct appeal outside of those intellectual circles Lenin himself dismissed as "useful idiots": the journalists and academicians who described "the future at work" to audiences largely unable to verify what they were told in classrooms, broadcasts, and the pages of popular literature. Between Adolf Hitler's accession to power in 1933 and the final destruction of Nazi Germany in 1945, however, the Union of Soviet Socialist Republics (U.S.S.R.) emerged as towering over a Western Europe that had exhausted its material and moral capital in the past half-century—the embodiment, indeed, of an alternative world order.

That order was disproportionately attractive outside of Europe. The undemocratic nature of Marxism-Leninism made it particularly appealing to local elites conditioned by imperialism and their own histories of authoritarian governance. Its model of rapid economic development by mobilizing indigenous resources in "developmental dictatorships" attracted graduates of Western business schools such as Harvard University and the London School of Economics that since the 1930s had taught the superiority of management over free markets. Finally, the anti-Western nature of Marxism-Leninism, more clearly and rapidly understood by non-Europeans than by Westerners themselves, was intellectually and psychologically appealing, while simultaneously offering solid prospects of direct support from the U.S.S.R. against former imperial powers.

Global strategic circumstances after World War II, in short, not merely favored but invited a Soviet offensive designed to take advantage of the capitalist West's vulnerabilities as defined by Marxism-Leninism. Direct armed conflict, particularly on nuclear levels, was unnecessary: the West would ultimately collapse because of its own internal contradictions. It was, however, necessary to maintain a massive military establishment to take specific advantage of Western vulnerabilities. From the perspective of communism, there was no harm in giving history a nudge here and there.

Beginning in the 1960s a conventional academic wisdom developed in the West that insisted on the mutuality of superpower responsibility. According to this model the United States and the U.S.S.R. shared responsibility for the genesis and the continuation of a conflict that seemed increasingly to put the human race at risk of thermonuclear annihilation, for reasons that appeared increasingly arcane to reasonable people. To a degree this analysis reflected a fundamental discrepancy in available sources. The Soviet Union guarded its archives and its press, while in the West both records and mouths were increasingly open. "Mirror-imaging," seeking points of similarity and convergence between the Soviet and Western systems, offered hope of understanding, albeit indirectly, the inner dynamics of a U.S.S.R. that throughout its existence remained a closed society. Asserting mutual responsibility also seemed a possible way of initiating dialogue between the superpowers, in the same way individuals may find discussion easier when they share ownership of the issue at stake.

Underlying all of these elements, however, was what in many cases amounted to a principled rejection by some nations of Western civilization—particularly in the forms represented by a United States that after 1945 emerged as the West's archetype and champion. The phenomenon is easier to illustrate than to explain. Admiration in non-communist countries for the Soviet Union as such soon became vestigial, replaced by alternate sites of what sociologist Paul Hollander describes as "political pilgrimages." From Mao Tse-tung's China to Fidel Castro's Cuba to Sandinistan Nicaragua and elsewhere, these areas grew progressively more squalid and less convincing even as benchmarks for misplaced idealism. More useful in understanding internal rejection of the West is reference to a universalist utopianism, fostered by an intellectual commu-

nity increasingly alienated from its particular roots, and indeed from any limitations whatsoever. A postmodernism predicated on the concept that reality is essentially a network of constructions determined by will can trace its antecedents further back than pseudo-philosophers Michel Paul Foucault, Jacques Derrida, and Paul de Man. Even in the 1950s the realities of American power and culture generated a mixture of aesthetic revulsion and moral guilt that facilitated not merely understanding but internalizing the rival viewpoint.

Thus far the Western/American position has been presented by inference. Throughout the Cold War the West's behavior was essentially reactive. The United States, to be sure, expected postwar tensions, but expected them eventually to be subsumed in a global free-trade economy with crisis management handled by the United Nations or its regional surrogates. An America impatient of ideology as opposed to idealism, inward-focused to the point of solipsism, and confident of its own merits beyond self-righteousness and arrogance was not by nature well equipped to meet the global, ideologically based challenge of the Soviet Union.

As the Cold War progressed, ideology became increasingly important to its continuation. The historian John Gaddis appropriately stresses the contingent importance of Joseph Stalin, insisting that as long as he was running the U.S.S.R., a cold war was unavoidable. Gaddis, however, understates ideology's ongoing central role in defining the Soviet system's legitimacy. Ideology grew even more important as the U.S.S.R. increasingly failed to meet the physical needs, much less the aspirations, of its people. Marxism-Leninism is a materialist system and is ultimately based on material. Fascism, with its principled emphasis on struggle, can proffer indefinite sacrifice and declare that it never promised its adherents "a rose garden." Socialist societies are more constrained; ultimately they must either deliver on their promises of "bread and roses too" or explain their failure.

The most obvious explanation for the shortcomings of the U.S.S.R. was the continued existence of the West. Western civilization was increasingly denounced less for any specific failings of attitude or behavior, but because it existed at all. When Soviet Premier Nikita Khrushchev said in 1956, "We will bury you," he enunciated the fundamental hope of the Cold War. When Ayatollah Khomeini of Iran denounced America in 1979 as the "Great Satan," he expressed the fundamental principle of the Cold War.

That the United States and its allies never fully understood the kind of mortal struggle they were waging may have been fortunate; otherwise the temptation to end the game might have dominated Western policies. Instead the West increasingly repudiated the authority of metaphysics and metahistory. As the chapters in this volume suggest, U.S. presidents, with the possible exception of Ronald Reagan, followed a strategy of coping with international challenges on an ad hoc basis. In the process the United States encouraged collaboration and cooperation with existing systems even when, as in dealing with South Vietnam or various Central American governments, that approach arguably damaged the immediate interests of America.

Conservatism was less a matter of principle than a reflection of the essential position of the United States as a status quo power. Sufficiently satisfied with the existing world order, the United States saw no need to risk more than surrogate confrontation with the U.S.S.R., to say nothing of "rolling back" the Soviet system. Nor did either the United States or its Western allies undertake military mobilization at the expense of economic sustainability or technological and cultural vitality. As a result, in the long run America's global presence had high and enduring levels of popular support. Local antagonisms tended to be anomalous and short lived. Where choice between the Cold War antagonists was clear and possible, the United States usually prevailed. Refugee streams in general flowed toward American spheres of influence rather than away from them. Few intellectuals who in principle rejected U.S. foreign policy were willing to exchange their Western passports for citizenship in Nicaragua, Cuba, or the German Democratic Republic.

This last point is a significant one: the essence of freedom is the ability to choose and the capacity to act on choices. The liberal multilateralism embodied by the United States may not have been especially inspiring, or especially heroic, but ultimately it was preferable to the real-world alternatives. Thereby hangs another paradox: the Soviet system, as indicated earlier, entered the Cold War with many distinct advantages. During the conflict not only did the communist leadership fail to build on them, but it also dissipated the ideological and material appeals it possessed. An arms race, pursued as a matter of principle as well as an issue of security, contributed to the process of bankrupting the U.S.S.R. and any other state that incorporated Soviet values. More significant, however, was an ideologically based commitment to a managed society whose consequences were gridlock and alienation.

Well before the Soviet Union's collapse, Marxism-Leninism was recognized as moribund by all but a hard core of adherents—themselves distinguished as much by opposition to the West and its values as by any affirmation of socialism. Instead of expanding, twentieth-century Marxism imploded. States outside its direct sphere of rule in Asia, Africa, and Latin America abandoned Marxism and its variants as too costly relative to probable results. As a final irony the West, freed from the burdens of the Cold War, is coming increasingly closer to securing that general level of abundance that is a prerequisite for the success of theoretical communism. It may be true that the United States and the West did not win the Cold War, but it is clear beyond question who lost it, and reasonably clear why it was lost.
—DENNIS SHOWALTER, COLORADO COLLEGE

CHRONOLOGY

1939

23 AUGUST
The Soviet Union and Nazi Germany sign a non-aggression pact, the Molotov-Ribbentrop Agreement. (*See* **Stalin**[1])
1 SEPTEMBER
Germany invades Poland. World War II begins.
30 NOVEMBER 1939 – 12 MARCH 1940
The Soviet Union and Finland fight the Winter War.

1940

27 SEPTEMBER
Germany, Italy, and Japan sign the Tripartite Pact, creating the Axis alliance.

1941

7 DECEMBER
Japanese planes attack U.S. forces at Pearl Harbor, Hawaii.
8 DECEMBER
The United States enters World War II.
11 DECEMBER
Germany and Italy declare war on the United States; the United States reciprocates.

1942

1 JANUARY
Twenty-six nations, led by the United States, Great Britain, and the Soviet Union, affirm the Atlantic Charter, issued by the United States and Great Britain in August 1941, pledging military and economic action against the Axis powers.

1943

30 OCTOBER
Allied foreign ministers meeting in Moscow call for an international organization to foster the principle of "sovereign equality of all peace-loving states." (*See* **Stalin**)

1944

21 AUGUST – 7 OCTOBER
The Dumbarton Oaks Conference lays the foundation for the United Nations. (*See* **Anglo-American Relations** and **Decolonization**)

1945

4–11 FEBRUARY
U.S. president Franklin Delano Roosevelt, British prime minister Winston Churchill, and Soviet premier Joseph Stalin meet at **Yalta.** (*See* **Anglo-American Relations** and **Stalin**)
6 MARCH
Petru Groza forms a communist-dominated government in Romania. (*See* **Monolithic Communism** and **Soviet Empire**)
25 APRIL – 26 JUNE
At the San Francisco Conference delegates from fifty nations create the United Nations Organization (U.N.). (*See* **Universalism**)
7 MAY
Germany surrenders unconditionally to the Allies.
16 JULY
The United States successfully explodes the first atomic bomb at the Alamogordo test

---

1. Boldface indicates a chapter title.

site in New Mexico. (*See* **Antinuclear Movement** and **Arms Control**)

17 JULY

U.S. president Harry S Truman, Churchill, and Stalin arrive at Potsdam. (*See* **Stalin**)

6 & 9 AUGUST

The United States drops the first two atomic bombs on Hiroshima and Nagasaki, Japan. (*See* **Antinuclear Movement** and **Arms Control**)

14 AUGUST

Japan announces its unconditional surrender. World War II ends.

2 SEPTEMBER

Ho Chi Minh proclaims the independence of **Vietnam** from France. (*See* **Decolonization, Diem, France, National Liberation,** and **Third World**)

18 NOVEMBER

The Communist Party wins communist-controlled elections in Bulgaria. (*See* **Monolithic Communism** and **Soviet Empire**)

29 NOVEMBER

The Yugoslav assembly, elected on 11 November, proclaims the Federal People's Republic of Yugoslavia and declares Marshal Josip Broz Tito prime minister. (*See* **Tito**)

1946

JANUARY–APRIL

The Soviet Union prompts a crisis in Iran by attempting to create an "autonomous" Azerbaijani republic that includes part of Iran. A military confrontation between the Americans and the Soviets is threatened. (*See* **Middle East** and **Soviet Empire**)

9 FEBRUARY

Stalin makes his "Two Camps" speech, declaring the impossibility of Soviet coexistence with the West.

22 FEBRUARY

George F. Kennan transmits his "Long Telegram" from Moscow to Truman. (*See* **Congress and Foreign Policy**)

5 MARCH

Churchill gives his "iron curtain" speech at Westminster College in Fulton, Missouri. (*See* **Monolithic Communism**)

28 MARCH

The Acheson-Lilienthal Plan, calling for international control of nuclear energy, is released. (*See* **Arms Control**)

14 JUNE

Bernard Baruch presents the **Baruch Plan** for international control of nuclear materials and destruction of nuclear arsenals to the

first meeting of the U.N. Atomic Energy Commission.

8 SEPTEMBER

The Republic of Bulgaria is declared, and the Bulgarian monarchy is abolished. (*See* **Monolithic Communism** and **Soviet Empire**)

19 NOVEMBER

The Communist Party wins communist-controlled elections in Romania.

23 NOVEMBER

France bombs Haiphong as the first military move to retain control of its colonies in Indochina. (*See* **Decolonization, Diem,** and **France**)

2 DECEMBER

The Americans and British agree to an economic merger of their zones of occupations in Germany. (*See* **Anglo-American Relations**)

1947

19 JANUARY

The Communist Party wins communist-controlled elections in Poland. (*See* **Monolithic Communism** and **Soviet Empire**)

FEBRUARY

Hungarians abolish their monarchy and declare their country a republic. (*See* **Hungary**)

12 MARCH

Truman announces his Truman Doctrine, declaring that Americans will support "free peoples who are resisting subjugation by armed minorities or by outside pressures," and requests $400 million in economic and military aid for Greece and Turkey.

22 MARCH

Truman bans communists from serving in the U.S. government. (*See* **McCarthyism**)

22 MAY

Truman signs a Greek-Turkish aid bill. (*See* **Middle East**)

5 JUNE

In a commencement address at Harvard University, Secretary of State George C. Marshall proposes the **Marshall Plan** for economic assistance to democracies of Europe.

JULY

"The Sources of Soviet Conduct," by "X" (Kennan), appears in *Foreign Affairs*, recommending U.S. **containment** of the Soviet Union. (*See* **Monolithic Communism** and **Soviet Empire**)

12 JULY

The **Marshall Plan** conference opens in Paris and is boycotted by the Soviet Union and eastern European countries.

26 JULY

Congress passes the National Security Act, creating the Central Intelligence Agency (CIA) and the National Security Council (NSC).

31 AUGUST

A Communist-led coalition wins a majority in Hungarian elections. (*See* **Hungary**)

2 SEPTEMBER

The United States and Latin American countries sign the Inter-American Treaty of Reciprocal Assistance in Rio de Janeiro, Brazil. (*See* **Third World**)

23 OCTOBER

Actor Ronald Reagan testifies before the House Un-American Activities Committee (HUAC) on communist influence in Hollywood.

30 OCTOBER

Brigadier General Leslie Groves, director of the Manhattan Project, testifies that the Soviet Union needs twenty years to develop its own atomic bomb. (*See* **Arms Control**)

4 DECEMBER

Bulgaria alters its name to People's Republic of Bulgaria. (*See* **Monolithic Communism**)

30 DECEMBER

King Michael of Romania abdicates, and the People's Republic of Romania is established.

1948

16 FEBRUARY

A people's republic is declared in North Korea. (*See* **Korean War**)

25 FEBRUARY

A bloodless communist coup succeeds in Czechoslovakia. (*See* **Monolithic Communism**)

17 MARCH

Great Britain, France, Belgium, the Netherlands, and Luxembourg sign the Brussels Treaty, the precursor of the Western European Union (WEU) and the North Atlantic Treaty Organization (**NATO**).

30 MARCH – 2 MAY

The Organization of American States is created during the Bogotá Conference.

6 APRIL

Finland signs a nonaggression treaty with the Soviet Union.

14 MAY

Israel proclaims its statehood and is invaded by seven Arab states the next day.

18 JUNE

Currency reforms are implemented in the American, British, and French occupation zones of Germany.

24 JUNE

The Soviet Union blockades land access to Berlin, and the United States responds by airlifting supplies to the city.

28 JUNE

Yugoslavia is expelled from the Cominform. (*See* **Soviet Empire**)

30 JUNE

British forces leave Palestine.

3 AUGUST

Whittaker Chambers testifies before the House Un-American Activities Committee (HUAC) and names Alger Hiss as a Soviet spy. (*See* **Hiss**)

15 AUGUST

The Republic of Korea (South Korea) is established. (*See* **Korean War**)

9 SEPTEMBER

The Democratic People's Republic of Korea (North Korea) is established.

15 DECEMBER

Hiss is indicted by a U.S. grand jury on two counts of perjury. He is eventually found guilty on 21 January 1950. (*See* **Hiss**)

1949

7 JANUARY

Secretary of State Marshall resigns after disagreements with Truman over U.S. interests in regard to **Israel** and its Arab neighbors.

8 FEBRUARY

Congressmen Karl E. Mundt (R-South Dakota) and Richard M. Nixon (R-California) introduce a bill to register communists in the United States.

15 FEBRUARY

Secreary of State Dean Acheson refuses new aid to Chinese Nationalists.

23 FEBRUARY

The National Security Council announces plans to study domestic communist subversion.

4 APRIL

Belgium, Canada, Denmark, France, Great Britain, Iceland, Italy, Luxembourg, the Netherlands, Norway, Portugal, and the United States form the North Atlantic Treaty Organization.

23 APRIL

The Truman administration cancels plans to build the supercarrier *United States,* sparking the **Admirals' Revolt** among top naval officers. (*See* **Arms Control**)

2 MAY

Chinese Nationalist leader Chiang Kai-shek flees to Formosa (Taiwan).

5 MAY

The Chinese communists and the North Koreans sign a mutual-defense treaty. The Federal Republic of Germany (West Germany) is established.

12 MAY

The Berlin Blockade ends; the U.S. airlift continues until 30 September.

30 MAY

The Soviet ambassador to the U.N., Andrey Y. Vyshinsky, rejects a Western proposal for German reunification. The German Democratic Republic (East Germany) declares its statehood. (*See* **Soviet Empire**)

19 JUNE

Communist leader Mao Tse-tung declares victory in China.

5 AUGUST

The State Department issues a white paper explaining the loss of China.

29 AUGUST

The Soviet Union explodes its first atomic bomb. (*See* **Antinuclear Movement** and **Arms Control**)

1 OCTOBER

The People's Republic of China is established.

8 DECEMBER

Chinese Nationalists abandon the mainland and flee to Formosa (Taiwan).

30 DECEMBER

Truman decides not to use American troops to defend Taiwan.

1950

JANUARY

The United States releases $1 billion in military aid to Western Europe. (*See* **Military Balance**)

11 JANUARY

The United States approves a plan to aid Tito if Yugoslavia is attacked by pro-Soviet eastern European armies. (*See* **Tito**)

3 FEBRUARY

Physicist Klaus Fuchs is arrested in London for spying for the Soviet Union.

9 FEBRUARY

Senator Joseph R. McCarthy (R-Wisconsin) charges that communists have infiltrated the State Department. (*See* **McCarthyism**)

14 FEBRUARY

The Soviet Union and the People's Republic of China sign a friendship treaty.

1 MARCH

Chiang establishes the Republic of China on Taiwan. Fuchs is sentenced to prison.

7 APRIL

An interagency committee guided by Paul H. Nitze produces National Security Council memorandum 68 (NSC-68).

15 JUNE

West Germany enters the Council of Europe.

25 JUNE

The North Koreans invade South Korea. (*See* **Korean War**)

27 JUNE

The U.N. Security Council approves military aid to South Korea and establishes a fifteen-nation U.N. force.

30 JUNE

U.S. troops enter the Korean War.

17 JULY

Julius Rosenberg is arrested for spying for the Soviets. His wife, Ethel, is arrested on 11 August.

9 SEPTEMBER

Truman announces a plan to increase the number of U.S. troops in Europe. (*See* **Military Balance**)

1 NOVEMBER

The People's Republic of China enters the war on the side of North Korea, and by 4 November U.N. troops are forced to retreat.

1951

6 MARCH

The Rosenberg spy trial starts. They are convicted on 29 March and condemned to death on 5 April.

21 JUNE

U.N. troops push communist forces out of South Korea. (*See* **Korean War**)

8 JULY

Truce talks start in Korea.

9 AUGUST

McCarthy charges twenty-nine State Department employees with disloyalty. (*See* **McCarthyism**)

1 SEPTEMBER

The United States, Australia, and New Zealand sign the ANZUS treaty.

8 SEPTEMBER

The United States and Japan sign a mutual security pact.

27 OCTOBER

A cease-fire line is established in Korea.

1952

10 MARCH

Fulgencio Batista y Zaldívar seizes power in Cuba. (*See* **Cuba**)

30 APRIL

Tito says Yugoslavia will not join **NATO**. (*See* **Tito**)

27 MAY

The European Defense Community (EDC) is proposed.

2 OCTOBER

Great Britain tests its first atomic weapon. (*See* **Arms Control**)

1953

7 APRIL

The Big Four foreign ministers meet in Berlin to discuss the status of Germany. (*See* **Ostpolitik**)

10 JUNE

President Dwight D. Eisenhower rejects the isolationist "Fortress America" doctrine.

18 JUNE

Soviet troops suppress anticommunist rioting in East Germany. (*See* **Soviet Empire**)

19 JUNE

The Rosenbergs are executed.

27 JULY

The P'anmunjon armistice ends the Korean War. (*See* **Korean War**)

12 AUGUST

The Soviet Union announces the test of its first hydrogen bomb. (*See* **Arms Control**)

19–22 AUGUST

A U.S.-sponsored coup in Iran topples Prime Minister Mohammad Mosaddeq and his government and installs Mohammad Reza Shah Pahlevi on the throne. (*See* **Middle East**)

1954

12 JANUARY

Secretary of State John Foster Dulles calls for a policy of massive retaliation against Soviet expansion.

10 FEBRUARY

Eisenhower opposes U.S. involvement in French Indochina.

18 FEBRUARY

McCarthy attacks the U.S. Army for promoting communists. (*See* **McCarthyism**)

1–28 MARCH

Delegates to the Caracas Conference discuss policies to stop communism in Latin America. (*See* **Third World**)

5 APRIL

Eisenhower declares that the United States will not be the first nation to use the hydrogen bomb.

7 APRIL

Eisenhower says a communist victory in Indochina would set off a chain reaction of disaster for the free world, a view that becomes known as the "domino theory."

23 APRIL

McCarthy accuses Secretary of the Army Robert Stevens of communist sympathies; Army-McCarthy hearings open and continue until 17 June.

7 MAY

Vietnamese forces defeat French troops at Dien Bien Phu.

27 JUNE

A U.S.-sponsored coup topples leftist Guatemalan president Jacobo Arbenz Guzmán.

20 JULY

The Geneva Accords divide Vietnam at the seventeenth parallel, creating North and South Vietnam.

2 AUGUST

The U.S. Senate votes to study possible censure of McCarthy. (*See* **McCarthyism**)

6–8 SEPTEMBER

The Southeast Asia Treaty Organization (SEATO) is established by the Manila Pact.

2 DECEMBER

The U.S. Senate condemns McCarthy. Responding to the Chinese shelling of the Nationalist Chinese islands of **Quemoy and Matsu**, the United States signs a mutual-defense treaty with Taiwan.

1955

17 FEBRUARY

The British announce their plan to build a hydrogen bomb.

18–24 FEBRUARY

The Middle East Treaty Organization (Baghdad Pact) is created.

17–24 APRIL

In Bandung, Indonesia, twenty-nine underdeveloped nations create the Non-Aligned Movement.

29 APRIL

Military clashes begin between North and South Vietnam. (*See* **Diem**)

5 MAY

The Allied occupation of West Germany formally ends as the Federal Republic of Germany becomes a sovereign nation.

9 MAY

West Germany formally joins **NATO.**

14 MAY

Responding to West German **NATO** membership, the Soviet Union, Albania, Bulgaria, Czechoslovakia, East Germany, Hungary, Poland, and Romania create the Warsaw Pact. (*See* **Soviet Empire**)

15 MAY

Representatives from the United States, the Soviet Union, Great Britain, France, and Austria sign the Austrian State Treaty, which results in Soviet troops being withdrawn from Austria. (*See* **Military Balance**)

20 SEPTEMBER

The Soviet Union grants East Germany sovereignty and membership in the Warsaw Pact.

26 OCTOBER

Ngo Dinh Diem declares South Vietnam a republic and himself premier. (*See* **Diem**)

29 DECEMBER

First Secretary Nikita Khrushchev of the Soviet Union rejects Eisenhower's Open Skies proposal.

1956

26 JANUARY
The Soviet Union returns Porkkala Peninsula to Finland.

14 FEBRUARY
Khrushchev denounces Stalin in a speech to the Twentieth Congress of the Communist Party. (*See* **Stalin**)

4 JUNE
The Voice of America broadcasts Khrushchev's "secret speech" of 14 February.

28–30 JUNE
More than one hundred people die during riots in Poznan, Poland.

26 JULY
Gamal Abdel Nasser nationalizes the Suez Canal. (*See* **Middle East**)

21 OCTOBER
The "Spring in October" revolution takes place in Poland.

23 OCTOBER
The Hungarian revolt begins. (*See* **Hungary**)

29 OCTOBER
Israel attacks Egyptian forces in the Sinai.

31 OCTOBER
Premier Imre Nagy asks the Soviet Union to leave Hungary. British and French troops land in the Suez Canal zone.

1 NOVEMBER
Hungary proclaims its neutrality and leaves the Warsaw Pact.

4 NOVEMBER
The Soviet Union invades Hungary. János Kádár is installed as premier. (*See* **Hungary**)

7 NOVEMBER
A cease-fire takes effect in the **Suez War**. (*See* **Middle East**)

8 NOVEMBER
Anti-Soviet fighting ends in Hungary.

15 NOVEMBER
A U.N. peacekeeping force arrives in Egypt.

1957

13 FEBRUARY
The Senate Foreign Relations and Armed Services Committees refuse Eisenhower's request to send American troops to the Middle East. (*See* **Congress and Foreign Policy**)

7 MARCH
The Eisenhower Doctrine, pledging U.S. aid to Middle Eastern countries resisting communism, is endorsed by a joint resolution of Congress. (*See* **Middle East** and **Military Balance**)

25 MARCH
The Treaty of Rome establishes the European Economic Community (EEC), to become effective 1 January 1958.

22 APRIL
John Foster Dulles announces his policy to "**roll back**" communism in Europe.

2 JULY
The United States proposes a ten-month nuclear weapons test ban. (*See* **Antinuclear Movement**)

5 OCTOBER
The Soviet Union launches its Sputnik satellite into orbit around the Earth.

1958

31 MARCH
The Soviet Union proclaims a unilateral halt to nuclear-weapons testing.

15 JULY
Eisenhower orders U.S. Marines into Lebanon. (*See* **Israel, Suez War**)

AUGUST
The Chinese resume the shelling of **Quemoy and Matsu.**

3 OCTOBER
The Soviet Union resumes nuclear tests after Americans and British refuse the proposed ban. (*See* **Arms Control**)

1959

1 JANUARY
Batista flees Cuba as rebel forces led by Fidel Castro Ruz advance on Havana. (*See* **Cuba**)

15 & 25–27 JANUARY
Eisenhower and Khrushchev hold summit conferences in Washington, D.C., and at Camp David.

19 AUGUST
The Baghdad Pact becomes the Central Treaty Organization (CENTO).

15–19 SEPTEMBER
Khrushchev visits the United States.

3 NOVEMBER
Charles de Gaulle declares that France will withdraw from the **NATO** military command. (*See* **France**)

1960

1 JANUARY
Khrushchev announces the Soviet Union will cut the number of its conventional troops even if arms-limitation talks fail.

19 JANUARY
Secretary of Defense Thomas Gates tells the House Defense Appropriations Committee that there are no bomber or missile gaps favoring the Soviet Union; in fact, correct estimates showed "a clear balance in our favor." (*See* **Military Balance**)

13 FEBRUARY

France explodes a nuclear device. (*See* **Arms Control** and **France**)

1 MAY

An American U-2 reconnaissance plane is shot down over the Soviet Union.

16 MAY

Summit talks in Paris break off after Khrushchev demands a U.S. apology for the U-2 affair.

SEPTEMBER

The Organization of Petroleum Exporting Countries (OPEC) is established.

11 NOVEMBER

President-elect John F. Kennedy disavows the "two-China" policy.

1961

3 JANUARY

Eisenhower cuts off diplomatic relations with Cuba.

1 MARCH

The Peace Corps is founded.

3 MARCH

President Kennedy proposes the **Alliance for Progress.**

15 APRIL

U.S.-trained Cuban exiles launch the Bay of Pigs invasion of Cuba. They are defeated by Cuban forces on 20 April. (*See* **Cuba**)

30 MAY

Dominican Republic ruler Rafael Leonidas Trujillo Molina is assassinated. (*See* **Third World**)

3 JUNE

Kennedy meets Khrushchev at a summit meeting in Vienna to discuss the American arms buildup and demilitarization of West Berlin. (*See* **JFK and LBJ**)

13 AUGUST

East Germany forbids its citizens to cross into West Germany.

15 AUGUST

Construction of the Berlin Wall begins. (*See* **Soviet Empire**)

10 DECEMBER

The Soviet Union and Albania sever diplomatic relations.

1962

2 MARCH

The United States resumes atmospheric nuclear testing. (*See* **Antinuclear Movement**)

22 OCTOBER

Kennedy announces a blockade of Cuba until the Soviet Union removes the missiles it

has installed there. (*See* **Cuban Missile Crisis**)

24 OCTOBER – 20 NOVEMBER

The U.S. Navy blockades Cuba.

27–28 OCTOBER

The United States accepts the Soviet offer to withdraw its missiles in exchange for an American guarantee that the United States will not invade Cuba, and the Soviets begin removing their missiles from the island.

1963

1 JANUARY

The Chinese Communist Party attacks Khrushchev's doctrine of peaceful coexistence with the West.

26 JUNE

Kennedy makes his "Ich bin ein Berliner" speech at the Berlin Wall. (*See* **JFK and LBJ**)

5 AUGUST

The United States, the Soviet Union, and Great Britain sign the Limited Test-Ban Treaty in Moscow. China has denounced the treaty, and France has refused to sign it. (*See* **Arms Control**)

30 AUGUST

A "hot line" goes into service between Washington, D.C., and Moscow.

22 NOVEMBER

President Kennedy is assassinated in Dallas and is succeeded by Vice President Lyndon B. Johnson.

1964

28 MAY

The Palestine Liberation Organization (PLO) is founded.

2–4 AUGUST

The USS *Maddox* and USS *C. Turner Joy* are attacked by the North Vietnamese in the Gulf of Tonkin.

7 AUGUST

The U.S. Senate passes the Tonkin Gulf Resolution.

16 OCTOBER

China detonates an atomic bomb. (*See* **Arms Control**)

1965

7 FEBRUARY

U.S. forces attack North Vietnam for the first time, following an attack on a U.S. base at Pleiku.

8 MARCH

U.S. combat troops land in Vietnam. (*See* **Diem**)

28 APRIL

Johnson sends marines to the Dominican Republic to quell unrest.

1966

3 FEBRUARY

An unmanned Soviet spacecraft lands on the moon.

7 MARCH

France formally announces that it will withdraw from the integrated military structure of **NATO.** (*See* **France**)

1967

27 JANUARY

Sixty-two nations sign a treaty prohibiting the military use of outer space.

21 APRIL

A coup topples the Greek government of Stephanos Stephanopoulos, preventing leftist Georgios Papandreou from coming back to power.

15 MAY

Egyptian forces move into the Sinai.

23 MAY

Egypt blocks the Strait of Tiran to Israeli shipping.

5 JUNE

The Six-Day War begins.

7 JUNE

Defeated Egypt accepts a cease-fire.

9 JUNE

Defeated Syria accepts a cease-fire.

23 JUNE

Johnson and Soviet premier Aleksey Kosygin meet in Glassboro, New Jersey. (*See* **JFK and LBJ**)

8 AUGUST

Indonesia, Malaysia, Thailand, the Philippines, and Singapore establish the Association of South East Asian Nations (ASEAN). (*See* **Third World**)

10 OCTOBER

Bolivia confirms the death of Latin American guerrilla Ernesto "Che" Guevara de la Serna.

1968

23 JANUARY

The USS *Pueblo* is seized by North Korea, which holds the crew for eleven months.

30 JANUARY

The Vietcong launch the Tet Offensive.

31 MARCH

Johnson announces a bombing halt in Vietnam and offers to open negotiations with the North Vietnamese; he also announces that he is dropping out of the presidential race. (*See* **JFK and LBJ**)

10 MAY

Paris peace talks open between the United States and North Vietnam.

1 JULY

The Nuclear Non-Proliferation Treaty (NPT) is signed. (*See* **Antinuclear Movement**)

15 JULY

General Secretary Leonid I. Brezhnev announces the Brezhnev Doctrine.

20 AUGUST

Warsaw Pact forces invade Czechoslovakia. (*See* **Soviet Empire**)

24 AUGUST

France explodes a thermonuclear bomb. (*See* **Antinuclear Movement** and **France**)

1969

18 MARCH

The United States begins secretly bombing **Cambodia.**

8 JUNE

President Richard M. Nixon announces his "Vietnamization" plan. (*See* **Nixon and Kissinger**)

25 JULY

In a speech in Guam, Nixon enunciates the Nixon Doctrine, a plan to reduce the U.S. military presence abroad by helping small nations to defend themselves.

1 SEPTEMBER

Mu'ammar al-Gadhafi stages a military coup, proclaiming the socialist Arab Republic of Libya. (*See* **Third World**)

24 NOVEMBER

The United States and the Soviet Union sign the NPT.

1970

30 APRIL

Nixon announces the invasion of **Cambodia** by U.S. troops.

4 MAY

Ohio National Guardsmen kill four students during an antiwar protest at Kent State University. (*See* **Antiwar Movement**)

29 JUNE

U.S. ground troops leave Cambodia.

1 OCTOBER

The Senate approves the building of antiballistic missiles. (*See* **Arms Control**)

7 OCTOBER

Nixon announces a new Vietnam peace plan.

15–19 DECEMBER

Rioting occurs in Polish cities.

1971

8 FEBRUARY
U.S. forces invade Laos.
25 OCTOBER
The U.N. admits China to membership and expels Taiwan. (*See* **China Policy**)
16 DECEMBER
Nationalists rebel in East Pakistan and establish Bangladesh.

1972

20 FEBRUARY
Nixon arrives in China, the first American president to visit that country. (*See* **Nixon and Kissinger**)
22–30 MAY
Pursuing a policy of **détente** with the Soviet Union, Nixon meets Brezhnev for a summit meeting in Moscow. They sign the Strategic Arms Limitations Talks (SALT I) interim agreement on 26 May.
5 SEPTEMBER
Members of the Black September faction of the PLO seize Israeli athletes at the Munich Olympics, killing eleven.
3 OCTOBER
SALT I and the ABM Treaty are signed in Washington. (*See* **Antinuclear Movement**)

1973

1 JANUARY
Great Britain joins the EEC.
27 JANUARY
The Vietnam peace accords are signed.
17–24 JUNE
A summit conference in Washington occurs between Nixon and Brezhnev. (*See* **Nixon and Kissinger**)
15 JULY
Congress imposes a halt on continued U.S. bombing of Cambodia.
11 SEPTEMBER
President Salvador Allende Gossens of Chile is ousted in a coup. (*See* **Democracy Imperiled** and **Third World**)
6 OCTOBER
The **Yom Kippur War** starts. (*See* **Middle East**)
30 OCTOBER
Mutual Balanced Force Reductions (MBFR) Talks open in Vienna.

1974

9 MAY
The U.S. House Judiciary Committee votes to impeach Nixon.
18 MAY
India explodes a nuclear device, which it describes as a "peaceful nuclear explosion" (PNE). (*See* **Arms Control** and **Third World**)
27 JUNE – 3 JULY
The Moscow summit conference between Nixon and Brezhnev takes place.
20 JULY
Turkey invades Cyprus.
9 AUGUST
Nixon resigns because of Watergate scandal. Gerald R. Ford becomes president.
14 AUGUST
Greece cuts **NATO** ties because of Turkish invasion of Cyprus.
4 SEPTEMBER
The United States establishes diplomatic relations with East Germany.
12 SEPTEMBER
Ethiopian emperor Haile Selassie is ousted in a military coup, whose leaders later declare the country a socialist state.
23–24 NOVEMBER
The Vladivostok summit conference between Ford and Brezhnev takes place. (*See* **Team B**)
26 DECEMBER
CIA director William Colby admits the agency spied on U.S. citizens.

1975

16 APRIL
The Khmer Rouge takes over **Cambodia.**
30 APRIL
Saigon falls to North Vietnamese forces. The **Vietnam War** is over.
1 AUGUST
The Helsinki Final Act is signed.
23 AUGUST
The Vietnamese-backed Pathet Lao takes over Laos.

1976

20 FEBRUARY
SEATO disbands.
2 JULY
Vietnam formally unites as one nation.

1977

27 JANUARY
President Jimmy Carter orders SALT II negotiations to proceed.

30 JULY
The U.S. government announces plan to deploy cruise missiles. (*See* **Arms Control**)

7 SEPTEMBER
Panama Canal treaties are signed in Washington, D.C.

23 SEPTEMBER
Secretary of State Cyrus Vance says the United States will abide by the expiring 1972 SALT I treaty.

25 DECEMBER
Israeli prime minister Menachem Begin and Egyptian president Anwar as-Sadat start peace negotiations in Egypt. (*See* **Middle East**)

1978

10 MARCH
Congress adopts the Nuclear Non-Proliferation Act of 1978. Carter signs Nuclear Non-Proliferation Treaty.

17 MARCH
Carter warns the Soviet Union against involvement in the domestic affairs of other countries.

7 APRIL
The United States defers production of the neutron bomb. (*See* **Antinuclear Movement** and **Arms Control**)

12 JUNE
Vance announces that the United States will not use nuclear weapons against nonnuclear powers that pledge nuclear abstinence.

5–17 SEPTEMBER
Sadat and Begin meet with Carter at Camp David and agree on an Egyptian-Israeli peace accord. (*See* **Middle East**)

1979

7 JANUARY
Vietnam invades **Cambodia,** replacing the regime of Pol Pot with a pro-Hanoi communist regime under Heng Samrin.

16 JANUARY
Reza Shah Pahlavi flees Iran.

1 FEBRUARY
Ayatollah Ruhollah Khomeini arrives in Iran.

26 MARCH
Sadat and Begin sign an Egyptian-Israeli peace treaty.

6 APRIL
U.S. aid to Pakistan is cut because of its nuclear-weapons program. (*See* **Arms Control**)

2 MAY
Undersecretary of State Warren Christopher says U.S. foreign policy will link aid with **human rights.**

18 JUNE
Carter and Brezhnev sign the SALT II agreement in Vienna.

19 JULY
Sandinista rebels take Managua and seize power in Nicaragua; President Anastasio Somoza Debayle flees. (*See* **Nicaragua**)

1 OCTOBER
The U.S. Panama Canal Zone accords from 1977 go into effect.

4 NOVEMBER
The U.S. embassy in Tehran is seized, and diplomats are taken hostage.

21 NOVEMBER
Muslim fundamentalists burn the U.S. embassy in Pakistan.

12 DECEMBER
NATO adopts the "two track" policy, uncoupling Europe, especially Germany, from U.S. protection.

25 DECEMBER
Soviet troops invade **Afghanistan.**

1980

24 APRIL
"Desert I" rescue raid by U.S. forces fails to free Iranian-held hostages.

21–27 MAY
About one thousand South Koreans die in political unrest following arrest of opposition leader Kim Dae Jung.

14 AUGUST
Massive strikes occur in Poland, led by Lech Walesa, at Lenin shipyards in Gdansk. (*See* **Soviet Empire**)

11 NOVEMBER
The Conference on Security and Cooperation in Europe meeting opens in Madrid.

1981

20 JANUARY
The Iranians release the U.S. embassy hostages.

6 OCTOBER
Sadat is assassinated in Cairo; he is succeeded by Muhammad Hosni Mubarak.

30 NOVEMBER
Intermediate-range Nuclear Forces (INF) talks open in Geneva. (*See* **Arms Control**)

10 DECEMBER

Spain joins **NATO** (effective 30 May 1982). (*See* **Military Balance**)

13 DECEMBER

Martial law is imposed in Poland, continuing until 21 July 1983.

1982

2 APRIL

Argentina seizes the Falkland Islands.

9 MAY – 14 JUNE

British forces retake the Falkland Islands.

6 JUNE

Israeli forces invade Lebanon.

30 JUNE

The Strategic Arms Reduction Talks (START) in Geneva opens.

AUGUST – SEPTEMBER

U.S. Marines arrive in Lebanon.

1983

23 MARCH

Reagan outlines the Strategic Defense Initiative (SDI). (*See* **Reagan Doctrine** and **Reagan's Transformation**)

18 APRIL

The U.S. embassy in Beirut is bombed, killing more than fifty people.

1 SEPTEMBER

The Soviet Union shoots down Korean Airlines flight 007.

23 OCTOBER

U.S. barracks are destroyed by a car bomb in Lebanon; 241 Marines are killed.

25 OCTOBER

U.S. troops invade Grenada.

23 NOVEMBER

Soviet delegation walks out of the INF talks in Geneva.

30 DECEMBER

The first nine Pershing II missiles in West Germany become operational. (*See* **Ostpolitik**)

1984

1 JANUARY

The first new U.S. cruise missiles are deployed in Great Britain. (*See* **Anglo-American Relations**)

26 FEBRUARY

U.S. troops withdraw from Lebanon.

29 JUNE

Soviets offer to negotiate with Americans about nuclear weapons in space. (*See* **Arms Control**)

1 AUGUST

Great Britain announces its plan to give up control of Hong Kong in 1997.

20 SEPTEMBER

The new U.S. embassy in Beirut is bombed.

20 OCTOBER

The Chinese Communist Party approves Deng's liberalization program.

1985

21 FEBRUARY

The Soviet Union agrees to international inspection of its civilian nuclear-power plants. (*See* **Antinuclear Movement**)

26 APRIL

Member states sign a twenty-year extension of Warsaw Pact.

10 JUNE

The United States announces it will abide by unratified SALT II treaty.

6 OCTOBER

The United States says SDI does not violate the 1972 ABM treaty. (*See* **Missile Defense**)

19–21 OCTOBER

Reagan and General Secretary Mikhail Gorbachev of the Soviet Union meet at the Geneva summit conference. (*See* **Gorbachev** and **Reagan Doctrine**)

1986

1 JANUARY

Spain and Portugal join the EEC.

15 APRIL

American planes attack targets in Libya in response to Libyan-sponsored terrorism.

5 OCTOBER

The *Sunday Times* (London) reports that **Israel** has been building nuclear weapons for twenty years.

11–12 OCTOBER

The Reykjavík Summit between Reagan and Gorbachev proposes a 50 percent cut in long-range missiles. (*See* **Gorbachev** and **Reagan Doctrine**)

17 OCTOBER

Congress approves aid to the contras in Nicaragua. (*See* **Congress and Foreign Policy** and **Nicaragua**)

3 NOVEMBER

The U.S. press breaks the Iran-Contra Affair.

28 NOVEMBER

The United States exceeds the weapon limits of the unratified SALT II treaty by deploying the B-52 bomber.

1987

26 FEBRUARY

The Soviet Union ends an eighteen-month unilateral moratorium on nuclear testing with an underground nuclear test. (*See* **Arms Control**)

17 MAY

Iraqi planes attack the U.S. frigate *Stark* in the Persian Gulf.

8-10 DECEMBER

Reagan and Gorbachev meet in Washington.

8 DECEMBER

The INF Treaty is signed, mandating the removal of 2,611 intermediate-range nuclear missiles from Europe.

9 DECEMBER

The Palestinian *intifada* against **Israel** begins.

1988

14 APRIL

The Geneva Accords on **Afghanistan** are signed; the Soviets agree to withdraw half their forces by 15 August 1988 and the remainder by 15 February 1989. (*See* **Gorbachev**)

27 MAY

The Senate approves the INF Treaty.

29 MAY – 2 JUNE

A summit between Reagan and Gorbachev is held in Moscow.

3 JULY

The U.S. cruiser *Vincennes* downs an Iranian commercial jet over the Persian Gulf.

20 AUGUST

A cease-fire is reached in the Iran-Iraq war.

6 DECEMBER

Gorbachev announces to the U.N. a plan to reduce the Soviet military by five hundred thousand men. (*See* **Glasnost and Perestroika** and **Gorbachev**)

14 DECEMBER

The U.S. government opens talks with the PLO.

1989

15 JANUARY

Demonstrations in Prague commemorate the twentieth anniversary of the protest-suicides by students after the 1968 Soviet invasion.

23 JANUARY

East German leader Erich Honecker announces a 10 percent cut in military spending by 1990.

20–21 FEBRUARY

The Hungarian Central Committee approves a new constitution, omitting mention of the leading role of the Communist Party. (*See* **Cold War Conclusion**)

21 FEBRUARY

Václav Havel is sentenced to nine months in prison for inciting protests against the Czech government. He is released on 17 May.

26 MARCH

Elections are held for a new Soviet Congress of People's Deputies. Many party and military officials lose to independent candidates. Boris Yeltsin wins an at-large seat for Moscow with 89 percent of the vote. (*See* **Glasnost and Perestroika**)

17 APRIL

The Solidarity trade union is legalized in Poland.

25 APRIL

One thousand Soviet tanks leave Hungary. (*See* **Cold War Conclusion**)

11 MAY

Gorbachev announces that the Soviet Union will unilaterally reduce its nuclear forces in eastern Europe by five hundred warheads. (*See* **Arms Control** and **Gorbachev**)

25 MAY

The Soviet Congress of People's Deputies elects Gorbachev as president.

3-4 JUNE

The Chinese government orders suppression of a prodemocracy demonstration by students in Tiananmen Square.

4 JUNE

Solidarity wins a decisive majority in the first free parliamentary elections in Poland for almost half a century.

19 JUNE

START negotiations resume in Geneva.

25 JULY

President Wojciech W. Jaruzelski of Poland invites Solidarity to join a coalition government.

17 AUGUST

The Soviet Politburo endorses a plan for limited economic autonomy for the fifteen Soviet republics. (*See* **Glasnost and Perestroika**)

7 OCTOBER

The Hungarian Communist Party formally disbands. (*See* **Cold War Conclusion**)

23 OCTOBER

Hungary adopts a new constitution, becoming the Republic of Hungary.

9 NOVEMBER

East Germany opens its borders, including the Berlin Wall.

20 NOVEMBER

Mass demonstrations are held in Prague.

1-3 DECEMBER

At the Malta summit between Gorbachev and President George Bush, Gorbachev says that "the characteristics of the Cold War should be abandoned." (*See* **Cold War Conclusion** and **Gorbachev**)

7 DECEMBER

East Germany announces multiparty elections for 6 May 1990.

22 DECEMBER

Nicolae Ceausescu is toppled after leading Romania for twenty-four years. He and his wife, Elena, are executed on 25 December. (*See* **Power Vacuum**)

1990

1 JANUARY

Poland enacts sweeping economic reforms.

11-13 FEBRUARY

At the Ottawa Conference foreign ministers of Warsaw Pact and **NATO** countries discuss Bush's "open skies" proposal and agree to formal talks on German reunification.

26 FEBRUARY

The Soviet Union agrees to a phased withdrawal of Soviet troops from Czechoslovakia, to be completed by July 1991. (*See* **Cold War Conclusion**)

11 MARCH

Lithuania declares its independence from the Soviet Union. Soviet troops begin withdrawal from Hungary.

3 MAY

NATO foreign ministers agree to allow full membership to a reunified Germany.

30 MAY – 3 JUNE

The Washington summit between Gorbachev and Bush is held.

8-9 JUNE

Havel's party captures a majority in parliamentary elections in Czechoslovakia.

12 SEPTEMBER

Meeting in Moscow, foreign ministers of the two Germanies and the Big Four powers agree to set 1994 as the date of withdrawal of Soviet troops from East Germany.

3 OCTOBER

West and East Germany unite as the Federal Republic of Germany.

22 DECEMBER

Walesa is sworn in as president of Poland. Slovenians vote for independence from Yugoslavia. (*See* **Power Vacuum**)

1991

2 JANUARY

Soviet elite forces capture buildings in Latvia and Lithuania and kill fifteen protesters in Vilnius on 13 January.

20 JANUARY

Hundreds of thousands march on the Kremlin to protest Soviet crackdown in the Baltic states.

21 JANUARY

The EEC suspends $1 billion in economic aid to the Soviet Union.

16 MARCH

Serbian president Slobodan Milosevic announces Serbia will no longer recognize the authority of the Yugoslavian federal government. (*See* **Power Vacuum**)

27 MARCH

The United States withdraws its medium-range missiles from Europe. (*See* **Military Balance**)

APRIL–SEPTEMBER

The Soviet Union disintegrates as its constituent republics declare independence. (*See* **Cold War Conclusion, Glasnost and Perestroika, Power Vacuum,** and **Soviet Empire**)

12 JUNE

Boris Yeltsin is elected president of the Russian Federation.

19 JUNE

Soviet troops complete their withdrawal from Hungary.

21 JUNE

Soviet troops complete their withdrawal from Czechoslovakia.

25 JUNE

Slovenia and Croatia declare independence from Yugoslavia. (*See* **Power Vacuum**)

1 JULY

The Warsaw Pact is formally dissolved. The Supreme Soviet permits the sale of state-owned enterprises.

19 AUGUST

In a coup attempt Gorbachev is held at his vacation dacha and replaced by Gennadi Yanayev. Yeltsin denounces coup leaders as traitors. (*See* **Gorbachev**)

21 AUGUST

The Soviet coup collapses; Gorbachev is released from house arrest.

24 AUGUST

Gorbachev resigns, disbands the Central Committee, and places Communist Party property under control of the Soviet parliament. (*See* **Gorbachev**)

29 AUGUST

The Supreme Soviet bans the activities of the Communist Party. The Russian republics sign political and economic treaties with Ukraine and Kazakhstan.

2 SEPTEMBER

The European Community recognizes the independence of the Baltic states, and the United States establishes diplomatic relations with them.

7 SEPTEMBER

Croatia and Slovenia declare immediate secession from Yugoslavia.

8 SEPTEMBER

Macedonia votes to declare independence from Yugoslavia.

27 SEPTEMBER

Bush announces unilateral dismantling of 2,400 U.S. nuclear warheads. (*See* **Arms Control**)

19 OCTOBER

Ethnic Albanian legislators declare Kosovo independent from Yugoslavia. (*See* **Power Vacuum**)

23 OCTOBER

Yugoslav forces attack Dubrovnik in Croatia.

8 NOVEMBER

The EEC imposes economic sanctions on Yugoslavia.

25 NOVEMBER

Soviet republics reject a union treaty proposed by Gorbachev. (*See* **Gorbachev**)

8 DECEMBER

The leaders of Russia, Ukraine, and Belorussia proclaim that the Soviet Union has ceased to exist and declare the creation of the Commonwealth of Independent States. (*See* **Cold War Conclusion, Glasnost and Perestroika, Gorbachev, Power Vacuum,** and **Reagan's Victory**)

19 DECEMBER

The EEC announces it will recognize Slovenia and Croatia by 15 January 1992.

20 DECEMBER

Bosnia-Herzegovina applies to the EEC for recognition as an independent state.

21 DECEMBER

Eleven former Soviet republics announce they constitute the Commonwealth of Independent States, to begin operations by 15 January 1992. Russia retains the permanent seat held by the Soviets at the U.N. Security Council.

25 DECEMBER

Gorbachev resigns as president of the Soviet Union.

CHRONOLOGY

AFRICA

Were the Reagan administration policies in Angola and Mozambique effective?

Viewpoint: Yes. Reagan administration policies in Angola and Mozambique successfully blocked the spread of communism in southern Africa.

Viewpoint: No. Reagan policies in Angola and Mozambique prolonged internecine warfare and helped South Africa maintain its apartheid-based regime.

Following a military coup in Portugal in April 1974, the ruling junta agreed to grant independence to Angola, a Portuguese colony. Three anti-Portuguese movements had been vying for power in the southwest African nation: the Marxist Popular Liberation Movement of Angola (*Movimento Popular de Libertação de Angola* or MPLA), led by Antonio Agostinho Neto; the National Front for the Liberation of Angola (*Frente Nacional de Libertação de Angola* or FNLA), headed by Holden Roberto; and the National Union for the Total Independence of Angola (*União Nacional para a Independência Total de Angola* or UNITA), founded by Jonas Savimbi. Different foreign powers supported each movement. The Soviets and Cubans backed the MPLA, while the Americans, South Africans, Chinese, and Zaireans supported the FNLA and, to a lesser extent, UNITA. When Angola became independent on 11 November 1975, the country was divided among the three movements, with the MPLA controlling the capital, Luanda.

The United States refused to recognize the MPLA government, although many African leaders did. Congress passed the Clark Amendment (1975), which prohibited the Ford administration from arming any faction in Angola. President Jimmy Carter continued Gerald R. Ford's policy of not recognizing the MPLA government, but distanced himself from active support of the FNLA-UNITA anti-MPLA front. Carter, who emphasized human rights in his foreign policy, was uncomfortable with the support UNITA received from the apartheid regime in South Africa. President Ronald Reagan's administration renewed U.S. involvement in Angola. The major reason for this move was the presence of about twenty thousand Cuban troops, who were fighting with the MPLA against UNITA. In 1985 the administration persuaded Congress to repeal the Clark Amendment, and the Central Intelligence Agency (CIA) began to supply UNITA with large quantities of advanced weaponry. In 1986 Reagan received Savimbi in the White House, treating him like a head of state.

The rise of Mikhail Gorbachev to power in Russia in 1985 and the relaxation of the Cold War led the United States to support a package deal for southwest Africa: Cuban troops would be withdrawn from Angola in exchange for a removal of South African soldiers and the granting of independence to Namibia. Withdrawal of foreign troops from Angola began in 1989; Namibia became independent in 1990; and the United States recognized the MPLA in 1993, after that government, now led by Jose Eduardo dos Santos (Neto had died in September 1979), won an internationally monitored election in September 1992.

The 1974 coup in Portugal also led to the independence, on 25 June 1975, of another Portuguese colony, Mozambique. The government of this newly independent state was formed by leaders of the Left-leaning Mozambique Liberation Front (*Frente da Libertação de Moçambique* or FRELIMO), headed by Samora Moisés Machel. Prior to and after independence, FRELIMO was engaged in a bitter fight with the right-wing movement Mozambique National Resistance Movement (*Resistência Nacional Moçambicana* or RENAMO), which was supported by the apartheid regime of South Africa and the white minority administration of Ian Smith of Rhodesia. The United States recognized the FRELIMO government and even provided economic assistance, but in 1977 Congress stopped the aid program, accusing FRELIMO of violating human rights in its fight against RENAMO. Mozambique turned to the Soviet Union for economic and military support, as relations with the United States deteriorated. The United States, worried about Soviet and Cuban inroads in Angola, and fearful of further expansion of Soviet influence on the continent, began, indirectly, to support RENAMO in its war against FRELIMO. In 1985, when the Clark Amendment, which prohibited U.S. military aid to the Angolan factions, was repealed, some in Congress tried to have the administration increase its involvement in Mozambique as well. By that time, however, the Reagan administration was already working on improving relations with the Mozambique government, leading Congress, in April 1984, to lift the 1977 embargo on aid to Mozambique.

Viewpoint:
Yes. Reagan administration policies in Angola and Mozambique successfully blocked the spread of communism in southern Africa.

In January 1981, when Ronald Reagan assumed the U.S. presidency, the noncommunist world faced many challenges in its attempts to resist communist expansionism. This situation was especially true in the Third World, where the Soviet Union and its allies intervened in local and internal conflicts to promote Marxist, or at least anti-Western and anti-American, political movements. Africa was fertile ground for Soviet attempts at aggrandizement. Growing civil strife across the continent created discernible opportunities for Soviet diplomacy, and by the mid 1970s thousands of Soviet military advisers, tens of thousands of Cuban combat troops, and tremendous amounts of military and economic aid were pouring into Africa.

The situation in the former Portuguese colonies in southern Africa was especially tense. Having been granted their independence from Lisbon in 1974, both Angola and Mozambique were divided by factional conflicts aggravated by Cold War tensions. In 1975 U.S. aid to Jonas Savimbi's anticommunist National Union for the Total Independence of Angola (*União Nacional para a Independência Total de Angola* or UNITA) had enabled him to maintain viable resistance to the pro-Soviet communist government of his country. Aid to anti-Soviet forces in Mozambique was also under serious consideration. Before more decisive steps in promoting noncommunist resistance could be taken, existing U.S. policies had to overcome serious domestic challenges. Many proponents of détente, a policy of relaxed diplomatic relations with the

Soviet Union, argued that resisting communist expansion in the Third World endangered this arrangement, while others feared that a continued pattern of economic aid would lead to the commitment of U.S. troops far from home in another Vietnam-like war. Just as Congress had cut funding to the beleaguered government of South Vietnam after the United States withdrew from that country in 1973, so too did it pass the Clark Amendment (1975) to cut funding to Savimbi's anticommunist movement in Angola.

Reagan was firmly resolved to reverse the advance of international communism. Indeed, the Soviet invasion of Afghanistan (December 1979) had already spelled out the diplomatic intentions of Moscow clearly to policymakers of the Carter administration, and fewer of them placed stock in détente as a viable option. The second round of the Strategic Arms Limitation Talks (SALT II) signed in the summer of 1979 remained unratified by the U.S. Senate. Over the course of 1980, Carter initiated a defense buildup that increased military spending and emphasized earlier administration decisions to reinforce American conventional and strategic forces around the world. The administration initiated what turned out to be long-term U.S. support for the Islamic resistance fighters (mujahideen) in Afghanistan.

Reagan determined to follow these measures, but found himself constrained in the implementation of "roll back" policies against the expansion of the Soviet Union. Although Carter had dramatically increased military spending during his last years in office, the U.S. military remained relatively weak compared to what it had been. Reagan appointed his close friend and political associate Caspar W. Weinberger, known for his administrative efficiency, as secretary of defense to facilitate the reconstruction of U.S. conventional forces and raise morale in the armed forces. Despite Reagan's bullishly anti-

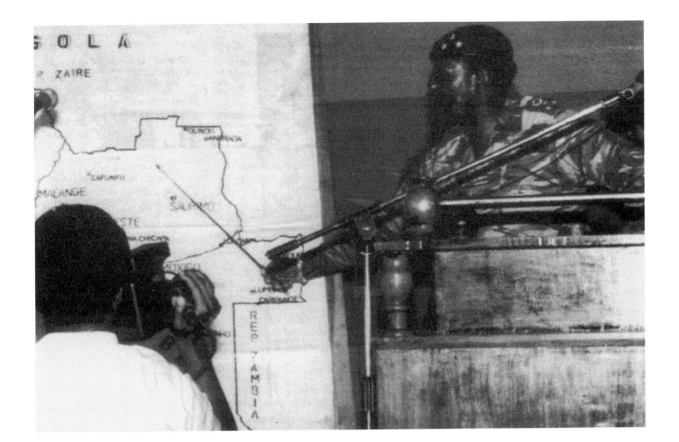

Angolan UNITA leader
Jonas Savimbi briefing
the press in late 1987

communist rhetoric and publicly stated view of the Vietnam War as "a noble cause," many within the military and foreign-affairs establishment were still plagued with fears that large-scale American involvement overseas would engineer another expensive, wasteful, and ultimately futile conflict such as the one in Vietnam, especially because of the poor state of the military.

For these reasons the Reagan administration waged its war with communism through a variety of means designed to be effective, yet fiscally and militarily prudent. As the conventional military was recovering in quantitative and qualitative terms, Reagan placed greater emphasis on relatively less expensive nuclear deterrence. By 1983 the administration had realized plans of the Carter administration to deploy Pershing II cruise missiles in Western Europe, and in March of that year Reagan announced that the United States would develop a space-based antiballistic missile defense system, the Strategic Defense Initiative (SDI). Through diplomatic channels the administration tried hard to break off or minimize the détente-era commercial relationships from which the Soviet Union had benefited economically and technologically. Dissident movements in Eastern Europe and the Soviet Union also received American support.

When it came to mounting resistance to Soviet expansion in the Third World, however, the Reagan administration initiated support to noncommunist governments and resistance movements in what were called "low-intensity conflicts" (LICs). While it avoided direct commitments of U.S. troops, a combination of financial support and American-led covert operations enabled many anticommunist movements to fight against Soviet-supported governments and organizations, as well as to challenge the ability of the Union of Soviet Socialist Republics (U.S.S.R.) to remain competitive as a superpower. Though ultimately successful in rolling back communist influence in the Third World, while condemning the Soviet Union to economic ruin on a wide and impressive scale, Reagan's policies suffered from serious domestic criticism and political opposition. A major scandal, the Iran-Contra affair, resulted from attempts by administration officials to find legal means of skirting congressionally imposed restrictions on American aid to the "contra" resistance fighters in Nicaragua.

When the Reagan administration formulated policy for Angola and Mozambique, political opposition became more pronounced. Earlier American involvement in Angola, in particular, prejudiced many legislators against either the renewal of aid to Savimbi or an extension of U.S. involvement in Mozambique. Despite repeated administration requests, Congress refused to repeal the Clark Amendment, which had outlawed aid to Savimbi, until late 1985. In the meantime, Reagan's commitment to fighting communism in Angola never flagged, and the president made repeated positive references to

AFRICA

the rebel cause. Rather than violate congressional restrictions, the administration funneled a great deal of support to the rebel leader through South Africa, which at times intervened directly in the conflict. In addition to direct support they were already receiving from Johannesburg, Angolan rebels now received U.S. supplies and funding that was in a purely technical sense intended for the South African army. Additional financial support to Savimbi was garnered through the close relationship of the Reagan administration with Saudi Arabia. In addition to matching U.S. funding to the mujahideen in Afghanistan, the Saudi monarchy willingly agreed to contribute funds to UNITA.

By the time the Clark Amendment was repealed, the situation in Angola had changed dramatically. Through indirect U.S. support and direct aid from its allies, Savimbi's forces had become a credible political force. After direct U.S. military aid was reinstated in November of 1985, Savimbi became still stronger and forced the communist sponsors of the Angolan regime to commit even greater resources for its defense. In broader geopolitical terms, Soviet power was on the wane and Premier Mikhail Gorbachev began to pursue policies designed to reduce the external security requirements and military expenditures of Moscow. In 1986 Gorbachev first began talking about withdrawing from Afghanistan. For Angola this development was especially important because Soviet economic support for Fidel Castro's regime in Cuba began to decline, and the ability of Havana to maintain its presence in Africa came into serious question even as Castro insisted that it needed to be larger. By December 1988, as the U.S. administration came to favor better relations with the declining U.S.S.R., Assistant Secretary of State for African Affairs Chester A. Crocker successfully negotiated a quid pro quo over Angola that established a schedule for the withdrawal of Cuban and South African troops from the country by 1991 and laid the groundwork for an agreement between Washington and Moscow to cut aid to their respective partisans after the Cubans were gone. Although the coalition government that Savimbi, acting on American encouragement, entered into ultimately degenerated into a renewed civil war, the Soviet and Cuban influence disappeared altogether. Had the Reagan administration ignored Savimbi's movement or allowed it to be crushed, it is conceivable that neither the negotiation of Cuban withdrawal nor the increased drain on the resources of the communist world would have been achieved.

An examination of the case of Mozambique, much more subtle than that of Angola,

reveals a highly nuanced and well-considered policy-making process that also enjoyed ultimate success. Despite many critiques that suggest the Reagan administration haphazardly labeled any government or political movement interested in social or political reform as a stooge of Soviet imperialism, Reagan's approach to Mozambique reveals that this was not necessarily the truth of the matter. While the Marxist movements against which the Reagan doctrine was applied had rather clear connections to the communist world, there were several cases where the administration pursued improved relations with communist governments when it was in its interest to do so.

The development of the U.S. relationship with China in the early 1980s is an excellent case in point, for the visit of Chinese leader Deng Xiaoping to the United States in 1982 presaged a period of favorable relations between the two countries that built on Richard M. Nixon's idea, stillborn in the détente era, of bringing communist China into a strategic relationship based on mutual antagonism toward the Soviet Union. The situation in Mozambique was not at all dissimilar. Although the postindependence government had fallen into the hands of the nominally Marxist president Samora Moisés Machel, there was evidence that his regime was not especially close to Moscow.

Reagan administration officials believed that the security of southeast Africa could best be ensured not by toppling Machel through an American-supported guerrilla struggle but by cultivating him diplomatically. It was also significant that apart from the relatively weak South African–supported Mozambique National Resistance (*Resistência Nacional Moçambicana* or RENAMO) there was no other substantial antigovernment resistance movement of any consequence operating within Mozambique. From a strategic perspective, both the ambivalence of Machel's regime toward the Soviet Union and its relative internal stability (compared with countries such as Nicaragua, Ethiopia, Afghanistan, Cambodia, and Angola, which were all consumed by open civil conflict) precluded any serious commitment of troops from the Soviet Union or Cuba, though Machel's government did receive some aid from the Soviets.

Reagan's strategy in this case was to gravitate Mozambique toward the United States by settling the internal conflict. Although members of the right wing of the Reagan administration continued to call as late as 1987 for a low-intensity conflict against Mozambique, no such activity was taken directly or indirectly by the United States, and Mozambique posed no threat to U.S. security interests in Africa. Partly in response to American diplomatic encouragement, South

U.S. POLICY IN MOZAMBIQUE

At a 24 June 1987 session of a U.S. Senate subcommittee, chaired by Senator Paul M. Simon (D-Illinois), Assistant Secretary of State for African Affairs Chester A. Crocker spoke about U.S. policy in Mozambique:

No country in southern Africa has worked more consistently than Mozambique with the United States to further the cause of peace and stability in southern Africa. Farther afield, Mozambique no longer votes with the USSR in the United Nations on such international questions of overriding importance to Moscow as Afghanistan and Kampuchea. In short, Mozambique has over the past 5 years evolved a more independent, nonaligned foreign policy course that has distanced it from Moscow. . . .

Our skepticism about RENAMO has sometimes been incorrectly portrayed as U.S. Government advocacy of a military solution to Mozambique's problems. I welcome the opportunity to refute this myth and reaffirm our consistent conviction, in Mozambique as elsewhere in southern Africa, that military conflict cannot solve political problems. Mozambique's pressing human and economic problems cannot be solved as long as the devastation of civil strife continues. It is the policy of the United States to use whatever influence is available to us, as we do everywhere in the region, to encourage an end to hostilities and peaceful solution of conflicts.

The United States has in the past, when circumstances were propitious for doing so, promoted contact between the Government of Mozambique and RENAMO. For example, we did so in connection with negotiations between them that followed the conclusion of the Nkomati Accord between Mozambique and South Africa. Should further opportunities arise for us to play a similar role in ending hostilities between the government and the insurgents in Mozambique, we will not hesitate to undertake that role. We must, none-theless, realize that Mozambicans themselves must be the primary architects of a peaceful future for their country. . . .

The fate of Mozambique is a critical issue for all of independent southern Africa and for U.S. interests in that key region. Even a quick look at a map of the region indicates why this is so. The road, rail, and pipeline corridors through Mozambique represent virtually the only transport egress for southern African countries that is not dominated by South Africa. All the independent countries of southern Africa, including democratic Botswana and staunchly pro-Western Malawi and Zaire have a vital stake in keeping those transport links open and in preventing the regional instability that would surely follow their closure by violent means. Mozambique is thus the key policy question by which southern Africans judge the intentions of the United States and other foreign countries toward the region.

Because of Mozambique's key position, the success of our efforts to promote peace and stability in southern Africa depend importantly on how we handle the critical issue of relations with that embattled country. The policy of the Reagan administration has helped to bolster a conscious decision by the Government of Mozambique to reduce its dependence on Moscow and a move toward genuine nonalignment and improved relations with the West. In doing so, we have reduced Soviet influence in southern Africa and advanced prospects for regional peace and stability. This successful course has the support of our Allies and our African partners and had placed the Soviets squarely on the defensive.

Source: *"U.S. Policy Toward Mozambique," U.S. Department of State,* American Foreign Policy: Current Documents 1987 *(Washington, D.C.: U.S. Government Printing Office, 1988), pp. 652–653.*

Africa and Mozambique concluded the Nkotami Accord (March 1984), which provided for an end to South African support for RENAMO in exchange for the expulsion of exiled African National Congress (ANC) militants who were operating from Mozambique. Although the two countries continued to distrust one another, particularly after Machel's death in a mysterious plane crash over South African territory in Octo-ber 1986, the declining fortunes of Soviet imperialism in any case reduced the internal situation in Mozambique to a civil conflict untouched by Cold War antagonism.

In both Angola and Mozambique the Reagan administration pursued the correct policies. Indirect support to Savimbi's forces, replacing direct aid that had been cut off in 1976 by a Vietnam-traumatized Congress,

AFRICA

enabled him to pose a credible challenge to communist expansion in southern Africa and to tie down Cuban and Soviet resources that could have been deployed elsewhere or husbanded to alleviate domestic economic problems. Despite renewed Cuban attempts to prop up the Marxist Angolan government after direct U.S. aid was resumed in 1985, Savimbi's military successes, impossible without this assistance, gave him the leverage he needed to force his opponents to negotiate and compel the Cubans to leave his country. In Mozambique the more subtle strategy of using diplomatic means to encourage a settlement of its internal conflict and bring an end to South African intervention succeeded in keeping Machel's government away from the Soviet Union. By resisting the recommendation of some of his advisers to support RENAMO, either directly or through South Africa, Reagan deftly avoided the unnecessary alienation of a regime that could be won over through other means. Toward both countries the right policy was adopted.

−PAUL DU QUENOY,
GEORGETOWN UNIVERSITY

Viewpoint:
No. Reagan policies in Angola and Mozambique prolonged internecine warfare and helped South Africa maintain its apartheid-based regime.

Reagan administration policies toward the former Portuguese colonies of Angola and Mozambique reflected the general policy of the United States in the 1980s: to win without betting. Both African countries had fought long and fratricidal wars of independence—which came less because of the success of the rebels themselves than as a consequence of a rebellion in Portugal. The new government in Portugal promptly abandoned the struggle for empire and left its former territories to their own devices. In Mozambique that meant a debilitating low-grade struggle for power between the Mozambique Liberation Front (*Frente da Libertação de Moçambique* or FRELIMO) and Mozambique National Resistance (*Resistência Nacional Moçambicana* or RENAMO). To describe them in "tribal" terms is tempting but incomplete. In addition to the ethnic differences between them, the first incorporated an official Marxist/Leninist ideology that gained it minimal support from the Soviet bloc; the second tended to be against anything FRELIMO was for and drew corresponding assistance from white South Africa.

The new government in Angola was formed by the Marxist Popular Liberation Movement of Angola (*Movimento Popular de Libertação de Angola* or MPLA), in principle at least a multiethnic party with a Marxist/Leninist cast. There the "outsiders" were the National Front for the Liberation of Angola (*Frente Nacional de Libertação de Angola* or FNLA) and National Union for the Total Independence of Angola (*União Nacional para a Independência Total de Angola* or UNITA). Both were regional/ethnic organizations with strong anticommunist rhetoric that during the 1970s earned them significant assistance from the Central Intelligence Agency (CIA) and from a South Africa increasingly concerned with establishing a security zone on its northern frontier. The MPLA was correspondingly able to draw on increasing amounts of military and economic aid from the Soviet Union and Cuba, the latter state even committing ground forces in support of its cause. It scarcely required advanced credentials in international relations to conclude that neither Angola nor Mozambique were promising venues for external involvement. In 1976 the U.S. Senate passed legislation outlawing any funding for Angola; RENAMO never succeeded in attracting significant U.S. attention, even on the far anticommunist right.

There matters more or less stood when the administration of Ronald Reagan took office in January 1981. Its particular concern was less with Angola and Mozambique than with stabilizing the security of a South Africa whose preservation was defined as a major U.S. strategic interest. That policy, it must be emphasized, did not mean approving existing patterns of race relations. Apartheid, however, represented in good part the white South African response to a legitimate external threat. Angola, the Reagan administration argument went, was for practical purposes a client of the Union of Soviet Socialist Republics (U.S.S.R.) and Cuba. Let Cuba withdraw from Angola, and South Africa would be in position to abandon its occupation of Namibia, a strategic glacis the Pretoria government had defined as indispensable to its security under current circumstances. Domestic changes could be left until later.

Mozambique escaped the worst consequences of the Reagan years. RENAMO never developed a strong enough American lobby to get its own aid programs. If anything, Reagan's administration tilted a bit in the direction of FRELIMO in the mid 1980s—again not enough to commit enough resources to destabilize a slowly emerging domestic balance

Things were different further west. The U.S. policy shift was welcome both in South Africa and to UNITA, whose leader, Jonas Savimbi, had spent years canvassing American conservatives for support. The fighting in southern Angola and northern Namibia had never really stopped. In the early 1980s it escalated sharply, with UNITA troops backed by small, high-tech South African forces gaining significant local successes.

UNITA was never strong enough to conquer enough of Angola to form even a shadow government. South Africa had a vested interest in seeing that UNITA never became that strong: its alliance with Savimbi was recognized on both sides as a marriage of immediate convenience. Then in December 1983 South Africa launched an independent operation to capture the Angolan capital of Luanda and dispose entirely of an MPLA that seemed increasingly vulnerable. The Soviet Union, kept informed of troop movements by its space satellites, responded decisively: an invasion would lead to a direct confrontation with Cuban forces and a fresh influx of Soviet arms and equipment.

The South African government had marketed its Angolan conflict as "war on the cheap." No significant domestic support existed for an all-out engagement with Fidel Castro's mechanized forces. UNITA soldiers were not up to it; South African expeditionary forces were configured for war on an altogether more modest scale. South Africa backed down as the United States in 1984 brokered talks that led to unilateral South African withdrawal from Angolan territory.

The Cubans, however, remained. The Reagan administration was unwilling, especially with a presidential election coming up, to engage itself in mediating a more comprehensive settlement. Nor, on the other side of the issue, was it willing to restrain South Africa from resuming the conflict, albeit on a smaller scale, within a year. By now, however, the war was becoming increasingly brutal—a fact Savimbi managed to camouflage sufficiently for Reagan to convince Congress to repeal the ban on military aid to Angola. However, UNITA, and not the legitimate government, benefited from the new legislation. MPLA struck back, invading UNITA-controlled territory in 1987 in the largest-scale fighting of the war to date. Savimbi's men held—just barely, with the aid of South African ground and air forces and supplies of American Stinger anti-aircraft missiles. UNITA and South Africa agreed on the necessity of counterattack. At the end of the year the allies drove for the MPLA stronghold of Cuito Canavale. They were met by more than fifty thousand Cubans, whose well-planned and neatly timed flank march cut South African supply lines and forced them to retreat.

By that time the status of South Africa as an international pariah was becoming embarrassing even to the Reagan administration, which was willing enough to twist Pretoria's arm to obtain a cease-fire. That proved unnecessary as South Africa was already cutting its losses. So was Castro. Apart from the increasing casualties suffered by his expeditionary force for a cause anything but popular in Cuba, the U.S.S.R. was no longer as generous as it once had been with direct and indirect subsidies. In December 1988 an agreement, signed in New York, provided for a series of phased withdrawals to take South Africa out of Namibia in 1989 and remove the Cubans from Angola by May 1991.

Both parties met their deadlines. That did not mean an end to U.S. involvement. Reagan's successor, George Bush, continued to provide UNITA with enough military aid to keep the war going, though on a reduced scale, until the middle of the decade. The Cold War was long over; a fundamental change of government in South Africa rendered the regional conflict moot; and the Angolan cease-fire of 1994 left another African burnout case, a "failed state" whose failure owed much to itself, much to its immediate neighbors—and much to a United States that did little or nothing to manage the behavior of its ostensible clients. Instead the United States committed just enough resources and influence during the Reagan years to sustain a broken-backed war, then relegated southern Africa to its historic place in U.S. diplomatic priorities—on the bottom.

DENNIS SHOWALTER, COLORADO COLLEGE

References

Chester A. Crocker, *High Noon in Southern Africa: Making Peace in a Rough Neighborhood* (New York: Norton, 1992);

Raymond L. Garthoff, *The Great Transition: American-Soviet Relations and the End of the Cold War* (Washington, D.C.: Brookings Institution, 1994);

Henry Kissinger, *Years of Renewal* (New York: Simon & Schuster, 1999);

Zaki Laïdi, *The Superpowers and Africa: The Constraints of a Rivalry, 1960–1990,* translated by Patricia Baudoin (Chicago: University of Chicago Press, 1990);

George P. Shultz, *Turmoil and Triumph: My Years As Secretary of State* (New York: Scribners, 1993);

Richard C. Thornton, *The Nixon-Kissinger Years: Reshaping America's Foreign Policy* (New York: Paragon House, 1989).

AFRICA

ANGLO-AMERICAN RELATIONS

Was there a mutual trust between the United States and Great Britain during the Cold War?

Viewpoint: Yes. The United States and Great Britain had a special relationship built on mutual self-interest and common heritage.

Viewpoint: No. The political and economic decline of Great Britain reduced its international status and weakened its relationship with the United States.

The concept of a "special relationship" between Great Britain and the United States was a product of World War II. It reflected the close personal relationship between President Franklin D. Roosevelt and Prime Minister Winston Churchill, as well as a common strategic environment that required close cooperation, especially in the European theater. It also reflected a mutual propaganda campaign designed to bridge a century and a half of mutual suspicion. After 1945 the concept was nurtured in a Britain increasingly aware of its objective decline in power: Britain hoped as well to play Greece to America's Rome by providing the finesse allegedly lacking across the Atlantic. Washington for its part was sufficiently uncomfortable with its new status as guarantor of the noncommunist world that British support, first in the Mediterranean and then in the organizing of the North Atlantic Treaty Organization (NATO), was a welcome given.

From the beginning of this postwar relationship significant differences existed between the English-speaking powers. Britain had little sympathy for U.S. policy with China and not much more for the Korean War (1950–1953). The United States remained distant from, when not suspect of, the increasingly vestigial British empire; yet, it expected consistent support for its own initiatives and responses. The Suez Crisis (1956), when the United States essentially left France and Britain to twist in the wind while it addressed the Hungarian revolution, epitomized a special relationship that in both American and British circles had become that of patron and client—a favored client to be sure, but a client nonetheless.

To a significant degree Britain acquiesced in its new status by abandoning a global role its economy could no longer support, concentrating instead on its European connections. Yet, in that sector Britain sustained a special role for the balance of the Cold War, supporting the United States on crucial issues from cruise missiles to flexible response. Elsewhere in the world, Britain maintained a bemused distance from the Vietnam imbroglio (ended 1975), while the United States attempted to maintain something like an even hand between Britain and Argentina (and by extension, Latin America) in the Falklands War (1983). A special relationship, however, that in many ways was the creation of personalities, Churchill's and Roosevelt's, was revitalized during the 1980s by two other personalities: Ronald Reagan and Margaret Thatcher. Sharing a broad spectrum of common values, the president and prime minister presided over the Cold War endgame and reestablished a connection that was later continued on a personal level by Bill Clinton and Tony Blair.

**Viewpoint:
Yes. The United States and Great
Britain had a special relationship
built on mutual self-interest and
common heritage.**

In 1946 Winston Churchill, then leader of
the opposition in the British parliament, went
to the United States to proclaim the need for a
"fraternal association of the English-speaking
peoples." He was quite clear about the foundations upon which this association would be
based. It was the "great principles of freedom
and the rights of man which are the joint
inheritance of the English-speaking world and
which through Magna Carta, the Bill of
Rights, the Habeas Corpus, trial by jury and
the English common law find their most
famous expression in the American Declaration of Independence." Churchill's great ora-
tion at Fulton, Missouri, on 5 March, sometimes
called the "Iron Curtain" speech, involved him
in the creation of a fiction: an ideal vision of
both the British Empire and Anglo-American
relations. It was not necessarily true that "a
special relationship between the British Commonwealth and Empire and the United States"
existed, however, or that many listeners were
confident "that half a century from now you
will . . . see 70 or 80 millions of Britons spread
about the world and united in defence of our
traditions, our way of life, and of the world
causes which you and we espouse." Yet, the
sentiments he expressed merely capped an honorable tradition that went back to before the
start of the century.

Indeed, one can best think about Anglo-
American relations since 1945 in terms of
three aphorisms. The first is the old adage:
"blood is thicker than water"; the second, by
the German leader Otto von Bismarck: "the
most important fact in modern history is that
North America spoke English"; and the third,
by the English statesman Lord Palmerston:
"states have permanent interests not permanent friends." In other words, the United
States and Great Britain have cooperated
closely because it was in both their best interests to do so, and they have found it much easier because of a shared language, shared modes
of thought, and shared operating procedures.

Churchill's "Iron Curtain" speech is a particularly important document because it cleverly tied together the two major issues in
Anglo-American relations, the Cold War and
the fate of the British empire, that pulled U.S.
foreign policy in different directions. Both the
British and the Americans were grappling with

the problem of how to deal with the Soviet
Union. On this issue their policies moved in
parallel. George F. Kennan delivered his
"Long Telegram" from Moscow (22 February)
only a few days before Churchill's speech in
Missouri. The telegram, which adumbrated
the policy of containment, was drawn up, it is
worth noting, in the light of conversations
between Kennan and the chargé d'affaires at
the British embassy, Frank Roberts. Roberts
sent a less celebrated but similar document to
his own government. Both governments
agreed that the Soviet threat existed and must
be resisted by a coalition of nations. At this
stage neither the British nor the Americans
wanted this coalition to be based around military force.

There was much less agreement about the
future of the British empire. Although both
Churchill and President Franklin D. Roosevelt
had agreed upon a set of joint principles,
known as the Atlantic Charter (1941), the
United States was committed to a policy of
anti-imperialism. If this strain of policy had
become dominant in U.S. foreign policy, then
Anglo-American relations would have been
forced back onto the rather frigid level that
had existed in the 1930s. Partly as a result of
Churchill's successful appeal, however, the
administration of Harry S Truman increasingly took the view that the struggle against
Soviet communism was more important than
the stand against British imperialism.

The way was thus paved for a geopolitical
coalition, which operated in 1947 under the
Truman Doctrine and the Marshall Plan; during the 1948–1949 Berlin airlift, as a joint
Anglo-American operation; and in 1949, during the formation of the North Atlantic Treaty
Organization (NATO). The signature of this
treaty turned Britain and the United States
into true military allies. It was an Anglo-American front that overrode French opposition to
German rearmament in 1950 and again in
1954. Anglo-American dialogue was the dominant feature in the formulation of a military
strategy for NATO in 1954, 1957, and 1967.
The strategy decided on in 1967, known as
"flexible response," so enraged French opinion against the partnership of "les Anglo-Saxons" that they withdrew from the military side
of NATO. This partnership survived the end
of the Cold War in the 1990s.

It is certainly true that it proved less easy
for the British and Americans to work in harmony outside Europe. Although Britain contributed forces to the U.S.-led armed effort in
Korea (1950–1953), that effort, although far
from negligible, was militarily unimportant.
British concern for the safety of her Asian col-

British prime minister Margaret H. Thatcher

(Fox)

increased caution explains the unwillingness of Britain to send troops to Vietnam during the 1960s, a refusal that caused tension between the administration of Lyndon B. Johnson and the government of Harold Wilson. However, Wilson's 1968 decision to withdraw British forces from "East of Suez" in some ways eased relations. Although Britain became a less important global partner, it was also freed of the taint of imperialism. In the short term the succeeding government of Edward Heath tried to live out the logic of Wilson's decision by reorientating policy to Europe and introducing a deliberate *froideur* (coldness) into Anglo-American discussions. Yet, the simple fact that Britain was reliant on the U.S. security umbrella ensured that in the meanwhile relations returned to normal. Margaret Thatcher's use of a language of presumed intimacy in the 1980s, which mirrored Churchill's rhetoric in 1946, did not indicate that she was sentimental but that such language was meaningful and useful. Visiting Washington in 1981, as recounted by Percy Cradock in his *In Pursuit of British Interests: Reflections on Foreign Policy under Margaret Thatcher and John Major* (1997), she said, "we in Britain stand with you. . . . Your problems will be our problems and when you look for friends we will be there." On another visit in 1985 she observed, "We see so many things in the same way and you can speak of a real meeting of minds." Even when she was displeased she used the same tone: "I feel I have been particularly wounded by a friend."

Such rhetoric was still meaningful because it was underpinned by a network of daily cooperation, which could be described as the "subcutaneous fat" of the relationship and can be illustrated by reference to two fields: nuclear weapons and intelligence. The atomic bomb was developed by an Anglo-American program. After World War II, however, the U.S. government tried to establish a monopoly on nuclear weapons. The McMahon Act (July 1946) cut off cooperation. Yet, this initial disagreement was progressively overcome. The provisions that related to Britain were repealed in 1958. After that date there was both coordinated nuclear-war planning and an exchange of nuclear and missile technology. In 1962 the United States agreed to supply Britain with its Polaris Submarine/Sea-Launched Ballistic Missile (SLBM). This missile was replaced in the 1980s by the Trident II SLBM: the United States did not supply these weapons to any other nation. The implication of such transfers was closer relations between the military and scientific establishments of both countries.

onies, such as Malaya, made it reluctant to follow the American anticommunist crusade in the region. Britain recognized the de jure existence of communist China in 1950, whereas the Americans refused to do so until the 1970s; Britain refused to assist the Eisenhower administration to intervene against communists in North Vietnam, and in doing so dissuaded the Americans from intervening unilaterally. Instead, the British cosponsored a peace conference for Indochina with the Soviets. The most spectacular falling out between the United States and Britain occurred in 1956 as a result of the Anglo-French invasion of Egypt, launched in an attempt to repossess the Suez Canal. The Eisenhower administration believed that the British had favored "neo-imperialism" over the Cold War struggle. This fundamental disagreement was exacerbated by an unusual breakdown in channels of communication. Yet, whereas the Suez crisis soured Franco-U.S. relations for a generation, much of the damage to Anglo-American cooperation was repaired at a hastily convened summit between U.S. president Dwight D. Eisenhower and British prime minister Harold Macmillan, held in March 1957.

Thereafter the British acted with more caution and in step with the Americans. This

British and American intelligence also established intimate collaboration. During World War II there was close cooperation in the fields of both human and signals intelligence. The latter was codified by the wartime British-United States Agreement (BRUSA). In contrast to the nuclear field, signals intelligence made a smooth transition into the postwar period. The agreement of 1948, an intelligence entente of "English-speaking" nations, persisted throughout the Cold War. Relations in human intelligence were also close. This cooperation was, paradoxically, revealed by intelligence failures: the "Cambridge Cell" spies Kim Philby, Guy Burgess, Donald Maclean, Anthony Blunt, and John Cairncross did so much damage because they had access to American as well as British intelligence. It was a tribute to the strength of the relationship that intelligence-sharing continued unabated despite these disasters.

The United States and Great Britain cooperated closely in the Cold War because it was in their interests to do so. Yet, the resilience of that relationship owed much to a network of formal and informal contacts working on a regular basis below the high-political level.

–SIMON BALL, UNIVERSITY OF GLASGOW, SCOTLAND

Viewpoint:
No. The political and economic decline of Great Britain reduced its international status and weakened its relationship with the United States.

The term "special relationship" referred to the view of British political leaders that their diplomatic and military relationship with the United States enjoyed certain privileges over other nations and gave Britain opportunities to exercise influence on world events. Although just what these privileges and opportunities were remained vague and uncertain, this idea did have a history. It began in 1945 when Britain emerged as one of the three victorious powers that, along with the United States and Soviet Union, sat down to negotiate the end of World War II and the terms under which a defeated Germany would be governed. It continued to develop during the years of the Labour Party government of Clement Atlee (1945–1950), which determined to have its own nuclear weaponry and maintain its Atlantic alliance through membership in the North Atlantic Treaty Organization (NATO). A permanent seat on the United Nations (UN) Security Council, carrying with it the right to veto actions recommended by another member, appeared to confirm the ability of Britain to maintain its status as an independent and influential player in international politics.

If the Atlantic Alliance and a nuclear deterrent supplied the structure of the special relationship, the events that defined the functioning of that arrangement told a different story. The demands of the war had taken a heavy toll on the British economy, leaving it unable to sustain an effective military presence to maintain the peace settlement. Thus, in 1948 the Atlee government was unable to intervene to support the Greek state against a communist insurgency. Eventually the United States, under the Truman Doctrine (1947), supplied the means to defeat the rebels. American power and influence were even more decisive during the Suez Crisis (1956). Under heavy diplomatic and financial pressure from the Eisenhower administration, Britain withdrew from an alliance with France and Israel, which was aimed at taking control of the Suez Canal from Egyptian president Gamal Abdel Nasser. The crisis was symbolic of the dependent relationship of Britain upon U.S. power. President Dwight D. Eisenhower and Prime Minister Anthony Eden had both played central roles in the wartime partnership against Germany, but a decade later that history did not translate into cooperation.

Eden's successor, Harold Macmillan, fared little better. Macmillan's government tried to develop an independent missile system (Blue Streak). Testing proved it inferior to a U.S. system (Skybolt), and Macmillan agreed to adopt the American alternative. The Kennedy administration then scrapped Skybolt in favor of a submarine-launched system (Polaris), and Macmillan agreed to open British ports in Scotland to base this system in Europe. The chain of events ended with the Nassau Agreement (21 December 1962), struck between the Macmillan and Kennedy administrations. The submarines would be British, and the agreement allowed Britain to use the missiles in an emergency affecting its "supreme national interests." There was, however, no imaginable circumstance that would justify British use of nuclear weapons without the concurrence of NATO and its U.S. leadership. Such was certainly the opinion of John F. Kennedy, who told his secretary of state that he wanted the agreement because the British "were nice people and we should try, if we could, to help them out."

In fact, the only person who took the special relationship seriously was French president Charles de Gaulle. Still smarting from the bad treatment he had received from the British dur-

NASSAU AGREEMENT

Joint U.S. and British statement on Nuclear Defence Systems, 21 December 1962

1. The President and the Prime Minister reviewed the development programme for the SKYBOLT missile. The President explained that it was no longer expected that this very complex weapons system would be completed within the cost estimate or the time scale which were projected when the programme was begun.

2. The President informed the Prime Minister that for this reason and because of the availability to the United States of alternative weapons systems, he had decided to cancel plans for the production of SKYBOLT for use by the United States. Nevertheless, recognising the importance of the SKYBOLT programme for the United Kingdom, and recalling that the purpose of the offer of SKYBOLT to the United Kingdom in 1960 had been to assist in improving and extending the effective life of the British V-bombers, the President expressed his readiness to continue the development of the missile as a joint enterprise between the United States and the United Kingdom, with each country bearing equal shares of the future cost of completing development, after which the United Kingdom would be able to place a production order to meet its requirements.

3. While recognising the value of this offer, the Prime Minister decided, after full consideration, not to avail himself of it because of doubts that had been expressed about the prospects of success for this weapons system and because of uncertainty regarding date of completion and final cost of the programme.

4. As a possible alternative the President suggested that the Royal Air Force might use the HOUND DOG missile. The Prime Minister responded that in light of the technical difficulties he was unable to accept this suggestion.

5. The Prime Minister then turned to the possibility of provision of the POLARIS missile to the United Kingdom by the United States. After careful review, the President and the Prime Minister agreed that a decision on POLARIS must be considered in the widest context both of the future defence of the Atlantic Alliance and of the safety of the whole Free World. They reached the conclusion that this issue created an opportunity for the development of new and closer arrangements for the organisation and control of strategic Western defence and that such arrangements in turn could make a major contribution to political cohesion among the nations of the Alliance.

6. The Prime Minister suggested and the President agreed, that for the immediate future a start could be made by subscribing to NATO some part of the forces already in existence. This could include allocations from United States Strategic Forces, from United Kingdom Bomber Command, and from tactical nuclear forces now held in Europe. Such forces would be assigned as part of a NATO nuclear force and targeted in accordance with NATO plans.

7. Returning to POLARIS the President and the Prime Minister agreed that the purpose of their two Governments with respect to the provision of the POLARIS missiles must be the development of a multilateral NATO nuclear force in the closest consultation with other NATO allies. They will use their best endeavors to this end.

8. Accordingly, the President and the Prime Minister agreed that the United States will make available on a continuing basis POLARIS missiles (less warheads) for British submarines. The United States will also study the feasibility of making available certain support facilities for such submarines. The United Kingdom Government will construct the submarines in which these weapons will be placed and they will also provide the nuclear warheads for the POLARIS missiles. British forces developed under this plan will be assigned and targeted in the same way as the forces described in paragraph 6.

9. These forces, and at least equal United States forces, would be made available for inclusion in a NATO multilateral nuclear force. The Prime Minister made it clear that except where her Majesty's Government may decide that supreme national interests are at stake, these British forces will be used for the purpose of international defence of the Western Alliance in all circumstances.

10. The President and the Prime Minister are convinced that this new plan will strengthen the nuclear defence of Western Alliance. In strategic terms this defence is indivisible, and it is their conviction that, in all ordinary circumstances of crisis or danger, it is this very unity which is the best protection of the West.

11. The President and the Prime Minister agreed that in addition to having a nuclear shield it is important to have a non-nuclear sword. For this purpose they agreed on the importance of increasing the effectiveness of their conventional forces on a world-wide basis.

Source: *Harold Macmillan, At The End of The Day, 1961–1963 (London: Macmillan, 1973), pp. 554–555.*

ANGLO-AMERICAN RELATIONS

ing World War II, de Gaulle used the Nassau Agreement as a sign that Britain was not sufficiently committed to European interests and vetoed Macmillan's application to join the European Economic Community (EEC). The subsequent proliferation of nuclear weapons left hollow the British claim that having them guaranteed its status as a great power.

By the end of Macmillan's premiership (18 October 1963) it was clear that the primary international role of Britain was European, as a member of NATO and the EEC—a course urged throughout the 1960s by American statesmen. This new direction became even more obvious and necessary as another theme of British national life asserted itself: decline. This theme had several aspects. First and foremost it meant economic and financial malaise. A trading gap, between goods sold abroad and those imported, continued to indicate that British industry was not paying its way in the national economy. Throughout the 1960s Conservative and Labour Party governments alternated between the implementation and relaxation of wage controls—a "stop and go" policy—that tried to keep domestic consumption from creating inflationary pressures. This instability in the domestic and international economy led to the devaluation of the pound sterling, another signal that the nation was having trouble paying its way. During the 1970s a rise in labor-union unrest, featuring strikes and demands for inflationary wage increases, supported the impression that Britain could not mount an independent role in foreign affairs.

The second feature of decline was the loss of traditional benchmarks of British prestige. Throughout the 1960s the African colonies achieved independence. The Commonwealth of Nations, an association of former members of the British empire, proved unable to deal with any controversial issue, such as the apartheid policy of South Africa, and ended up a vehicle for state visits and sporting events. By 1969 violence erupted in Northern Ireland, forcing the Labour government to suspend local government and impose direct military rule from London—a sign that even ancient colonial issues could not be settled. These instances of decline found confirmation in scholarly analyses. Titles such as Correlli Barnett's *The Collapse of British Power* (1972), Paul M. Kennedy's *The Rise and Fall of the Great Powers: Economic Change and Military Conflict from 1500 to 2000* (1987), and many social and economic histories containing chapters such as "The British Economy and its Problems" and "The Beginnings of Decline" chronicled the loss of British influence on the global stage. The spy scandals of the 1950s, which in turn inspired a variety of fictional and nonfictional accounts of

the failures of British intelligence operations, created the impression that Britain was a less-than-trustworthy ally. Even the eventual entry of Great Britain into the EEC (1973), however necessary, left a trail of partisan bickering and disruption. This struggle over "Euro-skepticism" culminated in 1990 when Conservative Party leadership forced the resignation of Prime Minister Margaret Thatcher, herself a critic of the EEC and a staunch supporter of the special relationship with the United States.

Thatcher had cultivated a strong and admiring relationship with President Ronald Reagan. For one moment it appeared that their good rapport would give the special relationship a concrete and positive meaning. In 1983 the military government of Argentina invaded British South Atlantic possessions in the Falkland Islands. The Thatcher government, with bipartisan and public support, dispatched a task force, and war followed. When the Argentines resisted U.S. efforts at mediation, the Reagan government agreed to veto any effort at the United Nations Security Council to condemn the British military action. The outcome of the conflict, resulting in the British recovery of the islands and the resignation of the Argentine government, appeared to confirm a close-working relationship between London and Washington.

In contrast to the cautious evenhandedness of U.S. diplomacy, the American people gave the British cause near-unanimous approval. Moreover, the nations of both the Commonwealth and the EEC initiated boycotts of Argentinean goods. For a British nation that had remained the staunchest European ally of the United States, including consistent support for its war in Vietnam, this was the least that might have been expected. Arguably the European connection proved more supportive to Britain than its special relationship with the United States. The response of the Reagan administration reflected the U.S. role as a superpower, concerned with matters affecting world order rather than the narrow concerns of a once-upon-a-time ally. When leading politicians of the Conservatives joined to force Thatcher from the premiership, they gave a clear indication that members of her own party agreed with this assessment.

The special relationship also fell prey to a shift in cultural perceptions. During World War II the American media had celebrated Britain for its traditions of free institutions, representative government, and respect for the individual. In the postwar world, writers on the English national decline tied its faltering economy to divisions of social class, particularly to an educational system that privileged traditional humanistic studies over technical ones and gave advantages to upper-middle-class children over working-class children of equal ability. Books such as Walter Allen's *Tradition and Dream: The English and American Novel from the Twenties to Our Time* (1964), Daniel Snowman's *Britain and America: An Interpretation of Their Culture, 1945–1975* (1977), and Jane Walmsley's *Brit-think, Ameri-think: A Transatlantic Survival Guide* (1986) set traditional, cozy, and deferential British values against optimistic, aggressive, and egalitarian American attitudes. Within U.S. higher education the teaching of British history was no longer guaranteed to be part of the curriculum; English literature departments expanded their offerings to emphasize a greater variety of American writers and even included concentrations on creative writing and moviemaking. As the U.S. outlook became increasingly global and multicultural, the special presence of a British heritage shrunk and retreated. By the end of the century it was across the English Channel toward Europe that Britain looked to define its role on the world stage.

–ROBERT MCJIMSEY, COLORADO COLLEGE

References

Walter Allen, *Tradition and Dream: The English and American Novel from the Twenties to Our Time* (London: Phoenix House, 1964);

Correlli Barnett, *The Collapse of British Power* (London: Eyre Methuen, 1972; New York: Morrow, 1972);

Winston Churchill, *The Sinews of Peace: Post-war Speeches,* edited by Randolph S. Churchill (London: Cassell, 1948);

Percy Cradock, *In Pursuit of British Interests: Reflections on Foreign Policy under Margaret Thatcher and John Major* (London: Murray, 1997);

Peter Jenkins, *Mrs. Thatcher's Revolution: The Ending of the Socialist Era* (London: Cape, 1987);

Paul M. Kennedy, *The Rise and Fall of the Great Powers: Economic Change and Military Conflict from 1500 to 2000* (New York: Random House, 1987);

Alan Sked and Chris Cook, *Post-War Britain: A Political History* (Sussex, U.K.: Harvester Press, 1979; New York: Barnes & Noble, 1979);

Daniel Snowman, *Britain and America: An Interpretation of Their Culture, 1945–1975* (New York: New York University Press, 1977);

Jane Walmsley, *Brit-think, Ameri-think: A Transatlantic Survival Guide,* cartoons by Gray Jolliffe (London: Harrap, 1986).

ANGLO-AMERICAN
RELATIONS

ANTINUCLEAR MOVEMENT

Did antinuclear-weapons protests affect Western arms-control policy?

Viewpoint: Yes. The antinuclear movements contributed to Western security by encouraging moderation in the negotiating strategies of the superpowers.

Viewpoint: No. The antinuclear protests were ineffective in altering the policies of the nuclear powers.

Nuclear weapons defined the Cold War in an historically significant way. For the first time competing nations had at their disposal the means to annihilate each other. As the nuclear-arms race between the superpowers intensified, it became an ever more important consideration in international politics, as alarmed populations and concerned leaders began to question whether increases in their nations' nuclear arsenals, or even the existence of nuclear arsenals at all, contributed or threatened world peace and the future of civilization. In the free societies of the West, these concerns often took the form of movements that demonstrated opposition to nuclear weapons through protests and strong government lobbying.

How did this opposition affect a Cold War strategic policy and international security? It may be argued that popular concerns about the devastating effects of nuclear warfare successfully persuaded governments to pursue more moderate foreign policies, which both averted international crises that could have resulted in nuclear war and markedly reduced superpower tension in general. On the other hand, scholars question the extent to which antinuclear protests contributed either to the aversion of crises or to reductions in superpower tension. Some believe that the antinuclear movement actually compromised international security by undermining the ability of Western governments to rely on the deterrent power of nuclear weapons.

Viewpoint:
Yes. The antinuclear movements contributed to Western security by encouraging moderation in the negotiating strategies of the superpowers.

Nuclear weapons are terrifying in their destructive power. During the Cold War most Western leaders shared Winston Churchill's belief that a "balance of terror" could preserve the peace and Western security. Millions of others around the world doubted the balance of terror could hold forever, and they engaged in various forms of protest against the further development and buildup of nuclear arms, as well as for nuclear-arms control and disarmament. Many conservative commentators feared the peace movements in Western Europe and the United States would undermine Western security, while academic social scientists largely ignored the protest campaigns as unlikely to make much difference either way. Both views were incorrect: antinuclear-weapon protest had a modest influence that added to security and stability.

ES GIBT NUR EINE NULL-LÖSUNG:

Advocacy for nuclear restraint was quite diverse. Because there is no way to distinguish the influence of different strands of protest activity, antinuclear-weapons activism must be assessed in its entirety. Such activism involved both mass-based, grassroots campaigns and advocacy by some of society's elites, especially many nuclear scientists. Most protest campaigns encompassed both more radical and moderate groups and individuals, and their activities tended to be complementary. Protest activity also waxed and waned over time. It peaked in the late 1950s, in response to the radioactive fallout being produced by atmospheric nuclear testing, and in the early 1980s, in response to the heating up of the Cold War, the collapse of existing arms control talks (especially the Strategic Arms Limitation Talks [SALT]), and various signals of an increased emphasis on nuclear war-fighting strategies. Protest levels also varied by country. Great Britain experienced perhaps the greatest average level of activism. The United States and Italy witnessed an intermediate amount of pro-

test, while France saw relatively limited protest. West Germany and the Netherlands were also the sites of extensive protest in the 1970s and 1980s, but not as much before then.

Before asking whether this activism was helpful or harmful to security, the obvious first question is whether it had any influence at all. Despite the neglect of protest campaigns in the mainstream international relations literature, many studies since the late 1980s have shown that antinuclear-weapons activism did have an impact. The key is not to view impact simply in terms of success versus failure. The major protest campaigns manifestly did not succeed in accomplishing their most cherished stated objectives. There was never an agreement to "ban the bomb"; the United States and the Soviet Union did not negotiate a nuclear freeze; and it took until after the Cold War was over to negotiate a comprehensive nuclear test ban. Failure to achieve their maximum objectives, however, does not mean such campaigns lacked any influence whatsoever. In fact, at several points they managed to affect policy in directions favorable to arms control.

The most sophisticated research in this area considers the ability of the movement to have influence to be a function of different countries' domestic structures. Both the possible access points to the political system and the chances of sustaining policy change have been shown to vary with prevailing institutional arrangements, political culture, and domestic divisions. In the United States, activist campaigns gained influence through generating electoral pressure, changing the balance among elite coalitions, or providing new ideas, depending on the time period in question. In Western European countries with strong party discipline, changing party platforms also proved an avenue for public influence.

Activism probably had its greatest influence on setting the agenda. Advocacy campaigns helped convince reluctant U.S. administrations to put certain specific items on the negotiating agenda with the Soviet Union, such as a nuclear test ban in the late 1950s and limits on anti-ballistic missiles (ABMs) in the late 1960s. At other times, especially the 1980s, protest put arms control in general on the agenda, pushing the United States to enter new talks at times when it wanted to engage in only a military buildup instead. On rare occasions opponents of existing U.S. policy were even a source of specific arms-control proposals that the United States agreed to place on the table and were eventually accepted. The most notable case was the "zero option" for intermediate-range nuclear forces, which was initially promoted by West European party activists and later became the basis for the INF (Intermediate-Range Nuclear Forces) Treaty.

In addition to influencing the agenda, activism sometimes had a profound effect on Western rhetoric and declaratory posture. Again, the most dramatic case occurred in the early 1980s. The Reagan administration entered office with a policy of talking openly about possible scenarios for fighting a nuclear war. Protest against contemplating such a possibility was so extensive that the administration completely clamped down on such rhetoric, and President Ronald Reagan even revealed himself to be a closet nuclear abolitionist. By 1985 he had made a joint statement with Soviet general secretary Mikhail S. Gorbachev that "a nuclear war cannot be won and must never be fought."

Although activists generally found it difficult to influence the actual course of arms-control negotiations, they did contribute to the successful ratification of some arms-control treaties by the U.S. Senate once the negotiations were finished. Protest efforts also sometimes helped limit certain planned weapons developments or deployments by Western countries. Domestic opposition played an important role in getting the United States to agree to limits on ABM systems, as well as to scale back the MX missile program and efforts to develop an anti-satellite weapon.

Interestingly, there is now considerable evidence that some Western peace and arms-control advocates also influenced Soviet policy. The centralized, authoritarian Soviet system made access difficult, but when arms-race opponents could gain the ear of a potentially sympathetic Soviet leader, such as Nikita S. Khrushchev or Gorbachev, the resulting policy change could be swift and far-reaching. Communist control of Soviet society made genuine grassroots peace activism largely impossible until the glasnost of the late 1980s (at which point a fairly significant campaign against nuclear testing arose), but a transnational network linking Western arms-control advocates to sympathetic Soviet scientists did enjoy influence on several issues.

Western advocacy proved most important as a source of new ideas in the Soviet system. Most importantly, much of Gorbachev's "new thinking" has been attributed to Western ideas transmitted through transnational channels. Transnational-advocacy networks also helped coordinate initiatives between Soviet and Western arms-control supporters, making it easier for each to overcome potential domestic opposition. Finally, activism on behalf of nuclear disarmament in the West reinforced certain norms in Soviet society that were favorable to such a course.

In sum, antinuclear-weapons activism at several points helped place the idea of initiating new arms-control talks onto the agenda, often shaping the topics and proposals that would be the focus of such talks; helped limit potential new weapons developments; and strengthened the rhetoric and norms in favor of nuclear abolition. At the simplest level, transnational networks of arms-control advocates often provided a means of communication between the Western and Soviet sides, and a forum for preliminary discussion of new ideas, at times when communication through official channels was effectively blocked.

The next question is whether this activism was a good thing or a bad thing. Many commentators during the Cold War argued that peace movements were harmful to Western security, because they imposed limits on Western defense efforts while placing no such restrictions on Soviet military power. Some, including presidents Dwight D. Eisenhower and Reagan, suggested the protest campaigns were either controlled by Moscow or unwittingly allowed themselves to be manipulated by the Soviets.

There is no denying that the Soviet Union sought to take advantage of Western peace movements, and there were some organizations, especially in the 1940s and 1950s, that were under communist control. The existence of Soviet efforts to manipulate the peace movement, however, does not prove the success of such efforts. In fact, most of the leading advocacy groups chose to keep their distance from communist-dominated peace groups and their platforms. They sought to make clear that their opposition to the nuclear-arms race applied to both sides. The nuclear-freeze campaign was especially explicit about this, always referring to the freeze as a bilateral proposal.

Moreover, the Western grassroots opinion that the Soviets occasionally sought to mobilize rarely responded to Soviet overtures that would be one-sided in their effects. For example, in the early 1980s the Soviets called for a freeze that would apply just to Euromissile deployments, which would have had the effect of keeping existing Soviet SS-20s in place while preventing planned NATO deployments of new INF systems. U.S. freeze advocates rejected the proposal because it would not apply to other nuclear systems, while Western European activists expressed their preference for proposals that would also remove the Soviet SS-20s.

The Soviets, however, could generate a positive response when they took concrete, costly actions that showed a willingness to make sacrifices in order to achieve cooperation. Two unilateral moratoria on nuclear testing, begun in 1958 and 1985, respectively, simultaneously reflected and stimulated Western activist efforts to ensure a favorable U.S. response (with greater success in the earlier case than the latter). In short, while blatant efforts at manipulation were largely ineffective, when the Soviets showed credible evidence of a genuine interest in mutual-arms control, Western arms-control-advocacy efforts were sometimes required to get the United States to join the Soviets in new talks—the agenda-setting influence noted above.

Even if activism against nuclear weapons did not generally have negative consequences, can one conclude that it actually had positive effects? In three distinct ways it did. First, activist influence sometimes produced a valuable note of reassurance. Security specialists, such as Janice Gross Stein, increasingly believe that, unless they are accompanied by reassurance measures, deterrence strategies can be dangerous and may actually provoke escalation rather than deter challenges. Activism sometimes helped produce reassurance in both directions. On the one hand, Western domestic politics often tended to pro-

duce rhetoric and actions designed to emphasize political leaders' hard-line, anticommunist credentials, creating an emphasis on deterrence with no leavening of reassurance. At some points when such policies were helping feed a potentially dangerous heating up of the Cold War, protest helped get Western leaders to ease back on their tough talk and show an interest in controlling the arms race.

This ability to moderate U.S. policy in particular, when it had moved toward the hard-line end of the spectrum, may have been most important in the early 1980s. By 1983 the *Komitet gosudarstvennoy bezopasnosti* (Committee for State Security or KGB) became convinced that the Reagan administration really was planning a nuclear first strike, and if peace-movement pressure had not convinced the administration to declare its desire to avoid nuclear war and to get arms control back on track, this mistaken impression may have lasted long enough to precipitate a dangerous Soviet miscalculation.

On the other hand, Soviet behavior also frequently alarmed the West. At times the transnational activist contacts helped convince the Soviets to take certain gestures—such as suspending nuclear tests, or allowing inspection of a radar site near Krasnoyarsk that was believed to be a violation of the ABM Treaty—that helped reassure Western governments. Finally, and most simply, protest was clearly responsible for placing on the agenda, and then maintaining the pressure to reach an agreement on, the issue—nuclear testing—that led to the first-ever nuclear-arms control treaty. The Limited Test Ban Treaty of 1963, though modest in its concrete effects, was symbolically important in showing both sides that mutually acceptable cooperation was possible, and this agreement almost certainly would not have arisen if it were not for widespread popular protest.

A second way in which activism contributed to peace and stability was by helping restrain deployment of weapons systems that had the potential to be destabilizing. Domestic U.S. opposition to ABM systems in the late 1960s and 1970s contributed significantly to the Nixon administration's decision to accept their mutual limitation in the ABM Treaty. This treaty helped prevent a competition in defensive and offensive weapons that could have reduced both sides' confidence in their second-strike capabilities. In the 1980s protest against the ten-warhead MX missile led Congress to cap deployment at fifty, a number too low to give the United States a theoretical first-strike capability. Both by getting the two sides to make useful signals of reassurance and by helping limit certain potentially destabilizing weapons developments, activism enhanced international stability. By contributing to actions and outcomes that reduced the probability of nuclear war, protest activity was clearly advancing Western security.

The third contribution to security is more speculative and is based on certain findings in bargaining studies. Several sympathetic analysts, for example David Cortright in *Peace Works: The Citizen's Role in Ending the Cold War* (1993), have argued that Western peace and human-rights groups helped bring about the end of the Cold War. They point to transnational contacts that supported dissidents in Eastern Europe and to pressures on North Atlantic Treaty Organization (NATO) governments that made arms control possible. Both arguments are plausible, but there is also a third way in which activism may have contributed to the end of the Cold War—by leading to policy shifts that produced an intermediate, compromise bargaining strategy between the preferred peace-movement approach and the previous hard-line government approach. Most studies of bargaining in international crises or conflicts have concluded that the best approach is a mix of coercive and accommodative gestures, including a strong emphasis on reciprocity. Such a "firm but fair" strategy signals both resolve not to yield and a willingness to recognize the other side's interests. Empirical research shows such an approach is better at avoiding war, while preserving one's core interests, than either a purely coercive or a conciliatory approach.

The Reagan administration entered office committed to a highly coercive "negotiating from strength" approach, in which it would seek leverage from a massive military buildup while offering no concessions to the Soviets. Evidence marshaled by bargaining studies suggests such a strategy was likely to fail and also increased the risk of war. Western peace movements forced an adjustment in the strategy, however. They got the administration to enter talks and express a willingness to compromise years earlier than it had originally planned, thus changing the Western bargaining posture from a purely coercive one to a mixed one that more closely resembled the firm but fair approach.

If this bargaining stance was indeed effective in helping bring about a favorable end of the Cold War for the West, this would be another way in which peace-movement influence contributed positively to Western security. The irony is that it would be a result of neither the peace movement nor its right-wing critics seeing their preferred policies enacted. Rather, the operation of democratic politics, by producing a compromise between the advocates of conciliatory and coercive approaches, may have led the West to inadvertently adopt an optimal bargaining strategy. An interesting counterfactual question is whether peace movement success in seeing its own proposals adopted would have led to even better results. The key point is that the influence that antinuclear-weapons activism exerted actually contributed to the peaceful course and resolution of the Cold War, and this result is one that both activists and their erstwhile critics surely are happy to live with.

–JEFFREY W. KNOPF, CENTER FOR
NONPROLIFERATION STUDIES,
MONTEREY INSTITUTE OF
INTERNATIONAL STUDIES

Viewpoint:
No. The antinuclear protests were ineffective in altering the policies of the nuclear powers.

As the development of nuclear arsenals became a more prominent feature in Cold War politics, many in the West came to believe that attempts by their own governments to gain an advantage in strategic weapons over the Soviet Union represented the greatest threat to peace and stability. Beginning in the early 1960s, and becoming especially pronounced in the 1980s, many concerned citizens responded to the threat of nuclear annihilation with mass protests calling for the reduction and even elimination of their countries' nuclear arsenals. Such protests, however, both were misguided and were potentially an agent of dangerous constraint on sound strategy and policy. The pressure and demands of the Western antinuclear movement, however, remained a largely irrelevant factor in strategic planning.

The most obvious reason the nuclear disarmament movement was not positive for international security and stability was its utter inability to change the minds of strategic thinkers or to slow, arrest, or reverse the growth of nuclear arsenals. No matter how many people marched in the streets, how many letters antinuclear activists wrote to politicians, and how much protestors turned their fear of a nuclear exchange into publicly expressed outrage, their efforts convinced none of the Western governments, which either had their own nuclear weapons or allowed those of other powers to be deployed on their soil, even once to change their policies on nuclear arsenals. In this sense the antinuclear movements remained far outside the political mainstream.

In a democracy, political radicalism never contributes much to government policy unless it can generate mainstream popular support or succeed in overthrowing the government and imposing its views on the country. The anti-

HOPES FOR PEACE

On 26 January 1977 newly elected U.S. president Jimmy Carter sent a letter to Soviet leader Leonid Brezhnev, stating the American foreign-policy position and his hopes for peaceful relations. Carter wrote:

Having assumed the position of President of the United States, I want to share with you my views about relations between our two countries. . . .

As I understand your highly important speech in Tula, the Soviet Union will not strive for superiority in arms, it will stand against such a conception, and that it will require only a defense which is strong enough to deter any potential enemy. The United States does not want anything less or more for itself either. Therefore, our two countries, with consistency and wisdom, should be able to avoid a new arms race. I declared to the American people that the elimination of all nuclear weapons is my firm goal. There are three areas in which progress can be made on the way to this goal. The most important first step must be the urgent achievement of an agreement on the second stage strategic weapons limitation, and also an agreement to move on in the direction of additional limitations and reductions in the sphere of strategic weapons. Moreover, I hope that we will soon be able to conclude a properly verifiable agreement on the universal banning of all nuclear tests, and that we also will strive to achieve more openness regarding the strategic policy of our countries. . . .

Nine days later, General Secretary Brezhnev responded:

I want on my own behalf and on the behalf of my colleagues in the leadership to congratulate you once more on your assumption of the position of the President of the United States. . . .

For objective reasons, at the present time the central sphere of relations between the USA and USSR really is to ensure cooperation between our two countries with the goal of stopping the arms race and of disarmament. Only in this way can the main task of our peoples, as well as that of all other peoples—elimination of the threat of war, first of all, of course, nuclear-missile war—be completed. As you also recognize, we have to finish the development of a new agreement on limitation of strategic offensive weapons without delays. We believe that this task is completely manageable. Because the main parameters of the agreement are, in fact, already determined on the basis of the agreement which was reached in Vladivostok. The successful conduct of this exclusively important and necessary affair to its conclusion would allow us to start hard work on more far-going measures in this area and, undoubtedly, would give a new impulse for a constructive development of Soviet-American relations in general. . . .

Source: *"The Carter-Brezhnev Letters, January-February 1977," CNN Cold War Historical Documents, Internet Web Page.*

nuclear movement never came remotely close to doing either. Commitment to nuclear deterrence was broadly represented across the political spectra of the major Western powers throughout the entire Cold War. Traditional parties of the Left in these countries—the Democrats in the United States, Labor in Great Britain, the French Socialists, or the German Social Democrats—as well as those of the Right, consistently supported the presence of nuclear weapons in their national arsenals. A Democratic president, Franklin D. Roosevelt, ordered the creation of the atomic bomb, and another Democratic president, Harry S Truman, authorized the only two wartime uses of it that the world has yet seen. The British Labor Party and West German Social Democrats willingly and happily signed agreements allowing for the deployment of the American Pershing II cruise missile, a major bugbear of the antinuclear movements in the 1980s, on their territory. Just as partisan politics had little to do with support for nuclear deterrence, neither did differences in strategic views. While proponents of both confrontational and relaxed relations with the Soviet Union found a home in parties to the right and left of center, none of the adherents to either of these divergent views seriously advocated the elimination of nuclear weapons.

Furthermore, American approaches to strategic-arms control, beginning in earnest with Dwight D. Eisenhower's "open skies" proposal of 1959–1960, followed over the next two decades by the Kennedy and Johnson administrations' initiatives on nuclear-testing bans and the Strategic Arms Limitation Talks (SALT) and other nuclear weapons agreements of the 1970s, preceded the beginnings of major domestic protests focused on nuclear disarmament. Revealingly, at the height of the protests in the early to mid 1980s, the Reagan administration actually ceased serious approaches to arms control after the Soviets rejected the president's "zero-zero" option to remove intermediate-range nuclear missiles from Europe in October 1981. Two years later, after Ronald Reagan implemented the Carter administration's agreements on the deployment of Pershing II cruise missiles in Western Europe and while the antinuclear protests reached their height both there and in the United States, the permanent arms-control talks in Geneva actually broke down when the Soviet delegation walked out in protest of the Pershing deployment. More interesting still, by the time the later Reagan, Bush, and Clinton administrations did conclude arms-control agreements with the Soviet Union/Russia, from the late 1980s on, the mass demonstrations of the Western antinuclear movements had already subsided.

The complete lack of strategic sense implicit in the antinuclear movements's demands allows

ANTINUCLEAR MOVEMENT

one to understand why they had so great an absence of impact on their countries' nuclear policies. Indeed, no sensible strategic planner could or did reach the conclusion that abandoning nuclear weapons or even freezing the growth of their nuclear arsenal in absolute terms would elicit similar measures or "good will" from Moscow. Despite the involvement of literally thousands of people from a wide range of backgrounds, political philosophies, and generations, few approached nuclear policy or even arms-control negotiations under the impression that the weakness of a non-negotiated arms reduction would command respect from Moscow. Indeed, it is now known that both superpowers looked for ways to get around almost every arms-control agreement they signed within a short time of their conclusion.

Why would a nation that many Western scholars identify with considerable justification as a "neo-feudal" state be amenable to anything but increasing its strength? Leonid Brezhnev, the Soviet leader at the height of the arms race, spoke enthusiastically about altering the global correlation of forces, while Nikita S. Khrushchev, his immediate predecessor, drafted a new program for the Soviet Communist Party in 1961 that in all seriousness announced the intention to overtake the United States by 1980. The fact that the Union of Soviet Socialist Republics (U.S.S.R.), like Imperial Russia before it, suffered tremendously from insecurity about its place in the world and even the stability of its own borders was highlighted for the Soviet government by the predication of its own rule on what amounted to a coup d'état sustained by the systematic murder of tens of millions of its own people. Weakness was no option for its leaders.

Even if strategic planners did believe that hardcore Kremlin leaders respected weakness, unilateral disarmament in the West would quite simply have left it dangerously exposed to Soviet superiority. When the USSR had pretensions to strategic-weapons superiority, as it did in the late 1950s in the shadow of the so-called "missile gap," it showed every sign of using it to improve its strategic position. In fact, Soviet commitment to arms control was only strong when Moscow needed it either to restrain Western strategic-weapons superiority (as it did in vain after the agreements governing the Pershing II deployments were made) or to promote an international environment favorable to the internal development of the USSR (as Khrushchev did by elaborating "peaceful coexistence" after the myth of his nuclear superiority had been revealed).

In addition to ignoring the fact that decades of history have proven that the only practical value of nuclear weapons in international politics is their coercive power, the antinuclear movement also failed to consider that any calculating hawk in Moscow or Washington would be forced to embrace his own death and the annihilation of his country in a nuclear war. Paradoxically the ability of both powers to remain competitive with each other depended on their possession of arsenals of weapons (conventional as well as nuclear) that could never be used. The competition in especially lethal nuclear weapons, furthermore, did much to keep a general state of peace since a major war spelled nuclear annihilation. In what was known as "the Cold War," after all, attempts to alter what Brezhnev had called the correlation of forces focused on peripheral issues that had only subtle strategic relevance, like whose influence predominated in Iran or what the complexion of the Guatemalan government was.

Perhaps the most significant fact that dismisses the view of antinuclear movements as something positive has only recently been revealed. Reagan administration defense secretary Caspar W. Weinberger recalls in his memoir, *Fighting for Peace: Seven Critical Years in the Pentagon* (1991), that it was suspicious indeed that Western European protestors could demonstrate at American military and diplomatic installations because Washington was deploying new missiles to defend them, while they never said a word or took even one step toward Soviet embassies and consulates at a time when Moscow was pointing missiles at them. It is now known from documentary evidence, together with memoirs and reflections from former Soviet officials, that the *Komitet gosudarstvennoy bezopasnosti* (Committee for State Security or KGB) funded the Western protest movements. It is not really known whether protest organizers knew the true source of the revenue, and it is almost certainly untrue that either they or the mass-popular support they generated were devoted communists, but the fact remains that Moscow believed funding antinuclear movements in the West would make a meaningful contribution to its strategic position. This situation was especially true in the 1980s, when the deployment of the Pershing II cruise missile and the prospect of a functional ballistic-missile-defense system underscored the Soviet Union's strategic inferiority.

Since the growing strategic imbalance was technological in nature, there was little else Moscow could do about it but try to disrupt the deployment of the new weapons. Its economic stagnation and oppressive police state left it woefully behind. A large portion of KGB covert operations in the 1970s and 1980s involved industrial espionage. The commercial transfer of technology in the trade deals of détente was an important reason why Moscow tried to preserve that relationship. The inability of the Soviets to do anything about the growing gap in strategic forces was especially true because of the Reagan administration's hard-line stance on arms control and its consistent refusal to give up the Strategic Defense Initiative (SDI) for concessions on other types of weapons. Shrewdly using the political liberties of the democratic West to remove its strategic advantage, though ultimately unsuccessful and a desperate measure in any event, was a brilliant way to approach an otherwise unsolvable problem.

–PAUL DU QUENOY, GEORGETOWN UNIVERSITY

References

Christopher Andrew and Oleg Gordievsky, *KGB: The Inside Story of Its Foreign Operations From Lenin to Gorbachev* (New York: HarperCollins, 1990);

David Cortright, *Peace Works: The Citizen's Role in Ending the Cold War* (Boulder, Colo.: Westview Press, 1993);

Matthew Evangelista, *Unarmed Forces: The Transnational Movement to End the Cold War* (Ithaca, N.Y.: Cornell University Press, 1999);

Thomas W. Graham, "The Politics of Failure: Strategic Nuclear Arms Control, Public Opinion, and Domestic Politics in the United States, 1945–1980," dissertation, Massachusetts Institute of Technology, 1989;

Jeffrey W. Knopf, "Domestic Politics, Citizen Activism, and U.S. Nuclear Arms Control Policy," dissertation, Stanford University, 1991;

Knopf, *Domestic Society and International Cooperation: The Impact of Protest on US Arms Control Policy* (Cambridge & New York: Cambridge University Press, 1998);

Walter LaFeber, *America, Russia, and the Cold War, 1945–1996,* eighth edition (New York: McGraw-Hill, 1997);

Thomas Risse-Kappen, "Public Opinion, Domestic Structure, and Foreign Policy in Liberal Democracies," *World Politics,* 43 (July 1991): 479–512;

Peter Schweizer, *Victory: The Reagan Administration's Secret Strategy That Hastened the Collapse of the Soviet Union* (New York: Atlantic Monthly Press, 1994);

Glenn H. Snyder and Paul Diesing, *Conflict Among Nations: Bargaining, Decision Making, and System Structure in International Crises* (Princeton: Princeton University Press, 1977);

Janice Gross Stein, "Deterrence and Reassurance," in *Behavior, Society, and Nuclear War,* edited by Philip E. Tetlock and others, volume 2 (New York: Oxford University Press, 1991), pp. 8–72;

Caspar W. Weinberger, *Fighting for Peace: Seven Critical Years in the Pentagon* (New York: Warner, 1991);

Lawrence S. Wittner, *The Struggle Against the Bomb,* volume 1: *One World or None: A History of the World Nuclear Disarmament Movement Through 1953* (Stanford, Cal.: Stanford University Press, 1993);

Wittner, *The Struggle Against the Bomb,* volume 2: *Resisting the Bomb: A History of the World Nuclear Disarmament Movement, 1954–1970* (Stanford, Cal.: Stanford University Press, 1997).

ANTINUCLEAR MOVEMENT

ANTIWAR MOVEMENT

Did the antiwar movement have a beneficial effect on U.S. policy toward Vietnam?

Viewpoint: Yes. Antiwar protesters changed domestic and foreign policy in a positive manner, and forced public officials to be more accountable.

Viewpoint: No. The antiwar movement undercut the government position on the Vietnam War and helped the North Vietnamese win the conflict.

U.S. military involvement in the Vietnam War (ended 1975) engendered domestic opposition of increasing size and ferocity. It was truly the first televised war; graphic images of Buddhist monks setting themselves on fire or of Vietcong irregulars attacking the American embassy in Saigon during the Tet Offensive (30 January–24 February 1968) helped consolidate antiwar sentiment, which was especially intense on college campuses. Large marches were staged in major cities and antiwar protesters burned draft cards and chanted "Ho, Ho, Ho, We Won't Go!" and "LBJ, LBJ, How Many Kids Did You Kill Today?" Students organized "sit-ins" on college campuses and occupied university buildings. There was violence, also. Extremist and revolutionary groups such as the Weathermen bombed college buildings (targeting laboratories or other structures in which military-funded research was done) and robbed banks to finance their activities. Following the invasion of Cambodia in 1970 protesting students were shot and killed by National Guard troops at Kent State University in Ohio (4 May) and at Jackson State College in Mississippi (15 May).

The antiwar movement had influence beyond the number of its followers, which remained small. In fact, solid majorities in Congress supported presidents Lyndon B. Johnson and Richard M. Nixon on the issue of U.S. involvement in Vietnam until nearly the end of the war and continued to appropriate funds for that intervention. There were three reasons, however, why the antiwar movement assumed importance greater than its dimensions. First, it went beyond criticizing a particular policy—U.S. military involvement in Vietnam— to raising fundamental questions about post–World War II containment and what it entailed; in this instance, the antiwar movement broke with the consensus on foreign policy that had prevailed since the late 1940s. Second, the movement also raised questions about the credibility and trustworthiness of American leaders and government (the term "credibility gap" was created to describe the lack of faith in Johnson's assurances that the United States was winning the Vietnam War), leading the media and public to adopt a more skeptical, even suspicious, attitude toward public officials. Third, antiwar protesters were part of a loose coalition of other 1960s protest movements, together called "the Movement," which challenged other American values. Although composed of different pedigrees, seriousness, appeal, and scope, with some groups promoting more audacious agendas than others, together they critiqued fundamental assumptions of the American way of life. Among their concerns were civil rights, women's liberation, gay rights, environmentalism, and the counterculture (fashion and drugs). The antiwar movement was invigorated by a membership largely composed of privileged, college-bound sons and daughters from the middle class, a fact not lost on its critics, who charged that its supporters were motivated mainly by the selfish desire to avoid the personal risks of having to fight for their country.

One unintended consequence of the antiwar movement was the Watergate break-in (1972), which resulted in the resignation of Nixon (9 August 1974). As the intensity of the antiwar protest grew, Nixon and advisers close to him began to suspect that the Soviet Union and Cuba were secretly funding some Movement activities, perhaps without the knowledge of their leaders and organizers. The Federal Bureau of Investigation (FBI) under J. Edgar Hoover was already involved in some spying on the leaders of the Movement, but Nixon wanted increased surveillance and also tried to involve the Central Intelligence Agency (CIA). Hoover and Richard M. Helms, the director of the CIA, objected and refused to cooperate. Nixon then decided to create the secret "Plumbers" unit, comprising Cuban émigrés who used to work for the CIA in the early 1960s when it was actively trying to destabilize the Castro regime in Cuba. Nixon turned to E. Howard Hunt, a retired CIA official who had supervised the Cuban operatives, to recruit some of his former charges. The Plumbers accomplished little in their campaign against the antiwar movement: they broke into the office of a psychiatrist—who had treated Daniel Ellsberg, a defense analyst who in 1971 leaked the *Pentagon Papers* to the press—and rummaged through Ellsberg's files hoping to find material to embarrass him. Then, in June 1972, they broke into headquarters of the Democratic National Committee (DNC) at the Watergate Building, bugging the office of DNC chairman Larry O'Brien and looking for evidence that foreign (probably Cuban) money was funding some Democratic Party activities. They were discovered by the night watchman and arrested. Nixon's press secretary, Ron Ziegler, described the break-in as a third rate burglary, but investigators soon traced the men to the Committee to Re-elect the President (CREEP), headed by former attorney general John N. Mitchell. Also implicated was Secretary of the Treasury Maurice H. Stans, who dispensed illegal campaign slush funds, and two of Nixon's closest advisers, White House chief of staff Harry R. Haldeman and domestic policy adviser John D. Ehrlichman.

Viewpoint:
Yes. Antiwar protesters changed domestic and foreign policy in a positive manner, and forced public officials to be more accountable.

In 1975 Saigon was captured by North Vietnam, ending a war that gripped the United States for nearly fifteen years. Although American troops had been withdrawn two years previously, the fall of Saigon encapsulated the failure of U.S. policy in Vietnam. For years the Vietnam War had been waged in the public domain. Occasionally, leaders sought to keep knowledge of the war restricted, but increasing casualties and the escalation of soldiers caught the attention of politicians, the media, and young Americans for whom the war was not simply waged in Pentagon conference meetings or on paper. These were the men who were expected to fight a conflict whose cause, nature, and resolution were unclear to them. Many understood that they were expected to defeat an insurgency, protect South Vietnamese democracy, and check international communist aggression, but the seeming perpetuity of the conflict produced doubt and eventually criticism of U.S. foreign policy in the region. In the early 1960s most U.S. citizens had favored involvement in Vietnam; as late as 1965, as antiwar protests gained momentum, most Americans polled were embarrassed by student conduct and continued to support the commit-

ment to the war. At the same time, however, the antiwar movement moved beyond college campuses and onto the streets of America. With some politicians and national figures openly challenging Johnson's policy, the protests now involved a larger audience that was critical of U.S. policies in Indochina.

It is difficult to assess whether the Vietnam protest movement shaped U.S. policy, especially on broader issues, in a positive manner, as the sole purpose of the movement was to end the war. Clearly, the antiwar movement and its public demonstrations raised questions about the resolve of the nation to pursue the conflict, perhaps hindering decision-making by political and military leaders. The protesters, however, put Vietnam at the forefront of the American political agenda; toppled the Johnson presidency, thus signaling the end of 1960s liberalism; and affected the Nixon administration. In the process young Americans demonstrated that they were a new political force in public life by demanding voting rights, which produced a constitutional amendment awarding the franchise to eighteen-year olds. The protest movement, however, left an ambiguous legacy whose impact on American politics cannot be ignored.

The antiwar movement was diverse, encompassing various classes, races, ethnic groups, and generations. Yet, any discussion of the Vietnam protesters must begin with the Baby Boomers who came of age in the 1960s, a time of political activism on college campuses. Following the

North Carolina sit-ins (February 1960), college students became more involved in political issues such as civil rights and university reform. The Civil Rights Movement, particularly the Freedom Rides (1961) and Freedom Summer (1964) inspired students to address college concerns such as in *loco parentis* (supervision by a school administration in the place of a parent) and campus-speech policies. Emboldened by the civil-rights spirit, students at institutions such as the University of California, Berkeley, used nonviolent protest tactics to reform campus policies. Not only did these activists credit the experiences of Student Nonviolent Coordinating Committee (SNCC) members for their accomplishments, but they drew upon that ethos to also challenge U.S. Vietnam policy. As campus demonstrations, such as the Free Speech Movement (1964), achieved their initial goals the activists were inspired to confront the Vietnam issue. Berkeley students marched upon the Oakland draft office within weeks after their victory over the university trustees. College students were at the forefront of the antiwar demonstrations, with institutions such as the University of Michigan holding teach-ins, modeled after the sit-ins.

The *Michigan Daily* reported that nearly three thousand students and faculty participated in these lectures, debates, and discussions. In April 1965 the first national antiwar demonstration was held at the National Mall in Washington, D.C., with civil-rights leaders such as Dr. Martin Luther King Jr., folk singers, and student activists participating.

For the Baby Boom generation the Vietnam War defined their lives, whether they supported U.S. policy or protested against it. It was the umbrella issue that united various constituencies on the political Left (including minorities, women, traditional liberals, and the New Left) and helped define the Right (with more blue-collar Americans supporting traditional conservative positions). This divide enabled rising conservatives such as Ronald Reagan to build new political coalitions and propel them into power and national prominence. The future president ran on a campaign of law and order, promising to stop the disorder at Berkeley, during the 1964 gubernatorial race in California. Antiwar activism and demonstration tactics, particularly at the Democratic National Convention in Chicago (1968), also contributed to the election of

National Guardsmen and students, following the shooting of Jeffrey Miller and other antiwar protesters at Kent State University on 4 May 1970

(John Filo)

ANTIWAR MOVEMENT

Richard M. Nixon, who won by a slim margin. Nixon could not avoid the growing criticism of U.S. involvement in Vietnam and promised during the campaign to bring the troops home—although he actually increased the number of soldiers in Southeast Asia and secretly launched a campaign against neutral Cambodia (1970).

The antiwar movement demonstrated the political power of young Americans. Nixon signed the Twenty-Sixth Amendment (1971) during his first administration, which reduced the voting age to eighteen years. Protesters' assertions of being young enough for military service but not old enough to vote had resonated. War demanded public sacrifice; the protesters believed that if they could be drafted to serve the nation, they should be able to influence national politics. Instead of vocalizing their demands from the streets, by 1972 they shaped policy with national leaders. While some argue that obtaining the franchise siphoned political activism, many young people enthusiastically entered into national politics, particularly in support of George S. McGovern's presidential campaign (1972).

The antiwar movement encompassed a wide spectrum of Americans. Although not officially associated with the movement, journalists were instrumental in sustaining antiwar sentiment. The publication of the *Pentagon Papers* (1971) seriously damaged U.S. involvement in the war. It exposed the secret war in Laos, deficiencies of the military, and the corruption of the South Vietnamese government. Published jointly in the *New York Times* and *Washington Post,* this collection of articles by Daniel Ellsberg publicized the confusion and ineptitude of the Kennedy and Johnson administrations. Moreover, they revealed how the government deceived the public throughout the 1960s. In the end, the *Pentagon Papers* did more to promote disapproval of the war than the antiwar activists did. As historian Terry H. Anderson notes in *The Sixties* (1999), after the publication of the Ellsberg articles, opinion polls revealed that only 15 percent of Americans supported the war and that more than 60 percent of the public thought that the war was "immoral." Publication of the *Papers* set the stage for journalism in the 1970s, which closely monitored national politics and eventually exposed the Watergate scandal.

Along with Watergate, the antiwar movement profoundly shaped American politics in the late twentieth century. Even before the Nixon scandal, Vietnam War protesters raised questions about government credibility. Their presence provoked media attention, but that scrutiny eventually was directed toward Johnson and Nixon and their handling of the war. The era of government trust and the rule of experts that signified the 1940s and 1950s was shattered in the late 1960s as the media and antiwar protesters exposed fallacies in national

policies. Watergate sealed public mistrust of political officials and a new period in politics emerged, in which Americans, like the antiwar protesters, believed less of what the politicians said and held them accountable for what they did.

–BRYAN ROMMEL-RUIZ, COLORADO COLLEGE

Viewpoint:
No. The antiwar movement undercut the government position on the Vietnam War and helped the North Vietnamese win the conflict.

Interpretations of the influence of the antiwar protest movement generate much heat with historians, especially those who came of age during the Vietnam War (ended 1975). College campuses were the focal point of the antiwar movement and the ground where the intellectual debate raged regarding the war. The movement had a profoundly negative effect on U.S. policy in relationship to Vietnam, by prolonging the conflict into a decade-long struggle that resulted in hundreds of thousands of combatant and civilian casualties, and afterwards the deaths of millions of innocent people throughout Southeast Asia.

Several background points are important to remember when considering the seeming paradox that an antiwar movement could actually result in the prolonging of a war. First, throughout the twentieth century the American concept of war focused on the mass application of force and matériel against the enemy, a mind-set that first began to evolve under Ulysses S. Grant in the final years of the American Civil War (1861–1865).

This strategy was coupled with a western democratic belief that war is an aberration from what should be a rational political process between nations. In other words, political intercourse and negotiations should be capable of solving any problem between rational nations; if it does not, then the full power of an industrial society should be applied against the opponent until he relents. Once the enemy has conceded, the normal process of peace and negotiations can be restored. This concept was markedly different from the Vietnamese perception, rooted in a communist doctrine that perceived war, politics, and peace as a continuum, in which war is not necessarily an aberration but instead yet one more path for the achievement of certain goals. Coupled with this attitude was the realization that mass, in terms of force and matériel, could not stand

SENATOR KENNEDY SPEAKS AGAINST THE WAR

Senator Edward M. Kennedy (D-Massachusetts) was a leading opponent of continued U.S. involvement in Vietnam. On 21 August 1968 he gave a speech at Holy Cross College in Worcester, Massachusetts, including a call for a halt in the bombing of North Vietnam:

This is a nation of confidence and compassion and high purpose. This is the only way we can live. All these are vital concerns. There is another. It is the war in Vietnam.

This war is the tragedy of our generation. Like most of you in the early years of our involvement, I hoped that we could help the South Vietnamese to help themselves. We hoped that a modest program of American advisors, equipment and aid would enable the Government of South Vietnam to build a nation and a government capable of attracting the support of its own people.

But those hopes are gone. They have foundered in miscalculation and self-deception; they have been stymied by the stubbornness of the foe, but above all, they have been buried by the incompetence and corruption of our South Vietnamese allies.

A Government that has consistently proved incapable or unwilling to meet the demands of its own people, a Government that has demanded ever more money, ever more American lives to be poured into the swamp of their failure. We, to our sorrow, have met almost every demand.

Almost 200,000 Americans have been killed or wounded, 25,000 have died, over a hundred billion of our tax dollars have been spent.

Here were the resources to have fulfilled the promise of American life. Here were the young men to have given leadership to a nation. Here were the energies and the labors of a Government of dedicated men. Here was progress to dream of and to work for and to hand down to our children.

Here was an America ready to give leadership to an entire world.

Old allies and new friends, former enemies and present adversaries, all might have looked at our country with warmth and respect and the knowledge that this is their model of the future. It was all here and now it is gone.

It is gone, that is, unless we now resolve to bring an end to this war, not five or 10 years from now, not after the expenditure of another hundred billion dollars and the lives of another 25,000 of our finest sons, but as quickly as it is physically possible to reach the essential agreement and extricate our men and our future from this bottomless pit.

Specifically, our Government should undertake these actions as soon as possible.

End unconditionally all bombing of North Vietnam.

Negotiate with Hanoi the mutual withdrawal from South Vietnam of all foreign forces both allied and North Vietnamese.

Accompany this withdrawal with whatever help we can give to the South Vietnamese in the building of a viable political, economic and legal structure that will not promptly collapse upon our departure.

To demonstrate to both Hanoi and Saigon the sincerity of our intentions by significantly decreasing this year the level of our military activity and the level of our military personnel in the South.

These steps would enable us to end our participation in this war with honor, having fulfilled our commitment to prevent a North Vietnamese military takeover of the South and having left the future of South Vietnam to the self-determination of the South Vietnamese people.

Source: Vital Speeches of the Day, *34 (15 October 1967 – 1 October 1968): 718.*

against the power of the U.S. military, and therefore victory must be achieved by other means.

Finally, there was the evolution of two different ways of thinking in terms of what could be called "the rules of war." Evolving out of eighteenth and nineteenth century western European traditions, the United States has tended to fight its wars in a manner that tried to limit the horrors.

Prisoners were to be treated humanely, civilians are noncombatants, women were not to be raped and children were not to be tortured, religious sites were to be respected and preserved—all of which were distinctions that could best be defined as conventional warfare.

Asian societies have rarely seen war in such a light. Japanese behavior during World War II

(1939–1945) is a clear example, as are the horrific acts of barbarism committed by North Korean forces in the 1950 invasion of South Korea. In Vietnam different wars would be fought by each side: the tragedy for U.S. forces being that the definitions they tried to maintain at the start of the conflict were impossible to keep when facing an enemy who fought outside the parameters as understood by the Americans.

Given these factors the paradigm was set for disaster when the United States initiated its escalation of involvement in Vietnam late in the summer of 1964 and went to a full scale intervention immediately after the election of Lyndon B. Johnson. From the beginning of the conflict the impact of the antiwar movement was negative.

Several crucial mistakes were made in the opening moves of the administration in its conduct of the war in Vietnam, all of which were in part a result of concern about public opinion and the small, but ever-increasing, antiwar movement. In an attempt to placate middle- and upper-middle-class society, draft deferments were automatically granted to anyone attending college. If the National Guard did not become a refuge, it was still rare for a college graduate to wind up as a "grunt" on the front line unless he volunteered to do so. Thus, the war was not fought by all of American society, who would then all have a stake in either seeing it through or stopping it before it started. This situation was unique in American history. The sons of Boston abolitionists and Southern planters died alongside one another in the Civil War (1861–1865); former slaves and sharecroppers fought in several conflicts; and Theodore Roosevelt Jr., the son of a former president, was one of the first men ashore at Utah Beach in the Normandy invasion (6 June 1944).

The system of military service designed for Vietnam seemed custom-made to divide the United States against itself and created, as well, an environment where it was socially "cool" to be part of the antiwar movement, while the burden of the conflict fell disproportionately on the working class and the poor. Antiwar protests rarely flourish in communities and schools where neighbors' sons and classmates are dying on the front lines. The irony is that as the antiwar movement gained strength the accusation was made by its leaders that the war was deliberately racist in its use of lower socio-economic groups as front-line troops, while the accusers were able to avoid service because they were primarily white middle- and upper-middle-class males.

The memory of this incongruity would linger, and President George Bush's decision to mobilize the National Guard and commit them to a combat role in Desert Storm (January 1991)

was, in large part, a political rather than a military decision to insure middle-class support for the effort. This move slammed shut the door of public acceptance of an antiwar movement and helped to create a unified front to see the war through to a speedy conclusion, something that never happened in 1965.

Concerned about American public opinion, the Johnson administration tried to fight a half-effort war while maintaining economic prosperity at home. Johnson hesitated, as well, to adapt the principle of mass application of force, in part out of fear of Chinese or Soviet intervention, but also to avoid arousing protest. The result was a half effort that increased the carnage to an unimaginable level. Rather than make a full commitment to force, which could very well have brought North Vietnam to its knees in a matter of weeks or months at most, the war dragged out for years, a slow bleeding that in the end became repulsive to the vast majority of Americans.

This decision was a result clearly calculated and designed by North Vietnamese leader Ho Chi Minh. Unable to win a direct-military conflict of massed attacks, what was sought instead was the eroding of the will of the United States to fight, a victory won not on the battlefield but through the political process . . . thus the realization of war, politics, and peace as a single entity to achieve a desired goal.

If, at any point in that conflict, but particularly in the first year of full scale commitment, North Vietnam had seen clearly a unified American war effort—a willingness to use the force necessary to achieve victory—the result would have been a collapse of the North Vietnamese incursion. Clear evidence to support this conclusion was the Christmas bombing campaign of 1972 when an unrelenting round-the-clock air offensive against Hanoi and Haiphong devastated the North Vietnamese air defense systems, leaving the capital and their primary port open to total annihilation if the United States had so desired.

The key point to consider is that the offensive was launched by Richard M. Nixon after the presidential elections of 1972 and was done in clear defiance of a concern about public opinion and the antiwar movement. The message clearly conveyed was that the offensive would continue, regardless of loss, regardless of protests, until the North Vietnamese negotiated a settlement and returned U.S. prisoners of war (POWs). If not, they would face total destruction. They chose negotiation, though in the long term even this acceptance was yet again undertaken with the realization that eventually American resolve would dissipate and the campaign of conquest of the South could continue, as it did in 1975.

The American antiwar movement clearly allied itself with the communists; many antiwar leaders openly declared their support of North Vietnam and hoped for eventual U.S. defeat. It is hard to imagine such open statements calling for the death of American troops if the soldiers had been middle-class and upper-class men.

This sentiment was turned against the U.S. military establishment with disastrous results. In their ignorance (or arrogance) many antiwar followers directly blamed drafted troops for what was happening, completely forgetting the fundamental point that in a free democracy the military must follow the orders of its civilian leaders. The vitriolic campaign of abuse heaped upon returning combat veterans is unforgivable.

The antiwar movement was created, in part, by the presence of modern media, in particular television. Images became reality in terms of how society perceived the conflict. An antiwar protest, even if it was nothing more than a crowd of college students out on a lark or a mindless rampage, had media presence, while those who supported the effort and quietly went about their daily lives had no media appeal. A riot not filmed was a nonevent, but the images of the National Guard attempting to stop a campus riot would sear the national conscience.

Rarely was it noted that the images of the war in almost all cases were freely generated by the United States, while those from the North Vietnamese were highly scripted and controlled. The image of the execution of a Viet Cong terrorist by the police chief of Saigon became a damning statement, impossible to counter since there were no images of the thousands of executions committed by the North Vietnamese, including the torture and murder of countless innocent civilians. The heartbreaking photo of a child, burned by napalm, should always be remembered as an indictment against all war, but was used by the antiwar movement as a statement that the United States alone was the perpetrator of tragedy in the region. The use of these images became so chic that Hollywood actresses would travel to North Vietnam for photo opportunities with POWs, where they would then lecture the prisoners about their war crimes. Images of POWs who were tortured and murdered because they refused to cooperate were not available.

The final irony is that in a military sense the United States actually reached a turning point with the defeat of the communist Tet Offensive (30 January–24 February 1968), but the images, the outcry over casualties, and the wave of protests (which ignored the fact that North Vietnam launched the offensive during a holiday truce) broke the back of American political resolve even as military victory was achieved. Surviving leaders of the Vietcong movement in the South testified after the war that the offensive had been a complete disaster and many of them thought the war was lost.

Two months after Tet, Johnson announced his decision to withdraw from the 1968 presidential campaign and to initiate political negotiations to end the war. Everything afterward was but a winding down that North Vietnam knew would eventually lead to victory. Although North Vietnam knew that it could not win a war, what it had to do was create an environment where the United States would lose the war. The antiwar movement made sure that defeat was possible, while more than fifty thousand Americans died in vain.

–WILLIAM R. FORSTCHEN,
MONTREAT COLLEGE

References

Terry H. Anderson, *The Movement and the Sixties* (New York: Oxford University Press, 1996);

Gerard J. DeGroot, ed., *Student Protest: The Sixties and After* (New York: Addison Wesley Longman, 1998);

Todd Gitlin, *The Sixties: Years of Hope, Days of Rage* (Toronto & New York: Bantam, 1987);

Charles Kaiser, *1968 In America: Music, Politics, Chaos, Counterculture, and the Shaping of a Generation* (New York: Weidenfeld & Nicolson, 1988).

ARMS CONTROL

Were nuclear-arms-control negotiations beneficial to the United States?

Viewpoint: Yes. Nuclear-arms-control negotiations lowered the risk of nuclear war, facilitated open communications, and provided an alternate arena for superpower conflict.

Viewpoint: No. Arms-control talks had relatively little practical significance and did not lead to better superpower cooperation.

The United States has been engaged in arms-control projects since the Washington Naval Treaty (1922). Nuclear-arms limitation, however, has attracted most of the attention and effort—specifically the bilateral discussions with the Union of Soviet Socialist Republics (U.S.S.R.) during the Cold War. The symmetry of the respective nuclear arsenals and the level of their destructive powers made them a focal point for hopes that negotiations might limit the destructiveness of any future conflict, or at least reduce the risk of a war that Western experts conceded would be one of mutual annihilation.

Early efforts at nuclear-arms negotiations during the Eisenhower administration foundered on the absence of any mutual ground. The Cuban Missile Crisis (October 1962), however, frightened both the U.S. and Soviet governments sufficiently that they agreed first to install a "hot line" for real-time communication, then to ban atmospheric nuclear testing. Efforts to build on those gains during the Johnson/Brezhnev years resulted in the Nuclear Nonproliferation Treaty, designed to limit the spread of nuclear weapons, and the beginnings of discussions on stabilizing the number of nuclear missiles in service and prohibiting the development of missile defenses. Conventional arms-control wisdom at this period was that holding each other's populations hostage was the most likely guarantor of peace.

Richard M. Nixon and Henry Kissinger saw strategic-arms limitation as part of a general strategy of détente, and they pursued it assiduously in the early 1970s. The Anti-Ballistic Missile Treaty (1972) allowed only limited defense by either party. In the event the United States eschewed that option entirely, putting more faith in an interim Strategic Arms Limitation Treaty (SALT) that fixed the number of nuclear-delivery platforms.

Verification, always a sticking point in arms-control negotiations, was greatly facilitated in the 1970s and 1980s by the development of satellite reconnaissance. In passing, critics of the "militarization of space" are flogging a long-dead horse, but might take some comfort in that the initial militarization served the end of arms limitation. Politics ended the golden era of arms-control negotiations. A Soviet Union confident of its destiny took umbrage at President Jimmy Carter's attempts to link nuclear negotiations with human-rights proposals. Simultaneously a resurgent American conservatism saw Carter as giving away the store in return for empty promises. The Soviet invasion of Afghanistan (December 1979) ended any hope for U.S. approval of a second SALT treaty.

Believing any kind of negotiations were best undertaken from strength, President Ronald Reagan initially pursued a military buildup. Not until 1985 did he begin working with Soviet premier Mikhail Gorbachev from the mutually acceptable premise that a nuclear war was unwinnable and therefore must never be fought. The result between 1987 and 1991 was a series of talks and agreements that instead of merely limiting or capping numbers of nuclear weapons, actually rolled them back. That process continued after the fall of Gorbachev and the collapse of the U.S.S.R., to the point where by the end of the twentieth century some U.S. generals were discussing the possibility of complete nuclear disarmament, with only the capacity to manufacture nuclear weapons in an emergency being maintained. Sharply criticized by more cautious pundits, it nevertheless represents a viewpoint unthinkable in such circles for a half-century. Who knows? Stranger things have happened.

Viewpoint:
Yes. Nuclear-arms-control negotiations lowered the risk of nuclear war, facilitated open communications, and provided an alternate arena for superpower conflict.

Nuclear-arms control has been a central feature of U.S. foreign policy since the end of World War II. In part this was connected with the founding of the United Nations (UN), whose lesser members through the General Assembly from the beginning expressed their discomfort with the growing militarization of the postwar world. Arms control reflected as well the concern of Americans with how best to manage the nuclear weapons that had given such convincing proof of their power at Hiroshima (6 August 1945) and Nagasaki (9 August 1945). The first U.S. proposal to "ban the bomb" involved prohibiting any other country from developing one by putting nuclear technology under control of the UN. The Soviet Union saw this initiative as a deception. The Americans, after all, would retain their nuclear know-how, and Soviet premier Joseph Stalin was unwilling to abandon his own chance to make the Union of Soviet Socialist Republics (U.S.S.R.) a nuclear power in its own right.

The initial Soviet nuclear tests (1949) put formal arms-control measures into the deepest freeze for more than a decade of the Cold War. During that time, however, two other factors began influencing U.S. policy. One was the exponentially increasing power of nuclear weapons and the improving sophistication of their delivery systems. The resulting synergy made the proposed strategies for using them in a hypothetical conflict increasingly detached from reasonable political and military calculation. The emergence of "deterrence theory," the postulate that neither the United States nor the U.S.S.R. could win a nuclear war, but

both would definitely lose it, developed into the concept of "mutual assured destruction," better known by its acronym of MAD. The central assumption of MAD was that the best guarantee of peace in a bipolar thermonuclear environment was the capacity of both adversaries to annihilate each other beyond any reasonable doubt. The possible consequences of this doctrine, best expressed in the movie classic *Dr. Strangelove or: How I Learned to Stop Worrying and Love the Bomb* (1964), seemed increasingly probable as nuclear technology continued its advance in the 1960s.

Related to the prospect of nuclear annihilation was the increasing commitment among international-relations theorists on all points of the intellectual and ideological spectrum to the idea that dialogue, however limited, could be decisive initially in preventing accidents and averting misunderstandings, then by establishing a structure of communication that might prove an entering wedge for wider agreements. Few except the most committed Cold War hawks protested when the "hot line" was opened between Washington and Moscow in 1963. The Cuban Missile Crisis (October 1962) had provided a healthy reminder that "fog and friction" continued to shape everyday events even in a nuclear environment. The United States had received two messages within a few hours, both supposedly from Soviet premier Nikita S. Khrushchev, one conciliatory and one assertive, and administration officials had no way of determining immediately which was operative to what degree. On the other side of the line, when a U.S. aircraft crossed into Soviet space in the arctic, the Kremlin had to decide whether this was a routine miscalculation or the first step in a nuclear attack.

First tested in the Arab-Israeli War of 1967 (Six Days War), the hot line became such an everyday instrument of clarification that it came to be taken largely for granted by the time the Cold War ended. Similar in concept was the Incidents at Sea Agreement (1972). Aggressive warship captains and pilots were harassing each other to a point where a serious

Soviet foreign minister
Eduard Shevardnadze
(left) and U.S. secretary of
state George P. Shultz
meeting shortly before
the December 1987 sum-
mit in Washington, D.C.

(Diana Walker)

ARMS CONTROL

collision was only a matter of time. The agreement essentially reasserted long-standing "rules
of the road" for maritime navigation and provided a means of bringing "cowboys" of both
navies back into line without loss of face.

These and similar agreements, official or
customary, that emerged during the final
decades of the Cold War benefited the United
States in two ways. First and specifically, they
limited the possibility of a situation generated
by accident escalating into something else—
always a greater risk in an open society, where
even high levels of policy making were characterized by conflict, than in a relatively more
hierarchic, controlled one, such as the
U.S.S.R. As a status quo power, moreover, the
United States had the most to gain by anything that reinforced existing behaviors and
kept them within existing parameters. The
"behavioral" agreements, however, were by the
specificity that made them successful a corre-

sponding dead end in terms of such wider consequences as limiting, or even ratcheting
down, the nuclear-arms race, to say nothing of
encouraging more general détente.

Some basic agreements, especially on the
atmospheric testing of increasingly "dirty"
thermonuclear weapons, were concluded in
the early 1960s. Not, however, until the end of
the decade, with the United States increasingly
mired in Vietnam and the U.S.S.R. facing the
domestic consequences of waging long-term
total war from a limited economic base, were
the superpowers willing to engage systematically in the process of considering when
enough was too much and more was less.
Issues of technical verification and scientific
progress complicated even the basic question
of who stopped first in the missile race. The
Soviet Union, a closed society in principle, had
no intention of exposing its nuclear war-making capacities to its ideologically defined mor-

tal enemy. An America whose identity was strongly based on the postulate that anything that could be investigated, should be investigated, was correspondingly unlikely to abandon research in both offensive and defensive nuclear technologies. Developments in electronics, in miniaturization, and above all in information technology during the 1970s further increased both the practical and political difficulties of implementing arms control as opposed to discussing it, or using the concept as a weapon in the war for people's minds.

In the United States, and in a Europe growing concerned with the risks of nuclear proliferation, arms control became a virtual shibboleth in intellectual circles. The Soviet Union as well possessed its own "concerned scientists" whose cautious initiatives during the 1970s were more independent of their government than U.S. conservatives were willing to admit. It was nevertheless state action that developed increasingly precise formal agreements: the Limited Nuclear Test Ban Treaty (1963), the Nuclear Non-Proliferation Treaty (1968), and above all the Strategic Arms Limitation Treaty (1972) created an environment that was more stable and easily verified thanks to developments in space-based photography. Western anxieties in particular were alleviated by the widespread belief that technology in the form of satellite photographs could replace James Bond's real-life counterparts in an intelligence war whose human ramifications seemed increasingly unacceptable in the aftermath of the Vietnam War (ended 1975).

The nuclear-arms-control treaties benefited the United States as well by providing an alternate forum for conflict. Instead of grappling with each other over fundamental issues, the United States and U.S.S.R. could discuss the arcana of throw weight verification systems, and on-site inspections. To a significant degree the attitudes and behaviors developed in this arena extended to others as well. By the mid 1980s it was a grim joke among international-relations specialists that both superpowers were so bound by the formalities of conference procedures and similar midlevel negotiations that crises defused themselves before either side was in a diplomatic position to push the nuclear button.

That behavior, in turn, reflected the underlying attitude on both sides of the table that their best interests were not served by running high risks of all-out war. For the Soviets that premise was at bottom ideological, reflecting the Marxist-Leninist postulate that the triumph of communism was inevitable. The West matched this level only in the 1980s, with Ronald Reagan's equally firm premise that the

Soviet Union could not endure because of its internal contradictions. What the arms-control negotiations of previous years had done was provide a structured matrix for testing both hypotheses. In particular, there were not two Reagans, the "Bad Ron" who spoke of evil empires and the "Good Ron" of the Reykjavik summit (11–12 October 1986). Nor did Mikhail Gorbachev suddenly have an epiphany sometime in 1987 and decide to fold his country's nuclear hand. Both heads of state, rather, pursued a strategy of moving away from the arms race as the focus of Soviet-American relations—each confident in the ability of his own system to prevail once the parameters were shifted. The results are a matter of record, but it must not be forgotten that the American triumph in the Cold War pivoted on the arms-control negotiations, much in the same way a massive door turns on ball bearings.

–DENNIS SHOWALTER,
COLORADO COLLEGE

Viewpoint:
No. Arms-control talks had relatively little practical significance and did not lead to better superpower cooperation.

At times in the history of the Cold War, especially in its latter half, the United States pursued policies that were intended to improve its contentious relationship with the Soviet Union. In what eventually came to fall under the rubric of détente, one of these policies, the entry into strategic-arms-control negotiations, had critical importance. Unfortunately for proponents of détente, however, such talks had relatively little practical significance in military terms and proved their ultimate uselessness as a focus of superpower cooperation. Indeed, all too often such negotiations proved themselves to be tools of the sharp and contentious realist approach to international disputes that they were supposed to be smoothing over.

Before the generally ineffective nature of arms-control negotiations becomes clear, however, it is necessary to point out that in its early stages such diplomacy produced some mutually beneficial results. During the Kennedy and Johnson administrations some of the first successful efforts to ban the atmospheric testing and proliferation of nuclear weapons proved helpful for environmental reasons. Apart from these apparent victories, the success rate of arms-control negotiations has

START I: STRATEGIC ARMS REDUCTION TREATY (1991)

The United States of America and the Union of Soviet Socialist Republics, hereinafter referred to as the Parties,

Conscious that nuclear war would have devastating consequences for all humanity, that it cannot be won and must never be fought,

Convinced that the measures for the reduction and limitation of strategic offensive arms and the other obligations set forth in this Treaty will help to reduce the risk of outbreak of nuclear war and strengthen international peace and security,

Recognizing that the interests of the Parties and the interests of international security require the strengthening of strategic stability,

Mindful of their undertakings with regard to strategic offensive arms in Article VI of the Treaty on the Non-Proliferation of Nuclear Weapons of July 1, 1968; Article XI of the Treaty on the Limitation of Anti-Ballistic Missile Systems of May 26, 1972; and the Washington Summit Joint Statement of June 1, 1990,

Have agreed as follows:

ARTICLE I

Each Party shall reduce and limit its strategic offensive arms in accordance with the provisions of this Treaty, and shall carry out the other obligations set forth in this Treaty and its Annexes, Protocols, and Memorandum of Understanding.

ARTICLE II

1. Each Party shall reduce and limit its ICBMs and ICBM launchers, SLBMs and SLBM launchers, heavy bombers, ICBM warheads, SLBM warheads, and heavy bomber armaments, so that seven years after entry into force of this Treaty and thereafter, the aggregate numbers, as counted in accordance with Article III of this Treaty, do not exceed:

(a) 1600, for deployed ICBMs and their associated launchers, deployed SLBMs and their associated launchers, and deployed heavy bombers, including 154 for deployed heavy ICBMs and their associated launchers;

(b) 6000, for warheads attributed to deployed ICBMs, deployed SLBMs, and deployed heavy bombers, including:

(i) 4900, for warheads attributed to deployed ICBMs and deployed SLBMs;

(ii) 1100, for warheads attributed to deployed ICBMs on mobile launchers of ICBMs;

(iii) 1540, for warheads attributed to deployed heavy ICBMs.

2. Each Party shall implement the reductions pursuant to paragraph 1 of this Article in three phases, so that its strategic offensive arms do not exceed:

(a) by the end of the first phase, that is, no later than 36 months after entry into force of this Treaty, and thereafter, the following aggregate numbers:

(i) 2100, for deployed ICBMs and their associated launchers, deployed SLBMs and their associated launchers, and deployed heavy bombers;

(ii) 9150, for warheads attributed to deployed ICBMs, deployed SLBMs, and deployed heavy bombers;

(iii) 8050, for warheads attributed to deployed ICBMs and deployed SLBMs;

(b) by the end of the second phase, that is, no later than 60 months after entry into force of this Treaty, and thereafter, the following aggregate numbers:

(i) 1900, for deployed ICBMs and their associated launchers, deployed SLBMs and their associated launchers, and deployed heavy bombers;

(ii) 7950, for warheads attributed to deployed ICBMs, deployed SLBMs, and deployed heavy bombers;

(iii) 6750, for warheads attributed to deployed ICBMs and deployed SLBMs;

(c) by the end of the third phase, that is, no later than 84 months after entry into force of this Treaty: the aggregate numbers provided for in paragraph 1 of this Article.

3. Each Party shall limit the aggregate throw-weight of its deployed ICBMs and deployed SLBMs so that seven years after entry into force of this Treaty and thereafter such aggregate throw-weight does not exceed 3600 metric tons.

Source: Arms Control Implementation & Compliance, Internet Web Site.

been rather low. One of the earliest approaches, President Dwight D. Eisenhower's proposal for "open skies," a policy of opening superpower strategic-weapons arsenals to mutual aerial observation, failed to achieve any positive Soviet response largely because Moscow already knew that American U-2 spy planes were flying over its territory and could not do much about it, at least not until one was shot down over Soviet territory in May 1960. Coming on the heels of much bluster about the nuclear capabilities of the Union of Soviet Socialist Republics (U.S.S.R.), Soviet leader Nikita S. Khrushchev's indignation about the incident at the subsequent Paris summit meeting with Eisenhower only disguised what must have been a humiliating truth: that the United States already knew with some degree of certainty that the "bomber" and "missile gaps" that plagued American strategic planners in the 1950s were myths and that the Soviets were on the losing end of the arms race. "Open Skies," the first meaningful step toward strategic-arms control, could only have confirmed that reality to Khrushchev's embarrassment. In other words, realism with regard to the correlation of strategic forces prevailed over the ideological draw of arms control.

The next meaningful proposition of arms control after the conclusion of negotiations that led to the atmospheric testing ban of the mid 1960s, the initiatives of the Nixon administration, were even more thoroughly grounded in strategic realism than Khrushchev's response to Eisenhower's approach had been. Such measures as the first round of Strategic Arms Limitation Talks (SALT I) of 1971 (signed in 1972) and the Anti-Ballistic Missile (ABM) Treaty of 1972 acknowledged and offered to preserve the rough strategic-weapons parity that had developed between the superpowers by the late 1960s. Nixon's motivation for adding this dynamic to superpower relations is interesting. It is difficult to believe that an administration generally characterized (especially in its early stages) by bitter opposition to communism and Soviet expansionism, a field in which Nixon had few equals, would lend itself so easily to the recognition of Soviet strategic, and by implication political and diplomatic, parity that the viable alternative of an arms race would be ignored. Indeed, the ABM treaty prevented both countries from developing ground-based anti-ballistic-missile defense systems, even though American technological superiority made it absolutely clear that Washington stood by far the most to lose. At a time when the administration was enticing China into rapprochement and attempting to assert American economic hegemony throughout the Western camp, however, the palliative of a favorable arms-control agreement may have eased these unfavorable geopolitical transitions for the Soviet Union.

As the administration began to move more toward détente, arms control came to occupy a more important place in American foreign policy. Under the direction of National Security Adviser, and later Secretary of State, Henry Kissinger, arms control became a critical tool for the creation of a cooperative international system built on mutual understanding and the respect of mutual interests. The series of arms-control talks through the 1970s, culminating in the more comprehensive SALT II agreement of 1979, conceded at least a strategic parity, if not actual superiority, to the Soviet Union in exchange for what were expected to be incidences of Soviet geopolitical restraint.

Such détente-era concessions, among which arms-control issues were only one category, were ultimately proven foolish. While the United States willingly surrendered ground to the Soviet Union over strategic weapons and other areas, Moscow demonstrated little willingness to restrain itself internationally. Throughout the 1970s communism blossomed in the Third World, with Marxist revolutionary movements receiving military and economic aid directly from the Soviet Union and its close allies, notably Cuba. Notions that détente would also work some sort of positive effect on the Soviet Union were dashed by increasingly harsher stances on issues that had the attention of strong American domestic constituencies, such as the imprisonment of political dissidents in the U.S.S.R., its oppressive Jewish emigration policy, and its relentless persecution of other people of faith. Even the arms-control process itself was tainted by what many believed to be Soviet aggrandizement when the Carter administration discovered in early 1977 that Moscow would soon begin testing an advanced ballistic-missile-guidance system that would give the Soviets a first-strike capability against the U.S. nuclear arsenal. Although talks continued, Soviet provocations led the Carter administration to conduct a conventional-forces buildup, which intensified after the Soviet invasion of Afghanistan in December 1979, and to gain the permission of West European governments to deploy Pershing II cruise missiles on their territory in the near future. At the same time the Soviet record on humans rights and the apparent expansion of communism throughout the Third World effectively killed SALT II, which the U.S. Senate had refused to ratify. Far from being the international relations panacea that many had believed, arms control merely allowed the Soviets to embark on an unprecedented geopolitical démarche while Western diplomats thought they were negotiating in good faith.

It came as no surprise that the Reagan administration, while remaining extremely skeptical of the "benefits" of arms control, moved forward the Carter administration policy of increasing the size and power of the military. At the same time the Soviets demonstrated little commitment to meaningful arms control. A Reagan administration proposal to bar intermediate-range nuclear forces from central Europe, the "zero-zero" option of October 1981, went unanswered by Moscow. Indeed, until the Soviet Union began to go through serious political upheaval in the late 1980s, the Soviet approach to arms control was to try to reduce U.S. strategic pressure on the U.S.S.R., which commanded it to maintain catastrophically high defense spending.

This need became especially acute when Reagan announced in March 1983 that the United States would begin research and development for the Strategic Defense Initiative (SDI), a space-based anti-ballistic-missile defense system that the Soviet Union had by its own admission no hope of countering. When Mikhail Gorbachev came to power two years later, a principle aim of his foreign policy was to persuade the United States to abandon SDI. In fact, at both the Geneva summit of November 1985 and the Reykjavik summit of October 1986, Gorbachev predicated any further arms-control discussion on an American promise to stop the development of SDI. In other words, he only pursued strategic interests conceived from a realist's perspective, and he failed when Reagan refused to dump SDI for more arms control. Concessions that Gorbachev eventually made on both nuclear and conventional forces over the course of 1987 had much more to do with the absolute necessity of reducing Soviet military investment than with "good will" or fostering broad understanding between the superpowers.

It is quite revealing that even past proponents of arms-control negotiations, and their contemporary apologists, often acknowledge that the minutiae over which the superpowers agreed or disagreed was not in and of itself of tremendous efficacy or importance. What they argue, however, is that the structure of arms-control negotiations were valuable because they created a network of working and personal relationships, as well as a substantial diplomatic conduit that could have acted as a safeguard in the event of a crisis. By keeping the Soviets talking, in this view, arms-control talks proved their worth even if they never succeeded in freezing the nuclear-arms race or bringing about meaningful disarmament.

What proponents of this view fail to realize, however, is that superpower communications during the Cold War were always rather good. No matter how serious matters became, even during such tense and confrontational "flashpoints" as the Korean War (1950–1953) and the Cuban Missile Crisis (October 1962), formal and functioning diplomatic relations remained in place. At no point since President Franklin D. Roosevelt's diplomatic recognition of the Soviet Union in November 1933 have relations between Washington and Moscow ever broken off. Furthermore, when it was in the interests of both countries to do so, even rosy diplomatic relations were not impossible to bring about. World War II cooperation between Roosevelt and Joseph Stalin, the bloodiest dictator in history and eventually the greatest opponent of the United States, had firm foundations in mutual trust and even friendliness. During the Cold War there were abundant examples of close talks between the superpowers and mutual visits of their leaders that existed independently of, and often had no connection at all with, the various arms-control negotiations.

Furthermore, the arms-control talks of the 1970s were ultimately self-defeating for improved relations because the approach of the Soviet Union came to be widely and correctly perceived as fundamentally dishonest. Even as American officials hungered for a breakthrough that would ease superpower tensions, the talks in which they sought that goal were being undercut by unmistakable patterns of Soviet-led and supported communist aggression throughout the world and by veiled challenges even to what the American negotiators hoped to achieve in the talks themselves. Wherefore arms control, indeed?

–PAUL DU QUENOY,
GEORGETOWN UNIVERSITY

References

Coit D. Blacker, *Reluctant Warriors: The United States, the Soviet Union, and Arms Control* (New York: Freeman, 1987);

Zbigniew Brzezinski, *Power and Principle: Memoirs of the National Security Adviser, 1977–1981* (New York: Farrar, Straus & Giroux, 1983);

John Lewis Gaddis, *We Now Know: Rethinking Cold War History* (Oxford: Clarendon

Press, 1997; New York: Oxford University Press, 1997);

Raymond L. Garthoff, *Détente and Confrontation: American-Soviet Relations From Nixon to Reagan* (Washington, D.C.: Brookings Institution, 1985);

Garthoff, *The Great Transition: American-Soviet Relations and the End of the Cold War* (Washington, D.C.: Brookings Institution, 1994);

Henry Kissinger, *White House Years* (Boston: Little, Brown, 1979);

Kissinger, *Years of Renewal* (New York: Simon & Schuster, 1999);

Kissinger, *Years of Upheaval* (Boston: Little, Brown, 1982);

Richard Rhodes, *Dark Sun: The Making of the Hydrogen Bomb* (New York: Simon & Schuster, 1995);

Peter Schweizer, *Victory: The Reagan Administration's Secret Strategy That Hastened the Collapse of the Soviet Union* (New York: Atlantic Monthly Press, 1994);

Richard C. Thornton, *The Carter Years: Toward A New Global Order* (New York: Paragon House, 1991);

Thornton, *The Nixon-Kissinger Years: Reshaping America's Foreign Policy* (New York: Paragon House, 1989);

Cyrus R. Vance, *Hard Choices: Critical Years in America's Foreign Policy* (New York: Simon & Schuster, 1983).

ARMS CONTROL

CHINA POLICY

What motivated the United States to strengthen its relations with China in the 1970s?

Viewpoint: The Sino-American rapprochement was a deliberate and provocative constriction of U.S. global containment of the Soviet Union that increased superpower tensions.

Viewpoint: The Sino-American rapprochement was part of a U.S. attempt to reduce tensions with the communist world.

The increasing tensions between the People's Republic of China (PRC) and the Soviet Union in the 1960s created an intriguing opportunity for American diplomacy. To many strategic thinkers in the West it seemed possible that Beijing could be drawn out of its once close relationship with Moscow and possibly even become a Cold War ally of the United States.

The election of Richard M. Nixon to the presidency in 1968 made that possibility into a reality. Despite his well-established credentials as a firm opponent of communism and defender of Chiang Kai-shek's Chinese Nationalist forces in Taiwan, Nixon moved to take advantage of Chinese disenchantment with the Union of Soviet Socialist Republics (U.S.S.R.). Nixon's political instincts were supported by the historical studies of his national security adviser, Henry Kissinger, who concluded that multipolar international systems were more stable than bipolar ones. After exploratory talks through the Chinese diplomatic mission in Warsaw, Kissinger made a secret visit to Beijing in July 1971. The positive outcome of these talks led to Nixon's own visit to China in February 1972 and to the evolution of Sino-American rapprochement. On a broader diplomatic level, the Nixon administration forged trade relations with Beijing, formally recognized separatist Taiwan as Chinese territory, favored the eventual reunification of the island with the mainland, and pursued a mutually agreeable outcome of the Vietnam War (ended 1975).

The implications of these events for international politics were legion. It seemed likely that the Soviet Union's largest ally, and the world's most populous country, might abandon its solidarity with the communist world and become an ally of its chief adversary. Many scholars and policymakers have pondered how wise these developments truly were for keeping the peace between the superpowers.

Henry Kissinger and Zhou Enlai conversing informally before the July 1971 summit in China

(Chinese government photo)

Viewpoint:
The Sino-American rapprochement was a deliberate and provocative constriction of U.S. global containment of the Soviet Union that increased superpower tensions.

The maintenance of a balance of power between the superpowers helped bring the Cold War to a "soft landing." Indeed, Mikhail Gorbachev and his reformers would never have embarked on their bold course in the 1980s had the Soviet leadership not felt the external environment to be relatively secure. In pondering why the Cold War continued as long as it did, however, it seems that continual, but often misguided, efforts at equilibration on both sides in turn triggered destabilizing "security dilemmas" that drove the conflict forward.

Even the master "equilibrator," Henry Kissinger, was unable to bring about anything more than a transient stability. Anxious about the impact of the Vietnam fiasco on perceptions of American power, U.S. leaders jumped at the first opportunity to reestablish the balance of power. By playing the China card in the 1970s, however, the United States initiated a dangerous game for higher stakes than were ever on the table during the Vietnam War (ended 1975). The world was fortunate that this policy only helped to scuttle détente, but did not precipitate crises of the magnitude of the Cuban Missile Crisis (October 1962), though the potential for such an event existed.

In order to grasp the significance of the ultimately destabilizing role China played in the balance of power during the 1970s, it is necessary to understand the basic concept of the "security dilemma," which ultimately explains how international conflict may be driven at root by fear and not just by "evil." Indeed, fear has been recognized as a cause of war at least since Thucydides asserted that Spartan fears of the growing power of Athens was the primary cause of the Peloponnesian War (431–404 B.C.). Lacking a world-state to enforce rules, countries in conditions of "anarchy" are forced to adopt a "self-help" posture toward their own security. These measures, however, ranging from building arms to searching for alliance partners, may inadvertently cause other states to fear. They in turn react with similar measures, resulting in a spiral of dangerous behaviors, and often, ultimately, in war. Even Hans Morgenthau, who maintained that international politics was simply a naked struggle for power, appeared to recognize the pernicious effects of the security dilemma when he enjoined Americans not to encroach on the vital interests of competing powers. Thus, instability is likely to result when a state acts to alter the balance of power, perhaps with the intention to equilibrate, but often provocatively "overshooting" in practice.

From the beginning of the Nixon administration the eventual goal of extrication from Vietnam was recognized. It was felt, however, that the military withdrawal could not be seen as a capitulation, lest adversaries of the United States, particularly the Soviet Union, be emboldened. Therefore, while gradually withdrawing American soldiers from combat, Richard M. Nixon ordered punitive actions, such as the bombing of Hanoi and the mining of North Vietnamese harbors, to induce cooperation at the negotiating table. In addition to North Vietnamese negotiator Le Duc Tho's stubborn and utterly uncompromising diatribes, the confidence of U.S. leaders in American power was additionally shaped by their impression of turmoil at home. Kissinger reports in *The White House Years* (1979) that Nixon "inherited near civil-war conditions." Hindsight, of course, is twenty-twenty, but it seems clear in retrospect that fears concerning domestic stability were exaggerated—there was no "crisis of capitalism," and normalcy returned to domestic politics quickly after the Vietnam commitment had been liquidated. It is easy to see how such concerns, however, might have affected perceptions concerning the external environment, precipitating a desperate search to redress the "balance," even if that meant dealing with the perpetrators of the Chinese Cultural Revolution (1966–1976). Thus, U.S. foreign-policy elites took from Vietnam a deep and abiding fear that Americans would not stand up to the "real test" to come.

If American leaders sought to rankle the Soviets, they found the right place in focusing on East Asia. Playing the China card forced Soviet strategists seriously to consider the discomforting scenario of fighting a two-front war. Other states facing similarly precarious strategic circumstances had undertaken such awesome projects as building the Panama Canal (1904–1914), but also extreme and tragic measures as carrying out

the notorious Schlieffen Plan prior to World War I. Moreover, underlaying the difficult Soviet strategic problem in the East was their pathological fear of Asians, occasioned by the premodern conquest of Muscovy (1223) by Genghis Khan—that this brute had also conquered China proved no particular comfort.

Twentieth-century history reinforced a sense that the eastern possessions of Russia were extremely vulnerable, beginning with its humiliation at the hands of the Japanese in 1904–1905. Vladivostok was occupied by the Allies after World War I, and the Bolsheviks only succeeded in recapturing the East after a long and difficult civil war. During World War II Joseph Stalin was preoccupied with the possibility of war on two fronts. Various crack units in Siberia were not brought west to combat the Nazis until the most desperate moment—when they were employed to great effect in the Battle of Moscow in the terrible winter of 1941–1942. Not completely trusting of a deal struck with the Japanese, Stalin cultivated and supported the virulently anticommunist Chiang Kai-shek, hoping that the Chinese Nationalist leader could keep the Japanese busy. Such historical legacies left Soviet leaders acutely sensitive to changes in the East Asian balance of power.

The material basis for this vulnerability was plainly apparent. The southeastern half of Russia is not only extremely remote and underpopulated, but the major cities from Novosibirsk to Vladivostok lie strung out west to east along a railroad that runs along the Chinese border. These "outposts," lacking any kind of possibilities for drawing on strategic depth, excepting the scenario of sending partisans into the vast northern forests, appeared to be all but sitting ducks for Mao Tse-tung's hordes. Indeed, this most precarious supply line could not be protected given the Chinese superiority in numbers, no matter what the technological disparity between the armies. Edward N. Luttwak explains in an article in *China, the Soviet Union and the West: Strategic and Political Dimensions in the 1980s* (1982), that the Soviet military in Siberia and the Russian Far East was not prepared for heavy combat at the end of the 1960s: "Soviet field formations found themselves at the thinly stretched end of very long supply lines. Far from being in 'jump off' positions, many of the Soviet divisions would have had a hard time operating in any kind of combat regime." This real vulnerability helps to explain much subsequent Soviet behavior, for example, the speed and urgency with which Moscow turned to making nuclear threats after the March 1969 border clashes. According to Luttwak, "the Soviet ability to wage nonnuclear war (against China) was quite small." In failing to grasp the extreme nature of

Soviet insecurity in the East, successive U.S. administrations guaranteed a return to superpower mistrust and instability.

Kissinger's memoirs suggest that he began to consider the "China card" as the Sino-Soviet crisis was unfolding on the remote Ussuri River in March 1969. Meeting an "emotional" Soviet ambassador, Anatoly F. Dobrynin, after the first clash, in which thirty-one Soviet border troops were thought to have been killed, Kissinger says that he made every attempt to change the subject rather than listen to the ambassador's description of Chinese atrocities. Despite a consensus among academic experts, including Kenneth Lieberthal, Harry Gelman, and Harold Hinton, Kissinger maintains to the contrary that the Soviets had instigated the clashes. Thus, while the Chinese were still castigating Nixon as the "notorious god of war," Nixon and Kissinger shocked senior U.S. officials at a 14 August National Security Council (NSC) meeting when they announced that the United States would lean toward China during the present crisis. This position was shocking, of course, because not only did the Chinese appear to be the instigators of the border clashes, but Mao's neo-Stalinist Cultural Revolution had made the Kremlin appear rather moderate by contrast.

Largely as a result of the debacle in the East, Moscow began to move swiftly toward détente with the West, far in advance of the development of American ties with Beijing. Indeed, the specter of war with China was quite sufficient to make the Soviets eager to enter the arms-control process with the United States. Détente appeared to be in full gear as diplomats succeeded in negotiating the first ever limits on levels of strategic-nuclear weapons, called SALT I. Here, however, American policy went astray. Instead of careful assurances with regard to Soviet security, the Americans chose to press their advantage, brandishing the China card in a menacing fashion. Historian R. Craig Nation, in *Black Earth, Red Star: A History of Soviet Security Policy, 1917–1991* (1992), describes the psychological result for Moscow: "Nixon was officially received in the Chinese capital en route to the Moscow summit in February 1972. The result encouraged the Soviets' worst fears. On the very eve of the greatest achievements of the détente era Washington betrayed its spirit . . ."

It can also be demonstrated that Soviet anxiety vis-à-vis China during this period was extremely high. As reported by Nation, the number of Soviet army divisions east of the Ural Mountains thus increased between 1969 and 1973 from twenty-three to forty-five, with tactical aircraft increasing sixfold. As these changes generally occurred prior to serious American overtures to the Chinese, it seems that Chinese hostility alone was quite sufficient to bring about progress in arms controls and serious anxiety in Moscow. American diplomatic, and later military, overtures toward the People's Republic of China (PRC), therefore, had the effect of pouring profuse quantities of gasoline on a previously manageable blaze. The argument can be made that the enormous Soviet buildup on the Sino-Soviet border represented an expenditure of resources that would otherwise have gone into Eastern Europe. While this assertion is probably correct regarding the viability of the long-term Soviet economy, it is important to note that Soviet forces facing the North Atlantic Treaty Organization (NATO) did not decrease during this period; rather, the number of divisions increased from twenty-six to thirty-one.

Given the effect of Nixon's visit to China on the Soviets, it is hardly surprising that in the subsequent years a resurgence of superpower competition occurred in the developing world. During the crisis surrounding the Yom Kippur War (1973), Kissinger played the American hand well, but then, once again overplayed that hand, choosing to exclude the Soviets from the peace settlement altogether. Where moderation was required to maintain détente, Kissinger went for an outright American political victory. Having lost in an area that mattered, the Middle East, the Soviets turned to making mischief elsewhere in Africa. Thus, the Soviets airlifted Cuban combat troops to Angola in 1974–1975, then to Ethiopia in 1978. While these interventions had little real effect on the balance of power, the experience of watching Soviet "power projection" in action played into the pathology that American elites took from Vietnam—that the Soviets were seeking to take advantage of post-Vietnam weakness of the United States. This situation may even have been true to some extent, but Soviet adventures in Africa should not have created the anxiety that they did in Washington.

Having created mistrust by playing the China card at a particularly inopportune moment, American leaders sought to retaliate for aggressive Soviet moves in Africa by endeavoring to construct a functioning Sino-American alliance. The first steps were taken down this road in December 1975 when Kissinger and President Gerald R. Ford decided to permit the sale of a jet engine factory and two Cyber 72 computers with military applications to the Chinese. Apparently there were voices within the Carter administration that recognized that military links with the Chinese could be counterproductive, and thus Presidential Review Memorandum 24, which was leaked to the press in June 1977, observed: "Moscow would then be compelled to make a fundamental reassessment of its policies toward the U.S. . . . At some undefined point, Soviet perceptions of the threat of U.S.-Chinese military collaboration would stiffen the Soviet positions."

In dramatically accelerating Sino-American relations, President Jimmy Carter made a fundamental mistake. He raised the temperature of the superpower competition considerably by retaliating for Soviet moves on the geopolitical periphery (the Horn of Africa) with U.S. initiatives aimed at the Soviet security core. In May 1978 Carter's national security adviser, Zbigniew Brzezinski, traveled to Beijing, where it was widely reported that arms transfers were discussed. For Americans to appreciate the significance of such steps, one would have to imagine the Soviets selling high-tech weapons to a hostile, nuclear-capable Mexico that possessed many times the American population and claimed parts of U.S. territory that were inherently difficult to defend. When Carter announced full normalization of Sino-American ties in December 1978, Secretary of State Cyrus R. Vance was apparently appalled at the implications for the SALT talks.

Rather than stabilizing the balance of power in Asia, the new Sino-American alliance helped to precipitate two dangerous crises in this region at the close of the decade, which had the cumulative effect of destroying what was left of détente. Despite Washington's protests to the contrary, this alliance seemed to be at work during the Chinese punitive attack on Vietnam in 1979 that occurred just after Deng Xiaoping's return from a visit to the United States. If the Vietnamese had not succeeded in blunting China's initial thrust so effectively, one wonders how a wider Sino-Soviet confrontation, potentially enveloping even the United States, could have been avoided.

By 1979 China had already succeeded in purchasing Western antitank weapons and surface-to-air missiles. Negotiations were ongoing for the purchase of ninety Harrier jump-jets, with the option of building two hundred more under license. The visit of Secretary of Defense Harold Brown during the summer of 1979 caused further anxiety in Moscow. In October 1979 a Pentagon report leaked to the press advocated that Chinese and U.S. forces undertake joint military exercises. Thus, by the time of the invasion of Afghanistan, the Soviets could claim with some justification, according to Nation, that "The occupation of Afghanistan did not occasion détente's failure. It was, rather, the product of that failure."

In playing the China card, American leaders successfully tipped the global balance of power in their own favor. They sought this advantage largely out of the humiliation and insecurity that

flowed from the Vietnam quagmire, but in pursuing the policy they aggravated a Soviet pathology of insecurity regarding the defense of Russia's far-flung eastern possessions against the "yellow peril." In a classic security dilemma, the reckless pursuit of unilateral advantage decreased the security of all. The opening to China might have been accomplished in a more subtle manner. The greatest mistake was Carter's setting in motion the establishment of Sino-American military ties. Seduced by Brzezinski, he recklessly answered Soviet meddling on the periphery with a body-blow to the core of Soviet security, ensuring that Cold War crises would continue for at least another decade.

–LYLE J. GOLDSTEIN,
PRINCETON UNIVERSITY

**Viewpoint:
The Sino-American rapprochement was part of a U.S. attempt to reduce tensions with the communist world.**

Did the balancing of Soviet power by the United States through strengthened U.S.-China ties work to stabilize the international system in the 1990s? The answer is the opposite. The balance-of-power strategy improved U.S.-China relations, but worsened Sino-Soviet relations, and left the stability of U.S.-Soviet relations short-lived. By the early 1980s all three bilateral relations were snared in tensions, and the international system became rather fragile.

The 1962 Cuban Missile Crisis triggered U.S. policymakers' thinking of a new international system, where bilateral confrontation between the United States and Soviet Union could be ameliorated. President Richard M. Nixon and National Security Adviser Henry Kissinger envisioned a multipolar world, for which the two statesmen adopted the classic balance-of-power strategy. Realizing the absence of some key elements of balance-of-power among major European powers in the nineteenth century, they applied the U.S.-Soviet-Chinese strategic triangle. The main feature of this strategy was to establish better relations with China, which was a rival of the Soviet Union. Then, two goals were attempted: stabilize the international system and obtain leverage to manipulate the three-power relations.

After the People's Republic of China (PRC) was established in 1949, it had encountered resistance from the United States from Korea to Vietnam. The hostile relationship showed visible signs of change by the end of the

1960s when the United States initiated with some peace feelers, such as allowing bank credits for China. In 1969 more tangible and predominant concerns about a massive Soviet attack on China made the latter edge quietly toward a close security relationship with the United States. China simply could not afford a confrontation with both superpowers, and the border conflicts with the Soviets that year convinced China about its vulnerability and the necessity of military collaboration with the United States.

In December 1969 diplomats from the United States and China met publicly in Warsaw. In early 1971 the United States ended its restrictions on travel to China, and the U.S. Ping-Pong team made a high-profiled tour of the country. In June the United States partially removed trade restrictions on China, and in July, Kissinger made a secret and historical visit to Beijing. After the road was paved, Nixon met with Chairman Mao Tse-tung and Premier Zhou Enlai in China in February 1972. The meeting of the two adversaries set the stage for Nixon-Kissinger's multipolar world based on the U.S.-China-Soviet triangle.

Between 1972 and 1980 U.S.-China ties warmed up. In 1973 the two countries signed agreements on trade, liaison offices, debt settlements, and the exchange of journalists. In 1976 both sides agreed on the construction of agrochemical complexes in China and on the export of U.S. computers to China for both civilian and military purposes. In 1979 President Jimmy Carter normalized relations with China, and Deng Xiaoping visited the United States to consult on a range of economic and security issues. After Deng's return, China launched a military attack on Vietnam, now a Soviet ally and Chinese enemy. In January 1980, after the Soviet invasion of Afghanistan, U.S. Secretary of Defense Harold Brown visited China and elaborated U.S.-China military cooperation. U.S. intelligence monitoring stations were set up in China along the Soviet border. The United States timely utilized the strategic environment around the world and significantly improved U.S.-China relations. The result from managing U.S.-Soviet relations, however, was a short-lived success and a decisive backfire.

As the United States and China entered a cooperative relationship, the United States also turned to open broader economic and security agreements with the Soviet Union in order to smooth interactions. The idea led to a major grain deal in July 1972 and a trade pact in October. Between May 1972 and May 1974 the Americans and Soviets signed forty-one treaties and agreements. Among them was the Basic Principles of Relations, signed by Nixon and Leonid Brezhnev in May 1972, to prevent the development of situations that would pull their relations into serious danger, to do their utmost to avoid military escalation and the outbreak of nuclear war, and to exercise mutual restraint and settle differences peacefully. In the same month the two countries signed the Strategic Arms Limitation Talks (SALT I) treaty and the anti-ballistic missile (ABM) treaty. In June 1973 the superpowers signed an agreement on the prevention of nuclear war.

Thereafter, the U.S.-Soviet relations deteriorated. During the Yom Kippur War (1973–1974) the Soviet Union provided arms to Egypt and Syria to fight a U.S. ally, Israel. In 1975 the Soviet Union assisted Cuban military intervention in Angola. The two events not only estranged the superpower relationship but also sent the Third World into turmoil. The Soviet Union complained about the link made between congressional approval of U.S.-Soviet trade relations and Soviet permission on the increase in the emigration of Jews.

In 1976 the Soviet Union warned against U.S. intervention in the Lebanese civil war, and the United States criticized Soviet involvement in Somalia and Angola. In 1977 Carter launched his human-rights campaign against the Soviets, while Moscow criticized proposed U.S. changes in the 1974 SALT II agreements. Although the two countries managed to sign SALT II in June 1979, the Soviet army invaded Afghanistan in December. As a result SALT II was pulled out of Senate ratification and the United States imposed a grain embargo on the Soviet Union, as well as boycotted the 1980 Moscow Olympics.

If U.S. strategy meant to stabilize the international balance-of-power system, the balancing of Soviet power through improved U.S.-China relations actually worsened Sino-Soviet relations. The 1950 Sino-Soviet military alliance evolved into mutual criticism by the late 1950s and border conflicts by the late 1960s. In 1968 the Soviet army invaded Czechoslovakia, which alarmed China. By the so-called Brezhnev Doctrine the Soviet Union possessed the right to intervene militarily in other communist states that were not following communist dictates. Beijing began to see the Soviets as the largest security threat. In March 1969 China and the Soviet Union fought a bloody war, resulting in hundreds of fatalities, over the islands in the Ussuri River. Later that year the Soviets even threatened to conduct a "surgical strike" to wipe out Chinese nuclear capabilities. The two countries were on the verge of a larger war.

Between the 1969 Sino-Soviet conflicts and the 1972 U.S.-China summit, however, Sino-Soviet relations were mixed with goodwill policies. The Soviets endorsed the Chinese application to join the United Nations (UN) and the two countries signed agreements on trade, navigation, and border protocols. Still, Sino-Soviet hostility left the window open for Washington to approach Beijing for a common strategy against Moscow. In January 1972 the Soviets criticized Nixon's upcoming visit to China. As a result of U.S.-China strategic cooperation, Moscow virtually faced a scenario of possibly having to fight on both European and Asian fronts. Indeed, Moscow deployed more troops along the Chinese border by reducing its forces in Europe. Between 1972 and 1975 Sino-Soviet relations remained tense, whereas the United States maintained better relations with China and the Soviet Union, respectively. Yet, both Moscow and Beijing were aware of the U.S. "card-playing" strategy and tried to raise their own positions within the triangle.

The Sino-Soviet hostility intensified during the late 1970s and the trend was not necessarily in favor of U.S. interests. China worried about Soviet moves to fill the power vacuum left by the United States in Vietnam. In May 1978 China accused the Soviet Union of supporting Vietnamese regional expansionism and criticized Soviet-Cuban actions in Africa. In November 1978, Moscow and Hanoi signed a treaty to provide Soviet access to Vietnamese ports and military bases, renewing Chinese fears of encirclement. In the wake of the Vietnamese invasion of Cambodia, China attacked Vietnam in February 1979.

If the balance-of-power strategy played a mixed role in stabilizing the international system in the 1970s, it scored almost a total failure in the first half of the 1980s and then became irrelevant when the Cold War came to an end in the late 1980s. In 1979 the Soviets invaded Afghanistan and the Carter administration immediately instituted a series of sanctions in response, including a grain embargo and sharp cut of exports of advanced technology. When Ronald Reagan came into office in 1981, he developed a series of strategies against the Soviet threat, including the deployment of new long-range missiles and ordering full neutron-bomb production. In 1983 the Soviet Union shot down South Korean airliner KAL 007, continued to occupy Afghanistan, and consolidated its influence in Vietnam. The Reagan Doctrine was then used by the Reagan administration to support "freedom fighters" in Nicaragua, Angola, Afghanistan, and Cambodia. After the U.S. invasion of Grenada in October 1983, the Soviet Union walked out of the intermediate-range nuclear force (INF) negotiations with the United States, and shortly thereafter, suspended the Strategic Arms Reduction Treaty

(START). In March 1984 a U.S. aircraft carrier collided with a Soviet submarine, and later that year two U.S. warplanes provoked nervous responses from the Soviets.

Entering the 1980s the U.S.-China rapprochement also showed signs of strain, especially over the Taiwan issue. The Taiwan Relations Act (1979) already made the Chinese unhappy. The U.S.-China relationship then slipped off the track designed as the triangular balance of power. In 1981 the United States decided to sell the sophisticated FX fighter plane and other advanced weapons to Taiwan. In 1982, as a response to the U.S. pro-Taiwan policy and overall U.S.-Soviet-Chinese relations, Beijing announced its "independent foreign policy," which essentially called for better Sino-Soviet relations while maintaining cooperative relations with the United States. Deng told U.S. Secretary of State Alexander M. Haig Jr. that China would not "beg" for U.S. military assistance or sacrifice Chinese interest to satisfy U.S. demands on Taiwan. By the mid 1980s, the United States and China continued their high level visits and military collaboration. Nevertheless, there was a strong momentum within the top Chinese leadership to distance themselves from the United States and improve Sino-Soviet relations.

Although the renewed Sino-Soviet tie took a slow start in the early 1980s, it eventually geared toward a new pattern of cooperation. The two powers were adjusting their strategic thinking more in terms of bilateral relations than in the triangular context. In 1982 the border negotiations resumed and two years later economic adviser Ivan Arkhipov went to China, the most senior Soviet official to visit that country in ten years. Both sides signed agreements on trade, technical cooperation, and scientific exchanges.

Global politics and security opened a new chapter when Mikhail Gorbachev came to power in 1985. He started unprecedented political reforms at home and called for East-West cooperation. The original balance of power lost relevance even in U.S. strategic thinking. The Union of Soviet Socialist Republics (U.S.S.R.) and the United States held a series of fruitful summits, often with the Soviet initiatives. In 1987 the two countries signed an INF treaty to eliminate medium-range nuclear missiles. The United States cautiously watched and assessed the Soviet change, but finally became convinced by the shift of the Soviet policy toward peace. The Cold War gradually faded into history by the end of the decade.

At the same time, Sino-Soviet relations made substantial progress as the Soviets cut troops along the Chinese border, withdrew

THE SHANGHAI COMMUNIQUÉ

After the early 1972 meetings between President Richard M. Nixon and Chinese leaders, the United States and China issued a joint message on 27 February, outlining areas of agreement and disagreement.

During the visit, extensive, earnest and frank discussions were held between President Nixon and Premier Chou En-lai on the normalization of relations between the United States of America and the People's Republic of China, as well as on other matters of interest to both sides. In addition, Secretary of State William Rogers and Foreign Minister Chi Peng-fei held talks in the same spirit. . . .

There are essential differences between China and the United States in their social systems and foreign policies. However, the two sides agreed that countries, regardless of their social systems, should conduct their relations on the principles of respect for the sovereignty and territorial integrity of all states, non-aggression against other states, equality and mutual benefit, and peaceful coexistence. International disputes should be settled on this basis, without resorting to the use or threat of force. The United States and the People's Republic of China are prepared to apply these principles to their mutual relations.

With these principles of international relations in mind the two sides stated that:

—progress toward the normalization of relations between China and the United States is in the interest of all countries;

—both wish to reduce the danger of international military conflict;

—neither should seek hegemony in the Asia-Pacific region and each is opposed to efforts by any other country or group of countries to establish such hegemony; and

—neither is prepared to negotiate on behalf of any third party or to enter into agreements or understandings with the other directed at other states. . . .

The two sides agreed that it is desirable to broaden the understanding between the two peoples. To this end, they discussed specific areas in such fields as science, technology, culture, sports, and journalism, in which people-to-people contacts and exchanges would be mutually beneficial. Each side undertakes to facilitate the further development of such contacts and exchanges.

Both sides view bilateral trade as another area from which mutual benefit can be derived, and agreed that economic relations based on equality and mutual benefit are in the interest of the peoples of the two countries. They agree to facilitate the progressive development of trade between the two countries.

The two sides agreed that they will stay in contact through various channels, including the sending of a senior U.S. representative to Peking from time to time for concrete consultations to further the normalization of relations between the two countries and continue to exchange views on issues of common interest.

The two sides expressed the hope that the gains achieved during this visit would open up new prospects for the relations between the two countries. They believe that the normalization of relations between the two countries is not only in the interest of the Chinese and American peoples but also contributes to the relaxation of tension in Asia and the world.

Source: Current History, *62 (September 1972): 131–132.*

---

troops from Afghanistan, and ended military support of Vietnam. Gorbachev visited Beijing in 1989. By the end of 1980s, for the first time since 1945, the United States, the Soviet Union, and China were in a cooperative relationship. There was no longer room for the balance of power.

The balance of power in the 1970s left important lessons for the future. First, as Nixon had suggested in 1971, all would be better off if there were a "strong healthy United States, Europe, Soviet Union, China, Japan, each balancing the other, not playing one against the other, an even balance." Nevertheless, that was not what had happened. Second, the structure of international systems did not necessarily determine cooperation or conflict among nations. The bipolar U.S.–Soviet Cold War was just as dangerous as the multipolar (triangular) U.S.-Soviet-Chinese balance of power. The stability of the international system can only be defined by cooperative or hos-

CHINA POLICY

tile behavior. Third, it was not the balance of power that brought the Cold War to an end. The most urgent driving force, among other factors, was economic restraints on global confrontation and common aspirations for economic prosperity. Gorbachev was right: we all lost the Cold War and we all won by ending it.

–MING ZHANG, ASIA RESEARCH INSTITUTE

References

"China Says Enough," *Economist* (24 February 1979): 11;

Gordon A. Craig and Alexander L. George, *Force and Statecraft: Diplomatic Problems of Our Time* (New York: Oxford University Press, 1983);

Raymond L. Garthoff, *Détente and Confrontation: American-Soviet Relations From Nixon to Reagan* (Washington, D.C.: Brookings Institution, 1985);

Joshua S. Goldstein and John R. Freeman, *Three-Way Street: Strategic Reciprocity in World Politics* (Chicago: University of Chicago Press, 1990);

Henry Kissinger, *Diplomacy* (New York: Simon & Schuster, 1994);

Kissinger, *The White House Years* (Boston: Little, Brown, 1979);

Walter LaFeber, *America, Russia, and the Cold War, 1945–1996,* eighth edition (New York: McGraw-Hill, 1997);

Richard Ned Lebow and Janice Gross Stein, *We All Lost the Cold War* (Princeton: Princeton University Press, 1994);

Edward N. Luttwak, "The PRC in Soviet Grand Strategy," in *China, the Soviet Union and the West: Strategic and Political Dimensions in the 1980s,* edited by Douglas T. Stuart and William T. Tow (Boulder, Colo.: Westview Press, 1982, pp. 263–274;

R. Craig Nation, *Black Earth, Red Star: A History of Soviet Security Policy, 1917–1991* (Ithaca, N.Y.: Cornell University Press, 1992);

William L. Scully, "The Military Dimension of Sino-American Relations," in *China Policy and National Security,* edited by Frederick Tse-shyang Chen (Dobbs Ferry, N.Y.: Transnational Publishers, 1984), pp. 31–51;

Richard C. Thornton, *The Nixon-Kissinger Years: Reshaping of American Foreign Policy* (New York: Paragon House, 1989);

Ming Zhang, *Major Powers at a Crossroads: Economic Interdependence and an Asia Pacific Security Community* (Boulder, Colo.: Lynne Rienner, 1995).

CHINA POLICY

COLD WAR CONCLUSION

Is the Cold War over?

Viewpoint: Yes. The Cold War is over because most communist states are defunct or struggling to survive in the international community.

Viewpoint: No. Although the United States stands as the most powerful country in the world, many Cold War antagonisms continue to pose difficulties for American leadership.

The dissolution of the Soviet Union in December 1991 left many hotly debated questions about what the political shape of the world would be in the future. Some students of global affairs argued that the values of liberal democracy and capitalism had triumphed and that the emergence of shared political values, a global economy, and international organizations spelled the end of the competitive approach to international relations. Others contended that the hegemony enjoyed by the United States over much of the globe would come to an end and that a more traditional multipolar world governed by concepts of national interest would reassert itself. Critics of this view believed that the United States would retain its leading role in world affairs into the foreseeable future.

Whatever shape the world takes, serious questions were raised about whether the collapse of the Union of Soviet Socialist Republics (U.S.S.R.) created chaos or harmony. The absence of the Soviet Union from the world stage and the relative weakness of the Russian Federation, its principal successor, altered the balance of power. While new centers seemed to be in the process of emerging, developing conflicts also had the potential to threaten international peace.

Many experts believe this situation resulted in a dangerous power vacuum that has been the agent of instability. Certainly, the world has had no shortage of wars and crises since 1991, problems that might not have emerged were there still a Soviet Union. Critics of this view argue that the collapse of the U.S.S.R. represented victory: a challenge to global security was defeated absolutely, whether by its own domestic problems, direct pressure from the rest of the world, or a combination of the two. While the post-Soviet world may have its problems, in this view the position of the United States in the world remains unchallenged, and structures of stability that developed in the postwar world continue to ensure global stability.

COLD WAR CONCLUSION

Viewpoint:
Yes. The Cold War is over because most communist states are defunct or struggling to survive in the international community.

To define the end of the Cold War, one must first describe what it actually was. This endeavor is difficult, in some respects, because the Cold War was many things to many people. It was a struggle between the forces of communism in the East and capitalism in the West. Primarily, it was a political competition defined by military deadlock, with economic conflict thrown in to make it interesting. No one should ever question the fact that it was indeed a war—one unlike any ever seen, but a war nonetheless. The struggle grew out of the opposition of capitalists who financed the building of the United States and western Europe in the nineteenth century against communists whose adherents were primarily the people who actually performed the labor—who actually built the industrial might that exemplifies the West.

There has always been a struggle between the haves and have-nots, but this particular competition goes much deeper. Western democracy was founded on the individual right to succeed or fail based on little-to-no input or interference from government. This orientation led to what many saw as a heartless and cruel exploitation of the workers. It is interesting to note that some of those same laborers who rose to become the great "captains of industry" were decried by their former compatriots as the worst examples of the abusers. In fact, rarely have workers-turned-managers advocated unionism or better working conditions.

In the early twentieth century communism promised equality—political as well as economic—for all. This goal was something that the capitalists did not promise; they only said that one would have equal opportunity to achieve, not succeed, nor would one have equal say until one achieved power. Conversely, the communist ideal was appealing to those who were unable or unwilling to take the risks necessary to succeed on the capitalist playing field. The promise of equality also proved attractive to women who were not allowed to vote and had limited rights in commerce.

The advent of the Soviet Union in 1917 was heralded by communists around the world as a triumph—they believed that it was just a matter of time before this heaven-sent achievement spread all over the world. Abuses of the Soviet system, which were horrendous even then, were largely unknown to the outside world. In fact, the Soviet ideal was held up as a model by many in the United States, especially during the Great Depression. Information that leaked out of the Union of Soviet Socialist Republics (U.S.S.R.) about the horrors of Soviet rule were believed to be propaganda created by capitalist opposition.

The extreme dislike of communism led business leaders early on to try and destroy it, especially as it appeared in the form of labor unions (although not all unions were communist, they shared many of the same ideas). This hostility continued into the political realm as well. Governments watched communists carefully, and after 1917 this scrutiny grew even more intense. Probably the greatest example of government fear of communism was in Germany during the early 1920s, when an Austrian-born sergeant (newly promoted) was sent to spy on the National Socialist Workers Party—the Nazis. The spy was one Adolf Hitler, who later came to power based partly on his hatred of the communists, who would also be among his first victims.

Western democracies remained vehemently anticommunist throughout the 1930s, condemning communism in all its forms and shunning the Soviet Union. While it is true that the Soviets joined the Allies during World War II, this alliance was done out of expediency rather than a lessening of the mutual animosity. The Cold War began shortly after the Japanese surrendered in 1945.

Relations between the victorious Allied powers grew strained after World War II. France, devastated physically, politically, and economically, set out to regain its former glory in the colonies. The British, breathing a sigh of relief, saw their empire disappear within fifteen years. The Soviets began to rebuild their country and establish a buffer zone to prevent being directly attacked ever again. This desire, as well as their ideological goals, drove the Soviets headlong into confrontation with the West.

While the Allies rapidly demobilized their military forces, the Soviets refused to do the same. Intent on protecting their borders, they established "independent" satellite states around them. From the Balkans to the Baltic, communism seemed to be winning the day. This movement was the "Iron Curtain" that Winston Churchill referred to in his 1946 speech in Fulton, Missouri.

The Soviets soon confronted the West in Berlin, instituting a blockade in 1948 that was answered by an American airlift. Chinese communists defeated the nationalists in 1949. That same year the Soviets tested their first nuclear weapon. It seemed to the West that the communists, a singular, unified entity in their minds, were spreading worldwide like a cancer.

In response to this perceived threat, the West decided to protect itself by forming the North Atlantic Treaty Organization (NATO). An attack on any member nation was taken as an attack against all, to be answered by an appropriate response. The U.S.S.R. retaliated by establishing its own defensive organization, the Warsaw Pact, which hardly allayed Western fears—nor did the Korean War (1950–1953), introduction of a Soviet long-range bomber capable of delivering a nuclear device, the so-called space race, the Cuban Missile Crisis (October 1962), and development of intercontinental ballistic missiles (ICBMs).

At the heart of all this competition was a fear of losing and being taken over by the other side. The Cold War was viewed as an "all or nothing," victory-or-death fight: a total war, but fought without the violent devastation of either side. Instead, the military aspect of the conflict typically was fought by proxy. Rarely, and secretly, did Western troops directly engage Eastern bloc forces. Most notably, this combat occurred with Soviet and American fighter pilots in the Korean conflict.

That is not to say that casualties did not occur. Many thousands of cold warriors died, especially reconnaissance and intelligence personnel, but the conflict was fought primarily through others. U.S. troops engaged the forces of communism in the uniforms of North Korea, Cuba, and North Vietnam. The Soviets fought capitalism in Africa and Afghanistan. The Cold War was fought on all continents and with most of the world taking part, with a few notable exceptions, such as India. From South Africa to Bolivia, Europe to Malaya, Vietnam to Angola, this conflict was fought by thousands.

In addition to military engagements, the Cold War was also an economic war. Western democratic capitalists lined up against Eastern totalitarian communists. The West tried to out-produce the East in weapons and matériel, as well as consumer goods. For their part, the East tried to keep up, but in the end could not. In the process the Soviet Union destroyed itself, while the West, and especially the United States, became stronger.

In many ways this war was also a cultural one, in which western European concepts of government, religion, justice, freedom, and culture ran headlong into that which developed in the East. This aspect of the conflict was not decided or resolved—who will win it is anyone's guess.

There can be no doubt that the West, headed by the United States, won the Cold War. The U.S.S.R. was defeated on every front, despite its tactical victories, most notably in intelligence and in Africa. President Ronald Reagan ended the Cold War by increasing the already high-level of military production, and in this case it was beneficial to the United States to prolong the conflict, as this was the greatest chance of success. For his part, Mikhail Gorbachev tried to stave off the collapse of the Soviet Union with glasnost and perestroika, but in the end the whole system crashed.

That the Cold War is over is readily apparent: virtually all of the communist states are gone, while those that remain are struggling to survive or change. Just because the world is now in a postwar era, however, does not mean the end of strife. In many ways the world is more dangerous than before. The Soviet Union, through its repression of ethnic, religious, and cultural differences, kept old hatreds and feuds from coming to the surface. This policy gave the veneer of calm and tranquility while these tensions were bubbling under the surface. One only has to look at the formerly communist region of the Balkans to understand just how dangerous this situation can be.

Perhaps the greatest failure of the United States at the end of the twentieth century was in not offering a new Marshall Plan to the defeated nations of the Cold War. While some were able to rebuild, most are unstable and in various stages of collapse. The Russians, who claimed that they always liked Americans, even during the Cold War, rapidly became angry at Western criticism of their methods of handling internal matters. They were left to fend for themselves, and the West criticized them anyway. Worse still, any offers of economic assistance came with the price tag of unwelcome, unrealistic, and unacceptable "advice" from the United States. This arrogance caused further alienation and the cooling of relations between the two countries.

The world was left with the United States as its sole superpower, or "hyperpower" as the French called it, at the end of the Cold War. How the United States will use this power and what influence it will have on the future remains to be seen. While there is an ongoing struggle, it is definitely not the Cold War. It is the international community trying to reestablish itself after the prolonged conflict stunted it. The Cold War ended when the communists were driven out of power in Moscow and the Supreme Soviet voted to disband the Soviet Union.

—WILLIAM H. KAUTT, SAN ANTONIO, TEXAS

Viewpoint:
No. Although the United States stands as the most powerful country in the world, many Cold War antagonisms continue to pose difficulties for American leadership.

In March 1998 the *Cold War International History Project Bulletin* published a piece by National Security Archive director Thomas Blanton that ruminates on the question of when the Cold War ended. Did it occur in 1988 when Mikhail Gorbachev renounced the Brezhnev doctrine or when the Berlin Wall fell in November 1989? Was it during the Malta summit between Gorbachev and President George Bush in December 1989, or when the Soviet Union was formally dissolved in 1991? Blanton argues that the Cold War ended on Christmas Eve 1989, when the United States let it be known that it would not object to Soviet military intervention on behalf of antigovernment protestors in hardline communist Nicolae Ceauçescu's Romania. While the speculations of Blanton and his colleagues are interesting, they ignore a fundamental feature of modern international politics: for all practical purposes the Cold War never ended.

A crucial factor that those who reflect on the history of the Cold War, and the scholarly debate about its "end," must realize is that many predictions about the future structure of the world made after 1989 show little promise of coming true. Optimistic analysts, such as Francis Fukuyama in *The End of History and the Last Man* (1992), argued that liberal capitalist democracy had triumphed in an intensely ideological structure and that this development represented the "end of history." Pessimists, such as Samuel P. Huntington in *The Clash of Civilizations and the Remaking of World Order* (1996), claimed that the world would not be dominated by one single ideology but would become divided along vaguely defined cultural fault lines that would replace Cold War bipolarity. Another school of thought posited that the authority of the nation state would decline in importance and be superseded by international organizations. Other observers contended that the collapse of the Soviet Union brought about a unipolar world in which no other nation posed a credible challenge to hegemonic U.S. leadership. Still others, such as former secretary of state Henry Kissinger, have argued from a realist perspective that the bipolar world will be replaced by a multipolar world in which emerging centers of power will become roughly equal players in a great power system dominated by interests.

Ten years after the fall of the Berlin Wall, none of these analyses were even close to describing international politics at the turn of the century, or even the way they were likely to develop in the foreseeable future. A cursory look at the complexion of world governments shows a surprisingly wide variety, even if some states had made a transition from authoritarianism (communist or noncommunist) to democracy. Most of the world population, however, still lived in countries that were either fundamentally undemocratic or whose democratic credentials were far from ideal. Incidences of ethnic and religious persecution persisted, often developing in places where they had not been a notable factor in recent history. While cultural factors remained important in international affairs, it is difficult to argue that nations believed to belong to a transnational cultural tradition would conduct themselves regularly and uniformly on that basis, to say nothing of the fact that diverse cultural traditions cannot be neatly delineated any more accurately now than when philosophers of the Romantic era tried to determine where "national character types" were located on the map.

Theorists who have suggested that international organizations were taking on greater importance cannot easily explain why the United Nations (UN) failed to stop literally dozens of conflicts since the end of World War II, many of which resulted in hundreds of thousands of deaths and destruction without parallel. The argument is even less convincing when one considers how inefficiently other serious issues such as concerns about terrorism, nuclear proliferation, environmental problems, and human rights were addressed by international organizations. Even the European Union (EU), the institution that came closest to creating a supranational political structure at the regional level, had to contend in 2000 with serious political and economic challenges that engendered much skepticism and opposition.

In many other cases the jealous protection of national sovereignty, especially by larger and more-powerful countries with strong domestic opposition to notions of "world government," turned international forums into little more than debating societies to which certain members were embarrassed about paying their dues. Indeed, perhaps the most effective way to argue against the radical American militiamen who insisted that there was a vast international conspiracy to impose a "new world order" over the United States was to ask them how UN forces could be expected to pull it off when they could not manage to control small villages in Bosnia or Rwanda.

POST–COLD WAR NUCLEAR WORRIES

Although the end of the Cold War reduced superpower tensions, regional and local conflicts continued, and the prospect of nuclear war or nuclear terrorism remains. On 5 December 1996 a group of international military officers called for efforts to reduce the dangers of nuclear war:

STATEMENT ON NUCLEAR WEAPONS BY INTERNATIONAL GENERALS AND ADMIRALS

We, military professionals, who have devoted our lives to the national security of our countries and our peoples, are convinced that the continuing existence of nuclear weapons in the armories of nuclear powers, and the ever present threat of acquisition of these weapons by others, constitute a peril to global peace and security and to the safety and survival of the people we are dedicated to protect. . . .

We know that nuclear weapons, though never used since Hiroshima and Nagasaki, represent a clear and present danger to the very existence of humanity. There was an immense risk of a superpower holocaust during the Cold War. At least once, civilization was on the very brink of catastrophic tragedy. That threat has now receded, but not forever—unless nuclear weapons are eliminated.

The end of the Cold War created conditions favorable to nuclear disarmament. Termination of military confrontation between the Soviet Union and the United States made it possible to reduce strategic and tactical nuclear weapons, and to eliminate intermediate range missiles. It was a significant milestone on the path to nuclear disarmament when Belarus, Kazakhstan and Ukraine relinquished their nuclear weapons.

Indefinite extension of the Nuclear Non-Proliferation Treaty in 1995 and approval of the Comprehensive Test Ban Treaty by the UN General Assembly in 1996 are also important steps towards a nuclear-free world. We commend the work that has been done to achieve these results.

Unfortunately, in spite of these positive steps, true nuclear disarmament has not been achieved. Treaties provide that only delivery systems, not nuclear warheads, will be destroyed. This permits the United States and Russia to keep their warheads in reserve storage, thus creating a "reversible nuclear potential." However, in the post–Cold War security environment, the most commonly postulated nuclear threats are not susceptible to deterrence or are simply not credible. We believe, therefore, that business as usual is not an acceptable way for the world to proceed in nuclear matters.

It is our deep conviction that the following is urgently needed and must be undertaken now:

First, present and planned stockpiles of nuclear weapons are exceedingly large and should now be greatly cut back;

Second, remaining nuclear weapons should be gradually and transparently taken off alert, and their readiness substantially reduced both in nuclear weapons states and in de facto nuclear weapons states;

Third, long-term international nuclear policy must be based on the declared principle of continuous, complete and irrevocable elimination of nuclear weapons.

The United States and Russia should—without any reduction in their military security—carry forward the reduction process already launched by START—they should cut down to 1000 to 1500 warheads each and possibly lower. The other three nuclear states and the three threshold states should be drawn into the reduction process as still deeper reductions are negotiated down to the level of hundreds. There is nothing incompatible between defense by individual countries of their territorial integrity and progress toward nuclear abolition.

The exact circumstances and conditions that will make it possible to proceed, finally, to abolition cannot now be foreseen or prescribed. One obvious prerequisite would be a worldwide program of surveillance and inspection, including measures to account for and control inventories of nuclear weapons materials. This will ensure that no rogues or terrorists could undertake a surreptitious effort to acquire nuclear capacities without detection at an early stage. An agreed procedure for forcible international intervention and interruption of covert efforts in a certain and timely fashion is essential.

Source: Coalition to Reduce Nuclear Dangers, Internet Web Page.

Assertions of sovereignty and independence also exposed the illusion that the United States enjoyed an historically unique role as world hegemon, or "the last remaining superpower." While the United States held an undeniably strong position, it was naive for strategic thinkers at the beginning of the 1990s to argue that Washington could effectively lead the world without opposition. In purely economic terms, the United States was challenged in fairly pronounced trade disputes with almost every other economic power. Even in the era when the Cold War was thought to be ending, America faced fresh challenges from several small countries, few of which were dealt with in an effective and lasting way. Solutions to broader international problems such as the Middle Eastern peace process, the spread of terrorism, and a plague of human rights violations, remained elusive under U.S. leadership, largely because Washington was neither powerful enough nor committed enough to bring them about.

Even the most pragmatic approach, the notion that the superpower struggle would fizzle and be replaced by global multipolarity, showed little sign of becoming reality. Many international-relations theorists, such as Paul Kennedy in *The Rise and Fall of the Great Powers: Economic Change and Military Conflict From 1500 to 2000* (1987), predicted that U.S. preeminence was approaching an "imperial sunset" and that other rising powers, such as the EU, China, and Japan, would become serious and equal contenders in the world arena. Kissinger predicted in *Diplomacy* (1994) that the United States would become only one of several major powers that would cooperate and compete with each other in a way not all that different from the European great powers of the nineteenth century. For a variety of reasons, these models have not become reality, either.

Although European integration was further along, several major member-states experienced serious and long-term economic difficulties caused by the drain of their expensive welfare states and the constrictive economic policies demanded by the process of integration. Their situation was still less promising from a military-strategic perspective because, despite rhetorical attempts to recast its role, the North Atlantic Treaty Organization (NATO) was still far and away the sole guardian of European security, and, despite some talk of a purely European collective-security alliance and perhaps integrated European armed forces, American leadership showed no sign of weakening. Indeed, the two major "post–Cold War" crises in Europe, in Bosnia-Herzegovina (1992–1995) and Kosovo (1998–1999), were only effectively dealt with by unmistakably United States–led diplomatic and military action after years of waffling and indecision by both the European NATO members and the international community.

In Asia, neither China, Japan, nor India, three countries identified by Kissinger as "emerging centers of power" (albeit India was only a possible center in his analysis), escaped from the roles they played during the Cold War. Japan was still the only regional partner of the United States in promoting security of the western Pacific rim and, despite much worry in the late 1980s, its economy faced serious structural challenges that prevented its rise to independence as a great power. China was developing economically, it is true, but not showing much more geopolitical ambition than fussing over Taiwan, trying to build a blue-water navy, engaging in nuclear espionage, and moving closer to Russia. Domestically, Beijing had serious problems dealing with growing political, religious, and ethnic dissent, as well as the burden of sustaining what was still a predominantly agrarian population. While India tested nuclear weapons in the summer of 1998 and passed the billion mark in population in 2000, its strategic policy had more to do with the security of its own borders and its relations with Pakistan and China than with making a bid for global influence.

In a world neither unipolar, multipolar, nor supranational—and that showed no signs of becoming so in the foreseeable future—what else can be said but that it was bipolar? American leadership in certain (but by no means all) situations far from its shores was discussed, but where was the other pole in the contemporary world to be found?

It is important for the observer of international affairs to realize that the relationship between Washington and Moscow did not depart from its Cold War antagonism in any meaningful way. Although there was a flurry of diplomatic activity and much talk of good relations in the late 1980s and early 1990s, in many ways the events from 1989 to 1991 created a situation in which that relationship in some ways became dramatically worse. The mantra that "post–Cold War" foreign investment in the Russian Federation and other successor states of the Soviet Union, so widespread in the Western international-studies community in the early 1990s, would magically produce benevolent liberal democracy was proven wholly fallacious. Despite tens of billions of dollars in loans from the International Monetary Fund, direct foreign aid from Western countries, and private or semiprivate investment from Western businesses and nongovernmental organizations (NGOs), the institutions of civil society and the rule of law upon which democracy relies were

COLD WAR CONCLUSION

tragically and embarrassingly weak or absent in Russia. The administration of foreign aid, in both the West and Moscow, was dogged by corruption and inefficiency, while the development of a free market was plagued by a variety of legal and ethical problems, including allegations that billions of dollars of foreign aid was stolen by Russian officials and laundered through Wall Street banks. In a society that was becoming increasingly disenchanted with democratic ideals, the popularity of the communist party and noncommunist "parties of order" far outpaced that of politicians and movements advocating further reform and democratization.

From a diplomatic perspective the failure to produce a government and society truly convinced of political democracy and capitalist economics has only enhanced the continuity of underlying tension in Russian international relations. Simply put, between 1989 and 1991 Russia lost almost everything it had gained territorially since the reign of Peter the Great (1682–1725), together with a great deal of foreign influence. Consciousness of these developments has driven Russian foreign policy since 1991. Despite its acute domestic political and economic problems, Moscow failed to renounce its historic pretensions to world-power status. Moscow still tried to retain a predominating influence through its leadership of the Commonwealth of Independent States (CIS) and had no compunction about intervening militarily and economically in several of them. A movement to reintegrate former Soviet territory into the Russian Federation was afoot and met with some success with regard to Belarus. Moscow also consistently objected to NATO expansion into Eastern Europe, behaving as if Western guarantees of East European freedom and security, literally trod upon by Russian armies time and again since the First Partition of Poland (1772), were an explicit threat to Russia. Taken as a percentage of its annual budget, the Russian Federation, despite its obvious domestic economic troubles and serious questions about the effectiveness of its military, was proportionally the second largest defense spender after China, devoting 16.3 percent of its budget in 1998 to the military. Over the same period the United States spent 5.7 percent of its budget on defense.

In addition to its military prowess, Russia tried fairly consistently to develop or improve diplomatic relations with countries that had contentious relations with the United States. The most notable example was Moscow's support for Yugoslavia, first during the bloody wars in the former provinces of that country and then during the Kosovo Crisis. The choice to side unabashedly with a dictator associated with genocide, criticize the West and the United States for intervening against him, and insist on playing a role in the peace process to which it was patently not entitled illustrated that Russia was more concerned with its own status as a world power than with genuine cooperation with the international community.

Further afield, relations with Saddam Hussein's Iraq, which fought a United States–led coalition in 1990–1991, were warmed by periodic Russian denunciations of the UN-sponsored economic embargo of Baghdad, even though this measure was taken to pressure Iraq into abandoning its genocidal attacks against its Kurdish minority and its attempts to develop weapons of mass destruction. This connection was enhanced by a reported $800,000 payment from Saddam to former Russian prime minister and popular political figure Yevgeny Primakov. There were further allegations that the Iraqi nuclear-weapons program may have been enhanced by Russian scientists and technology. Other "rogue states" at odds with the United States, such as Iran, Syria, Lybia, and North Korea, were courted by Moscow after the Gorbachev era, while "post–Cold War" governments or pseudo-governments that grew out of political movements not always in favor in Washington, such as the postapartheid government of South Africa and the autonomous authority of the Palestine Liberation Organization (PLO), developed warm relations with Russia. The marked improvement in Sino-Soviet relations that followed Gorbachev's visit to Beijing shortly before the Tiananmen Square Massacre (3–4 June 1989) proceeded apace. Both countries signed a treaty normalizing their long and contentiously disputed frontier and were found on the same side of the Kosovo Crisis, especially after U.S. bombs fell on the Chinese embassy in Belgrade.

While Moscow successfully gained ground in the developing world and posed a credible strategic challenge to the United States, many of its Cold War antagonisms remained firmly in place. Although relations with Western Europe improved dramatically after 1989, with many bitter critics of the Soviet Union (such as British prime minister Margaret Thatcher and German chancellor Helmut Kohl) moving steadily toward cooperation, irresponsible Russian fiscal policies, leading up to the financial crisis of August 1998, endangered Western European investments while its stance over NATO intervention in Kosovo by and large alienated Western Europe diplomatically. The situation in the Far East was much worse, for Japan refused to accept Russian occupation of part of its northern territories and dramatically increased its attention to its mutual-defensive relationship with the United States.

With certain exceptions (notably Eastern Europe) the general geopolitical situation that existed throughout the Cold War endured. A distinctive bipolarity existed in that the United States and Russia were the only two poles that attracted other countries diplomatically, regardless of serious internal difficulties in Russia. The traditionally large and strong network of U.S. allies around the Sino-Russian periphery remained largely intact and expanded in the wake of the successful rolling back of Soviet influence in Eastern Europe. Superpower posturing in parts of the Third World where the influence of the other superpower was weak continued, and Beijing, despite its recent tilt toward Moscow, remained fickle in its orientation and continued to do whatever it perceived to be in its own strategic interest. The slow proliferation of nuclear weapons notwithstanding, nuclear deterrence and nuclear-arms control as strategic options remained the province of policy makers in Washington and Moscow alone.

Although the ideological component of the Cold War changed with the collapse of Soviet communism, the government of the Russian Federation was dominated by unrepentant former communists who had the largest parliamentary presence (for whatever that is worth in Russia) for most of the brief history of the federation. Like the Soviet Union, Russian pretensions to world power status and the actions that followed were of vastly more importance to the rest of the world than the political philosophy on which the power of the Russian state rested at home. Indeed, observers of the long-term foreign policy of great powers have argued convincingly that those goals (and the internal debates surrounding them) generally survive radical changes in regime. As Woodruff D. Smith thoughtfully posited in *The Ideological Origins of Nazi Imperialism* (1986) regarding imperialism in early-to mid-twentieth-century German history, they can even gain strength as new regimes come

to power. Besides, if ideology alone defined the Cold War, why did no one seriously contend that it started with the inception of Bolshevik government in Russia in 1917? How, moreover, can one explain the downright cordial cooperation between the democratic West and the Soviet Union despite their obvious ideological differences during World War II if antagonism is a function of ideological conflict? If the Cold War was the expression of bipolar antagonism between Washington and Moscow—born of pretension to world leadership, kept cold by the specter of nuclear war, and fought through subtle diplomacy, small conventional conflicts on the geopolitical sidelines, as well as competition for influence in the developing world—one can only conclude that it continues on.

–PAUL DU QUENOY, GEORGETOWN UNIVERSITY

References

Francis Fukuyama, *The End of History and the Last Man* (New York: Free Press, 1992);

Samuel P. Huntington, *The Clash of Civilizations and the Remaking of World Order* (New York: Simon & Schuster, 1996);

Paul Kennedy, *The Rise and Fall of the Great Powers: Economic Change and Military Conflict From 1500 to 2000* (New York: Random House, 1987);

Henry Kissinger, *Diplomacy* (New York: Simon & Schuster, 1994);

Henry R. Nau, *The Myth of America's Decline: Leading the World Economy into the 1990s* (New York: Oxford University Press, 1990);

Woodruff D. Smith, *The Ideological Origins of Nazi Imperialism* (New York: Oxford University Press, 1986).

COLD WAR CONCLUSION

CONGRESS AND FOREIGN POLICY

Did Congress have a positive effect on U.S. diplomatic efforts during the Cold War?

Viewpoint: Yes. Congressional assertion of its authority in U.S. foreign affairs had a positive effect by reviewing and modifying executive initiatives.

Viewpoint: No. Congress undermined presidential leadership and hampered diplomatic efforts.

The often-cited "comeback" of Congress as a positive factor in U.S. foreign policy during the 1970s is better understood in terms of the retort: "What comeback? Congress never went away." Even during World War II it played a vital role as a sounding board and informal advisory body for a Democratic president always aware of the Republican minority in both houses. The "bipartisanship" of such Republican stalwarts as senators Robert A. Taft and Arthur H. Vandenberg was based on regular consultation and concessions. Franklin D. Roosevelt's successor in the White House, Harry S Truman, also discovered the limits of presidential autonomy, particularly in his policies first toward China, then Korea. During the Eisenhower and Kennedy administrations congressional involvement in foreign affairs seemed muted, which reflected in part the skill of both presidents in mouthing differences of opinion. It also illustrated the development of what might be called a Cold War consensus on the floors of both the House and Senate, as well as a growing experience, both congressional and presidential, in managing differences of perspective on foreign-policy matters. An accompanying recognition was that domestic rather than foreign affairs determined the outcome of elections.

A corresponding paradox emerged: Cold War issues were considered primary in terms of national survival, but secondary in terms of party interest. That view persisted through most of the Vietnam War, and the war itself did less to change it than the election of Richard M. Nixon as president in 1968. The voters also continued to return Democratic majorities to Congress—and the visceral antagonism widely felt toward Nixon in Democratic circles tended to generate interest in better ways of exercising opposition. Party dynamics were reinforced by academic developments. Since the New Deal and World War II, the focus of optimistic opinion among the intelligentsia had been in favor of expanding presidential power. The joint impact of the Vietnam War and the Nixon presidency highlighted a growing school critical of what was called the "Imperial Presidency" by no less an authority than historian Arthur M. Schlesinger Jr.

The role of the executive branch in foreign policy attracted particular attention. The Constitution said little about it—a logical consequence of the subject's relative unimportance to the framers. "Loose construction" of the issue during and after World War II, combined with the acknowledged extensive powers of the president as commander in chief of the armed forces, had combined since 1940 to create a situation that could legitimately be described as extraconstitutional, independently of which parties controlled what branches. During the Ford and Carter administrations Congress increasingly asserted its right not merely to debate policy, but to control action. Cold War realists argued, on the contrary, that discussion meant delay and openness meant exposure.

The foreign policy of the Reagan era, with its strong emphasis on assertiveness through proxies, focused the argument. The White House confronted a Congress increasingly prone to question either the merits of particular involvements or the goals of the local interests the United States was supporting. The Contras in Nicaragua offer the most familiar example, but after four decades of the Cold War, few innocents of any stripe were left anywhere in the world. The degree to which the Reagan administration was blocked in developing and implementing foreign policy remains open to debate. What cannot be challenged is that between 1980 and 1988 foreign affairs became the stuff of public controversy in ways unheard of in the history of the republic. The Iran-Contra Affair, a complex issue of clandestine arms exchanges supported by the executive branch in defiance of the spirit, if not always the letter, of congressional intention, epitomizes a pattern that did not disappear with the end of the Cold War. The dialectic between Congress and the presidency over the making of foreign policy has constitutional and historical roots too deep to disappear merely because specific circumstances change.

Viewpoint:
Yes. Congressional assertion of its authority in U.S. foreign affairs had a positive effect by reviewing and modifying executive initiatives.

The relationship between Congress and the presidency in making foreign policy is rooted in the history and Constitution of the United States. James Madison in *Federalist,* number 51 made the point that the legislative branch naturally predominates in republican governments. Through most of the nineteenth century, Congress and its leaders overshadowed the executive branch. Exceptions—specifically during the Civil War (1861–1865)—were just that. Even during this war, Abraham Lincoln was closely watched by a variety of congressional agencies— and by individual senators and representatives as well. Once the guns fell silent, Congress sought to reassert its traditional primacy by means that included the impeachment of Lincoln's successor, Andrew Johnson. The failure of the process, rather than its audacity, was what amazed contemporaries.

In the twentieth century the balance shifted, but slowly and by degrees. During World War I Woodrow Wilson asserted a degree and an extent of control over foreign policy arguably greater than that of any Allied executive. He received his comeuppance when Congress repudiated his League of Nations by refusing to sanction U.S. entry into the body, again as much because of Wilson's failure to consult with the legislature over that organization. During the interwar years even Franklin D. Roosevelt deferred to congressional insistence that the United States do everything possible to avoid involvement in the wars that loomed in Asia and Europe. FDR's approach to U.S. entry into World War II has been accurately described as "one step forward, two

steps back." During the war the legislative branch authorized a national mobilization supervised by an executive branch that faced virtually no oversight on matters ranging from the internment of Japanese Americans to the development of the atomic bomb. That situation, however, was at the time generally regarded as an anomaly. Only after the war, with the emergence of a major and growing threat from the Union of Soviet Socialist Republics (U.S.S.R.), did the "bipartisan foreign policy" of 1941 to 1945 come to be described as normative. Only in the 1940s did Congress authorize the creation of large and overlapping agencies of foreign policy— such as the Department of Defense, National Security Agency (NSA), and Central Intelligence Agency (CIA)—that stood essentially under executive control and increasingly cloaked even their ordinary operations under a mantle of secrecy justified by national security. Presidents put their individual stamps on foreign-policy events, assisted by a developing media culture that found it easier to focus on one symbolic figure than a hydra-headed bicameral legislature.

The rise of what Arthur M. Schlesinger Jr. called the "Imperial Presidency" did not simply represent usurpation of power. The Constitution says little about the president's role in international affairs, but the Tenth Amendment has generally been interpreted as supporting federal aggrandizement. Even more significant has been the unquestioned constitutional role of the president as commander in chief of the armed forces. From the Korean War (1950–1953) to the Vietnam War (ended 1975), and in dozens of threats and confrontations in between, the executive branch exercised no more than its admitted constitutional rights to deploy or withdraw U.S. forces as seemed appropriate.

Congress, for its part, reviewed and reacted to executive initiatives, modified and focused courses of action, and pointed with pride or viewed with alarm foreign-policy decisions as the demands of the next election seemed to suggest. Even before U.S. involvement in Vietnam, the concept of bipartisanship in foreign policy was giving way to "me-tooism," with the party out of power insisting it could achieve national goals more effectively and less expensively than its rival. That mentality persisted through much of America's longest war, as congressmen of both parties proved reluctant to put themselves in a position of opposing the president and by extension denying support to U.S. servicemen in combat.

The 1968 election of Richard M. Nixon marked the beginning of a tectonic shift in foreign policy making. Nixon, at best a controversial figure, was an object of such existential loathing to so many senior Democratic congressmen—and to a corresponding number of Democratic voters—that it became easier to risk charges of partisanship in opposing a war whose futility had alienated many Republican legislators as well. The War Powers Resolution (1973), setting temporal limits on presidential authority to commit U.S. forces without congressional approval, was in some ways a bipartisan measure. Tested two years later as the fall of Saigon loomed, it endured as the Senate Foreign Relations committee refused then-president Gerald R. Ford's request for military aid to a collapsing South Vietnam.

Congressional involvement characterized Ronald Reagan's two terms as well. The Boland Amendments (1982, 1984) in particular curbed U.S. aid to the guerrillas fighting a Soviet-backed regime in Nicaragua. Unable to convert his congressional opponents, Reagan took the desperate step of evading their restrictions by a complex structure of secret initiatives that were eventually brought to public view as the Iran-Contra scandal (1986–1988). Charges and investigations dogged the final years of Reagan's presidency and continued into the 1990s. A case can be made, indeed, that only the collapse of the Soviet Union (December 1991) averted a major constitutional crisis over not merely the issue of aid to the Contras but also the question of control of foreign policy that Iran-Contra represented.

As Reagan's vice president and former director of the CIA, George Bush was sufficiently singed by the Iran-Contra affair that he chose not to challenge its paradigms during the Persian Gulf Crisis (1990–1991). While believing he had the constitutional right to impose sanctions, deploy troops, and ultimately go to war on his own authority, Bush accepted the decision of Congress to debate a resolution of support. Nor did he have any illusions about the depth of the support he eventually received from a Congress that throughout remained collectively lukewarm

in its enthusiasm for another military adventure on the far side of the world. Bush's decision to close down the fighting against Iraq, with Saddam Hussein still in power, owed a good bit to concern over probable criticism from a Congress less and less reluctant to micromanage foreign affairs in ways that created no-win situations for any president.

The election of Bill Clinton in 1992 was the first time since 1936 that a domestically oriented candidate won the White House. Clinton campaigned on domestic issues such as lifestyles and the economy. His growing international involvement was ad hoc and involuntary, often as much a response to specific domestic pressures, as in the case of sending troops to Haiti in September 1994, as to any calculated determination of U.S. vital interests. Clinton was handicapped as well by the lack of a high-quality foreign-policy team— a consequence of the twelve year exclusion of Democrats from the levers of foreign policy. His foreign policy was subjected to corresponding criticism as being random and ineffectual, although its venues have scarcely been as threatening, or dramatic, as those that made Cold War headlines. Nor has the Clinton administration been willing to risk the casualties that in the past have bought support for presidential policies.

As a consequence, Congress has increasingly challenged the conduct of foreign policy. The Senate rejection of the Comprehensive Test Ban Treaty (1999) is paradigmatic. The original Test Ban Treaty (1963) had been approved by a four-to-one majority, despite significant criticism of the agreement as a leap in the dark, unjustified by the previous Cold War behavior of the Soviet Union. Support for the president as commander in chief and foreign-policy arbiter, however, is no longer automatic. Indeed, overt antagonism and efflorescent resistance from Congress may well become near routine aspects of U.S. foreign-policy formation—not as a manifestation of partisan politics, but as part of the wider process of reasserting an historic balance between the executive branch and legislature.

–DENNIS SHOWALTER,
COLORADO COLLEGE

Viewpoint:
No. Congress undermined presidential leadership and hampered diplomatic efforts.

When Richard M. Nixon entered office in 1969, few realized that the dynamics of the American system of government would change

CONGRESS AND
FOREIGN POLICY

significantly by the time of his resignation five years later. By the mid 1970s much of the initiative and authority in foreign policy making had been taken from the hands of the executive branch. While disagreements over foreign-policy decisions of the Nixon administration had a great impact and were the original impetus, congressional imperatives led the legislative branch to exceed its constitutional mandates in foreign affairs and endanger the successful execution of U.S. foreign policy.

Nixon found himself confronted by a situation that no previous Cold War president had encountered. While his predecessors had built progressively upon the initial structure of containment established by the Truman administration, Nixon had to modify structural problems that had developed within it. The policies of the Johnson administration, and the changing dynamics of international politics and diplomacy, had created serious problems for U.S. strategy vis-à-vis the Soviet Union. By the late 1960s the Soviets had overcome earlier difficulties and reached parity with the United States in strategic weapons. The postwar recoveries of Western Europe and Japan allowed these countries increasing political independence from American foreign pol-

icy. West German chancellor Willy Brandt's *Ostpolitik* (Eastern policy) led his country, and much of Western Europe, into rapprochement with the Soviet Union. These developments were worsened by President Lyndon B. Johnson's firm commitment to the war in Indochina, which tied down substantial U.S. military resources and became extremely costly. Combined with the costs of Johnson's domestic social programs, America became less prosperous domestically and less competitive internationally.

Nixon had to counter each of these steps. In addition to ending the expensive and unpopular conflict, Nixon viewed the creation of an independent and self-sustaining South Vietnamese state as both a major victory for containment and a pacification of threats to China, which Nixon wished to draw into an anti-Soviet alliance. Achieving that end had long been elusive because the Johnson administration had a fundamental inability to produce a winning strategy. Despite the massive buildup of American forces, the strategic doctrine of Secretary of Defense Robert S. McNamara did not allow for anything beyond a defensive stance in Vietnam. Massive bombing attacks against North Vietnam, the main

U.S. soldiers removing a cache of supplies from a landing zone during the controversial 1970 Cambodian incursion

(U.S. Army photos— J. D. Coleman collection)

CONGRESS AND FOREIGN POLICY

KNOWLAND CALLS FOR CONGRESSIONAL REVIEW

The struggle over control of foreign policy during the Cold War between the president and Congress did not begin with the Vietnam War. For instance, in a 15 November 1955 speech on "peaceful coexistence" and "atomic stalemate," Senator William F. Knowland (R-California) called for greater congressional oversight—this time for a more aggressive check of communism.

Certainly they are so important and the results of the decisions made and to be made are so far-reaching that the Congress and the American people must be taken into the confidence of the administration.

No matter what the decisions are in the elections of 1956, a Republican administration and a Democratic-controlled Congress in the months immediately ahead share a heavy responsibility, for the survival of this Republic and the possibility of a free world of free men hangs in the balance. . . .

Coexistence and atomic stalemate will result in ultimate Communist victory, unless one believes that the men in the Kremlin have completely changed their long-term strategy of ultimately having a Communist world, and no longer follow the doctrine that in order to achieve their ends anything is allowable (including deception and treachery). We must face up to the fact that the Communist concept of "peaceful coexistence" means that the United States or other free nations of the world will be allowed to exist only until communism is able to subvert them from within or destroy them by aggression from without. . . .

Before our eyes the people of the United States would see nation after nation nibbled away and when the realization finally dawned that this policy would inevitably result in our country becoming a continental Dien Bien Phu in a Communist totalitarian world, the chances of our winning such a struggle would be so lessened and the Soviet world so extended that they then would be prepared for an all-out challenge to us wherein we would be allowed the choice to surrender or die.

It seems to me that the responsible committees of the Congress should promptly summon the State and Defense officials and the Joint Chiefs of Staff to fully inquire into our foreign and defense policy to find out where in their judgement it will take us and whether this clear and present danger which appears to me to exist is such that a basic change in the direction of our policy is warranted.

Time is running out and I would remind the Senate that in this day and age of the airplane and the atomic weapon, time is not necessarily on the side of the free world.

Source: *Current History*, 28 (January 1955): 57–58.

aggressor and adversary, did not begin until March 1965. Nothing at all had been done about the blatant violation of Laotian and Cambodian neutrality by communist forces and the use of "sanctuary" bases on the territory of those countries to prosecute the war in South Vietnam. Supply routes to the North, through which most of the military hardware of the communist forces poured, were not blockaded even though the Sino-Soviet split had confined them to seaports in North Vietnam (Haiphong) and Cambodia (Sihanoukville, now Kompong Som). Even when the North Vietnamese suffered an unmitigated military defeat during the Tet Offensive (1968), the Johnson administration utterly failed to follow up on it and gain a strategic advantage.

Nixon entered office on the promise of having a winning strategy. In theory it was quite simple. Deploying U.S. military power into Cambodia would deprive the communists of the use of both their previously untouched base camps along its border with South Vietnam and access to their supply port at Sihanoukville. At the same time bombing raids on the North were to be accelerated and the approaches to Haiphong, the main supply port in North Vietnam proper, were to be mined. With their supply routes cut and their refuges in "neutral" Cambodia annihilated, it was believed that the communist forces would concede to a peace agreement favorable to the United States.

At precisely this point, however, Nixon's policies were sidelined. The growing unpopularity of the war was such that any prospect of widening it, even if there were compelling tactical and strategic reasons to do so, was instantly regarded with suspicion. With the country in what seemed to be increasingly difficult straits, Congress became more assertive in foreign affairs. When the bombing campaign against the Vietnamese communists operating from Cambodia (begun in March 1969) and the ground-based incursions into the country in May 1970 were announced, public reaction was stormy. Within days after Nixon's public announcement of his Cambodia policy, radical antiwar groups launched massive demonstrations and called for a general strike. At Kent State University in Ohio, four students were killed in a confrontation with National Guardsmen.

It was by the vocal protest and bloodshed of the student protestors that Congress was emboldened to assert its authority over prerogatives that the Constitution delegated to the executive branch. The Cooper-Church amendment (July 1970), named after Senators John

Sherman Cooper (R-Kentucky) and Frank Church (D-Idaho), prohibited further American involvement in Cambodia. Even though the president is constitutionally in command of U.S. armed forces, and American commitment to the preservation of South Vietnamese independence was a long established principle, Congress curtailed his ability to use it. The tragedy was that despite the uproar over the incursion, substantial progress had been made toward routing communist forces from Cambodia before U.S. troops were compelled to withdraw not by military reverses but by congressional decree. Perhaps significantly, when the House Judiciary Committee voted on four articles of impeachment against Nixon, the only one to be defeated had to do with his "secret" bombing of Cambodia.

In this instance Congress had derailed the only hope of ending the war on terms acceptable to the United States and achieving what Nixon proudly called "peace with honor." Worse was yet to come, however. After the efforts of National Security Adviser Henry Kissinger had achieved the January 1973 peace settlement, one that could do little but collapse (as it did when North Vietnam conquered the South two years later), congressional machinations once again went to work. The War Powers Resolution, passed later that year, deprived the executive branch, of the power to use the armed forces for longer than sixty days without congressional approval.

Although it was a well-intentioned bill designed to prevent the United States from becoming embroiled in another Vietnam scenario, its practical effects on U.S. military policy have been quite serious. One central problem has been that congressional approval for the use of the military has become a tool of partisan politics. This situation almost precipitated a crisis during the Persian Gulf War (1991), when congressional Democrats who opposed Republican president George Bush's military solution held up approval of the commitment of troops, in some cases to gain concessions on other issues. Although Bush was enjoying overwhelming public support, was acting decisively to liberate the innocent victims of naked aggression, and was protecting American interests in the Middle East, crucial U.S. military action was delayed and even threatened altogether.

The same scenario was almost repeated with regard to Democratic president Bill Clinton's handling of the Kosovo Crisis in the spring of 1999. Once again, although the executive was acting with tremendous public support in an attempt to eliminate a threat to European stability and stop what appeared to be a genocidal conflict, the Republican majority in the House of Representatives, with some Democratic support, passed a resolution calling for an end to U.S. involvement in the conflict.

Even in instances in which direct military conflict has not been used, Congress has meddled in foreign affairs. In 1976 the legislature passed a law forbidding any American military or intelligence body from assassinating foreign leaders. Although seemingly reasonable, one must not forget that this legislation is a major reason why the world still has Saddam Hussein, who has ruled Iraq for the past twenty years through political terror, murdered tens of thousands of Kurdish and Shiite Muslim civilians, destabilized the Middle East, and ruthlessly victimized Kuwait. It has also frustrated policies designed to free several Third World countries from communist dictatorships, which had generally been established by force. Had it been in effect during the Roosevelt administration, attempts on the lives of Adolf Hitler and other Nazi officials would have been illegal.

While the Reagan administration remained reluctant to commit troops to major wars, its reliance on covert operations also became a target of what increasingly came to be called the "Imperial Congress." Even though the National Security Act of 1947 gave the executive clear authority over the Central Intelligence Agency (CIA), the main actor in Reagan's covert operations, Congress bitterly resented the independence of the administration. Although its earliest and most prominent activities provided support to the Nicaraguan "contra" freedom fighters in their struggle against the communist regime of the Sandinistas, Congress imposed a series of measures to restrict the administration's policy. Known collectively as the Boland Amendments, after Representative Edward Patrick Boland (D-Mass.), these laws at different times restricted or outlawed covert American support to the contras. In addition to perpetuating the ruthless Sandinista regime by limiting the operations of the contras, Congress demanded the investigation and trial of administration officials who were believed to have continued to funnel support to the rebels. The resulting scandal paralyzed the administration and the presidency.

Congressional reassertion of authority over foreign policy has been negative for the United States. Since the Nixon presidency the legislative branch has gone far beyond the constitutional limitations on its authority and in the process crippled or threatened to cripple decisive action that was essential for American security interests and for peace.

—PAUL DU QUENOY, GEORGETOWN UNIVERSITY

References

James MacGregor Burns, *Roosevelt: The Soldier of Freedom* (New York: Harcourt Brace Jovanovich, 1970);

Arthur M. Schlesinger Jr., *The Imperial Presidency* (Boston: Houghton Mifflin, 1973);

Peter Schweizer, *Victory: The Reagan Administration's Secret Strategy That Hastened The Collapse of the Soviet Union* (New York: Atlantic Monthly Press, 1994);

Richard C. Thornton, *The Carter Years: Toward A New Global Order* (New York: Paragon House, 1991);

Thornton, *The Nixon-Kissinger Years: Reshaping American Foreign Policy* (New York: Paragon House, 1989);

Caspar W. Weinberger, *Fighting For Peace: Seven Critical Years in the Pentagon* (New York: Warner, 1990);

Bob Woodward, *Veil: The Secret Wars of the CIA, 1981–1987* (New York: Simon & Schuster, 1987).

CUBA

Was Cuba an independent participant in world politics?

Viewpoint: Yes. Cuba sought support from the Soviet Union only after being rejected by the United States and has since practiced an anti-American foreign policy as much for domestic reasons as for international considerations.

Viewpoint: No. Cuba supported communist revolutions in the Third World with Soviet direction and aid, but the fiction of independent Cuban action allowed the U.S.S.R. to maintain détente with the West.

Cuba has a singular place in the history of the Cold War. In 1962 the Soviet decision to deploy nuclear missiles and tactical nuclear weapons to the island nation nearly caused a war with the United States. In later years the Cuban communist regime played a crucial role in supporting movements of national liberation all over the Third World. By the end of the 1970s Cuban troops and supplies had been sent as far away as Cambodia and Ethiopia, as well as to a host of other developing nations in Africa and Latin America. Cuban support for Third World revolutionary movements and communist governments lasted until late in the Cold War and often proved decisive in their military victories.

Much scholarly debate has centered on the prominent activist role of Cuba in the international communist movement. The Soviets and Cubans consistently maintained that the global projections of military power from Havana were born of revolutionary Marxist zeal and carried out independent of the Soviet Union. Sometimes, the Soviets claimed, Fidel Castro's activities embarrassed Moscow and jeopardized its effort to build détente with the United States. While some Western scholars support this argument, others argue that the volume of Soviet assistance, first to secure Cuba in its early communist history and then to support it in its overseas adventures, was too substantial to allow for independent Cuban military and strategic activity on a global stage.

Viewpoint:
Yes. Cuba sought support from the Soviet Union only after being rejected by the United States and has since practiced an anti-American foreign policy as much for domestic reasons as for international considerations.

On New Year's Eve 1958 Fidel Castro forced the corrupt Cuban dictator Fulgencio Batista y Zaldívar into exile, successfully completing the first guerrilla war of national liberation in the Western Hemisphere. The revolution was initially celebrated in all strata of society, except perhaps by those individuals who most closely identified with the fallen government.

Castro had succeeded, moreover, without major outside help from the United States, the Union of Soviet Socialist Republics (U.S.S.R.), or anyone else. While organizing a working government from scratch, he held several constitutional conventions with representatives from across the Cuban political spectrum: labor unions, government workers, farmers, land owners, and the Communist Party, which had existed in Cuba since 1923. During these meetings the only ones Castro kept at arm's length, and later banned, were the communists.

Castro in the early days of his revolution does not appear to have planned a set political agenda beyond winning the war. His only two platforms were to raise wages and introduce land reforms. He sought recognition from the other countries of North and South America. The Eisenhower administration refused to recognize Castro's government and began planning for a counterrevolution among the disaffected, self-imposed exiles who mainly settled in Miami, Florida.

The United States has had a catastrophic record of supporting the wrong governments in Latin America: Batista over Castro, Augusto Pinochet Ugarte over Salvador Allende Gossens in Chile, the Somocistas over the Sandinistas in Nicaragua. In general, if the opposition was military, that was good for U.S. foreign policy goals; if it was any popular group that gave off a whiff of reform, that was considered bad.

A review of Cuban foreign policy shows that Castro has been driven less by ideology than economics. He did not act as a client of the U.S.S.R. except when it suited Cuban interests. With the end of the Cold War, Castro's main motivation seems to be whatever will irritate the Yankees the most. Some writers even suggest that this enmity dates back to prerevolutionary years when a promising baseball pitcher named Fidel Castro was cut in spring training by the Washington Senators—a never-forgotten blow to his pride. A more cogent chronology seems to be the disillusion that came from the cold shoulder of Dwight D. Eisenhower's State Department, a policy that was continued by John F. Kennedy.

Both U.S. administrations were engulfed in the darkest period of the Cold War. Eisenhower had been embarrassed by the U-2 spy plane incident (May 1960); the Berlin Wall was constructed (1961); and Vietnam was beginning to be seen as the most vulnerable piece in the "domino theory." The last thing any U.S. administration needed or wanted was a revolutionary government in its own backyard. Communist or not, Castro represented a destabilizing factor in an otherwise stable hemisphere—stable largely because of dictatorships or oligarchies that were richly subsidized by American companies who depended on a cheap and complacent labor force supplying resources from copper to bananas.

Restoring the status quo in Cuba seemed a simple plan. The United States would train, arm, and transport a small army of dissidents from Miami back to the island, land them, and supply protective air cover. The dissidents would rouse the countryside and march triumphantly into Havana, the roads lined with their cheering, liberated countrymen. It did not quite work out that way. The only changes brought about by the Bay of Pigs fiasco (April 1961) were intensified anger and mistrust on the part of the Cubans, as well as embarrassment and irritation on the part of the United States.

Seeing that there was no chance of rapprochement with the Americans, Castro chose that moment to do what he knew would antagonize them the most. He declared that he was a communist, always had been, and always would be. This act was waving a red flag in front of his defeated enemy. Castro knew that from then on, Cuba was in danger of invasion by the United States. He also learned to beware of assassination attempts—Central Intelligence Agency (CIA) or otherwise generated. Badly in need of economic and technical assistance, Castro more and more had to rely on the U.S.S.R., but Cuba never became a true client. There were several reasons for this situation. Logistically it was impossible for Russia to create a satellite so far away, whose problems were completely foreign to the Soviet experience, and that was so close to the United States. Moreover, there were strong ideological differences between the Cuban and Soviet governments. The Soviets needed a strong Communist Party to head the government; Castro, despite his declaration of allegiance, still held the Cuban Communist Party at a distance and staffed his government with his trusted revolutionaries who had been hunted alongside him. After the Bay of Pigs the United States imposed an economic quarantine, conducted large-scale naval maneuvers just off Cuban waters, strengthened its force at Guantanamo Bay, and otherwise manifested a hostile attitude, including sponsoring overflights by U-2 spy planes.

In October 1962 the U-2s photographed the construction of launch sites for intermediate-range nuclear weapons. Cuba, seeking protection, had gone to the Soviet Union. Nikita S. Khrushchev saw it as an opportunity to secretly deploy missiles off the coast of America and present it as a fait accompli. It became a Bay of Pigs in reverse, with everything going terribly wrong for the side taking the initia-

tive. From the withdrawal of the missiles, and the fall of Khrushchev, the increasingly conservative governments of Russia were wary of supplying Cuba with any type of military aid and regarded Castro as a loose cannon. The U.S.S.R. continued to be Cuba's main trading partner—in large part because the United States maintained an economic embargo and has treated Cuba as an enemy state to the point of sustaining a de facto commitment to overthrowing the Castro government by isolating it. The question thus becomes whom is the embargo really damaging?

–JOHN WHEATLEY, BROOKLYN
CENTER, MINNESOTA

❋

Viewpoint:
No. Cuba supported communist revolutions in the Third World with Soviet direction and aid, but the fiction of independent Cuban action allowed the U.S.S.R. to maintain détente with the West.

After the emergence of Fidel Castro's revolutionary government in Cuba (1959), its apparent weakness mandated close collaboration with the Soviet Union. In its turn this collaboration, together with unsuccessful American attempts to remove Castro from power, led to the communization of both the revolutionary party and the island nation as a whole. Despite its early status as a de facto Soviet protectorate, Cuba blossomed into something that in many ways resembled a great power. Beginning in the mid 1970s, tens of thousands of Cuban troops actively supported communist movements in many Third World nations as far apart as Angola and Cambodia. Many who reflect on the place of Cuba in the Cold War world, including Castro himself, maintain that the less-than-expected geopolitical gambit of Havana in the 1970s had no connection at all to its relationship with the Soviet Union. Purely out of his own ideological zeal, and not as a function of the alliance with Moscow, it is often argued, Castro devoted the resources of his small country to spreading Marxism around the world wherever the opportunity presented itself.

This argument was of crucial importance within the U.S. policymaking community. In the era of détente, officials and academics who were eager to see Henry Kissinger's idea of relaxing relations with the Soviet Union come to fruition had an increasingly difficult

Cuban health delegation arriving in Managua, Nicaragua, on 25 May 1979

(UPI/Bettman Archive)

time explaining to their critics, and those of unformed opinions, why their favored strategy was viable despite the generally open expansionism of world communism that culminated in the Soviet invasion of Afghanistan (December 1979). For a time their explanation was that Cuban interventions in the Third World, a major target for critics of détente prior to Afghanistan, not only were independent of Soviet strategy but actually embarrassed Moscow at a time when it was trying to reciprocate American overtures to relax tensions between the two countries. Some have even suggested that evidence of Soviet support for Marxist revolutionary movements originally aided by Castro came not out of the desire of the Kremlin to challenge the United States in the Third World but as a result of pressure from Havana; in other words, the tail wagged the dog. Castro denied any attempt to coordinate his activities with Soviet geopolitical strategy; he argued on the popular CNN *Cold War* television series that if there had been a broader plan organized by Havana and Moscow, it would surely have succeeded. Ascribing Castro's troublesome "independent" action to his genuine enthusiasm for Marxism in this way gave Moscow enough plausible deniability for American proponents of détente to insist that their ideas were viable.

Although much new information about the Soviet-Cuban relationship is emerging from formerly closed archives, there can be little doubt that Castro's actions were strongly oriented toward supporting Soviet aggrandizement. The clearest argument refuting the assertion that Cuba moved on its own militarily and strategically comes from a careful consideration of the island nation itself. By the late 1970s experts estimate that Havana sustained as many as fifty thousand to sixty thousand troops all over the Third World, in as many as ten countries.

For a nation of slightly more than ten million people, this activity was a remarkable achievement. These types of interventions made no less powerful a country than the United States worry about the size and expense of its own foreign involvements. President Dwight D. Eisenhower ran most of his administration on the principle of avoiding large military deployments overseas. Apart from sending thirteen thousand Marines to Lebanon in 1958, American strategy relied mainly on relatively less-expensive measures, such as nuclear deterrence and covert operations. When John F. Kennedy followed Eisenhower into the White House in 1961, he centered his strategic approach around a "flex-ible response" to communist pressure; that is, he avoided the same kind of costly entanglements that Eisenhower had avoided in order to devote American resources in a less pronounced capacity on a global scale. By the fall of 1963, shortly before Kennedy's assassination, the presence of approximately sixteen thousand U.S. military personnel in South Vietnam was sufficient to cause the president concern. Although his successor, Lyndon B. Johnson, deployed significantly larger military forces to defend South Vietnam and made other military commitments to places such as the Dominican Republic, Johnson did so only at the cost of tremendous financial pressure, social unrest, and, ultimately, the end of his own political life when he withdrew from the 1968 presidential campaign. If the United States, arguably the greatest power of the age, vastly larger and wealthier than Cuba, winced at major military deployments, one can only marvel at Castro's ability to do so by himself apparently with impunity.

The communist history of Cuba also makes specious the assertions of its diplomatic independence. Although Castro's revolutionary movement came to power in 1959 and successfully defended itself against the Bay of Pigs invasion (April 1961), the new regime predicated many of its subsequent actions on the notion that it was extremely vulnerable and needed to be protected. The Soviets later claimed this assertion as justification for constructing nuclear missile bases in Cuba in 1962, the action that precipitated the Cuban Missile Crisis (October 1962). Thirteen years later, though, Castro apparently felt so secure that he sent a large contingent of Cuban forces to fight in distant Angola, even though the Soviet Union had been foiled in its attempt to establish a missile base to "protect" its Cuban ally.

Unless the situation changed dramatically, it is far from likely that any responsible leader would go to the expense of making so great a commitment without a combination of previous assurances for security in the future and without a degree of pressure. Revealingly, the Soviet Union subsidized Cuba from the time of Castro's revolution until the collapse of the Union of Soviet Socialist Republics (U.S.S.R.) in 1991. Withdrawal of those subsidies had a deleterious effect upon the Cuban economy. Since its largest traditional trading partner, the United States, was separated from it by a comprehensive economic embargo, it is easy to see that Soviet subsidies could have been translated into diplomatic pressure. By the late 1970s, furthermore, the departure of so many troops from Cuba had created a situa-

CASTRO ON IMPERIALISM

At the 1973 meeting of nonaligned nations in Algiers, Cuban leader Fidel Castro spoke about his view of the Cuban relationship with the Soviet Union:

There are some who, with patent historic injustice and ingratitude, forgetting the real facts and disregarding the profound, unbridgeable abyss between the imperialist regime and socialism, try to ignore the glorious, heroic and extraordinary services rendered to the human race by the Soviet people, as if the collapse of the colossal system of colonial rule implanted in the world up to World War II and the conditions that made possible the liberation of scores of peoples heretofore under direct colonial subjugation, the disappearance of capitalism in large parts of the world and the holding at bay of the aggressiveness and insatiable voracity of imperialism—as if all that had nothing to do with the glorious October Revolution!

How can the Soviet Union be labeled imperialist? Where are its monopoly corporations? Where is its participation in multinational companies? What factories, what mines, what oilfields does it own in the underdeveloped world? What worker is exploited in any country of Asia, Africa or Latin America by Soviet capital?

The economic co-operation that the Soviet Union provides to Cuba and many other countries comes not from the sweat and the sacrifice of the exploited workers of other peoples, but from the sweat and efforts of the Soviet workers.

Others regret the fact that the first socialist state in history has become a military and economic power. We underdeveloped and plundered countries must not regret this. Cuba rejoices that it is so. Without the October Revolution and without the immortal feat of the Soviet people, who first withstood imperialist intervention and blockade and later defeated the fascist aggression at the cost of 20 million dead, who have developed their technology and economy at an unbelievable price in efforts and heroism without exploiting the labour of a single worker of any country on the face of the earth—without them, the end of colonialism and the balance of power in the world that favoured the heroic struggles of so many peoples for their liberation wouldn't have been possible. Not for a moment can we forget that the guns with which Cuba crushed the Playa Girón mercenaries and defended itself from the United States; the arms in the hands of the Arab peoples, with which they withstand imperialist aggression; those used by the African patriots against Portuguese colonialism; and those taken up by the Vietnamese in their heroic, extraordinary and victorious struggle came from the socialist countries, especially from the Soviet Union. . . .

What state have those resolutions condemned from Belgrade to Lusaka for its aggression in Vietnam and all Indo-China? The imperialist United States. Whom do we accuse of arming, supporting and continuing to maintain the Israeli aggressor state in its rapacious war against the Arab countries and in its cruel occupation of the territories where the Palestinians have the right to live? We accuse U.S. imperialism. Against whom did the non-aligned countries protest over the intervention in and blockade of Cuba and the intervention in the Dominican Republic and for maintaining bases at Guantánamo, in Panama and Puerto Rico against the will of their peoples? Who was behind the murder of Lumumba? Who supports the killers Amícal Cabral? Who helps to maintain in Zimbabwe a white racist state and turn South Africa into a reserve of black men and women in conditions of semi-slavery? In all these cases, the culprit is the same: U.S. imperialism, which also backs Portuguese colonialism against the peoples of Guinea-Bissau and Cape Verde, Angola and Mozambique.

Source: Phillippe Braillard and Mohammad-Reza Djalili, Tiers Monde et relations internationales, *translated as* The Third World and International Relations *(London: Pinter, 1986; Boulder, Colo.: Lynne Rienner, 1986), pp. 136–137.*

tion in which Castro needed some kind of security assurance, and the Soviet Union promptly supplied this pledge in the form of combat troops, the so-called Soviet brigade, which became a point of contention in summit meetings between the Soviets and the Carter administration.

Indeed, the Soviet Union historically was by no means immune from using economic and military assistance as a lever in diplomatic relations with smaller and less-powerful countries. Only five years before Cuban involvement in Angola, moreover, the Soviet Union attempted to buttress its strategic position by creating a supply base for its nuclear submarines at Cienfuegos. Although the United States successfully resisted this endeavor, it is clear that the Cuban government colluded with Moscow to advance the strategic interests of the Soviet Union. Why that should have changed within the next few years, when regular Cuban troops assisted pro-Soviet (as opposed, interestingly, to pro-Chinese or nonaligned) Marxist movements in such strategic locations as Angola, Ethiopia, Cambodia, and Nicaragua, is difficult to imagine.

Further, an examination of Cuban interventions in the context of the character of the leadership of Leonid Brezhnev leaves little doubt that Castro's activities, regardless of their origins, benefited Soviet strategic policy. There is much evidence to suggest that Nikita S. Khrushchev's downfall in 1964 was at least in part the result of what others in the Soviet leadership believed to be ineptness in foreign affairs. Following the Cuban Missile Crisis, Khrushchev began to pursue a course that many saw as an attempt to return to "peaceful coexistence" with the United States. Whatever the precise rationale behind Khrushchev's removal, it is well worth noting that the more conventional-minded leadership that replaced him made clear its intention to "alter the global correlation of forces" and maintain a confrontational character in superpower relations, while undoing most of Khrushchev's domestic program of economic liberalization and political de-Stalinization. Moreover, as the Brezhnev leadership sought what it called "stability in cadres," or the general ossification of the administrative apparatus of the Soviet government and Communist Party, ideological Marxism was replaced by a far more cynical worldview dominated by characteristic undertones of Soviet patriotism and Great Russian nationalism. In other words, the Soviet position as a world power was now interpreted in the vanguard as being a function of its ability to hold on to and expand what it already had acquired.

To such a leadership the sort of détente that many American strategic planners were coming to believe in appealed only as a device to neutralize U.S. strategic advances and benefit commercial relationships with the West in exchange for vague promises of geopolitical restraint. Ideologists in Moscow were certainly under no illusions when they characterized proponents of détente within the American business community as being so greedy that they would sell the Soviet Union the materials with which it would build the gallows of capitalism.

The only problem with the Soviet approach was that any direct provocation on the geostrategic level would be harmful to the development of those relations. Maintaining the fiction of independent Cuban action allowed them to play a relatively passive role in encouraging Marxist revolutionary struggle throughout the Third World. Indeed, by minimizing their exposure to Western criticism, the Soviets continued to enjoy the benefits of détente for years, even as international communism became more prevalent in the Third World and a more serious strategic threat to the West. Only specific challenges from Moscow, such as that presented by its development of a perfected guidance system in 1977 and its blatant invasion of Afghanistan, finally caused that to change.

For a variety of reasons, the Cuban role in world affairs was anything but independent. Its relative size and power make it difficult to accept that Castro acted purely on his own through the 1970s. It is equally unlikely that the Soviet Union, which stood to benefit both strategically and materially from its relationship with the West and saw itself as a great power on the rise, would in any circumstances have been Castro's bag carrier whenever he desired to support a Third World revolutionary movement. Cuban claims of vulnerability in the early 1960s are exceedingly difficult to square with Castro's allegedly freestanding decision to export much of his military power in the following decade. Soviet policies of geopolitical aggrandizement in the Brezhnev era, furthermore, stood to benefit enormously from Cuban activities, while Cuba itself merely became impoverished, bound up in several overseas entanglements that had serious consequences for Cuban society.

–PAUL DU QUENOY,
GEORGETOWN UNIVERSITY

CUBA

References

Raymond L. Garthoff, *Détente and Confrontation: American-Soviet Relations from Nixon to Reagan* (Washington, D.C.: Brookings Institution Press, 1994);

Jim Hershberg, "New East-Bloc Evidence on the Cold War in the Third World and the Collapse of Détente in the 1970s," *Cold War International History Project Bulletin,* 8–9 (Winter 1996/1997);

Henry Kissinger, *Years of Renewal* (New York: Simon & Schuster, 1999);

Bruce D. Porter, *The USSR in Third World Conflicts: Soviet Arms and Diplomacy in Local Wars, 1945–1980* (Cambridge & New York: Cambridge University Press, 1984);

Richard C. Thornton, *The Carter Years: Toward A New Global Order* (New York: Paragon House, 1991);

Thornton, *The Nixon-Kissinger Years: Reshaping of America's Foreign Policy* (New York: Paragon House, 1989).

CUBAN MISSILE CRISIS

Did the Kennedy administration handle the Cuban Missile Crisis effectively?

Viewpoint: Yes. The Cuban Missile Crisis was handled effectively because the Kennedy administration avoided all-out nuclear conflict with the Soviet Union through quiet negotiations combined with a strong, public stand.

Viewpoint: No. The Kennedy administration could have adopted policies in the Cuban Missile Crisis that would have left the United States in a better strategic position vis-à-vis the Soviet Union.

The Cuban Missile Crisis (October 1962) was the most serious Cold War crisis, the closest the United States and the Soviet Union came to a nuclear war with each other. Following a July 1962 visit by Cuban foreign minister Raúl Castro Ruz and finance minister Ernesto "Che" Guevara de la Serna to Moscow, the Soviet Union decided to place ballistic missiles in Cuba. American U-2 reconnaissance planes detected an increased number of ships sailing from the Soviet Union to Cuba, and flights over Cuba between 29 August and 6 September revealed that the Soviets were building a defensive missile system on the island. President John F. Kennedy informed Soviet premier Nikita S. Khrushchev that the American government would not tolerate turning Cuba into a base for offensive military capabilities aimed at the United States. Khrushchev assured Kennedy that the Soviet Union had placed only defensive, short-range, surface-to-air missiles in Cuba to augment Cuban air defenses. In fact, in addition to twenty-four surface-to-air missiles, Khrushchev had sent forty-two offensive, nuclear-armed, medium-range missiles and ordered the shipment of twenty-four additional long-range missiles (they never arrived). He also sent forty-five thousand Soviet troops and technicians to the island.

The hurricane season delayed further intelligence-gathering flights over Cuba until after 11 October. Flights conducted between 11 and 14 October revealed that the Soviet Union was busily building launching pads for offensive ballistic missiles at San Cristóbal. Intelligence reports also said that Soviet ships carrying ballistic missiles had left their Black Sea ports and were heading toward Cuba, where they were due in about ten days. U.S. intelligence assessed that, by December 1962, the Soviet Union would have fifty operational strategic nuclear missiles in Cuba. On 23 October four of the medium-range missiles were already operational.

Kennedy convened a group of advisers, known as the Executive Committee of the National Security Council (ExComm), to assess U.S. options. The choices they discussed ranged from invading Cuba with troops or attacking the missile bases with surgical aerial strikes, on one extreme, to accepting the Soviet offensive presence, on the other. Eventually the ExComm agreed on an air and maritime blockade of the island, which would prevent the Soviets from delivering additional missiles to Cuba. Blockade supporters pointed to several advantages of their proposal over other options. An invasion might be costly in American lives, while an aerial strike might not destroy all the launch pads and would leave intact Soviet nuclear-armed bombers on the runways. An invasion or air strike might also cause Soviet casualties, and with or without such losses, it was difficult to imagine that the Soviet Union would passively watch a U.S. attack on a Soviet ally—it was more reasonable to assume that they might retaliate either by attacking the United States directly or, more likely, by capturing West Berlin or some other Western asset of high value.

A blockade appeared to be the less provocative, but equally firm, option: it would prevent the Soviets from moving more missiles onto the island, but allow them several days (the time it would take the Soviet cargo ships to reach the blockade line) to consider their own options and negotiate with the United States. On 24 October, two days after Kennedy announced the blockade, Pentagon officials reported that twelve of the twenty-five Soviet ships sailing toward Cuba had changed course to avoid the blockade. When one of the cargo ships reached the blockade line and was discovered to carry missiles, it was turned away. Another ship, the tanker *Bucharest,* was stopped by U.S. Navy vessels and allowed to continue to Havana when it was ascertained that it was carrying only oil. The next day, all remaining ships turned back. "We were eyeball to eyeball," Secretary of State Dean Rusk was reported to have said, "and the other fellow just blinked." Behind-the-scenes negotiations between Kennedy and Khrushchev produced a compromise on 28 October: the Soviet Union would withdraw its missiles from Cuba in exchange for a U.S. pledge not to invade Cuba and a tacit understanding that the United States would withdraw the aging U.S. medium-range Jupiter missiles from Turkey.

Viewpoint:
Yes. The Cuban Missile Crisis was handled effectively because the Kennedy administration avoided all-out nuclear conflict with the Soviet Union through quiet negotiations combined with a strong, public stand.

The Cuban Missile Crisis (October 1962) began when U.S. military reconnaissance flights provided proof that the Soviets were placing medium-range nuclear missiles in Cuba, ninety miles from Florida. This move was a destabilizing one as it reduced dramatically the flight time of, and hence the reaction time to, nuclear missiles that might be used to attack the United States. The United States was not friendly with Cuba, and the possibility of a communist regime in the Western Hemisphere possessing nuclear weapons was unacceptable. President John F. Kennedy decided to assert U.S. rights under the Monroe Doctrine (1823) to prevent this circumstance from happening.

The situation in Cuba was tense because, having just finished its revolution, it was not exactly stable. Still, the communists in Cuba continued to ride a wave of popularity and Cuban armed forces were enthusiastic, if not well-trained. Fidel Castro was no friend of the United States; after all, the Kennedy administration had tried to overthrow him in the failed Bay of Pigs invasion (April 1961), and it was fairly obvious to all that he was a true communist. The United States decided to undertake action to prevent the further placement of nuclear missiles in Cuba, by military force if necessary.

What the Americans did not know was that the Soviets already had nuclear weapons in

Cuba, which they planned to use to repel a possible invasion—this fact only became known in the West after the Cold War ended. Soviet doctrine allowed for the use of, and a willingness to use, tactical nuclear weapons in these circumstances. Of course, their use would have caused a general, almost undoubtedly nuclear, war. At the same time, the U.S. Army was preparing an invasion from Florida—moving tens of thousands of men and tons of matériel to the state—and was ready to attack if called upon. Both sides were ready for a confrontation.

Hawks on both sides pushed for war, even the possible use of nuclear weapons. Many people within the defense establishment believed that the best way to deal with the Soviet Union was to launch an all-out attack, including nuclear weapons, in a first strike. This assault would decide the Cold War all at once, in their opinion, and the victorious West could move on.

U. S. Air Force general Curtis E. LeMay, the architect of the most devastating air attacks in history—the fire bombing of Tokyo (9–10 March 1945)—and the nuclear attacks in Japan (August 1945), had no qualms about nuclear war. He believed not only that it was possible to win a nuclear exchange, but that the resulting millions of friendly casualties from such a confrontation would be acceptable. On the Soviet side, there also were many hawks who wanted war, especially since they believed that the United States would invade Cuba. While Nikita S. Khrushchev did not agree, he was willing to fight if necessary. Clearly both sides were "eyeball to eyeball."

The situation escalated, however, when the Cubans shot down a U-2 reconnaissance aircraft on a spy mission in their airspace. Cuba was perfectly within its rights to do this as the overflight was a violation of its national sovereignty. The fact that the United States did not know that

Cuban air defenses were capable of this action and the pilot was killed only added ammunition to the hawks in Washington.

There was only one method short of war, however, to prevent the placement of nuclear missiles in Cuba—a blockade, which is in fact an act of war. On the other hand, a "quarantine" (a blockade by another name) is not. By "quarantining" Cuba the United States could achieve its goal, using an extreme measure without the negative consequences attached to it. Still, the strategy was dangerous, for both sides clearly had no real idea of the motives or resolve of their opponents. The Kennedy administration announced that U.S. naval forces would stop, board, and search ships approaching Cuba in international waters and turn back those carrying offensive weapons. While this was a more "peaceful" solution, Kennedy made it clear that he would attack Cuba if the missiles already on the island were not removed.

Nevertheless, during the crisis the leadership in the United States and the Soviet Union realized that they were on the brink of a nuclear exchange and that, if they wanted to avoid it, they would have to negotiate. The problem was that they were so used to being enemies, after the end of World War II, that they did not really know how to talk to each other, especially since this situation had already proved how incorrect their concepts of each other were. Despite these difficulties, however, they negotiated.

The Soviet position, that they had a right to place missiles in Cuba, was not unreasonable as the United States had medium-range nuclear missiles in Europe pointed directly at the Union of Soviet Socialist Republics (U.S.S.R.). The reality was that the Soviets were simply doing what the Americans had already done and they misjudged U.S. intelligence capabilities, never expecting to get caught. Further, Khrushchev was honestly surprised by the U.S. reaction, for he had miscalculated U.S. resolve in this matter. Again, this blunder only demonstrates how little the two sides understood the motives and goals of the other.

Both sides worked together, for the first time since World War II, for a common goal and a common good, and reached equitable terms. The Soviets agreed to publicly pull out their nuclear weapons from Cuba, while the United States said it would secretly remove its medium-range missiles from Turkey. This agreement was a victory for both sides. The United States was able to save face with the secrecy clause, while the U.S.S.R. got the Americans to remove their weapons from the Soviet border.

In all, the crisis was successful in that both sides walked away from it with concessions at the cost of few lives. There was no world war, and the crisis set the stage for future relations. The United States and the U.S.S.R. came to the realization that having these weapons on the border of their enemy was a dangerous and destabilizing strategy. They also discovered that they needed greater communication with each other to prevent these misunderstandings and avoid a nuclear conflict. Finally, they recognized that perhaps they should consider working together to reduce their vast nuclear stockpiles.

Yet the United States and Soviet Union did not become friends after this incident. Both sides intensified their efforts to nullify the actions of the other, but with less directly confrontational means. The Soviets gave greater support to countries fighting U.S. interests, while the Americans reciprocated, giving rise to fighting each other by proxy.

The Soviets also made some crucial military decisions as a result of this confrontation. Most notably, they recognized that the U.S. quarantine was effective because the Soviet navy was unable to compete with its U.S. counterpart. This realization led to an intense period of naval construction in the Soviet Union to create a truly blue-water navy that could deal with this newly discerned threat. The Cold War was not over after the Cuban Missile Crisis, but the crisis was the last time that both sides stood on their highest nuclear alert status.

–WILLIAM H. KAUTT, SAN ANTONIO, TEXAS

Viewpoint:
No. The Kennedy administration could have adopted policies in the Cuban Missile Crisis that would have left the United States in a better strategic position vis-à-vis the Soviet Union.

One of the great questions of Cold War historiography is whether or not the resolution of the Cuban Missile Crisis (October 1962) was a victory for the Kennedy administration. Most scholars are familiar with the story of how the Soviet Union began placing offensive weapons in Cuba while assuring the United States that it was only providing defensive assistance to the Cubans. In August 1962 Director of Central Intelligence (DCI) John A. McCone noted that Soviet surface-to-air missiles (SAMs) in Cuba must be there to protect something far more valuable and began to suspect that they were protecting nuclear missiles. During August and September, Senator Kenneth B. Keating (R-New York) warned that the Soviets were sending missiles to Cuba. The Kennedy administration monitored developments, and both President John F. Kennedy and Congress delivered warnings in September against the introduction of offensive missiles into Cuba. Kennedy made public statements on 4 and 13

September warning the Soviets; Congress later backed him up with a joint resolution authorizing the president to take steps to prevent Cuba from becoming a threat. On 16 October evidence from U-2 overflights was presented to Kennedy showing that the Soviets had placed missiles on the island. During the next week an ad hoc advisory committee known as the Executive Committee of the National Security Council (ExComm) met in secret to devise the U.S. response, taking care not to tip off the press or public to the nature of their deliberations. On 22 October, Kennedy spoke to the nation about the nature of the Soviet missiles in Cuba and the measures he was instituting to meet the threat, including a naval "quarantine" of the island. The blockade effectively ended the supply of these weapons to Cuba, but did nothing to remove existing missiles. Diplomatic wrangling ensued in which the Soviets appeared to want either a no-invasion pledge by the United States or one coupled with the removal of U.S. missiles from Turkey, in return for withdrawal of its missiles. Just when it looked like the United States might have to make further concessions or invade Cuba, the Soviets on 28 October agreed to remove their missiles in return for a promise by the Americans not to invade Cuba (subject to United Nations [U.N.] inspection and verification that the missiles were removed). The Kennedy administration also quietly assured the Soviets that it already was committed to removing the missiles from Turkey a satisfactory amount of time after the crisis was over.

Soviet premier Nikita S. Khrushchev's gambit of placing nuclear-capable missiles in Cuba ended in failure for the Soviets, who were forced to withdraw their weapons while exacting only a public pledge that the U.S. would not invade Cuba. While this was undeniably a defeat for Khrushchev, it is less clear that this was a victory for Kennedy. A conventional interpretation is that Kennedy scored an impressive diplomatic triumph. By responding initially with a quarantine to prevent the introduction of further weapons to Cuba, he showed the firmness that convinced Khrushchev to back down before the United States resorted to more drastic military measures. Such dramatic actions as air strikes against the missile sites or an invasion of Cuba, however, might have triggered a Soviet response in Berlin or elsewhere that could have escalated to a nuclear exchange between the superpowers. There are, therefore, important criticisms of Kennedy's performance during and after the crisis that cast doubt on the assertion that he handled the crisis with consummate skill and won an important victory.

One of the initial critiques of Kennedy's performance stressed the dangers inherent in pushing the world to the precipice of nuclear

CUBAN MISSILE CRISIS

CUBAN MISSILES

On 22 October 1962 President John F. Kennedy, on radio and television, told the American people of the presence of Soviet nuclear missiles on the island of Cuba.

Within the past week, unmistakable evidence has established the fact that a series of offensive missile sites is now in preparation on that imprisoned island. The purpose of these bases can be none other than to provide a nuclear strike capability against the Western Hemisphere.

Upon receiving the first preliminary hard information of this nature last Tuesday morning at 9:00 a.m., I directed that our surveillance be stepped up. And now having confirmed and completed our evaluation of the evidence and our decision on a course of action, this Government feels obliged to report this new crisis to you in fullest detail.

The characteristics of these new missile sites indicate two distinct types of installations. Several of them include medium range ballistic missiles capable of carrying a nuclear warhead for a distance of more than 1,000 nautical miles. Each of these missiles, in short, is capable of striking Washington, D.C., the Panama Canal, Cape Canaveral, Mexico City, or any other city in the southeastern part of the United States, in Central America, or in the Caribbean area.

Additional sites not yet completed appear to be designed for intermediate range ballistic missiles—capable of traveling more than twice as far—and thus capable of striking most of the major cities in the Western Hemisphere, ranging as far north as Hudson Bay, Canada, and as far south as Lima, Peru. In addition, jet bombers, capable of carrying nuclear weapons, are now being uncrated and assembled in Cuba, while the necessary air bases are being prepared.

This urgent transformation of Cuba into an important strategic base—by the presence of these large, long range, and clearly offensive weapons of sudden mass destruction—constitutes an explicit threat to the peace and security of all the Americas, in flagrant and deliberate defiance of the Rio Pact of 1947, the traditions of this Nation and hemisphere, the joint resolution of the 87th Congress, the Charter of the United Nations, and my own public warnings to the Soviets on September 4 and 13. This action also contradicts the repeated assurances of Soviet spokesmen, both publicly and privately delivered, that the arms buildup in Cuba would retain its original defensive character, and that the Soviet Union had no need or desire to station strategic missiles on the territory of any other nation.

The size of this undertaking makes clear that it has been planned for some months. Yet only last month, after I had made clear the distinction between any introduction of ground-to-ground missiles and the existence of defensive antiaircraft missiles, the Soviet Government publicly stated on September 11, and I quote, "the armaments and military equipment sent to Cuba are designed exclusively for defensive purposes," that, and I quote the Soviet Government, "there is no need for the Soviet Government to shift its weapons . . . for a retaliatory blow to any other country, for instance Cuba," and that, and I quote their government, "the Soviet Union has so powerful rockets to carry these nuclear warheads that there is no need to search for sites for them beyond the boundaries of the Soviet Union." That statement was false.

Only last Thursday, as evidence of this rapid offensive buildup was already in my hand, Soviet Foreign Minister Gromyko told me in my office that he was instructed to make it clear once again, as he said his government had already done, that Soviet assistance to Cuba, and I quote, "pursued solely the purpose of contributing to the defense capabilities of Cuba," that, and I quote him, "training by Soviet specialists of Cuban nationals in handling defensive armaments was by no means offensive, and if it were otherwise," Mr. Gromyko went on, "the Soviet Government would never become involved in rendering such assistance." That statement also was false.

Source: *John F. Kennedy Library, Boston, Massachusetts, Internet Web Page.*

annihilation. Some critics even argue he primarily wanted to demonstrate his "toughness" as the 1962 midterm elections approached. Not only did this response to the crisis involve great risk of nuclear war, but it also brought unnecessary humiliation to Khrushchev and was a contributing factor to his ouster from power in 1964. In place of Khrushchev, who challenged the Stalinist legacy and was open to genuine efforts to reduce tensions with the West, the Soviets installed a leadership troika that eventually was dominated by Leonid Brezhnev, who was more Stalinist than Khrushchev and less interested in genuinely easing tensions than in a détente framework that permitted the Soviets and their proxies to gain from Western restraint. The second critique is that Kennedy, in fact, gave too much away, that beneath the appearance of a successful resolution of the crisis was the surrender of important issues of U.S. strategy.

The first critique of Kennedy is customarily associated with liberals and leftists, and it basically challenges the wisdom of Kennedy's confrontational response. Adlai E. Stevenson, the ambassador to the United Nations, and respected columnist Walter Lippman both advocated resolution of the crisis through a trade in which the United States would remove its Jupiter missiles from Turkey in return for a withdrawal of the Soviet missiles from Cuba. Kennedy met in the Oval Office with Soviet foreign minister Andrey Gromyko during the week that ExComm was considering the U.S. response, and Kennedy could have brought up the issue. The Soviet Union would have had no interest in publicizing these discussions, as that would have forced Kennedy to take a more confrontational policy in public for political reasons. Had the administration attempted to resolve this issue through quiet diplomacy, the Soviet Union and Khrushchev would have been spared the humiliation that contributed to two developments that worked against Western interests in the long run: the replacement of Khrushchev by a more hardline leadership and a renewed Soviet commitment to build up its nuclear forces just as Defense Secretary Robert McNamara was reasoning that the United States had attained strategic sufficiency and did not need further building of its strategic forces.

It has come out that Kennedy was prepared to trade the missiles in Turkey for the Soviet ones in Cuba. According to an administration plan, former U.N. official Andrew Cordier was to present to Secretary General U Thant a message that the Kennedy administration approved of a possible U.N. initiative calling upon the Americans and Soviets to remove their respective missiles. The Kennedy administration reasoned publicly, and in its back-channel contacts with the Soviet Union, that it could not trade the Jupiter missiles in Turkey because that would embolden potential adversaries to seek other means of blackmailing the U.S. into removal of other weapons from other friendly countries, thereby undermining U.S. reliability as a security guarantor. Revelations about the proposed Cordier gambit, however, reveal that the Kennedy administration was prepared, with the proper window-dressing, to make the trade as a gesture to world peace. Kennedy could have attempted such a resolution quietly through negotiations; although the administration would have taken a public-relations hit, had details of such arrangements been leaked by any government official who felt the United States was being blackmailed, it could have responded that the missiles in Turkey were already rendered obsolete by those carried on Polaris submarines that routinely sailed in the Mediterranean Sea. The Soviets could not replace their missiles in Cuba with any comparable weapons system. In effect, Kennedy could have argued, the United States and Western Europe would be more secure after the trade than before it.

A critique of the Kennedy response offered by more hardline critics is that it was too weak. Dean Acheson, secretary of state under President Harry S Truman, was brought in during the Cuban Missile Crisis as an informal adviser to the ExComm. Acheson argued that the Soviet missiles in Cuba were a direct threat that should be removed forcibly. Attorney General Robert F. Kennedy countered that an attack on the missile sites would make the president the moral equivalent of Japanese World War II leader Hideki Tojo. Acheson rejected this argument, citing President Kennedy's public comments in September and the subsequent resolution of Congress; he also pointed out that the Monroe Doctrine served notice to foreign powers that the United States would consider their adventures in the Western Hemisphere a hostile act. Having given these warnings, Acheson contended, the United States could act against the Soviet missiles without forfeiting the moral high ground.

Questions arising out of the Monroe Doctrine, in fact, provide some of the strongest grounds of criticism for the performance of the Kennedy administration. In December 1823 President James Monroe pronounced that the United States would regard interference by European nations in the Western Hemisphere as an unfriendly act. While the United States lacked the force to back this pronouncement and relied on the strength of the British navy to keep Europeans out of the hemisphere for most of the nineteenth century, the Monroe Doctrine had been invoked and backed forcibly with some frequency in the twentieth century. While such events were not always happy from the perspective of the Latin Americans or Americans involved, this doctrine was a cardinal principle of U.S. policy and one that had not been renounced. Kennedy's promise not to invade Cuba in return for the removal of the Soviet missiles, however, conceded that a hostile foreign power, motivated by an ideology implacably hostile to the United States, could act in the Western Hemisphere in contravention of American interests and the United States would accept it. Even if the United States had no intention of invading Cuba, its renunciation of the Monroe Doctrine marked a significant ideological retreat in the face of Soviet power.

Whether one criticizes or praises Kennedy in his handling of the Cuban Missile Crisis, he clearly benefited from considerable good fortune in its resolution. The media never learned about the secret deliberations of the ExComm and accepted the offered explanations for the forces moving into the southeastern United States leading up to 22 October. The Soviets did not hold off announcing their final capitulation until Kennedy authorized the Cordier mission to proceed. As it was, the crisis left several lingering effects that worked against U.S. interests. The Soviet failure contributed to the replacement of Khrushchev by a leadership more hard-line, shrewd, and successful. The Soviets also learned the importance of building a large nuclear arsenal quickly, precisely at the moment that McNamara was erroneously concluding that the Soviets knew they could not match the United States and would not attempt to do so. The push to the abyss of nuclear destruction left European allies of the United States displeased, even though they remained supportive during the crisis. Nonetheless, the realization that the United States could place them in mortal danger over an issue so far removed from them posed important complications for future relations between the allies, especially with France. The imminent problem of Soviet missiles in Cuba had been resolved in part because of abundant good for-

tune, but the seeds of future problems were sown amid the triumphalist rhetoric.

It is understandable that Kennedy has been credited for rejecting either more pacifistic or more warlike recommendations in selecting his course. Yet, his performance was too flawed to warrant celebration. He might have assumed a more confrontational posture, struck militarily, and left no room for doubt about U.S. strength and willingness to defend its allies and cardinal tenets of foreign policy. Or he might have engaged in quiet negotiations designed to facilitate the trade he was ready to make, and essentially made anyway, which would have avoided the humiliation of Khrushchev and the Soviet Union that led to the ascension of political forces more astute and resistant to meaningful accommodation with the West. In seeking to appear tough but restrained, Kennedy passed up policies that could have left the United States in a better position vis-à-vis the Soviet Union.

–JOHN A. SOARES JR., GEORGE
WASHINGTON UNIVERSITY

References

Michael R. Beschloss, *The Crisis Years: Kennedy and Khrushchev, 1960–1963* (New York: Edward Burlingame, 1991);

James Blight and David Welch, *On the Brink: Americans and Soviets Reexamine the Cuban Missile Crisis* (New York: Hill & Wang, 1989);

Dino Brugioni, *Eyeball to Eyeball: The Inside Story of the Cuban Missile Crisis*, edited by Robert F. McCort (New York: Random House, 1991);

Aleksandr Fursenko and Timothy Naftali, *One Hell of a Gamble: Khrushchev, Castro, and Kennedy, 1958–1964* (New York: Norton, 1997);

Raymond L. Garthoff, *Reflections on the Cuban Missile Crisis* (Washington, D.C.: Brookings Institution, 1989).

DECOLONIZATION

Should the United States have pressured Britain and France to decolonize?

Viewpoint: Yes. U.S. pressure on Britain and France to dismantle their colonial systems opened the door to freer international trade.

Viewpoint: No. It was poor diplomacy for the United States to push France and Great Britain to decolonize; the Americans needed the support of these allies in confronting the Soviet Union.

The United States, itself created after a war of independence against the British Empire, had always been disposed against imperial acquisitions, by itself or others. There are but few ventures in American history that were similar to the imperial drive of the European powers, and these endeavors (the Philippines and Cuba) did not last long. Explicit expression of this anti-imperialism is found in President Woodrow Wilson's "Fourteen Points" plan for post–World War I Europe, and his calls for the self-determination of peoples. After World War II the United States began to apply pressure on its two allies, Britain and France—but also on the Netherlands, Belgium, and Portugal—to dismantle their colonial holdings in Africa, Asia, and the Western Hemisphere.

Was the United States correct in pressuring its allies to abandon their colonies? Some historians and economists question not so much the ultimate correctness of that policy, but its timing. First, they argue that it made little sense to weaken two strong allies of the United States at the time when they were standing shoulder to shoulder with America in its global effort to contain the Soviet Union. They point out that in many of the former colonies regimes came to power that were not always friendly to the West and its interests. The second argument holds that the United States did not do any favors to many of the developing countries by pressuring the European colonizing powers to leave too early. In many cases the newly independent states found themselves without the physical or administrative infrastructure, as well as political and economic institutions, to allow them to function effectively as modern states.

On the other side of the debate is the argument that colonialism was an archaic system that was bound to be swept away under the pressure of nationalism and modernity. In addition, the European powers did much to plunder their colonies, and there was no reason to believe that they would now begin to be more attentive to nation-building and development. The United States was thus wise to stand on the side of inevitable change. In addition, U.S. history and values left it no choice but to support self-determination and freedom. Perhaps, this argument goes, had the United States been more energetic in distinguishing itself from its colonial allies, it would have had less trouble in recruiting the support of Third World countries in its campaign against the Union of Soviet Socialist Republic (U.S.S.R.).

Viewpoint:
Yes. U.S. pressure on Britain and France to dismantle their colonial systems opened the door to freer international trade.

Following the end of World War II, many American policy makers feared a return to the economic chaos, high-tariff walls, and regional trade blocks that characterized the Great Depression. The danger for the United States was that restoration of the beggar-thy-neighbor protectionist policies of the 1930s threatened its recovery. The economy of the United States was dependent on foreign markets and overseas investment opportunities as an outlet for its domestic surplus. For this reason, the United States opposed any state that espoused economic nationalism and preferential trading (communism and Third World nationalist revolutions were especially dangerous—both called for a closed trading system, rejected private property, and favored a centralized system of production and distribution).

In 1932 Britain adopted imperial preferences at the Imperial Economic Conference in Ottawa, Canada, which produced a network of twelve bilateral agreements among the commonwealth countries, granting each special trading privileges. Britain offered imperial preferences in return for concessions (the exchange was primarily foodstuffs from the dominions for British manufactured goods). The Ottawa agreements were followed by seventeen trade agreements (1932–1935), creating a vast "Sterling Area," which was a group of countries that chose to base their economies on the pound sterling. These countries were heavily dependent on the British market, did most of their trade in sterling, and/or fixed their own currency exchange rates in relation to the pound, and held some or all of their reserves in sterling. During the 1930s Britain resisted pressure for an Anglo-American accord to reduce the imperial preference system.

As a commercially liberal hegemon, the United States established a liberal multilateral trading system benignly through the Bretton Woods system. The conferences at Bretton Woods, New Hampshire (1–22 July 1944), known formally as the United Nations Monetary and Financial Conference, created an international monetary system to promote stable economic exchanges. The International Monetary Fund (IMF) and International Bank for Reconstruction and Development (IBRD, or World Bank) were established to help finance the reconstruction after the war. The IMF created fixed exchange rates to keep currency values within specific ranges (making the dollar the key currency against which other currencies were measured) and advanced credits to countries with balance-of-payments deficits to discourage them from unilaterally devaluing their currency. In 1947 the General Agreement on Tariffs and Trade (GATT) was founded to reduce tariffs and other nontariff barriers on trade.

The United States also established a liberal multilateral trading system coercively through the Atlantic Charter (Anglo-American declaration of war aims that was signed on 12 August 1941), Lend Lease Act (11 March 1941), Anglo-American Mutual Aid Agreement (28 February 1942), and post–World War II loans to Britain and France. The British imperial preference system was seen as a barrier to American economic recovery from the Great Depression since foreign markets could provide an outlet for surplus agricultural and manufactured products. U.S. secretary of state Cordell Hull believed the Ottawa agreements to be one of the greatest commercial injuries ever inflicted on the United States.

Britain and the United States jointly signed the Atlantic Charter with the goal of reconstructing the postwar multilateral trading order. The United States used the agreement to force Britain to reverse its imperial preference system, and also wrote a nondiscrimination clause into the document. A draft of the fourth "condition," as cited by Lloyd C. Gardner in *Sterling-Dollar Diplomacy: Anglo-American Collaboration in the Reconstruction of Multilateral Trade* (1956), dealt with economic matters following the war:

> Fourth, they will strive to promote mutually advantageous economic relations between them through the elimination of any discrimination in either the United States of America or in the United Kingdom against the importation of any product originating in the other country; and they will endeavour to further the enjoyment by all peoples of access on equal terms to the markets and to the raw materials which are needed for their economic prosperity.

For the sake of good Anglo-American relations, President Franklin D. Roosevelt agreed to Prime Minister Winston Churchill's request to water down the original accord. The redrafted paragraph included "with due respect for their existing obligations."

The Anglo-American Mutual Aid Agreement outlined the provisions of the lend-lease of supplies. Article VII was less vague about the intent of eliminating discriminatory trade policy in the reconstruction of the postwar multilateral trading order. The United States and Britain agreed to

... the elimination of all forms of discriminatory treatment in international commerce, and to the reduction of tariffs and other trade barriers; and, in general, to the attainment of all the economic objectives set forth in the Joint Declaration made on August 12, 1941, by the President of the United States of America and the Prime Minister of the United Kingdom.

The goal of Article VII was to destroy the British imperial economic bloc and break up the sterling area. Similarly, the intention of the Lend Lease Agreement with the French (signed on 28 February 1945), much like the accord with Britain, was the "elimination of all forms of discriminatory treatment in international commerce." With such a policy the United States often operated at cross purposes with Britain and France in the Middle East and Asia.

After World War II the United States made its foreign aid conditional upon the acceptance of the open-door trading principle of equal opportunity to global markets and raw materials. The Anglo-American Financial Agreement (6 December 1945) extracted several painful concessions from the British. In 1945, in exchange for a loan of $3.8 billion, London agreed to dismantle much of its imperial trading bloc in eighteen months, including a British commitment to end the sterling area dollar pool and quantitative import controls on American goods. In addition, Britain was required to restore sterling convertibility in mid 1947, allowing countries enjoying export surpluses with the United Kingdom to exchange sterling for scarce dollars. A devastated England had no choice but to retreat from its imperial preference system.

In addition to destroying the British system of imperial preferences, the United States sought to dismantle the empire (at least until the rise of the Cold War rivalry with the Soviet Union), by promoting a policy of self determination. Article III of the Atlantic Charter called for "sovereign rights and self-government restored to those who have been forcibly deprived of them." Roosevelt repeatedly offered advice to Churchill on the desirable steps toward Indian independence.

France received the same treatment from the United States. In 1945 the French leader Charles de Gaulle received a $1 billion loan from the United States in exchange for his promises to curtail government subsidies and currency manipulation that had given advantages to its exporters in the world markets.

Concerned about a return to the economic blocs of the 1930s and about its own postwar economic recovery, Washington used the leverage created by the dependence of London on American financial assistance to destroy the British imperial economic bloc, dismantle the Ottawa system of imperial preferences, and break up the sterling area. The postwar American objectives of fostering stability were also political in nature since tensions between the trading blocs had contributed to World War II and would preclude world peace. Hull pre-

Algerian protestors jeering a French paratrooper guarding a town hall in Algiers, circa 1960

(Keystone Press)

DECOLONIZATION

dicted in 1938, "I know that without expansion of trade, based on fair dealing and equal treatment for all, there can be no stability and security either within or among nations."

–STEVEN E. LOBELL AND BRENT STEELE,
UNIVERSITY OF NORTHERN IOWA

Viewpoint:
No. It was poor diplomacy for the United States to push France and Great Britain to decolonize; the Americans needed the support of these allies in confronting the Soviet Union.

The future of the British and French colonial empires was a major point of contention between the United States and its Western allies during World War II. Knowing that both Britain and France would have a difficult time reestablishing control over their colonies immediately after the war, President Franklin D. Roosevelt categorically refused to promise to help them do so. Roosevelt's successors embraced this position and even enhanced it by frequently pressuring U.S. allies, both through quiet diplomacy and direct power politics, to free their colonies. By the early 1960s the colonial empires of both Britain and France were mostly gone. Although the policy was founded in the belief that the United States would live up to the idealism of its own past and become more influential in the Third World by distancing itself from the imperialism of its allies, American pressure for decolonization had far more liabilities than benefits.

One of the chief problems with pushing for decolonization was that it opened the United States to justifiable criticism about its own policies in the Third World. Even as Washington was preaching its solidarity with Third World revolutionaries and forcing the hand of Britain and France to let go of their sizable colonial holdings, the United States was vulnerable to its own critics. Although it allowed its major overseas colony, the Philippines, to become independent in 1946, Washington exercised a great amount of control over a considerable amount of territory in the Third World. At a time when the place of the Third World on the geopolitical chessboard was far from clear, U.S. economic and political influence in many developing countries was a marked target for the propaganda of revolutionary movements and the Soviets, who came to support such movements. Many Latin American revolutionaries focused on U.S. economic (and implicitly, political) domination as an important

cause of the woes of their countries. In many ways persuasive revolutionary propaganda capitalized on what was at the least a semantic inconsistency in U.S. policy toward colonialism after the war. Many in the Third World asked themselves how the United States could champion national independence and political freedom for oppressed peoples while it supported dictators who ruled their countries in accordance with U.S. interests while suppressing political liberty and social justice. Some came to believe that the United States was merely trying to move its allies out of strategic parts of the world in order to move in itself. In an ideologically charged superpower struggle, the seemingly quixotic commitment of Washington to the liberation of colonies opened it to accusations of hypocrisy that were not unjustified.

The U.S. position on colonies also had a desultory effect on its alliance relationships. Containment of the Soviet Union, the dominant Cold War strategy pursued by the United States, relied on a global network of allies. Britain and France were both charter members of the North Atlantic Treaty Organization (NATO), the first and strongest of these alliances, while they were simultaneously the largest colonial powers. Tension came to a head in 1956 when Washington withdrew support from Anglo-French intervention in Egypt, where President Abdel Gamal Nasser had just nationalized the European-controlled Suez Canal, even though President Dwight D. Eisenhower had promised French and British leaders that he would support a military solution if peaceful alternatives failed. Indeed, the United States voted with the Soviet Union and against its own allies in support of a United Nations (U.N.) resolution calling for a cease-fire and withdrawal of European troops.

Although British politicians had a relatively easier time reconciling themselves to the loss of their overseas possessions, granted most of them independence in an orderly manner, and weathered the storm in Anglo-American relations, France had serious problems divesting itself of its empire, and related factors seriously affected its relationship with the United States. After losing its struggle against the Marxist-nationalist forces of Vietnamese leader Ho Chi Minh in 1954, the French faced a much more serious problem in Algeria. Regarded as an integral part of metropolitan France and inhabited by more than one million European settlers and their descendants who claimed French citizenship, Algeria dominated French politics. Difficulties in dealing with this issue created widespread domestic unrest, nearly resulted in a dangerous military intervention in French politics, and led directly to the collapse of the Fourth Republic (the postwar constitutional order of the country) in 1958. All the while the Eisenhower administration, and prominent politicians such as Democratic senator and future president John F. Kennedy, called for France to depart. When French president Charles de Gaulle was forced to abandon Algeria in 1962, he did so at risks that were both political and personal (the decision led to more than one assassination attempt). The international stature of France declined further and the country was forced to integrate most of the Europeans who subsequently fled from Algeria as refugees. By 1966 de Gaulle's consciousness of the decline of France as a world power and his sense that the United States had betrayed French interests led him to withdraw his armed forces from the integrated command structure of NATO and embark on a policy of "détente, entente, and cooperation" with the Soviet Union. While U.S. opposition to French colonial policies were not the only factor that led de Gaulle to a more independent foreign policy, they nevertheless weakened the solidarity of the Atlantic alliance and encouraged de Gaulle to disengage from a close relationship with the United States.

American pressure on the colonial powers to abandon their overseas possessions affected alliance stability at another level. Many European governments were actually able to rationalize decolonization as beneficial, since it eliminated serious drains on their economic and military resources and reduced their vulnerability to international crises. Many Europeans argued that the period of colonization had built up economic infrastructures and markets that would remain profitable after the colonies achieved political independence and that continued political domination was actually becoming unprofitable. While this theory met with mixed results, decolonization allowed the colonial powers to husband their economic resources domestically and accelerate their postwar recovery and growth. As a result of the loss of their overseas possessions, European politicians looked more constructively at European integration and its strong economic benefits.

Withdrawal from world-power status also meant that individual European NATO members would benefit from U.S. military protection. Defended by the American nuclear umbrella and a strong U.S. conventional commitment to Western Europe, the Europeans were free to spend proportionally much less on their own defense and devote these resources to domestic growth. Over time these pragmatic considerations translated into a determined effort on the part of many Europeans to decouple Western Europe from the United States and cast an integrated Europe in

the role of an independent world power. Although American influence was once again not the only decisive factor, the opposition of Washington to colonialism contributed to its European allies realizing that their colonial empires had no future and that their energy and ambition would best be directed toward integration and independent diplomacy.

Decolonization harmed U.S. security interests in more direct ways as well. In a general sense the departure of European powers from their colonies created power vacuums that destabilized entire regions and opened vast amounts of new territory to superpower confrontation. The bloodiest battles of the Cold War were fought in the Third World. Nowhere was this fact more true than in Southeast Asia, where the failure of the French to defeat the Vietnamese insurgents and its subsequent departure (actually urged by the United States) left Washington with the painful choice of allowing the region to fall under communist domination or picking up where the French had left off. The tortured involvement of the United States in Vietnam began in large measure with its own calls for decolonization in Indochina.

Though Vietnam was singular in its costs to the United States, the absence of European control allowed emerging states to do as they pleased with regard to strategic relations. Often nationalist Third World leaders sought to play the superpowers off against each other, always with their own interests in mind. Though some Mobutu Sese Seko's in Zaire and Suharto's in Indonesia after 1965) became firm U.S. allies, in many cases emerging Third World nations pursued policies that compromised American strategic interests, and the earlier anticolonial rhetoric of Washington did nothing to prevent it after independence had been achieved. Even Nasser, whom the United States had supported over its own allies during the Suez Crisis, kept Egypt in a de facto alliance with the Soviet Union until his death in 1970. After gaining its independence from Britain in 1947, India moved from its position as a colony of the closest U.S. ally to a close relationship of its own with Moscow. Dozens of other Third World leaders were happy to invite Soviet advisers and capital into their countries to facilitate modernization programs that the former colonial powers had been in the process of carrying out when they left.

These events dovetailed with Soviet strategy in the Cold War. Taking his cues from Lenin's prediction that nationalist revolution in the Third World was the first step toward world communist revolution, Soviet leader Nikita S. Khrushchev carried out an active policy of providing moral, material, and financial support to

DECOLONIZATION

DECLARATION ON GRANTING INDEPENDENCE TO COLONIAL COUNTRIES AND PEOPLES

United Nations General Assembly Resolution 1514 (XV), December 14, 1960

Mindful of the determination proclaimed by the peoples of the world in the Charter of the United Nations to reaffirm faith in fundamental human rights, in the dignity and worth of the human person, in the equal rights of men and women and of nations large and small and to promote social progress and better standards of life in larger freedom,

Conscious of the need for the creation of conditions of stability and well-being and peaceful and friendly relations based on respect for the principles of equal rights and self-determination of all peoples, and of universal respect for, and observance of, human rights and fundamental freedoms for all without distinction as to race, sex, language or religion,

Recognizing the passionate yearning for freedom in all dependent peoples and the decisive role of such peoples in the attainment of their independence,

Aware of the increasing conflicts resulting from the denial of or impediments in the way of freedom of such peoples, which constitute a serious threat to world peace,

Considering the important role of the United Nations in assisting the movement for independence in Trust and Non-Self-Governing Territories,

Recognizing that the peoples of the world ardently desire the end of colonialism in all its manifestations,

Convinced that the continued existence of colonialism prevents the development of international economic co-operation, impedes the social, cultural and economic development of dependent peoples and militates against the United Nations ideal of universal peace,

Affirming that peoples may, for their own ends, freely dispose of their natural wealth and resources without prejudice to any obligations arising out of international economic co-operation, based upon the principle of mutual benefit, and international law,

Believing that the process of liberation is irresistible and irreversible and that, in order to avoid serious crises, an end must be put to colonialism and all practices of segregation and discrimination associated therewith,

Welcoming the emergence in recent years of a large number of dependent territories into freedom and independence, and recognizing the increasingly powerful trends towards freedom in such territories which have not yet attained independence,

Convinced that all peoples have an inalienable right to complete freedom, the exercise of their sovereignty and the integrity of their national territory,

Solemnly proclaims the necessity of bringing to a speedy and unconditional end colonialism in all its forms and manifestations;

And to this end Declares that:

1. The subjection of peoples to alien subjugation, domination and exploitation constitutes a denial of fundamental human rights, is contrary to the Charter of the United Nations and is an impediment to the promotion of world peace and co-operation.

2. All peoples have the right to self-determination; by virtue of that right they freely determine their political status and freely pursue their economic, social and cultural development.

3. Inadequacy of political, economic, social or educational preparedness should never serve as a pretext for delaying independence.

4. All armed action or repressive measures of all kinds directed against dependent peoples shall cease in order to enable them to exercise peacefully and freely their right to complete independence, and the integrity of their national territory shall be respected.

5. Immediate steps shall be taken, in Trust and Non-Self-Governing Territories or all other territories which have not yet attained independence, to transfer all powers to the peoples of those territories, without any conditions or reservations, in accordance with their freely expressed will and desire, without any distinction as to race, creed or colour, in order to enable them to enjoy complete independence and freedom.

6. Any attempt aimed at the partial or total disruption of the national unity and the territorial integrity of a country is incompatible with the purposes and principles of the Charter of the United Nations.

7. All States shall observe faithfully and strictly the provisions of the Charter of the United Nations, the Universal Declaration of Human Rights and the present Declaration on the basis of equality, non-interference in the internal affairs of all States, and respect for the sovereign rights of all peoples and their territorial integrity.

Source: *Internet Modern History Sourcebook, Internet web site.*

Third World nationalists. Soviet support reached scores of non- and even anticommunist governments and political movements that had liberation from colonialism and Western influence as their goal. In the process the American containment structure was breached in disparate parts of the world and U.S. support and intervention (almost always without European assistance) became the only answer to Soviet expansionism. In a plethora of cases, noncommunist governments in strategically situated countries that had formerly been European colonies tilted toward the Soviet Union (for example, Egypt, Algeria, India, and Indonesia before 1965), while others were ruled at one time or another by hostile communist regimes (Vietnam, Cambodia, Angola, South Yemen, and Grenada). By removing political stability from much of the world, however oppressive it may have been, decolonization as it was encouraged by Washington only helped the Soviets achieve their ends to the detriment of the U.S. strategic position.

Finally, the Third World itself has suffered tremendously from the domestic political consequences of decolonization. While bad situations were made worse by civil conflicts fought between rival indigenous movements that enjoyed superpower support, many other problems that colonial rule had kept under control exploded. For all its flaws, colonial rule generally managed to keep ethnic and religious strife from developing into violence. Decolonization had the opposite effect from the beginning. The partition of the British Raj into a Hindu India and Muslim Pakistan in 1947 was followed almost immediately by religious violence and the horrible population transfer between those two countries, in which millions died or lost their homes after having lived in relative security during 150 years of British rule. Tension in the subcontinent has remained strong, leading both states to develop nuclear weapons. British withdrawal from its mandate in Palestine in 1948 left the young Israeli state vulnerable to the three major wars Arab states waged against it over the next twenty-five years. In central Africa the genocidal slaughter of the Tutsi population of Rwanda in 1994 stands out as an example of unrestrained intolerance, while much of the rest of Africa struggled to solve contentions arising from ethnic and religious diversity. Many newly independent Third World nations have also been plagued with such problems as massive overpopulation, famine, AIDS, economic difficulty of all types, and environmental catastrophe.

Social difficulties aside, political stability and human-rights abuses were more the rule in former colonies than the exception. Despite the quixotic rhetoric of anticolonialists, few colonies achieved independence with either the institutional basis or economic infrastructure necessary to develop stable governments and societies. Indeed, the expediency that American critics of colonialism demanded with regard to decolonization often led European powers to withdraw from colonies without having had the time or power to establish stable postcolonial governments. Colonies often emerged as independent nations with little more than small, poorly organized rebel movements in charge. This lack of experienced leadership often led to military governments and the establishment of police states that were as brutal as they were incapable of running a country. In one case—the British withdrawal from Rhodesia (now Zimbabwe)—militant settlers led by open white supremacist Ian Smith seized control of the decolonization process and declared its independence in 1965 as a racist state governed by its tiny European minority.

Many former colonies have spent much of their histories as independent nations ruled by corrupt and ruthless dictatorships, the crimes of some of which have no parallel even in colonial history. In Cambodia, formerly part of French Indochina, Pol Pot's communist regime murdered as many as one-third of its citizens in a bizarre attempt at social architecture. Idi Amin's regime in the former British colony of Uganda systematically murdered hundreds of thousands of political opponents. In part of what used to be French Equatorial Africa, an army officer named Jean Bédel Bokassa crowned himself emperor of the Central African Empire in 1977 and is rumored to have eaten children who refused to wear school uniforms bearing his picture. With few exceptions (notably Botswana) the history of decolonization is not one of peaceful transitions to stable, healthy, and democratic societies.

American pressure on its allies to let their colonies go had few benefits. It exposed the United States to charges of hypocrisy and alienated close allies, as well as helped persuade European leaders to pursue competitive economic development within the Western camp and the integration of Europe as a world power in its own right, while the United States provided much of their military security and was left trying to replace their presence in strategic parts of the Third World. Decolonization, and U.S. support for it, also fed into Soviet attempts to expand communist influence globally. In a superpower conflict that could not be allowed to escalate to nuclear confrontation, the postcolonial Third World became the principal battlefield of the Cold War. In a broader sense, European withdrawal from the Third World brought with it many problems that were never adequately addressed.

—PAUL DU QUENOY,
GEORGETOWN UNIVERSITY

References

P. T. Bauer, *Equality, the Third World, and Economic Delusion* (Cambridge, Mass.: Harvard University Press, 1981);

Bauer, *United States Aid and Indian Economic Development* (Washington, D.C.: American Enterprise Association, 1959);

P. J. Cain and A. G. Hopkins, *British Imperialism: Crisis and Deconstruction, 1914–1990* (London & New York: Longman, 1993);

Karen Dawisha, *Soviet Foreign Policy Toward Egypt* (London: Macmillan, 1979; New York: St. Martin's Press, 1979);

James J. Dougherty, *The Politics of Wartime Aid: American Economic Assistance to France and French Northwest Africa, 1940–1946* (Westport, Conn.: Greenwood Press, 1978);

Lloyd C. Gardner, *Sterling-Dollar Diplomacy: Anglo-American Collaboration in the Reconstruction of Multilateral Trade* (Oxford: Clarendon Press, 1956);

Gardner, Walter F. LaFeber, and Thomas J. McCormick, *Creation of the American Empire: U.S. Diplomatic History* (Chicago: Rand McNally, 1973);

Paul Kennedy, *The Rise and Fall of the Great Powers: Economic Change and Military Conflict from 1500 to 2000* (New York: Random House, 1987);

V. G. Kiernan, *European Empires From Conquest to Collapse, 1815–1960* (Leicester, U.K.: Leicester University Press, 1982);

Warren F. Kimball, "Lend-Lease and the Open Door: The Temptation of British Opulence, 1937–1942," *Political Science Quarterly,* 86 (June 1971): 232–259;

Kimball, *The Most Unsordid Act: Lend-Lease, 1939–1941* (Baltimore: Johns Hopkins Press, 1969);

Henry Kissinger, *Diplomacy* (New York: Simon & Schuster, 1994);

LaFeber, *America, Russia, and the Cold War 1945–1996,* eighth edition (New York: McGraw-Hill, 1997);

Bruce D. Porter, *The USSR in Third World Conflicts: Soviet Arms and Diplomacy in Local Wars, 1945–1980* (Cambridge & New York: Cambridge University Press, 1984);

Peter W. Rodman, *More Precious Than Peace: The Cold War and the Struggle for the Third World* (New York: Scribners, 1994);

Tony Smith, *America's Mission: The United States and the Worldwide Struggle for Democracy in the Twentieth Century* (Princeton: Princeton University Press, 1994);

William Appleman Williams, *The Tragedy of American Diplomacy* (Cleveland: World, 1959);

Fareed Zakaria, *From Wealth to Power: The Unusual Origins of American's World Role* (Princeton: Princeton University Press, 1998).

DECOLONIZATION

DEMOCRACY IMPERILED

Did the foreign diplomacy of the Nixon administration violate democratic principles?

Viewpoint: Yes. The Nixon/Kissinger method of conducting foreign policy undermined democratic principles with excessive secrecy and clandestine operations against elected Third World governments.

Viewpoint: No. The effective diplomacy of Richard M. Nixon and Henry Kissinger depended on timing and confidentiality that precluded congressional debates and media investigations.

Richard M. Nixon's 1968 election as president reflected ambition, hard work, and the discrediting of Democratic rival Hubert H. Humphrey by his close association with the Vietnam War (ended 1975). Nixon, under no illusions about his personal popularity with an increasingly influential media, was correspondingly determined to bring America's longest war to an end—but not as an end in itself. Nixon sought above all to develop a national strategy that would free the United States from the bipolar rigidity of the Cold War and the accompanying high risks of nuclear and conventional confrontation in places such as Vietnam. As his right hand, and eventual secretary of state, he chose Harvard professor Henry Kissinger.

Both men were committed to a new course. Ending the war was only the first step—but it took five years to accomplish. As Nixon reduced U.S. troop levels and sought to improve the self-sufficiency of South Vietnam, Kissinger fought diplomatically for a comprehensive withdrawal of all foreign forces from the country, followed by free elections. Both Vietnamese governments were sufficiently unhappy with those prospects, and that peace negotiations remained in gridlock. In turn this stalemate did nothing for the domestic credibility of the Nixon/Kissinger team—particularly in light of Nixon's campaign promise that he had a plan to end the war. It was not exactly a lie, but the extension of the time frame left the president vulnerable to revived charges of being "Tricky Dick," dishonest and conniving.

On other fronts Nixon and Kissinger achieved significant successes. Determined pursuit of détente seemed to soften U.S.-Soviet relations for the first time in decades. Arms-limitation talks were capped by a nuclear nonproliferation treaty, whose conclusion was facilitated by the unprecedented thawing of relations with China. Beginning with a ping-pong match, the process culminated in February 1972 with Nixon's state visit to Beijing. For a while it seemed that the bipolar Cold War might mutate into a three-way balance of power.

That prospect, however, was too Orwellian for increasing numbers of domestic critics. On one level they opposed the clandestine nature of Nixon administration diplomacy. On a deeper plane they criticized what they called its amoral nature—its indifference, for example, to human-rights issues in the Soviet Union and its willingness to make deals with the most unsavory of Third World regimes. Nixon and Kissinger were both elitists. Neither was good at self-explanation. Their appeals to pay more attention to product than process rang hollow as the Watergate affair

(1972) engulfed the administration and the emptiness of the finally signed Vietnamese peace accords (January 1973) became apparent. In the end Kissinger returned to Harvard, while Nixon resigned rather than face impeachment. Whether their foreign-policy achievements merited a better fate is the subject of this dispute.

Viewpoint:
Yes. The Nixon/Kissinger method of conducting foreign policy undermined democratic principles with excessive secrecy and clandestine operations against elected Third World governments.

President Richard M. Nixon and Henry Kissinger, first as national security advisor and then as secretary of state, followed a foreign policy that they saw as pragmatic and appropriate for the United States in a world where the war in Vietnam had proved American power had limits. Their pragmatism, however, was not tempered by principle. As a result, both within the United States and abroad, their foreign policy, successful or not, proved antithetical to democratic principles.

Nixon's foreign policy began undermining democracy in the United States prior to his election in 1968. During his campaign he claimed to have a "secret plan" to end the war in Vietnam, but he could not reveal the details because that would tip his hand to the Vietnamese leaders. In reality he had no such plan, beyond a vague hope that he would be able to end the war quickly, much as President Dwight D. Eisenhower, under whom Nixon had served as vice president, was able to end the fighting in Korea shortly after his election. This lie deprived the American people of the opportunity to make an informed choice between Nixon and his Democratic opponent, Hubert H. Humphrey, who, as Lyndon B. Johnson's vice president, supported the continuation of the war. All politicians promise more than they can deliver during an election campaign, but Nixon disguised his lie by proclaiming that national-security interests were involved. It was the first time Nixon's penchant for secrecy would prove incompatible with participatory democracy, but not the last.

Electoral politics again led to deceit during Nixon's reelection campaign in 1972. With the election fast approaching, the Vietnam peace talks stalled. Afraid that voters might reject a president who proved unable to end the war in four years, Kissinger made public pronouncements implying progress was being made and a final end to the war could be expected soon. This reassurance, which in no way represented the reality of the talks, again deprived the American people of the information they needed to choose a president.

Nixon's most egregious assault on democracy occurred between the two elections. In 1969 Nixon, responding to the advice of U.S. military leaders to attack the supply lines leading from North to South Vietnam, authorized the secret bombing of Cambodia. As the assault could hardly have been kept veiled from opposing military forces, the only ones deceived were the American people. The ability to decide between war and peace is at the heart of sovereign power. American citizens have chosen to exercise that power through the mechanism of the Constitution, which requires congressional consent to go to war. While the president holds constitutional authority as commander in chief, Nixon's use of that power to expand the war to Cambodia, without even informing Congress or the people, was an abuse of that authority and antithetical to democracy.

The Nixon/Kissinger way of conducting foreign policy also proved antithetical to democracy abroad, an ironic result given that the promotion of the democratic way of life, as opposed to totalitarian communism, was in theory a chief aim of U.S. foreign policy. Around the world the United States supported anticommunist thugs and compliant dictators, acting to promote what Nixon and Kissinger considered to be the chief American interest abroad: stability, not democracy.

The most infamous assault on democracy abroad during the Nixon/Kissinger years was the overthrow, and possible murder, of Salvador Allende Gossens, the democratically elected president of Chile. In 1970 Allende formed a coalition of socialist and other Marxist parties to support his campaign for president. Seeing not a nation searching for answers to pressing social and economic questions but rather a challenge to American authority—a dubious concept at best outside the United States—Nixon ordered that the election of Allende be stopped. He applied economic pressure by cutting off aid. The Central Intelligence Agency (CIA) began pouring money into Chile, both as bribes and to buy anti-Allende propaganda. The CIA even made contact with conservative military leaders in hopes that someone could be persuaded to stop Allende's election by force of arms. None of these efforts had its desired impact, and Allende was elected in a narrow race.

DEMOCRACY IMPERILED

"Chile voted calmly to have a Marxist-Leninist state, the first nation in the world to make this choice freely and knowingly," cabled the American ambassador, as quoted by Walter LaFeber in *The American Age: United States Foreign Policy at Home and Abroad Since 1750* (1989). In the opinion of the official U.S. representative on the scene, democracy was in effect in Chile. Nevertheless, Nixon was outraged by Allende's election and was determined to overthrow him. The CIA continued to channel funds to anti-Allende forces and launched an all-out propaganda blitz, supporting anti-Allende newspapers and politicians. Nixon increased economic pressure by blocking loans to Chile. The CIA worked with U.S. businesses to stop the shipment of spare parts for American-built machinery. Allende was unable to weather the storm and fell to a coup in 1973. He either committed suicide or was murdered shortly thereafter. American money and pressure had overturned the results of a democratic election. Nixon and Kissinger, not the people of Chile, had won.

In the case of Africa, Nixon and Kissinger ignored the principles of democracy in establishing their policies. Officially, U.S. policy was to encourage racial harmony in the white-minority-dominated states of Portuguese Angola, South Africa, and Rhodesia. Nixon and Kissinger, however, strengthened political and economic ties with such minority regimes, even going so far as

to violate the United Nations (U.N.) embargo of Rhodesia. Many were aware of the hypocrisy of American policy in Africa, which prompted one resignation from the U.S. delegation to the United Nations.

Even after Nixon's resignation from the presidency on 9 August 1974 as a result of the Watergate scandal, Kissinger continued to exercise a great deal of control over U.S. foreign policy, continuing as secretary of state under the new president, Gerald R. Ford. Kissinger was the key figure in the increasing U.S. involvement in Angola, as Portugal abandoned its attempts to maintain control and the country moved toward independence. Three factions in Angola, separated by ethnic and ideological differences, battled for control. The United States, along with China, South Africa, and several other countries and private organizations, covertly aided one faction, the National Front for the Liberation of Angola *(Frente Nacional de Libertação de Angola* or FNLA) against a Marxist-Leninist group, the Marxist Popular Movement for the Liberation of Angola *(Movimento Popular de Libertação de Angola* or MPLA). The third faction, the National Union for the Total Independence of Angola *(União Nacional para a Independência Total de Angola* or UNITA), also received support from China and South Africa. None of these groups had particularly strong democratic credentials. Instead, Kissinger sought to make the expansion of Soviet influ-

Chilean soldiers observing the bombing of La Moneda presidential palace in Santiago on 11 September 1973 during the coup against Salvador Allende Gossens

(Anonymous photo from private archive)

DEMOCRACY IMPERILED

ence expensive, both in money and lives, again without informing the American people. Even had the U.S.-backed faction triumphed, which it did not, it seems unlikely that a democratic regime would have been established.

Many historians consider Nixon and Kissinger's foreign policy to have had two great triumphs: the opening of China and détente with the Soviet Union. Whether or not one considers those two achievements to have been successful in the long term, it is clear that democratic principles played no part in their development. To make his approach to China, Kissinger went through such questionable channels as the leader of Romania, Nicolae Ceausescu, and the president of Pakistan, Agha Mohammad Yahya Khan, neither of whom had any democratic credentials. All approaches were conducted in secret. Once again Nixon and Kissinger deprived U.S. citizens of the opportunity to judge the policies of their leaders. Instead, the two policy makers presented America with an already accomplished fact when Nixon announced he would go to China.

In achieving détente with the Soviet Union, Nixon and Kissinger saw the relationship solely in terms of power politics. Both were surprised, and Kissinger was outraged, when members of Congress declined to make unconditional deals with an authoritarian, communist state. Congress's chief concern was the right of Jews to emigrate from the Soviet Union to Israel or other more hospitable areas. The Nixon/Kissinger team found it simply incomprehensible that some would place the rights of Soviet citizens above a deal that had the potential to stabilize Soviet-American relations.

Nixon and Kissinger considered themselves realists or pragmatists, adapting to the changing world of limited U.S. power. The way they practiced power politics, however, proved antithetical to democracy, both abroad and in the United States.

–GRANT T. WELLER, U.S. AIR FORCE
ACADEMY, COLORADO

Viewpoint:
No. The effective diplomacy of Richard M. Nixon and Henry Kissinger depended on timing and confidentiality that precluded congressional debates and media investigations.

The question of the "undemocratic" nature of the Nixon/Kissinger approach to U.S. foreign policy owed something to Henry Kissinger's doubly alien status, as a Harvard professor and an immigrant with a German accent. His Jewishness, in passing, played almost no role—a sign of the virtual disappearance of anti-Semitism from the public discourse. Of more significance in structuring the myth of damage resulting from the foreign policies of the Nixon administration was the near-existential loathing many Americans, not all of them liberals, felt for Richard M. Nixon—to the point that it was seriously discussed in certain faculty circles whether he might not seek to suspend the presidential elections in 1972. More specifically, "Tricky Dick" was widely associated with unspecified dark deeds done in secret—somewhat in the pattern of Harvard faculty meetings. In short, the two men were natural magnets for the kinds of anxieties fostered by the Vietnam War (ended 1975) and its aftermath.

In hindsight, and in the light of the tawdry realities of Watergate, the attacks on the alleged antidemocratic nature of Nixon's foreign policy may have a strong touch of melodrama. Yet, they were not whole-cloth invention. Nixon and Kissinger, his chief adviser and later secretary of state, shared a belief in the importance of leadership, insisting on the necessary role of great men in shaping events. They believed in the importance of doctrine, principle, and planning—all requiring high levels of intellectual ability—as opposed to the bureaucratic/pragmatic approach Kissinger in particular considered characteristic of former Cold War policy makers. Nixon and Kissinger were unabashed elitists who consistently asserted that the egalitarianism characteristic of American domestic life was a recipe for international disaster. Finally, both men downplayed the value of charisma—arguably because neither possessed it in any conventional sense. Kissinger said it best when asked about his relationship with a starlet decades his junior: "power is the best aphrodisiac." For Kissinger, the exile, and for Nixon, whose entire life was an uphill struggle against himself, approval came not for who one was, but from what one did.

Nixon's choice of Kissinger as his chief foreign-policy adviser reflected the new president's conviction that the bipolar world of the Cold War was changing, in good part because of the growing mutual weariness of the superpowers. The challenge was to use that tectonic shift to create and stabilize a new world order friendly to the United States, and more generally to those Western moral and political values Nixon and Kissinger both prized over anything else.

In a post-Vietnam America, where appeals to "come home" were reiterated as far up the political ladder as 1972, Democratic presidential candidate George McGovern, Nixon, and Kissinger spoke for involvement. Army Chief of Staff and

KISSINGER REPORTS FROM CHINA

After his fourth trip to Beijing, from late February to early March 1973, Henry Kissinger sent a memorandum covering his conversations with the Chinese, including discussions about the U.S.S.R., to President Richard M. Nixon.

The next day I purposely detailed our proposed force reductions on Taiwan and then made a more sweeping analysis of our policy toward the Soviet Union. I said that the nature of our relationship meant that we had to pursue a more complicated policy than the PRC which could oppose the Soviet Union outright on issues. We were making several agreements with Moscow, but we would not let these constrain us in the event that our interests were jeopardized. I pointed out that the USSR could follow one of two courses. If they truly wanted peace, we would welcome that course, and the agreements we were making, might contribute to that end. If, however, as seemed more likely, they were bent on a more threatening road, we had shown in the past that we would react strongly if our interests were jeopardized. In any event, I emphasized, we should maintain strong defenses and improve our strategic forces so long as the Soviet buildup continued. And on issues of direct concern to Beijing we would take Chinese interests into account, such as on the Soviet initiative on a nuclear understanding, where we have been fighting a delaying action ever since last spring.

Zhou and then Mao, however, both replayed the theme that we might be helping the Soviet Union, whether or not purposely. Whereas we saw two possibilities, i.e. that the Soviet Union would either pursue a peaceful or menacing course, the Chinese saw only the latter. They were spreading their influence everywhere with the help of their satellites, like India, and were out to isolate the Chinese. The "new czars" were neurotic and omnipresent. It was the Chinese duty to try and expose their designs wherever possible, however lonely their efforts in a world enamored with false détente.

Mao even went so far as to suggest that we might like to see the Russians bogged down in an attack on China; after wearing themselves out for a couple of years, we would then "poke a finger" in Moscow's back. I rejoined that we believe that a war between the two Communist giants was likely to be uncontrollable and have unfortunate consequences for everyone. We therefore wished to prevent such a conflict, not take advantage of it.

Given Mao's and Zhou's skeptical comments on the issue, I treated it at considerable length the day after my meeting with the Chairman. I said there were three hypothetical US motives in a policy that contributed to pressures on the PRC from the USSR. First, we might want the Soviet Union to defeat China. I stressed emphatically that whether Moscow defeated China or Europe first, the consequences for us would be the same; we would be isolated and the ultimate target. Thus this could never be our policy.

The second possible motive was the one Mao mentioned—our wish for a stalemated Moscow attack on Beijing, so as to exhaust the Soviet Union. I pointed out that even partial Soviet dominance of China could have many of the consequences of the first option. In any event, such a major conflict would have unpredictable consequences. The Soviet Union might take rash actions if they were stymied as the Chairman claimed we had been in Vietnam. And we would be forced either to demonstrate our impotence and irrelevance, or make a series of extremely complex decisions.

The third possibility was that we might contribute to a war between China and the Soviet Union through misjudgment rather than policy. This I recognized as a danger despite our intentions. I then analyzed at length our policy around the world, with emphasis on Europe, to demonstrate that we plan to maintain our defense, continue a responsible international role and work closely with our allies. In short, while seeking relaxation with Moscow, we would also ensure that if it did not choose a peaceful course we and our friends would be in a position to resist and defend our national interests. And I made it evident that we would consider aggression against China as involving our own national security.

It is not clear that we have fully allayed Chinese suspicions. While they have nowhere else to go in the short term, they will certainly watch our Soviet moves with wariness, and take out insurance with Japan and Europe.

Source: *William Burr, ed.,* The Kissinger Transcripts: The Top Secret Talks With Beijing and Moscow *(New York: New Press, 1998), pp. 113–114.*

later Secretary of State George C. Marshall once declared that no democracy could fight a seven-year war. Vietnam seemed to prove that at least a democracy could not win such a war as long as it depended on certain kinds of crusading zeal to generate public support. Often criticized by contemporaries, and later critics, for abandoning the moral basis of U.S. foreign policy, Kissinger and Nixon instead sought to redefine that basis by pruning the sentimentality that had grown around it since World War II. To recognize the principles of proportion and double effect was not to cast aside morality but to return it to philosophical and metaphysical roots that were starkly unsympathetic to feelings as opposed to reason. It was no less moral to insist on a cohesive worldview based on the interaction of events than it was to stigmatize particular events as unique manifestations of evil, to be eradicated whatever the potential cost.

Neither Nixon nor Kissinger accepted the concept of "convergence," made popular during the 1960s by scholars such as Daniel Bell and exemplified in the novels of John Le Carré. Instead they regarded Soviet and American systems as fundamentally different. Because of that difference, their diplomatic relationship was best managed by agreements that were best negotiated on specific issues. Progress in one area could then be extended to others—a concept given the name "linkage." As linkage developed, the Union of Soviet Socialist Republics (U.S.S.R.) would be enmeshed in a web of its own consensual weaving, whose rupture would cause losses demonstrably greater than the projected gains of a return to confrontation.

This scenario was just one side of détente. Simultaneously—and the credit for this contribution belongs to Kissinger—the United States would abandon its historical traditions of commitment followed by isolation, of enthusiasm giving way to cynicism. Instead Americans, or their leaders, would come to realize that impetuosity of any kind was counterproductive in a nuclear age. They would realize as well that, to borrow Sigmund Freud's aphorism, much may be achieved in a state of moderate misery. Superpower détente was only part of a new flexibility in international relationships. In Europe, in northern Asia, and throughout what was then called the Third World, nations were developing their own identities and strengths. As they became better able to act autonomously on their own behalf, so too must the United States tailor its commitments to its interests, rather than the other way around.

That approach marked the end of an "era of containment" based heavily on the combined threat of conventional intervention and nuclear retaliation. Neither Nixon nor Kissinger expected the Soviet Union to abandon, on its own accord, international behavior patterns generated by its domestic structure. Instead détente would encourage modifying aggressive behavior on grounds of rational self-interest. Should those incentives prove insufficient, Nixon and Kissinger proposed to develop a system in which the United States stood at the center of a network of relationships involving both allies and adversaries. Not merely flexible but consistently changing, that network would be the matrix of a world order stable enough to defy even nuclear-tipped challenges.

Implementing the vision required not merely activist diplomacy but also activist statecraft. Nixon and Kissinger ignored the traditional foreign-policy agencies in favor of a system focused on the National Security Council (NSC). That body drew on information gathered by the bureaucracy to develop proposals for action that were presented to the president and implemented in contexts of shuttle diplomacy, back-channeling, and general secrecy that generated drama and surprise that Nixon and Kissinger in turn used to increase their own auras as statesmen. The 1972 "opening" to China was marketed as a personal tour de force by the president. Kissinger was featured briefly in a nationally syndicated comic strip as superhero "Hennery the K," complete with cape. The Strategic Arms Limitation agreements (1972) and the Middle East negotiations (1973–1974) seemed, at least to their supporters, almost to justify the appellation.

The concept of a bipartisan foreign policy was eroding even before Vietnam. Afterward no president, especially one with Nixon's list of domestic enemies, could expect simple admiration for his pattern of virtuoso performances. Apart from criticism of particular policies, a general question emerged. How could Congress, which represented the American people, judge the appropriateness of a foreign policy whose formulation and postulates they barely understood? The answer was that effective diplomacy in the new contexts depended on degrees of timing and levels of confidentiality that precluded congressional debates and press investigations. Fewer and fewer people were willing to listen to this argument. Nevertheless, as Watergate engulfed his administration—and after Kissinger left a sinking ship and returned to Harvard—Nixon continued to follow his chosen approach to foreign policy. By the time of his resignation in 1974 it had become shadow diplomacy for a shadow president.

The Nixon/Kissinger team had pushed the envelope of the conduct of international affairs. It was open to the charge of substituting logic for observation: not for more than another decade would the Soviet Union seriously consider détente as anything more than another ploy in a mortal contest for supremacy. In a new century "multipolarity" remains an unrealized abstraction. While Nixon and Kissinger's methods made them objects of suspicion abroad as well as at home, being considered too clever for everyone else's good is a long way from subverting the democratic process. In the final analysis, the team of Nixon and Kissinger did the right thing from the wrong postulates. They maintained U.S. global involvement at a time when history and experience indicated a return to isolation—a return that, however temporary it may have been, might well have ended too late in the context of Soviet ambitions.

–DENNIS SHOWALTER,
COLORADO COLLEGE

References

Warren I. Cohen, *The Cambridge History of American Foreign Relations,* volume four, *America in the Age of Soviet Power, 1945–1991* (Cambridge & New York: Cambridge University Press, 1993);

Joan Hoff, "Nixon's Innovative Grand Design and the Wisdom of Détente," in *Major Problems in American Foreign Relations: Documents and Essays,* volume two, *Since 1914,* fifth edition, edited by Dennis Merrill and Thomas G. Patterson (Boston: Houghton Mifflin, 2000), pp. 496–511;

Walter LaFeber, *The American Age: United States Foreign Policy at Home and Abroad Since 1750* (New York: Norton, 1989).

DEMOCRACY IMPERILED

DIEM

Was it wise for the United States to assist in deposing Ngo Dinh Diem?

Viewpoint: Yes. The administration of Ngo Dinh Diem was corrupt and oppressive, and it threatened U.S. policy in Southeast Asia.

Viewpoint: No. The removal and murder of Ngo Dinh Diem, with U.S. complicity, was a moral and political blunder that contributed to American involvement in the Vietnam War.

Viewpoint: No. Despite Ngo Dinh Diem's abuses and excesses, his unified leadership was crucial to maintaining the war effort; the coup simply contributed to the defeat of the noncommunist South.

Ngo Dinh Diem, the first president of South Vietnam, remained until the day of his murder an enigma to the U.S. government that first supported him and then stood aside, ostentatiously looking the other way, as he was deposed and assassinated. Scion of wealth in a country of peasants and Roman Catholic in a nation largely Buddhist, Diem made his mark under French rule—first as a civil servant, then as a stubborn nationalist. Appointed Indochina's Minister of the Interior in 1933, he promptly resigned when the French refused to increase the autonomy of the colony. Diem remained outside of public life for twenty years, though active behind the scenes in the bourgeois section of the national movement. His opposition was personal as well as political; he had lost relatives at the hands of the Vietminh. In the 1950s, Diem cultivated extensive U.S. contacts, which facilitated his appointment in 1954 to what became the Republic of South Vietnam.

What this embryonic country needed was a revolution—what Diem offered was administration. He had early success establishing what amounted to a negative base of support built around objections, of whatever kind, to Ho Chi Minh. He sought, however, to centralize his control rather than expand his base. The Diem regime instituted neither fundamental land reforms nor progress toward industrialization. Local government was emasculated in favor of rule by increasingly indifferent, corrupt bureaucrats. The armed forces became alienated from the people they ostensibly defended. An emerging insurgent movement, partly indigenous and partly supported from Hanoi, found fertile ground in the late 1950s, moving from strength to strength as South Vietnamese security forces failed to meet each new challenge.

As his country eroded, Diem grew ever more remote and dependent on his immediate family. His sister-in-law, Madame Ngo Dinh Nhu, gained international notoriety. It was Diem's male relatives, however, especially his brothers, who by 1961 were transforming South Vietnam into a kleptocracy and generating, at the higher levels of government, increasing opposition based on fear of who would be next on the president's list of victims.

Except for public consumption, neither the Eisenhower nor Kennedy administrations entertained significant illusions about their ally. At the same time neither administration knew enough about South Vietnam to consider, much less agree on, an appropriate replacement. The final coup against Diem was a consequence of his summer 1963 attack on Buddhist dissidents. Opposition elements in the military—who by this time had at least faces and identities to their American counterparts—signaled that enough was enough. Washington responded through its Saigon embassy that it would provide direct support should an "interim period" of disorder follow Diem's removal.

This was not the same as suborning murder. Nevertheless, few Americans on the spot had any illusions about the outcome of the coup that began on 1 November 1963. Diem and one of his brothers were shot; the conspiring generals had a free hand to fight the war their way; and the United States had taken one more long step into a quagmire.

Viewpoint:
Yes. The administration of Ngo Dinh Diem was corrupt and oppressive, and it threatened U.S. policy in Southeast Asia.

The fall of South Vietnamese president Ngo Dinh Diem in November 1963 marked a major point of departure for American policy in Indochina. Although the U.S. government, and many scholars, long claimed that "neither the American Embassy nor the CIA were involved in [the] instigation or execution" of the coup that led to Diem's ouster and death, it has come to light that indeed Washington played a role in at least encouraging the military leaders who replaced Diem. American participation in his death is far from clear and, judging from accounts of John F. Kennedy's reaction to the news, may not have been an intended consequence of Diem's removal from power. Regardless of how pronounced U.S. participation in the coup was, however, it was a wise decision to remove Diem and offered the best possible solution at the time.

Diem's authoritarian government had no resonance in South Vietnam. Unlike other regimes that have been able to marshal the resources of their populations behind them, there were crucial factors that separated Diem personally, and the South Vietnamese elite generally, from the rest of the population. Like other colonial powers, France had trained a professional civil service, an intelligentsia, and a business elite from among the indigenous population of its colonies. This policy created problems after the French left Indochina in 1954, because the route to upward social mobility in the region lay through the willingness to assimilate at least partially into French culture. Diem and many other Vietnamese, Cambodians, and Laotians practiced Roman Catholicism, studied at Western universities, adopted Western fashions and ideas, and spoke French because it assured them a better place in the society of French Indochina. By independence, at least in noncommunist South Vietnam, the institutions of government remained dominated by this assimilated elite. South Vietnam as a whole, though, remained predominantly rural, agricultural, and about 80 percent Buddhist. Much of the population did not identify with Diem's regime, culturally or philosophically; this fact, and the elitist nature of South Vietnamese government and society, came to have great consequences when Saigon began to be challenged by the insurrection of communist guerrillas, the Viet Cong.

Several government policies alienated the general population even further, leading many citizens to support the guerrillas actively and many more to become apathetic. Since the success of any guerrilla movement rises and falls on its support from local populations, this was an unforgivable mistake by South Vietnamese leaders. Despite the pressing grievances of the rural population, Diem refused to initiate any meaningful land reform. The countryside was also subject to serious dislocation by the forced movement of people to accommodate the "strategic hamlets" policy of fortifying rural areas against rebel activity. In contrast, communist promises of giving land "to the people" had considerable appeal. Few of the illiterate Vietnamese peasants could have known what that had meant in every other communist country, but even if they did, many did not believe that their current situation could be much worse. Diem's military policies against the insurrection also fortified the alienation of the population. Regions that had experienced significant Viet Cong activity were treated with punitive expeditions in which many innocent people, suspected of aiding the rebels, were arrested or murdered. In a recently declassified record of their conversations, North Vietnamese leader Ho Chi Minh actually remarked to Soviet premier Nikita S. Khrushchev that he welcomed Diem's "wolfish image" because it would only continue to push the rural population toward communism.

Religious differences between the Catholic regime and Buddhist population also became a serious problem. In addition to the legal discrimination against Buddhists, many of them were rigid pacifists, particularly with regard to the struggle in which Vietnamese countrymen were fighting one another. The Western styles and sympathies of Diem's regime left Buddhists with the impression that the government represented imperialism after the fact and that Western involvement in their country was unnatural and the true source of the conflict. While these conclusions were debatable and the subject of per-

DIEM

A PLEA FOR HELP

On 7 December 1961 South Vietnamese president Ngo Dinh Diem sent a message to President John F. Kennedy, requesting help in the war against North Vietnamese communists. A portion of the letter appears below.

In the course of the last few months, the Communist assault on my people has achieved high ferocity. In October they caused more than 1,800 incidents of violence and more than 2,000 casualties. They have struck occasionally in battalion strength, and they are continually augmenting their forces by infiltration from the North. The level of their attacks is already such that our forces are stretched to the utmost. We are forced to defend every village, every hamlet, indeed every home against a foe whose tactic is always to strike at the defenseless. . . .

Mr. President, my people and I are mindful of the great assistance which the United States has given us. Your help has not been lightly received, for the Vietnamese are proud people, and we are determined to do our part in the defense of the free world. It is clear to all of us that the defeat of the Viet Cong demands the total mobilization of our government and our people, and you may be sure that we will devote all of our resources of money, minds, and men to this great task.

But Viet-Nam is not a great power and the forces of International Communism now arrayed against us are more than we can meet with the resources at hand. We must have further assistance from the United States if we are to win the war now being waged against us.

We can certainly assure mankind that our action is purely defensive. Much as we regret the subjugation of more than half of our people in North Viet-Nam, we have no intention, and indeed no means, to free them by use of force.

I have said that Viet-Nam is at war. War means many things, but most of all it means the death of brave people for a cause they believe in. Viet-Nam has suffered many wars, and through the centuries we have always had patriots and heroes who were willing to shed their blood for Viet-Nam. We will keep faith with them.

When Communism has long ebbed away into the past, my people will still be here, a free united nation growing from the deep roots of our Vietnamese heritage. They will remember your help in time of need. This struggle will then be a part of our common history. And your help, your friendship, and the strong bonds between our two peoples will be part of Viet-Nam, then as now.

Source: "WE MUST HAVE FURTHER ASSISTANCE FROM THE UNITED STATES IF WE ARE TO WIN THE WAR NOW BEING WAGED AGAINST US": Message from the President of the Republic of Viet-Nam (Diem) to the President of the United States (Kennedy), December 7, 1961 (Excerpt), U.S. Department of State, American Foreign Policy: Current Documents 1961 (Washington, D.C.: U.S. Government Printing Office, 1962), pp. 1053–1054.

spective, Diem's regime did little to dispel them. Diem himself was reputedly a relatively considerate individual, but he surrounded himself with people who clearly were not. His brother and main adviser, Ngo Dinh Nhu, was notoriously cruel and over time came to have more and more influence over his older brother.

On 8 May 1963 growing mutual resentment and mistrust erupted into violence when South Vietnamese troops fired on a peaceful mass celebration of Buddha's birth, aspects of which were forbidden by rigid laws against the waving of nongovernment banners in mass demonstrations. Riots spread during the summer, provoking more reprisals and alienating even more of the population from Diem's regime. The communist guerrillas were quick to take advantage of the situation, and tempered their Marxist rhetoric about reli-

gion. Ominously, members of the urban elite, and even the regime itself, began to go over to the opposition. During the riots the South Vietnamese foreign minister resigned and symbolically shaved his head in the fashion of a Buddhist monk. At almost the same time, Saigon's ambassador to Washington, Nhu's father-in-law, angrily resigned and denounced his daughter, Nhu's wife, who was known to applaud with glee the "barbecue show" whenever Buddhist monks immolated themselves to protest the war.

Although Diem resisted his decidedly less conciliatory associates and made some concessions, the damage was already done. The military, which had launched an unsuccessful coup in January 1960 and was ruthlessly purged of disloyal elements by the regime, began to show signs of wavering in their support. Much of the officer corps was frustrated with the self-serving inability of the regime to act decisively in military affairs. Since the coup promotions and assignments were based more on personal loyalty to the president than ability, and, like a tottering Roman emperor, Diem played the officers off against one another to sow distrust and prevent another rebellion. Many of his supporters in the upper echelon of the military were more interested in self-preservation and short-term gains in Saigon intrigues than in stabilizing their country and winning the war.

A parade of American visitors, inclined to commit firmly to the preservation of South Vietnam, including Vice President Lyndon B. Johnson, Defense Secretary Robert S. McNamara, Secretary of State Dean Rusk, General Walt W. Rostow, and General Maxwell D. Taylor, reported that South Vietnam was reaching stability with continued American assistance but needed more aid. They also noted that although the South Vietnamese administration worked hard, even using some unethical means, to deflect hawkish criticism that claimed more decisive American action was needed to shore up Saigon, the plain fact was that Diem was losing. In the process Kennedy's effort to stabilize South Vietnam and its ability to resist communism without a massive American military presence was undermined. The prospect of a major military commitment was untenable, given the low military spending of both his and Dwight D. Eisenhower's administrations. When a large military commitment was eventually supplied by Johnson after 1965, the economic, strategic, and social consequences of this decision were legion.

A function of Kennedy's strategy, especially after the summer of 1963, came to involve the removal of Diem from power. By late August military opposition to Diem began to take shape. In addition to all of the problems Diem had created for South Vietnam, the military increasingly shouldered the blame for the repression of his government. The American ambassador, Henry Cabot Lodge, asked for instructions about how to respond to soundings from the South Vietnamese generals about what the U.S. reaction to an attempted coup would be. Lodge made it understood that the Diem government still enjoyed Washington's support as long as he began to undertake meaningful reforms to stabilize his society. Diem's administration, however, continued its brutal repression of civic dissent. Being in a position to see the physical deterioration of Diem's regime, and its complete lack of any commitment to stabilizing reform, Lodge became convinced that it was untenable. Slowly he persuaded the U.S. administration that Diem had to go.

What, however, would come in Diem's place? In the early fall of 1963 important signals were given to Saigon to suggest that it change its ways. McNamara, to begin with, announced that American advisers would be withdrawn by the end of the year: South Vietnam would be on its own. In October, Kennedy approved some cuts in foreign aid to South Vietnam. Toward the end of that month Diem showed strong signs in meetings with Lodge of his willingness to engage in the kind of reform that the United States insisted he implement to secure his country. Yet, it was already too late. With the knowledge and approval of Lodge and the Kennedy administration, a military coup arrested Diem and took power on 1 November 1963. It was later announced that Diem had committed suicide, neither the first nor last time coup plotters used that device to cover up what was almost certainly murder.

Despite the ugliness that U.S. involvement in the removal of a foreign head of state seemed to imply, Diem's overthrow was fully justified. Kennedy's strategy was to use a limited commitment to train and equip the South Vietnamese army so that it could put down the communist insurrection and hold its own against North Vietnam should it ever attempt a direct attack. The policies of the Diem regime, which included mass arrests and imprisonment, gross violations of human rights, denial of even the most elementary civil and religious liberties, and the embarrassingly ineffective use of the military, made Kennedy's plan impossible. The only way for Kennedy's strategy in Southeast Asia, and indeed globally, to succeed was to put power in the hands of the South Vietnamese opposition. This option was neither difficult nor unwise, since that category included almost everyone in South Vietnam except Diem, his brother, and his brother's wife. Furthermore, there is no proof that the U.S. role in the coup included the approval or order of Diem's death. To have him and his closest associates out of power was enough for Kennedy.

Had the U.S. role been more pronounced, paradoxically, Diem would have had a better chance of surviving. Leaving the coup in the hands of Vietnamese generals, who had deep-seated emotional reasons to want to see Diem die, almost certainly did more to condemn him. To intervene to save Diem, following up on what Lodge had been counseled to tell the South Vietnamese generals two months before the coup, would almost certainly have led to the kind of major military commitment Kennedy so wished to avoid. Three weeks after the coup Kennedy was dead, and U.S. policy changed fundamentally for the worse—now including a major military commitment to South Vietnam.

–PAUL DU QUENOY,
GEORGETOWN UNIVERSITY

Viewpoint:
No. The removal and murder of Ngo Dinh Diem, with U.S. complicity, was a moral and political blunder that contributed to American involvement in the Vietnam War.

To call the intrigues surrounding Ngo Dinh Diem's last six months before he was assassinated by a coup instigated by the United States, albeit in a supposedly deniable manner, a snake pit does dishonor to snakes. Diem had been president of South Vietnam for eight years, largely because of U.S. support. He was an intense nationalist and anticommunist and had maintained a shaky, but fairly effective, coalition of Catholics, Buddhists, nationalists, the military, and several dozen other factions. Even though his regime depended on the United States, he was determined not to be seen as a puppet.

"Determined," however, is too light a word to describe Diem. "Stubborn," "egocentric," and "paranoid" (the latter with good reason) are more realistic epithets. He was an archetypical Cold War Third World autocrat. His advisory council consisted primarily of his family, whom he vaulted to positions of extraordinary power. He handpicked all generals and personally directed or approved all military activities against the Viet Cong (VC), composed primarily of South Vietnamese insurgents and former South Vietnamese natives who had fled to North Vietnam during the partition after the French had left in 1954. The VC were under operational control of the nationalist-communist government of North Vietnam. The war, which had started in 1945, had seesawed back and forth—with the VC controlling about a third (sometimes up to half) of the countryside. The South Vietnamese army was on the strategic and operational defensive. U.S. involvement, beginning with the presidency of Dwight D. Eisenhower, supplied equipment and advisers who were limited to training and noncombat roles. By the summer of 1963 the United States had committed between 25,000 and 29,000 advisers. Increasingly, many of those advisers began accompanying Vietnamese troops into combat, and some in turn became casualties. Whether this battlefield involvement was done in violation of official Washington policy, or whether it was carried out with a wink and a nod, remains uncertain. The major point is that American blood had been spilled, inflaming the hawks in Washington.

In the spring of 1963 the patchwork fabric of South Vietnamese society began ripping apart. Buddhists actively protested against the Diem administration. Ngo Dinh Nhu, Diem's brother, ordered a raid on their temples. Several Buddhists, mostly women and children, were killed. On 11 June, after notifying American television crews, an elderly, frail monk sat cross-legged in the middle of traffic on one of the busiest streets in Saigon, doused himself with gasoline, and set himself afire. This scene, endlessly rebroadcast throughout the world, precipitated the first serious discussions in the National Security Council (NSC) of the necessity of a coup to remove Diem. Feelers were put out cautiously through a Central Intelligence Agency (CIA) agent, who reported only to U.S. ambassador Henry Cabot Lodge, to the South Vietnamese generals—all of whom owed their rank and wealth to Diem.

The appointment of Lodge as ambassador was both cunning and shrewd on the part of President John F. Kennedy. Lodge had been Richard M. Nixon's running mate against Kennedy in the 1963 presidential election. Descended from two of the oldest patrician families in America, Lodge had an uprightness that was beyond question. If things went wrong, who was better to take the blame? Lodge was initially against the coup, until he had been in Vietnam for three days. Then he became its chief advocate, to the point of defying the president at the last second, when Kennedy became squeamish about becoming involved. Lodge had not yet even met Diem.

It must not be imagined that the NSC was solidly in favor of a coup. General Maxwell D. Taylor, chairman of the Joint Chiefs of Staff, spoke in opposition to an overthrow, pointing out that the South Vietnamese military was split different ways over Diem, and, in any event, the United States should not turn over the job of choosing a head of state to the military. In addition, curiously, there were only two voices for withdrawal of American forces. Robert F. Kennedy, the attorney general, suggested the United States could use current events to provide the motivation for withdrawal. An outraged secretary of state, Dean Rusk, batted the suggestion aside. The second official who favored the withdrawal of troops was a diplomat of vast experience in Vietnam, Paul Kattenburg, who had just returned from Saigon and was appalled by potential U.S. military involvement in the country. His next assignment was Guyana—a few miles from the former French penal colony called Devil's Island.

The debate dragged on into the fall: the participants feared the consequences of a coup, whether it failed or succeeded. The South Vietnamese generals, worried about Diem's intelligence network, waffled hot and cold. They would not proceed without full assurance of backing from the United States; the United States wanted complete deniability. Meanwhile, civil unrest went on unabated. Diem started secret talks with French president Charles de Gaulle, who dreamed of recovering some of the influence France enjoyed in colonial days, and with the North Vietnamese. There was a series of what Madame Ngo Dinh Nhu, sister-in-law of Diem and a Dragon Lady of the first order, termed "Buddhist barbecues." The Viet Cong were making important advances, and the generals were told that "the United States would do nothing to thwart the coup." On 3 November 1963, Diem was overthrown and murdered. The murders of Diem and his brother do not seem to have been part of Kennedy's game plan, but no arrangements had been made to provide them protection or exile.

The United States did not just make a misjudgment in policy, or err in understanding the true nature of the situation. What happened is best explained in terms of Greek tragedy. The United States committed an act of hubris, which is generally translated as "overweening pride" but really indicates an act so far beyond the natural moral order that it loosens "fate," that is, it releases forces of doom that are the inevitable and unstoppable consequences of that act. The United States had the chance to withdraw with honor. Instead, it fell ever deeper into the pit. When the U.S. administration assented to the assassination of Diem, it chose ever-enmeshing involvement that resulted in continuing instability in the South Vietnamese government (five changes of leadership in the first year after the coup) and Vietnamese military, as well as the eventual commitment of five hundred thousand U.S. ground troops, countless national treasure, the fall of two presidencies, an unhealed rent in the social fabric, and, not the least, fifty-five thousand American dead.

–JOHN WHEATLEY, BROOKLYN CENTER, MINNESOTA

U.S. ambassador Henry Cabot Lodge meeting with South Vietnamese president Ngo Dinh Diem in Siagon on 26 August 1963

(UPI/Bettman Newsphotos)

DIEM

**Viewpoint:
No. Despite Ngo Dinh Diem's abuses and excesses, his unified leadership was crucial to maintaining the war effort; the coup simply contributed to the defeat of the noncommunist South.**

The United States became involved in Vietnam during World War II when it established ties with the Viet Minh under Ho Chi Minh. Sending money, arms, and advisers, the United States used the Viet Minh from 1944 until the end of the war to gain intelligence about the Japanese, to conduct sabotage, and to assist in the recovery and escape of downed Allied airmen. This relationship was maintained by the Office of Strategic Services (OSS), which trained, equipped, and, in some cases, led their Viet Minh allies in battle.

After the war the United States broke its promise to Ho and the people of Indochina by supporting the French in their bid to return as a colonial power. In the ensuing conflict (the First Indochina War, 1946–1954), the United States supplied more than 80 percent of the funds and much of the equipment for the French effort. The war ended badly for the French, when they were forced to leave Indochina in September 1954. As part of the peace treaty, however, Vietnam was divided in two, with a communist government in the north and democratic, pro-French government in the south. This division would set the stage for the Second Indochina War (ended 1975), which engulfed the United States in political turmoil and a military quagmire for the better part of a decade.

Ho became ruler of the North, while Ngo Dinh Diem was made president of the South. Diem had already technically been in power, having been appointed by the French through Emperor Bao Dai. With U.S. support, Diem refused to accept the treaty-mandated elections on the future unification of Vietnam. Between 1956 and 1961 both sides prepared for war, the North with the support of the communist bloc and the South with the aid of the West—primarily the United States (although there were half a dozen other countries that assisted). The only common political trait the Vietnamese on both sides shared was ardent nationalism. This sentiment was a problem for any leader of either side, as it was difficult for them to be seen as not acting for outside interests.

Diem was hardly an ideal candidate for leading a struggling, divided nation through what would be a long, hard war. He was French-speaking, which automatically put him at odds with more than 75 percent of the population; he was also Catholic, which was even more problematic, as the majority of the people were Buddhists. Both of these traits made him appear as a sell-out to the former French masters. Indeed, he acted in a similar manner as the former rulers of Vietnam. He repressed the Buddhists, whom he suspected as being procommunist; replaced local leaders with French-speaking Catholics, further alienating the population; and worse still, brutally crushed any opposition to his rule, real or imaginary.

These issues did not concern the United States, but his growing corruption and inefficiency worried officials in Washington, who saw these problems as directly affecting the war effort. Coup plotters in the South Vietnamese Army (the Army of the Republic of Vietnam or ARVN) approached the U.S. ambassador in Saigon informing him of the plan, and President John F. Kennedy decided to go along with it. This decision was a crucial error, as it was the beginning of a series of lies and deceits that would eventually bring an end to U.S. involvement in the conflict. What the Americans did not know, nor approve of, however, was Diem's summary execution on 2 November 1963—which had been apparently planned all along.

For all his faults, Diem was decidedly anticommunist. This trait was one of his strongest qualities: for new nations to survive they need strong leaders in their early years, especially when at war. Individual freedoms and institutions usually take a back seat in any democracy during war, and South Vietnam was no different. Diem was steadfast in his convictions, which made him difficult to deal with at times, but also prevented his being seen to be a U.S. puppet or stooge. It was this same trait that made the Kennedy administration approve his removal.

Strangely enough, Diem gave the government of South Vietnam something that it never had after his death—legitimacy. Even though he was a dictator, he was a civilian and therefore independent from the military. Interestingly the very traits of "corruption" that the United States decried were the institutions that made his government more effective than those that followed. Nepotism breeds corruption, but it also promotes loyalty to the leader, which, in turn, creates unity. While this strategy is not the best way to achieve cohesion, it is better than no unity at all, which is exactly what happened after Diem's murder.

The important factor to remember is that the coup against Diem did not change any of the problems of his regime. In fact, these difficulties became more pronounced than before. The leaders who followed Diem were simple "yes men" to

DIEM

the United States and were not well regarded in the South; and their military regime was unstable. These officers did not know how to deal with civil problems, and as a result, the country and government was destabilized at a time when communist attacks and aggression were increasing. Worse still, ARVN leadership was also hindered, leading to an increasingly ineffective South Vietnamese war effort.

While the military felt it could run the war more efficiently than Diem, the truth was, it did not. What soldier has not felt that way at times? When South Vietnamese military leaders took those beliefs too far and proved miserable failures when in charge of the government, the result was repeated coups and attempted coups—hardly the stable environment necessary to win against a determined foe.

Of course the North was paying close attention to the situation in the South and used the disharmony and confusion to launch an offensive. Coincidentally, shortly after Diem's murder the United States was dragged deeper into the war. The elimination of Diem demonstrated the shallowness of the U.S. war effort. That the Kennedy administration had resorted to this type of action was seen—rightfully so—as hypocritical. The United States was so focused on preventing the spread of communism that it failed to notice that democracy does not work in all societies and that the American way is not always the best system. If the promoters of democracy undermine democracy elsewhere, or are seen as supporting anything other than the democratic ideal, they are a failure. Ironically, it was this type of action that actually hastened the end of South Vietnam.

The United States therefore assumed a greater responsibility for the war effort from 1965 onward. Yet ARVN troops were poorly trained, equipped, led, and motivated. Why should individual troops fight for something they did not have or could not expect to have? Their combat effectiveness was correspondingly low, so U.S. forces took over, giving ARVN troops even less reason to become involved. It is a wonder that South Vietnamese forces fought at all.

The murder of Diem did not come without a cost in the United States either. The increase in U.S. military action led to a rise in American casualties, causing mounting political opposition to the entire war. President Richard M. Nixon was actually elected on a platform to get the United States out of the war. His strategy was to help the ARVN take greater responsibility for the war in what was termed "Vietnamization." Eventually, the United States would simply "cut bait" and leave.

The Second Indochina War turned out badly all around. Far too many people died in a dubious and half-hearted effort that was doomed to failure because of the people in charge. The responsibility for this situation lies squarely on the Kennedy and Johnson administrations, as well as those selected to lead in Vietnam. Diem may have been a ruthless dictator, but he was no worse than those who followed him, while he was, in the long run, probably a more effective leader. From the U.S. standpoint, it would probably have been easier to work with Diem and his forces rather than repeatedly supplanting those who followed. If the United States had supported Diem rather than overthrowing him, Vietnam might have been able to shoulder more of the burden of the war before it was too late. Perhaps the conflict would have turned out differently, although it can never be known.

–WILLIAM H. KAUTT, SAN ANTONIO, TEXAS

References

David Halberstam, *The Making of a Quagmire: America and Vietnam During the Kennedy Era*, revised edition, edited by Daniel J. Singal (New York: McGraw-Hill, 1988);

Walter LaFeber, *America, Russia, and the Cold War, 1945–1996*, eighth edition (New York: McGraw-Hill, 1997);

John M. Newman, *JFK and Vietnam: Deception, Intrigue, and the Struggle for Power* (New York: Warner, 1992);

The Pentagon Papers: As Published by the New York Times (New York: Quadrangle, 1971);

Arthur M. Schlesinger Jr., *A Thousand Days: John F. Kennedy in the White House* (Boston: Houghton Mifflin, 1965).

DIEM

FRANCE

Was France a reliable Cold War ally of the United States?

Viewpoint: Yes. Although there were many differences of opinion and strategy between the French and American policy makers, France was a strong, consistent ally of the United States during the Cold War.

Viewpoint: No. Especially under Charles de Gaulle, the French undermined U.S. foreign policy in Europe and the world.

The relationship of the United States with its European allies was not always on the best of terms. Conflicts of interest and perspective often existed within World War II alliance relationships, particularly with regard to France. Struggling to maintain its colonial empire after the war, as well as its image of itself as a great power, France was confronted by American pressure to withdraw from its overseas possessions. As France recovered political stability and entered into a period of economic prosperity in the late 1950s, it felt increasingly constrained by American political and economic hegemony. By the mid 1960s French president Charles de Gaulle worked to restore the independent position of France in the world; he advocated reconciliation with the Soviet Union, as well as an expansion of diplomatic and economic relations with the Eastern bloc. In 1966 de Gaulle withdrew the French military from the integrated command structure of the North Atlantic Treaty Organization (NATO). After he left office, his successors pursued the same course to varying degrees.

Many have speculated whether de Gaulle's policy undermined French reliability as an ally of the United States. De Gaulle's critics in that regard argued that his goals were irreconcilable with that of the role as junior partner in the Atlantic alliance and that France would not prove dependable in the event of a major war. Indeed, France sharply criticized American involvement in Vietnam. Some wondered what it would do in the event of a major military confrontation between the superpowers. De Gaulle's defenders, on the other hand, point out that France maintained an informal military commitment to NATO and made a determined effort to balance its reemerging international role with its place in the strategy of containing the Soviet Union. In the post–Cold War world, these defenders of the French position argue, France made significant contributions to the United States–led military efforts in the Persian Gulf War (1991) and against Serbia (1999).

**Viewpoint:
Yes. Although there were many differences of opinion and strategy between the French and American policy makers, France was a strong, consistent ally of the United States during the Cold War.**

In 1966, when French president Charles de Gaulle insisted on the removal of all American forces from France as part of its severance of military ties to the North Atlantic Treaty Organization (NATO), U.S. secretary of state Dean Rusk asked him if that included the soldiers who were killed during World War II and buried at Normandy and elsewhere in France. This exchange is a good metaphor for many American perceptions of relations with the French; invariably, their conduct seems to embody a combination of ingratitude and determined efforts to defeat the clever, if imagined, machinations of the "Anglo-Saxons" who stood between the French and their lost imperial grandeur. While there is much validity to the notion of Franco-American friction, especially during the period when the United States was fighting in Vietnam and France was cutting ties to NATO, the reality is a good deal more complicated.

The French emerged from World War II in a situation unlike any other major European nation. While on the winning side, French military performance had done little to make its people proud, particularly during the early phases of the war. France lacked the linguistic and cultural ties Britain had to the United States and the heroic legacy of British resistance to the Nazis. Russia, the historic ally of France against Germany, had adopted an ideology and approach to international relations that raised doubts about its suitability as a future partner. Unlike the Germans, the French were not appalled by the evil done in their name. In short, the French were a fiercely proud people trying to reassemble the pieces of their imperial glory and recover from a humiliating performance in World War II. While they needed American assistance and support, the French, like other Europeans, did not seek to subordinate themselves to U.S. control. Accordingly, there were going to be clashes between French and American aims. Yet, despite differences in temperament and quarrels over national interest, France was a reliable ally for the United States during the Cold War. This position is especially clear when considering important Cold War episodes such as the Marshall Plan, the establishment of the Federal Republic of Germany, the formation of NATO, the battle

against communism in Asia, the Cuban Missile Crisis, and the deployment of Pershing II missiles.

When the United States offered the Marshall Plan (April 1948 – December 1951) to all of Europe in language that suggested openness to Soviet participation, the French worked with the British to ensure that the European request for American assistance would be unpalatable to the Soviets. The cooperation of British foreign secretary Ernest Bevin and French foreign minister Georges Bidault led Soviet foreign minister Vyacheslav M. Molotov to walk out of the tripartite conference, which was set up to organize the European response to the American invitation and began in Paris on 27 June 1947. The Soviet decision not to participate increased the likelihood that a workable plan could be produced and permitted the Truman administration to sell the Marshall Plan to the American public as an anticommunist measure.

While the French were reluctant to see the restoration of German power in any form, they agreed with the Americans and British to merge their zone of occupation in Germany with Bizonia in April 1949, creating Trizonia, and in May helped create the Federal Republic of Germany (FRG). In the negotiations that led up to the London Recommendations (1 June 1948), which established procedures for creating the republic, the French sought and obtained concessions from the United States and Britain, particularly concerning the permanent American involvement in a security structure for Europe. France was active in the Brussels Pact, pursuant to which Britain, France, and the Benelux countries agreed to plan a common defense; the French were an important advocate of the addition of the United States and Canada in the establishment of NATO (4 April 1949). The French had good reason for participation in these defense agreements, gaining an American presence that secured France against both the Soviets and Germans. This action should not obscure the fact, however, that French contributions to the establishment of the FRG and a credible Western defense posture were crucial to American efforts to lead the Western world in its containment of Soviet communism. French attempts to distance themselves from NATO during the 1960s were less crucial than its endeavors to construct the alliance in the first place.

Much attention has been focused on the fact that the United States provided ample economic and military assistance to the French in their effort to reassert imperial control over Indochina. This aid contrasted with French attempts to undermine the post-1954 American effort to build a noncommunist South Viet-

French president Charles de Gaulle inspecting a Soviet guard of honor during his 1966 visit to Moscow

(Popperfoto)

nam. Such a focus, however, obscures the fact that U.S. leadership saw the French as supporting American aims in Indochina until 1954. The United States encouraged them initially as part of a strategy to restore France as a counterpoise to Soviet power in Europe. Especially after the invasion of South Korea by communist North Korea in 1950, the French effort in Vietnam was seen by Americans as part of the worldwide battle against communism. While the French were obnoxiously self-serving in criticizing American efforts to succeed where they had failed, their warnings proved accurate. The United States would have done better to heed them and seek some approach to dealing with Vietnam that did not involve the massive commitment of ground forces.

During the long U.S. march to disaster in Vietnam, President John F. Kennedy faced the

Soviets during the Cuban Missile Crisis (October 1962) and was supported by French president Charles de Gaulle in his efforts to force removal of Soviet missiles from Cuba. De Gaulle's concerns about the possibility that the United States might get the French incinerated because of events in another part of the world subsequently led him to revise relations with NATO, but he was firmly on the side of the United States while the crisis was unfolding.

Another crucial element of French support for the United States occurred during the 1980s when French president François-Maurice Mitterand supported the deployment of Pershing II missiles in Europe, including an appearance to promote them before the West German *Bundestag* (Federal Diet) in January 1983. Mitterand warned German legislators of the dangers of divisions within NATO and spoke of the importance of a U.S. connection with Europe, and also defended the decision to deploy the Pershings. These missiles were an especially controversial component of the growing Western force structure that was challenged by many in Western Europe and the United States, who saw the deployment as reckless warmongering or nuclear overkill despite recent Soviet deployment of similar missiles. The deployment and resulting improvement of the Western military position forced the Soviet leadership to reconsider its policies in 1985 and elevate Mikhail Gorbachev to leadership. Support of this crucial initiative at an important time in the Cold War needs to be remembered in assessing French reliability.

Not only were the French reliable in these crucial issues, but policies that were seen as inimical to American interests were often far less harmful than is sometimes supposed. The United States opposed the development of an independent French nuclear arsenal, but this arsenal actually worked to the advantage of the United States and Western democracies. French weapons did not factor into U.S.-Soviet arms-control talks, while they contributed to deterrence of the Soviets. French attempts at détente in the mid 1960s undermined Western unity but accomplished far less than de Gaulle might have hoped simply because the Soviets understood that West Germany and the United States were the key nations with which any meaningful détente would have to occur. The most crucial problem threatening Western unity during the 1960s was the deterioration of the American strategic position occasioned by the stripping of military forces in Europe and Secretary of Defense Robert S. McNamara's conclusion that the United States had already achieved a sufficiency of nuclear weapons that made further building unnecessary. Whatever de Gaulle's diplomacy contributed to the weakening of the Western alliance was overshadowed by the strategic incompetence of the Johnson administration. Even the French severance of ties to NATO, while not helpful, permitted a U.S. response that compares favorably with the Soviet reaction to events in Hungary in 1956 and Czechoslovakia in 1968.

While French actions frequently irritated their American allies, U.S. conduct often heightened reasonable French suspicions and concerns. As France sought to restore control over its colonial possessions in Indochina and Algeria, U.S. policy seemed designed to replace French domination with American. In the case of Indochina, once the anticommunist Vietnamese were relieved of the legacy of French colonialism, the Americans believed they would be able to build them into a force capable of resisting North Vietnamese communism. In Algeria the French were

subject to American rhetorical complaints and also had to accept the insult inherent in American and British arms sales to the Tunisians, who were believed to be supplying arms to the Algerians. The Americans and British reasoned that failure to sell arms would force Tunisia to seek weapons from the Eastern bloc. Not only were the British and Americans assisting its opponents, these arms sales undermined French efforts to defend their action in Algeria with the rhetoric of anticommunism.

Additionally, the French grew concerned that American policies would place all of Europe at risk of nuclear reprisals by the Soviet Union because of issues in other parts of the world. In 1958 U.S. and British intervention in Lebanon occurred without sufficient French consultation or opportunity for participation, despite the involvement of France in the Tripartite Declaration of 1950, concerning the future of the Levant, and the historic French role in Lebanon. Although the French were not permitted to participate, they were on the receiving end of Soviet warnings that Western intervention might precipitate nuclear war. Also in 1958, Chinese Communist shelling of Quemoy and Matsu threatened to escalate into a nuclear war that could have engulfed Europe despite its distance from the conflict. After the Cuban Missile Crisis, in which de Gaulle supported Kennedy, the French had an even better understanding of how American actions elsewhere could threaten European security. De Gaulle also worried that the United States had not devoted sufficient thought to the defense of Europe had the Soviets opted to move against Western Europe in retaliation for American efforts in the Caribbean. Perhaps most alarming to the French were the growing indications that the United States was retreating from its nuclear commitment to Europe. As the Soviet nuclear arsenal grew, and especially after the Johnson administration decided to focus on the Vietnam War in lieu of upgrading its strategic forces, the French had reason to doubt the American resolve to incite the incineration of its own cities in defense of Europe.

The United States emerged from World War II victorious and largely unscathed; France was, meanwhile, a humbled, once-great power looking to regain its status and international importance. The two nations had a vested interest in limiting the influence of the Soviet Union and seeing the eventual triumph of Western democracy but also had different understandings of their own best interests. These departures often led to strained relations and diplomatic squabbles. They did not, however, prevent the French from being strong, reliable allies to the United States on the most important Cold War matters.

–JOHN A. SOARES JR., GEORGE WASHINGTON UNIVERSITY

FRANCE

Viewpoint:
No. Especially under Charles de Gaulle, the French undermined U.S. foreign policy in Europe and the world.

France may have been a nominal ally of the United States during the Cold War, but it was an irksome and unreliable one. On some important issues it sided with the United States—for example, the Berlin crises (1958–1961) and Cuban Missile Crisis (October 1962)—but the strategic goal of France, especially after Charles de Gaulle returned to power in 1958, was to create a world structure much different from the one the Americans promoted and become a "third force" between the United States and the Soviet Union. France worked to limit U.S. influence in Europe and to exclude from European institutions close U.S. allies such as Britain. It undermined many U.S. initiatives such as the Nuclear Non-Proliferation Treaty, isolation of countries that support terrorism, and coordination of Western policy vis-à-vis oil producers. Relations between the two countries improved somewhat in the 1970s, during the presidencies of Georges-Jean-Raymond Pompidou and Valéry Giscard d'Estaing. During the 1980s, with François-Maurice Mitterand and Ronald Reagan in power, the two countries appeared to agree even more on strategic issues, such as the placing of intermediate-range nuclear missiles in Europe. In the 1990s, however, France again emerged as one of the more outspoken critics of what its politicians called American "hegemony" and cultural "imperialism." Many Americans were convinced that the French were ungrateful, selfish, and petulant; unreconciled to the decline of France as a world power; and vainly determined to resuscitate their fading glory and regain the influence they had lost.

Relations between the two countries seemed auspicious from the start. France, smarting from its defeat at the hands of Britain and Prussia in the Seven Years' War (1756–1763), searched for ways to punish Britain. France had to give up its possessions in North America (except for two small islands off the shore of Newfoundland), and it was here that the first opportunity to redeem some of its tarnished honor—and perhaps some lost territory—presented itself. In order to pay for its war expenses and the maintenance of troops in North America, Britain imposed heavy taxes on the colonies. In response, during the decade following the Treaty of Paris (10 February 1763), the colonists grew more determined to seek independence. On 29 November 1775 the Continental Congress established a secret committee for the purpose of seeking aid from other countries for the struggle against British rule. France was only too eager to oblige—helping the Americans free themselves from Britain would be a fitting punishment for expulsion of the French from North America. In May 1776 Louis XVI authorized French assistance to the colonists. France provided the independent fighters with ten million livres in grants and thirty-five million livres in loans; they also enlisted the help of Spain, and their combined fleets in spring 1779 represented a major threat to the Royal Navy. French forces played a major role in the American victory over the British at Yorktown, Virginia, in October 1781. Spanish armies fought the British in Florida, forcing the diversion of British troops to the defense of the southern flank. French assistance to the revolutionaries, however, did not translate into a close relationship between the two countries. Secretary of the Treasury Alexander Hamilton and other U.S. leaders were suspicious of French intentions, believing they harbored a desire to regain their possessions in the Western Hemisphere. The violent turn that the French Revolution (1789–1799) took also made Americans, especially Federalists, suspicious of France and eager to reestablish good relations with Britain.

Cordial, but cool, relations between the two countries existed over the next century and a half. Things did not improve much during and after World War II. The Free France forces were allies to Britain and the United States against Nazi Germany, but the hauteur of the Free France leader, Charles de Gaulle, irritated Winston Churchill and Franklin D. Roosevelt to no end, and his insistence on being treated as a major player on the world scene caused both to view him more often than not as a nuisance. Both were afraid that if he remained the leader of the resistance, thus bolstering his claim to lead France after the war, it would be more difficult to form a stable Western security and political structure in Europe. In 1943 Churchill tried to persuade his own cabinet and FDR that it would be better to force de Gaulle to resign and appoint someone more agreeable as the putative leader of France.

Frictions between the United States and France continued after the war, even as the Western alliance was being formed. There were disagreements on how France should use the money it had received from the Marshall Plan (April 1948 – December 1951), as well as profound discord on whether Germany (then West Germany) should be allowed to rearm. In the face of a growing Soviet threat, the United States did not see an alternative to arming Germany. France, having just emerged from four years of occupation, would have none of it. Another

FRANCE

DE GAULLE SEEKS INDEPENDENT ROLE FOR FRANCE

In the late 1950s and early 1960s, French president Charles de Gaulle sought a more independent foreign policy for France and loosened the bonds with NATO. In the following passage from his memoirs, de Gaulle reveals his thinking on Europe and NATO.

In 1958 I considered that the world situation was very different from what it had been at the time of the creation of NATO. It now seemed fairly unlikely that the Soviets would set out to conquer the West, at a time when all the Western nations were back on an even keel and making steady progress. Communism, whether it rises from within or irrupts from without, has little chance of taking root without help of some national calamity. . . .

On the Western side, too, the military conditions of security had altered profoundly in twelve years. For, from the moment when the Soviets had acquired the wherewithal to exterminate America, just as the latter had the means to annihilate them, it was unimaginable that the two rivals would ever come to blows except as a last resort. On the other hand, what was to prevent them from dropping their bombs in between their two countries, in other words on Central and Western Europe? For the western Europeans, NATO had thus ceased to guarantee their survival. But once the efficacy of the protection had become doubtful, why leave one's destiny in the hands of the protector?

Finally, something had recently happened to alter France's international role. For this role, as I conceived it, precluded the Atlantic docility which yesterday's Republic had practised during my absence. In my view, our country was in a position to act on its own in Europe and the world, and must so act because, morally speaking, this was an essential motive force for its endeavors. . . .

My aim, then, was to disengage France, not from the Atlantic alliance, which I intended to maintain by way of ultimate precaution, but from the integration realized by NATO under American command; to establish relations with each of the States of the Eastern bloc, first and foremost Russia, with the object of bringing about a *détente* followed by understanding and co-operation; to do likewise, when the time was ripe, with China; and finally, to provide France with a nuclear capability such that no one could attack us without running the risk of frightful injury. But I was anxious to proceed gradually, linking each stage with overall developments and continuing to cultivate France's traditional friendships.

As early as September 14, 1958, I hoisted my colors. In a memorandum addressed personally to President Eisenhower and Mr. Macmillan, I called into question our membership of NATO which, I declared, was no longer adapted to the needs of our defense. Without explicitly casting doubts on the protection afforded to continental Europe by the British and American bombs, my memorandum pointed out that a genuine organization of collective defense would need to cover the whole surface of the earth instead of being limited to the North Atlantic sector, and that the world-wide character of France's responsibilities and security made it essential for Paris to participate directly in the political and strategic decisions of the alliance, decisions which were in reality taken by America alone with separate consultation with England. France's accession to this summit would be all the more appropriate because the Western monopoly of atomic weapons would very soon cease to belong exclusively to the Anglo-Saxons, now that we were about to acquire them. I therefore proposed that the alliance should henceforth be placed under a triple rather than dual direction, failing which France would take no further part in NATO developments and would reserve the right, under article 12 of the treaty which had inaugurated the system, either to demand its reform or to leave it. As I expected, the two recipients of my memorandum replied evasively. So there was nothing to prevent us from taking action.

Source: Charles de Gaulle, Memoirs of Hope: Renewal and Endeavor, translated by Terence Kilmartin (New York: Simon & Schuster, 1970), pp. 200–203.

major contention had to do with the French empire. Since its inception the United States opposed colonialism. After World War I, President Woodrow Wilson had enunciated his "Fourteen Point" peace plan in which self-determination by peoples was a major tenet. The United States was uncomfortable with Britain and France hanging on to their colonial possessions and at various points pressured both to give them up. The ongoing French—and, in the U.S. view, futile—war against Viet Minh forces in Indochina was thus a major early source of contention between the two countries. The U.S. view changed after the outbreak of the Korean War in June 1950; by 1954 the United States considered more direct military help after a large French contingent came under siege at Dien Bien Phu (1953 – 7 May 1954).

A major disagreement between the two countries was the status of Algeria. The vast desert territory was not considered a colony, but an integral part of France—it was a *département*, with its own representatives in the National Assembly. A bloody war erupted in the early 1950s between the Front Liberation National (FLN), the pro-independence Algerian movement, and the French army, with brutalities and atrocities committed by both sides. Partly in order to stem the flow of support to the FLN from Egyptian president Gamal Abdul Nasser, France joined with Britain and Israel in the October 1956 Suez Campaign. The failed operation led to an intensification of the war in Algeria to the point where it threatened to spread to neighboring Tunisia and Morocco. In 1958 the exhausted French government accepted an American offer to mediate, but commanders of the powerful French garrison in Algeria refused and staged a coup in which they seized governmental authority in the territory. Threatening to attack Paris, they demanded that de Gaulle, whom they saw as an ally of their cause of keeping Algeria in French hands, be returned to power.

De Gaulle had left government in 1946 in frustration with what he perceived as the chaotic ineffectiveness of the political system under the Fourth Republic. He retreated to his country home and wrote his memoirs. After more than a decade in the political wilderness, he was called back as the savior of France. He agreed to return on condition that the constitution be changed to create a much stronger and more independent executive. He became prime minister, oversaw the writing of a new constitution, and then became the first president of the Fifth Republic. Rebellion leaders, whose threats brought their fellow officer to power in Paris, soon learned that his ideas of how to solve the Algerian problem were different from theirs. To buy time he went to Algeria—one of his first acts in office—

and, standing on a balcony facing thousands of cheering French settlers, declared "Je vous ai compris" (I understand you), but he was already moving in another direction. Realizing the war was not winnable, he initiated talks with the FLN, and by 1962 Algeria gained its independence. The angry rebels did not go down without a fight; they carried out several attempts on his life, and one was nearly successful.

The United States, whose mediation effort indirectly contributed to de Gaulle's return to power, now found itself again facing its old nemesis—the stubborn Frenchman who saw it as his life's mission to return his country to its old grandeur. De Gaulle's policies contradicted U.S. interests in important ways, but none more than his belief that in a bipolar world France would always be a secondary power, following the lead and dictates of the Americans. De Gaulle's conclusions were clear: France should lead the effort to replace the bipolar with a multipolar world, in which France was one of the "poles."

De Gaulle pursued his ambitious goal with single-minded persistence and discipline, with reinforcing policies in different realms. One such objective was to equip France with nuclear weapons, both as a compensation for the gradual loss of the French empire and as a means to put France on an equal footing with the United States and the Union of Soviet Socialist Republics (U.S.S.R.), as well as with Britain, which already possessed a small nuclear arsenal. In 1960 France conducted its first nuclear test and in 1968 exploded its first hydrogen bomb. France was not content merely to become a nuclear power. It also worked hard to undermine U.S. nuclear nonproliferation policies that became the basis for the 1968 Nuclear Non-Proliferation Treaty (NPT)—which France, until 1994, refused to sign. France helped other countries to acquire nuclear know-how and technology, constructing nuclear reactors without safeguards preventing them from being used for potential weapons-related activities. It helped Israel build its nuclear reactor at Dimona and Iraq with its reactor at Osiraq as well as assisted Taiwan and other countries.

De Gaulle's European policies were not more hospitable to U.S. allies. In 1963 he vetoed British membership in the European Economic Community (EEC, or Common Market). In 1966 France withdrew from the integrated military command of the North Atlantic Treaty Organization (NATO). De Gaulle also worked hard to prevent the political integration of Europe, which he saw as an American ploy to weaken the power of individual European nations. He said that his vision for Europe was not one of a "United States of Europe" but rather one of *Europe des parties,* that is, a loose federation of sovereign states. De Gaulle's definition of Europe was also different from that of the United States: while the Americans worked to cement relations among western European nations, de Gaulle, who believed that the United States was unduly obsessed with communism, announced his vision of a Europe "from the Atlantic to the Urals."

De Gaulle was an open critic of U.S. policies in Vietnam. He had good relations with Ho Chi Minh and recognized Communist China at a time when the United States was still working to isolate that nation. In the Middle East, U.S. and French policies clashed more directly. France was a major arms supplier to Israel from the mid 1950s until 1967, when de Gaulle imposed an arms embargo, claiming it precipitated the Six-Day War; in a press conference he accused Jews of being "arrogant and stiff-necked people." France, however, continued to supply arms to Iraq, Libya, and Algeria. During the early days of the Yom Kippur War (1973), as Israel appeared to be facing a military defeat, France refused to allow U.S. transport planes, rushing emergency supplies to the beleaguered nation, to land and refuel on French soil or even fly through French airspace. In fact, of all the U.S. European allies, only Portugal agreed to assist the American airlift. This stand would be reminiscent of a similar French refusal, in 1986, to allow American planes to fly over France on their mission to bomb targets in Libya in retaliation for its support of terrorism. In 1973 the Arab oil-producing nations imposed an oil embargo on Western countries, causing oil prices to quadruple. After the war France led an effort by some European countries to isolate the United States and bargain directly with the Organization of Petroleum Exporting Countries (OPEC) for a better oil deal for Europe.

If the French did not hesitate to undermine U.S. policies on important issues, they also irked the Americans on less important, but emotionally charged, topics. After the 1979 Soviet invasion of Afghanistan, the Carter administration announced that the United States would boycott the 1980 Moscow Olympic Games. The United States persuaded several other countries not to attend, but France sent its athletes to Moscow. During 1980 the French continued to trade with Iran despite the American-led embargo because of the seizure of the U.S. embassy in Teheran and the keeping of American diplomats as hostages.

There is little doubt that, if push came to shove, France would have stood with the United States against the Soviet Union. It proved this during the Berlin and Cuban crises. It is also true that there were many differences between the two countries beginning in the immediate aftermath of World War II, and indeed during the war, that were elevated to a level of doctrine when de Gaulle came to power in 1958. His grand purpose—what he called his "certain idea of France"—was to weaken U.S. sway and influence in world affairs and again make France a major player. Mired in colonial wars throughout the 1950s, however, France was never powerful enough economically or politically to become the leader of a third force between the superpowers. It was strong enough, though, to be a source of irritation and unpredictability in world affairs. Florence Nightingale once said that "whatever else hospitals do, they should not spread disease." Whatever else an ally does, they should not add to one's aggravation. France failed that test of alliance during the Cold War.

–BENJAMIN FRANKEL, SECURITY STUDIES

References

Charles G. Cogan, *Oldest Allies, Guarded Friends: The United States and France since 1940* (Westport, Conn.: Praeger, 1994);

Frank Costigliola, *France and the United States: The Cold Alliance since World War II* (New York: Twayne; Toronto: Macmillan; New York: Macmillan, 1992);

Jean-Baptiste Duroselle, *France and the United States: From the Beginnings to the Present,* translated by Derek Coltman (Chicago: University of Chicago Press, 1978);

Philip H. Gordon, *A Certain Idea of France: French Security Policy and the Gaullist Legacy* (Princeton: Princeton University Press, 1993);

Gordon, *France, Germany, and the Western Alliance* (Boulder, Colo.: Westview Press, 1995);

Michael M. Harrison, *The Reluctant Ally: France and Atlantic Security* (Baltimore: Johns Hopkins University Press, 1981);

Jean Lacouture, *Charles de Gaulle,* 3 volumes (Paris: Seuil, 1984–1986);

John Newhouse, *De Gaulle and the Anglosaxons* (New York: Viking, 1970).

GLASNOST AND PERESTROIKA

What was Mikhail Gorbachev's motivation for initiating glasnost and perestroika?

Viewpoint: Mikhail Gorbachev was a sincere reformer who wanted to protect his country from U.S. aggression.

Viewpoint: Mikhail Gorbachev was a dedicated communist who saw a need to restructure the Soviet Union.

The emergence of Mikhail Gorbachev as Soviet leader in 1985 marked a turning point in the Cold War. Realizing that the Soviet Union was becoming less productive domestically and less competitive economically, Gorbachev advocated policies of broad liberalization to encourage economic efficiency and preserve the viability of the communist system. Gorbachev's reforms were characterized by two broad concepts. Glasnost, or "openness," referred to the introduction of government accountability to the people and entailed greater freedom of the press and public speech. Perestroika, or "restructuring," referred to fundamental reforms in the political and economic life of the country.

It is difficult to determine exactly what Gorbachev wanted. Both of his initiatives faced substantial resistance from the bureaucracy of the Communist Party and Soviet state and were in different ways prevented from reaching their full development. Reaction to increased political liberty galvanized popular support not to repair or conciliate with the Soviet system but to seek to overthrow it. By the late 1980s Moscow was confronted with national independence movements in the Soviet republics (including Russia) and ever-increasing calls for democratization and capitalist economic reforms for the entire country. Progressively, the Soviet Union disintegrated; despite Gorbachev's reforms and a last-minute attempt by his hardline opponents to remove him from power, he had no choice but to resign and announce the dissolution of the Union of Soviet Socialist Republics (U.S.S.R.) on Christmas Day 1991.

Viewpoint: Mikhail Gorbachev was a sincere reformer who wanted to protect his country from U.S. aggression.

The Soviet system was one of the most democratic ever devised, on paper; in reality, it was one of the most corrupt, inefficient, and disastrous ever implemented. For seventy years the Soviets destroyed their population, economy, and country trying to make this flawed system work. The problem they never understood was that communism does not work and will not work because it drains the creativity and motivation of the common man, who is the greatest innovator of any society.

Early on, Vladimir Ilich Ulyanov Lenin seemed to have understood (or at least grudgingly realized) that there was a problem with the road he was leading his country down. Instituting limited free trade and enterprise, he discovered that capitalism was stronger economically and that communism would have to learn to deal with this reality to succeed. However, this small experiment died along with Lenin in 1924, as Joseph Stalin set out to rule with a brutality that made Lenin's iron fist seem soft in comparison. The resulting economy was a disaster.

The late 1920s and the 1930s were periods of massive public works projects throughout the Soviet Union. These feats of engineering were created on the backs of laborers conscripted to construct them. What is even more amazing is that they were built with little or no modern machinery. Trading the toil and lives of hundreds of thousands of workers for the convenience of these dams and bridges and other public works might have been worth it, but the Soviets did not build them in areas where they would do any good. It is almost as if they were built just to prove that it was possible, for they have never really made a positive difference to the regions in which they were built. Worse still, many projects, such as the irrigation systems in Central Asia, have actually destroyed the ecology there. Probably the most infamous example is that of the Aral Sea, which will all but disappear within the next twenty years.

Moreover, literally hundreds of thousands perished in these ill-conceived projects. While it is true that working undesirables to death in a sort of massive mobile gulag was part of the Soviet master plan, it does not explain the true horror of what happened to these people in this forgotten holocaust. They died from overwork, starvation, brutality, disease, and exposure—all because they did not meet Stalin's vision of the ideal communist and therefore represented a threat.

The situation worsened during World War II (1939–1945), when survival meant taking these types of risks. The gambles continued during the atomic buildup of the late 1940s to the mid 1970s, when the Union of Soviet Socialist Republics (U.S.S.R.) irradiated Central Asia to obtain "strategic materials" and to test weapons. Kazakhstan is just one of the five Central Asian former Soviet republics that still endures the legacy of Soviet nuclear testing. This callous disregard for ecological science and for human life created the "nuclear lake" there.

Economically, the U.S.S.R. fared no better. With its command economics and shoddy workmanship, it is a wonder that the country lasted seventy years. There is an old U.S. Navy joke about why Soviet ships had so many guns onboard: the law of probabilities stated that at least one would work. Soviet vessels needed to pull into port to perform basic maintenance, but frequently the harbor facilities could not handle even the simplest of repairs. No one was lining up to buy Soviet products out of choice. The Soviets

themselves were in line only because they had no such choice, and those who did, the *nomenklatura* (ruling elite), chose Western goods. Perhaps the most damning indictment of all was that no one around the world would even trade for Soviet currency, it being almost totally worthless.

The results of the Soviet Union's quest for a communist paradise since 1922 were the deaths of tens of millions of innocent people and devastation from which land (altogether about the size of Texas) as made incapable of ever supporting any life. Yet, one man in the post–World War II era represented a chance to change. Mikhail Gorbachev was young, charismatic, and full of new ideas on how to overhaul the Soviet state when he became general secretary of the Soviet Communist Party in 1985. Hitherto unknown, Gorbachev set to work with a vigor that the people had never seen before. He, unlike any other secretary general before him, actually seemed to listen to the people's troubles, and more importantly, actually seemed to care. The people responded to this enlightening leadership, and to the reforms designed to counter the stagnation and decay of the previous seventy years. Gorbachev's reforms were also designed to counter the growing threat from the United States. This threat was embodied in the form of President Ronald Reagan, who, with his inflammatory rhetoric against the "evil empire" and massive increases in defense spending, strapped the Soviets' already weakened economy.

Reagan himself received a military force that had hit rock bottom under the administration of Jimmy Carter (1977–1981). Reagan immediately turned the tide when he increased defense spending by 100 percent during his two terms (1981–1989). This increase helped boost morale, which, in turn, was a boon to military recruiting and retention. With an increase in manpower, U.S. armed forces were able to focus on training and preparing for whatever they might be called upon to do.

Reagan also began a program of upgrades and modernization in the form of new research, development, and acquisition. He planned to build a six-hundred–ship navy and then pushed to meet that goal. He introduced new systems such as the Aegis class destroyers and cruisers as well as bringing old ships out of moth bails, such as the *New Jersey* class battleships. He also revived the B-1B "Lancer" supersonic nuclear bomber project and pushed for stealth technology research. Similar advances were made with ground forces.

The Reagan years were also the time of the creation of the Strategic Defense Initiative (SDI) or "Star Wars" antiballistic missile program. While this project itself never came to fruition, it did spur new research that brought into being other advances that drove American technology

Boris Yeltsin giving an address at the Russian White House during the August 1991 coup attempt

(Photo by Yuri Feklistov)

further than ever. However, SDI had a darker side too, as it caused great concern among the Soviets. For if a country can defend against incoming intercontinental ballistic missiles (ICBMs), then it could conceivably launch a first strike with an expectation of the enemy not being able to make a successful retaliatory attack. With his increased rhetoric and seemingly bellicose actions, the Soviets were truly concerned, early on, that Reagan would launch such an assault.

Not only were the Soviets taken aback by this massive increase after so many years of neglect by the Americans, but they also had serious troubles of their own in Afghanistan, where they were barely holding their own against rebel forces. This unpopular war had started in late 1979 and was beginning to divide Soviet society.

In addition, the U.S.S.R. was having trouble with its satellite nations in the Warsaw Pact, especially Poland. The Polish freedom movement, Solidarity, headed by Lech Walesa, was pushing the Communist Party in Poland for major reforms. The more the government pushed back, the stronger the movement became. However, Gorbachev decided not to invade Poland

as his predecessors had done in Czechoslovakia and Hungary decades earlier.

Gorbachev came in as a reformer, but he was still a communist brought up in the old system, and he believed that it could be made to work. When he assumed leadership, he was not strong enough to make all of the sweeping changes he wanted to, so he set about consolidating his power base. Within three years he achieved this goal and was able simply to remove Soviet military forces from Eastern Europe (excluding East Germany) with little or no internal opposition, forward his ideas of glasnost and perestroika (literally meaning "openness" and "restructuring," respectively), and make economic reforms as well. These reforms were designed to solidify his domestic power to give him the support he needed to make the next series of changes: political and social reforms. Yet, Gorbachev never got the opportunity, for events overtook the process.

Seeing a weakening of the Soviet position, reformers in Eastern Europe decided to make their move. Beginning in Poland, where the struggle had been ongoing for almost a decade, then moving to East Germany and then south, the populations simply seemed to rise up in 1989. The communist leadership, with no Soviet support forthcoming, put up a half-hearted resistance and then crumbled. The Berlin Wall, so long the symbol of the Cold War, came down in November 1989.

Gorbachev and the Soviet Union struggled on for another two years, but their power and influence were gone. Unable to complete the reforms, Gorbachev's country collapsed. Had he appeared on the scene a decade earlier, Gorbachev may have been able to save the entire system, but coming when they did, his actions were doomed to failure.

–WILLIAM A. KAUTT, SAN ANTONIO, TEXAS

Viewpoint: Mikhail Gorbachev was a dedicated communist who saw a need to restructure the Soviet Union.

After Mikhail Gorbachev was named general secretary of the Communist Party of the Soviet Union in March 1985, he embarked on a program of broad reform in the Soviet government, economy, and society. There were two major elements of these reforms. Glasnost, or "openness," was intended to unmask the heretofore secret administration of the Soviet Union and create greater accountability to the public. Perestroika, or "restructuring," involved structural reforms in the Soviet government and economy that were intended to promote greater efficiency and initiative. Despite much optimism about Gorbachev's personal commitment to peace, freedom, and democracy (some communist extremists have even labeled Gorbachev a Western secret agent!) the principal objective of his reforms was to ensure the future domestic stability and international competitiveness of his country and its communist system.

It is important to note that the common Western image of Gorbachev—that of an urbane, smiling man who loved children and played tennis—has concealed important facts that are relevant for any sophisticated discussion of his beliefs and goals. First and foremost, Gorbachev always was and remains a committed communist whose belief in the superiority of doctrinaire Marxism has yet to wane. Much of his approach in the late 1980s was based on the belief that effective reform of the problems faced by communist systems would generate support and even enthusiasm from the ordinary people who lived in them.

To accomplish that end, Gorbachev embarked on a course of reform designed to correct the structural problems of communism. When he came to power, these difficulties were pronounced. Most of the previous two decades had been characterized by the *zastoi* (stagnation) of the Leonid Brezhnev era. Selected chiefly as a compromise candidate to replace Nikita S. Khrushchev in October 1964, Brezhnev focused on promoting stability. Ambitious restructuring of the Soviet government, such as Joseph Stalin's purges and Khrushchev's effective yet much less bloody reform of the state administration and Communist Party apparatus, was avoided. This stability, however, resulted in a tendency toward inertia. Few Soviet apparatchiks were replaced under Brezhnev, and their average age crept upward as time went on. Many had been young party members when Stalin promoted them in the 1930s. By the 1980s many observers began to characterize the Soviet elite as a "gerontocracy" of old, self-interested men who lacked any serious initiative and remained in their jobs because of the leadership's stagnant approach to rule. The senile Brezhnev and his old, sickly, and short-lived successors Yuri Andropov (1982–1984) and Konstantin Chernenko (1984–1985) did little to improve the image of the system.

The aging face of Soviet leadership had a negative effect on the country at large. Corruption grew as the Brezhnevite elite increasingly followed a "stability in cadres" policy that suggested that political stability should supersede efficiency. This view trickled down to every level of Soviet society, prompting the joke that the guiding principle of Soviet economics was "you pretend to pay us and we pretend to work." The enhanced prestige of the military in the post-Khrushchev period, and the generally more aggressive approach of the Union of Soviet Socialist Republics (U.S.S.R.) to international relations under Brezhnev, caused military spending to remain at dangerously high levels, which prevented meaningful domestic economic reform. Khrushchev-era economic experiments that suggested more liberal and initiative-based market policies were shut down. By the time Brezhnev died in November 1982, the Soviet economy was approaching stagnation and the administrative structure was marred by corruption.

Even before Gorbachev came to power, some Soviet leaders had become aware of the systemic problems at work in the U.S.S.R. and began to take cautious steps toward their resolution. When he served as the head of the *Komitet gosudarstvennoy bezopasnosti* (KGB or Committee for State Security) before succeeding Brezhnev, Andropov had embarked on an anticorruption drive. Once he became general secretary, he initi-

GORBACHEV LOOKS BACK

On 25 December 1991 Mikhail Gorbachev spoke to the Russian people and announced his resignation as president of the U.S.S.R. after eleven former Soviet republics withdrew from the union.

I understood that initiating reforms on such a large scale in a society like ours was a most difficult and risky undertaking. But even now, I am convinced that the democratic reforms started in the spring of 1985 were historically justified.

The process of renovating this country and bringing about fundamental changes in the international community proved to be much more complex than originally anticipated. However, let us acknowledge what has been achieved so far.

Society has acquired freedom; it has been freed politically and spiritually. And this is the most important achievement, which we have not fully come to grips with, in part because we still have not learned how to use our freedom. However, a historic task has been accomplished.

The totalitarian system, which prevented this country from becoming wealthy and prosperous a long time ago, has been dismantled.

A breakthrough has been made on the road to democratic reforms. Free elections, freedom of the press, freedom of worship, representative legislatures, and a multi-party system have all become realities.

We have set out to introduce a pluralistic economy, and the equality of all forms of ownership is being established. In the course of the land reform, the peasantry is reviving, individual farmers have appeared and millions of hectares of land have been allocated to the urban and rural population. Laws were passed on the economic freedom of producers, and free enterprise, shareholding and privatization are under way.

Shifting the course of our economy towards a free market, we must not forget that this is being done for the benefit of the individual. In these times of hardship, everything must be done to ensure the social protection of the individual—particularly old people and children.

We live in a new world: An end has been put to the "Cold War," arms race and the insane militarization of our country, which crippled our economy, distorted our thinking and undermined our morals. The threat of a world war is no more. . . .

The August coup brought the overall crisis to a breaking point. The most disastrous aspect of this crisis is the collapse of statehood. And today I watch apprehensively the loss of the citizenship of a great country by our citizens—the consequences of this could be grave, for all of us.

I consider it vitally important to sustain the democratic achievements of the last few years. We have earned them through the suffering of our entire history and our tragic experience. We must not abandon them under any circumstances, under any pretext. Otherwise, all our hopes for a better future will be buried.

Source: Mikhail Gorbachev, Memoirs (New York: Doubleday, 1996), pp. xxvi–xxviii.

---

ated a broader campaign against inefficiency and social problems (especially alcoholism) that were beginning to affect the performance of the Soviet government and economy. Andropov also began attempts to engage the United States in a meaningful relaxation of relations between the superpowers. At one point he declared that "détente is by no means a thing of the past. It is the wave of the future!"

Gorbachev dramatically expanded all of these policies, though his approach to reform was constrained by the large and powerful party apparatus that was becoming increasingly resistant to change. Nevertheless, Gorbachev managed to cashier some eighty thousand apparatchiks, some 20 percent of the total, in the first few months of his rule. This action was significant since the major center of opposition to meaningful domestic reform was being challenged in a serious way; Khrushchev's attempts at reshuffling personnel had contributed to his removal from power. Though it proved less successful and actually created more problems for Soviet society, Gorbachev expanded on

Andropov's antialcoholism campaign in the hope that it would lead to greater efficiency.

Starting with these initiatives, Gorbachev also adopted meaningful reforms to reenergize the Soviet economy. Although such reforms as the decentralization of production decisions and the introduction of a limited social market economy did not generally meet with much success early on, Gorbachev's feeling was that they would ultimately make the socialist economic system of the Soviet Union function better and provide for the needs of the people in abundance and efficiency. Many drew the comparison to the New Economic Policy (NEP) of another committed communist, Vladimir Ilich Ulyanov Lenin.

Gorbachev's foreign policy was also an important element in his reforms. In the 1980s the Soviet Union spent between 15 and 25 percent of its Gross National Product (GNP) on the military. The hostile international situation prevented any meaningful shift of resources to domestic economic reform and modernization, and Gorbachev believed that détente would ease relations enough to allow him to focus on recovery without exposing the security of the U.S.S.R. Like many others in the Soviet leadership, he also realized that the technological advantages held by the West would ultimately spell doom for Soviet competitiveness in the international arena. It was impossible for him to reconstruct the viability of the Soviet Union as a major economic power if the technical aspects of development were ignored. The main goal of Gorbachev's foreign policy, then, was not to bring about vaguely defined "good will" or "world peace" but to increase his own country's chances for survival and prosperity through a period of truce in the Cold War. It goes without saying that the Soviet leader both planned on and received massive infusions of capital, foreign investment, and technology transfers from his new friends in the West.

This development should not have been surprising, for the Khrushchev era had supplied antecedents to this approach, especially Khrushchev's attempts to free up resources for domestic investment by encouraging "peaceful coexistence" with the West. When Gorbachev wrote in *Perestroika: New Thinking For Our Country and the World* (1987) that Soviet foreign policy "had to be radically reformed," he had much on his mind, indeed. In addition to his overtures to the United States, especially those after 1986, Gorbachev began to indulge in rhetoric about "a common European home." He also tried to repair relations with China, visiting Beijing only weeks before the massacre at Tiananmen Square, and improve relations with other neighboring states, such as Iran and Japan. As early as 1986, Gor-bachev announced his intention to withdraw Soviet troops from Afghanistan, and in 1988 he renounced the use of force in the internal affairs of other communist nations.

While these events were designed to create a stable and peaceful international environment, Gorbachev needed to ensure successful domestic development and modernization, as they reflected broader realities about the progress of political reform at home. The pace of domestic reform, especially in the economy, was relatively slow and unsuccessful at first. Though Gorbachev was able to force many oppositionist bureaucrats into retirement, there still remained much resistance within the state apparatus and communist party. By introducing glasnost policies of bureaucratic transparency, dissenting elements in the Soviet Union were actually made into tacit allies of Gorbachev since they were freely able to criticize the problems that the regime was beginning to confront. By the late 1980s, however, this situation created serious problems for Gorbachev himself. Few in the dissent community, it turned out, were willing to support a reformed communist regime. Glasnost-era revelations about the crimes of the Stalin era, and other eras besides, subject to only limited discussion during Khrushchev's reform period, alienated increasing numbers of people from the Soviet system and caused many to object on a fundamental level to its "restructuring." The high standard of living in the West left many Soviet citizens feeling cheated and let down by their government and its philosophy. New freedoms that allowed national and ethnic minorities, as well as Great Russian nationalists, to explore their cultural identity in a political context also presented a serious challenge to the imperial nature of the Soviet polity.

Inevitably, Gorbachev's reforms undermined his position. As economic reform stalled and enjoyed relatively limited success, political reform served only to place Gorbachev between the jaws of a vice. On the one hand, reformist elements to which he had hoped to appeal by and large rejected the idea that communism could be made serviceable and effective. While some remained socialist and even Leninist in orientation, few reformers did not call for free elections and an end to the monopoly on power held by the Communist Party, positions that Gorbachev only supported with much hesitation and pressure. In fact, Gorbachev removed many high-ranking government and party officials (such as Boris Yeltsin) from positions of power because they wanted to go too far in reforming the country. He also adopted coercive measures, including violent police and military actions, to control forces of ethnic dissent. On the other hand, as the reform process seemed to be spinning out of control, many members of the party and state administration,

GLASNOST AND PERESTROIKA

even some who had initially supported Gorbachev, came to believe with justification that the country was unraveling and that his reforms were jeopardizing the future of the U.S.S.R. In August 1991 an impressive group of Kremlin insiders, including the vice president of the U.S.S.R., the minister of defense, and the head of the KGB among others, organized a coup d'état that placed Gorbachev under house arrest in the Crimea and attempted to suppress the increasingly separatist government of the Russian Federation, led by Yeltsin. Although the coup failed, thanks to its inept organization, the resolve of pro-reform Russians—especially Yeltsin—and the unwillingness of the military to back the plotters, Gorbachev's position as head of state became untenable. As the reformers flocked to Yeltsin over the next few months, the Soviet Union broke up into its constituent republics and Gorbachev was compelled to resign.

Although Gorbachev will be remembered in history for how miserably he failed to reach his goals, it is nevertheless important to identify what they were. Gorbachev was not a democrat, nor was he ever convinced that the communist system in which he believed was born with fundamental flaws that almost certainly predestined it for destruction. Simply put, he wanted to restore a sense of confidence and initiative in the people and institutions so that they would support the continuation of Soviet communism. Though Gorbachev's approach involved greater political freedom and an attempt to create a limited social market economy, as did Lenin's New Economic Policy of the 1920s, he found that the vast majority of his people intended to use their new freedoms to tear down a system that had positively no democratic or moral legitimacy and try to replace it with one that did. Paradoxically, in trying to make his country more stable and competitive, he set in motion a process that led to its demise.

–PAUL DU QUENOY, GEORGETOWN UNIVERSITY

References

Jonathan R. Adelman, *Torrents of Spring: Soviet and Post-Soviet Politics* (New York: McGraw-Hill, 1995);

Raymond L. Garthoff, *The Great Transition: American-Soviet Relations and the End of the Cold War* (Washington, D.C.: Brookings Institution, 1994);

Mikhail Gorbachev, *Memoirs* (New York: Doubleday, 1996);

Gorbachev, *Perestroika: New Thinking For Our Country and the World* (Cambridge & New York: Harper & Row, 1987);

Jerry F. Hough, *Democratization and Revolution in the USSR, 1985–1991* (Washington, D.C.: Brookings Institution, 1997).

GORBACHEV

Did Mikhail Gorbachev betray the communist government in East Germany?

Viewpoint: Yes. Mikhail Gorbachev sold out the communist government of East Germany in an effort to gain economic and political concessions for the Soviet Union.

Viewpoint: No. Flaws within the German Democratic Republic itself generated a popular revolution that played the major role in the collapse of East Germany.

By the late 1980s the Soviet Union was in a desperate situation. Facing increasingly serious domestic political turmoil, its ability to defend its global strategic positions was coming into doubt. In 1989 Soviet control in Eastern Europe began to crumble. Realizing that he lacked the diplomatic and political strength to support communist regimes in the region, Mikhail Gorbachev allowed them to go their own way and hoped that they would remain friendly toward the Soviet Union. One of these states, East Germany, was in an anomalous position. Artificially separated from the West after World War II, it owed its unique existence to Soviet support and its stability to Soviet troops and tanks. Despite Western recognition of its political legitimacy during the détente era and the continued presence of Soviet military forces, its leadership remained concerned about its future once Soviet support was no longer forthcoming.

Without any prospect of help from Moscow, the East German regime faced popular demonstrations that it could not hope to control on its own. When it agreed to domestic political reform, including the opening of the Berlin Wall in November 1989 and free elections in March 1990, opposition parties devoted to national reunification captured 75 percent of the vote. Seeing that German reunification was probably an inevitability, the leaders of the occupying powers had to negotiate the process and control conditions. In the end, Gorbachev consented to reunification and the removal of Soviet troops in exchange for a fantastic number of concessions from the West, which promised to help his own ailing country and address its security concerns. In addition to guaranteeing its eastern border, the new Germany financed both the reform of the Soviet economy with the proportional equivalent of a Marshall Plan and the relocation of Soviet troops in East Germany. Bonn also sponsored Soviet membership in every major international economic organization, agreed to uphold all East German economic agreements with the Union of Soviet Socialist Republics (U.S.S.R.) in perpetuity, swore off weapons of mass destruction, and promised not to allow North Atlantic Treaty Organization (NATO) military exercises on former East German territory.

Viewpoint:
Yes. Mikhail Gorbachev sold out the communist government of East Germany in an effort to gain economic and political concessions for the Soviet Union.

The relative economic and geopolitical decline of the Soviet Union in the closing years of the Brezhnev era necessitated a fundamental revaluation of Soviet global strategy. In the Gorbachev era the Soviet Union encouraged policies of liberalization designed to preserve the continued independence and viability of the German Democratic Republic (GDR) and other Eastern European satellites without the heretofore necessary and exorbitant military and economic commitments. The failure of this policy when it was implemented in East Germany placed Gorbachev in a situation where he was able to use the jettisoning of that country from the Soviet orbit as a lever to extract concessions from the West and build the foundation of what many believed would be the recovery and modernization of the Union Soviet Socialist Republics (U.S.S.R).

By the early 1980s, aggressive Soviet attempts to "alter the global correlation of forces" and their corresponding high material costs had created a general stagnation in the Soviet economy. Even as the Soviet Union appeared to be extending its power and influence at an unprecedented pace, virtually all of its leading economic indicators were registering significant declines in the generally rosy rates of growth enjoyed since the end of World War II.

While new economic relationships arising from détente benefited the Soviets in some areas, they exacerbated problems in others. The growing importation of grain and high technology from the West increased an already negative trade balance and drained hard currency reserves at an unprecedented rate. Between 1975 and 1977 the Soviet hard-currency foreign debt increased by 60 percent, from $10 billion to $16 billion. At the same time traditional sources of hard currency revenue were drying up. After the oil crisis of 1979, market prices of oil and natural gas began to fall, in anticipation of a trend that only accelerated in the 1980s, and adversely affected Soviet earnings from their most vital export commodity. Saturation of Third World countries with Soviet weaponry led to a general leveling-off of Soviet arms exports at the same time. By the early 1980s Moscow was resorting to the increased sale of gold and other precious metals to make up the shortfall.

The overextended Soviet position within its "empire" proved to be a serious economic mill-

stone. Similar problems affecting the Soviet economy were magnified in its Eastern European satellites, countries naturally predisposed to greater dependence on military and material aid from the Soviet Union. Since the end of World War II, the general unpopularity of the puppet regimes in Eastern Europe had mandated a large, permanent Soviet military presence there, particularly after the Hungarian and Czech uprisings of 1956 and 1968. The costs of this forward position were substantial: an estimated $13 to $15 billion per year. Western analyses of Soviet military expenditures range them between 17 percent and 25 percent of the $1.4 trillion Gross National Product (GNP) of the U.S.S.R., compared with 6 to 8 percent of the $5 trillion U.S. GNP, the latter figure spent at a time of unprecedented military buildup.

Further afield the Soviet occupation of Afghanistan had degenerated into an unwinnable guerilla war, a veritable "Soviet Vietnam." In addition to their general economic plight, the Soviets also found themselves faced with a new and bullishly anticommunist American administration, led by Ronald Reagan, that quickly resolved to worsen their condition and roll back Soviet positions on a global scale.

Gorbachev's selection as Communist Party general secretary in March 1985 marked a renewed point of departure for the reforms advocated by a faction of the Soviet leadership, led at first by Gorbachev's mentor Yuri Andropov, that promoted renewed détente with the West. Just as Andropov began his tenure as general secretary in 1982 with attempts to ease tension with the West and create an environment favorable to the promotion of future Soviet viability, so too did Gorbachev begin to move toward a posture of engagement and relaxation. The first step in that direction, the replacement of the Brezhnevite Andrey Gromyko with the reformist Eduard Shevardnadze as foreign minister in July 1985, was candidly admitted by Gorbachev to be a political ramification of a foreign policy that had to be radically reformed.

Given the domestic constraints on Gorbachev's initiatives in the early perestroika period, it is plain that his true intentions toward Germany and Eastern Europe had to remain masked for the moment. From a strategic perspective, however, it is unlikely that Gorbachev's plan for détente and development could easily continue to accommodate the draining Soviet military presence and economic subsidization in Eastern Europe. The generally slow response of the Soviet economy to Gorbachev's economic reforms made these relationships even more untenable.

By the spring of 1987, Gorbachev was freed from constraints on the elaboration of his policy

GORBACHEV

for a restructured Eastern Europe. In a speech given in Prague in April of that year, Gorbachev referred to a new promise of national equality and independence within a socialist world. The practical translation of this example and many other rhetorical reductions in military and economic commitments came only in Foreign Ministry spokesman Gennadi Gerisamov's September 1989 statement characterizing Soviet policy as a "Sinatra Doctrine," allowing Eastern European nations to do things "their way." Since the Soviet position could no longer be maintained by hundreds of thousands of troops and expensive remedies for regional economic problems, Gorbachev sought to transform Eastern Europe into a belt of benevolent, self-sustaining regimes of a broadly socialist complexion.

Beginning in late 1986 the Soviets began to drop subtle hints concerning the future of the German question. Gorbachev's restructuring of the Soviet diplomatic corps enabled him to place a firm supporter, Yuli Kvitsinsky, at the embassy in Bonn. In February 1987 Nikolai Portugalov, one of Gorbachev's senior advisers on Germany, made the novel affirmation (for the U.S.S.R.) that citizens of the two Germanies belonged to the same nation. A former Soviet ambassador to the Federal Republic, Valentin Falin, suggested that the transit access agreement of 1971 might not be the last word on the future of Berlin. The Gorbachev-dominated Soviet press was replete with references to

future possibilities, all of which seemed to involve some change in the German question.

Despite some initial resistance these overtures bore fruit. West German chancellor Helmut Kohl's visit to Moscow in October 1988 was complemented by the largest extension of credit ever made from the West, 3 billion deutsche maarks from West German banks, together with scores of private deals made between the Soviet government and the phalanx of German businessmen who accompanied Kohl. With both a full relaxation in tension with the West and an unprecedented financial relationship with which to modernize his country, Gorbachev was now ready to proceed with the implementation of his strategy, the deconstruction of the Soviet position in Eastern Europe.

At the same time, East German leader Erich Honecker began to worry about what that would mean for his own country, and he reshuffled the East German leadership, tending to promote conservative adherents to the regime rather than reformists. In late 1987 and early 1988 government efforts against the East German dissent movement, especially its patriotic, but Leninist and pro-Gorbachev mainstream, reached new heights in the form of waves of arrests and confiscations of sensitive published material. Censorship of foreign publications and broadcasts, including even Soviet and reformist East European periodicals, increased dramatically, even though much of the population could follow

Soviet premier Mikhail Gorbachev answering reporters' questions in November 1990

GORBACHEV

Gorbachev simply by tuning in West German television and radio stations. Despite rhetoric about peaceful conflict resolution and official assertions to the contrary, the order to shoot would-be émigrés apparently remained in effect at least until February 1989, the last time an East German fugitive was murdered while trying to get over the Berlin Wall.

Since example and indirect appeals had only hardened Honecker's resolve to resist change, by the spring of 1989 Gorbachev's efforts began to become oriented toward destabilizing the East German regime. In July 1988 Gorbachev affirmed his renunciation of the Brezhnev doctrine—first before a session of the European Parliament in Strasbourg and then before a summit meeting of the Warsaw Pact. Honecker continued to resist. Perhaps most important of all was the laudatory attention given on 13 August 1989 to the twenty-eighth anniversary of the construction of the Berlin Wall, an event credited by Honecker with "'stability, security, [and] the continuation of socialist construction.'"

It cannot be known whether or not Gorbachev came to the same conclusion earlier, but Honecker's statement about the Wall was an implicit admission that East German political stability was a function of how effectively it could prevent its population from fleeing. The partial deconstruction of the Iron Curtain along the Austro-Hungarian frontier in May 1989, furthermore, had already resulted in the illegal emigration of several hundred East Germans through Hungary. What better lever for forcing reforms on the GDR could there have been than a destabilizing crisis on the order of the one that had necessitated the sealing of its border with the West in the first place?

Hungary happened to be at the top of the small list of foreign travel destinations where East Germans were permitted to go on vacation. In the last two weeks of August, one scholar has claimed, there were secret high-level talks among Hungarian, West German, and Soviet diplomats in which the Soviets supported, or perhaps even encouraged, the Hungarians to allow the East German vacationers to go to the West. It is clear, at least, that Gorbachev had endorsed the physical opening of the Hungarian border as early as March 1989 in a meeting with Prime Minister Miklós Németh, and it is difficult to see how he could not have perceived the problem that such a situation would create for Honecker. In the event, within three days of the Hungarian announcement on 11 September that it would not prevent the movement of foreign citizens to the West, some thirteen thousand restless East Germans poured into Austria. In Prague and Warsaw thousands more flooded the West German embassies and were eventually permitted to travel to the West. The stream of refugees out of Hungary, meanwhile, showed no sign of diminishing: more than one hundred thousand fled by the end of September.

As events were unfolding in Hungary, the Leninist opposition in the GDR began to form bona fide political parties and reinvent existing communist-dominated ones along reformist socialist lines. Gorbachev's visit to commemorate the fortieth anniversary of the founding of the GDR gave the opposition the impetus to bring its criticism of the Honecker regime to the forefront. Despite Honecker's authorization of force against a large demonstration in Leipzig, evidence shows that Soviet military and diplomatic pressure was brought to bear on the East German military not to intervene.

As a result of the deterioration of the situation, and probably with Soviet acquiescence, Honecker was removed as first secretary of the Socialist Unity Party on 18 October. His successor, Egon Krenz, is perhaps best viewed as a transitional figure; he had enough clout to claim continuity from Honecker, yet not enough to consolidate control of the state in a crisis situation. Though Krenz sounded more conciliatory than his predecessor, he nevertheless spoke firmly about continuity with the past and refused categorically to make any political concessions to the opposition. This stand was hardly pleasing to the protestors, and the demonstrations only increased in size and volume. By the end of October, Krenz reversed course and began to make small concessions.

An insipid concession spelled the end for Krenz. On 9 November Politburo member and Socialist Unity Party (SED) party boss of East Berlin Günter Schabowski announced on East German television that special permission to travel to the West was no longer necessary. Among a tumult of official misunderstanding and popular enthusiasm the gates of the Berlin Wall were flung open, and the entire city rejoiced as one. It is unlikely that the defining feature of East German history was nullified by an inexperienced nonentity responding to whimsical popular confusion in a police state. Nor is it likely that a regime that had lost so much control over events would have been able to survive in their aftermath. Krenz's eleventh hour hints at reform simply could not give him credibility either in the eyes of the opposition or Gorbachev. What seems most likely, then, is that Gorbachev gave Krenz the green light in order to undermine his position so completely that he could not hope to recover.

Indeed, within days the Socialist Unity Party all but collapsed. Amid resignations, firings, and suicides, Krenz was speedily removed from leadership and replaced by

GORBACHEV

GORBACHEV ON EUROPEAN RELATIONS

Mikhail Gorbachev struggled to redefine the Soviet role in Europe as his country began to fall apart. Before a 6 July 1989 meeting of the Council of Europe, Gorbachev called for a continued role for his country in European affairs and for a reduction in nuclear weapons. A portion of his remarks are presented here.

Social and political orders in one country or another changed in the past and may change in the future. But this change is the exclusive affair of the people of that country and is their choice. Any interference in domestic affairs and any attempts to restrict the sovereignty of states—friends, allies or any others—is inadmissible.

Differences among states are not removable. They are, as I have already said on several occasions, even favorable, provided, of course, that the competition between the different types of society is directed at creating better material and spiritual living conditions for all people.

It is time to deposit in the archives the postulates of the cold war period, when Europe was regarded as an arena of confrontation, divided into "spheres of influence," and somebody's "outpost," and as an object of military rivalry, a battlefield. In today's interdependent world, the geopolitical notions born of another era turn out to be just as useless in real politics as the laws of classical mechanics in quantum theory.

Meanwhile, it is on the basis of outdated stereotypes that the Soviet Union is suspected of planning domination and intending to tear the United States away from Europe. There are some who would like to place the U.S.S.R. outside Europe from the Atlantic to the Urals, by limiting its expanse "from Brest to Brest." The U.S.S.R., it is alleged, is too big for coexistence. Others would feel ill at ease with it. The present-day realities and prospects for the foreseeable future are obvious. The U.S.S.R. and the United States constitute a natural part of the European international-political structure. And their participation in its evolution is not only justified, but is also historically determined.

The philosophy of the "common European home" concept rules out the probability of an armed clash and the very possibility of the use of force or threat of force—alliance against alliance, inside the alliances, wherever. This philosophy suggests that a doctrine of restraint should take the place of the doctrine of deterrence. This is not just a play on words but the logic of European development.

Our goals at the Vienna talks are well known. We consider it quite attainable— and the United States President, too, supports this—to secure a substantially lower level of armaments in Europe in the course of two-three years, with the elimination of all asymmetries and imbalances, of course. And I emphasize—all asymmetries and imbalances. No double standards are admissible here.

We are convinced that it is also time to begin talks on tactical nuclear systems between all countries concerned. The ultimate objective is to fully remove the weapons, which threaten not only Europeans, who by no means intend to wage war on one another. Who then needs them, and what for?

Source: Current History, *88 (October 1989): 347.*

Dresden party boss Hans Modrow, an ardent reformer whom Honecker had accused of being another Alexander Dubček, the Czechoslovakian communist leader whose liberal reforms led to the Soviet invasion of his country in 1968. At last Gorbachev had the opportunity to create the reformist regime he had desired all along. Valentin Falin and the pro-Gorbachev former security official Markus Johannes Wolf were instrumental in coordinating the transfer of power to Modrow in an attempt to stabilize the situation so that a liberalized regime could be established.

Modrow entered power on the crest of a wave of reform and had five months before the national elections slated for March 1990 to build public confidence, but the limitations of the changes at once became apparent. From Moscow it was made clear that the leadership approved of what was happening because its members believed that Marxism and reform communism would play a leading, if not monopolistic, role in the future development of East Germany. Within the GDR the opposition was in full agreement with Modrow's affirmation of socialist principles, rejection of a West German–style social market economy, and commitment to creating a viable "third way" socialist state. Even in West Germany talk of speedy reunification, or indeed of any reunification at all, was not believed to be realistic.

What Gorbachev failed to consider, in his own country as much as in East Germany, is that popular democracy cannot be directed from above. The involvement of West German party organizations in the East German political process in the winter of 1989–1990 complicated the matter further. In the event, the free elections held in March 1990 demonstrated that the "third-way" platforms of the oppositionist political parties that had sprouted up during the emigration crisis the previous September in fact bore no relation at all to the political complexion of the East German electorate. Put together they polled less than 10 percent of the vote, while pro-unification parties modeled after, and in conjunction with, Western counterparts commanded about 75 percent.

Even before the March elections set Germany firmly on the course to reunification, the situation of the reformed former communists, now calling themselves the Party of Democratic Socialism, had been so damaged by the crisis, revelations about decades of corruption, and the visible disparity between East and West, that they were for the moment relegated to the political margin. This shift, and the sagging popularity of the lukewarm Marxist parties of the former opposition, demonstrated to Gorbachev that his strategy of creating a stable, reform socialist regime in East Germany had been illusory and that the reemergence of a unified German state was unavoidable. Ironically, Honecker had been right all along.

The collapse of Gorbachev's aim of creating a benevolently independent and socialist regime in East Germany and the inevitability of German reunification forced a reevaluation of his policy toward Germany. If he could not prevent the rebirth of what could only be Europe's preeminent power, he would extract the greatest possible price for it, using the Soviet military position in East Germany as leverage. Specifically, Gorbachev reoriented his German policy toward maximizing the financial aspect of the Soviet–West German relationship and minimizing security challenges that a reunified Germany would entail for Soviet military strategy in the future.

In this approach Gorbachev was far more successful. With the encouragement of the détente-oriented Bush administration, and in pursuit of his own goals for filling the developing power vacuum in eastern Europe, Kohl made enormous concessions on all the Soviet conditions. Toward the first condition Kohl pledged

70 billion deutsche marks, about 3 percent of the West German GNP, for the modernization of the Soviet Union, a figure roughly equal to the Marshall Plan in the 1940s. Bonn also sponsored Soviet membership in the International Monetary Fund (IMF), the World Bank, and the European Bank for Construction and Development. In addition Kohl pledged an additional 15 billion deutsche marks to finance the withdrawal and future housing costs of Soviet troops stationed in East Germany. Long-term trade agreements between the Soviet Union and East Germany were to be honored by the reunified nation in perpetuity.

In talks at Gorbachev's hometown of Stavropol in July 1990, Kohl affirmed that the renunciation of chemical, biological, and nuclear weapons by the Federal Republic would continue after reunification. The unified armed forces, furthermore, would be limited to 370,000 personnel, a 25 percent reduction in the size of the West German prereunification military. Forces in the integrated NATO command structure were banned from being deployed or conducting exercises in the former GDR. Finally, in the weeks following the official reunification of 3 October 1990, Germany reaffirmed the Oder-Neisse frontier as final, and the constitutional clauses that provided for the incorporation of historically German territory into the Federal Republic were declared irrelevant and deleted from the Basic Law. Gorbachev's strategic gains vis-à-vis Germany and in terms of the Soviet, and later Russian, position in the post–Cold War world were legion.

–PAUL DU QUENOY,
GEORGETOWN UNIVERSITY

Viewpoint:
No. Flaws within the German Democratic Republic itself generated a popular revolution that played the major role in the collapse of East Germany.

The decline and fall of the German Democratic Republic (GDR) began in 1985, when newly appointed Soviet premier Mikhail Gorbachev launched the stagnant Soviet system on a new course. His policies of "openness" and "reconstruction" also marked an about-face in the alliance/client system the Union of Soviet Socialist Republics (U.S.S.R.) had maintained in Eastern Europe since the end of World War II. Gorbachev made no secret of his conviction that the Soviet Union could no longer sustain the military spending that had de facto guaranteed existing domestic orders with Soviet garrisons. Nor did the premier hide his conviction that the governments and peoples of Eastern Europe must be in a position to find their own ways to socialism. In the latter context Gorbachev had no notion of dismantling the system that provided a strategic and diplomatic glacis for the U.S.S.R. Instead, he was convinced that that system was sufficiently established and that any disruptions would be temporary. Taken a step deeper, as a still-believing communist, Gorbachev found it intellectually and emotionally impossible to believe that the Eastern European states would turn their back on history and abandon the future for an inevitably doomed Western capitalist present.

Gorbachev's approach came as a general shock to the governments of the Warsaw Pact. Nowhere, however, was the impact greater than in East Germany. In the preceding decade the GDR and its ruling Socialist Unity Party (SED) had established themselves in a comfortable diplomatic and political niche. The Federal Republic of Germany (FRG), the exponentially more prosperous neighbor of the GDR, was increasingly subsidizing the East with hard-currency payments for everything from dissident release to pollution control. A West German intelligentsia obsessed with utopian illusions and delusions turned consistently to the GDR as a stick with which to berate their own society for its imperfections. If the East German economy had stagnated since the 1970s, the drain of supporting Soviet-inspired African adventures had also ended. East German athletes continued to demonstrate the merits of modern sports chemistry by bringing home a disproportionate number of medals from athletic competitions in which they participated. A few dissident groups existed: clergy, students, and intellectuals interested in environmental issues and human rights—the kind of people who exemplified German poet Heinrich Heine's nineteenth-century aphorism that the natural habitat of the Germans was the airy empire of dreams. Open protests, even a few street demonstrations, had become more frequent than in the past, but the prison system still functioned well, and for lesser offenses, job loss or exile to the West served to maintain the status quo without significant extra effort. When Premier Erich Honecker proclaimed that the Berlin Wall would stand for another century, he hardly seemed, to those on either side of that barrier, like a facile optimist.

Through the first half of 1989 the GDR showed no inclination to change and seemed to have no reason to do so. The regularly scheduled elections in May gave the government slate of candidates the predictable 98 percent. Officials praised the Chinese People's Republic for crushing the Tiananmen Square demonstrations in June. Other officials and theorists openly criticized, in speech and print, Gorbachev's policies and capacities. Paradoxically, this hardline attitude made increasing numbers of East Germans anxious that the next step might involve closing even such limited windows to the outside world as foreign vacations, or the right to apply for immigration to West Germany. By the end of summer West German embassies everywhere in the Warsaw Pact were filled with GDR citizens wanting to switch their allegiance. Hundreds of others simply left—most through Hungary that in May opened its border with Austria. By September so many "Ossis" (slang for East Germans) were arriving in the West that the Bonn government requested them to stay home because of a lack of accommodations.

The government of the GDR faced an impasse. It did its best to plug the leaks on its frontiers, but could do nothing about the television that broadcast to Europe and the world reports of the East German population hemorrhage. That same publicity made Honecker and his colleagues reluctant to turn loose the police and army. Nor were these the Cold War years, when tanks could be used with impunity against demonstrators. The GDR had by now a self-image as a "state of law" as well as a party state.

There were thousands of people on the street daily, protesting recent policies of the GDR government. It had begun in May, as a reaction to election results. By July "civic action groups" (ad hoc organizations) were built around existing dissident groups. Their demand for public dialogue on public issues resonated in the shops and factories. By September, East Germany possessed a flourishing system of de facto political parties. If as yet they had no power, they compensated by taking full advantage of the free publicity they received, in both German states and the world. Dissidents enjoyed as well automatic media sympathy—not least for the environmentalist, feminist, pacifist, and anticapitalist sentiments that formed so much of their public discourse.

The GDR government could not match the media savvy of its opponents—in part because it was distracted by preparations for its fortieth anniversary, to be celebrated in October. As the demonstrators kept the streets, the guest of honor, none other than Gorbachev, clashed with his hosts in public by indicating sympathy with the dissidents. Behind closed doors he urged party and government leaders to make terms with the people before events ran beyond their ability to control them. The dressing down was not well received by GDR officials, used by now to more moderate and conciliatory tones from their Soviet counterparts. Open comparisons were drawn between the respective purity of communism and the respective state of civilization in the GDR and the U.S.S.R. The police received a freer hand against dissidents and demonstrators—who as they were clubbed down, driven off the streets, or herded into vans shouted, "Gorby, help!"

It was a chant that shook the state to its foundations. A not-too-subtle source of GDR legitimacy had been its status as a preferable alternative to direct Russian rule. Now its citizens were calling on a Soviet premier for aid. It was a far cry from 1945. Nor were the police and army enthusiastic at the prospect of being used against their own people. On 9 October a mass rally in Leipzig, in the heart of "red Saxony," nearly sparked a confrontation. Then a series of speakers called for moderation and dialogue. The tension dissipated; security forces kept their truncheons holstered and rifles on "safe"; and the regime lost its last prospect of employing force successfully.

Within days Honecker was deposed. His successor, Egon Krenz, opened borders and sought to open dialogue. East Germans, however, saw Krenz as just another faceless apparatchik. The demonstrations by now were attracting as many as two hundred thousand marchers in the larger cities. With what Karl Marx might have called the cunning of history, that German quality that has been called "love of order" kept even the biggest rallies nonviolent and nondestructive, removing any pretext for intervention. A desperate Krenz further reduced travel restrictions on 6 November. In Berlin, citizens began challenging the guards at border checkpoints. Then the bolder among them challenged the Wall itself, as West Berliners cheered and went home for hammers. In one night the Berlin Wall became a source of souvenirs. Political infighting bled white a government and party now suffering from daily revelations of corruption and favoritism that had

characterized life at the top in the GDR. On 1 December East Germany became a parliamentary democracy when the previously marginal People's Chamber struck the monopoly of SED power from the constitution. Within a year the GDR itself would be absorbed into a Germany that was both more, and less, than the former Federal Republic written large.

Gorbachev played a marginal role in the collapse of East Germany. He had no desire to confront a united Germany and no desire to lose the "special relationship" that existed between the GDR and U.S.S.R. Nor did Gorbachev somehow betray an East German leadership that was well on its way to losing control before he arrived in Berlin. GDR leadership was a victim of a toxic mix of complacency, rigidity, and arrogance at the top. No government, and in particular no authoritarian government, can afford those flaws for any length of time. The GDR also fell to one of the few genuine popular revolutions of modern history—a sustained manifestation of the kind of civic courage sometimes said not to exist among Germans, and rare in any culture.

—DENNIS SHOWALTER,
COLORADO COLLEGE

References

Jeffrey Gedmin, *The Hidden Hand: Gorbachev and the Collapse of East Germany* (Washington, D.C.: American Enterprise Institute Press, 1992);

David H. Shumaker, *Gorbachev and the German Question: Soviet-West German Relations, 1985–1990* (Westport, Conn.: Praeger, 1995);

Michael J. Sodaro, Moscow, *Germany, and the West: from Khrushchev to Gorbachev* (Ithaca, N.Y.: Cornell University Press, 1990).

GORBACHEV

Was Alger Hiss guilty of spying for the Soviet Union?

Viewpoint: Yes. The evidence in Soviet government archives and the memoirs of high Communist Party officials prove that Alger Hiss was a spy.

Viewpoint: No. Alger Hiss was not guilty, and the accusations made against him were the product of public hysteria and political opportunism.

One of the most controversial issues in Cold War history focuses on the activities of one man: State Department official Alger Hiss. A close associate of many U.S. leaders (including President Franklin D. Roosevelt and Supreme Court justice Oliver Wendell Holmes), founding General Secretary of the United Nations (U.N.), and president of the Carnegie Endowment for International Peace, Hiss had a high profile in the American international-affairs community and access to a considerable amount of sensitive information. When Congress began to investigate subversive activity in the United States in the late 1940s, a former American communist named Whittaker Chambers claimed to have known Hiss years earlier as a member of Communist Party USA (CPUSA) and accused him of having spied for the Soviet Union.

While Hiss denied before Congress and in court that he had spied for the Union of Soviet Socialist Republics (U.S.S.R.), that he was or had ever been a communist, and that he had even known Chambers, his accusers produced circumstantial evidence that implicated Hiss in espionage. Amid a media storm defined by passionate invective on both sides, Hiss was acquitted of espionage but found guilty of perjury in his denial of having known Chambers.

Although much evidence about Soviet espionage in the United States, not available at the time of Hiss's trial, has emerged, scholars continue to debate whether he was in fact a spy. Many argue that such revelatory evidence as the National Security Agency (NSA) Venona documents prove Hiss's guilt beyond a shadow of a doubt, but others contend that the recently released evidence is not sufficiently conclusive to demonstrate his complicity.

Viewpoint:
Yes. The evidence in Soviet government archives and the memoirs of high Communist Party officials prove that Alger Hiss was a spy.

The conviction of Alger Hiss on perjury charges in January 1950 was one of the most controversial issues in the United States during the early Cold War. Throughout the trial and afterward, Hiss's supporters claimed that the affair was a vindictive and slanderous crusade. These claims can no longer be taken seriously. Evidence presented at the Hiss trial, materials from Federal Bureau of Investigation (FBI) files that were opened in the 1970s, additional documents released by the FBI in the 1990s, sensitive papers declassified by the U.S. National Security Agency (NSA) in 1995–1996, and selected items from secret police archives in Russia and Hungary all confirm that Hiss was, as alleged, an agent of the *Glavnoye Razvedyvatelnoye Upravleniye* (GRU), or the Main Intelligence Directorate of the Soviet army general staff.

The Hiss case began on 3 August 1948 when Whittaker Chambers, a senior editor at *Time* magazine, testified before the Un-American Activities Committee of the U.S. House of Representatives (HUAC). Chambers told the committee that he had been part of an underground communist conspiracy to infiltrate the U.S. government. Hiss, a former high-ranking State Department official who, since 1946, had been president of the Carnegie Endowment for International Peace, was one of the coconspirators named by Chambers, and the only one who vigorously denied the charges. As the controversy grew, Hiss sued Chambers for slander, prompting Chambers to reveal that the conspirators had been engaged in espionage on behalf of the Soviet Union. Chambers disclosed notes and microfilm that he said Hiss had delivered to him in 1938. Following these revelations, the slander trial was suspended, and the federal government brought charges against Hiss. Although the statute of limitations for espionage had expired, Hiss was convicted of perjury and sentenced to forty-four months in prison.

The jury that convicted Hiss was presented with strong evidence, including uncontested proof that several of the notes turned over by Chambers were in Hiss's handwriting, while others were produced on the Hiss family's typewriter. A former maid for the Chambers family testified that both Alger and Priscilla Hiss repeatedly visited the Chamberses' house in the mid 1930s. She also stated that Priscilla visited on several occasions without her husband, thus refuting Hiss's testimony that his family did not socialize with Chambers or his wife. Other important factors leading to conviction included inconsistent testimony by the Hisses about what happened to their old car and an alleged $400 loan made by Hiss to Chambers in 1937. Furthermore, Hiss's testimony was made less credible because his denials were far too sweeping. It was extremely difficult for the jury to accept his assertion that he had worked at the Agricultural Adjustment Administration (AAA) in the 1930s without ever discussing communism with his coworkers, several of whom were known to have been sympathetic to that doctrine. Taken together, this evidence was sufficient to convince the jury that Hiss had been a communist and engaged in espionage for the Soviet Union. His denials under oath made him guilty of perjury.

Despite the conviction, many people remained skeptical about Hiss's guilt, and doubts about the verdict continued to resurface even in the early 1990s. After Hiss was released from prison in 1954, he continued to insist that he was the innocent victim of a conspiracy. Throughout the 1960s, and especially the 1970s, his claims were supported by several prominent intellectuals. Because of Richard M. Nixon's key role in the HUAC investigation of Hiss in 1948, the Watergate scandal in the 1970s led to a resurgence of support for Hiss. Many of Nixon's opponents argued that Hiss's account of a government conspiracy against him was plausible. A final expression of doubt about Hiss's guilt came in 1992 after a cursory search of the former *Komitet Gosudarstvennoy Bezopasnosti* (KGB, or Committee for State Security) archives resulted in a statement by Russian military historian Dmitri A. Volkogonov that no evidence had been found linking Hiss with Soviet intelligence. A short while later, Volkogonov disavowed this statement and acknowledged that neither he nor anyone else had yet checked the GRU archives where most of the relevant files on Hiss would have been kept. He also acknowledged that the search of KGB archives had been superficial and that his comments had been intended mainly to propitiate Hiss's attorneys, who had been pressuring him to issue such a statement.

These doubts about Hiss's guilt notwithstanding, evidence available since the mid 1970s clearly shows that he spied for the Soviet Union. New documentation that emerged in the 1990s not only corroborates this analysis but also indicates that Hiss most likely continued to spy for the Soviet Union until just before his departure from the State Department in 1946.

In the 1970s the FBI released most of its files on the Hiss-Chambers controversy. This material confirms much of the evidence pre-

sented at the trial and adds several important new details. One revelation was a statement by Hede Massing, a former Soviet courier, that she had met with Hiss and discussed his efforts to recruit one of her agents, Noel Field, for the GRU. This testimony provided corroboration of Chambers's description of Hiss as a spy for Soviet military intelligence. FBI files also provided evidence that the Hiss defense team had tracked down, and then attempted to conceal, the whereabouts of the typewriter used by Hiss in the 1930s, an action that indirectly cast doubt on Hiss's veracity. Finally, the newly released

records showed that the FBI had suspected Hiss of spying several years before Chambers testified; this suspicion had been relayed to the State Department and was the main reason for Hiss's departure in 1946. Although none of this new information amounted to conclusive proof that Hiss was a spy, it confirmed key evidence presented at the trial. Following the end of the Cold War, a large quantity of additional material pertaining to the Hiss case became available. The opening of archives in Hungary and Russia, the release by the NSA of transcripts of Soviet intelligence cables intercepted by the United States, and the publication of several memoirs by former Soviet intelligence operatives have contributed new evidence reinforcing the conclusion that Hiss was a spy.

Documents in the former Central Party Archive in Moscow, which became available in the early 1990s, corroborate essential aspects of Chambers's testimony, including his description of an underground Communist Party network in the United States with direct ties to Soviet intelligence services. The documents show that members of this network sought to penetrate the U.S. government and copy sensitive State Department materials. This evidence undermines claims by Hiss's supporters that the documents produced by Chambers were forgeries and part of a conspiracy to implicate Hiss. Other archival materials implicate Hiss even more directly in Soviet espionage. In 1993 a Hungarian researcher, Maria Schmidt, came across previously unavailable materials in the Hungarian archives that confirmed Massing's account of Hiss's attempt to recruit Field. The record of Field's interrogation by the Hungarian secret police in the early 1950s includes a statement that Hiss had been working for the Soviet Union and that in 1935 Hiss attempted to persuade Field to join the Soviet espionage network. Field said he had informed Hiss that he (Field) was already working for Soviet intelligence, thus setting up the exchange between Hiss and Massing, as Massing had described. Although Hiss's defenders claimed that the Field transcript was suspect because it was compiled while Field was imprisoned and that he might have been coerced, Schmidt persuasively responded that a false confession could not possibly have been in the Soviet Union's interest at that time. Furthermore, Schmidt pointed out that the Hungarian archive contains multiple copies of a letter written by Field to Hiss in the 1950s offering to make a public statement that Hiss was not a spy. This letter, she noted, was "part of the Soviet disinformation campaign on Hiss's behalf."

Further confirmation of Massing's testimony is provided by KGB archival materials that were declassified in the late 1990s for an American historian, Allen Weinstein, and his Russian coauthor, Alexander Vassiliev. These materials include a series of cables between Massing's superiors in New York and Moscow, discussing how their operations in the United States might be impaired by the breach of security stemming from Field's disclosure to Hiss that he was a Soviet agent. The cables clearly indicate that Hiss contacted Field to recruit him, that Field told Hiss that he was already an agent, and that they then had an exchange at Field's apartment

about Hiss's efforts. Massing's trial testimony is thus fully confirmed by archival materials.

KGB archives provide several other references to Hiss's career as a GRU agent. One cable from a KGB station chief in New York that listed Soviet agents in the State Department noted that Hiss had been recruited by the GRU. A 1938 memorandum from Yitzhak Akhmerov, the KGB station chief at the time, about efforts by a Soviet agent, Michael Straight, to recruit Hiss, affirms that "Hiss belongs to our family." A 1994 memoir by Pavel Sudoplatov, a high-ranking Soviet intelligence official from the 1930s through the early 1950s, provides further confirmation that Hiss was a spy. Sudoplatov maintains that a former GRU station chief in New York had told him that Hiss was a member of the Silvermaster spy cell in Washington, D.C. through the mid 1930s and that Chambers's testimony in 1948 was considered a great setback for the GRU. All this additional evidence leaves no doubt that Hiss was guilty both of spying for the Soviet Union and of committing perjury.

The latest evidence also shows that Hiss almost certainly remained a Soviet agent after Chambers left the party in 1938. The first indication of this came from Oleg Gordievsky, a high-ranking KGB officer who defected to the West in 1985. In 1990 Gordievsky wrote that Hiss was an agent during World War II and that his code name at the time was ALES. The release in 1995–1996 of decoded Soviet intelligence cables, which had been intercepted in the late 1930s and 1940s by the U.S. Army Signal Corps under the Venona project, confirmed Gordievsky's account and provided additional evidence that Hiss remained a Soviet spy until the end of his tenure at the State Department. A cable dated 30 March 1945 stated that ALES had been working for the GRU continuously since 1935, that for the last several years he had worked with Nathan Silvermaster, and that he had been at the Yalta Conference (4–11 February 1945). They showed that Hiss went on to Moscow, where he met with Soviet deputy foreign minister Andrey Yanuaryevich Vyshinsky and received a medal. Independently of Gordievsky's account, the Venona transcript identified ALES as "probably Alger Hiss." Hiss himself had acknowledged that only four Americans traveled to Moscow after the Yalta Conference. Of the four, only Hiss ever came under suspicion of spying. A second, partially deciphered Venona cable, dated 28 September 1943, indicates that the GRU was still interested in Hiss during World War II.

Hiss's presumed spying activities after 1938 are further highlighted in evidence from the former KGB archives that underscores his links with a known Soviet agent, Harold Glasser, who stated that ALES "is aware that he is a Communist with all the consequences of illegal status." Pavel Fitin, the head of the First Directorate of the Soviet state security apparatus, noted that Glasser (code named RUBLE) should be awarded the Order of the Red Star because he had just learned from ALES that several GRU agents had recently received decorations.

The combination of all this mutually corroborating evidence from such disparate sources as KGB and NSA archives, as well as several memoirs by well-placed Soviet officials, leaves little doubt that Hiss continued to spy for the Soviet Union at least through 1945. Even if a small degree of uncertainty remains about the precise duration of Hiss's espionage activities, there is no longer any doubt that he was a spy.

—MARK KRAMER, HARVARD UNIVERSITY

Viewpoint:
No. Alger Hiss was not guilty, and the accusations made against him were the product of public hysteria and political opportunism.

On 25 January 1950 Alger Hiss was convicted of perjury. Hiss had been accused of spying for the Soviet Union, but the statute of limitations for prosecuting espionage had expired. Hiss denied the charges under oath and was then charged with perjury. His pursuers, however, including Whittaker Chambers, the chief witness against him, were either lying or mistaken. Hiss was not a spy.

The case began when Chambers, himself an admitted former communist agent, named Hiss as a fellow communist during testimony before the House Un-American Activities Committee (HUAC). Initially, Chambers only identified Hiss as a communist and denied that Hiss had any role in espionage. Only later did Chambers accuse Hiss of being a spy. Chambers claimed to have had a long relationship with Hiss, during which the Hiss and Chambers families had become close. Hiss denied more than a passing familiarity with Chambers, whom he had known under a false name. The question of this relationship became the focus of the perjury case. If it could be established that Chambers and Hiss had in fact been close, then to most people it followed that Chambers was being truthful and Hiss was a communist.

Chambers presented many details of Hiss's life in his testimony, which convinced many observers that the two men must indeed have been close. Descriptions of the Hiss home and Hiss's bird-watching hobby soon filled the record.

The nature of the format—HUAC hearings, not a judicial proceeding—however, denied Hiss the opportunity to face his accuser. HUAC representatives confronted Hiss with portions of Chambers's statement, but never with its entirety. As a result, several errors and omissions in Chambers's recollections about Hiss's life, home, and family went unnoticed until most had already made up their minds. Public opinion and HUAC found the points where Chambers was correct, for example regarding Hiss's ornithological enthusiasm, more convincing than they merited. One of the most compelling moments was Chambers's description of Hiss's sighting of a prothonotary warbler, a rare bird. Many were convinced that only a close friend would be aware of such an event. In reality, Hiss told anyone who would listen about the experience, even dropping into reverie on the stand until the questioner cut him off. Another detail missing from Chambers's account was Hiss's son's near-fatal encounter with a car while riding his bike. Surely a close friend would know of such an event. By the time careful cross-checking revealed the omissions, the prothonotary warbler had already convicted Hiss in the eyes of many Americans.

Chambers gained more credibility as a witness than he could possibly have deserved. He admitted to repeatedly perjuring himself, and yet his supporters always accepted the most recent statement as the truth. Somehow, his testimony that Hiss was a spy canceled out his previous solemn declaration that Hiss was involved in no such activities. At several other points Chambers changed his story to suit circumstances, citing either a faulty memory or offering no explanation at all for the contradictions.

While many supported Chambers's allegations, it appeared for some time that his words would not have any concrete impact without physical evidence. When Hiss sued Chambers for libel, however, Chambers produced microfilm containing photographs of classified State Department documents and handwritten memos. Together, these became known as the Pumpkin Papers, as Chamber had hid them for a time in a hollowed-out pumpkin in the garden of his farm. Examination showed the typing to be consistent with a typewriter owned by the Hiss family and the handwriting to be that of Hiss. Solid proof had at last been obtained, it seemed.

The introduction of the documents, however, cast further doubt upon the credibility of Chambers as a witness. Chambers never adequately explained why he had held back the documents until he himself was in danger of losing the libel suit. The best explanation seemed to involve a sort of anticommunist intervention, where Chambers exposed Hiss in hopes of forcing him to confront and renounce his communist

CHAMBERS THE SPY

Although the accusation against Alger Hiss, that he was a spy for the Soviet Union, is still controversial and disputed, there is little doubt that Whittaker Chambers spied against the United States. A portion of his testimony, recounted in the Washington Daily News *and entered into the* Congressional Record *by Senator John E. Rankin (D-Mississippi), is presented below.*

Chambers testified that he had two sources of information in the State Department. His principal source, from which he obtained most of the strictly confidential documents, operated in the following manner:

The source would bring the documents out in a brief case and take them home. There, Chambers would take over the brief case and go on to meet a photographic expert at a prearranged place. The expert would take the brief case and documents to a laboratory in Baltimore, put the documents on film, and would return the brief case and contents to Chambers the same night.

Sometimes Chambers stated it would be as late as 1 in the morning before he got the brief case back. He would then proceed to the home of his source, deliver the brief case, and the documents would be returned to the State Department files.

Chambers would then pick up the microfilms in Baltimore, place them in a tobacco pouch, and carry them to New York, where he would deliver them to a Colonel Bykov, of the Soviet espionage system, who was at that time known to Chambers as Peter. . . .

Chambers testified that between 1932 and 1933 he obtained documents from the State Department, the Bureau of Standards, the Aberdeen Proving Ground, and certain information from the Navy; also that the same ring with which he worked got vital information from key United States industries. The documents pictured on the microfilm, which had been developed at the time we secured them from Chambers, were highly confidential and classified documents from the Department of State, the most important of which came from the office of Assistant Secretary of State Francis B. Sayre.

These documents bore the official stamp of Mr. Sayre and have been identified by him as having been taken from his office. Four people had access to these documents once they arrived at Sayre's office, namely Francis B. Sayre, Alger Hiss, his first assistant; Eunice Lincoln, his administrative assistant; and Anna Belle Newcomb, secretary and stenographer for the office. . . .

Mr. Chambers also testified that he received and transmitted to Russian agents information concerning a new self-sealing aviation tank developed by the Navy, the metallurgical formula dealing with the Norden bomb sight, and the lists of foreign intelligence agents and naval intelligence reports.

Source: Appendix to the Congressional Record, 94, part 12, 30th Congress, 2nd Session *(19 June 1948–31 December 1948), pp. A5354.*

beliefs. When Hiss denied being a communist, Chambers announced he was also a spy. When Hiss denied being a spy, Chambers introduced the documents. Every time Chambers's story started to crack, he raised the stakes. Chambers explained that he still considered himself Hiss's friend and would only introduce enough evidence to force Hiss back to the side of the angels. This reasoning is questionable at best.

The documents also introduced another inconsistency into Chambers's story. He had long maintained that he left the communist underground in 1937, but the State Department documents were from 1938. Over the course of several interviews, Chambers went from his story of having left the underground in 1937, to expressing doubt over the exact time frame (as if such a semi-

nal event in a life could be readily forgotten), to being unshakably certain that he had renounced communism in 1938, shortly after Hiss provided him with the classified material. Unfortunately for Chambers's credibility, all the evidence to be had regarding Chambers's defection supports the initial 1937 date. While on the run from his former communist comrades, Chambers supported his family through translation work. His lack of a fixed address distressed his employers, who kept records showing their traveling translator to have been on the payroll in 1937.

This leads to the most basic mystery of the Hiss case. Why were Americans so ready to believe Chambers, a *Time* magazine editor who in the past had authored a play condemned as blasphemous and poems that can only be described as pornographic, and was by his own admission a perjurer many times over? Why were they so ready to condemn Hiss, a respected former member of the State Department who had served as the secretary general at the San Francisco conference that created the United Nations and, at the time of the accusation, served as the president of the Carnegie Endowment for International Peace? The answer lies in the time period in which the Hiss case emerged, the second Red Scare in the United States.

The emergence of the Cold War changed the U.S. wartime ally, the Soviet Union, into America's chief rival in the postwar world. Most Americans saw domestic communists as tools of Moscow, blindly obedient and a threat to national security. The chief threat from these communists came through subversion, rather than force of arms, and many Americans believed they had to be vigilant to root out these secret traitors. In 1948 Chambers's initial accusation found an audience ready to hear and believe that a respected member of the government could have been an agent of international communism.

There were also those who were ready not only to believe, but to profit from, Chambers's allegations. HUAC, having failed to turn up any communists in its many investigations, was in disrepute for its questionable investigative tactics. If Hiss were indeed a communist, then HUAC would have a long future ahead of it, sniffing out subversion and communists in high places.

The Republican Party as a whole was inclined to believe Chambers. Republicans had been out of power since 1933, when Franklin D. Roosevelt entered the White House. Roosevelt's New Deal had struck many Republicans as near-socialism, and many sought to discredit the agencies Roosevelt had created, as well as the men and women who had served in them. Hiss first came to Washington as a New Deal bureaucrat, before moving on to the State Department, and was thus a prime target.

Finally, there was Richard M. Nixon, a first-term Republican congressman from California and a junior member of HUAC. The Hiss case was Nixon's path to fame and power. Nixon gained notoriety as the man who would not give up, who always kept searching until new evidence was found to move the case forward. A famous news photograph showed Nixon examining a role of microfilm from the Pumpkin Papers through a magnifying glass. Though one cannot read microfilm in such a manner, the photo gained Nixon publicity and helped him run for and win a Senate seat in 1956. Nixon had personal as well as professional reasons to attack Hiss. A Harvard educated lawyer, Hiss had elite tastes and a superior air. Nixon, the son of a grocer and a graduate of the little-known Whittier College, resented Hiss's type. Proving Hiss a liar, and therefore a communist spy, would justify a lifetime of resentment against his presumed social betters.

Hiss had the misfortune to be accused of being a communist spy during a time when his accuser found powerful, motivated allies, and when the American public was primed by their fear of communist subversion to accept such accusations at face value. During the second Red Scare, HUAC, Nixon, and Chambers attacked, hounded, and ultimately convicted Hiss, not for espionage, but for perjury—for saying he was innocent.

–GRANT WELLER, U.S. AIR FORCE ACADEMY, COLORADO

References

Christopher Andrew and Oleg Gordievsky, *KGB: The Inside Story of Its Foreign Operations From Lenin to Gorbachev* (New York: HarperCollins, 1990);

Whittaker Chambers, *Witness* (New York: Random House, 1952);

Fred J. Cook, *The Unfinished Story of Alger Hiss* (New York: Morrow, 1958);

John Earl Haynes, Harvey Klehr, and Fridrikh Igorevich Firsov, *The Secret World of American Communism* (New Haven: Yale University Press, 1995);

Haynes and Klehr, *Venona: Decoding Soviet Espionage in America* (New Haven: Yale University Press, 1999);

Alger Hiss, *In the Court of Public Opinion* (New York: Knopf, 1957);

Hiss, *Recollections of a Life* (New York: Seaver Books/Holt, 1988);

Tony Hiss, *The View From Alger's Window: A Son's Memoir* (New York: Knopf, 1999);

Ethan Klingsberg, "Case Closed on Alger Hiss?" *Nation,* 8 November 1993, pp. 5–9;

Maria Schmidt, "The Hiss Dossier," *New Republic,* 8 November 1993, pp. 10–13;

Pavel Sudoplatov and Anatoli Sudoplatov, with Jerrold L. and Leona P. Schecter, *Special Tasks: The Memoirs of an Unwanted Witness, A Soviet Spymaster* (Boston: Little, Brown, 1994);

Sam Tanenhaus, *Whittaker Chambers: A Biography* (New York: Random House, 1997);

U.S. National Security Agency, "VENONA Papers," available on-line at http://www.nsa.gov;

Allen Weinstein, *Perjury: The Hiss-Chambers Case* (New York: Knopf, 1978);

Weinstein and Alexander Vassiliev, *The Haunted Wood: Soviet Espionage in America—The Stalin Era* (New York: Random House, 1999).

Should the West have intervened in the Hungarian uprising of 1956?

Viewpoint: Yes. If the United States had assisted the Hungarian insurgents in 1956, the Soviets would likely have backed down in the face of unified American-Hungarian opposition.

Viewpoint: No. The United States had pressing concerns in the Middle East and was reluctant to intercede in what seemed to be an internal Hungarian dispute.

Hungary was occupied by the Red Army during the last months of World War II. In the immediate aftermath of the conflict the Soviets allowed a measure of political democracy, but by 1949 the Hungarian communists had taken over the government and declared Hungary a Socialist People's Republic. In 1955 Hungary joined the Warsaw Pact, the military organization led by the Soviet Union.

Agitation for political freedom continued, however. It reached its peak in October 1956, when a popular insurrection toppled the communist government and placed Imre Nagy in power. He announced that Hungary would withdraw from the Warsaw Pact and become neutral. In response, Soviet troops invaded Hungary, and in a bloody battle, which cost the lives of thousands of Hungarians, crushed the insurrection and replaced the reformist Nagy with the more docile János Kádár.

The United States and its West European allies did not come to the aid of the Hungarian freedom fighters and were criticized for their inaction during the revolt and subsequent suppression. Some claim that the Hungarian uprising was inspired in large measure by Secretary of State John Foster Dulles's remarks about "rolling back" Soviet domination of Eastern and Central Europe, and that the rebels expected the United States to come to their assistance. In addition to facing elections in November 1956, however, the administration of Dwight D. Eisenhower was preoccupied with the Suez Crisis in the Middle East and was unwilling to confront the Soviet Union in Hungary.

Viewpoint:
Yes. If the United States had assisted the Hungarian insurgents in 1956, the Soviets would likely have backed down in the face of unified American-Hungarian opposition.

By the mid 1950s Soviet rule over Eastern Europe was beginning to experience serious challenges. In both Poland and Hungary national leaders sought to chart a new course for their countries that had the potential of separating them from control of the Soviet Union. Although the Soviets were able to rein in secretary of the Polish Workers Party Wladyslaw Gomulka's attempts to depart from their influence, they were markedly less successful in Hungary. In October 1956 the reformist government of Imre Nagy determined to undertake domestic reforms and break ranks with its communist neighbors by leaving the Warsaw Pact. Although the less-than-cooperative approach was crushed by Soviet tanks, the Hungarian people proved more than willing to take a stand for political movements that would have led to greater political freedom. Despite the impressive enthusiasm of these popular demonstrations, the West offered little support to the Hungarian insurgents. There were, however, many compelling reasons why that support should have been forthcoming.

Perhaps the most practical reason why the West, and particularly the United States, should have intervened to defend the Hungarians against renewed Soviet aggression is that such an action would have rested on unimpeachable diplomatic grounds. The wartime settlements among the victorious allies in World War II had provided for the existence of states around the Soviet periphery that were "friendly" to Moscow. This palliative gesture, designed to quench Joseph Stalin's thirst for lasting security of Soviet borders, was unambiguously reciprocated by the Soviet leader with a promise to hold free and democratic elections throughout Eastern Europe shortly after the end of the war.

These elections never took place. Although there were democratic processes in the Eastern European countries liberated by the Red Army, they were from the outset patently unfair in that parties of the Right, and often even the center, were excluded from the elections because of their past associations, real or imagined, with fascist or counterrevolutionary elements. Political resources were, as a matter of Soviet occupation policy, distributed in a biased fashion that unfairly benefited national communist parties and their fellow travelers. With broad sections of the electorate legally excluded from expressing their voice in the democratic processes and manifest Soviet interference in elections in Eastern Europe, Soviet assertions that they had held up their end of the bargain were and remain difficult to support. Furthermore, when even the tarnished results produced by unmistakable Soviet interference resulted in leftist coalition governments that were neither completely loyal to Moscow nor dominated by the communist element within them, Stalin had no compunction about imposing his will. No method, including kidnapping, blackmail, or murder, was considered out of bounds in the Soviet-directed exclusion or sidelining of noncommunist parties and politicians that was completed by early 1948. In this situation neither the fundamentally illegitimate communist governments of Eastern Europe nor the Soviet government, which so jealously protected them for its own strategic and ideological reasons, would have had an ethical leg to stand on should they have been confronted with the prospect of Western intervention in 1956.

The particular situation in Hungary makes the case for Western intervention even more compelling. The struggle surrounding resistance to hardline communism and the Soviets was much more pronounced in Hungary than anywhere else in Eastern Europe at any time in the history of the Cold War. Quite unlike Czechoslovakia in 1968, or the whole of Eastern Europe in 1989, Hungarian citizens challenged and fought against the Soviet military. Despite the desperation that resulted from the isolation in which the rebels fought, the Soviet army was actually forced to make a tactical retreat before completing its brutal suppression of the uprising in Budapest. Many were killed in the fighting and more than two hundred thousand people fled to the West. Far more, including such prominent figures as József Cardinal Mindszenty, the Roman Catholic Primate of Hungary, sympathized vocally with the rebellion and the policies that had given birth to it, and embraced the suffering that their stand would entail.

Had the West chosen to intervene, it would undoubtably have found widespread popular support. Even if the intervention did not involve North Atlantic Treaty Organization (NATO) troops marching into Hungary, the ground was fertile for precisely the kind of native anti-Soviet and anticommunist resistance movements that the Eisenhower administration in particular had no problem supporting. Indeed, in many ways Hungary was much more promising than the Third World in that regard. Many other anti-Soviet moves made or planned on the initiative of the administration, particularly in Iran in 1953 and Guatemala in 1954, rested on granting limited covert support to such seemingly specious agents as tiny mercenary forces, small cliques of disgruntled army officers, and unarmed and untrained exiles.

Interestingly, these interventions, or "low-intensity conflicts" (LICs) as they came to be called, were on balance successes, not only during the Eisenhower administration but throughout the Cold War. With the notable exception of the Bay of Pigs invasion in Cuba (April 1961), supporting anti-Marxist factions worked well for the United States and cost the Soviets dearly. The destabilization and eventual loss of friendly governments in Guatemala (1954), and later Nicaragua (1990), to guerrilla fighters deprived Moscow of potential strategic positions in Central America, while the toppling of Mohammad Mossadeq's regime in Iran (1953) kept that country from drifting further toward Moscow. Support

Russian tanks on a Budapest street during the October 1956 invasion of Hungary

(The Photo Source)

HUNGARY

from the Carter and Reagan administrations for the mujahideen resistance fighters in Afghanistan, after the Soviet invasion of that country in 1979, not only cost the Soviets a strategic position, but created far-reaching problems for its military that continue to plague the successor states of the Union of Soviet Socialist Republics (U.S.S.R.) In addition, Reagan administration support for opposition movements in Poland and Czechoslovakia were critical in keeping them functioning through the 1980s. There is no reason to assume that similar measures in Hungary would not have been effective or worthwhile. While some make the argument that Hungarian geography was not conducive to guerrilla fighting in quite the same way as the Third World, it should not be forgotten, as it so often and conveniently is, that anticommunist resistance fighters within the Soviet Union, particularly in Ukraine and the Baltic States, fought against the Soviet regime for several years after their "liberation" with no help at all from the outside world. From Washington's perspective, moreover, intervention involving the delivery of weapons and supplies to the rebels in Hungary, and the use of the Central Intelligence Agency (CIA) to train and organize them, would in no way have violated the New Look doctrine of avoiding expensive localized conflicts while relying on relatively less-expensive covert operations and nuclear deterrence.

Another common argument against intervention was that the West could not credibly have afforded to challenge the Soviet Union strategically or militarily, and that it was better not to risk that sort of confrontation. Yet, intervention on the behalf of the rebels had every diplomatic justification and would not have been out of step with Dwight D. Eisenhower's general approach to the Cold War. On the broader strategic level it is highly unlikely that a general crisis would have resulted if the West had taken a firm stance in support of Hungarian freedom. In the rawest military terms the United States was far and away in the lead, and both sides knew it at the time.

Despite Soviet leader Nikita Khrushchev's 1955 attempt to dupe American observers into believing that the U.S.S.R. had strategic air superiority by having a rather small number of Soviet bombers fly in circles over the Kremlin, American aerial reconnaissance had dispelled that illusion at least several months before the Hungarian uprising. Khrushchev's bluster about Soviet nuclear capabilities, becoming prominent for the first time during the Suez Crisis of 1956, which occurred at almost the same time as the events in Hungary, were confined to threatening Britain, France, and Israel. Even when he was at his most dramatic in this period, the vainglorious Soviet leader did not even pretend that his nuclear arsenal could touch the United States. Unfortunately

for him, the United States could have used the proximity of its strategic air bases to the U.S.S.R. to lay large parts of it to waste. It is incredible to believe that men as cunning as Khrushchev, whose entire lives were devoted to advancing themselves into leadership and making the Soviet Union the dominant power in global affairs, would have risked its destruction and quite possibly their own lives in order to prevent Hungary from at most becoming neutral.

Finally, the United States actually stood to lose a great deal by not intervening on behalf of the Hungarian insurgents. Even though the Eisenhower administration was loath to become involved, it nevertheless directed Radio Free Europe and other American radio programs aimed at audiences within the communist bloc to broadcast messages of hope and encouragement. These messages left many in Hungary to believe that Western help was forthcoming and that they should become more bold. Whether or not explicit promises were made, the unmistakable impression was that they could expect something from the West greater than brave words and no action. Many refugees and Hungarian citizens expressed their unabashed disappointment about the absent fruits of what they had on a wide scale interpreted to be pledges of Western support. By allowing this situation to develop, the Eisenhower administration seriously risked American credibility abroad. After standing up vigorously for the rights of West Berlin in 1948–1949, had the United States now decided that freedom was secondary to dry strategic calculations and fiscal policies? At a time when decolonization was opening large parts of the Third World as Cold War battlegrounds, it was a question that many non- or anticommunist Third World politicians had to answer.

–PAUL DU QUENOY,
GEORGETOWN UNIVERSITY

Viewpoint:
No. The United States had pressing concerns in the Middle East and was reluctant to intercede in what seemed to be an internal Hungarian dispute.

Nikita Khrushchev's February 1956 speech on the deleterious effects of Stalinism (indeed, of Joseph Stalin himself) shook the communist world to its foundations. Renewed hope of personal liberty, both in the general public, who soon learned of the "secret" speech, and within Party organizations, sparked a wave of emotional responses. Reaction varied throughout Soviet-influenced Eastern Europe, ranging from release of religious leaders from imprisonment and increased "democratization" in Poland to outright rejection of Krushchev's "betrayal" of socialism in hardline Albania. In Hungary, the government of Stalinist Mátyás Rákosi was constitutionally dismantled from within in July of 1956. This dismantlement took place under Soviet supervision with Soviet deputy premier Anastas Mikoyan himself attending the sessions of the Hungarian Central Committee that brought about Rákosi's removal.

Unrest within the Party itself continued to mount, however, throughout the summer and autumn, building eventually into increasingly organized popular protests. Security police in Budapest violently dispersed several protests in October, which in turn provoked a massive popular uprising on 23 October. More than two hundred thousand Hungarians took to the streets of their capital, demanding greater liberty and supporting the assumption of power by Imre Nagy, himself an anti-Stalinist moderate communist. Nagy was also supported by the Soviets, at least at first, in the hope he would secure Party rule. Hungarian Party secretary Erno Gero called for Soviet troops to quell the "revolt," and Soviet occupation forces fired on some of the protesters. Nagy emerged with support from virtually all Hungarians, and called for the evacuation of Soviet troops from Budapest and eventually from all of Hungary. In the confusion the Soviets at first complied, but returned just a week later in overwhelming force to crush the revolt and install pro-Soviet János Kádár, who ruled Hungary for another thirty years. Nagy and his followers were tried and executed.

Many people, including Khrushchev, accused the North Atlantic Treaty Organization (NATO) powers of "adding fuel to the flames of a civil war" in Hungary. Some sources attest to the widely held belief among Hungarians that the United States, at least, would intervene militarily on their behalf in any struggle against the Soviet Union. Perhaps even more important than an examination of the reasons underlying this belief is an analysis of the feasibility, or even desirability, of such an intervention from a Western point of view.

Several questions must be answered regarding possible Western intervention in the Hungarian uprising. First, was it clear to the West that this revolt was, in fact, against Soviet domination or was it seen merely as an internal squabble among communists with differing thoughts on Stalinism? Second, did the timing of the October 1956 uprising favor a potential Western military response? Third, and most crucial, was the West prepared to fight a war against the Soviets over Hungary at this time?

The NATO powers had witnessed a series of miniature rebellions throughout the Soviet bloc in 1956. Up until the eve of the Hungarian uprising most observers had fixed on Poland, where Wladyslaw Gomulka had faced down the Soviets by threatening to rebel and pursue an independent course, á la Marshal Josip Broz Tito of Yugoslavia. The embers of that revolt were banked by the Poles themselves: having reached an accord with the Soviets, Gomulka and his allies brutally suppressed a student demonstration on 22 October. The Polish situation was resolving itself more into an ideological rift within communist ranks than a rebellion against the Soviets. In Hungary, however, the situation was almost reversed. The early stages of the revolt consisted of the Communist Party of the Soviet Union sending a representative to oversee the removal of an undesirable, pro-Stalin Hungarian Communist Party leader—everything pointed toward another internal political shift in the communist world, with little opening for exploitation by the West. As unrest spread from within the Communist Party, and wider segments of the population became involved, something of a nationalist character emerged. Nagy was portrayed as a Hungarian patriot as often as he was as a moderate communist (though he did not classify himself as anything other than a communist until the Soviet reprisals had begun). When the storm finally broke, crowds chanted anti-Soviet slogans and called for Nagy's reinstatement as premier, as well as tore down a huge statue of Stalin; as Hungarian army and police units turned their weapons over to the protesters, it became clear that more than internal policy issues were at stake. It also became obvious that Nagy did not consider it necessary to stay within the communist umbrella in order for Hungary to prosper. One day after assuming the post of premier he declared the new government ought to have "the broadest national basis" and, in fact, the Hungarian Revolutionary Committee, established at this time as a provisional government, included members of noncommunist political parties. This policy was further than Polish autonomous impulses had led Gomulka's party—it was the first significant crack in the Soviet bloc since the Soviet Union broke with Yugoslavia in 1948.

The other crucial difference between the Hungarian uprising and "Polish October" was the matter of timing, both internal to the revolt and in terms of world events. The Polish "rebellion" gradually changed shape over the course of the year, from January to October. There was time for analysis and reflection, as well as prediction of the course of events. Not so in Hungary: the tempo of unrest quickened from late July through mid October, until the explosion on 23

EISENHOWER APPEALS TO THE SOVIETS

On 4 November 1956, President Dwight D. Eisenhower sent a letter, concerning Soviet actions in Hungary, to Marshal Nikolai A. Bulganin. The text of the note appears below.

I have noted with profound distress the reports which have reached me today from Hungary.

The Declaration of the Soviet Government of October 30, 1956, which restated the policy of non-intervention in internal affairs of other states, was generally understood as promising the early withdrawal of Soviet forces from Hungary. Indeed, in that statement, the Soviet Union said that (quote) it considered the further presence of Soviet Army units in Hungary can serve as a cause for an even greater deterioration of the situation (unquote). This pronouncement was regarded by the United States Government and myself as an act of high statesmanship. It was followed by the express request of the Hungarian Government for the withdrawal of Soviet forces.

Consequently, we have been inexpressibly shocked by the apparent reversal of this policy. It is especially shocking that this renewed application of force against the Hungarian Government and people took place while negotiations were going on between your representatives and those of the Hungarian Government for the withdrawal of Soviet forces.

As you know, the Security Council of the United Nations has been engaged in an emergency examination of this problem. As late as yesterday afternoon the Council was led to believe by your representative that the negotiations then in progress in Budapest were leading to agreement which would result in the withdrawal of Soviet forces from Hungary as requested by the government of that country. It was on that basis that the Security Council recessed its consideration of this matter.

I urge in the name of humanity and in the cause of peace that the Soviet Union take action to withdraw Soviet forces from Hungary immediately and to permit the Hungarian people to enjoy and exercise the human rights and fundamental freedoms affirmed for all peoples in the United Nations Charter.

The General Assembly of the United Nations is meeting in emergency session this afternoon in New York to consider this tragic situation. It is my hope that your representative will be in a position to announce at the session today that the Soviet Union is preparing to withdraw its forces from that country and to allow the Hungarian people to enjoy the right to a government of their own choice.

Source: U.S. Department of State, American Foreign Policy: Current Documents 1956 *(Washington, D.C.: 1957), pp. 467–468.*

October that startled even the participants. The Soviets withdrew from Budapest on 30 October, but within a few days returned and systematically annihilated the revolutionaries. There was little time for NATO to predict what was going to happen, less time to prepare for intervention, and still less to execute any incursion strategy to support the revolutionaries before they had been overrun by Soviet tanks. American propaganda radio in Europe could only urge the Hungarians to resist—there would be no help coming from NATO.

It is well to remember that October 1956 was a busy month for the NATO powers. The smoldering dissension in the Soviet bloc was vastly overshadowed by the war in the Middle East. Arab League powers had not ceased their machinations against non-Islamic states and throughout the summer had increased their pressure on Israel, instigating several border inci-

dents and generally heightening tension in the region. On 26 July, Egypt nationalized the Suez Canal, prohibiting international traffic along the Anglo-French maintained waterway; this development prompted both the British and French to formulate covert plans to recapture the canal. Rapid deployment forces were marshaled on Cyprus and Malta, ready to seize the Suez in conjunction with an Israeli military advance into the Sinai Peninsula. United Nations cease-fire proposals were rejected by Israel (under pressure from London and Paris) to allow the British and French time to land, which they did by sea and air on 5–6 November. With such well-laid plans and massive political intrigue, it is difficult to picture the British or French suddenly canceling their Suez operations in favor of, for example, an airborne reinforcement of Hungarian positions in the suburbs of Budapest. Clearly their priorities were elsewhere.

American military preparedness was less of an issue than for other NATO allies. There was an increasing amount of American military aid being given to Yugoslavia, as part of Tito's successful efforts to play the East off against the West. In addition, Austria was permitted to rearm, and Soviet forces were withdrawn from their forward positions. Finally, plans had just been approved to rearm Germany, only a matter of days prior to the Hungarian uprising: American bases were already fully manned and enough matériel stockpiled to handle many weeks of fighting. All this points toward an increasing readiness on the part of American armed forces to fight a protracted struggle against the Soviet Union, both in terms of their own preparedness and that of American allied or potential satellite states in Central Europe. When examining American military adventurism, however, it is always necessary to include domestic political factors.

If the timing of the Hungarian uprising was not inauspicious for the Pentagon, it certainly was for other segments of the American decision-making apparatus. The presidential election was less than a week away when the Hungarians asked the U.N. for assistance against the Soviet assault. President Dwight D. Eisenhower had been severely criticized during the campaign for his seemingly flippant attitude toward nuclear war. As a result, American strategy makers had recently reversed their positions on a "winnable" nuclear war—at least in public. This policy understandably limited the range of response options given the necessity or desirability of military engagement in Europe or elsewhere. In addition, the United States had suffered more than 136,000 casualties in the Korean War, the vast majority of which occurred after the Chinese communists had entered the war. American public opinion might back intervention on behalf of a small nation beset with internal political problems, but was it ready to face a war on a grander scale than Korea? Supporting the Hungarians would almost certainly have led to armed conflict with the Soviets, which would spread far beyond downtown Budapest and involve the majority of American service personnel. Furthermore, unlike China in 1950, the Soviets had the atomic bomb.

The Western political dilemma went beyond the possible concerns of the American public regarding nuclear war and its expression in the 1956 presidential elections. In a larger sense, the timing of the Hungarian revolt was unfortunate: Britain and France had engaged roughly six thousand men in the Middle East, and these were all the troops they had to spare for power projection. Britain had announced plans to cut its military by up to one half, which were eventually implemented in early 1957. Since the end of World War II, Britain had turned over most of its worldwide defense commitments by default to the United States. Britain had relied heavily on its commonwealth and dependent nations to fight the last two wars, and now those countries were pursuing largely independent foreign and military policies. Australia, Canada, South Africa, New Zealand, and India had contributed greatly to British forces up through the Korean War, but they could not be relied upon to support another world war should the British wish to engage the Soviet Union.

France was in a different position. More than half of the French army was drawn into Algeria by 1956 in an effort to quell a revolt that had begun before the end of World War II. More than ten thousand French soldiers died by the time Algeria was granted independence. Thousands more were wounded—and they returned home angry. France was split over the Algerian question as it had not been since the Dreyfus Affair (1894). Algeria was a *département* (state) of France, and many Algerians lived happily as French citizens on both sides of the Mediterranean. An almost equal number of Algerians favored independence, an end to French influence, and a return to a more-rigid Islamic culture. This division mirrored the one in French society. Algeria, coupled with the losses incurred almost simultaneously in Indochina—it had been little more than two years since Dien Bien Phu (1953 – 7 May 1954)—more than occupied the attentions of France.

The rest of the NATO alliance was also still recovering from World War II, and though their populations might have been prepared for a defensive war against the Red Army, they could not be expected to make the sacrifices necessary to support a sustained offensive against all of Eastern Europe. This last issue is an important factor to weigh when considering the feasibility of Western military intervention in Hungary: would it be a war solely against the Soviets, supported by indigenous populations all the way into the Ukraine, or would it also entail fighting the East Germans, Czechoslovaks, Romanians, Bulgarians, and Poles? If all the turbulence following Krushchev's anti-Stalin speech was revolution within, and not against, a communist system, would not the nations of Eastern Europe band together against an outside threat to their newfound life of socialism? Complaining about Stalinist excesses was one thing—discarding the workers' paradise was another. Furthermore, the unity of the socialist world, while not necessarily taken for granted for ideological reasons, was (at least in Eastern Europe) based on other factors as well. Newly rearmed Germany, with or without communism, might give Poles and Czechs reason enough to stand with the Russians against the Germans, especially a Germany recently deprived of one-fourth of its territory and whose citizens had been ethnically cleansed from Poland and the Czech lands. The West had sold out the people of Eastern Europe for political gains in the recent past: who would not believe the possibility of NATO promising territorial gain in exchange for German support in a war against the Soviets?

There was little chance that the United States would militarily support the Hungarian rebels. Internal problems in Hungary seemed to be the result of a power shift within the communist world in the aftermath of the death of Stalin. The dissimilarity to Poland or other less turbulent states was not immediately clear. Timing of the revolt, both the speed with which it developed, erupted, and was crushed, and the general time frame relative to events elsewhere in the world, was unfavorable for a Western military intervention. The United States was at odds with its major partners, Britain and France, concerning their invasion of Egypt. Within the United States there was concern that any war must be conventional, ruling out any "surgical strike" option; even a conventional war was a public-relations risk because of recent losses in Korea. The American president faced an election where one of the major topics was the way in which the United States should conduct foreign relations, and any intervention could be seen as an aggressive move, not only by the socialist world, but by American voters. Even had the United States, Britain, and France not been occupied elsewhere, the rest of Western Europe could not be counted upon to supply the support required of a major new war. Even Germany had only begun to rearm, and it was unclear whether this development was to be an asset or a liability for the Western Alliance vis-à-vis Eastern Europe. In summation, when the world of 1956 is seen as a whole, it becomes clear that the Western powers had neither the opportunity nor ability to intervene militarily on the side of the Hungarian rebels.

–LARRY HELM,
GEORGE WASHINGTON UNIVERSITY

References

J. F. Brown, *Eastern Europe and Communist Rule* (Durham, N.C.: Duke University Press, 1988);

R. Ernest and Trevor N. DuPuy, *The Encyclopedia of Military History: From 3500 B.C. to the Present* (New York: Harper & Row, 1970);

Robert H. Ferrell, *American Diplomacy: A History* (New York: Norton, 1959);

John Lewis Gaddis, *Strategies of Containment: A Critical Appraisal of Postwar American National Security Policy* (New York: Columbia University Press, 1972);

Gaddis, *We Now Know: Rethinking Cold War History* (Oxford: Clarendon Press, 1997; New York: Oxford University Press, 1997);

Charles Gati, *The Bloc That Failed: Soviet-East European Relations in Transition* (Bloomington: Indiana University Press, 1990);

Gati, *Hungary and the Soviet Bloc* (Durham, N.C.: Duke University Press, 1986);

Hans-Georg Heinrich, *Hungary: Politics, Economics and Society* (London: Pinter, 1986);

Townsend Hoopes, *The Devil and John Foster Dulles* (Boston: Little, Brown, 1973);

Nikita Khrushchev, *Khrushchev Remembers,* translated by Strobe Talbot (New York: Little, Brown, 1970);

György Litván, ed., *The Hungarian Revolution of 1956: Reform, Revolt and Repression 1953–1963,* translated by János M. Bak and Lyman H. Legters (New York: Longman, 1996);

Thomas W. Simons Jr., *Eastern Europe in the Postwar World* (New York: St. Martin's Press, 1991);

Adam B. Ulam, *Expansion and Coexistence: Soviet Foreign Policy, 1917–73* (New York: Praeger, 1974);

Jiri Valenta, "Soviet Policy Toward Hungary and Czechoslovakia," in *Soviet Policy in Eastern Europe,* edited by Sarah Meiklejohn Terry (New Haven: Yale University Press, 1984), pp. 93–124;

Vladislav Zubok and Constantine Pleshakov, *Inside the Kremlin's Cold War: From Stalin to Khrushchev* (Cambridge, Mass.: Harvard University Press, 1996).

JFK AND LBJ

Did the Johnson administration continue the policies of the Kennedy presidency?

Viewpoint: Yes. Johnson administration policies, both foreign and domestic, furthered John F. Kennedy's anticommunist and social agenda.

Viewpoint: No. Lyndon B. Johnson departed significantly from John F. Kennedy's strategic policies, especially in escalating the Vietnam War.

The assassination of John F. Kennedy on 22 November 1963 stunned the world. The implications of this tragedy for U.S. diplomatic history, however, remain far from clear. Kennedy's vice president, Lyndon B. Johnson, entered office claiming that his policies would continue those of his predecessor. The defining issue of the Johnson administration, the conflict in Vietnam (ended 1975), became a major factor in American life within the first year of his presidency. At Johnson's urging, Congress made a firm and open-ended military commitment in August 1964 to the defense of South Vietnam. U.S. troops, starting with a contingent of marines, were deployed to defend that country the following March. By the end of the conflict more than five hundred thousand U.S. troops were serving in Indochina; the defense budget was higher than ever before; and the conflict had become the dominant issue not only in American strategic thought but also in domestic political discourse.

Is this the course upon which Kennedy had embarked before his assassination? On the one hand, Kennedy had criticized the Eisenhower administration for its failure to prevent a communist takeover in Cuba and blamed it for what appeared to be dangerous gaps in strategic weapons. He also began his administration intent on raising the defense budget and increasing the size of the military. At the time of his assassination, moreover, sixteen thousand U.S. military advisers were already serving in South Vietnam. On the other hand, the depth of Kennedy's commitment to the defense of South Vietnam was coming seriously into question. Earlier in his administration he had been reluctant to commit U.S. forces and resolve firmly other conflict situations. The relation of Johnson's policies to those of his predecessor remains a subject for ample debate.

Viewpoint:
Yes. Johnson administration policies, both foreign and domestic, furthered John F. Kennedy's anticommunist and social agenda.

The Vietnam War (ended 1975) will forever mark Lyndon B. John-

son's administration. Among the defining points of the 1960s, participation in the conflict is perceived as a failed U.S. initiative and Johnson's responsibility. As a new generation of Americans begin to study this problematic and controversial event from a more removed historical perspective, they are presented with many mass media projects, such as Oliver Stone's *JFK* (1991), that misinterpret the Cold War presidential

agenda of both John F. Kennedy and Johnson. In truth, they were guided by the same anticommunist impulse and domestic agenda. No doubt Johnson's escalation of troops in Vietnam, and the Gulf of Tonkin Resolution (1964), represented direct U.S. involvement in international Cold War policies. Perhaps the immediacy of American casualties accentuates one's historical sensibility. Nonetheless, Johnson's Cold War agenda, like his domestic Civil Rights program, reflected a continuation of Kennedy's policies. Both men fought the not-so-subtle Republican reproach that Democrats were "soft on communism," embodied in the oft-repeated aphorism "Truman Lost China." JFK and LBJ were quick to combat such claims, and their Cold War agendas—reflected in Kennedy's encounters with the Soviets and Cubans and Johnson's Vietnam initiatives—were efforts to demonstrate their vigorous anticommunism.

The Kennedy mystique was shrouded in youth, vigor, and the belief in new possibilities. Of course, this image was the public one the president cultivated, but his administration was quite conservative when dealing with the Cold War and domestic issues. In this respect Kennedy must be viewed as a transitional president, and not one whose agenda was radically different from Dwight D. Eisenhower's (as is often portrayed). Cuba is the prime example. Eisenhower's administration began funding and training a paramilitary operation to overthrow Fidel Castro. Once in office Kennedy continued the operation and also pursued covert strategies after the Bay of Pigs fiasco (April 1961). Cuba became the touchstone for Kennedy's Cold War policies, encapsulated in the Cuban Missile Crisis (October 1962). Although the president's anticommunist rhetoric never paralleled that of the Joseph R. McCarthy era, the nuclear standoff with the Soviet Union over Cuba and the promotion of bomb shelters opened a new phase of the Cold War. Whereas communist subversion was the menace of the 1950s, the fear of nuclear holocaust characterized Kennedy's anticommunist campaign.

Presidential candidate John F. Kennedy during the 1960 campaign restraining his running mate Lyndon B. Johnson as he gestures for a nearby plane to cut its motor

(Photograph by Richard Pipes)

JFK AND LBJ

Kennedy's Cold Warrior mentality was best reflected in his first State of the Union address (1961). He announced that:

> Our greatest challenge is still the world that lies beyond the Cold War—but the first great obstacle is still our relations with the Soviet Union and Communist China. We must never be lulled into believing that either power has yielded its ambitions for world domination—ambitions which they forcefully restated only a short time ago. On the contrary, our task is to convince them that aggression and subversion will not be profitable routes to pursue these ends.

During the Kennedy administration, defense spending was increased in order to make up for the armaments gap the president claimed existed between the United States and Soviet Union. Not only did the defense budget expand by nearly $6 billion, but new sectors of the military also emerged, such as the U.S. Army Special Forces (SF or Green Berets), to deal with communist insurgencies, such as the growing conflict in Vietnam. Like other facets of his administration, Kennedy's military initiatives reflected the complexity of his liberalism. The promotion of the Green Berets was in consonance with other "progressive" programs, such as the Peace Corps, just as the defense budget was connected with the space program in counteracting Soviet advances. The Peace Corps and Green Berets were part of the same anticommunist worldview: they were designed to send experts abroad to promote democracy and technology and to secure a U.S. political presence in areas—particularly Third World nations in the case of the Peace Corps—not already controlled by either superpower.

In 1963, months before his assassination, Kennedy ordered the escalation of U.S. advisers in Vietnam from 1,600 to 16,000. Hoping to secure the Diem administration, the president found himself doubting the South Vietnamese leader, especially after Ngo Dinh Diem's brutal crackdown of a peaceful demonstration was exposed to the American public. As historian Terry H. Anderson notes in *The Sixties* (1999), Kennedy found himself frustrated with Diem, who was not combating the Vietcong effectively, and he approved a plot to overthrow the South Vietnamese president. As with Castro, Kennedy was not above initiating removal of the South Vietnamese head of state once he represented a threat to U.S. interests.

While the Vietnam War and the Civil Rights movement directly connect the two Democratic administrations, it is worth noting Johnson's activities in the Carribean. In April 1965 rumors of a coup d'état in the Dominican Republic prompted Johnson to direct his atten-

tion to this crisis. Intelligence reports accused Castro of encouraging civil unrest and preparing troops for an invasion of the neighboring country. According to Christopher M. Andrew in his *For the President's Eyes Only: Secret Intelligence and the American Presidency from Washington to Bush* (1995), Johnson sent the marines to the Dominican Republic nominally to "give protection to hundreds of Americans." Whether communist insurgency was at the heart of the Dominican crisis is debatable, but Johnson treated it as if it were his Bay of Pigs. Indeed, as presidential special assistant Jack Valenti warned Johnson, "One fact is sure . . . if the Castro-types take over the Dominican Republic, it will be the worst domestic political disaster any Administration could suffer." Moreover, Johnson assumed command of U.S. military involvement in Santo Domingo. As Andrew notes, Johnson "astonished both the State Department and the CIA by his determination to take personal charge of almost every detail of the handling of the Dominican" situation. Clearly, Johnson's attitude was to prevent the Dominican Republic from becoming another Cuba. His Texas-size inferiority complex matched his ego, and he was determined to outdo Kennedy in every way possible. Johnson was nearly successful: his domestic agenda, particularly his Civil Rights agenda, was more extensive, and his small victory in the Carribean suggested what resolute anticommunist initiatives could accomplish.

The Vietnam War, of course, changed all that he accomplished. Although Johnson would bear ultimate responsibility for escalating the conflict, Kennedy's policies left him little room to maneuver. With American aid and personnel already invested in South Vietnam, any attempt by Johnson to withdraw would have been viewed as defeat—a label no U.S. president wanted attached to his record. Johnson later said that he had no alternative if he wanted his true concern, the Great Society, to be implemented. Given the world he inherited, one is not surprised by his actions. Johnson claimed, as recorded by Anderson, that

> I knew from the start that I was bound to be crucified either way I moved. If I left the woman I really loved—the Great Society—in order to get involved with that bitch of a war on the other side of the world, then I would lose everything at home. All my programs. All my hopes. . . . But if I left that war and let the Communists take over South Vietnam, then I would be seen as a coward and my nation would be seen as an appeaser.

In 1963 Johnson took over Kennedy's Cold War agenda, as he did the Civil Rights program. Just as Johnson intended to continue and then expand Kennedy's domestic initiatives, he did

JFK AND LBJ

the same with Cold War policies. Between 1963 and 1965 Johnson drew upon optimism in the country to promote his War on Poverty and support for South Vietnam. As the former was designed to eliminate poverty in America, the latter was expected to end the communist insurgency in Indochina. These twin and inseparable programs represented the apex of American liberalism in the 1960s, and they collectively went up in flames with the riots in Watts and Detroit, as well as the napalm bombs in Vietnam. Together, Kennedy and Johnson represented the hopes and dreams of the Cold War era: freedom at home and abroad. So too must they be held accountable for its failures.

–BRYAN ROMMEL-RUIZ,
COLORADO COLLEGE

Viewpoint:
No. Lyndon B. Johnson departed significantly from John F. Kennedy's strategic policies, especially in escalating the Vietnam War.

The U.S. strategic policy of President Dwight D. Eisenhower (1953–1961) was based on the so-called New Look, characterized by relatively low military spending, a reliance on less-expensive nuclear technology, and avoidance of costly conventional military conflicts. Rather than expanding the military at a rate that was economically unsound, Eisenhower and his strategic planners laid the groundwork for a broad and stable domestic base that would become a major advantage later in the Cold War. During the presidential election campaign of 1960, John F. Kennedy sharply criticized Eisenhower's approach to military and strategic policy. Kennedy accused the administration of losing Cuba to Fidel Castro's revolutionary movement. Further, he reproached Eisenhower's handling of the "missile gap," which allegedly threatened to give the Soviet Union a clear advantage in nuclear weapons, even though the administration could not reveal that it knew from intelligence sources that there was no such gap.

Although he appeared to be more hawkish than his Republican predecessor during the election, President Kennedy's approach to military and strategic policy closely resembled what he had criticized. After his inauguration Kennedy discovered the true complexities of the international situation. He faced crises in three parts of the world that could not have been further apart. In Europe, Soviet premier Nikita S. Khrushchev's 1958 ultimatum calling

for the withdrawal of Western military forces from West Berlin was still in effect. Only a few months after Kennedy entered office the city was physically divided and split from East Germany. In Asia the revolutionary Pathet Lao movement threatened to topple the government of Laos. In Latin America, as has already been stated, the Cuban revolutionary movement had taken power and was veering sharply away from the pro-American alignment of Castro's predecessor, Fulgencio Batista y Zaldívar.

Kennedy was reluctant to commit forces decisively to any one of these regional crises lest U.S. military power be overtaxed. While the relative weakness in conventional U.S. military capabilities somewhat validated the criticisms of Eisenhower's defense policy and caused Kennedy to begin a conventional-forces buildup, his immediate capabilities were constrained to what came to be called the "flexible response" policy. In addition to its foundations in necessity, flexible response also continued Eisenhower's cautious approach to the delicate balance between military spending and the health of the domestic economy. Kennedy, a realist in regard to fiscal as well as foreign policy, understood the benefits of avoiding the militarization of the economy, which had plagued the development of the Soviet Union.

The factors contributing to flexible response, as the main feature of Kennedy administration foreign policy, were strongly reflected in its activities. Kennedy allowed anti-Castro Cuban exiles, trained by the Central Intelligence Agency (CIA) in Guatemala, to make a full-scale amphibious assault at the Bay of Pigs (April 1961), but this incursion was only the fulfillment of a plan developed by the less-than-committed Eisenhower administration. Its origins, and its continuation within the matrix of Kennedy's flexible response, moreover, left the invasion devoid of direct U.S. military participation at every stage. Even the limited air support that Kennedy promised to the exile forces was withdrawn at the last moment, dooming them to defeat.

The main pressure point for the United States in Europe, West Berlin–which Khrushchev had described as "the testicles of the West"–posed another problem. The precarious access of the West to the city, illustrated by the Berlin blockade of 1948–1949, remained in dispute during the Kennedy administration. That situation became more acute when Khrushchev demanded the West withdraw its forces from the city in November 1958. By August 1961 the failure of the West to comply with this demand, intricacies in the alliance relationship between Moscow and its East German ally, the massive flight of East German citizens to the West through Berlin, and a desire on Khrushchev's part to test the new president led to the Soviet construction of the Berlin Wall and the physical separation of West Berlin from surrounding East German territory. Despite this provocative attempt to maneuver the United States out of the city and undermine European confidence in the U.S. commitment to Europe, Kennedy resisted any rash action that could have led either to a direct confrontation or increased U.S. military presence in Europe.

Just as Kennedy avoided a conventional imbroglio against Castro's seasoned revolutionary army in Cuba and a confrontation with the Soviets over Berlin, he deftly sidestepped military involvement half a world away in Indochina. Since the Geneva agreement (1954) "temporarily" divided Vietnam into a noncommunist South and communist North, the entire region had been subject to North Vietnamese attempts to establish communist hegemony. In 1961 the Pathet Lao, the revolutionary movement in Laos, was threatening to destabilize that country just as the Vietcong communist guerrilla movement in South Vietnam raised serious questions about the ability of Saigon to control its hinterlands.

In both these cases Kennedy made only minor commitments to shore up these noncommunist countries. Although nearly sixteen thousand U.S. military advisers were sent to South Vietnam by the time of Kennedy's assassination, significantly fewer were sent to Laos. That country came progressively under the influence of the Pathet Lao, and as the war in Vietnam escalated, its formal neutrality was made ridiculous by the constant flow of troops and supplies from North Vietnam through Laotian territory, down the so-called Ho Chi Minh Trail to the communist cadres operating in South Vietnam. American advisers only trained the South Vietnamese army and were ordered not to engage in combat. Though in practice this situation was not always avoided, it is significant that Kennedy never committed regular ground troops to the country. He assertively resisted the recommendations of many high-ranking military officers to do so and rejected other hawkish criticism of his Vietnam policy with the simple argument that if the United States was not engaged in nearby Cuba, there was no logical reason for it be engaged in distant Vietnam. He publicly stated that the conflict with the communist forces was Saigon's to win or lose. The appalling inability of South Vietnamese president Ngo Dinh Diem either to put down the communist uprising or maintain the stability of his own regime actually pushed Kennedy away from what U.S. involvement there was in Indochina. After Diem resisted American pressure to introduce stabilizing reforms, the U.S. Defense Department announced a tentative plan to steadily reduce and then withdraw all U.S. military forces in South Vietnam by the end of 1965. In October of 1963 economic aid to Saigon was dramatically reduced, portending what U.S. policy might have become.

After Kennedy was assassinated on 22 November 1963, he was succeeded by Vice President Lyndon B. Johnson, and U.S. foreign policy changed dramatically. Despite Johnson's assiduous claim that his policies represented continuity, within a week of Kennedy's death, plans to withdraw U.S. troops and reduce financial support to South Vietnam were abruptly forgotten. Johnson had no history of affinity for his president. It was rumored, with substantial credibility, that the two men actively disliked each other and that Kennedy had only taken Johnson on as his running mate in order to carry Texas, Johnson's home state, in the 1960 presidential election. Although both men, when they were senators in the 1950s, had been critical of Eisenhower's defense policy, Johnson was substantially more vocal and much more closely identified with the conservatism of the "Dixiecrat" wing of the Democratic Party and the interests it represented. Despite his criticism of Eisenhower and his pragmatism in office, Kennedy's identification with more liberal constituencies, and his Roman Catholic faith, had alienated many Democrats, especially in the predominantly Protestant South. What appeared to be indecisiveness in foreign affairs aroused emotionally charged reactions from people who believed that leaving Cuba in Castro's hands, and not drawing a firm line against communism in Indochina or throughout the world in general, betrayed weakness, inexperience, and even a lack of patriotism. The potential danger presented by the Cuban Missile Crisis (October 1962) reinforced that perception. Many of the conspiracy theorists who argue that there was more to Kennedy's assassination than a lone gunman have put forward (albeit without conclusive proof) that the true impetus for the president's death came from a cabal of individuals and groups who believed vital U.S. interests abroad were being sold out, had material interests in a defense buildup, and thought Johnson's ascendancy would mark a radical departure from Kennedy's policies.

Regardless of what may or may not have laid behind the assassination of Kennedy, Johnson's entry into office marked a significant departure from previous strategic policies. This change was true not only in foreign affairs but on the homefront as well. While Kennedy's policies on civil rights, themselves broadly supported by both political parties, were continued by the Johnson administration, his general domestic policies certainly were not. Beginning

JOHNSON ON FOREIGN POLICY

In his first State of the Union address in 1964, Lyndon B. Johnson presented his vision of American foreign policy:

For our ultimate goal is a world without war, a world made safe for diversity, in which all men, goods, and ideas can freely move across every border and every boundary.

We must advance toward this goal in 1964 in at least 10 different ways, not as partisans, but as patriots.

First, we must maintain—and our reduced defense budget will maintain—that margin of military safety and superiority obtained through 3 years of steadily increasing both the quality and the quantity of our strategic, our conventional, and our antiguerrilla forces. In 1964 we will be better prepared than ever before to defend the cause of freedom, whether it is threatened by outright aggression or by the infiltration practiced by those in Hanoi and Havana, who ship arms and men across international borders to foment insurrection. And we must continue to use that strength as John Kennedy used it in the Cuban crisis and for the test ban treaty—to demonstrate both the futility of nuclear war and the possibilities of lasting peace.

Second, we must take new steps—and we shall make new proposals at Geneva—toward the control and the eventual abolition of arms. Even in the absence of agreement, we must not stockpile arms beyond our needs or seek an excess of military power that could be provocative as well as wasteful.

It is in this spirit that in this fiscal year we are cutting back our production of enriched uranium by 25 percent. We are shutting down four plutonium piles. We are closing many nonessential military installations. And it is in this spirit that we today call on our adversaries to do the same.

Third, we must make increased use of our food as an instrument of peace—making it available by sale or trade or loan or donation—to hungry people in all nations which tell us of their needs and accept proper conditions of distribution.

Fourth, we must assure our pre-eminence in the peaceful exploration of outer space, focusing on an expedition to the moon in this decade—in cooperation with other powers if possible, alone if necessary.

Fifth, we must expand world trade. Having recognized in the Act of 1962 that we must buy as well as sell, we now expect our trading partners to recognize that we must sell as well as buy. We are willing to give them competitive access to our market, asking only that they do the same for us. . . .

Seventh, we must become better neighbors with the free states of the Americas, working with the councils of the OAS, with a stronger Alliance for Progress, and with all the men and women of this hemisphere who really believe in liberty and justice for all.

Eighth, we must strengthen the ability of free nations everywhere to develop their independence and raise their standard of living, and thereby frustrate those who prey on poverty and chaos. To do this, the rich must help the poor—and we must do our part. We must achieve a more rigorous administration of our development assistance, with larger roles for private investors, for other industrialized nations, and for international agencies and for the recipient nations themselves.

Ninth, we must strengthen our Atlantic and Pacific partnerships, maintain our alliances and make the United Nations a more effective instrument for national independence and international order.

Tenth, and finally, we must develop with our allies new means of bridging the gap between the East and the West, facing danger boldly wherever danger exists, but being equally bold in our search for new agreements which can enlarge the hopes of all, while violating the interests of none.

In short, I would say to the Congress that we must be constantly prepared for the worst, and constantly acting for the best. We must be strong enough to win any war, and we must be wise enough to prevent one.

We shall neither act as aggressors nor tolerate acts of aggression. We intend to bury no one, and we do not intend to be buried.

We can fight, if we must, as we have fought before, but we pray that we will never have to fight again.

Source: A Hypertext on American History: From the Colonial Period Until Modern Times, on-line website.

JFK AND LBJ

in 1965 administration-sponsored legislation provided for massive federal social programs that Kennedy had never contemplated. Accompanied by dramatic tax increases and increased government spending, both of which flew in the face of Kennedy's fiscal conservatism, the "Great Society" programs eventuated an economic downturn while failing to reach many of its intended goals. Indeed, since 1965 such social problems as violent crime, out-of-wedlock birth, and drug abuse have increased dramatically, while a slightly larger percentage of Americans live in poverty at the turn of the millenium than before the much heralded "war on poverty" began more than thirty years ago.

Domestic differences between the two administrations are often overlooked because of the much more significant alteration of foreign policy. While Johnson's social programs did not do much to help the domestic economy or solidify American society, his approach to foreign affairs was perhaps even more damaging to the United States. Kennedy's modest increases in conventional forces paled in comparison to Johnson's dramatic defense buildup. Between 1950 and 1970 the national defense budget increased from $13 billion to $70 billion, the most dramatic increase coming in the last five years of that period, when U.S. involvement in Vietnam escalated. Indeed, after the Korean War (1950–1953) the Eisenhower administration had reduced the military budget and maintained it at a level 20 percent lower than it had been in the last year of Harry S Truman's presidency.

Spending as freely as he was on the military, Johnson was much less bashful than his immediate predecessors when it came to its use. Although Johnson hesitated over whether or not the United States should have moved decisively into Vietnam, he was both predisposed to greater involvement and rather early on, at least as early as February 1964, decided in favor of expanding the U.S. role in Indochina. In August 1964 a small North Vietnamese attack on U.S. naval units in the Gulf of Tonkin, an incident that Secretary of Defense Robert S. McNamara years later admitted was initiated by U.S. forces, prompted Congress to approve defense-budget increases to "take all necessary steps" to defend South Vietnam.

With congressional consent, and the support of a wide majority of the American people, Johnson's decision to make the sort of commitment that Kennedy wished to avoid was swiftly put into effect. The first marines waded ashore in South Vietnam on 8 March 1965. The essentially defensive strategy that the administration employed, however, perhaps in an effort to minimize the costs of its commitment, forever spoiled the prospect of a victory. Under the plan

elaborated by McNamara, the main goal was to prevent the fall of South Vietnam to the communists. North Vietnamese resolve to unify the Vietnamese people under communism and dominate Indochina, egged on as it was for its own reasons by the Soviet Union and (reluctantly at first and later not at all) by China, left Hanoi with the advantage. Johnson's unwillingness to move against Vietcong bases in Cambodia and Laos, which supported all communist military operations in South Vietnam before Hanoi sent troops directly across the 17th parallel in April 1970—more than five years after American involvement began—paralyzed Johnson's attempts to create a stable and self-sufficient South Vietnam. Until Richard M. Nixon entered office (1969) and ordered troops to attack these bases, the only solution Washington would countenance was to increase the U.S. military presence to nearly five hundred thousand troops and hope that their numbers would make up for the inherent flaws in military strategy. As history tells us, they did not.

The magnitude of Johnson's departure from Kennedy's approach to foreign affairs, similar as it was to Eisenhower's, was so great that it resulted in many of the problems that strategists had predicted increased spending would cause and that both Eisenhower and Kennedy had deftly avoided. The increasing orientation of domestic production toward military spending, something the national economy was not structurally prepared for and could not bear easily at that time, created inflation at home and precipitated the flight abroad of the dollar and the gold reserves upon which the currency was based. The combination of this development with the continuing export-led economic growth of Western Europe and Japan undermined the dollar-based system of international finance established at the Bretton Woods Conference in 1944. By August 1971 this system of currency exchange was abandoned by Nixon's decision to move the dollar off the gold standard.

Strategically, the expense of the conventional military buildup led to the relative neglect of the development of the U.S. nuclear arsenal. By the late 1960s the decisive advantage in strategic weapons, one of the pillars of the Eisenhower-Kennedy approach, had eroded with the development by the Union of Soviet Socialist Republics (U.S.S.R.) of a functional Intercontinental Ballistic Missile (ICBM) system. The surging economic strength of Western Europe and Japan led them to seek increasingly independent roles in international politics. The pretensions to power implicit in economic strength was a major factor behind the West German decision to pursue *Ostpolitik* (eastern policy), a course of relaxing tensions and increasing contacts with Eastern Europe and the Soviet Union, with full and undisguised vigor. Under Charles de Gaulle, the French policy of "détente, entente, and cooperation" with the U.S.S.R. was inspired by a desire for a more independent role and led France to leave the integrated command structure of the North Atlantic Treaty Organization (NATO) in 1966. Remembering the none-too-helpful reactions of the United States to British and French problems in the Third World in the 1950s, U.S. allies were not too inclined to help the United States out of its difficulties in the 1960s.

Johnson's policies also had many consequences that analysts had not predicted. The costs to American society were particularly serious. Introduction of the draft to raise the necessary troops for service in Vietnam was highly unpopular. People resented having their sons sent to fight in a far-off place that many had never even heard of—for strategic reasons that were not easily explained or understood even by specialists. Press coverage of the war, something that had been controlled rather strictly during previous conflicts, went unchecked and was amplified greatly by the use of televised reports. The appearance on the evening news of daily "body counts" of soldiers killed in Vietnam demoralized the country.

Popular opposition to the war contributed to the radicalization of American political thought. Not unlike the situation in other countries strained by war, a significant segment of society, especially students and other young people, found common ground in the antiwar movement with extremists who questioned the values and institutions that made the United States great. As the war dragged on, radicals and their supporters became increasingly vocal—not only in their opposition to the war but also in their advocacy of revolutionary social and political change—which divided the country along the lines of race, class, age, and even gender; destabilized society; and created near-civil-war conditions. For the first time in the Cold War, the resolve of the United States to be a world power was brought into question.

In 1968 the much-despised Johnson decided not to seek reelection. In addition to all of the other problems his marked policy departure from the Kennedy administration had created, he could not bring himself even to try to keep his office. Johnson's decisive break with his predecessors created problems for the United States that have bedeviled it ever since. The specter of Vietnam haunts military planners; social and political institutions are ominously weakened; and domestic problems that Johnson tried to spend away are in many ways worse. Had America remained committed to a less activist form of containment until its economy could bear an interventionist "roll back" approach, this result might not have been the case.

–PAUL DU QUENOY, GEORGETOWN UNIVERSITY

References

Terry H. Anderson, *The Sixties* (New York: Longman, 1999);

Christopher M. Andrew, *For the President's Eyes Only: Secret Intelligence and the American Presidency from Washington to Bush* (New York: HarperCollins, 1995);

Michael R. Beschloss, ed., *Taking Charge: The Johnson White House Tapes, 1963–1964* (New York: Simon & Schuster, 1997);

Robert Dallek, *Flawed Giant: Lyndon Johnson and His Times, 1961–1973* (New York: Oxford University Press, 1998);

Townsend Hoopes, *The Devil and John Foster Dulles* (Boston: Little, Brown, 1973);

Walter LaFeber, *America, Russia, and the Cold War, 1945–1996,* eighth edition (New York: McGraw-Hill, 1997);

H. R. McMaster, *Dereliction of Duty: Lyndon Johnson, Robert McNamara, the Joint Chiefs of Staff, and the Lies That Led to Vietnam* (New York: HarperCollins, 1997);

Arthur M. Schlesinger Jr., *A Thousand Days: John F. Kennedy in the White House* (Boston: Houghton Mifflin, 1965);

Richard J. Walton, *Cold War and Counterrevolution: The Foreign Policy of John F. Kennedy* (New York: Viking, 1972).

KOREAN WAR

Was U.S. military intervention in Korea in 1950 justified?

Viewpoint: Yes. Military intervention in Korea was necessary because it demonstrated that the United States would resist communist aggression.

Viewpoint: No. Although support of South Korea prevented a communist takeover, U.S. intervention in Korea was outside the boundaries of strategic containment policy and led to the support of a tyrannical regime.

Franklin D. Roosevelt, Winston Churchill, and Chiang Kai-shek met at the Cairo Conference in Egypt from 22 to 26 November 1943 to discuss peace terms to be imposed on Japan at the end of World War II. One of their important decisions was to grant independence to Korea, which had been occupied by Japan since 1905. Following the surrender of the Japanese, Korea emerged in 1946 divided at the Thirty-eighth Parallel into a Soviet-controlled north and U.S.-controlled south. The division was meant to be temporary, but by 1948, after no agreement was reached on unification and general elections, the two Koreas declared their separate status as independent republics.

On 25 June 1950 North Korea invaded South Korea, capturing the capital, Seoul, within three days. President Harry S Truman announced that the United States would resist the North Korean aggression, and the United States received support in the United Nations (UN) to put together an international (mostly American) military force to repel North Korean forces. On 15 September 1950 UN forces under the command of General Douglas MacArthur made a surprise landing at Inchon, recapturing Seoul on 25 September. American-led forces pushed into North Korea, taking the capital of Pyongyang on 19 October, and kept advancing north, forcing the retreating North Koreans all the way to the Yalu River, which separates Korea from China. U.S. policymakers believed that China would stay out of the war, and Truman issued veiled warnings that the United States might use nuclear weapons if China intervened. On 26 November, however, Chinese forces crossed the Yalu and forced UN soldiers to retreat southward. By 24 December the Chinese forces reclaimed all of North Korea and began crossing the Thirty-eighth Parallel into South Korea, capturing Seoul on 4 January 1951. UN forces regrouped and fought back, recapturing Seoul on 14 March. Truman, impatient with MacArthur's public calls for a war on China, dismissed the general on 11 April. MacArthur's successor, General Matthew B. Ridgway, led UN forces north across the Thirty-eighth Parallel, and on 13 June captured Pyongyang again.

On 23 June the Soviet Union called for a cease-fire. Over the next two years, however, on-again, off-again talks between the two sides were accompanied by constant skirmishing along the Thirty-eighth Parallel, with UN and North Korean forces pushing each other back and forth. During the election campaign of fall 1952, Republican presidential candidate Dwight D. Eisenhower vowed to end the war, and upon assuming office in January 1953, set out to do so. He increased the military pressure on the Chinese by announcing that the United States was placing nuclear weapons in Okinawa;

increased U.S. air power on the Korean peninsula; and removed the Seventh Fleet from the Formosa Straits, where it had served as a barrier preventing Taiwanese Nationalist forces from attacking the Chinese mainland. At the same time, Eisenhower pressured Syngman Rhee, the South Korean leader, to soften his demands for an immediate reunification of Korea. On 27 July 1953 an agreement was signed putting an end to the fighting. The Korean War claimed two million lives, including 54,246 Americans.

Viewpoint:
Yes. Military intervention in Korea was necessary because it demonstrated that the United States would resist communist aggression.

Controversy surrounds President Harry S Truman's decision to commit U.S. resources to the defense of South Korea following an attack by communist North Korea in June 1950. Many analyses hold Truman's order to be inconsistent with American strategic policy on the basis of a statement made by Secretary of State Dean Acheson in January 1950 that appeared to establish a U.S. defensive perimeter that excluded South Korea. Scholars have argued that the bloodshed and expense of the Korean conflict (1950–1953) were both unnecessary from a strategic perspective and unjustified according to public statements of the administration itself.

Acheson's statement notwithstanding, U.S. intervention on the Korean peninsula was not only justified, but essential. The strategic position of the peninsula was of vital importance to U.S. security policy from any rational perspective. Its proximity to Japan cannot be ignored. Indeed, the history of northeast Asia has often been determined by who controlled this strategic peninsula. Shortly after its emergence as a world power in the late nineteenth century, Japan colonized Korea both to safeguard its own shores and create a foundation for the extension of its influence in Asia, particularly into Manchuria.

The strategic relevance of Korea was not lost on the Truman administration as World War II drew to a close in the Pacific. Although Franklin D. Roosevelt had made loose agreements to allow an extension of Soviet influence into China, the new president was far less enthusiastic about cooperation with the Soviet Union in general, to say nothing of conceding particular strategic advantages to it in the immediate postwar world. When the spectacular successes of the Red Army against the Japanese in Manchuria appeared to suggest that Soviet troops might also take control of Korea, Truman hastily dispatched a diplomatic mission to secure the division of the peninsula at the Thirty-eighth Parallel. Shortly thereafter, the Allied adminis-

tration of the defeated Japanese empire, almost certainly not on purely its own initiative, risked direct confrontation with Moscow when General Douglas MacArthur categorically refused to allow the Soviet Union to share in the occupation of Japan (they wanted Hokkaido) and threatened to jail the Soviet delegation in Tokyo if the Red Army landed in the Home Islands uninvited. There can be no logical reason why this same administration would seriously intend to abandon a strategic position to the communist world only a few years after having gone to great pains to secure it and, further, retreat in the face of communist military pressure only a year after it forced Soviet premier Joseph Stalin to end his blockade of West Berlin.

Ideology also played a serious role in Truman's decision to defend South Korea. Just as was the case with West Berlin, America could not lead the noncommunist world by caving in to demonstrations of strength from the opposition. Indeed, allowing South Korea to fall was an even riskier proposition than giving in to the Soviets in Berlin, because the communist attack was ostensibly the sole initiative of North Korean leader Kim Il-Sung. Although new evidence suggests that Moscow and Beijing played roles in Kim's decision to attack the South, the fact of the matter is that before the "unofficial" entry of China into the conflict in November 1950, the entire communist offensive was carried out by North Korean troops. For the United States to stand idly by while one of the weakest communist powers conquered a small and otherwise defenseless country was not an acceptable option for an administration that had defined its main foreign-policy doctrine by its resolve to resist communist expansion on a global scale. How far, indeed, would American prestige have fallen if Kim's repressive regime had been allowed to rule all of Korea!

The ideological approach found further resonance in developing international standards of behavior. It is important to remember that the defense of South Korea was not merely a unilateral American initiative. The North Korean attack received formal censure from the international community, and a United Nations (UN) resolution approved defensive military action. In addition to the United States, more than a dozen nations sent contingents to fight against the advancing communist forces. In addition to the

U.S. Marines withdrawing from the Chosin Reservoir in December 1950 after being attacked by Chinese troops

obvious strategic considerations, Washington was operating under the aegis of a mandate from the international community, which rejected aggressive war in principle. Interestingly enough, the Soviet Union could easily have deprived the United States of that moral justification by ending its boycott of the institution (over the refusal to allow the communist Chinese to exercise China's rights in the UN) and using its Security Council vote to veto the resolution calling for the defense of South Korea.

Another critical justification for U.S. involvement in Korea was that intervention was in many ways the linchpin in the evolution of Truman's strategic anticommunist design. Confronted with a Soviet Union that had begun to promote its own aggrandizement even before World War II had ended, Truman had little choice but to resist Soviet attempts to push the limits of what Roosevelt had conceded through wartime diplomacy. Increasingly, this stance took on a military character as the West perceived a Soviet hand in favor of the postwar communist insurrection in Greece, saw the tenuous democracies of postwar Eastern Europe blotted out by violent and extralegal means sponsored

by Moscow, and had its diplomatically unassailable occupation rights in West Berlin challenged by the Soviet military.

As these developments unfolded, however, real U.S. military power actually declined immediately after the war because of domestic political pressure for demobilization and reductions in the defense budget. The deceiving perception that the world was now in the hands of the Western allies dramatically undercut the ability of the United States to resist increasingly bold assertions of communist influence. Even the Marshall Plan (1947), the administration program of economic assistance for the postwar recovery of Europe, remained a controversial domestic political issue until the balance of American politicians were convinced that West European communist parties had serious potential for success in times of economic hardship and political instability.

Moving from economic aid to increased military expenditures was a much more difficult sell, especially in light of the relatively difficult U.S. domestic economic situation immediately after the end of the war. Truman's championing of Greek and Turkish efforts to resist communist expansion and his successful challenge to the Soviet blockade of West Berlin, incredibly enough, did not result in the kind of military buildup that one might expect. Indeed, the defense budget for fiscal year 1950, immediately before the United States became involved in Korea, stood at $13 billion, just 30 percent more than the dangerously low amount spent annually on the military before World War II, when the U.S. Army was the eighteenth largest in the world, ranking just after the Bulgarians.

If America was to continue its role as a superpower and present a credible military challenge to Soviet expansionism, its defense budget had to be increased. Tepid responses to more subtle moves from the communist world could only be improved upon if these provocations became blatant and direct military threats. Whether Acheson cleverly left South Korea out of the defensive perimeter to dupe the communists into believing that the North could conquer the rest of the peninsula with impunity or they came to that mistaken conclusion on their own, the attack unified the United States in favor of both the war and the steady military buildup that accompanied it. Even though the Eisenhower administration sought to end the war quickly and then reduce conventional expenditures in favor of the financially cheaper doctrine of massive retaliation, U.S. armed forces were for the rest of the Cold War substantially stronger than they were in the early postwar years.

On a broader geopolitical level Truman's decision to intervene in Korea was beneficial to the U.S. global position. While the international community showed quite forcefully that it was unwilling to countenance naked aggression, the resolve, quantity, and quality of U.S. military deployment to Korea demonstrated that the United States was firmly committed to the defense of its allies and strategic interests. This reaction was particularly important because the communist invasion of South Korea was the first true test of that commitment. It came slightly more than a year after the creation of the North Atlantic Treaty Organization (NATO), a defensive alliance dependent on U.S. military power, and at a time when proponents of European integration were already beginning to look toward an alternative. Such projects as the European Defense Community, a West European defensive alliance designed to exclude the United States, were already on the drawing board. The use of U.S. military power in Korea showed many European politicians that Washington could be relied upon to defend their countries against aggression. This belief, together with the realization that Western Europe could spend far less on defense and devote more resources to recovery

from World War II and for further economic development if it were protected by U.S. forces, led to the demise of early plans for an independent European defense; only recently have such notions been revived.

The cohesion that resulted from continued U.S. military and strategic leadership of the West was augmented by other positive benefits of the commitment to Korea. In Asia the principle of U.S. commitment to Seoul led to precisely the same kind of American-led collective security alliance that involvement on the peninsula had fortified in Europe. The South East Asia Treaty Organization (SEATO), formed in September 1954, combined under U.S. strategic leadership countries as far flung as the Philippines and Pakistan. Commitment to South Korean security also convinced Japan of the reliability of the United States as a protector so much that it abjured major defense spending until after 1976, recovered and prospered economically in the postwar era, and, despite some furtive overtures in the détente era, remained antagonistic toward the Soviet Union and its Russian successor state. In the Third World, furthermore, noncommunist and anti-Soviet governments and political movements came to believe in the 1950s and later, albeit with mixed prescience, that they could rely on Washington to support them. The fires of the Korean battlefields welded the structures of containment firmly in place.

–PAUL DU QUENOY,
GEORGETOWN UNIVERSITY

Viewpoint:
No. Although support of South Korea prevented a communist takeover, U.S. intervention in Korea was outside the boundaries of strategic containment policy and led to the support of a tyrannical regime.

The assertion that the Korean War (1950–1953) was a "wrong war" for the United States has tended to be the province of the intellectual and political Left. Old-line domestic leftists such as journalist I. F. Stone dismissed it as exporting to Asia an aggressive Cold War against an essentially passive, if not peace-loving, Soviet Union. British and Continental commentators wrote the war off as another example of U.S. fecklessness, combining febrile anticommunism with an unsophisticated approach to geopolitics that equated the Korean peninsula with the Fulda Gap (a major potential invasion route for the Soviets if they were to attack Europe). In the post-Vietnam

THE KOREAN WAR TRUCE

The truce was signed at ten in the morning, on June 27th, 1953. The news was relayed at once to all unit commanders. After 10 P.M. no one was to fire his weapon. Even an accidental discharge, we were told, would mean a court-martial. Throughout the hot sunny afternoon the Chinese sent over barrage after barrage of propaganda pamphlets. The projectiles exploded hundreds of feet in the air; the cannisters would open and the papers would flutter down to earth like snow. The papers would sometimes fail to separate and an entire packet would streak downward, landing hard. Judging from the height of the trajectory and the angle of the smoke trails, the projectiles were probably artillery. The smaller ones—mortars—made a peculiar noise before they detonated, like a loon. Sometimes they went WHOOP-WHOOP in a kind of falsetto. These harmless barrages were mingled with accurate artillery and mortar bombardments. No one was interested in chasing around the paddies looking for pamphlets. It seemed as though the Chinese were merely trying to expend all of their heavy ammunition and pamphlets before the cease-fire went into effect. . . .

At 10 P.M. the hills were illuminated by the light of many flares; white star clusters, red flares, yellow flares and other pyrotechnics signifying the end of a thirty-seven-month battle that nobody won and which both sides lost. The brilliant descending lights were probably visible all along the 150-mile front, from the Yellow Sea to the Sea of Japan. The last group of shells exploded in the distance, an 82mm. landed nearby, the echoes rumbled back and forth along the Changdan Valley and died out.

A beautiful full moon hung low in the sky like a Chinese lantern. Men appeared along the trench, some of them had shed their helmets and flak jackets. The first sound that we heard was a shrill group of voices, calling from the Chinese positions behind the cemetery on Chogum-ni. The Chinese were singing. A hundred yards or so down the trench, someone began shouting the Marine Corps hymn at the top of his lungs. Others joined in, bellowing the words. Everyone was singing in a different key, and phrases apart. Across the wide paddy, in goonyland, matches were lit. We all smoked for the first time in the MLR trench. The men from outpost Ava began to straggle back, carrying heavy loads. Later in the night a group of Chinese strolled over to the base of Ava and left candy and handkerchiefs as gifts. The men that were still on Ava stared, nothing more. So ends the Korean conflict. . . .

Source: Martin Russ, The Last Parallel: A Marine's War Journal (New York & Toronto: Rinehart, 1957), pp. 317–320.

years a school of historians, best represented by Bruce Cumings, denounced U.S. action in Korea as unwarranted intervention on the wrong side of a civil conflict, in support of a murderous tyrant, Syngman Rhee, whose provocations essentially initiated the war in the first place.

The end of the Cold War and the corresponding revelations from former Soviet archives have done much to discredit the first two lines of criticism. Evidence is clear that while the timing of the North Korean attack might have been influenced by the withdrawal of the last U.S. troops from South Korea in the spring of 1950, the attack itself had been planned independently of any American behavior. Far from being a response to provocation or a North Korean leap through a window of opportunity, the offensive was the product of extensive negotiation among Kim Il-Sung, Joseph Stalin, and Mao Tse-tung. If both of the latter rulers saw the risks of Kim's proposed initiative, in the final analysis they nevertheless backed his play. The Cumings school of argument for its part has been discredited—except in the most rarefied of academic circles—by the course of events. South Korea may not be a Jeffersonian idyll, but its development into an economically prosperous and politically open society is nevertheless a sharp contrast to the squalid tyranny perpetuated north of the Thirty-eighth Parallel.

That the Korean War may have been criticized for the wrong reasons does not, however, automatically make it a "good war" or in the best interests of the United States. Several factors combined to encourage the position expressed in the famous speech to the National Press Club by Secretary of State Dean Acheson in January 1950: namely, that Korea (along with Taiwan) was not a part of the primary U.S. defense perimeter. First and foremost was the earlier comprehensive and expensive failure of U.S. policy on the Asian mainland from 1941 to 1949. Nationalist China had absorbed increasing material and moral resources in its fight with the communists without anything resembling corresponding returns. As early as 1945 the Truman administration seriously considered leaving the Nationalists to their own devices and hoped for collaboration between the Nationalists and Communists. Instead, it inherited a diplomatic debacle that in turn generated the first major breach in the bipartisan approach to foreign policy that had been at least the public-relations norm since the attack on Pearl Harbor (7 December 1941). The eventual controversy over "who lost China" also served as an entering wedge for critics of the Democrats as either soft on communism or naive as to its nature. By no means were all of these critics followers of Senator Joseph R. McCarthy (R-Wisconsin), and their attacks bit deeply into an administration already seen by many of its ostensible supporters as abandoning the New Deal (1933–1940). Deliberately accepting another Asian involvement seemed correspondingly foolish.

Related to the unstable Korean situation was the anxiety that open support for Rhee might encourage the Nationalist refugee government on Taiwan to make similar claims for assistance—perhaps even to imitate Rhee by a campaign of provocation against the Chinese mainland designed to force America's hand. Neither the state department nor the Pentagon believed Taiwan could withstand an attack by the People's Liberation Army—an assault that was widely expected before the end of 1950 in high Washington circles, with the hope that it could be kept off the front pages of U.S. newspapers.

Korea was also a distinctly unpromising ally. The U.S. forces that occupied the southern half of the peninsula in the autumn of 1945 had no mission beyond a vague one of restoring Korean independence. Even without local and great-power rivalry, that was a tall order. A half-century as a Japanese colony had left Korea without a significant administrative apparatus, middle class, economic structure, or indeed anything else that seemed to offer promises of future contribution to order and prosperity. The rapid establishment under Soviet auspices of a communist client state north of the Thirty-eighth Parallel helped create a certain negative consensus, as Koreans unwilling to test their future under that system migrated to a South that by 1948 had established, under U.S. and United Nations (UN) auspices, its own government, right-wing and nationalist, under Rhee. Even by the most relaxed standards of the Cold War, Rhee was a hard man. While the new Republic of Korea claimed, as did its northern counterpart, to represent all of Korea, Rhee's treatment of dissidents reflected his conviction that the struggle between the two halves was mortal—and he intended the South to survive at whatever cost.

Rhee was encouraged in this view by a series of insurrections that staggered the new country from its inception. The exact mix of indigenous initiative and support from Pyongyang remains undetermined. What was noticed by the U.S. occupiers was the brutality with which Rhee's army and police, both poorly trained and ill disciplined, proceeded against the insurgencies. On the other hand, as the military aspect of the counterinsurgency succeeded, the South Korean government began offering and implementing small-scale reforms, particularly in land ownership and tenure. In the final analysis, while the Rhee government was neither universally accepted nor generally popular, the alternative offered by the North was not sufficiently appealing to spark a general uprising in its favor.

That negative, however, did not make South Korea prima facie alliance-worthy. In 1949 the last U.S. occupation forces, by then no more than a token, withdrew. The Central Intelligence Agency (CIA) predicted the incompetent authoritarianism of the Republic of Korea (ROK) would lead to eventual takeover of the peninsula by communist forces. General Douglas MacArthur, supreme American commander in the Far East, for once agreed with the Joint Chiefs of Staff that Korea could not defeat a Northern invasion without a substantial infusion of U.S. forces—which should not be made available. In case of an invasion the United States would evacuate its nationals and submit the issue to the UN where the Soviet Union was expected to block action by exercising its Security Council veto.

That limited-risk policy reflected a third set of strictures against making war in Korea. U.S. armed forces had been drawn down to the danger point. Even the nuclear deterrent was hollow at the core, with planes described as atomic bombers in fact unable to deliver the weapons. The garrison of Germany consisted of a single division, plus another division's worth of lightly armed constabulary troops. The deployable strategic reserve in the United States consisted of another single division, the 82nd Airborne. The four divisions occupying Japan were at two-thirds or less of their full war strength, while their operational readiness was generally recognized as deficient by any reasonable standards. Korea, moreover, was an unpromising theater relative to armed forces doctrines that, based on recent experience, continued to emphasize decisive operations. To the army and air force in particular, "limited war" was barely a theoretical concept, while Korea was a virtual definition of a geostrategic dead end.

Acheson was not alone in his exclusion of South Korea from the sphere of U.S. vital interests. In the spring of 1950 Democratic Senator Thomas T. Connolly (D-Texas), chairman of the Senate Foreign Relations Committee, predicted the eventual abandonment of South Korea and denied it was essential to U.S. security. The ambassador to the ROK, John J. Muccio, predicted a Northern victory in any general conflict. Military advisers to the embryonic army of South Korea were more optimistic, but primarily for career reasons as opposed to professional convictions. They were, after all, assigned to teach the South Koreans to fight and win American-style. It is not good for a professional soldier to admit in public that he is failing in his mission.

Despite all the prewar reservations, the United States eventually committed itself to a large-scale limited war in Korea, and eventually gained an operational stalemate that in time became a grand strategic victory. It did so, however, against its own well-considered and well-conceived policies, developed over a period of several years. Such reactions to circumstance were characteristic of U.S. foreign policy after 1945. In this case the results spoke for the behavior. That does not make the commitment wise.

–DENNIS SHOWALTER,
COLORADO COLLEGE

References

Dean Acheson, *Present at the Creation: My Years in the State Department* (New York: Norton, 1969);

Clay Blair, *The Forgotten War: America in Korea, 1950–1953* (New York: Time Books, 1987);

Bruce Cumings, *The Origins of the Korean War,* volume 1, *Liberation and the Emergence of Separate Regimes, 1945–1947* (Princeton: Princeton University Press, 1981);

Cumings, *The Origins of the Korean War,* volume 2, *The Roaring of the Cataract, 1947–1950* (Princeton: Princeton University Press, 1990);

Rosemary Foot, *The Wrong War: American Policy and the Dimensions of the Korean Conflict, 1950–1953* (Ithaca, N.Y.: Cornell University Press, 1985);

John Lewis Gaddis, *Strategies of Containment: A Critical Appraisal of Postwar American National Security Policy* (New York: Oxford University Press, 1982);

Gaddis, *We Now Know: Rethinking Cold War History* (Oxford: Clarendon Press; New York: Oxford University Press, 1997);

Chen Jian, *China's Road to the Korean War: The Making of the Sino-American Confrontation* (New York: Columbia University Press, 1994);

Walter LaFeber, *America, Russia, and the Cold War, 1945–1996,* 8th edition (New York: McGraw-Hill, 1997);

Vojtech Mastný, *The Cold War and Soviet Insecurity: The Stalin Years* (New York: Oxford University Press, 1996);

David McCullough, *Truman* (New York: Simon & Schuster, 1992);

William Stueck, *The Korean War: An International History* (Princeton: Princeton University Press, 1995).

McCARTHYISM

Was there a legitimate basis for the Red Scare encouraged by Senator Joseph R. McCarthy's investigation of communist infiltration of U.S. government agencies?

Viewpoint: Yes. McCarthy was right to challenge communists in the U.S. government, because they had infiltrated important positions and had subversive potential.

Viewpoint: No. Although there were some spies, McCarthyism led to a greater danger from an anticommunist witch-hunt that undermined civil liberties, damaged innocent lives, and narrowed legitimate political discourse.

In February 1950, during a speech in Wheeling, West Virginia, Senator Joseph R. McCarthy (R-Wisconsin) waved a piece of paper in front of his audience claiming it was a list of names of 205 members of the U.S. Communist Party who were employed in important positions in the federal government. The Senate Foreign Relations Committee created a special subcommittee to look into McCarthy's allegations, and in July 1950 announced that the charges were false.

Undeterred, McCarthy continued his attacks, supported by the political conservatives alarmed by the liberal influences in American government. Reelected to the Senate in 1952, McCarthy became chairman of the Permanent Investigations Subcommittee of the Senate Government Operations Committee. From that position he launched a series of investigations into alleged communist infiltration of the government. Adept at the art of innuendo and insinuation, he continued his public attacks on leading public officials in the administrations of both Harry S Truman and Dwight D. Eisenhower. He accused General George C. Marshall of treason for his China policy; attacked Eisenhower for not being vigorous in rooting out communist subversion, thus reducing the United States to a "state of whining and whimpering appeasement"; and charged that Secretary of State John Foster Dulles had doctored the records of the Yalta Conference (4–11 February 1945).

By 1954 even Republicans had grown tired of McCarthy's conduct and began to distance themselves from his tactics. Following a series of accusations McCarthy leveled against the U.S. Army, the Senate began an investigation into his methods. McCarthy was subsequently censured by the Senate on 2 December 1954, on a vote of sixty-seven to twenty-two. His influence evaporated almost overnight, and he died on 2 May 1957 of an alcohol-related liver ailment.

Critics of McCarthy described him as a cynical and ruthless opportunist, fanning irrational fears about the influence of communism in the United States and exploiting the resulting fears to advance himself politically. In the process, he helped to create a climate of suspicion and terror in which many ordinary Americans paid a heavy price merely for having their names mentioned as possible communist sympathizers. Despite his constant references to communists in high places, he never exposed a single active communist, although he did uncover government employees and other individuals who in their youth had been members of the Party or were in sympathy with it. Supporters of McCarthy, while condemning his tactics, argued that for all his crudeness he was influential in alerting Americans to the communist menace and in drawing their attention to the dangerous naiveté of many liberals in their benign view of the Soviet Union and communism.

Viewpoint:
Yes. McCarthy was right to challenge communists in the U.S. government, because they had infiltrated important positions and had subversive potential.

The American Left tirelessly defended members of the U.S. Communist Party; fellow travelers; alleged communist spies such as Alger Hiss, Julius and Ethel Rosenberg, and Harry Gold; and several Moscow-directed infiltrators who occupied senior positions in the FDR administration, Manhattan Project, and other sensitive spots. This background allowed a reckless Republican senator from Wisconsin, Joseph R. McCarthy, to launch a campaign against communist influence in the United States. In his famous speech of 9 February 1950, in Wheeling, West Virginia, he waved a sheet of paper at the audience, proclaiming: "I have here in my hand a list of 205 . . . a list of names that were made known to the Secretary of State as members of the Communist Party, and who nevertheless are still working and shaping policy in the State Department." This speech marked the beginning of a communist witch-hunting era in the United States, during which hundreds of people in academe, Hollywood, and journalism lost their jobs and were ostracized.

Half a century later, with Soviet-era archives open, it turns out that there was a list—not the one brandished by McCarthy, but a real one nonetheless—with code names, salary receipts, and copies of sensitive materials from the Manhattan Project and U.S. State Department. The appearance of Soviet evidence, starting in the early 1990s after the breakup of the Soviet Union, coincided with the 1995–1996 declassification of American intelligence files known as the Venona Files, which contain intercepts of Soviet spy cables. Materials in these files provide details of widespread Soviet penetration of a variety of U.S. agencies and government offices. Newly available materials have not settled the ideological battles that raged in the United States in the 1940s and 1950s. Historian Arthur M. Schlesinger Jr., for example, argued in *The Vital Center: The Politics of Freedom* (1949) that there were only about one hundred thousand communists in the United States, and that they were on the margins of American life. This argument misses the point, because many American communists were part of the elite deployed in every key juncture of American life: academia, journalism, and other opinion-molding positions. Their positions allowed even a few communists and communist sympathizers to wield influence out of proportion to their actual numbers, especially in major American cities, trade unions, and professional guilds.

Some historians argue that these individuals were idealists who believed that what was going on in the Union of Soviet Socialist Republics (U.S.S.R.) was no more than a Soviet-style New Deal. There is no doubt that some Soviet sympathizers were naive and others were duped, but many in the pro-Soviet elite were aware of the nature of the Soviet system and the help they were providing it. The case of the Spanish Civil War (1936–1939) demonstrates the role the Communist Party of the United States of America (CPUSA) played in organizing the Lincoln Brigade and how it colluded with the Soviet Union. Rather than naiveté one should assume that they were loyal to what they perceived as the international socialist movement, although they knew that the Comintern was an agency of Joseph Stalin. Moreover, it has long been known that the CPUSA had been funded by the U.S.S.R., the proof coming from Soviet archives.

There is little doubt that McCarthy exploited events that created the impression the Soviet Union and communist movement were on the move (for example, the Soviet 1949 nuclear test, the fall of China, and the Korean War), and that he had little knowledge of communism or of the workings of the communist movement, but he was on to something. McCarthy exaggerated the scope of the problem, was careless with the facts, and had no compunction about destroying reputations with vicious innuendos. The fact remains, however, that from the mid 1930s through the mid 1940s, there were high-level Soviet sympathizers in the administration of Franklin D. Roosevelt, and that, during World War II, the Soviets relied on many spies in sensitive spots to provide them with a wealth of military information, including early designs of the nuclear bomb.

McCARTHYISM

McCarthy was wrong and irresponsible in leveling charges of disloyalty against three American presidents and two secretaries of state for being lax on U.S. security. Staff members of these high officials, however, did entertain ideas about the Soviet Union that were manifestly inaccurate. The most significant adviser on Soviet affairs to Roosevelt was Harry L. Hopkins, a radical New Dealer who believed that the U.S.S.R. was not only a World War II ally, but a postwar ally as well. He believed the Soviet Union would become a liberal state. He pushed through the idea that U.S. relations with the U.S.S.R. could be based on generosity without reciprocity, leading to massive U.S. support for the Soviet Union during the war. The U.S.S.R. was never questioned about what it did with the aid and never gave any information either. No U.S. military representative was ever invited to observe any major Soviet campaign. The six-volume study of British military intelligence shows that the British spied on the U.S.S.R. throughout the war because the Soviets refused to supply any information about their war plans.

The first year of the Truman administration was similar to the Roosevelt period in spirit and deeds. Truman soon realized, though, that he was surrounded by advisers who were genuinely friendly to the U.S.S.R. This realization dawned on him especially after the Potsdam Conference (July–August 1945), during which Truman, a graduate of the famed Thomas Joseph Pendergast political machine in Missouri, had little difficulty in identifying Stalin for what he was, something Roosevelt was never able to do. Truman was thus keener to uproot pro-Soviet influence in his administration, initiating a series of steps that some of his supporters thought were excessive, such as convening the loyalty boards. McCarthy began his anticommunist campaign in the middle of Truman's anticommunist purges of the administration, paying little attention to the fact that Truman was already moving vigorously to correct whatever problems there were with Soviet sympathizers in positions of influence. Unlike Truman, Dwight D. Eisenhower was the first true Cold War president, and there was no one in his circle of advisers, or in his administration, who harbored any illusions about the Soviet Union or the nature of the competition between the two countries.

McCarthy was an opportunist who never showed any interest in educating himself about the communist movement, but he was a patriot, even if a misguided one. Whether or not he truly believed that there was a communist conspiracy in high places and that there was, indeed, a communist infiltration into every position of influence, he must have, in the end, persuaded himself that this was the case. It is not likely that anyone could have pursued the cause with such an unrelenting zeal and at such a high cost to himself and his career. McCarthy came from the isolationist Midwest, with constituents who were suspicious of cosmopolitanism and foreign involvement. It is not a paradox that he was an isolationist and a fanatical anticommunist at the same time: his reasoning was that, had it not been for the evil influence of communists abroad and their sympathizers at home, there would not be a need for the United States to become heavily involved in the world.

McCarthy was not always right, and his methods were mostly reprehensible. In hindsight, however, he was more perceptive than the Left about the nature of the Soviet system, the competition between the U.S.S.R. and the United States, and about how far some Soviet sympathizers in the United States would go to help the Soviet Union.

-AMOS PERLMUTTER,
AMERICAN UNIVERSITY

Viewpoint:
No. Although there were some spies, McCarthyism led to a greater danger from an anticommunist witch-hunt that undermined civil liberties, damaged innocent lives, and narrowed legitimate political discourse.

The sudden end of the Cold War between 1989 and 1991, stunning almost everyone, spurred a new wave of interpretive contention about the history of the East-West conflict. The collapse of the Soviet empire also made possible the previously unimaginable reality of access to the former state secrets of the Communist Party regimes. Not surprisingly, the first wave of reconceptualization in the West promoted a "vindicationist" or "triumphalist" interpretation of Cold War history. The essence of this reductionist argument was that the West had ultimately "won" the Cold War because of its superior way of life. The unconcealed corollary of this argument, trumpeted by national-security elites and establishment scholars, was that they had been right all along in advocating a hard-line policy toward the Soviet Union and its allies.

The triumphalist mentality had a particularly pronounced impact on debate over the ever-neuralgic subject of the history of domestic communism and spying within the United States. New documentation from the Soviet

McCARTHY CENSURE

Sen. Joseph R. McCarthy's (R-Wisconsin) bullying tactics intimidated both fellow senators and individuals brought before his committee. In December 1954 his colleagues struck back. Following is a portion of Senate Resolution 301, offered on 2 December by Sen. Ralph E. Flanders (R-Vermont) to the Senate Select Committee, which was considering censuring McCarthy for his abusive conduct.

"*Resolved,* That the Senator from Wisconsin, Mr. McCarthy, failed to cooperate with the Subcommittee on Privileges and Elections of the Senate Committee on Rules and Administration in clearing up matters referred to that subcommittee which concerned his conduct as a Senator and affected the honor of the Senate and, instead, repeatedly abused the subcommittee and its members who were trying to carry out assigned duties, thereby obstructing the constitutional processes of the Senate, and that this conduct of the Senator from Wisconsin, Mr. McCarthy, is contrary to senatorial traditions and is hereby condemned.

Sec 2. The Senator from Wisconsin, Mr. McCarthy, in writing to the chairman of the Select Committee to Study Censure Charges (Mr. Watkins) after the Select Committee had issued its report and before the report was presented to the Senate charging three members of the Select Committee with 'deliberate deception' and 'fraud' for failure to disqualify themselves; in stating to the press on November 4, 1954, that the special Senate session that was to begin November 8, 1954, was a 'lynch-party'; in repeatedly describing this special Senate session as a 'lynch bee' in a nationwide television and radio show on November 7, 1954; in stating to the public press on November 13, 1954, that the chairman of the Select Committee (Mr. Watkins) was guilty of 'the most unusual, most cowardly things I've ever heard of' and stating further: 'I expected he would be afraid to answer the questions, but didn't think he'd be stupid enough to make a public statement'; and in characterizing the said committee as the "unwitting handmaiden,' 'involuntary agent' and 'attorneys-in-fact' of the Communist Party and in charging that the said committee in writing its report 'imitated Communist methods—that it distorted, misrepresented, and omitted in its effort to manufacture a plausible rationalization' in support of its recommendations to the Senate, which characterizations and charges were contained in a statement released to the press and inserted in the *Congressional Record* of November 10, 1954, acted contrary to senatorial ethics and tended to bring the Senate into dishonor and disrepute, to obstruct the constitutional processes of the Senate, and to impair its dignity; and such conduct is hereby condemned."

Source: Congressional Record, 83rd Cong., 2nd Sess., 1954, 100, pt.12: 16394–16395.

archives has indeed revealed that Premier Joseph Stalin's agents worked tirelessly to infiltrate the American government and its most sensitive institutions, especially during World War II. New evidence confirms the guilt of some celebrated U.S. spies, such as Julius and Ethel Rosenberg, and strongly—though not conclusively—establishes the guilt of others, such as Alger Hiss.

Triumphalist scholars, national-security elites, and sympathetic journalists have used this information as part of the effort to rewrite the history of the Cold War in such a way as to vindicate U.S. actions. Domestic anticommunism—long perceived as an excessive assault on civil liberties, an American "nightmare in red"— is hence transformed into an honorable crusade born of the necessity to rid the nation of genuine threats to internal security.

Despite the undeniable significance of the revelations from the Soviet archives, this vindicationist spin on the issue of domestic communism makes for bad history. The demonstrable existence of scores of communist spies in the United States does not change the reality that the nation indulged in a wave of anticommunist hysteria, undermining civil liberties and constitutional rights, destroying the lives of thousands of citizens, and narrowing the boundaries of legitimate political discourse in America.

Clearly the most significant source of new information on the issue of domestic spying has stemmed from declassification of top-secret records of the Venona Project—a program of U.S. government-decoded intercepts of Soviet intelligence transmissions during World War II. Ironically, American scholars began to learn about Venona not in Washington, the capital of

the "free" world, but in the Moscow archives. Only after these scholars and public officials pointed out this embarrassing irony in the mid 1990s did the Federal Bureau of Investigation (FBI) and National Security Agency (NSA) cooperate in declassifying thousands of World War II–era records documenting the history of domestic spying and subversion.

The Venona documents, FBI files, and Russian records clearly reveal a substantial Soviet campaign of espionage against the United States during World War II. Moreover, perhaps two hundred to more than three hundred members of the Communist Party United States of America (CPUSA), rather than being content merely to advocate an ideological position, participated directly in Soviet espionage activities. They did so because, naive about the true horrors of Stalinism, they remained true believers in the legitimacy and historical inevitability of communism, with the Soviet Union as its vanguard.

Several key points must be kept in view when evaluating the new evidence and in challenging the legitimacy of the revisionist history of domestic communism. While espionage is illegal, and rightfully so, students of history nonetheless should bear in mind that the transgressions of American communists in government and industry were performed in behalf of a U.S. ally in wartime. It is easy to forget, under the long shadow cast by the subsequent Cold War, that the United States and Soviet Union

McCARTHYISM

worked in tandem to defeat fascist aggression. As millions of Soviet troops perished in bearing the brunt of fighting Adolf Hitler's armies, American leaders, the press, and public cast "Uncle Joe" Stalin and the Red Army in the most favorable light. Thus, although U.S. communists knew they were divulging state secrets, they may not have viewed their actions as unpatriotic insofar as they acted in support of a close military ally in a mutual struggle against fascist aggression.

Communist spies in the United States did real damage, however, by enhancing the Soviet capability of competing with the West in the arena of military technology. There seems little doubt that spying by Klaus Fuchs, Rosenberg, and others enabled the Union of Soviet Socialist Republics (U.S.S.R.) to avoid many of the time-consuming mistakes and trial-and-error procedures that American scientists weathered in the ultimately successful quest to develop atomic weapons. Estimates vary, but it appears that spies enabled the U.S.S.R. to develop the bomb at least two to three years in advance of what might otherwise have been expected. Spies also helped the Soviets bridge a technological gap in the development of jet engines and aircraft. Radar was yet another Western technological advantage that the Soviets closed in on as a result of espionage. Earlier-than-expected Soviet development of such technology does not appear to have altered history to any significant degree, although such a statement is bound to produce argument based on counterfactual scenarios of what might have been. In any case, no one questions that the Soviets would have, eventually, developed all of these technologies.

The real interpretive core of the history of domestic communism, however, is not the activities of U.S. spies but the repressive crusade against the American Left that came in tandem with the Cold War. Focus on the reality of domestic spying, which occurred primarily before and during World War II, conveniently diverts attention from successful state-centered drive to extirpate the Left and enforce ideological orthodoxy throughout the history of the Cold War, especially during its first decade of existence. By controlling communism at home, national security elites reinforced the new foreign policy of containing communism across the globe. Proponents of the new orthodoxy equated dissent with treason as a means of discrediting legitimate political discourse.

U.S. national security policy rejected the very concept of diplomacy with the Soviet Union, China, and other communist states. Countersubversives blamed a group of diplomats, the "China hands," for the "loss" of China to communism in 1949, a development that flowed in actuality from the superior organization and tactics of Mao Tse-tung's communists over the hapless regime of Chiang Kai-shek.

Anticommunist crusaders depicted the Yalta Conference (4–11 February 1945), once considered a great triumph of wartime diplomacy, as a forum of appeasement, darkly suggesting that President Franklin D. Roosevelt's aides present at the conference, such as Hiss, had spurred a sell-out of the national interest. Hiss had also played a part in establishing the United Nations (UN), whose role the United States would consistently downplay in deference to a system of multilateral anticommunist alliances.

The anticommunist movement served the purposes of political conservatism on domestic issues as well. Conservative elites had been badly unnerved by the New Deal, which they equated with creeping socialism. Roosevelt's program had, of course, lacked any such consistent focus, having constituted a hodgepodge and somewhat desperate effort to achieve some relief and recovery in the midst of the Great Depression (1929–1941). Nevertheless, by conducting an all-out purge of Leftists from government, schools, business, and industry, the conservative forces behind the anticommunist crusade diverted American politics sharply to the Right. Liberals emphasized that they represented the "vital center" rather than the Left, which effectively ceased to exist in mainstream American politics.

The federal government—and especially J. Edgar Hoover's FBI—drove the countersubversive movement. More than any other department or agency, the FBI led the campaign of hearings, prosecutions, and loyalty reviews designed to extirpate Leftists from government. The federal government itself orchestrated repression and denial of civil liberties to thousands of Americans, the overwhelming majority of whom were not and never had been spies or criminals. Indeed, for every genuine spy such as Fuchs or Rosenberg, hundreds of people guilty only of ideological deviation became victimized. Prominent, patriotic Americans—men such as physicist Robert Oppenheimer and diplomat John Paton Davies who had worked tirelessly for their country during the war—were discredited and driven out of government service for past Leftist affiliations or, in the case of Davies, trumped-up allegations.

For every well-known victim, however, there were hundreds of obscure men and women driven from their jobs, and even from their homes, solely on the basis of their past Leftist affiliations. The knock on the door by an FBI agent could mark the end of a career and one's life. Anticommunist hysteria of postwar America indeed became a nightmare of jobs lost, families divided, blacklists compiled, hear-

McCARTHYISM

ings held on trumped-up charges, constitutional rights denied, and—in some respects most odious of all—intense pressure to ensure the misery of others by "naming names."

Senator Joseph R. McCarthy (R-Wisconsin) was a late entrant, though a most spectacular one to be sure, into the arena of anticommunist hysteria. McCarthy's spurious and sensational campaign, abetted by the FBI, the highest U.S. public officials, and the press, debuted in 1950 and lasted until 1954. Given McCarthy's use of the "big lie," the ruthless tactics he and his associates employed, the excesses and instability that he and his movement represented, it is remarkable that "McCarthyism" lasted four years—before the junior senator's Waterloo in the Army-McCarthy hearings.

McCarthy had served his purpose, however. The postwar campaign had succeeded in purging the Left, not just from government, but throughout American society. Excesses of the movement, so clearly evident by the mid 1950s, could now be attributed to a single unstable individual without discrediting the movement as a whole. Damage done by the wave of anticommunist hysteria in the United States exceeded that perpetrated by American and Soviet spies in wartime. The countersubversive crusade destroyed thousands of lives, compromised civil liberties, reinforced ideological orthodoxy in a supposedly free country, and encouraged anti-intellectualism, primitivism, and fear of foreign contacts.

The right-wing backlash ensured that a variety of progressive causes that American communists and Leftists had long advocated—civil rights for African Americans, rights for labor, national health care, and other social reforms—were put on the back burner. Blacklists, bans, and book burnings stifled dissent and artistic expression. Far from a justifiable response to threats to national security, the anticommunist hysteria of the postwar period represents the most sustained era of political repression in American history.

–WALTER L. HIXSON,
UNIVERSITY OF AKRON

References

Albert Fried, ed., *McCarthyism: The Great American Red Scare: A Documentary History* (New York: Oxford University Press, 1997);

Richard M. Fried, *Nightmare in Red: The McCarthy Era in Perspective* (New York: Oxford University Press, 1990);

John Earl Haynes and Harvey Klehr, *Venona: Decoding Soviet Espionage in America* (New Haven: Yale University Press, 1999);

David M. Oshinsky, *A Conspiracy so Immense: The World of Joe McCarthy* (New York: Free Press, 1983);

Arthur M. Schlesinger Jr. *The Vital Center: The Politics of Freedom* (Boston: Houghton-Mifflin, 1949);

Richard Rovere, *Senator Joe McCarthy* (New York: Harcourt, Brace, 1959);

Ellen Schrecker, *Many Are the Crimes: McCarthyism in America* (New York: Little, Brown, 1998);

Athan G. Theoharis, *Seeds of Repression: Harry S Truman and the Origins of McCarthyism* (Chicago: Quadrangle Books, 1971).

MIDDLE EAST

Did the Soviet Union pose a major threat to the Middle East during the Cold War?

Viewpoint: Yes. The Soviets pursued an aggressive foreign policy in the Middle East that not only helped destabilize the region but compromised the U.S.S.R. as well.

Viewpoint: No. The Soviet threat to the Middle East was greatly exaggerated; the U.S.S.R. simply desired to create a regional balance of power and secure its periphery.

As the Cold War progressed, the global competition between the United States and Soviet Union spilled into many parts of the Third World. Time and again, the Middle East was beset by bloody conflicts. The founding of the Jewish state of Israel in 1948 provoked several of its Arab neighbors to challenge its very existence and go to war several times. American support for Israel (especially after the 1967 War), the vestiges of European colonialism, continuing poverty and inequality, the toppling of traditional regimes and their replacement with military juntas, and the growth of Islamic fundamentalism all contributed to the development of anti-American sentiment in the region, as well as to the militarization of Middle Eastern politics.

The Soviet Union had always been outspoken in its political and material support for movements of national liberation and had inherited the Russian legacy of pursuing a strategically advantageous position in the Near East. Throughout the Cold War, and especially after the Suez Crisis of 1956, several important states in the region gravitated toward the Soviet Union and pursued anti-Israeli and anti-Western policies with military and economic support from Moscow. Many scholars speculate, however, that ties between the Soviet Union and some Middle Eastern states did not represent a significant strategic threat to the stability of the region or to U.S. interests there. Others have made the argument that the Soviets were consistently searching for opportunities to expand their influence in the region and that these attempts were built on policies that destabilized the region and challenged the American presence there.

**Viewpoint:
Yes. The Soviets pursued an aggressive foreign policy in the Middle East that not only helped destabilize the region but compromised the U.S.S.R. as well.**

It was once fashionable in the field of history to discuss the so-called science of geopolitics and its shaping of foreign policy. Though the validity of some of the theories of geopolitics might be debated, when it comes to the expansionist designs of the Soviet Union into the Middle East there is no doubt that the Kremlin dreamed of hegemony in the region and saw it as a key component to their overall plan. Fantasies of dominance by particular nations usually transcend the tenure of a political

party or ideology, and thus it was with Russia and the Soviet Union.

Starting with Ivan the Terrible in the sixteenth century and ending with Nicholas II in the early twentieth century, the foreign policy of the tsars in relationship to the Middle East was an aggressive one, formed by religious issues, desire for warm water access, expansionism, and as a counterbalance to English and French efforts in the region. The change in who ruled Russia did not affect these designs, which were compounded by the rise of Arab nationalism, the collapse of Western imperialism, and the transformation of the region due to the wealth generated by oil.

The post-1945 environment in the Middle East was a situation ripe for Soviet adventurism. Apologists for Joseph Stalin might argue that the good intentions of the Union of Soviet Socialist Republics (U.S.S.R.) were clearly demonstrated by its voluntary withdrawal from Iran after World War II. The obvious response to this argument is that any attempt to hold northern Iran was impossible given the nearby British military presence in what was still colonial India and the American projection of power into the Persian Gulf as part of the logistical buildup in support of the Soviet Union during the war.

Iran was a potential battle Stalin knew he could not win, and thus he turned it into a propaganda show of peaceful withdrawal. At the same time, Soviet support of communist movements in Greece and Turkey were a clear attempt to forward their political and military control of the region, a situation that directly resulted in the implementation of the Truman Doctrine (1947).

A long list of Soviet maneuvers to expand their influence and power in the Middle East now unfolded. Egyptian president Gamal Abdel Nasser's attempt in the mid 1950s to form an Arab League was directly fronted by the Soviets with significant financial, technical, and military support. This aid continued throughout the 1960s and into the 1970s. While Soviet advisers provided training in the Middle East, within the Soviet Union thousands of Arab military and political personnel were indoctrinated.

If ever there is an example of the true level of the threat generated by the Soviet Union in the Middle East it is the 1973 Yom Kippur War. A powerful surprise assault by the Egyptians and Syrians all but overwhelmed the Israeli Defense Forces (IDF). The American response to this aggression was the initiation of an airlift of supplies that depleted most U.S. military stockpiles in Western Europe. A proxy

Presidium chairman Nikolay V. Podgorny (l) and Vice President Anwar as-Sadat signing the Soviet-Egyptian Treaty in May 1970

(Photo provided by Mohamed Heikal)

MIDDLE EAST

war between the United States and the Soviet Union then ensued, a conflict that came dangerously close to an inferno. As Israeli forces turned the tide in the Sinai and crossed the Nile in a brilliant counterattack, Soviet troops started to prepare for a possible intervention in Egypt. At the same time American military forces went on full alert and Israel indicated that it might feel compelled to unleash its nuclear arsenal if the Soviets interfered. One of the finer moments of U.S. president Richard M. Nixon and National Security Adviser Henry Kissinger was their containment of this crisis that could have resulted in nuclear war.

In some ways the Soviets initially won the gambit, with America paying a terrible price for its intervention through the rise of terrorism and an oil embargo that helped to trigger nearly a decade of inflation. Yet, in the long run the events of 1973 started a profound shift in the western Middle East, especially in terms of Egypt's relationship to Israel and the United States.

Egyptian leader Anwar as-Sadat's break from Soviet influence in the 1970s was perhaps the greatest power shift in the Middle East of the entire postwar period. Disgusted with what he saw as Soviet duplicity and believing that Soviet designs ran counter to the needs of the region, as-Sadat had the courage to shatter the paradigm, a move that transformed Egypt and Middle East politics.

The history of Soviet adventurism in the 1980s in the Middle East was one of disaster. The Iran-Iraq War (1980-1988) threatened to destabilize the entire region, and because of its support of Iraq, the Soviet Union became a target for Iranian-inspired fundamentalism. Far worst for the U.S.S.R. was the invasion of Afghanistan in December 1979.

The relative ease of the Soviet retaking of Central Asia republics in the 1920s had reinforced among European Russians a contempt and a dismissal of the fighting ability of the various ethnic groups of the region. As a result, a military campaign that the Soviets assumed would be finished in less than three months became a ten-year debacle that directly contributed to the destabilization of the gerontocracy in the Kremlin, unleashed some of the same social ills that America experienced after Vietnam, and smashed any lingering dreams of hegemony in the region. At the same time rising ethnic tensions in the Trans-Caucasus Region generated additional pressures, many of the problems a direct result of Iranian-backed fundamentalism that had come to define the Soviet Union as one of the two Great Satans.

For nearly fifty years Soviet foreign policy in the Middle East was an unrelenting attempt to fulfill the dream going back to the early tsars: expansion of influence, projection of military power, and control of resources. The Persian Gulf War (1991) was the final closure on this chapter. Soviet efforts in the region had proven to be such an abysmal failure that all the U.S.S.R. could do was be a mute witness while a former client state was defeated. Although the Soviet Union had posed a threat to stability in the Middle East, in the end it was the Middle East that became a major contributor to the downfall of the Soviet Union.

–WILLIAM R. FORSTCHEN,
MONTREAT COLLEGE

Viewpoint:
No. The Soviet threat to the Middle East was greatly exaggerated; the U.S.S.R. simply desired to create a regional balance of power and secure its periphery.

The Union of Soviet Socialist Republics (U.S.S.R.) inherited an important concern faced by Imperial Russia: the obsession for security. Nowhere was this desire more evident than in the Middle East, where the Soviet Union pursued a practical and cautious policy while attempting to create regional balance and, most of all, security along its periphery. Though the unease with which the United States regarded Soviet behavior in the Middle East in the 1970s is understandable, it was unwarranted. The U.S.S.R. did not stray remarkably from the course it had followed in the region, or for that matter in other areas, during previous decades.

Obviously the Middle East possesses great strategic importance given that it is the land bridge to Europe, Africa, and Asia. Since World War II the Soviet Union adhered to the position of "peaceful coexistence" while conducting a gradual courtship of its neighbors in the Middle East. The U.S.S.R. would react to events but did not initiate them. Actions instigated by the Arabs or Israelis, however, were often shaped and directed by the United States, leaving the Soviet Union desperate to prevent the erosion of its position in the Arab states. Frequently, what appeared to be Soviet intervention or expansion on the surface, when examined more closely, was actually defensive aggression in the attempt to maintain the status quo. The foremost interest for the U.S.S.R. was its traditional border security.

The Soviet Union would have found the Middle East infertile ground for expansion.

Arab nationalism, Islamic unity, and regional rivalry rendered impossible any consistent policy for the Soviets, who discovered their clients to be as shifty as sand dunes, and found themselves used by—instead of using—the Middle Easterners.

The Arab-Israeli War of 1973 (Yom Kippur War or War of Ramadan) evidenced the erosion of the Soviet position in the Middle East. Egyptian leader Anwar as-Sadat realized that he could not rely upon the Soviets to recover the territories seized by the Israelis in 1967 during the Six-Day War. Emboldened by the fact that the United States was the key to the Egyptian-Israeli stalemate, Sadat expelled Soviet advisers, limited Soviet military presence in Egypt, and resumed communications with the United States. The U.S.S.R. insisted that the situation could be resolved by peaceful means, but started to cultivate relations with Syria, Libya, Iraq, and the Palestine Liberation Organization (PLO) to serve as a counterweight to the possible loss of Egypt as an ally. This action was not motivated by expansion but by the need to retain some sort of a foothold in the area. At the Nixon-Brezhnev summit (17–24 June 1973), Leonid Brezhnev urged the Americans to cooperate to resolve diplomatically the Egyptian-Israeli matter in order to avoid war. Secretary of State Henry Kissinger admitted that the United States had no interest in negotiating with the Soviets, stating "We were not willing to pay for détente in the coin of our geopolitical position." Americans knew that their ally, Israel, was stronger and that the United States was the answer to the settlement.

On 6 October 1973 Egypt and Syria attacked Israel. By 21 October Kissinger presented a plan for a cease-fire to the Soviets that they accepted, asking only that the United States and U.S.S.R. jointly introduce the proposal to the Security Council. Kissinger flew to Israel to put forth the details of the cease-fire, apparently indicating that it would be understood if a "few hours of 'slippage' in the cease-fire deadline" occurred. To term the continued Israeli attacks as "slippage" was an understatement. Although Resolution 338 passed in the United Nations on 22 October putting into effect the cease-fire, the Israelis continued to violate it based on unconfirmed, alleged Egyptian offensive behavior. The U.S.S.R. was in dire straits. The Soviets were not following any sort of offensive strategy, but merely attempting desperately to hold onto their credibility, as well as diplomatic and political survival, in the Middle East. United Nations (U.N.) Resolution 339, "urging" a return to positions held by Israel and Egypt at the time of the implementation of the cease-fire, did not halt Israeli attacks. Brezhnev

was forced to threaten Israel with the "gravest consequences" if it did not adhere to the resolutions. Kissinger informed Israeli leader Golda Meir that "there were limits beyond which we could not go, with all our friendship for Israel, and one of them was to make the leader of another super power look like an idiot." Soviet ambassador Anatoly Dobrynin requested that U.S. and Soviet troops should be dispatched through the Security Council to enforce the cease-fire. Kissinger's answer was a flat-out "no." According to Kissinger, the Americans were not about to reintroduce Soviet troops into Egypt through the U.N. after they had labored for years to reduce Soviet military presence. Any participation in such a joint effort would legitimize the Soviet role in the region, which was exactly what the U.S. wanted to prevent. Brezhnev responded with the threat that the U.S.S.R. would be coerced into unilateral action if it could not act with the cooperation of the United States. The U.S. response was to issue a military alert short of full readiness, Defense Readiness Condition (DEFCON) III. The Soviets were stunned at the disproportional reaction on the part of the Americans and retreated. U.N. Resolution 340 followed and "demanded" that the Israelis return to positions they held on 22 October. The United States had achieved its objectives: American influence with the Arabs had expanded at a cost to the Soviets, and an Arab or Israeli victory had been prevented, meaning that the United States was in the dominant position and the Soviets cut out of the situation.

The Soviet Union did not initiate the October War nor was it able to aggrandize its influence in the Middle East by manipulating its outcome. Rather, the United States orchestrated the conclusion of the Arab-Israeli conflict to its advantage, and definitely to the detriment of the Soviet Union. The United States, not the Soviet Union, took the initiative in the Middle East and the rest of the Third World.

Conventional wisdom says that as-Sadat had the bright idea of reaching out to Israel and Prime Minister Menachem Begin, but the reality is that the American hand was pushing the two together. The Israel-Egyptian relationship in 1978 was reversible and temporary. U.S. strategy was to forge an irreversible and permanent relationship between the two nations, in order that: Egypt would be firmly ensconced in the U.S. camp; the United States would obtain a political base in both Israel and Egypt, to fall back upon when Iran, the forwardmost position of the containment structure, collapsed; and Israel would never be confronted with a two-front conflict again. Besides a long-term Israeli-Egyptian peace treaty, the United States wanted a statement of

THE SOVIET UNION AND THE MIDDLE EAST

On 30 March 1971 Leonid Brezhnev, General Secretary of the Communist Party of the Soviet Union, delivered his annual report to the 24th Congress of the CPSU. A portion of his remarks pertained to Soviet policy in the Middle East.

The Middle East is another "hot spot" in world politics.

The crisis which has arisen as a result of Israel's attack on the UAR, Syria and Jordan has been one of the most intense in the development of international relations over the past period.

Together with the fraternal socialist countries we did everything necessary to stop and condemn the aggression. We raised this question in the UN Security Council in the most resolute terms. An extraordinary session of the General Assembly was called on our demand. The USSR and other fraternal countries have broken off diplomatic relations with Israel, which has ignored the UN decision for a ceasefire. Our country has helped to restore the defense potential of the Arab states which were subjected to invasion, the UAR and Syria in the first place, with whom our co-operation has been growing stronger from year to year.

The United Arab Republic recently came out with important initiatives. It announced its acceptance of the proposal put forward by the UN special representative, Dr. Gunnar Jarring, and readiness to conclude a peace agreement with Israel once the Israeli troops are withdrawn from the occupied Arab territories. The UAR has also proposed steps to resume navigation along the Suez Canal in the very near future. Thus, the attitude of the Arab side provides a real basis for settling the crisis in the Middle East. The Israeli Government's rejection of all these proposals, and Tel Aviv's now openly brazen claims to Arab lands clearly show who is blocking the way to peace in the Middle East, and who is to blame for the dangerous hotbed of war being maintained in that area. At the same time, the unseemly role of those who are instigating the Israeli extremists, the role of US imperialism and of international Zionism as an instrument of the aggressive imperialist circles, is becoming ever more obvious.

However, Tel Aviv ought to take a sober view of things. Do Israel's ruling circles really expect to secure for themselves the lands of others they have occupied and to go scotfree? In the final count, the advantages obtained by the invaders as a result of their piratical attack are illusory. They will disappear as mirages pass from view in the sands of Sinai. And the longer the delay in reaching a political settlement in the Middle East, the stronger will be the indignation of world public opinion, and the Arab people's hatred of the aggressor and its patrons, and the greater the harm the Israeli rulers will inflict on their country.

The Soviet Union will continue its firm support of its Arab friends. Our country is prepared to join other powers, who are permanent members of the Security Council, in providing international guarantees for a political settlement in the Middle East.

Once this is reached, we feel that there could be a consideration of further steps designed for a military detente in the whole area, in particular, for converting the Mediterranean into a sea of peace and friendly co-operation.

Source: 24th Congress of the Communist Party of the Soviet Union: March 30–April 9, 1971: Documents *(Moscow: Novosti Press Agency Publishing House, 1971), pp. 30–31.*

principle concerning the Palestinian question, in order to placate Saudi Arabia—to maintain ties with that nation and access to its oil.

Firstly, the United States prodded Israel into negotiating with Sadat; secondly, it increased pressure and conflict in the Horn of Africa. Arms that were denied to Ethiopia were made available to Somalia. The Middle Eastern nations, especially Saudi Arabia, were concerned with events in Africa, as they did not desire to be encircled by pro-Soviet states. Thirdly, the United States announced the Geneva Conference to pressure both Egypt and Israel into negotiations. The possible addition of the Soviets would only have complicated matters and shifted the goal from a separate peace to a comprehensive settlement. The United States managed to outmaneuver and exclude the U.S.S.R. from Middle East affairs.

Using détente in order to buy time, the United States attempted to preserve its preeminence by taking the initiative to actively undercut the Soviet Union at every turn. In the Middle Eastern theater, it would do so by excluding the

Soviet Union from such vital issues as the afore-mentioned resolution of the Arab-Israeli conflicts, luring Soviet clients into the U.S. camp with various means of assistance, addressing issues that seemed to possess minimal U.S. interest, and eventually becoming the "chief power broker" in the region. The Soviet Union acted in response to these American initiatives. As Minister of Defense Marshal Andrei Grechko declared in 1974, as reported by Raymond L. Garthoff, in *Détente and Confrontation: American-Soviet Relations From Nixon to Reagan* (1985), "The Soviet state in its foreign policy actively and purposefully opposes the export of counterrevolution and the policy of oppression, and supports the national-liberation struggle, resolutely resisting imperialist aggression in whatever distant part of the globe it appears."

The U.S.S.R. had no interest in exporting revolution; however, it did oppose counterrevolution. In Angola, the United States first supported the Portuguese suppression of the national liberation movement and then assisted Holden Roberto's National Front for the Liberation of Angola (Frente Nacional de Libertação de Angola, or FNLA), while its Western allies aided Jonas Savimbi's National Union for the Total Independence of Angola (União Nacional para a Independência Total de Angola, or UNITA). In response, the Soviet Union and Cuba supported Antonio Agostinho Neto's Marxist Popular Movement for the Liberation of Angola (Movimento Popular de Libertação de Angola or MPLA). Motivated by irredentist claims to the Ethiopian territory of Ogaden, Somalia attacked Ethiopia in 1977, but only after the United States, in an attempt to woo the Somalis away from the Soviets, promised arms. The Soviet Union had ties with both Ethiopia and SomaliA and were forced to choose in order to respond to the conflict. They supported Ethiopia and displayed remarkable restraint by stopping the Ethiopian counteroffensive into Somalia. The United States utilized surrogates, what the Soviets deemed as U.S. paladins, such as Iran and Saudi Arabia in a manner that was certainly not defensive, but offensive to the Soviet Union. Saudi Arabia helped win over Sudan from the Soviet sphere, supported the Eritreans against the Ethiopians, and facilitated U.S.-Somali relations. The Soviets realized that the United States did not see détente in the 1970s as a departure from the direct, proxy, and allied interventions that occurred in the 1950s and 1960s.

The Soviet Union had used direct power only in its security zone (Hungary in 1956, Czechoslovakia in 1968, and Afghanistan in 1979) and, therefore, considered these operations as defensive. In comparison, the United

States was more active. U.S. troops pushed north of the 38th parallel in Korea in 1950, occupied the Dominican Republic in 1965, bombed North Vietnam from 1964 until 1972, invaded Cambodia in 1970, bombed Kampuchea in 1975, targeted Libyan fighters flying over the Gulf of Sidra in 1981, and invaded Grenada in 1983. The United States exaggerated the Soviet propensity to resort to force. Yet, the U.S.S.R. was cautious and discriminatory in its use of force.

Afghanistan was the first instance in the Middle East in which the Soviets directly intervened with troops since the occupation of Iran immediately following World War II in 1945–1946. On 9 December 1979 Soviet forces assembled along the Soviet-Afghan border. They launched a full-scale invasion by the end of the month. Why did they invade Afghanistan at such an unsuitable moment? Brezhnev said the invasion "was no simple decision" for the Soviets. Their reasoning focused on the internal situation in Afghanistan and its possible effects. Hafizullah Amin was found to be a most unsatisfactory ruler in the eyes of the Soviets, because he was unable to consolidate the communist factions. According to Henry S. Bradsher, in *Afghanistan and the Soviet Union* (1983), the Soviet Union believed itself in "danger of losing its grip [that it had] gained in the April 1978 coup." It was also afraid of the establishment of an anticommunist, or rather anti-Soviet, regime with strong Islamic overtones in a country bordering disaffected, traditionally Islamic peoples of the Soviet Union. The driving force behind the invasion was to stabilize the situation in Afghanistan and as a result to secure Soviet borders.

From the French to Mongol to German incursions, the Russians had suffered enough invasions to create a national paranoia, which resulted in a Soviet obsession to create a *cordon sanitaire* (buffer zone) of neutral or friendly states surrounding its borders. The loss of Afghanistan would mean encirclement by "hostile nations." The Islamic nationalism that Ayatollah Ruholla Khomeini was propagating only added fuel to the fire of Muslim fanaticism brewing in Afghanistan. Afghan rebels, mujahideen, were fighting a jihad and if they succeeded, Central Asian Muslims might be more than tempted to follow a like path. Therefore, the Soviet Union pursued a plan of "defensive aggression."

Arguments that the Soviet Union wanted to prove their superpower status by direct military intervention in Afghanistan are absurd. Weighing their past actions and capabilities, it is unlikely that the world considered the Soviet Union as anything other than a superpower. Also, such arguments, nor the accusation that the Soviet Union was on an "imperialistic roll" of successes, do not explain the timing of the invasion.

When Mohammad Reza Shah Pahlavi was deposed in Iran (1979), a geopolitical opportunity to alter the correlation of forces to the Soviet advantage materialized. The hostage crisis (1979–1980) threatened to wipe away this opportunity. The Soviet Union assumed that the United States would assemble enormous military power near Iran, overthrow Khomeini, and recover Iran as a client. The Soviets needed to deter the Americans from action and prevent Iran from falling into U.S. clutches and to draw it somehow into the Soviet camp. The sole answer was military power. From the Soviet perspective Afghanistan had to be stabilized and leverage increased on Iran. The supreme irony was that the Carter administration had decided not to militarily pressure the Iranians.

"That dirty little war" as the Soviets began to refer to their action in Afghanistan, cost the U.S.S.R. dearly. The Soviet Union was dragged into the Afghan quagmire to receive blow after blow, and suffered economically, militarily, and politically because of its preoccupation with Afghanistan. According to Thomas T. Hammond, in *Red Flag Over Afghanistan: The Communist Coup, the Soviet Invasion, and the Consequences* (1984), the Soviets came to understand well the old Hindu saying, "O Gods from the venom of the cobra, the teeth of the tiger, and the vengeance of the Afghan deliver us."

The 1978 coup in Afghanistan resulted in a state that identified with communism and thus the Soviet Union. This development was accepted by the United States. Therefore, the U.S.S.R. considered Afghanistan a Soviet interest, and any Soviet involvement there would be a move to consolidate the status quo with respect to international geopolitics. In the context of the bipolar power system, this Soviet action was comparable to the U.S. role in the Dominican Republic. In order to retrieve interests that were quickly slipping away and address the security imperative, the Soviet Union felt that it had no other alternative than to act in Afghanistan, even though the timing was inopportune.

Again, the U.S. reaction was disproportional to the Soviet action. National Security Adviser Zbigniew Brzezinski went on record to state that the United States wanted to "ostracize and condemn the Soviets." President Jimmy Carter and Brzezinski proceeded to do just that, and discarded all détente "Marquess of Queensberry" rules. Carter transformed the image of Amin into the leader of a "freedom-loving people" struggling for independence and nonalignment, and remarked how the presence of Soviet troops was reminiscent

of the dark days during the power struggle in Czechoslovakia. Of course, Amin was a communist and Afghanistan was far from nonaligned. Various penalties were levied against the Soviet Union, such as a U.N. condemnation of the invasion, the boycott of the Moscow Olympics, a grain embargo, postponement of Senate consideration of SALT II, suspension of the sale of highly technological items, and a halt of economic and cultural exchanges. China and the United States, furthermore, coordinated assistance to the Afghan resistance. Much more crucial, however, was the Carter Doctrine, the military buildup that ensued, and rapprochement with China.

The United States used the Soviet invasion of Afghanistan to dismantle détente. The administration did not respond militarily to what Carter absurdly called the "greatest threat to peace since the second world war," but rather adopted a new and preferred policy. Were the moves made by the United States solely in response to the Soviet military presence in Afghanistan, it could be said that the Americans overreacted. It appears that Washington, however, was prepared to embark on a new policy and that the Soviets conveniently provided the justification and explanation. The United States pursued a drive for superiority over the Soviet Union. In addition to the massive military buildup, the United States abandoned arms control and modified its military doctrine, as evidenced in Presidential Directive (PD) -59, the Carter Doctrine, and Ronald Reagan's National Security Decision Directives (NSDD) -13, -32, and -82. The United States was determined to force the Soviet Union to overextend itself. This "gunboat diplomacy" led the United States into new areas of the world, even where its interests were minimal, in order to undercut the Soviet Union.

In the 1970s Soviet behavior in Middle Eastern interstate and internal conflicts consisted of one direct military intervention in Afghanistan in 1979, one threat of direct intervention in the 1973 October War, one intervention by proxy in the Ethiopian-Somali crisis from 1977 to 1988, as well as naval activity, participation of military advisers, direct and indirect arms supplies, training, political involvement, diplomacy, and propaganda. Starting with the 1973 October War, the grasp of Moscow on the Middle East slipped, never to be reestablished. Turmoil within states, as well as regional rivalry and foreign interference, prevented the Soviets from establishing a firm foothold in the Middle East despite their efforts. The Soviet Union found itself forced to react to U.S. proactive policies and maneuvers instead of just ensuring its national security with friendly or neutral states and maintaining a balance of power. The threat to the Middle East from the Soviet Union during the 1970s was no greater than in the past nor more dangerous than that posed by any other "great" power. It has been greatly exaggerated.

—JELENA BUDJEVAC, GEORGE WASHINGTON UNIVERSITY

References

Anwar as-Sadat, *In Search of Identity: An Autobiography* (New York: Harper & Row, 1978);

Henry S. Bradsher, *Afghanistan and the Soviet Union* (Durham, N.C.: Duke University Press, 1983);

Philippe Braillard and Mohammad-Reza Djalili, eds., *Tiers monde et relations internationales,* translated as *The Third World and International Relations* (London: Pinter, 1986; Boulder, Colo.: Lynne Rienner, 1986);

George W. Breslauer, ed., *Soviet Strategy in the Middle East* (Boston: Unwin Hyman, 1990);

John C. Campbell, "The United States and the Middle East," in *Crisis and Conflicts in the Middle East: The Changing Strategy: From Iran to Afghanistan,* edited by Colin Legum (New York: Holmes & Meier, 1981);

Jimmy Carter, *Keeping Faith: Memoirs of a President* (New York: Bantam, 1982);

Joseph J. Collins, *The Soviet Invasion of Afghanistan: A Study in the Use of Force in Soviet Foreign Policy* (Lexington, Mass.: Lexington Books, 1986);

Frederic J. Fleron Jr., and others, eds., *Contemporary Issues in Soviet Foreign Policy: From Brezhnev to Gorbachev* (New York: De Gruyter, 1991);

Robert O. Freedman, *Moscow and the Middle East: Soviet Policy Since the Invasion of Afghanistan* (Cambridge & New York: Cambridge University Press, 1991);

Raymond L. Garthoff, *Détente and Confrontation: American-Soviet Relations From Nixon to Reagan* (Washington, D.C.: Brookings Institution, 1985);

Galia Golan, "The Soviet Union in the Middle East," in *The Soviet Union and the Third World: The Last Three Decades,* edited by Andrzej Korbonski and Francis Fukuyama (Ithaca, N.Y.: Cornell University Press, 1987), pp. 178–207;

Thomas T. Hammond, *Red Flag Over Afghanistan: The Communist Coup, the Soviet Invasion, and the Consequences* (Boulder, Colo.: Westview Press, 1984);

Henry Kissinger, *Diplomacy* (New York: Simon & Schuster, 1994);

Kissinger, *Years of Upheaval* (Boston: Little, Brown, 1982);

Neil Matheson, *The "Rules of the Game" of Superpower Military Intervention in the Third World, 1975–1980* (Washington, D.C.: University Press of America, 1982);

Alfred L. Monks, *The Soviet Intervention in Afghanistan* (Washington, D.C.: American Enterprise Institute for Public Policy Research, 1981);

A. F. K. Organski, *The $36 Billion Bargain: Strategy and Politics in U.S. Assistance to Israel* (New York: Columbia University Press, 1990);

William B. Quandt, *Decade of Decisions: American Policy Toward the Arab-Israeli Conflict, 1967–1976* (Berkeley: University of California Press, 1977);

Quandt, *Peace Process: American Diplomacy and the Arab-Israeli Conflict Since 1967* (Washington, D.C.: Brookings Institution; Berkeley: University of California Press, 1993);

Alvin Z. Rubinstein, *Red Star on the Nile: The Soviet-Egyptian Influence Relationship Since the June War* (Princeton: Princeton University Press, 1977);

Rubinstein, *Soviet Foreign Policy Since World War II: Imperial and Global* (Cambridge, Mass.: Winthrop Publishers, 1981);

Oles M. Smolansky, *The Soviet Union and the Arab East Under Khrushchev* (Lewisburg, Pa.: Bucknell University Press, 1974);

Richard C. Thornton, *The Carter Years: Toward A New Global Order* (New York: Paragon House, 1991);

Thornton, *The Nixon-Kissinger Years: The Reshaping of American Foreign Policy* (New York: Paragon House, 1989).

MILITARY BALANCE

Did the conventional military force of NATO deter a Soviet invasion of Western Europe?

Viewpoint: Yes. NATO acted as an effective conventional deterrent during the forty-five-year standoff against the Warsaw Pact nations.

Viewpoint: No. The threat of nuclear weapons, not conventional forces, ensured the military balance in Europe.

The military balance in Europe during the Cold War was a study in disconnects and dissonances. A fundamental imbalance in the capacities of the former World War II allies existed as early as 1945. The Soviet Union, battered though it was by the war and its antecedents, possessed in the final analysis the conventional military capacity to extend to the English Channel and the Pyrenees against a network of states disarmed, disarming, and disorganized as much by victory as by defeat. The U.S. nuclear capacity was a "hollow deterrent," at best able to set the stage for a repetition of D-Day (6 June 1944) that was likely to leave nothing in its aftermath for either superpower to assimilate. A European community well aware of this possibility eventually supported, as the least-worst alternative, the creation of a common-defense system intended to keep "the Americans in, the Russians out, and the Germans down." The North Atlantic Treaty Organization (NATO) of the 1950s, however, retained its essential dependence on nuclear retaliation—in good part because of the reluctance of the rapidly recovering European states to devote significant resources to conventional defense. NATO's counterpart and counterpoint, the Soviet-directed Warsaw Pact, put significantly more effort first into developing a conventional military capacity with an offensive focus, then into integrating nuclear capabilities into that structure. Through the 1960s Warsaw Pact doctrine stressed a fast-paced offensive, designed to neutralize U.S. thermonuclear capacities in part by surprise, in part by holding Western Europe hostage, and in part by making the casus belli itself a moot point. The often-raised question of U.S. willingness to exchange Chicago for Munich lost a good deal of its meaning should Munich be under Soviet occupation.

The nuclear dimension of Western defense was challenged in the 1960s with the rise of the Federal Republic of Germany (FRG) to a central position in the councils of Western Europe and the Atlantic Alliance. Itself denied a nuclear capability by its own legislation—and the collective memories of the Third Reich—the West German government and its citizens were well aware that NATO nuclear scenarios had in common the reduction of the FRG to a radioactive wasteland. Clear as well was that the West German population and economy were expanding from their original centers in the Rhine and Ruhr toward an eastern frontier that in 1945 had been essentially rural. The new demographic and industrial configuration offered limited room for maneuver warfare. Yet, at the same time, the Warsaw Pact was bringing on line successive new generations of conventional weapons systems that at least matched anything the vaunted western technological superiority could offer.

The geostrategic position of West Germany, and its political implications, increasingly shaped the military discourse in NATO. How best to meet the challenge of stopping the Warsaw Pact at the frontier without immediate recourse to nuclear options? By themselves the NATO states could find no answer they were willing to pay for. The threat was met by a U.S. Army eager to return to conventional-war parameters after its Vietnam excursion. An initial foray into an "active defense" that critics excoriated as resembling static warfare without permanent fortifications, the new solution became "AirLand Battle." Introduced in the 1980s, this concept combined flexible forward defense with massive air strikes against Warsaw Pact follow-on forces. As applied to Europe, Air-Land Battle was designed less to win the conventional battle than to "not lose" it, buying time for diplomats to negotiate an end to the conventional fighting before the missiles began flying—and before NATO exhausted its limited conventional resources. Even that modest vision disturbed some NATO soldiers and politicians, who disliked the implications of air strikes into Warsaw Pact territory. Like its nuclear-dependant predecessor, however, AirLand Battle held the field as the least-worst alternative until the collapse of the Warsaw Pact and the Soviet Union made the issue of conventional war in Europe moot—for a time.

Viewpoint:
Yes. NATO acted as an effective conventional deterrent during the forty-five-year standoff against the Warsaw Pact nations.

The ultimate objective of all military operations, from the tactical level through the strategic, is to convince an opponent that he has lost or at least cannot win. Historian Geoffrey Blainey makes the case succinctly, in *The Causes of War* (1973), that war occurs when two nations disagree in their assessments of their relative strengths and believe that they can gain more from fighting than through negotiations. Over the course of the more than forty-year existence of the North Atlantic Treaty Organization (NATO) this idea was the underlying principal at work. NATO succeeded in convincing the Soviet Union and its client states within the Warsaw Pact that they could not win conventionally in Europe and reap any benefit from the victory. This belief, in the end, was the cold fact that won the Cold War. The Soviet assessment had four components: an accurate figuring of the costs of invading the more heavily populated territory of Germany, a recognition of the relative fragility of their own alliance, an appreciation for the effects of new weapons technology, and a realistic understanding of the time-space factors involved in an invasion.

From the beginning the Russians were aware of the true cost of their final push into Germany in 1945. In the closing days of World War II, by prior agreement, the Western allies stopped their own offensive. Although it was probably feasible for the British, Americans, and French to continue their eastward advance, the conferences of the "Big Three" had established the lines upon which postwar Germany would be divided. Rather than continue to fight for territory he later would have to cede to the Russians, General Dwight D. Eisenhower quite correctly pulled his forces up short. This infuriated some, as it allowed the Russians to capture the crown jewel of the German Reich, Berlin.

For years it was known that the final battle for Berlin had been costly for the Russians. They immediately acknowledged that they had taken hundreds of thousands of casualties. It is only since the fall of the Soviet Union that a more accurate assessment of losses appeared. The number of Soviet casualties in the final push toward and capture of Berlin appears to have been more than one million, although even the Russians cannot determine an exact figure. In their own assessment of future operations the Soviets surely took this heavy loss into consideration. Moreover, these casualties were not ones that could have been avoided through developing technology. This massive sacrifice was, at least partially, a result of the nature of the ground over which the Soviets fought in those final days of World War II. Military operations in "urban terrain" (MOUT in Western military parlance) are extremely expensive in terms of human lives. This was a lesson the Russians relearned in their 1994 and 1999 operations in Grozny, the capital of the breakaway Russian state of Chechnya.

Berlin prefigured the other major cities of West Germany in representing a formidable obstacle. Cities are the worst barrier, but even small towns can slow down an offensive. Urban defenders can operate in three dimensions: that is, they can be above ground in buildings, dug in at ground level, and below ground in the pipes and tunnels that exist beneath all modern towns. Securing a MOUT objective means clearing the enemy room-by-room from the whole area. This is time consuming and expensive when the defenders are determined, as they had been in Berlin in 1945. Thus, the memory

MILITARY BALANCE

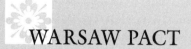

WARSAW PACT

The Warsaw Treaty Organization (WTO), commonly known as the Warsaw Pact, was formed in 1955 by the Soviet Union and its Eastern European satellites to counter the entry of West Germany into the North Atlantic Treaty Organization (NATO). It also allowed the Soviets to have a legitimate military presence in Eastern Europe as well as answered the creation of Western-backed alliances in Southeast Asia and the Middle East.

STATEMENT ON THE FORMATION OF A JOINT COMMAND OF THE ARMED FORCES OF THE WARSAW TREATY STATES

14 May 1955

Under the Treaty of Friendship, Cooperation and Mutual Assistance between the People's Republic of Albania, the People's Republic of Bulgaria, the Hungarian People's Republic, the German Democratic Republic, the Polish People's Republic, the Rumanian People's Republic, the Union of Soviet Socialist Republics and the Czechoslovak Republic, the states that are parties to the treaty have taken the decision to form a joint command of their armed forces.

This decision envisages that general questions pertaining to the strengthening of the defence capacity and to the organization of the joint armed forces of the states that are parties to the treaty will be examined by the Political Consultative Committee, which will take appropriate decisions.

I. S. Koniev, Marshal of the Soviet Union, has been appointed commander-in-chief of the joint armed forces allotted by the states that are signatories to the treaty.

The assistants appointed for the commander-in-chief of the joint armed forces are the Ministers of Defence and other military leaders of the states that are parties to the treaty, who are vested with the command of the armed forces of each state that is a party to the treaty, allotted to the joint armed forces.

The question of participation of the German Democratic Republic in measures pertaining to the armed forces of the joint command will be examined later.

A staff of the joint armed forces of the states that are parties to the treaty will be set up under the commander-in-chief of the joint armed forces and this staff will include permanent representatives of the general staffs of the states that are parties to the treaty.

The headquarters of the staff will be in Moscow.

Distribution of the joint armed forces on the territories of states that are parties to the treaty will be carried out in accordance with the requirements of mutual defence, in agreement among these states.

Source: Lawrence Freedman, ed., Europe Transformed: Documents on the End of the Cold War (New York: St. Martin's Press, 1990), p. 47.

---

of Berlin represented an obstacle the true scale of which the allies of NATO did not fully comprehend in the same way that the Russians apparently did.

The Soviets also recognized the relative weakness of the Warsaw Pact in a conventional supporting role, as well as its susceptibility to United States– and NATO–led "unconventional" rear-area warfare along lines from the U.S.S.R. to the inter-German border, let alone in newly captured territory. The military leadership of the Soviet Union was generally inclined to distrust even their own allies in most cases, and in Poland this misgiving was largely justified. Many Poles viewed their nation as one that had been conquered and forced into communism. This sentiment, coupled with strong cultural ties to the Catholic Church, meant that

the U.S.S.R. was probably correct in its assessment that Poland was not the steadiest of allies. Events in the 1980s bore this out.

The specific threat to Soviet military lines of communication across Poland came from NATO "unconventional" warfare troops. Although they truly came into their own in Vietnam, the U.S. Special Forces (SF) were originally created with NATO in mind. Popularly known for the headgear, the green beret, the initial SF charter was for rear-area operations in Europe. The SF deliberately recruited East German defectors and Polish expatriates in the 1950s to create a force capable of covert insertion behind Soviet lines in East Germany and Poland. Once inserted, these small twelve-man teams were designed to engage in diverse missions ranging from interdiction (blowing

American and Soviet tanks face off at Checkpoint Charlie in Berlin on 28 October 1961

(AP/Wide World Photos)

up bridges and dams to cut major routes from Russia to Germany) to recruiting Poles into larger guerrilla units. Awareness of this NATO capability and their own weakness in this area gave the Soviets reason to pause.

A window of opportunity opened, in a conventional sense, in the late 1960s and through the mid 1970s. The largest and strongest member of NATO, the United States, stood weakly upon shaky legs after pulling out of Vietnam in 1973. As one celebrated U.S. commander, Lieutenant General Harold Moore, noted, "The whole U.S. Army was just a replacement pool for the forces in Vietnam." After Vietnam the social interaction of the military with the nation-

at-large required abandonment of the draft and adoption of an all-volunteer force. Associated with this policy was a decrease in the size of the army and an increase of many social problems (drugs, alcohol, and a culturally based distrust of authority) that undercut the effectiveness of the U.S. military for ten years (1968–1978).

Two conflicts that took place in the Middle East played a large role in the conventional defense of Western Europe at that point, the Six-Day War (1967) and Yom Kippur War (1973). Nobody could ignore the lessons of these wars. Israel, using NATO-supplied arms, decisively defeated the much larger Soviet-equipped armies of their Arab

MILITARY BALANCE

opponents on both occasions. In 1967 Israel had started with a preemptive air attack and employed an offensive war of maneuver. This engagement alone was an impressive display of tactical and operational prowess, as well as a demonstration of the effectiveness of Western weapons. It was, however, the initial successes of the Egyptians in the 1973 war that gave the most pause.

Egypt had learned from the preceding conflicts that a war of open maneuver against the Israelis could be suicidal for its largely conscript army. Moreover, the drubbing repeatedly handed out by the Israeli Air Force (IAF) suggested that control of the skies was an unobtainable goal unless something changed the equation. That "something" came in the form of air-defense missiles. Egypt purchased heavily in this area. They also developed a limited operational plan that envisioned only a short thrust across the Suez and then holding on in prepared defensive positions with wire-aimed Anti-Tank Guided Missiles (ATGMs) against the inevitable Israeli armored counterattacks. In this phase of the war the Egyptians were hugely successful. The IAF battered itself against Egyptian air defenses, and the initial Israeli armor attacks suffered huge casualties from Soviet-built ATGMs. From this conflict both NATO and the Warsaw Pact arrived at the Clausewitzian conclusion that defense was once again the stronger form of warfare. Thus, while the United States was undergoing a significant "rebuilding" period, technology appeared to pick up the load of deterrence.

In the end it all came down to a time-space analysis by the Soviets. The question they needed to answer in the affirmative was, "Can we reach the Rhine before the United States can bring her full conventional strength to bear?" Several factors contributed to this answer never being given in the positive. Over the course of the standoff in Western Europe several factors rose and fell in importance, but the response was always in the negative.

The first factor was Soviet awareness of the cost of invasion in a heavily populated area such as Western Europe. The 1945 experience brought that lesson home to them. The next element was generally geographic: most rivers in the area of contention run at right angles to the planned Soviet approaches. Blowing up bridges is far easier than crossing them under fire. The Soviets could not ignore that the terrain in their planned areas of offensive would canalize them into smaller and smaller areas. Another element adding to the NATO side of the equation was an acknowledgment that the defensive is a stronger form of warfare. This

becomes especially important when the Soviet strength in armor and aircraft was theoretically neutralized (or at least minimized) with the development of ATGMs and air defense. The Soviets also recognized the weakness (or susceptibility) of some of their allies to unconventional warfare and the potential effects of this vulnerability upon their own rear areas. Finally, and perhaps most tellingly, when the United States placed "pre-positioned" armored equipment (entire divisions) in Europe, the Soviets realized that they could not stop the near instantaneous arrival of U.S. ground reinforcements by air. Prior to the development of long-range commercial and civilian passenger or cargo jets, "pre-positioning" was not practical. Reinforcing units had to come by sea, and therefore they might as well bring their equipment on the same ships. After that point, however, entire divisions could fly in over the course of a few days to "marry up" with equipment already located in Europe. This reduced the time available for the Soviets to achieve their objectives. In the end it was obvious that, independently of the threat of nuclear weapons, NATO fielded an effective conventional deterrent during the forty-five-year standoff of the Cold War.

–ROBERT L. BATEMAN, U.S. MILITARY ACADEMY, WEST POINT

Viewpoint:
No. The threat of nuclear weapons, not conventional forces, ensured the military balance in Europe.

The Cold War in Europe was waged bitterly on a daily basis for nearly fifty years—yet waged to the sound of silence. Not a shot was officially fired. Not a casualty was officially inflicted. Never before in history have two hostile forces with so much destructive power failed to use it. There are multiple reasons for this extraordinary situation.

The West learned soon after the last shot of World War II was fired in 1945 that it faced an aggressive and dangerous enemy in the Soviet Union. In the early years of the Cold War confrontation, conflict was avoided through a combination of diplomacy and bluff. The West was in no condition to fight a full-scale land war so soon. The U.S.S.R. was not either, having suffered much devastation of its prime agricultural land and industrial facilities, as well as huge losses of people, and it faced the postwar need to rebuild its infrastructure while at the same time occupy and consolidate its hold on newly conquered lands of Eastern Europe. Still the Soviets presented a formidable army along and behind what Winston Churchill had recently called the Iron Curtain (1947).

The United States was in a quandary. Rapid demobilization had cut the size of its armed forces to dangerously low levels. Politicians at home called for withdrawal from Europe. The economy was still adjusting from its wartime production, and Ford cars now took precedence over Sherman tanks. Logistically and politically it was impossible to maintain in Europe an effective military counterforce. The only effective means to protect Western Europe was to establish the nuclear umbrella.

Two things happened to change this strategy radically. Russia blockaded Berlin (1948–1949) and exploded an atomic bomb (10 July 1949). The former demonstrated the will of the West to deter aggression; the latter negated the U.S. threat of first use of atomic weapons by creating the certainty of retaliation. The great standoff had begun.

In order to understand how the Western, or after 1949 the North Atlantic Treaty Organization (NATO), allies planned to defend Western Europe, one must comprehend the probable Soviet battle plan. Based upon their World War II field experience, the Soviet army believed in massive armored and mechanized forces supported by huge amounts of artillery. Soviet planners reasoned that if enemy defenses destroyed the first three lines of attack, the fourth and fifth lines would punch through, and reserve forces could quickly exploit the breach. They were willing to sacrifice men and material for speed and mobility. The Soviets calculated that they had nine to twelve days to reach the Atlantic coast and close off its harbors before the United States could respond with an equalizing force.

As surveillance techniques became ever more sophisticated, however, the element of surprise became harder to achieve. Any suspicion of a buildup would heighten readiness and trigger reinforcements. NATO forces could double their number of fighter and tactical aircraft within twenty-four to forty-eight hours. The United States could probably have at least one battle-ready division at sea in the same time frame. Thus the Soviets developed the concept of war from a standing start; in other words, come as you are.

The main difficulty with this strategy is over-reliance on the follow-up forces and their logistic support. As demonstrated in the Persian Gulf War (1991), modern large-scale armored battle is fast, furious, and appallingly destructive, with little opportunity to adapt to circumstances. The winner had better get it right the first time. The first phase of the NATO defense strategy in Europe was similar to its nuclear strategy. Recognizing that it was politically and economically impossible to match the Russians tank for tank, the alliance partners planned to make a Soviet offensive from a standing start so expensive that prudence would dictate careful thought about the wisdom of any such move. The threshold of ignition was raised to a point where no particular incident sparked a military response from either side for the duration of the Cold War in Europe. This situation proved especially valuable during the periods when the attention of the United States was being distracted by conflicts in Korea (1950–1953) and Vietnam (ended 1975).

The United States has, since World War I (1914–1918), preferred expending firepower to committing men, and to that end it has spent countless resources in developing ways and means of creating maximum destruction with the fewest casualties. This policy has led to such marvels as smart bombs, cruise missiles, and laser-sighting systems. The U.S. military went away from establishing a static-defense line to employing mobility in depth to allow its armor to do what it does best—fight on the move.

Weapons systems such as the A-10 tank buster, and later the integration of antitank helicopters such as the Cobra and Apache, went a long way to equalizing the balance of forces. In the Persian Gulf War, for example, helicopters were credited with half the tank kills. NATO air forces always believed, perhaps optimistically, that they could attain battlefield air superiority within three to four days even though they faced better than two-to-one odds. This belief was not merely bravado, but a close calculation of the quality of their aircraft and crew training, as well as the introduction in the 1980s of the Airborne Warning and Control System (AWACS), to which the Soviets had no effective equivalent. AWACS enabled NATO to strategically control the sky above the battlefield.

As new weapons technology and a new generation of conventional weapons began to arrive on line in the 1980s, most notably the M-1A1 heavy tank, and as continual satellite surveillance made it practically impossible for the Soviets to change a battery without it being seen and evaluated in real time in Washington, the defensive strategy evolved once again to one of stopping them in their tracks. This strategy posited that the frontline forces could contain or control the initial attack long enough to gain air superiority, which in turn would allow for the massive destruction of the second and third assault lines caught in a massive traffic jam. The battle against the first-line assault weapons of the Soviet arsenal would be close, with a slight edge to NATO because of superior technology. Against the second-line forces, however, Western aircraft would enjoy a turkey shoot along lines later experienced in the Persian Gulf.

In this mad world, Mutual Assured Destruction (MAD) was the main deterrent to war in Europe. The Cuban Missile Crisis (October 1962) had convinced the Soviets of the will of the Western allies to use atomic weapons if they felt the necessity. To avert the ultimate showdown, however, NATO needed a flexible-response system, and they found it in the axiom: "speak softly and drive a U.S. M-1A1 or a German Bundeswehr Leopard."

-JOHN WHEATLEY,
BROOKLYN CENTER, MINNESOTA

References

Geoffrey Blainey, *The Causes of War* (New York: Free Press, 1973);

Robert A. Doughty, *The Evolution of US Army Tactical Doctrine, 1946–76* (Fort Leavenworth, Kans.: Combat Studies Institute, U.S. Army Command and General Staff College, 1979);

Paul H. Herbert, *Deciding What Has to Be Done: General William E. DePuy and the 1976 Edition of FM 100–5, Operations* (Fort Leavenworth, Kans.: Combat Studies Institute, U.S. Army Command and General Staff College, 1988);

Allan R. Millett and Peter Maslowski, *For the Common Defense: A Military History of the United States of America* (New York: Free Press, 1984; London: Collier-Macmillan, 1984).

MILITARY BALANCE

MONOLITHIC COMMUNISM

Was communism a monolithic movement?

Viewpoint: Yes. Communism was a pervasive threat that was not stopped until the 1990s.

Viewpoint: No. Communism in the twentieth century lacked cohesiveness because Soviet interests frequently differed from those of other communist states.

At the end of World War II, Joseph Stalin's Soviet Union stood as both the first and most-powerful country with a communist government. In addition to being powerful in its own right, the Union of Soviet Socialist Republics (U.S.S.R.) held a preponderance of influence over the rest of the communist world. As the Cold War became the dominant factor in post–World War II international relations, the communist world was widely perceived as a well-coordinated, centrally controlled, monolithic international movement led by Moscow.

This view was challenged by scholars and area specialists, who argued that the national interests of the different communist countries, to say nothing of the traditional suspicion with which some of them viewed the others, would be more powerful than adherence to a common ideology. Indeed, over time, differences among communist states began to develop. Some communist leaders began to feel that the Soviet Union was pursuing policies not designed to bring about the world revolution that Karl Marx and Vladimir Illych Ulianov Lenin had predicted, but was rather interested in pursuing more-traditional Russian policy objectives, albeit with a rhetorical veneer that paid lip service to socialism. The communist governments of Yugoslavia and China, later to be followed by Albania and Romania, maintained relations with Moscow that were openly strained. Additional Soviet policies alienated communist governments and movements in other countries.

Many scholars have reached the conclusion that these developments represented deep and irreparable fissures in what had been thought to be a monolithic communist world. Others, though, argue that apparently unbridgeable ideological differences were merely disputes over tactics and that the ultimate aim of international communism had a coherent and well-defined objective.

Viewpoint:
Yes. Communism was a pervasive threat that was not stopped until the 1990s.

Communism developed from the utopian idealism of the nineteenth century at a time when the rich were obscenely wealthy and the poor were horrendously destitute. Power was for those with wealth, and those without money and land had no real chance of acquiring it. Karl Marx and Friedrich Engels were writing for an appreciative audience, one that had suffered at the hands of capitalism. The working conditions for common laborers was no better than that of slaves; in many cases, they were physically worse off.

As a result, when the idea that workers could (and should) have some political and economic power started to arise, the laboring classes were ecstatic although guarded about their chances of success, while the ruling classes were alarmed. Union busting became a fact of life for many, but it was more because of economics and power than ideology. The atheistic message of communism did not sit well with most Christians, and while in some places communists even developed a pseudo-Christian message, it was still soundly condemned by virtually all Christian denominations. As unions survived attempts, legal and otherwise, to destroy them, their leaders realized that they not only had economic bargaining power with the employers, but they could exploit a similar capability in politics as well. The advent of universal male suffrage in Western countries helped solidify the possibilities.

World War I (1914–1918) was a difficult time for the communists as much of Europe was destroyed and a generation of young men went off to die on the Western Front. Throughout the Allied nations, communists were viewed as traitors if they did not support the war, which most did not. The Central Powers treated communists even more harshly. It is strange, then, that Germany employed a "biological weapon" in the form of Vladimir Illych Ulianov or Nikolai Lenin by sending him back to Russia, sparking the plague of revolution and thereby removing that country from the war.

The one success of the communists in the early part of the last century was the victory over the tsars in 1917. The Russian Revolution and the ensuing civil wars and strife until 1923 kept Russia out of the important development of the Treaty of Versailles (1919) and its clauses, which virtually guaranteed another world war. In fact Russia's situation caused it to lose large amounts of territory even though it actually had been on the winning side.

Germany was destroyed by the war even though little or no fighting actually took place within its borders. Socialists and communists became the targets of roving bands of former soldiers called *Freikorps*. The Weimar Republic turned to these right-wing radical former soldiers to put down rebellions by communists and socialists against its rule in 1919. Hatred of the communists in postwar Germany was popular as many felt that the soldiers on the Western Front had been "stabbed in the back" by the socialists and communists. These sentiments were so prevalent that they, in part along with the horrendous inflation of the 1920s and the later Great Depression, helped elect the Nazis to the Reichstag and specifically helped propel Hitler to the chancellorship in 1933. In addition, Hitler first attacked the communists upon assuming power after the suspicious Reichstag fire.

The Soviet Union, a pariah state in the 1920s and 1930s, was nevertheless seen by many idealists in the West as a workers' paradise. They knew nothing of the strict control of news and information; all they knew was that the workers looked happy and supposedly controlled the government. What greater utopia could be found? The reality that they did not know was that conditions there were horrendous beyond belief.

This type of idealism led otherwise democratic people to support the so-called Republicans in the Spanish Civil War. The Republicans were actually socialists to the point of being communist. The Soviets supported the Republicans, while the Nazis aided and fought alongside their fellow fascist, Francisco Franco. American leftists even fielded the Abraham Lincoln Brigade to fight for the Republicans in Spain. Perhaps if they had known the realities of communist rule, these more moderate leftists might not have been such ardent supporters or might even have stayed out of the war altogether.

These activities were monitored carefully by the governments of the West, especially the anticommunist United States. A decidedly Christian and capitalist nation, most Americans were offended by the atheistic communist message. As communism was viewed as a cancer, which could spread quickly and devastatingly, governments paid close attention.

Still, many people, especially out-of-work and working class, supported the communist cause because of its idealistic promises. There were those who were "card carrying" communists who were either true believers, idealists, or adventurers. A great many more people were

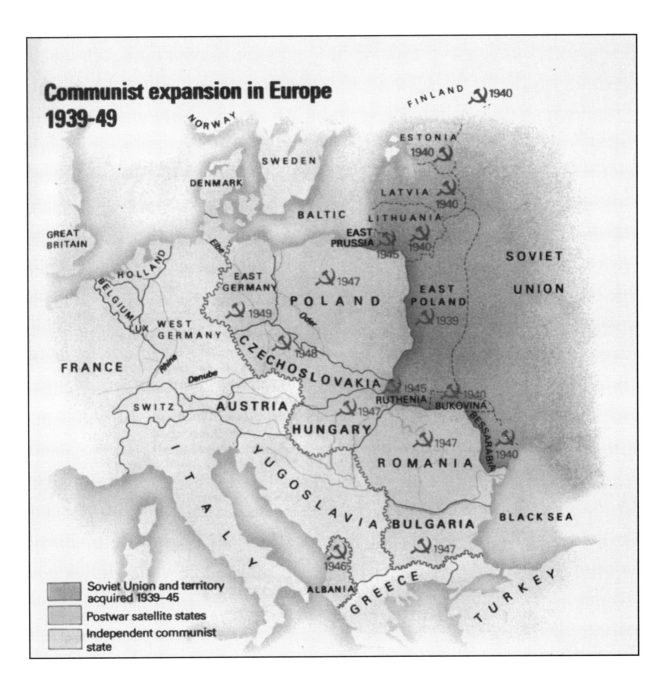

Communist expansion in Europe 1939-49

Soviet Union and territory acquired 1939–45

Postwar satellite states

Independent communist state

A map of Soviet-backed regimes, designated by the sickle and hammer of the U.S.S.R. and the dates of communist takeover

(Robert Thompson, War in Peace, *[1983]), p. 23)*

sympathetic with the stated goals of communism—political and economic equality for all—an attractive message, especially during the privation of the Great Depression.

Many of these communists would be well placed later to cause considerable harm to U.S. national security. For instance, while the United States went to incredible lengths to ensure the absolute secrecy of the Manhattan Project to build the first atomic bomb, it is now known that at least two high-level members of the bomb team were giving secrets to the Soviet Union from 1941 until 1947.

The threat of communism became even more apparent after World War II. With the increasing bellicosity of the Soviets, many nations were beginning to realize that the workers' paradise was a lie. The spread of communism

to the Eastern bloc (1945), the Berlin Blockade and Airlift (1948–1949), the Chinese Revolution (1949), the Soviet detonation of a nuclear device (1949), the Korean War (1950–1953), and the establishment of the Warsaw Pact (1955) all served to make Americans and other Westerners aware of the dangers of communism.

The case of Julius and Ethel Rosenberg deserves special attention. They both were executed in 1953 for giving atomic bomb secrets to the Soviet Union. Supporters asserted their innocence (and still do), but with the fall of the Soviet Union, the *Komitet gosudarstvennoy bezopasnosti* (Committee for State Security, or KGB) agent that worked with them has confirmed that they were guilty. However, one official went on to say that the United States only caught the middlemen, that the true agents

A map of Soviet-backed regimes, designated by the sickle and hammer of the U.S.S.R. and the dates of communist takeover

(Robert Thompson, War in Peace, *[1983]), p. 23)*

MONOLITHIC COMMUNISM

were in the Manhattan Project and that one was still alive in 1998.

The case became a cause célèbre for liberals who wanted to believe that the Rosenbergs were not guilty or that the government went too far. The case remains important because it demonstrates the fear and threat that communism engendered in the United States. The continuing debate confirms the passion of the situation.

These types of problems and fears spurred Joseph R. McCarthy (R-Wisconsin) to use the House Un-American Activities Committee (HUAC) to further his career by hunting down communists in the United States (1950–1954). The problem is that there actually was widespread communist sympathy in the United States even after the Korean War (although by then it had begun to fade). The witch-hunt that McCarthy unleashed not only damaged the lives of innocent people but also probably helped to mask the activities of real communist agents within the American establishment.

What, then, was the exact threat from communism? The stated goal of communism is to free the world from capitalist imperialism and any other form of government by any means necessary. What the communists meant was to conquer the world, and they were perfectly willing to do anything to achieve this goal.

In the 1920s and 1930s the Soviet Union concluded two agreements with its archenemy, Germany. They first assisted the Germans in developing their tanks and combat aircraft inside the Soviet Union—secretly—as Germany was restricted by the Versailles Treaty from possessing these weapons of aggressive war. In 1939 Foreign Minister Joachim von Ribbentropp concluded a nonaggression pact, meaning that the two countries would not go to war with one another. That same year they invaded Poland together, but in 1941 Nazi dictator Adolf Hitler turned on Soviet leader Joseph Stalin and started one of the most brutal and devastating military campaigns in history. Nevertheless, the Soviets came back from the brink of defeat and swallowed up most of eastern Europe. They took the Baltic states of Lithuania, Latvia, and Estonia and, at the end of the war, spread their revolution to Poland, Czechoslovakia, Hungary, Romania, and East Germany. The Soviets supported the Chinese Communists, the North Koreans, and the North Vietnamese.

It was Soviet premier Nikita S. Khrushchev who said in November 1956, "We will bury you!" The Soviets then went on to support wars in Cuba, Malaya, Angola, South Africa, Bolivia, and elsewhere. While there was no world communism and no unified control, there was cooperation.

While many now deny the true threat of communism, the reality is that it was a real and pervasive threat throughout the twentieth century. The Soviets were beaten in a series of bloody and vicious wars culminating with the Cold War. They also destroyed themselves and their country in their attempt at world domination—all in the name of communist revolution.

–WILLIAM H. KAUTT, SAN ANTONIO, TEXAS

Viewpoint:
No. Communism in the twentieth century lacked cohesiveness because Soviet interests frequently differed from those of other communist states.

Seventy-two years after the publication of Karl Marx's *Communist Manifesto* (1848) the Communist International (Comintern) attempted to unite, in purpose and course of action, the communist movements from all over the world. Yet, communism was no more a united front in 1920 than it had been in 1848, to say nothing of 1948. The disunified, often feuding, factions of malcontents striving for a contradictory dictatorship of the proletariat, and a workers' and peasants' paradise, could hardly be called "monolithic."

The Comintern was actually the Third International. In 1864 the International Working Men's Association, or First International, was led by Marx, whose goal was a unifying ideology that would bring organized world revolution. This first group consisted of Bakuninist anarchists, socialist Proudhonists and Blanquistes from France, nonsocialist democrats from Italy, and a variety of other radicals. After a more than ten-year search for cohesiveness, the International died in Philadelphia in July 1876. The Second International, or Socialist International, founded in 1889, was longer lived but no less heterogeneous. This disunity became glaringly obvious by the onset of World War I (1914–1918) as some members chose nationalism over socialism and internationalism, and joined their countrymen in battle. Lenin later led others to form the Third International in 1919 in an effort to rise above the "Great Capitalist War."

This new organization differed from its predecessors. With the undeniable success of the Russian Communist Party in 1917 as the first "national" Communist Party to seize the reins of power at home, the communist movement now had a recognized leader. In 1919 the Comintern was formed by the Soviet Union with the intent of fostering revolution elsewhere. In the invitation to the founding of the new International, as reported by Branko Lazitch and Milorad M. Drachkovitch in *Lenin and the Comintern* (1972), Lenin wrote, "the congress must establish a common fighting organ for the purpose of maintaining permanent coordination and systematic leadership of the movement, a center of the Communist International, subordinating the interests of the movement in each country to the common interest of the international revolution." Lenin stated clearly that this movement was one with a goal. It frequently was the case that the West willingly accepted the communists' own self-description, and the movement was monolithic according to its organizational statement. Perhaps the acceptance of this statement was as close as the movement ever got to solidarity.

During its early years not even the Communist Party of the Soviet Union (CPSU) could be considered monolithic, as there were a variety of ideological and power issues yet unresolved. Lenin's succession was bitterly contested. The Internationalists, led by Leon Trotsky, found themselves battling the adherents of "socialism in one country," led by Joseph Stalin and Mikhail Aleksandrovich Bakunin. Conflicts within the CPSU were frequently mirrored in the Comintern itself. By the 1930s, as the CPSU internal struggle was resolved, it appeared that under Stalin's "guidance" the Comintern had become increasingly homogeneous.

The Comintern existed, so far as Stalin was concerned, to further his own ends and consequently those of the Union of Soviet Socialist Republics (U.S.S.R.). Using his position as a virtual dictator over several political parties outside his own borders, Stalin could play the Comintern card in any high-stakes diplomatic game. Thus, after the Ribbentrop-Molotov Pact, or Nazi-Soviet Non-Aggression Pact (1939), the Comintern was used as a forum to criticize the "underground" activities of the German and Italian communist parties. In an effort to cement the pact, Stalin dropped the German Communists like hot rocks; left to fend for themselves, they quickly evaporated under Gestapo pressure. The Italians (as well as Hungarians, Czechs, Slovaks, Bulgarians, Romanians, and Austrians) did not fare much better. Similarly, communist parties in other states, such as France and Britain, were encouraged to promote German friendship and peace among all nations—effectively joining the profascist parties in their respective countries. This situation changed in June of 1941, however, when Stalin showed his ideological flexibility: the Comintern was used as a tool to whip up support in the Allied countries for the Soviet Union. Suddenly the various communist parties around the world were antifascist, and many leaders of party organizations in occupied Europe returned to join, infiltrate, or even take over and lead resistance movements (as in Yugoslavia). As if this about-face were not enough, in an effort to appease his new allies, Stalin dissolved the Comintern entirely in 1943. No outward support now came from the Soviet Union for these increasingly outspoken, and politically exposed, national communist parties.

With the entry of the Soviet Union into World War II as an Allied power, Stalin totally switched gears on several fronts. His main goal became defeating Germany, and everything that did not contribute to this result took a backseat. He quickly concluded that the assistance of Britain and the United States was essential. Thus, communist revolutionary zeal was downplayed. National communist parties were encouraged and left to fight the enemy any way they could. Suddenly diversity was the order of the day, out of which emerged several powerful communist parties with their own leadership structures and regional power bases. The postwar period is a history of increasingly ineffectual attempts to reverse these trends and complete the unification of purpose and action that had seemed within reach before the war.

When only the CPSU had achieved political power, world communist interest was equal to the national interest of the U.S.S.R. It was easier to convince the international communist movement that the continued existence and success of the Soviet Union, as the only socialist state, was paramount. After the war, however, when the number of ruling communist parties increased, conflicts arose as each of these parties, fighting to maintain power, began to look to their own national interest. Political success carries with it that which is incomprehensible without (or before) it: "you can't go home again." Suddenly, the goal changes: power must be maintained, not merely achieved. The precedence of this new goal requires different behavior. The communist world discovered that conflicts between states were not limited to the capitalist world.

The Communist Information Bureau (Cominform), created in 1947, served from the beginning as a window displaying the disunity of world communism. One of its earliest sessions was used to criticize and berate French and Italian communist parties for cooperating with other local political parties. During the war the communist parties had been instructed by Moscow to cooperate with local nationalists in the Resistance. Now, however, diversity was no longer tolerated. This attack was instigated by Stalin and carried out by the Yugoslav Communist Party (CPY). Ironically, the Yugoslavs found themselves next on the list.

MONOLITHIC COMMUNISM

THE CHINESE CRITICIZE THE SOVIETS

Not all ran smoothly within the communist camp. There were frequent squabbles among these nations, particularly between China and the U.S.S.R. In 1964 the Chinese Communist Party condemned their counterpart in the Soviet Union:

The events of the recent years show that the leaders of the C.P.S.U. headed by Khrushchev have become the chief representatives of modern revisionism as well as the greatest splitters in the international Communist movement.

Between the 20th and 22nd congresses of the C.P.S.U., the leaders of the C.P.S.U. developed a rounded system of revisionism. They put forward a revisionist line which contravenes the proletarian revolution and the dictatorship of the proletariat, a line which consists of "peaceful coexistence," "peaceful competition," "peaceful transition," "a state of the whole people," and "a party of the entire people."

They have tried to impose this revisionist line on all fraternal parties as a substitute for the common line of the international Communist movement which was laid down at the meetings of fraternal parties in 1957 and 1960. And they have attacked anyone who perseveres in the Marxist-Leninist line and resists their revisionist line.

The leaders of the C.P.S.U. have themselves undermined the basis of the unity of the international Communist movement and created the present grave danger of a split by betraying Marxist-Leninism and proletarian internationalism and pushing their revisionist and divisive line.

Far from working to consolidate and expand the Socialist camp, the leaders of the C.P.S.U. have endeavored to split and disintegrate it. They have thus made a mess of the splendid Socialist camp.

They have violated the principles guiding relations among fraternal countries as laid down in the declaration and the statement, pursuing a policy of great-power chauvinism and national egoism toward fraternal Socialist countries, and thus disrupted the unity of the Socialist camp.

They have arbitrarily infringed the sovereignty of fraternal countries, interfered in their internal affairs, carried on subversive activities and striven in every way to control fraternal countries.

In the name of the "international division of labor," the leaders of the C.P.S.U. oppose the adoption by fraternal countries of the policy of building socialism by their own efforts and developing their economies on an independent basis, and attempt to turn them into economic appendages. They have tried to force those fraternal countries which are comparatively backward economically to abandon industrialization and become their sources of raw materials and markets for surplus products.

The leaders of the C.P.S.U. have openly called for the overthrow of the party and Government leaders of Albania, brashly severed all economic and diplomatic relations with her and tyrannically deprived her legitimate rights as a member of the Warsaw treaty Organization and the Council of Mutual Economic Assistance.

The leaders of the C.P.S.U. have violated the Chinese-Soviet treaty of friendship, alliance and mutual assistance, made a unilateral decision to withdraw 1,390 Soviet experts working in China, to tear up 343 contracts and supplementary contracts on the employment of experts and to cancel 257 projects of scientific and technical cooperation, and pursued a restrictive and discriminatory trade policy against China. They have provoked incidents on the Chinese-Soviet border and carried out large-scale subversive activities in Sinkiang.

On more than one occasion, Khrushchev has gone so far as to tell leading comrades of the Central Committee of the C.P.C. [Communist Party of China] that certain anti-party elements in the Chinese Communist party were his "good friends." He has praised Chinese anti-party elements for attacking the Chinese party's general line for Socialist construction, the big leap forward and the people's communes, describing their action as a "manly act."

Source: Current History, *47 (September 1964): 173–176.*

The first indication that the West had that something was awry in the communist world occurred on 28 June 1948. The CPY received and ignored a summons to a meeting of the Cominform; when its delegates did not appear, they were expelled, and the break with Moscow became public. Stalin denounced the Yugoslavs, accused them of ideological mistakes, and castigated them for not appearing before the Cominform to accept the criticism of their fellow socialist nations. Over the next year the public debate raged back and forth and eventually led to a permanent split. Yugoslavia never again was part of the communist "family." The results of this schism were manifold. There was a crackdown throughout Eastern Europe in an effort to enforce uniformity of thought and action. Stalin feared that Yugoslavia would serve as an example, leading other communist parties to stray. In order to defend itself as a "true" Marxist-Leninist country, Yugoslavia was forced to develop its own brand of socialism. In the international arena, with the founding of the Non-Aligned Movement, Yugoslavia provided an alternative to those who wanted to distance themselves from Moscow and still avoid the capitalist world.

Stalin died in 1953, and the Soviet Union once again faced a succession crisis. In 1956 the new First Secretary, Nikita S. Khrushchev, delivered his "Secret Speech" to the Twentieth Party Congress and with it ended the possibility of a monolithic communist movement. The admission that Stalin had committed "excesses" and "perversions of Party principles" accompanied by Khrushchev's changes in both foreign and domestic policy, caused an uproar in the communist world. Polish communists began their own "national road to socialism," followed by a similar upsurge of popular resentment against Soviet domination in Hungary. Though both movements were suppressed, the former by a domestic reaction and the latter by Soviet tanks, neither country ever became a carbon copy of the Soviet Union. Poland never fully collectivized, and Hungary maintained enough liberal economic reforms of 1956 to carry into the postcommunist world forty years later a stronger economy than its Eastern-bloc compatriots. Diversity had returned to communist Europe, but there were limits to what kinds and levels Moscow would accept.

As Yugoslavia had once attempted to emulate the Soviet Union and had fallen in love with all things Russian, so too, by the 1950s, had China; Russian had even become their official second language. The relationship between the Soviet Union and the Chinese Communist Party (CCP) began at the party's inception. The evolution of the CCP followed a pattern that was similar to many other communist parties. To achieve

power there were several years of cooperation with nationalists of some stripe; then, during the period of consolidation and centralization of power there was war with the nationalists; finally, after the party gained power for itself, competition escalated between party members with different regional intranational support centers. At this last stage, relations with outside communist forces became important—they may even have been the deciding factor determining who will lead the party. Because of the close ties between the CPSU and CCP, the internal struggles both of the Soviet Union and China frequently became interrelated. There were many shifts in alliances between the CPSU and CCP that were sometimes a result of domestic power struggles and practical considerations, and other times the result of ideological concerns. The career of Mao Tse-tung, with its myriad successes and reversals, is a prime example.

When Stalin died, the Chinese backed Georgey Maksimilianovich Malenkov as his successor, believing he would continue Stalin's policies. In only a matter of months, however, they shifted their support to Khrushchev for the same reason. Imagine their surprise three years later when Khrushchev denounced Stalin. The two countries began to drift apart; there was even, according to Richard C. Thornton in *China, a Political History, 1917–1980* (1982) a "gradual phasing out of Soviet military aid and training programs." In an attempt to break free of Soviet control and establish an independent Chinese economy, the Great Leap Forward (1958–1960) was formulated. When Khrushchev began to criticize this movement, the relationship unraveled quickly. Mao's plans to bombard Quemoy, an island in the Formosa Strait garrisoned by Nationalist Chinese troops, further upset the relationship with Moscow: Mao considered this matter a domestic one, and it seems to have escaped him that this move was likely to worsen relations with both the U.S.S.R. and the United States—neither of which saw it as a purely "domestic" issue. Eventually the split grew public and deteriorated to ideological name-calling, not unlike the recriminations that had flown back and forth between the CPY and CPSU in 1948. Each side saw the other as a traitor to the ideals of Marxism-Leninism.

An "independent" China gave world communists one more example to follow. In 1961 Albania shifted its allegiance from the Soviet Union to China. Described by J. F. Brown in *Eastern Europe and Communist Rule* (1988) as the "last Stalinist paranoid," Albanian dictator Enver Hoxha followed a nationalist policy that maintained the independence of his country through alliances with whomever would safeguard Albania against any current threat. In the mid 1940s the perceived threat was from Greece, and the support came from Josip Broz Tito's communist Yugoslavia; when Tito became the threat, the Soviets appeared to be the natural ally; after the 1956 Soviet invasion of Hungary, and subsequent de-Stalinization process, it was time once again time to find a new supporter. A distant China seemed to be the perfect candidate. This approach can be seen as formal recognition that the U.S.S.R. was no longer the accepted leader of the communist movement, even by its protégés.

From this time forward there was increasing distance between the CPSU and many other communist parties. Though some remain loyal, such as those in Cuba and East Germany, the invasion of Czechoslovakia in 1968 was, for most, the last straw. In general, throughout Western Europe what survived of the movement fragmented after Stalin and Khrushchev's 20th Party Congress speech. Walter Laqueur noted in *Europe in Our Time: A History, 1945–1992* (1992) that "Gradually West European communism began to show 'revisionist' symptoms; the gulf between revolutionary theory and reformist practice grew steadily wider." New, noncommunist, leftist political parties appeared, and alternatives to Soviet communism proliferated.

From the creation of the Soviet Union, the international communist movement was ruled by Soviet interests: first, as the only existing socialist state, and later as the bulwark against capitalist imperialism of the West. At its most "monolithic," world communism reflected more of Stalin's personality than of any inherent cohesiveness. At first it was "obvious" that Soviet national interest was virtually synonymous with the interests of all communist parties. The U.S.S.R. never ceased following its own national interest; its client states gradually began to do the same. The less dependent national communist parties became, the less frequently their interests coincided with those of the CPSU. According to Laqueur, even with nonruling communist parties, where "Pro-Soviet enthusiasm . . . usually grew with distance," there came an eventual realization, not unlike that arrived at by members of the Second International, that national concerns made a uniformity of ideology and action impossible and even undesirable. A united communist front has been as ephemeral and unattainable as communism itself.

–JULIJANA BUDJEVAC, GEORGE WASHINGTON UNIVERSITY

References

C. E. Black and E. C. Helmreich, *Twentieth Century Europe; A History,* fourth edition (New York: Knopf, 1972);

J. F. Brown, *Eastern Europe and Communist Rule* (Durham, N.C.: Duke University Press, 1988);

Zbigniew K. Brzezinski, *The Soviet Bloc, Unity and Conflict* (Cambridge, Mass.: Harvard University Press, 1967);

John King Fairbank, *The Great Chinese Revolution, 1800–1985* (New York: Harper & Row, 1986);

François Furet, *The Passing of an Illusion: The Idea of Communism in the Twentieth Century,* translated by Deborah Furet (Chicago: University of Chicago Press, 1999);

Charles Gati, *The Bloc that Failed: Soviet-East European Relations in Transition* (Bloomington: Indiana University Press, 1990);

Barbara Jelavich, *History of the Balkans* (Cambridge & New York: Cambridge University Press, 1983);

Walter Laqueur, *Europe in Our Time: A History, 1945–1992* (New York: Viking, 1992);

Branko Lazitch and Milorad M. Drachkovitch, *Lenin and the Comintern,* volume 1 (Stanford, Cal.: Hoover Institution Press, Stanford University, 1972);

Joseph Rothschild, *Return to Diversity: A Political History of East Central Europe Since World War II* (New York: Oxford University Press, 1989);

Sarah Meiklejohn Terry, ed., *Soviet Policy in Eastern Europe* (New Haven: Yale University Press, 1984);

Richard C. Thornton, *China, a Political History, 1917–1980* (Boulder, Colo.: Westview Press, 1982).

MONOLITHIC COMMUNISM

NATIONAL LIBERATION

Did national liberation movements of the Third World aid either of the superpowers during the Cold War?

Viewpoint: Yes. National liberation movements, even if they were not instigated by the Soviets, allowed the U.S.S.R. to challenge American interests throughout the world.

Viewpoint: No. The national liberation movements proved to be of little value to the superpowers. They were expensive drains on the U.S. and Soviet treasuries, and their leaders pursued independent action when it suited them.

World War II seriously weakened the colonial powers, three of which—Belgium, the Netherlands, and France—had been defeated and occupied by German arms. Britain, although it was on the winning side in the conflict, faced serious questions about its ability to maintain its empire. At the same time the United States, now the preeminent Western power, was systematically pressuring its allies to abandon their colonial legacies. In addition to American pressure, popular movements within European colonies were advocating independence. Having contributed to the war efforts of their ruling powers and seeing their relative weakness, their position in 1945 was strong, but in many cases the European colonial powers were unwilling to let go. Over time, these liberation movements also began to work against national governments that were strongly aligned with the United States and which refused to undertake social and political reform. The Third World emerged as one of the leading battlegrounds in the postwar world.

Like all other Cold War conflicts, wars of national liberation were dramatically influenced by the global competition of the United States and Soviet Union. A source of debate in Cold War studies is to what extent superpower conflict created the animus for these conflicts. Many scholars argue that national liberation movements existed independent of any geopolitical aspiration on the part of the superpowers and were relatively untouched by their competition. In other words, they believe that leaders of such movements were driven purely by a desire to be free of foreign control and to implement reform. Other scholars believe that the amount of support the movements received from the Soviet Union caused them to become functions of precisely that global conflict, and that their causes usually became mere vehicles for Soviet geopolitical aggrandizement in the Third World.

**Viewpoint:
Yes. National liberation
movements, even if they were not
instigated by the Soviets, allowed
the U.S.S.R. to challenge American
interests throughout the world.**

Recent revelations found in documents from archives of former Soviet-bloc nations show that the relationship between the Soviet Union and its satellites and allies were far more complicated than the term "communist monolith" suggests. National liberation movements had their own motivations and internal dynamics, which did not always fit neatly with Soviet plans. Despite these complications, however, the Soviets recognized that they could profit greatly from the triumph of these movements, even where leaders were not selected or installed by the Soviet Union. Connection to these movements gave the Union of Soviet Social Republics (U.S.S.R.) opportunities to challenge Western interests, threaten Western access to vital natural resources, complicate planning by Western nations in the event of any international crisis, and contribute to the perception that Western democracy was headed for the scrap heap, as well as suggesting that nations and political movements wishing to be at the forefront of international politics in the future would do best to align with Soviets and their friends.

Scholars have debated the precise importance of Nikita S. Khrushchev's January 1961 speech in which he pledged Soviet support for wars of national liberation. Soviet assistance grew slowly at first, but by the mid 1970s pro-Soviet Marxists scored gains that cast doubt about the ability of Western democracies to meet the Marxist-Leninist challenge. In 1976 Soviet leader Leonid Brezhnev boasted that "the general crisis of capitalism is continuing to deepen" and "no impartial person can deny that the socialist countries' influence in world affairs is becoming stronger and deeper." The new Soviet Constitution of 1977 specified among the aims of Soviet foreign policy, "strengthening the positions of world socialism, supporting the people's struggle for national liberation and social progress." One index of this activity was the increase in military advisers sent from the Soviet Union and Warsaw Pact nations to Third World countries. From fewer than four thousand in 1965, the number escalated to between eight thousand and ten thousand from 1970 to 1975, to almost sixteen thousand by 1979. This number did not include Cuban military forces, of whom there were up to sixty

thousand in Angola after 1975 and another twelve to fifteen thousand sent to Ethiopia in late 1977 and early 1978. During the détente era in the mid 1970s, many Americans expected a reduction of international tension, including the exercise of restraint by the two superpowers. In 1976, however, Brezhnev explained to the Twenty-Fifth Party Congress that "We make no secret of the fact that we see détente as the way to create more favorable conditions for peaceful socialist and communist construction." Any observer in the mid to late 1970s could see that conditions were becoming more favorable to "communist construction" and to the Soviet Union, in large part because of their support for national liberation movements and the impact this policy had in the West.

Between 1945 and 1975, many newly independent nations emerged from the former colonies of the European imperial powers. As these new nations set about organizing their political affairs, both superpowers hoped to find new friends. While the United States had certain advantages in this quest, historical fact and ideological opportunities combined to make the Soviets seem a particularly inviting sponsor for rising elites in the new nations. The Soviet Union, even its tsarist predecessor, lacked the Western European history of colonialism in Africa and Asia; they also were free of the U.S. connections with Britain, France, Belgium, and the Netherlands, which were the greatest of the imperial powers. Perhaps more importantly, the Soviet Union offered an appealing explanation of imperialism as the last stage of capitalism and presented Soviet communism as the vanguard of the revolutionary movement that would ride the forces of history to triumph over Western imperialism and capitalism. In particular, as communist regimes friendly to the Soviet Union came to power in an increasing number of Third World nations, they carried with them a momentum that seemed to suggest that the Soviet Union was the wave of the future.

In the early 1960s, two apparent opportunities presented themselves to the Soviet Union. One was Vietnam, where communists were attempting to unify their country, which had been divided in 1954; the other was the Congo. The Soviets met with little success in the latter and did not support further African adventures until the effects of the Vietnam War were being felt in the United States and around the world. Soviet support, however, was crucial to the North Vietnamese; without Soviet matériel, especially sophisticated anti-aircraft weaponry, the insurgents would have had a much more difficult time involving so many American troops at such high cost in a misadventure that accomplished little that the U.S. leadership sought.

The Vietnam War hobbled the Americans in several ways. It stripped the U.S. force structure in Europe, weakening the deterrent value of forces there and raising doubts about American reliability. U.S. spending on Vietnam instead of on strategic weapons permitted the Soviets to attain nuclear parity with the United States and opened possibilities to attain superiority in the 1970s. President Lyndon B. Johnson's efforts to finance the war without adequate funding, in hopes of maintaining public support for both the conflict and his Great Society social programs, undermined the American-dominated Bretton Woods financial system that had been the linchpin in Western economic arrangements since the end of World War II and assured American global economic predominance. At comparatively low cost to themselves, the Soviets were able to greatly obstruct the United States, in the process assisting the successful reunification of Vietnam under a pro-Soviet communist government that later extended to dominate Laos and Cambodia.

Perhaps even more importantly, the fear of future "Vietnams" and the general weakening of resolve among the American public paved the way for the Soviets to act without meaningful competition from pro-American forces in several nations in the late 1970s. This activity contributed to the ascension to power of as many as eleven pro-Soviet governments. By the end of the decade, Soviet-friendly "liberators" had taken charge of such countries as Angola, Ethiopia, South Yemen, Afghanistan, and Nicaragua. Angola, Afghanistan, and Nicaragua are particularly instructive in illustrating how the Soviets could capitalize upon and profit from situations that they did not create.

A driving force behind Soviet involvement in Angola was Fidel Castro and the Cubans, who saw an opportunity in that former Portuguese colony to burnish their credentials as leaders of revolutionary socialism by sending forces to assist the Popular Movement for the Liberation of Angola (MPLA, the acronym for *Movimento Popular para a Libertação de Angola*) in its civil war. American restraint, rather than leading to reciprocity by the Soviets, led only to an increase in Soviet and Cuban activity on behalf of the MPLA. After the Tunney Amendment prohibited U.S. funds in fiscal 1976 from being sent to Angola, the Cuban presence increased from four thousand to around twelve thousand troops. The Clark Amendment, indefinitely extending the Tunney prohibition, did nothing to weaken Cuban or Soviet interest in aiding the MPLA, which established control of

Vietnamese civilians cheering a convoy of Vietminh soldiers in October 1954

the country and proclaimed the People's Republic of Angola (1975). With Cuban and Soviet support and American indifference, Angola had gone communist. International observers looking at Indochina and Angola in 1975–1976 noted that American friends were losing, while Soviet allies were winning.

Afghanistan, historically a neutral nation serving as a buffer between competing powers, was reduced to communist domination in an April 1978 coup. While the Soviet invasion in December 1979 garnered more attention and headlines, the earlier coup moved Afghanistan from neutrality into the Soviet sphere where it was poised to threaten not only a Pakistani government friendly to the U.S. and China, but also Iran. In 1978 Iran still looked like a reliably pro-American nation, although the Soviets gained from a pro-Soviet presence on Iran's border, whether it was firmly in the U.S. camp or racked by later revolutionary instability.

In Nicaragua a group of Cuban-trained revolutionaries successfully established themselves at the head of what was designed to be a Marxist-controlled movement with close ties to Cuba and the Soviet Union but with sufficient moderate participation to disarm potential critics. The Sandinista strategy was helped inadvertently by the United States. The Americans actively intervened to cut off the supply of arms to Somoza from all sources, leaving him isolated, desperate, and increasingly brutal in his backlash against the guerrillas who were receiving steady inflows of supplies. This backlash polarized the country and was helped further by the failure of a U.S.-sponsored mediation effort that had encouraged moderate opponents of Somoza to reveal their opposition. Exposed as critics of Somoza, they had little choice but to cut the best possible deal with the Sandinistas and join the anti-Somoza movement. This situation permitted the Sandinistas to pose as leaders of a broad-based coalition even while they planned to dominate the resulting government. With the collapse of the Somoza government the Sandinistas took power in July 1979, quickly moving to establish control of the country down to the neighborhood and city-block level. Within a year they restructured the government to ensure permanent Sandinista control of Nicaragua. Despite their claims of moderation, the Sandinistas made clear that they intended to establish a Castro-like dictatorship—and to assist Marxist guerrillas in neighboring countries in doing likewise.

The success of these revolutionary movements threatened important lines of communication and access to natural resources for the United States and its allies. Vietnam was important for its rubber and tin. The naval base at Cam Ranh Bay permitted the projection of Soviet naval power into the South China Sea toward the Philippines and Taiwan. Ethiopia and South Yemen made possible a Soviet presence close to the Suez Canal, a vital shipping lane for the Middle Eastern petroleum that was essential to the Western industrial economies. Angola gave the Soviets and Cubans a position of power in close proximity to the abundant resources of Zaire (formerly the Congo) and also permitted projection of Soviet naval power into vital sea lanes. Nicaragua gave the Soviets an opportunity to reconnoiter the Pacific Coast of the United States and ensured the complication of U.S. military planning for any crisis, even one outside of the hemisphere. Efforts by like-minded Marxists, with Cuban, Soviet, and Sandinista support, to re-create the Nicaragua model in Guatemala, El Salvador, and even Colombia, threatened instability near the petroleum-rich nations of Mexico and Venezuela, to say nothing of the Panama Canal.

In addition to their capacity to threaten natural resources vital to the economies and defense efforts of the United States, Western Europe, and Japan, these revolutionary movements had considerable impact on perceptions of the international situation. One "Somali official" told an American journalist that "We have learned that there is only one superpower." Jose Lopez Portillo, president of Mexico from 1976 to 1982, reportedly believed the United States ultimately could not win the Cold War.

Former National Security Council staffer Peter W. Rodman correctly pointed out in *More Precious Than Peace: The Cold War and the Struggle for the Third World* (1994) that the pro-Soviet regimes coming to power in Africa, Asia, the Middle East, and Latin America "were not only accomplished facts; they and their Soviet patrons could honestly imagine them to be the wave of the future. Their internal opponents were demoralized and in disarray, seemingly abandoned by the West."

This seeming abandonment by the West was reversed, with particular fanfare when, during the years of the Reagan Doctrine, the United States sought to assist armed challengers to many of these newly communist states. That, however, does not alter the fact that during the 1960s and 1970s the Soviet Union made strong gains and contributed to the weakening of the United States economically, strategically, and militarily by supporting wars of national liberation in emerging nations. The Soviet Union did not create the sources of discontent to which the pro-Marxist "liberation" movements appealed, but it profited from them just the same.

–JOHN A. SOARES JR.,
GEORGE WASHINGTON UNIVERSITY

Viewpoint:
No. The national liberation movements proved to be of little value to the superpowers. They were expensive drains on the U.S. and Soviet treasuries, and their leaders pursued independent action when it suited them.

Myths die hard. One such myth is that the various national liberation movements that fought for the independence of their countries from colonial rule were helpful to the Soviet Union and injurious to U.S. interests. Such a view, especially in retrospect, does not have much to support it.

There are two things over which there is no debate. The first is that Soviet premier Nikita S. Khrushchev, in a secret speech in January 1961, outlined an ambitious plan to shift the battle against the capitalist world from the developed, industrial nations of the West to the poor, emerging countries of the Third World. On its face this shift in Soviet strategy made sense, for four reasons. First, capitalism had proven much more resilient

ASIAN INDEPENDENCE

On 23 March to 2 April 1947, delegates from twenty-nine countries met at a conference in New Delhi, from which a declaration on national independence movements was issued. Extracts from that document are presented here.

The liberation movements in Asia have been motivated by the human desire to be free, as well as by the example of revolutionary developments in neighboring regions and in other parts of the world. An Indonesian delegate pointed out that the independence movement in his country was set in motion by the Russian and Chinese revolutions—as well as by Japan's victory over Russia.

The events of the Second World War drew further attention to liberation movements in Asia. The slogan "Asia for the Asians," launched by Japan for its own ends, gave an increased impetus to the liberation movements in the countries of South-East Asia.

There is in the countries of Asia an intense general need to put an end to foreign domination. It is recognised that for many reasons the colonial powers, and particularly Great Britain, are no longer in a position to hold the countries of Asia in political subjugation. Such a question may therefore find a rapid solution with the transfer of political power.

There was a recognition and a deep concern that Asia as a whole should adopt the view that imperialism must not continue to dominate any region of Asia for any given period of time. . . .

The Burmese, Indonesian and Malay delegates requested that no Asian country should agree to give direct and indirect assistance to the colonial powers in their attempts to keep Asian countries in subjection. Particular reference was made to the necessity for every Asian country to refuse transport facilities, the use of airports or any other provision of military support to the colonial powers for the purpose of the domination of other Asian countries. . . .

After a brief preliminary discussion on the concepts of "race" and "racial discrimination," the Chairman stated the principles which ought to govern relations between racial groups in Asia.

Complete equal rights for all citizens.

Complete religious freedom for all citizens.

No exclusivity of a social nature or in the public sector to the detriment of any racial group.

Equality under Law for any person of foreign origin who is resident in the country. . . .

Source: *Phillippe Braillard and Mohammad-Reza Djalili,* Tiers Monde et relations internationales, *translated as* The Third World and International Relations *(London: Pinter, 1986; Boulder, Colo.: Lynne Rienner, 1986), pp. 24–25.*

---

than communist theoreticians had believed. Karl Marx had proclaimed that capitalism carried within it the seed of its own destruction, but there was no evidence for that in the late 1950s. Marx was led to believe that capitalism was doomed because he assumed that the twin processes of the accumulation of capital in the hands of the few and the evisceration of the exploited masses would continue unabated, until a breaking point was reached. Western societies were smarter than that. Beginning in the 1920s, different governments enacted various social welfare laws that ameliorated the harsher aspects of the free market. Social democratic governments in Europe and Canada, and the Democrats in the United States, introduced measures such as social security, unemployment benefits, government jobs, greater access to health and education, and more. These measures blunted whatever revolutionary fervor there was, making a democratic transition in the West to communism more and more remote.

Second, the leaders of the capitalist world—the United States and Britain, soon to be joined by France—possessed nuclear weapons. Any direct assault by the Soviet Union on Western Europe in order to hasten the spread of communism would have resulted in the destruction of the Union of Soviet Socialist Republics (U.S.S.R.) itself. Third, the emerging countries in Africa, Asia, and Latin America, mired in poverty and misery, offered more opportunities for a revolutionary socialist message. What was more, many leaders of the national liberation movements, who led the anticolonial fight, were themselves socialists, genuinely believing that the socialist model of a centrally planned economy was more suitable to their conditions than the

NATIONAL LIBERATION

free-market model the United States was pushing. Fourth, the major colonial powers—Britain, France, Belgium, the Netherlands, and, to a lesser extent, Spain and Portugal—were part of the Western, anti-Soviet camp. There was a natural animosity among the liberation fighters toward these Western countries, and the Soviet Union had every reason to believe that it could exploit this hostility toward the West for the benefit of the Soviet Union.

It was because of this line of thinking that President John F. Kennedy, who learned of Khrushchev's speech from the Central Intelligence Agency (CIA), whose agents were able to get the text, attached great importance to it. So much so, in fact, that he ordered Khrushchev's speech copied and disseminated within the administration.

Were Kennedy administration fears about Soviet aid to national liberation movements well founded? Should the United States have worried about greater Soviet influence in the emerging countries of the Third World? Was there anything meaningful the United States could have done about it?

The liberation of African and Asian countries from colonial rule was inevitable. No one could have expected the native populations in Kenya, Mozambique, and Algeria—or India, Laos, and Cambodia—to agree to remain forever under European rule. The United States, itself the result of a rebellion against colonialism, had always understood that, and was uncomfortable with the imperial possessions even of close allies. American support for the self-determination of peoples had been so pronounced that it played a major role in President Woodrow Wilson's plan for peace in post–World War II Europe. As World War II came to a close, at least some U.S. policies in the Pacific theater were aimed to make it more difficult for Britain to add colonial possessions to its empire. In the late 1940s the United States refused to help the French in their effort to keep Indochina; when Britain and France, in collaboration with Israel, launched the Suez campaign in 1956, the United States vigorously objected, seeing in the action a last-ditch effort by decaying colonial powers to reassert themselves; also in the late 1950s the United States increased its pressure on France to find a negotiated settlement to the war in Algeria.

Supporting the colonial powers against the forces of national liberation was thus not an option for the United States. It would not have made sense politically and was against American principles. Actively assisting such movements was not an option either. It would have pitted the United States against important Western European allies. The last thing in U.S. interests was to increase the battle effectiveness of national liberation movements, thus causing even more British, French, Belgian, and Dutch soldiers to be sent to the colonies, making their countries even less capable of contributing manpower and means to the North Atlantic Treaty Organization (NATO) as it was building the structures to defend Western Europe against Soviet encroachment.

The main options—actively supporting the colonial powers against liberation movements or supporting the liberation movements against the European colonial powers—were thus largely foreclosed to the United States. In several places it pressured the colonial powers to negotiate (for example, in addition to Algeria, in Palestine). In most other places it stayed aloof from the battle.

The Third World, where national liberation movements were most active during the 1950s and early 1960s, was not that important to U.S. interests. Countries that were of interest to the United States—for example, the oil-producing monarchies of the Middle East, or archipelago nations of Indonesia and the Philippines—had either gained independence earlier in the century or faced problems other than national liberation. Most other Third World nations were poor, had no natural resources, and were located in places distant from important sea lanes or industrial centers. It thus did not make much difference, as far as U.S. interests were concerned, who ruled many of these countries.

Those Third World countries that became "clients" of the United States proved to be a drain, requiring massive economic aid (much of which never reached the citizenry but ended up in the Swiss bank accounts of the rulers), political support, and military assistance. The same was true for those countries in the Third World in which pro-Soviet movements came to power, often with the assistance of the Soviet Union: these nations became a burden on the Soviet treasury. Indeed, among the first initiatives of reformist premier Mikhail Gorbachev, after coming to power in 1985, was to cut off the massive Soviet subsidies to a host of Third World countries—among them Cuba, Angola, Ethiopia, and Afghanistan—in which the Soviets had helped bring to power leftist movements. A sober analysis of Soviet interests taught Gorbachev what the United States should have realized at the outset—that most Third World countries were liabilities, not assets.

The most important argument against worrying too much about whether or not national liberation movements were aided by Moscow was raised by George F. Kennan when he argued that the United States should be less concerned with ideology and more willing to cooperate with left-leaning regimes. He made this argument in the late 1940s, when people saw the

NATIONAL LIBERATION

communist bloc as monolithic and directed from Moscow. Kennan contended that leaders of independence movements, even if they shared an ideological affinity with the communist regime in Moscow, would be more powerfully motivated by their own national interests to break away from Moscow when it suited them. He used this argument to push for the containment of the Soviet Union: if Soviet-bloc countries were contained long enough, the natural differences among them—differences that communism could not paper over—would in time cause the bloc to disintegrate.

The same logic applied to whatever gains the Soviet Union made in the Third World national liberation movements. There was no reason to believe that the leaders of the newly independent countries of Africa and Asia—individuals who led long, hard, and costly battles to achieve precious national independence—would consent to replace one colonial power (say, Britain or France) with another (the Soviet Union). It was more realistic to anticipate that they would shrewdly exploit the Soviet Union for aid and support as long as it suited their national needs, or, as occurred more often, would cleverly play West and East against each other to gain maximum support from both sides.

In sum, national liberation movements spearheaded the inevitable and entirely understandable battle against colonialism and for self-determination. The Soviet Union extended support to some of these movements because it saw it as a way to weaken Britain and France, and because some of these movements were led by Left-leaning leaders. The United States was too concerned about this aspect of the anticolonialist struggle, fearful that the U.S.S.R. would materially gain in the Cold War competition if leftist, pro-Soviet movements came to power in Third World countries. Most of these nations were of no strategic or economic value to the United States; most were so poor that they were a net drain rather than a net gain to whichever superpower won their allegiance. As was proven in the cases of other left-leaning regimes, communists were nationalists first and were more likely to pursue their own national interests than slavishly follow Moscow.

—BENJAMIN FRANKEL,
SECURITY STUDIES

References

Ted Hopf, *Peripheral Visions: Deterrence Theory and American Foreign Policy in the Third World, 1965–1990* (Ann Arbor: University of Michigan Press, 1994);

Jeane J. Kirkpatrick, *Dictatorships and Double Standards: Rationalism and Reason in Politics* (New York: Simon & Schuster, 1982);

Douglas J. MacDonald, *Adventures in Chaos: American Intervention for Reform in the Third World* (Cambridge, Mass.: Harvard University Press, 1992);

Constantine C. Menges, *The Twilight Struggle: The Soviet Union v. The United States Today* (Washington, D.C.: AEI Press, 1990);

Peter W. Rodman, *More Precious Than Peace: The Cold War and the Struggle for the Third World* (New York: Scribners, 1994);

Tony Smith, *America's Mission: The United States and the Worldwide Struggle for Democracy in the Twentieth Century* (Princeton: Princeton University Press, 1994).

NICARAGUA

Was the Reagan administration policy on Nicaragua successful?

Viewpoint: Yes. U.S. policy toward Nicaragua during the Reagan administration halted the spread of communism and encouraged the development of democracy in Central America.

Viewpoint: No. Reagan administration policies damaged U.S. credibility and led to protracted civil war in Nicaragua.

Nicaragua, a small Central American country once considered a potential site for a canal that would connect the Atlantic and Pacific Oceans (the canal was eventually built in Panama), was ruled by the Somoza family since 1934, when General Anastasio Somoza García took power after deposing President Juan Bautista Sacasa. During the Sacasa presidency Somoza had arranged the murder of Augusto César Sandino, who since 1926 had led a rebellion against the U.S.-supported government of Nicaragua. Somoza himself was assassinated in September 1956 and was succeeded by his son, Luis Somoza Debayle, who in turn was succeeded by his brother Anastasio Somoza Debayle in 1967.

The Somozas ruled Nicaragua as if it were their private estate. Resentment among the masses grew, and in 1961 the left-leaning *Frente Sandinista de Liberación* (FSLN, or Sandinista National Liberation Front) was created, a movement named for the murdered rebel leader. For the first ten years of FSLN existence, the U.S.-trained Nicaraguan National Guard managed to control the activities of various antigovernment movements. In 1972, however, the Somoza regime began to lose control. That year a powerful earthquake shook Managua, the capital city, killing more than six thousand residents and rendering more than three hundred thousand homeless. International relief agencies immediately began to send money and other assistance to the victims, but it was soon learned that Somoza, who took charge of the relief effort, stole a large portion of the money. Many more people died as hunger worsened, disease spread, and the rubble remained uncleared. Resentment against the regime increased as well.

In 1976 Jimmy Carter was elected U.S. president, and he placed the pursuit of human rights at the center of his foreign policy. American support for Somoza declined, and his continued repression at home further weakened his position. The Sandinistas, under the leadership of Daniel Ortega Saavedra, controlled ever larger sections of the Nicaraguan countryside, and on 19 July 1979 they entered Managua. Somoza fled the country the same day and was killed in Paraguay in September 1980.

The Carter administration initially welcomed the Sandinistas and offered Nicaragua a generous economic aid package of $75 million. It was not too long, however, before Sandinista domestic and foreign policies gave the U.S. administration pause. When Ronald Reagan became president in January 1981, he froze the unpaid portion of Carter's economic package and in April, saying that the Sandinistas were aiding left-wing antigovernment forces in El Salvador, suspended it altogether. Relations between the United States and

Nicaragua continued to deteriorate, and in 1983–1984 the Reagan administration imposed a boycott on trade with that Central American nation.

During the early phase of the Sandinista reign, a group of about two thousand former members of Somoza's National Guard organized a military opposition (known as the Somocistas) to the new regime. Operating out of bases in neighboring Honduras, they launched attacks against targets important to the government. They were soon joined by an anti-Sandinista rebel group made up of members of the English-speaking Miskito tribe, who were resentful of government efforts to force them to become more integrated into Nicaraguan society. In 1981 they combined to form a counter-revolutionary group commonly called the Contras.

Congress initially agreed to Reagan administration requests to support the Contras. That changed, however, after the Sandinistas won the November 1984 elections, which were held under international supervision. Covert involvement of the administration with the anti-Sandinista cause continued and was a central part of the 1986 Iran-Contra affair. Following mediation efforts by Costa Rican president Oscar Arias, the Sandinistas agreed to hold free elections on 25 February 1990. They lost the election to the *Unión Nacional Opositor* (National Opposition Union, or UNO), led by Violeta Barrios de Chamorro, and handed over power. After the elections, U.S. president George Bush lifted the economic sanctions on Nicaragua.

Viewpoint:
Yes. U.S. policy toward Nicaragua during the Reagan administration halted the spread of communism and encouraged the development of democracy in Central America.

U.S. actions in Nicaragua, including support for anti-Sandinista Contra guerrillas, were perhaps the most controversial aspects of Reagan administration foreign policy. The United States suffered international disrepute because of its role in mining Managua Harbor in 1984. The Iran-Contra scandal (1986) wracked the administration when it was revealed that proceeds from secret arms sales to Iran were intended for diversion to the Contras in apparent violation of a congressional ban on Contra aid. This scandal paralyzed the administration for months before it was able to regain its footing and conclude nuclear-arms-reduction agreements with the Soviet Union. The disregard for congressional will suggested by the Iran-Contra scandal seemed to some a veritable shredding of the Constitution. These concerns, however, should not obscure the fact that Ronald Reagan's Nicaragua policy was a necessary and largely successful attempt, conducted in the face of inconsistent and often opportunistic congressional obstructionism in order to combat radical totalitarianism.

Five main facts need to be remembered in evaluating Reagan's Nicaragua policy. First, the Sandinistas, members of *Frente Sandinista de Liberación* (FSNL, or Sandinista National Liberation Front), were determined to impose a totalitarian government on Nicaragua; even U.S. congressional opponents of Contra aid had little positive to say about the Sandinistas. Second, the Sandinistas saw no distinction between their domestic and foreign policies and were committed to encouraging revolutions in neighboring countries that would defeat not only right-wing dictatorships but "bourgeois" democracies as well. Third, the Carter administration set the tone for creativity in devising ways around clear congressional mandates concerning Nicaragua. Fourth, the majority of congressmen did not consistently oppose Contra aid nor offer a coherent alternative. Throughout the 1980s, congressional restrictions on Contra aid varied widely, generally based upon whatever parliamentary maneuvers opponents were able to execute to overcome their lack of voting strength. Prior to the Iran-Contra scandal, fiscal 1985 was the only year that Contra aid was prohibited; variations in congressional restrictions made it extremely difficult for the administration to develop a consistent policy. Fifth, significant attention has been paid to Contra atrocities and weaknesses; less recognition has been given to the popularity they maintained among the Nicaraguan people. When the Sandinistas finally permitted an open election, confident of victory, the opposition candidate who was linked to the Contras and the United States won a smashing victory. Reagan's Nicaragua policies were part of a successful strategy to halt the spread of communism and encourage the development of democracy in Central America.

The totalitarian tendencies of the Sandinistas are sometimes obscured because they came to power at the head of a coalition opposing Anastasio Somoza Debayle and were part of a government junta that included moderate elements. Sandinistas, however, made tactical alliances to gain power and never

THE CONTRAS

The United States supported the anti-Sandinista rebels (the Contras) in their war to regain control of Nicaragua. Marine colonel Oliver L. North, who helped supply the rebels, described life in the base camps in Honduras in his memoirs.

During the day, the camps were a hub of activity. As the men trained for incursions back into Nicaragua, the women washed clothes in the river, collected wood for the fire, and carried water from the purification system. They also prepared the meals—black beans and rice in the morning, and then, for variety, rice and black beans at night. The dining area was often no more than an open pavilion with a plastic sheet overhead to keep out the rain. By the end of the day, everyone was exhausted from the spartan labor of survival.

When times were good, the soldiers had boots. For everyone else, it was bare feet, sneakers, or sandals. The fighting men wore whatever would pass for a uniform: it wasn't unusual to come across a formation that included Honduran army fatigues, Guatemalan khakis, U.S. Army-type camouflage outfits, and even Cuban army clothes, captured from a warehouse in Nicaragua. Some of the best uniforms were dark-blue work suits that Calero had ordered from Sears—right out of the catalogue.

Many of the camp residents wore clothes donated by American philanthropic organizations, and I would see kids wearing the most incongruous T-shirts: Alcatraz Prison, Minnesota Twins, Esprit, Harvard University, even "Kiss me, I'm Irish."

No matter how often I visited the camps, the resistance fighters were always younger than I expected. At Yamales, the largest of the camps, I met a dark-eyed ten-year-old named Tomás who had arrived at the camp with his teenage brother. Their parents were described as "missing"—probably detained, or worse, by the Nicaraguan authorities. Tomás had a child's eagerness for what his older brother was doing, and when he insisted that he, too, wanted to fight the Sandinistas, the officers allowed him to tag along with his brother during the training. He was quite a sight with his heavy AK-47, which was almost as big as he was.

When his brother's unit left the camp and went back into Nicaragua, Tomás had to be restrained from going with them. He was crushed: the only real connection he had left in the world was leaving, and Tomás knew that his brother night never return. That night, Tomás ran away from the camp. They found him in the morning, safe—but still furious that his brother had gone off without him.

In one respect, however, Tomás was fortunate. At least he and his brother were fighting on the same side. As in any civil war, there were families in Nicaragua where brothers were actually shooting each other.

The White House and the State Department's Office of Public Diplomacy did what they could to make Americans aware of the conditions in the camps, but it was never easy. In 1991, when the Kurds started fleeing Iraq, I was reminded all over again of what the Contra camps were like. Americans are a generous people. We send relief to earthquake victims and refugees all over the globe. But the Contras, most of whom were refugees from Sandinista oppression, were largely ignored.

Source: *Oliver L. North, with William Novak,* Under Fire: An American Story *(New York: HarperCollins, 1991), pp. 263–265.*

intended to permit "bourgeois democracy" to hijack their revolution. In their first weeks in power the Sandinistas established Civil Defense Committees to be organized street by street throughout Nicaragua to identify potential opponents. Leading Sandinistas explained their intention to keep power until completion of their revolutionary program. In the spring of 1980 the Nicaraguan Council of State was expanded and membership altered to ensure a permanent Sandinista majority. Sandinista leaders on many occasions denigrated the elections they had promised the Organization of American States (OAS) they would hold. In August 1980 they announced that elections would not be held until 1985, and opposition political activity was prohibited before 1984 to ensure time for the proper indoctrination of the Nicaraguan people. In September 1980 the governing junta officially announced its subservience to the Sandinista directorate.

A logical adjunct of the commitment to Marxist revolution, and their ties to Cuban dictator Fidel Castro, was the Sandinista friendship with the Soviet Union. The late 1970s and early 1980s looked like a propitious time for close ties to the Soviets. Several pro-American regimes had been replaced by pro-Soviet governments during the 1970s; these losses and the apparent lack of U.S. resolve contrasted sharply with Soviet gains and growing confidence. With the U.S. economy suffering from stagflation that defied conventional economic logic and appeared unsolvable, the comparative economic weakness of the Union of Soviet Socialist Republics (U.S.S.R.) eluded many observers. Internal considerations, not U.S. pressure, led the Sandinistas to seek close ties with the Soviets and the Cubans. By the time Jimmy Carter left the U.S. presidency the Sandinistas were openly supporting Marxist guerrillas in El Salvador, and Guatemalan Marxist guerrillas had established their headquarters in Managua. Sandinista support for the unsuccessful "final offensive" launched by Salvadoran guerrillas in January 1981 led Carter to suspend aid to Nicaragua that had been part of his unsuccessful program to try to moderate the revolution; the offensive also led Carter to renew military shipments to El Salvador that previously had been terminated for human-rights reasons.

Despite Reagan's antipathy to communism and Sandinista support for the Salvadoran guerrillas, the Reagan administration in 1981 gave the Sandinistas two opportunities to focus on domestic concerns and refrain from revolutionary ferment abroad in return for improved relations with the United States. On both occasions the Sandinistas were unwilling to abandon their commitment to revolution. Only after these two efforts failed did the Reagan administration opt to support the armed anti-Sandinista resistance. The administration expected that this backing would prevent the Sandinistas from consolidating their control internally and limit their ability to support subversion in neighboring countries.

Reagan's support for the armed resistance was different from Carter's initial approach to the Sandinistas. Carter hoped cordial relations and aid would either moderate the Sandinistas or encourage sources of moderation within Nicaragua. Even though his policy differed from that ultimately followed by Reagan, Carter also encountered congressional prohibitions that hindered his ability to pursue his foreign policy. Congress imposed conditions on Carter's aid program before passing it in 1980; one condition required Carter to certify that the Sandinistas were not supporting guerrilla movements in other countries. Although U.S. government analysts concluded that the Sandinistas were supporting the Salvadoran guerrillas as a matter of policy, administration lawyers reasoned that the absence of "conclusive proof" of official Sandinista involvement permitted Carter to certify Sandinista nonsupport for guerrillas in order to comply with the law. Thus, even before Reagan took office the executive branch had resorted to evasive measures in an attempt to develop a coherent policy in the face of legislative challenges.

When Carter was looking for ways to influence the new Managua government, moderate and conservative Democrats were among those suspicious of the Sandinistas; such Democrats also were crucial to Reagan-era debates on Contra aid. Arguments between Democrats and Republicans were only part of this contention; liberal, moderate, and conservative Democrats argued with each other, and older intelligence-committee members sought to protect their prerogatives against younger legislators who were concerned about the U.S. role in Central America. This infighting did not yield a clear, coherent alternative to the Reagan policy. Supporters and opponents of Contra aid engaged in a series of clashes over the amount and type of aid to be dispensed and the restrictions to be placed on it. The Sandinistas themselves were never popular with the members of the U.S. Congress, even when they were not flying to Moscow or sending military forces into Honduras just days after votes against Contra aid. The Democrats never committed to anything approximating support for the Sandinistas; 1984 Democratic presidential nominee Walter F. Mondale said during the campaign that he might "quarantine" Nicaragua if he were elected. The fact that many opponents of Contra aid also disliked the Sandinistas led liberal representative Michael D. Barnes (D-Maryland) to point out that moderate and conservative Democrats sought "a way to be on both sides of the issue." Their lack of voting strength forced leading Contra-aid opponents to employ creative parliamentary maneuvering that further muddied the picture. Barnes said, "Our whole strategy was to postpone an up-or-down vote for two years. We just didn't have the votes if Reagan ever presented it that way." There also were elements of opportunism in some opposition to assistance to the Contras. Some Democrats hoped to deal a decisive defeat to Reagan to blunt his legislative momentum; James C. Wright Jr. (D-Texas) saw Contra aid as an avenue he could utilize to prove to liberal Democrats that he was not too conservative to succeed Thomas P. "Tip" O'Neill Jr. (D-Mass.) as Speaker of the House.

The law banning Contra aid at issue in the Iran-Contra scandal was the Boland Amend-

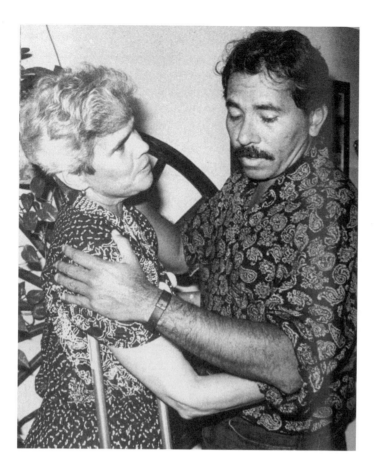

President-elect Violeta Barrios de Chamorro and President Daniel Ortega Saavedra embracing after the February 1990 election in Nicaragua

(Mario Tapia)

The Contras themselves are crucial to any assessment of Reagan's Nicaragua policy. Much attention was paid to their atrocities, U.S. support, and the former members of Somoza's National Guard among them. Far less attention has been devoted to their battlefield successes, the amount of territory they were able to seize and hold, their popularity among the peasantry and Indians, and Reagan administration efforts to ensure that the Contras served as a force for Nicaraguan democracy. By 1988 the U.S. State Department estimated that fewer than two hundred out of sixteen hundred Contras had served in the National Guard; moreover, one-fifth of the officer corps consisted of former Sandinistas. Many who had supported the overthrow of Somoza were displeased that the Sandinistas were replacing a *Somocista* dictatorship with a Sandinista dictatorship. Reagan's support for the resistance was part of a strategy for not only confronting the Soviet Union but also advancing democracy. Support for the anti-Sandinista resistance, armed and political, was part of a strategy that included pressure on communist nations such as Afghanistan, Cambodia, and Angola; forcible eviction of the communist government from Grenada (1983); and diplomatic efforts to encourage transitions toward democracy in such countries as Chile, the Philippines, Haiti, Argentina, Guatemala, El Salvador, and Honduras. As part of this strategy, the United States did not support diplomacy for its own sake but sought to encourage the Contadora and Arias peace processes when they gave promise of moving Nicaragua toward democracy. In the context of this strategy, support for the Contras was a means of pressuring the Sandinistas to permit genuine pluralistic democracy in keeping with their promises to the Organization of American States (OAS).

The Reagan administration sought to encourage democracy in Nicaragua, not fraudulent elections that conferred respectability on a Marxist dictatorship. Accordingly, the U.S.-backed opposition did not participate in the 1984 elections. The violence by Sandinista mobs and police, and Sandinista domination of media outlets and their restriction of campaigning opportunities, made participation by the opposition pointless. By 1990, however, the situation had changed. The Sandinistas had been prevented from consolidating their control because of the efforts of the Contras and the related political opposition in Nicaragua. The United States appeared tired of the issue, and the Bush administration suggested that it would recognize the Sandinistas if they won fair, open elections. Moreover, the loss by the Soviet Union of its Eastern European sat-

ment, which went through various iterations during the decade. The initial amendment passed the House of Representatives unanimously in December 1982 as the result of a compromise in which it was understood that the administration was permitted to continue its policy. At the time this bill was passed, Congress rejected a more stringent ban on funds to the Contras, proposed by Representative Thomas R. Harkin (D-Iowa). Also at this time the Senate defeated a measure proposed by Christopher J. Dodd (D-Connecticut) that would have banned support for any Central American paramilitary groups. The Boland Amendment was later tightened for fiscal 1985 to prohibit all Contra aid; the administration and Congress, however, continued to fight over the issue, and Congress approved various forms of assistance in subsequent years.

A few facts about Congress and the Contras should be emphasized: Democrat opponents of aid offered neither a clear alternative policy nor a particular solicitude for the Sandinistas; fiscal 1985 was the only year in which Congress banned aid prior to the Iran-Contra scandal; and the extensive parliamentary maneuvering required to ban Contra aid was a credit to the legislative skill of its opponents but undercuts claims that the ban was an authoritative statement of national or congressional will.

ellites and the liquidation of its war in Afghanistan showed its limitations as a future patron. The prospect of improved relations with the West and their confidence of victory led the Sandinistas to hold a fair election and invite large numbers of international observers to vouch for its legitimacy. In the end, however, Sandinista confidence was misplaced.

The Reagan policy of supporting the armed resistance in Nicaragua kept the pressure on the Sandinistas and prevented the consolidation of their revolution. As former State Department and National Security Council official Peter W. Rodman argued, in *More Precious Than Peace: The Cold War and the Struggle for the Third World* (1994), "In the end, the United States kept the Contras alive long enough to extract from the diplomatic process and from the Sandinistas a crucial quid pro quo—a sufficiently free election in which the core issue of Nicaragua's destiny would be addressed." That election demonstrated the success of Reagan policy. The opposition candidate, Violeta Barrios de Chamorro, made no effort to dissociate herself from the Contras or the United States and was even photographed with George Bush. On election day in Nicaragua, 90 percent of registered voters cast ballots. Chamorro received 55 percent of the vote to Sandinista Daniel Ortega Saavedra's 41 percent; she carried eight of nine administrative regions. The Nicaraguan people freely had chosen a democratic alternative to *Somocismo*—and to the Sandinistas.

–JOHN A. SOARES JR., GEORGE WASHINGTON UNIVERSITY

Viewpoint:
No. Reagan administration policies damaged U.S. credibility and led to protracted civil war in Nicaragua.

The presidency of Ronald Reagan (1981–1989) earned respect for its contributions to the downfall of communism and the withering away of undemocratic leftist, authoritarian governments. Reagan possessed a clear vision for the promotion of democratic freedoms: his rhetoric was rooted in solid plans and realized in extraordinary achievements. Throughout the decade, however, Reagan administration policies in Nicaragua were marked by undeniable inconsistencies and antidemocratic ironies. International supporters, such as former British prime minister Margaret Thatcher, emphasize that Reagan restored confidence in the American experience and rendered the

U.S. voice in global affairs more powerful and clearly understood. The circumstances of U.S. involvement in Nicaragua in the 1980s, however, damaged American credibility.

To characterize Reagan's vision as an amalgamation of Francis Bacon, John Locke, and trendy 1960s modernization theorists would be to underestimate its potency. In fact, the "hard-liners" who dominated U.S. foreign policy relative to Latin America consciously framed their arguments and plans on Reagan's expressed views. One of the clearest ironies is that a president so widely criticized as dissociated from significant policy decisions was shielded in the context of special congressional and independent prosecutorial investigations by the evidence of this pattern, while proponents of the controversial barter with the Iranians in 1984, in order to resupply the Contras, considered the plan a sincere and noble application of theory to practice.

The key to Reagan's view of the future was his abiding belief that growth and human progress can make the greatest strides in countries that encourage economic freedom. Prosperity depends on the ability of individual citizens to fulfill their needs and pursue their ambitions. In other words, freedom begins in the daily lives of individuals. As Reagan noted in 1981:

> Trust them, because whenever they are allowed to create and build, whenever they are given a personal stake in deciding economic policies and benefiting from their success, then societies become more dynamic, prosperous, progressive, and free.

In his 1989 farewell address to the nation, Reagan described "a city teeming with people of all kinds . . . with free ports that hummed with commerce and creativity." Reagan considered that in order for the United States to approach the ideal of his "shining city on the hill," it also had to serve as inspiration to travelers who would participate in its commerce as well as foster similar cities in other lands.

Reagan's vision contained a set of mutually reinforcing goals: to promote economic prosperity by protecting the freedoms of individual Americans and to increase the potential of U.S. prosperity by expanding the push for freedom into international affairs. His prime directive to promote democracy abroad was less a moralistic crusade than a pragmatic plan to preserve American economic and security interests, which was certainly what Reagan was elected to do. In pursuit of these goals in Nicaragua, however, his administration worked in contradiction to the will of Congress, which put up roadblocks—particularly the Boland Amendments (1983, 1984) to the War Powers Act (1973)—that had to be circumnavigated. Ironically, the battle for democracy abroad, Reagan administration officials decided, supposedly required some accommodation to undemocratic methods.

American economic assistance to developing countries is intended to increase the level of material benefits provided to the populace. Because the reduction of poverty levels undercuts the popular tendency (or necessity) to revolt, foreign aid can also serve to undermine the international labor movements that are frequently organized and joined by socialist-leaning individuals. The dampening of social unrest serves to sustain the global markets needed by growing industrialized capitalist economies.

Latin America was a proving ground for the battle between the spreading forces of global capitalism and world socialism. Although Vladimir Ilich Ulyanov Lenin had predicted such developments in the international political economy, the most practical strategy he could propose to combat imperialism was to best the opponent at his own game. As did the United States throughout the Cold War, the socialist Soviet empire steadily pushed resources into Latin America in order to stake claims to the territory.

The promotion of democracy did not mesh consistently with these concerns. On significant occasions the U.S. government chose to work with undemocratic dictatorial leaders, as long as these authoritarians supported anticommunism. The democratic good of the foreign peoples weighed less heavily in the balance-of-power calculations. In a 1982 address to the nation, Reagan emphasized the importance of viewing specific policies from a broad perspective:

> We desire peace. But peace is a goal, not a policy. Lasting peace is what we hope for at the end of our journey. It doesn't describe the steps we must take nor the paths we should follow to reach that goal.

The fact that the Reagan administration short-changed democracy in order to crush world socialism detracts from the moral value of the ultimate victories. At best, these contradictions are ironic; at worst, they raise questions that may damage American credibility.

"Never give up the fight for freedom, a fight which, though it may never end, is the most ennobling known to man," Reagan declared in 1990, upon the presentation of a section of the Berlin Wall at the presidential library established in his honor. A look at the methods used in advancing guerrilla warfare in Nicaragua, however, reveals a distinctive, and perhaps regrettable, lack of "nobility."

Historical authoritarian traditions in Nicaragua were distinguished by the lack of accepted political institutions or mechanisms for balancing social groups, as well as the dearth of established legal norms for competition and development. The anticommunist plans of certain individuals in the U.S. government was to support the movement of "national liberation" in Nicaragua to drive out the communist leaders. Although the provision of military equipment, training, or other support to the anti-Sandinista rebels by any U.S. intelligence agency had been forbidden by Congress, the National Security Council (NSC) deemed itself exempt from this law, and staff members continued to route support to the Contras. Marine colonel Oliver L. North secretly raised more than $34 million for the Contras in 1984 and added to that total by syphoning profits from the clandestine sale of American missiles to Iran in 1985–1986.

After years of civil war the Nicaraguan people were decimated. Currency devaluation, continued property expropriation, and the militarization of the economy crippled their ability to meet rudimentary needs of the population. War service reduced the productivity of individuals needed for family income and pitted classes against one another. In other words, the "psychological operations" of the Contras and the Reagan administration were successful. From the U.S. perspective, the decade of war was worthwhile not merely because it finally achieved the installation of democratic elections but because future socialist efforts were effectively undermined. The inevitable by-products of a successful war effort (profits of middlemen, extraction of surplus value, and privileges of state bureaucrats) eroded the possibilities for a developed unity among classes that could have led to the return of communist leaders.

Out of true respect for the democratic achievements of the Reagan presidency arise deep concerns with the contradictions inherent in the policies in Nicaragua. The lofty goals of "democracy promotion" exist a bit uncomfortably alongside angry frustrations with an obstructionist Congress, inconsistencies in the application of theory to practice, and brutal results of a protracted civil war. In 1959 Henry Cabot Lodge wondered, "The U.S. can win wars, but the question is, can we win revolutions?" The extant case raises the question of how to measure a win or a loss in a revolution.

–EMILY CUMMINS, WASHINGTON, D.C.

References

E. Bradford Burns, *At War in Nicaragua: The Reagan Doctrine and the Politics of Nostalgia* (New York: Harper & Row, 1987);

Thomas Carothers, *In the Name of Democracy: U.S. Policy Toward Latin America in the Reagan Years* (Berkeley: University of California Press, 1991);

Roy Gutman, *Banana Diplomacy: The Making of American Policy in Nicaragua, 1981–1987* (New York: Simon & Schuster, 1988);

Robert Kagan, *A Twilight Struggle: American Power and Nicaragua, 1977–1990* (New York: Free Press, 1996);

Amos Kiewe and Davis W. Houck, *A Shining City on a Hill: Ronald Reagan's Economic Rhetoric, 1951–1989* (New York: Praeger, 1991);

Peter Kornbluh, ed., *Nicaragua: The Making of U.S. Policy, 1978–1990* (Alexandria, Va.: Chadwyck-Healey, 1991) [microform];

Kornbluh, *Nicaragua, the Price of Intervention: Reagan's Wars Against The Sandinistas* (Washington, D.C.: Institute for Policy Studies, 1987);

Anthony Lake, *Somoza Falling* (Boston: Houghton Mifflin, 1989);

Robert A. Pastor, *Condemned to Repetition: The United States and Nicaragua* (Princeton: Princeton University Press, 1987);

Peter W. Rodman, *More Precious Than Peace: The Cold War and the Struggle for the Third World* (New York: Scribners, 1994);

Peter H. Smith, *Talons of the Eagle: Dynamics of U.S.–Latin American Relations* (New York: Oxford University Press, 1996);

Lawrence E. Walsh, *Final Report of the Independent Counsel for Iran/Contra Matters* (Washington, D.C.: U.S. Court of Appeals for the District of Columbia Circuit, 1993).

NICARAGUA

NIXON AND KISSINGER

Were Richard M. Nixon's and Henry Kissinger's approaches to foreign policy unified?

Viewpoint: Yes. The foreign policy of Nixon and Kissinger consistently applied the theories of multipolarity and balance of power.

Viewpoint: No. Nixon and Kissinger disagreed significantly on foreign policy. Their unlikely pairing was primarily a result of internal Republican Party politics.

In the administration of President Richard M. Nixon, the formulation of foreign policy was dominated by two individuals—the president himself and his national security adviser (and later secretary of state) Henry Kissinger. The two statesmen came from much different backgrounds. Nixon had made his political career largely by means of his vociferous opposition to communism. At the time of his election to the presidency in 1968, Nixon's credentials as a cold warrior were well established. Kissinger, on the other hand, took a much more subtle approach to statecraft and international affairs. Having argued that the careful management of diplomacy among the major powers of nineteenth-century Europe had kept the peace for a considerable time, he sincerely believed that well-managed relations between the superpowers and other emerging centers of power in the world was crucial to peace in the modern world.

The foreign policy of the Nixon administration employed elements of both approaches to strategy. While it decidedly escalated the war in Vietnam to check communist expansion in Asia and tried hard to bring China into the American camp, it also engaged in arms control and summit talks with the Soviet Union. Did these events represent a harmonization of foreign policy between the two leaders, or were they merely pursuing disparate goals in isolation from each other?

Viewpoint:
Yes. The foreign policy of Nixon and Kissinger consistently applied the theories of multipolarity and balance of power.

It is not easy to maintain a consistent and steady foreign policy in a democracy, susceptible as it is to the shifting moods and preferences of public opinion. The American system of government, with its separation of powers and checks and balances, makes it more difficult

still. There are also the complications that the pluralistic nature of American society adds. This is a country of immigrants whose groups ably use opportunities the political system affords them to press for policies that address their views; businesses and industries hire lobbyists to persuade elected officials to vote in favor of interests that concern them. It is little wonder that a prominent analyst of American foreign policy, Harvard professor Samuel P. Huntington, writing in *Foreign Affairs*, chose the title "The Erosion of American

National Interest" to describe this system.

Henry Kissinger himself wrote on the difficulties of maintaining steadiness and coherence in U.S. foreign policy by pointing to the nature of the policy-making bureaucracy and the professions from which presidents usually recruited secretaries of state and defense. Since most individuals in charge of foreign-policy making came from law or business backgrounds, they brought with them the attitudes and experiences of these professions. The presence of legally trained officials in policy making circles tended to give U.S. policy its formalistic and legalistic coloration, with a strong belief in the power of contracts and agreements and the tendency for an ad hoc, case-by-case approach to solving problems. Many successful businessmen brought with them an optimistic, can-do approach, undergirded by the assumption that there were no intractable problems, that even the most difficult situation could be resolved by throwing enough money and energy into solving it, and that people were mostly motivated by rational, cost-benefit calculations. Kissinger argued that the legalistic and business approaches were not suitable training for navigation in a complex and tragic world in which people are driven by all kinds of motives, agreements do not have the same force as contracts, and the competition for power and resources is fierce and largely unregulated.

When Richard M. Nixon and Kissinger assumed the responsibility for American foreign policy in 1969, they faced all these difficulties—plus one more: the Vietnam War, which they had inherited from the departing Johnson administration. They inherited not only the war but also an agitated, edgy, and deeply divided public, suspicious of government and mistrustful of its leaders. To have maintained a consistent and steady foreign policy under these circumstances was a remarkable achievement.

The Nixon and the Ford administrations owed this consistency to the conceptual framework that Kissinger, Nixon's national security adviser, provided. Kissinger developed this framework while he was a Harvard academic, studying nineteenth-century diplomacy, and a Council of Foreign Relations scholar, writing about the nuclear policies of the United States and the North Atlantic Treaty Organization (NATO). He argued that for an international order to be stable it must be "legitimate." By legitimate Kissinger did not mean that world order must necessarily be just. He only meant that the leading powers in the system accepted that order and abided by its norms. Making an international order legitimate required that all the leading countries were status quo powers

and that there were no revolutionary powers bent on subverting the system.

To achieve a legitimate order, there was a need to "de-ideologize" the foreign policies of countries and make the powers concentrate on interests rather than philosophical or ideological goals. Pursuing philosophical preferences and a sense of justice might lead to ideological crusades and prevent the establishment of a legitimate order. Ideological crusades were especially dangerous in the nuclear age, in which a total victory over a nuclear-armed adversary was no longer possible. Concentration on interests, on the other hand, would make it easier to reach necessary compromises. A legitimate order would limit not only the goals states would pursue in their foreign policies but also the means they would employ. Kissinger believed that states should be more circumspect in how they went about achieving their goals.

Kissinger also believed that a multipolar world would be more stable than a bipolar one: the main advantage was that in the former it was more difficult for any one country to become hegemonic. With a few powers of roughly equal strength, a multipolar world offered powers the option of creating an alliance to check the rise of a potential hegemon. Multipolarity was especially appealing to Kissinger in the late 1960s. American public opinion was more and more critical not only of the costly Vietnam War but of U.S. global involvement generally. Kissinger feared that under the continuing pressure of a disaffected public, American leaders would begin to pull back from the high level of international engagement that characterized U.S. policies in the 1950s and 1960s. In the bipolar world then in place, if the United States were to retrench, there would be no power to contain the spread of Soviet influence. There was thus a need to encourage the rise of other powers—for instance, China or a united Europe—that would be in a position to help the United States continue its containment policies, even as the U.S. contribution to such an effort diminished somewhat as a result of domestic political pressures.

Kissinger believed in the possibility of creating a legitimate international order, but he was not naive or sentimental. Competition and conflict were still at the core of the relations among states, and there was a need for credible military capabilities as bases for any foreign-policy initiatives. Thus, recognizing both the impatience of a restive public opinion with foreign entanglements and the need to make sure Western interests were not sacrificed as a result of reduced American involvement, Nixon announced in July 1969 the Nixon Doctrine,

President Richard M. Nixon and Secretary of State Henry Kissinger conferring at the White House, 16 September 1972

(White House Photo)

also known as the Guam Doctrine, when he made the speech highlighting the new approach. He declared that the United States would help regional powers economically and militarily so they could not only defend themselves more effectively against Soviet threats but also become regional policemen, making sure that U.S. interests were not victimized even if it became less involved.

Kissinger was not confident that a democracy, because of its open, pluralistic nature, could sustain a steady foreign policy. He thus wanted to create a policy-making apparatus that would shield it, to a degree, from the vagaries of shifting public opinion. An examination of Nixon-Kissinger policies shows that these principles guided and informed administration policies, lending them coherence and legibility.

The first and most important effort by the new administration was to turn the Soviet Union from a revolutionary to a status-quo power by launching broad détente policies to try to bring the U.S.S.R. into the family of nations. The United States opened credit and technology mar-

kets in the West to the communist regime, conferred political legitimacy on it, and negotiated a series of agreements to regulate better the relationship between the two countries. As part of this process the administration toned down its criticism of human-rights violations in the Soviet Union and was careful not to be associated with dissenters such as Aleksandr Solzhenitzyn. This does not mean that behind the scenes the administration was not pressing for greater openness and tolerance in the U.S.S.R. and for greater freedom for Soviet citizens to emigrate (for example, allowing Jews to immigrate to Israel). During the Ford administration Kissinger also oversaw the Helsinki Accords (1 August 1975), which addressed human-rights issues in the Soviet Union. The purpose, however, was to work to advance U.S.-supported norms and principles in a less confrontational way—more quietly, behind the scenes, and in an agreed-upon fashion. This approach was derived directly from Kissinger's belief in the need to de-ideologize U.S. foreign policy: one could not expect the U.S.S.R. to support an international system in which the leading powers constantly criticized it.

That Nixon and Kissinger placed less importance on ideology and more on power calculations also led them to the "opening" of the People's Republic of China. After more than twenty years of estrangement between China and the United States, Nixon and Kissinger made the historical visit to Beijing in February 1972, ushering in a new era in international relations. The opening to China was inspired by three of Kissinger's guidelines: first, as was the case with the Soviet Union, there was a need to engage major powers in the system if a legitimate international order were to be established. The isolation of China had to end. Second, as the United States was retreating under the pressure of domestic public opinion, there was a need to find another power that would help contain the potential expansion of Soviet power, especially in Asia. China was an ideal "balancer," especially as its own relations with the U.S.S.R. had been steadily deteriorating since the early 1960s. Third, even beyond the immediate need to find a balancing partner in Asia, Kissinger wanted to replace the bipolar with a multipolar structure to allow for future flexibility in American foreign policy. Allowing China to assume its rightful place in the world was a step in this direction.

The Nixon administration also increased military and economic aid to selected friendly countries—for example, Israel, Iran, and Pakistan—in order to make them more capable not only of defending themselves, but also of helping America secure its interests in their regions. A perfect example was the crisis in Jordan in September 1970, when Palestinian Liberation Organization (PLO) guerrillas hijacked and blew up several airplanes. When Syria, upset with King Hussein's campaign against the PLO, began to move its troops in preparation for an invasion of Jordan, the United States encouraged Israel, a strong U.S. ally, to place its forces on alert and warn Syria not to intervene. The United States, deeply enmeshed in Vietnam at the time, did not have the capability or will to aid Jordan. Of course, preventing a Syrian invasion of Jordan was also in Israeli interests.

Even the manner in which the administration pursued the war it had inherited in Vietnam was in keeping with the principles Kissinger developed. The war was continued not because Nixon or Kissinger believed that there was a way to "win" it in any meaningful sense. Rather, it was pursued because Kissinger believed that U.S. reputation for determination and resolve was important, and since it had undertaken the commitment to South Vietnam the United States had to see it through. Second, Kissinger initiated secret talks with the

North Vietnamese. Kissinger believed in talks and negotiations, but he was not naive—he would later criticize Carter administration cuts of defense programs by saying that perhaps military power no longer bought one as much influence as it once did, "but weakness still gets you nothing." There was a need to convince the North Vietnamese that they would lose if they just sat and waited for domestic public opinion in America to force the United States to leave Vietnam without North Vietnamese concessions. Nixon and Kissinger also relied heavily on "back channels" to advance their goals, trying to shield U.S. policymaking from the emotions that were engulfing America in reactions to the Vietnam War.

To say that the policies Nixon and Kissinger pursued were consistent and part of a larger, well-thought-out framework, is not to say that these policies were always right. The two misunderstood the degree to which the American public and its representatives would resent the excessive secretiveness of the policy process they had established; they also misjudged the degree to which a policy—any policy—had to be shown to adhere to deeply held American values and principles. Talk of balance of power, multipolarity, and legitimacy are not the most inspiring in the American political lexicon, especially not during passionate, contentious times. The Nixon and Kissinger policies were consistent, however, and well-grounded in an explicit and well-articulated view of history and the world.

—BENJAMIN FRANKEL,
SECURITY STUDIES

Viewpoint:
No. Nixon and Kissinger disagreed significantly on foreign policy. Their unlikely pairing was primarily a result of internal Republican Party politics.

When Lyndon B. Johnson left office in January 1969, the new administration of Richard M. Nixon had to contend with an unenviable legacy. The containment structure around the periphery of the communist world had begun to show signs of weakening. Crucial allies in Western Europe, especially France and West Germany, were departing from their previously strong pro-American positions to establish economic and diplomatic ties with Eastern Europe and the Soviet Union. Both implicitly and explicitly, this meant the emergence of a gap between them and the United States. At

NIXON ON DETENTE

President Richard M. Nixon, during a 25 February 1971 address to Congress, revealed his views on détente.

The cruel and unnatural division of Europe is no longer accepted as inevitable or permanent. Today there is a growing impatience with confrontation. We and our allies seek a European détente. But we know that we cannot achieve it if we let slip away the close friendships in the West and the basic conditions of stability which have set the stage for it. This obligates our allies and ourselves to conduct our diplomacy in harmony as we jointly and severally seek concrete negotiations on the range of issues in order to make détente a reality. . . .

In our view, détente means negotiating the concrete conditions of mutual security that will allow for expanded intra-European contact and cooperation without jeopardizing the security of any country. Soviet policies and doctrine, however, too often interpret détente in terms of Western ratification of the status quo and acknowledgment of continuing Soviet hegemony over Eastern Europe. Beyond this, Soviet policy has been tempted to offer a relaxation of tension selectively to some allies but not to others, and only on limited issues of primary interest to the U.S.S.R. In view of this fundamental difference, a major question for the alliance to face is whether we can overcome the East-West stalemate while maintaining unity among ourselves and avoiding internal divisions in our countries.

Obviously, the Western countries do not have identical national concerns and cannot be expected to agree automatically on priorities or solutions. Each ally is the best judge of its own national interest. But our principle objective should be to harmonize our policies and insure that our efforts for détente are complimentary. A differentiated détente, limited to the U.S.S.R. and certain Western allies but not to others, would be illusory.

The U.S.S.R. has frequently proposed a general conference on European security. But such a conference, in the Soviet formulation, would not address the main security issues—the German question, Berlin, mutual force reductions—but only very general themes. We and our allies are prepared to negotiate with the East in any forum. But we see little value in a conference whose agenda would be unlikely to yield progress on concrete issues but would only deflect our energies to drafting statements and declarations the interpretation of which would inevitably be a continuing source of disagreements. Once a political basis for improving relations is created through specific negotiations already in process, a general conference might build on it to discuss other intra-European issues and forms of cooperation.

Any lasting relaxation of tension in Europe must include progress in resolving the issues related to the division of Germany.

Source: Current History, *60 (May 1971): 302.*

---

the same time, Johnson's large-scale commitment to Vietnam had bogged down American military power in a war that seemed unwinnable. The economic consequences of high military spending, coupled with increased domestic government expenditures, created inflation, a decline in domestic civilian production, and drained American precious-metal and hard-currency reserves. At the nuclear level, American superiority in strategic weapons began to erode as the Soviet Union developed and deployed a fully functional intercontinental ballistic missile (ICBM) system, which allowed the Soviets by the end of the decade the capability to strike the continental United States from bases in Soviet territory.

The new administration had to decide how best to counter this deterioration of the American strategic position. Conventionally speaking, it would perhaps be easy to assume that a democratically elected government would adopt a unified approach to foreign affairs and, for that matter, to all other questions of state. America's political system, dominated as it is by two large umbrella parties, has, however, never lent itself to anything but a wide range of intra-party disputes on many political issues. Foreign policy was, and is, no exception.

This was a fact that Nixon had to face from the moment he declared his candidacy. Strongly identified with the conservative wing of the Republican Party, Nixon had to remain conscious of the more moderate element, led by New York governor Nelson A. Rockefeller, in order to unify it behind him in the 1968 election and to maintain its support for his reelection in 1972. Rockefeller had twice campaigned unsuccessfully for the Republican presidential nomination—against the outspokenly conservative Senator Barry Goldwater of Arizona in 1964 and Nixon in 1968—but, despite his losses, he nevertheless retained great influence in the party. Largely in order to accommodate the moderates, upon his election to the presidency Nixon was compelled to share power in foreign-policy making with Rockefeller's intellectual protégé Henry Kissinger, who became national security adviser.

There was no other logical reason to ask Kissinger to join the administration. Nixon had met him only once, briefly, at a cocktail party in 1967. Kissinger was a bona fide member of the Eastern establishment and its leading institutions—Harvard University and the Council on Foreign Relations. He thus fit the description of the Ivy League intellectual that Nixon viscerally resented and, some would say, pathologically distrusted. Having risen to prominence under Rockefeller, furthermore, Kissinger was estranged by association from Nixon and his firm commitment to reenergizing containment. Indeed, Kissinger's approach to global politics was firmly rooted in the notion that the best hope for stability was a managed peace based on shared understanding of the rules of the international game, commercial ties, and high-level diplomatic cooperation with the Soviet Union. He had elaborated this view in his Harvard dissertation, a study of the nineteenth-century Concert of Europe, a diplomatic order that held the peace for several decades on the foundations of the same sort of managed peace that Kissinger now advocated. In addition to what came to be called détente with the Soviet Union, Kissinger's strategy also involved the promotion of a multipolar world in which the major pitfall of bipolarity—the fact that a gain for one power was always a loss for the other—would be avoided.

Nixon's own strategy was the absolute opposite. With a background rooted in firm anti-communism and distrust of the Soviet Union, Nixon placed little faith in the concept of a managed peace. It was the Eisenhower administration, in which he had served as vice president, that had expanded the boundaries of containment to a global scale. In sharp contrast to Kissinger, who favored reaching out to Moscow with diplomatic and economic ties, Nixon's approach was based on the predication of negotiations on American strategic superiority.

To achieve that end Nixon determined to reinforce containment as a viable policy. Even before his election he had made clear that he wanted to establish diplomatic relations with China. Although Nixon had called Mao Tsetung a "monster" in the 1950s, and Beijing's commitment to communism had not changed since then, the future president presciently believed that the geopolitical and ideological factors that had led to Mao's estrangement from Moscow could work strongly in America's strategic favor. By bringing China into the containment structure, Nixon believed that the U.S. position vis-à-vis the Soviet Union would be dramatically improved; the largest and most powerful ally of the U.S.S.R. would be jumping ship to join its largest and most powerful adversary.

Vietnam played a crucial role in this approach. Historically, China had tried to establish hegemony over Southeast Asia. Its conversion to communism had brought with it no desire to see Vietnam unified. This conviction was actually reinforced in Chinese strategic thought as the Cold War developed, because Ho Chi Minh's regime in North Vietnam was pro-Soviet at a time when China and the Soviet Union were not friends. Ho's domination of Southeast Asia could only turn it into the other side of a geopolitical vice for Beijing: an unattractive prospect for Mao. In addition to their mutual antipathy to the Soviets, the preservation of a divided Indochina was another coincidence of interests upon which Sino-American rapprochement could be based. It ensured a part of the containment structure—the security of South Vietnam, Laos, and Cambodia being guaranteed by the Southeast Asia Treaty Organization (SEATO), established in 1954—and extricated China from the prospect of its own "containment" by the Soviet Union. Cooperation over Indochina was to be the cement of the Sino-American strategic relationship.

The near-war situation that existed between China and the Soviet Union in the first half of 1969, and the virtual closing of the supply route to Hanoi through Chinese territory, unequivocally illustrated the extent of their estrangement. It was an opportunity Nixon did not miss. By trying to stabilize the South Vietnamese regime, eliminate the communist positions in Cambodia and Laos, block the supply ports through which most Soviet support for the North Vietnamese arrived, and achieve a peace settlement that reestablished the antebellum status quo, Nixon moved to resolve the conflict on terms favorable to both the United States and China.

Kissinger's approach was radically different. Since his strategy involved drawing Moscow into friendly relations, it made no sense for him to support policies that made an ally of one of the Soviet's most bitter antagonists. Working with Nixon to reach a settlement in Indochina that was favorable to both the United States and China, and to use that settlement as the basis for making China an integral part of the containment structure, could not have any logical appeal for the national security adviser. As Kissinger's power in the foreign-policy making establishment of the administration grew, stimulated by Nixon's personal and professional entanglement in the tremendous intricacies of the Watergate scandal, his goals diverged ever more widely from Nixon's aspirations.

The final peace settlement that was signed in January 1973 was a farce as far as South Vietnamese independence was concerned. Although Kissinger had been instructed by Nixon to achieve a peace agreement according to which all communist and American forces would be withdrawn from South Vietnamese territory, he instead agreed to a plan that required the withdrawal of all American forces but only those communist forces that had crossed the seventeenth parallel directly. This concession left more than one hundred thousand communist troops, who had entered South Vietnam circuitously through Laos and Cambodia, on South Vietnamese soil after America withdrew. The disastrous results, culminating with the final conquest of the South by the North in April 1975 and Hanoi's partially successful attempts to dominate its much smaller neighbors around the same time, are known only too well.

In the broader strategic context China perceived the American activity that led to this turn of events to represent precisely the unified approach to foreign policy that did not exist within the administration. The resulting alienation soured the initially positive opening in Sino-American relations that began with Nixon's February 1972 visit. Kissinger's growing control over foreign policy (he was appointed secretary of state in September 1973 and still held the post of national security adviser until he stepped down in November 1975—significantly, he was the only person in American history to hold the two major foreign-policy posts) did nothing to help. By April 1974 the "tripolarity" that Kissinger had advocated as an element of his strategy, and that was manifested implicitly in his Vietnam peace negotiations, became a reality when Deng Xiaoping, a leading opponent of Mao's strategy of aligning closely with the United States, elaborated a similar "three worlds" strategy in a speech at the United Nations. The apparent failure of the United States in South

Vietnam, together with the progressive decline of Mao's health (he died in September 1976), gave Deng's faction significant ground in the Chinese strategic debate.

Another major point of divergence between the president and Kissinger was the question of détente with the Soviet Union and the future role of U.S. allies in international politics. In his first term Nixon had tried to reestablish American primacy in the West. The drift of West Germany (and, centrifugally, Western Europe) and Japan away from containment policies and toward favorable relations with the Soviet Union was a function of their tremendous export-led economic growth. As their economic power grew, increasingly wealthy U.S. allies began to assert their geopolitical independence. By definition this implied a movement toward a middle position in the superpower conflict. The Bretton Woods system of international finance had been designed in 1944 to keep these developments in check, but by the time Nixon entered office, the economic problems caused by the fiscal policies of the Johnson administration had led to the collapse of the system. Rather than allow economic dislocation to cause the unraveling of containment, Nixon abandoned the Bretton Woods system by removing the dollar from the gold standard in August 1971 and adjusting its value (now based on faith in the government of the United States) to equilibrate foreign-economic growth. This measure worked for a while and was helped by the rise in oil prices after the Yom Kippur War (October 1973, when Israel defeated Egypt and Syria). Despite weak attempts to continue their movement toward a middle position thereafter, both West Germany and Japan continued to be firmly in the American orbit at least until the late 1980s.

Kissinger's strategic thought differed radically. Just as he introduced the concept of tripolarism into the U.S. relationship with China, so did he also advocate "trilateralism" with regard to Western Europe. The movement toward the Soviet Union that was obviously present in West German "Eastern policy," or *Ostpolitik,* was encouraged by Kissinger. His ideas about the suitability of a multipolar world could lead him to no other conclusion but to support the drift of American allies toward the geopolitical center even while Nixon manipulated financial policy to try to prevent it.

It is clear that Nixon and Kissinger were influenced by different worldviews and that their otherwise unlikely coexistence in power was the result of Republican Party politics. Their competing strategies of containment and détente could not have been more opposite in their approaches to world politics. Interestingly, the same differentiation existed within other administrations, both before and after. At the beginning of the Cold War, the succession of President Franklin D. Roosevelt by Vice President Harry S Truman illustrated doubtlessly that a broad divergence of opinion on foreign affairs could exist within a political party, and even within an administration as entrenched as Roosevelt's was by its fourth term. At the end of the Cold War, the same basic difference on strategy emerged when Republican vice president George Bush, who was closely associated with Kissinger's approach to foreign policy, succeeded Ronald Reagan, who certainly was not. Nixon's relationship with Kissinger was not unique.

–PAUL DU QUENOY,
GEORGETOWN UNIVERSITY

References

Samuel P. Huntington, "The Erosion of American National Interest," *Foreign Affairs,* (September–October 1997), pp. 28–49;

Henry Kissinger, *White House Years* (Boston: Little, Brown, 1979);

Kissinger, *Years Of Upheaval* (Boston: Little, Brown, 1982);

Richard M. Nixon, *RN: The Memoirs of Richard Nixon* (Boston: Grosset & Dunlap, 1978);

John G. Stoessinger, *Henry Kissinger: The Anguish of Power* (New York: Norton, 1976);

Richard C. Thornton, *The Nixon-Kissinger Years: Reshaping American Foreign Policy* (New York: Paragon House, 1989).

NIXON AND KISSINGER

OSTPOLITIK

Was *Ostpolitik* in the strategic interests of the West?

Viewpoint: Yes. *Ostpolitik* was a useful and prudent response to the circumstances in central Europe during the 1970s and 1980s, leading to improved relations between the two German states.

Viewpoint: No. *Ostpolitik* weakened the Cold War Western alliance and legitimized a brutal communist state.

By the late 1960s the government of West Germany began to open diplomatic channels with the Soviet Union and its East European satellites. In 1967 Bonn concluded a trade agreement with Romania. After the Social Democrat Willy Brandt became chancellor of the Federal Republic in 1969, he pursued more sweeping policies of rapprochement with the countries of Eastern Europe, policies known collectively as *Ostpolitik* (eastern policy). In the latter half of 1970 West Germany negotiated treaties of friendship and nonaggression with Poland and the Soviet Union and ended more than two decades of cold relations with the two. In the following year transit rights to West Berlin, a Western "island" inside East Germany, were normalized. In 1972 additional West German talks with East Germany led to a treaty between the two states that normalized intra-German relations and led to full mutual diplomatic recognition for the first time in their history. All the while trade and commercial relationships between Bonn and the communist world increased greatly.

The easing of relations was not without controversy. Brandt's approach to the East depended on the permanent recognition of the division of Germany and the loss of the eastern territories that were annexed by Poland and the Soviet Union after 1945. Although Ostpolitik was launched against the backdrop of détente, the policy initiated by Richard M. Nixon and Henry Kissinger with the aim of easing East-West tensions, and was similar to it in some respects, many, both in West Germany and abroad, believed that overtures of the Federal Republic of Germany (FRG) to the East went too far too soon. It ran the risk of weakening West Germany's commitment to the North Atlantic Treaty Organization (NATO) and undermining American-led efforts to contain the spread of Soviet power and influence. On both sides of the Iron Curtain, observers read Ostpolitik as an attempt by Germany to use its economic might in an effort to play a more independent political role in central Europe. At the same time, Brandt's initiatives established channels with both East Germany and the Soviet Union that later facilitated German reunification, although this development could not have been anticipated almost until it happened and was not without a price when it came.

Viewpoint:
Yes. *Ostpolitik* was a useful and prudent response to the circumstances in central Europe during the 1970s and 1980s, leading to improved relations between the two German states.

Ostpolitik, the "opening to the East," that characterized the foreign policy of the Federal Republic of Germany (FRG) in the 1970s and 1980s, had its roots in a four-way interaction of pragmatism and principle in foreign and domestic politics. The Grand Coalition of Christian Democrats, Free Democrats, and Social Democrats that governed West Germany from 1966 to 1969 marked a transition from a Cold War era, when FRG foreign policy was shaped by Atlanticism and domestic policy was molded by democratization and regionalism. The former stressed West German identification with the West, including the United States, and its values. In practice that meant anticommunism and a low diplomatic profile. The latter emphasized drawing as firm a line as possible through the Nazi past, still perceived as too close for detailed scrutiny, and legitimating that decision by stressing the relative innocence of west and south Germany for crimes committed in Berlin with the connivance of Prussians.

This blend of myths was effective in the first stages of nation building. Willy Brandt, leader of the Social Democrats and Foreign Minister in the Grand Coalition, however, saw this stance as incomplete. On one level, after 1945 the Social Democrats had historically stood for Germany as a whole, challenging the Rhenish-Bavarian particularism of Konrad Adenauer, Franz Josef Strauss, and their largely Catholic supporters. On another, the Grand Coalition was the first time the Social Democrats had been part of the government. Brandt did not intend it to be the last. In practical terms, the limited international role of the FRG seemed out of balance with its growing economic power, while the Cold War appeared at a dead end. Not least in Brandt's calculations were moral factors. He believed decades of silence about German behavior in World War II was proving as damaging at home and abroad as any dwelling on that behavior could be.

Ostpolitik was Brandt's comprehensive answer to specific issues. It was both necessary and desirable, he argued, for the Federal Republic to normalize and extend its relations with the Union of Soviet Socialist Republics

(U.S.S.R.) and the states of Eastern Europe. In economic terms this meant reestablishing ties with a traditional German hinterland that otherwise would be left entirely to an East Germany that seemed on the point of its own economic takeoff. Politically Ostpolitik offered an opportunity to defuse tensions that placed the Federal Republic on the front line of any future conflict, nuclear or conventional. In the long run Ostpolitik might even prepare a path to German reunification by diminishing Soviet anxieties. Finally, Ostpolitik offered a chance to open the door of German memories on what had happened in the east from 1939 to 1945—and to give the Social Democrats a moral high ground currently held by conservatives in the Federal Republic.

Ostpolitik also involved modifying, when not abandoning, the strong arguments against Soviet global and regional policies that the West, including the FRG, had been making for a quarter century. Brandt's position was that the Russians would not have been where they were in 1945, and done what they did afterward, had it not been for the previous actions of Germany. It is a difficult argument to refute, no matter how strong the evidence from Russian archives of Joseph Stalin's ideologically based hostility to the West.

As foreign minister and later as chancellor, Brandt pushed Ostpolitik on every front despite U.S. opposition and North Atlantic Treaty Organization (NATO) suspicion. He knelt publicly at the Warsaw ghetto memorial—the first time an FRG chancellor had made that kind of dramatic acknowledgment of German behavior in the east during World War II. He also achieved some success in commercial negotiations with states of the Warsaw Pact. Politically, Brandt was less successful. Cultural exchanges and trade agreements brought him no further along in thawing East-West hostilities. It was increasingly apparent that he had exaggerated the potential of West Germany as a power broker: the U.S.S.R. paid attention when it wanted to. On the specific issue of unification, Russia remained predictably adamant. In a general context Ostpolitik nevertheless served notice that the Federal Republic accepted the postwar map of Europe and the postwar balance of power. Increasingly "German revanchism" became a propaganda slogan, rather than a sustainable anxiety, east of the Oder-Neisse Line that marked the new frontier between Teuton and Slav.

Ostpolitik was more effective in the limited context of inter-German relations. Brandt's political mantra that Germany was "two states in one nation" signaled practical abandonment of the previous Hallstein Doctrine, which asserted only the Federal Republic represented Germans internationally. An increasing number of states recognized the German Democratic Republic (GDR) de facto or de jure. Ostpolitik, however, was also intended to liberalize the GDR by small-scale rapprochement: agreements on issues of traffic, pension exchanges, and environmental issues. The ploy was obvious enough to generate significant response in the GDR. Critics even argued that Brandt had exacerbated the division of Germany by compelling the Soviet Union to become more public and positive in supporting East Germany.

Again, however, what began as doctrine evolved into policy, then became custom. Brandt's successor as chancellor, Social Democrat Helmut Schmidt, took a significantly more robust stand on the prospects of modifying Soviet policies and intentions. He nevertheless continued what might be called the "atonement" aspects of Ostpolitik, repeatedly affirming and regretting German atrocities committed against Eastern Europe during World War II. Schmidt also found it prudent to cooperate with the GDR on matters of human rights and human compassion, assuming the pension payments of elderly East Germans allowed by their government or paying what amounted to ransom for certain political prisoners. When Helmut Kohl became chancellor in 1982, he expanded the degree and level of cooperation. Even archconservative Strauss helped the GDR secure major loans.

In the context of the 1970s and 1980s such specifics were part of the normalization of the Cold War—perhaps indeed of its desensitization. The Pershing II missile crisis of the early 1980s indicated that when it came to a choice between NATO and U.S. connections or the extension of ties to the East, German governments and voters ultimately faced little difficulty choosing the former. That choice, however, did not exclude doing what could be done to ameliorate specific tensions between the two Germanies, and between the FRG and Warsaw Pact. As the 1980s progressed, and the financial aspects of the former process grew increasingly one-sided, both West German political parties tended to write off the costs in the same way a prosperous individual rationalizes continued assistance to a poor and feckless relative. Significant as well was the continued enthusiasm for the GDR among West German intellectuals disproportionately ready to seize upon any "hawkish" behavior by the Federal Republic as sure proof of a Nazi comeback.

If such people were impossible to conciliate, it was correspondingly prudent not to give them any extra ammunition. Moreover, neither the GDR nor its Soviet patron showed any obvious signs of weakness, let alone collapse. The Kohl government tolerated President Ronald Reagan's "evil empire" rhetoric, supported NATO, and continued to work under the table for everyday rapprochement with a counterpart Germany that at best understood the rules of the game and at worst allowed itself to be paid off.

In the aftermath of the collapse of the GDR, critics, by no means all of them from the Right, excoriated the Kohl government in particular for ignoring the dirtier laundry of East Germany: particularly its unsavory record on human rights and environmental issues. These were the same people, sometimes literally, who had called for reconciliation when confrontation appeared to carry risks. In fact, under Brandt, Schmidt, and Kohl, Ostpolitik modified by circumstances was a reasonable, pragmatic approach to an inherently unstable situation. It generated no great triumphs, but by helping to normalize the Cold War and routinize inter-German relations, it facilitated the unexpected developments of 1989, which could only have occurred in a relatively placid European environment.

–DENNIS SHOWALTER,
COLORADO COLLEGE

Viewpoint:
No. *Ostpolitik* weakened the Cold War Western alliance and legitimized a brutal communist state.

After Willy Brandt, the leader of the Social Democratic Party, became chancellor of West Germany in 1969, he initiated a policy of rapprochement with the Soviet Union and its East European allies. By Brandt's resignation in 1974, Bonn and Moscow had concluded treaties of friendship and nonaggression, and had recognized each other fully. West Germany also formally acknowledged the full sovereignty and legitimacy of the East German state and the loss of the historic German territories east of the Oder and Neisse rivers. Largely as a result of these diplomatic accords, West German trade with Eastern Europe and the Soviet Union increased dramatically. From the American perspective, however, there was little appeal in these developments. Although

National Security Adviser (and, later, Secretary of State) Henry Kissinger approved of Brandt's policies, believing them to fit in with his own vision of détente with the Soviet Union, they were only a long-term threat to American security interests and detracted from the ability of Washington to win the Cold War.

The evolution of the economic and political complexion of the world created serious challenges to U.S. Cold War strategy by the late 1960s. In Western Europe steady economic growth, beginning in earnest in the 1950s, was leading to precisely the same kind of political ambition that such observers as Paul Kennedy have associated with increased national wealth. In France, especially, this intent was enforced by its legacy as a great power and a widespread desire to maintain its influence in world affairs. At a time when it was steadily losing its grip on its colonial empire (beginning with Indochina in 1954 and then spreading throughout its possessions in Africa) and having its independent political action curtailed by American opposition (especially during the Suez Crisis of 1956), France sought a solution that would enable its pretensions to world power status to continue

while its international position was unquestionably in decline. For Charles de Gaulle, president of France from 1958 to 1968, the road to French exceptionalism lay largely in the reemergence of his country as an independent center of power. What could not be achieved by military might had to be achieved through diplomacy. When de Gaulle began to elaborate his program of "détente, entente, and cooperation" with the Soviet Union, he was consciously trying to bring France into a middle position from which it could maintain its independence. A critical function of this policy came to light in 1966, when de Gaulle withdrew French armed forces from the integrated military command structure of the North Atlantic Treaty Organization (NATO). Within Europe, moreover, de Gaulle tried to ensure French hegemony by excluding Britain from membership in the European Economic Community (EEC), which the French president vetoed in 1963.

De Gaulle was not alone in attempting to revive the diplomatic independence of his country. West Germany, with the greatest economic and industrial potential in Western Europe, was also moving toward a middle position between the United States and the

West German chancellor Willy Brandt praying at the Warsaw Ghetto Memorial on 7 December 1970

(Ullstein Bilderdienst, Berlin)

OSTPOLITIK

BRANDT-BREZHNEV PACT

When West German leader Willy Brandt signed a separate accord with the Soviets in 1970, it sent strong reverberations through Washington. Some commentators predicted that the United States would be excluded from Europe. Portions of a 25 August 1970 National Review *editorial, later reprinted in the* Congressional Record, *are presented here.*

What are the shades of Ribbentrop and Molotov murmuring as they look over the shoulders of their Minister-successors? Still further back in the darkness, what flickers through the ghostly minds of Adolf Hitler and Joseph Stalin? Did not that protocol of 31 years ago also "pledge both sides to renounce force in settling disputes" and look forward, "through an improvement in bilateral relations," to peace and advancing well-being in all Europe?

But Willy Brandt is no Hitler, and Leonid Brezhnev no Stalin. . . . Let us not skip quite so fast. . . .

The long-term aim of the Soviet Union, implicit in the accord, is thus strategically offensive: the progressive isolation and exclusion of the U.S. from Europe, with (whatever the illusions of German Socialists) the consequent extension of Soviet domination over all Europe. Meanwhile, for the nearer term, there are other substantial gains in prospect. The Soviet empire, with its economy of late faltering even more badly than usual, needs the infusions of advanced machines, products and technology that Germany can supply. The Presidium has not forgotten Lenin's dictum that German technology plus Russian space, resources and manpower would rule the world.

And this accord, Moscow believes and hopes, will help complete the process she deems essential but had been unable to complete even after a full generation: the legitimization of her empire. That the empire exists in fact is sufficiently demonstrated whenever a colony or vassal state acts in a manner that breaches the imperial discipline. But in the eyes of the Kremlin the de facto relation is too bare and even precarious. The Kremlin desires that the imperial order—formulated in its political essence as "the Brezhnev doctrine"—should be accepted as legitimate and unchallengeable by the non-Communist world.

Up to now one of the plainest standing challenges to the imperial legitimacy has been West Germany's "Hallstein doctrine," refusing diplomatic recognition to all states that recognize East Germany, thus to all the vassal nations. In signing this new Moscow accord, the German Socialists complete the slow burial of the Hallstein doctrine that began two years ago.

Third, and surely not last in importance: along three major fronts: the European (southwestern), Mideastern (actually, southern), and Far Eastern . . . the Kremlin is getting a German promise of all quiet on the Eastern front, so that attention may be focused on the present and potential troubles on the other two.

All in all, not a bad deal for Brezhnev.

Source: *Congressional Record, 116, part 22, 91st Congress, 2nd session (17 August 1970–31 August 1970), p. 30305.*

Soviet Union. The dilemma in Bonn, however, was that the legacy of Germany as a troublemaker in European politics had placed constraints upon it that sharply precluded any aggressive movement away from its Western orientation. Indeed, the Federal Republic of Germany (FRG) was required by its own constitution, the Basic Law, to use its military defensively, and later swore off permanently the development of nuclear, chemical, and biological weapons. Other European powers, it is also true, had been deeply suspicious of West Germany, particularly over the question of its rearmament in 1955. The first movement toward a collective security alliance in Western Europe, the Dunkirk Treaty of 1947, was an Anglo-French entente directed against a resurgent and revanchist Germany.

For roughly the first decade and a half of its existence, under the government of the outspokenly pro-Western chancellor Konrad Adenauer, the Federal Republic had remained firmly and faithfully disposed against the Soviet Union. Guided by the Hallstein Doctrine, named for the Foreign Ministry official who developed the concept, the standing policy of Bonn was to refute the legitimacy of the East German state and break relations with any country other than the Union of Soviet Socialist Republics (U.S.S.R.) that maintained diplomatic relations with it. As Adenauer aged, however, his associates in government became more and more disenchanted with his policy toward the East and began to realize that it was accomplishing little. This belief was especially true with regard to economic policy, for the Federal Republic was beginning to reap the benefits of its *Wirtschaftswunder* (economic miracle) of the 1950s, and many observers realized that the future of the FRG as an economic power would be enhanced by serious export-led growth. As early as June 1963, three months before Adenauer's resignation, West German foreign minister Gerhard Schröder publicly ruminated on the desirability of increased commercial contact with the East. Adenauer's successors, Ludwig Erhard (1963–1966) and Kurt Kiessinger (1966–1969), moved the country further in that direction, concluding informal trade agreements with the Eastern bloc and negotiating formal diplomatic relations with Romania in January 1967.

By the time Brandt came to power in 1969, the stage was set for further developments in the relationship of Bonn with Eastern Europe and the Soviet Union. The relatively innocuous course established by his predecessors now enabled Brandt to pursue

OSTPOLITIK

treaties of friendship and nonaggression with the Soviet Union (August 1970) and Poland (December 1970). The process was dominated throughout by Brandt's personal contrition (he fell on his knees and wept in Warsaw) about the aggressive past of Germany and his earnest desire to improve relations. *Ostpolitik* (eastern policy), as it came to be called, by 1972 had resulted in treaties at last normalizing the status of West Berlin, providing for Federal Republic diplomatic recognition of East Germany, and establishing diplomatic relations between the two German states.

The implications of these developments for an American strategic policy based on the containment of the Soviet Union were quite serious. Under the leadership of Brandt and his like-minded antecedents in the Bonn government, the neutralization of West Germany as an anchor of the Western alliance became a true possibility. By reciprocating Brandt's initiatives, and even facilitating their development by such actions as removing the Stalinist Walter Ulbricht from his leading position in East Germany in 1971, Moscow expressed its clear understanding of what decoupling West Germany, and perhaps all Western Europe, from the United States could mean for its position in the Cold War. As much recent work on Soviet occupation policy and diplomatic handling of the German question immediately after World War II shows, Soviet strategy had antecedents for desiring at least to neutralize Germany and prevent its inclusion in the Western camp. Since the Federal Republic was, relatively speaking, much stronger in 1970 than it was at its founding in 1949, the prospect of drawing Bonn into a neutral middle position was even more attractive. The fact that West Germany was strongly linked economically and politically to most of Western Europe by its membership in the EEC offered an enhanced prospect of using Bonn as a bridge to draw the rest of Europe centrifugally away from its alignment toward the United States.

Although many American strategists began to believe that a multipolar world was unavoidable and that the United States should get used to being one of several powers, it is difficult, indeed, to see how the potential loss of firm and economically strong allies could have had any particular benefit. If European movements toward diplomatic independence continued apace, Washington stood to lose everything it had gained strategically from its Marshall Plan investments in Western Europe and from bearing the lion's share of the bur-

den of defending Western Europe in the postwar era. Brandt's drift into a middle position between the superpowers was, then, no attractive prospect for an America that still faced down a brutal communist dictatorship that never missed a step when it came to forwarding international communism and challenging the strategic superiority of Washington. There is absolutely no argument to suggest that American strategic interests would have been served if the United States were divested of its strongest allies.

Ostpolitik was not good for the Germans, either. Although it normalized access rights to West Berlin and eased legal emigration from East Germany, the costs were significant. Brandt's initiative, first of all, legitimized the brutal expulsion of literally millions of Germans, most of whom were now West German citizens, from their homes at the end of World War II and renounced all hope of them either being allowed to return or receiving compensation. In short, Brandt condoned what a later generation called "ethnic cleansing" for the prospect of limited improvements in relations.

Although relations improved somewhat, Brandt's initiative offered perhaps even less of a chance of bringing about German reunification than Adenauer's policy had. By recognizing the East, Brandt announced to the world that he held the German Democratic Republic (GDR), an oppressive police state utterly devoid of historic, geographic, or democratic legitimacy, suddenly to be a legitimate country. If having "two states of one German nation," as the West German government put it, were an acceptable international settlement for both Bonn and East Berlin, why would the two states ever have to be reunified? Indeed, despite the normalization of relations and some improvements in GDR emigration policy, it remained a brutal police state. Political dissidents were subject to intense persecution, the economy remained under strict government control, ideological strictures were not loosened, and as late as February 1989 illegal émigrés were still shot for trying to leave the country.

When East European communism began to decline in the late 1980s, the regime of Erich Honecker, ironically chosen by the Soviets to succeed Ulbricht because of his more flexible approach to improving relations with the West, remained a steadfast opponent of Mikhail Gorbachev's reformist course in the U.S.S.R. Realizing the possible implications of Gorbachev's renunciation of Soviet military intervention in Eastern Europe for his country and position in the future, Honecker actively opposed political liberalization in his own country. Glasnost, the Soviet policy of openness in government, was even described as "counterrevolutionary" by his regime. Hints from both the West and Soviet Union about the future of a unified Germany were strongly resented by the East German government. In the end Honecker and his associates were not saved by the earlier attempts of Bonn to grant them legitimacy. Ultimately, the reunification of Germany in 1990 had greatly more to do with the domestic crisis of the Soviet Union, the collapse of the communist regimes in Eastern Europe, and the diplomatic responses of Moscow to these developments in 1989–1990 than it did with Brandt's naive maneuvers in the early 1970s. *Ostpolitik* was an ineffectual policy for everyone involved.

–PAUL DU QUENOY,
GEORGETOWN UNIVERSITY

References

Willy Brandt, *My Life in Politics* (London & New York: Hamilton, 1992);

Jeffrey Gedmin, *The Hidden Hand: Gorbachev and the Collapse of East Germany* (Washington, D.C.: American Enterprise Institute Press, 1992);

David H. Shumaker, *Gorbachev and the German Question: Soviet-West German Relations, 1985–1990* (Westport, Conn.: Praeger, 1995);

Michael J. Sodaro, *Moscow, Germany, and the West: from Khrushchev to Gorbachev* (Ithaca, N.Y.: Cornell University Press, 1990);

Richard C. Thornton, *The Nixon-Kissinger Years: Reshaping America's Foreign Policy* (New York: Paragon House, 1989).

OSTPOLITIK

POWER VACUUM

Did the collapse of the Soviet Union cause a dangerous vacuum in world politics?

Viewpoint: Yes. The change from a bipolar to a multipolar worldview caused significant destabilization because many nations resented the increased power and influence of the United States.

Viewpoint: No. The United States with its strong economy and resolve to use military power has filled whatever void in world politics the collapse of the Soviet Union caused.

The collapse of the Soviet Union in 1991 and its reconfiguration as a congeries of middle-sized regional powers generated as much anxiety as gratification among diplomats, soldiers, politicians, and intellectuals in the rest of the world. In forty years the Cold War had become familiar enough to seem the natural order of things. Even the threat of thermonuclear conflict was increasingly an abstraction. Particularly in hindsight, the bipolarity that developed after 1947 seemed accompanied by clarity, at least on major issues. Now every state faced a prospect of autonomy that tended to be more frightening than reassuring.

The situation of the United States as "the world's only remaining superpower" was another source of concern. To a degree it was generated by a cliché drummed for generations into the heads of students in basic history courses: the balance of power. This concept, reduced to its simplest terms, asserts that a state whose strength is disproportionate to that of its neighbors objectively encourages them to band against it. Where, in a global context, would the challenge to U.S. hegemony emerge, and what would be the consequences? The most likely challenger, moreover, the People's Republic of China, was scarcely a solid candidate for the moral high ground in a contest for world leadership. On the other side of the equation, concern was widespread that "American exceptionalism," the U.S. belief in its own moral and institutional superiority, would be given free rein.

That concern highlighted another contribution to post–Cold War angst: the power of disappointment. Generations of critics, domestic and foreign, who were influenced by varying compounds of Marxism, idealism, and malice, had predicted, if not the collapse of the United States, then at least its eclipse as the rest of the world marched triumphantly up the people's way into the sun. Instead the United States not only survived but flourished under a revived global capitalism. Their success just did not seem fair, and the use of its new position came under correspondingly intense scrutiny.

The results have been paradoxical. The United States has been simultaneously charged with seeking to impose a Pax Americana by unilateral initiatives in Haiti, Cuba, and Iraq and accused of callous indifference to poverty and injustice from Tibet to Timor and from Rwanda to Bosnia. Meanwhile, the Atlantic alliance tied itself in knots in the Balkans, ending almost a decade of muddle with nothing to show but a marginally effective protectorate over one of the more turbulent backyards in the world. Meanwhile, India and Pakistan, and China and Taiwan, continue to exchange threats—and in the former case, bullets as well. Yet, in the decade since the collapse of the Soviet Union, conflicts have remained restricted in area if not in violence. The world may be longing, in Norman Graebner's words in a Winter 2000 *Virginia Quarterly Review* article, for an "unobtrusive, reassuring, potentially stabilizing" presence, but it also seems able to struggle along without it—as has been the case for the past several millennia.

Viewpoint:
Yes. The change from a bipolar to a multipolar worldview caused significant destabilization because many nations resented the increased power and influence of the United States.

The end of the Cold War left the United States as the sole superpower. To win the Cold War, the United States greatly outstripped the Union of Soviet Socialist Republics (U.S.S.R.) both militarily and economically. It went on a weapons building spree that the Soviets could not match while at the same time producing an ever-increasing amount of consumer goods. The Soviets tried, but just could not keep pace with the United States and the West. In part, it was this fact that led to the Soviet defeat in the Cold War. Also during this time the United States outpaced its own European allies. However, the West, and specifically the United States, was left with a huge military arsenal and an industrial capacity that was simply enormous. Conversion of the industrial base was not too difficult, but what of the military capability?

Many Americans were uncomfortable with their country's role as the sole superpower. This situation gave rise to the so-called neo-Isolationists who believed that the United States was taking on too much responsibility in the post–Cold War world, and that its involvement should be greatly reduced. The greatest difficulty with this hegemony is that, unlike previous ones, it yielded no clearly defined Pax Americana, nor was there the expected "peace dividend" (expected reductions in defense spending would allow this money to be used elsewhere, according to the theory). There was no decline in violence around the world; in fact, there was an appreciable increase. One reason for this growth is that the power and influence of the United States, while usually mismanaged, was also greatly resented around the globe by both ally and foe alike as an unnecessary and unwanted intrusion into their affairs. With France leading the way, the world began to question the propriety and the right

of the American "hyperpower" to meddle in other countries' affairs.

The dramatic increase in U.S. military operations in the decade of the 1990s is both a symptom and an illness—symptom in that there was a substantial increase in trouble around the world after the fall of the U.S.S.R., and illness as these actions only increase resentment felt around the world. Unfortunately, there was some validity in the resentment, for the countries and regions were rarely better off after U.S. intervention. This increase in operations, more than 300 percent accompanied by a one-third reduction in personnel, made the U.S. forces more depleted, run-down, and ineffective. This situation, in turn, created even greater tension within the U.S. government and armed forces. Clearly they could not indefinitely operate as they had.

By far the most dangerous area of the post–Cold War world was that of nuclear weapons safeguards. The U.S.S.R. was one large nuclear power, but with its collapse, it became four nuclear powers (with another eleven non-nuclear states). Where the international community was used to dealing with one government with a unified leadership and goals, it now had four to contend with. To their credit, three of these new countries opted to accept generous aid packages and relinquished the nuclear weapons. As a result, Russia became the sole former Soviet nuclear power.

Nevertheless, the desire of other nations to develop nuclear weapons did not end, and these nations brought all their resources to bear. The problem was that the main successor state to the U.S.S.R.—Russia—had a terrible economy. The results were severe unemployment, payroll problems, and massive inflation. In such a situation the possibility and probability of personnel with access to weapons of mass destruction (nuclear, biological, and chemical) who were in serious financial hardship was on the rise. Grave violations of security occurred and continue to the present.

With nuclear weapons it was not just the uranium or plutonium that was the problem because weapons components and plans were also at risk. Worse still were the former Soviet scientists who, unable to earn a living at home, would accept positions (and high pay) from

POWER VACUUM

"rogue" states wishing to develop their programs. The countries with these programs were rapidly gaining what they needed to create these weapons. The outcome was a much more dangerous world.

The evidence of this dangerous world abounds. In 1998 India and Pakistan joined the nuclear club, confirming the long-time rumors that they were close to developing nuclear weapons. The list of countries working on this project was long, including such countries as Brazil, Iran, Iraq, Israel, North Korea, South Africa, and Syria.

Another cash-flow problem connected to this issue was that of nuclear surety—safeguarding these weapons from accidental or unintentional use. While Ukraine, Kazakhstan, and Belarus gave up their 2,822 nuclear weapons, the question remained: who was guarding the 5,326 nuclear weapons still in Russia? For instance, in the era of declining budgets and economic turmoil in Russia, and as the equipment aged, was there enough money to ensure proper maintenance or replacement of these weapons? What about the training of the operators and maintenance personnel? They frequently went for months without being paid. Were they working at peak efficiency?

Then there were early-warning radars and other systems to detect enemy missile launches. Did the Russians have enough money to maintain or replace these to ensure no false indications of an incoming attack? If not, the consequences could have been catastrophic, both for the United States and Russia as well as the world.

The breakup of the Soviet Union caused trouble outside as well. In Western countries there was a problem of division of resources. Where they had to watch and deal with one country and its goals, the countries of the world now had to deal with fifteen countries of the former Soviet Union, each with their own, sometimes competing, interests.

Another problem of the breakup of the U.S.S.R. was that it left Western Cold War institutions still in existence and floundering for a purpose. The North Atlantic Treaty Organization (NATO), for instance, became a superfluous entity with no raison d'être. Its actions in Kosovo in 1999 and beyond demonstrated this problem. It was a classic example

Joint Chiefs of Staff Chairman General Colin Powell briefing the Pentagon press corps on Iraqi air defenses during Operation Desert Storm in January 1991

(RD Ward/Department of Defense)

POWER VACUUM

of an organization trying to justify its continued existence by not taking serious risks.

A serious challenge came to the future status of the NATO alliance when the European Union (EU) announced that it was creating a rapid reaction force to deal with European matters and concerns—thereby leaving the United States conspicuously absent. This plan was a deliberate attempt by Europeans to keep the United States from meddling in their affairs. Perhaps it was to be a check to the American "hyperpower." Was it that the world was beginning to see the United States as the global threat? Only time will tell.

The United Nations (U.N.) also had difficulty defining its post–Cold War function. It attempted to assert control and power but was continually checked by states whose interests ran counter to such an organization. This development caused serious questions of status of national sovereignty, interestingly guaranteed in the U.N. Charter. Another obstacle for the U.N. was in defining its legal roles and responsibilities. In the late 1990s it established a war crimes tribunal to deal with the slaughter of thousands in Africa and the Balkans. It proposed an international criminal court for such matters, but this proposal was hotly contested by the United States and some nations usually at odds with America such as Iran and North Korea. Moreover, some of the rulings of the war crimes tribunal actually ran counter to established international law—such as the 1995 ruling that the Hague and Geneva Conventions apply to internal wars rather than just international conflict, as these documents themselves state.

During this time there was also an increase in terrorism. To be fair, much of this violence was because of the increase of narco-terrorism, but then, how does one classify terrorism at the hands of drug traffickers who are also "freedom fighters"? How to deal with terrorism, both unilaterally and as groups of nations, was a question hotly debated on both sides of the Atlantic.

One benefit of the Soviet Union and its system that went unrecognized for years was that internal ethnic, religious, and cultural struggles and disputes were suppressed and rarely came to the surface. Unfortunately for the innocents, most countries were unable to separate as peacefully as the Czechs and the Slovaks did. These disputes simply seemed to erupt in the decade following the Cold War, sending the United States and its allies scrambling to find a response.

Despite the stopgap measures of various organizations and governments and the supposed globalization of the international community, the world clearly became a more dangerous place with the demise of the U.S.S.R. This statement does not mean that the world was not better off without Soviet threats and influence. At least the planet was no longer under the threat of all-out nuclear war between superpowers. While there was a problem of nuclear weapons proliferation, at least it seemed to be under control. At the same time, there was a dramatic increase in lower-level warfare around the world mixed with terrorism. Only time will tell which threat was greater, and whether the responses were the correct ones.

–WILLIAM H. KAUTT, SAN ANTONIO, TEXAS

Viewpoint:
No. The United States with its strong economy and resolve to use military power has filled whatever void in world politics the collapse of the Soviet Union caused.

The end of the Cold War radically changed structures of international politics that had existed for nearly half a century. In the absence of the superimposition of superpower conflict over global affairs, many feared that local conflicts would reemerge and pose serious dangers for peace and security in the future. It was also widely believed that the collapse of the Soviet position in Eastern Europe would create a vacuum of influence that would eventually have to spread. The internal disintegration of the Union of Soviet Socialist Republics (U.S.S.R.), moreover, led to great worries about what a truncated and unstable Russia would do in the future if it were not adequately conciliated; about new ethnic conflicts within the former Soviet Union; and about the proliferation of Soviet nuclear-weapons technology abroad. Despite all the prognostications about how unstable the world could become after the Soviet collapse, however, nothing occurred to suggest that the absence of the U.S.S.R. has been at all destabilizing.

Perhaps the most significant change outside the territory of the former Soviet Union was the liberation of Eastern Europe from communist domination. Despite dire predictions about the desperate need in the region for economic and political reform and modernization, the countries that were formerly in the Soviet orbit show remarkable signs of progress. Most of them have adopted democratic governments and are well on their way to having broad-based civil society institutions. They enthusiastically covet membership in both the North Atlantic Treaty Organization (NATO) and European Union (EU), both of which have guaranteed peace and stability in Western Europe for decades. The so-called fast adjusters—Poland, Hungary, and the Czech Republic—have reached political and economic standards for NATO membership and were admitted to the alliance in March 1999.

With the exception of the former Yugoslavia, which despite its communist government spent most of its Cold War history as far outside the Soviet orbit as any country in Western Europe, the ethnic conflicts that plagued Eastern Europe historically have not posed much of a problem. The status of large Hungarian minorities in Romania and Slovakia, and even within the former Yugoslavia, has been more or less normalized. The Hungarians in those countries have yet to revolt. Ethnic German minorities that remained in Poland, Hungary, and Romania, as well as in the former Soviet Union after World War II have largely immigrated to Germany under its ethnicity-based citizenship laws. The question of the German-Polish frontier, which has no historical legitimacy and resulted in the brutal expulsion of millions of German civilians after 1945, has been sanctified both by the international community and Germany itself, as have legal issues concerning the expulsion of the Sudeten Germans from Czechoslovakia. At reunification, language providing for the incorporation of historically German territory into the Federal Republic, which had been applied to East Germany, was deleted from the German constitution. If the point is of any interest, the residency provisions of the Maastricht Treaty (Treaty on European Union; approved 1991, ratified 1993) allows any German citizen to move to their historic home should Poland and the Czech Republic join the European Union (EU).

The apparent success of the EU as an agent of economic and political integration effectively defuses another potential problem for Eastern Europe. Historically, that relatively underdeveloped region either came under the domination of one power (as it did during the Cold War) or was the object of dispute (as it had between the Hapsburg and Russian Empires in the nineteenth century). After the collapse of the Soviet Union, however, traditional patterns of hegemonic domination have not applied. Rather than facing economic and political penetration by a single country, the recent history of the region suggests that its countries will become integral parts of the

supranational EU with their security guaranteed by NATO membership.

Conflicts surrounding the post–Cold War fragmentation of Yugoslavia, which had been outside Soviet influence, has presented challenges to regional stability, but after nearly a decade the conflict has not gone beyond the former borders of that country. Its disintegration along ethnic lines, moreover, resulted from problems that have plagued that part of the world for the past thousand years and that historically presented challenges to the Yugoslav state. The decline of its cohesion began to reemerge after Josip Broz Tito's death in 1980, when the U.S.S.R. was still regarded as one of the two superpowers, and accelerated not as a result of events in Moscow but simultaneously with them. The resulting conflict in Bosnia-Herzegovina seems to have been ended by a U.S.-led NATO peacekeeping force, which entered that country in 1995 after U.N. peacekeepers failed to make an impact. In the wake of a U.S.-led aerial offensive against Yugoslavia in 1999, more NATO peacekeepers were poised to enter Kosovo, where ethnic conflict had broken out.

Further afield, potential trouble spots and "rogue" states have been checked by unilateral American action or by multinational efforts. Since its military defeat by a U.S.-led coalition in 1991, Iraqi chemical, nuclear, and biological weapons facilities have been dismantled by U.N. inspectors, while the U.S. Air Force enforces a "no-fly zone" that prevents Saddam Hussein from attacking Kurdish and Shiite Muslim minorities. In 1994 U.S. troops ousted a military junta in Haiti and restored pretensions to democratic government. That same year Washington reached an agreement with Japan and South Korea providing for a military solution should North Korea not acquiesce to UN inspection of its nuclear facilities. The United States has also demonstrated a willingness to take unilateral action against international terrorism, through both economic sanctions against countries that sponsor terrorists (such as Lybia and Iran) and military strikes against terrorist installations (such as the 1998 bombings in Sudan and Afghanistan).

The situation within the former Soviet Union presents problems, but hardly a challenge to world stability. Despite widespread popular resentment about having lost the Cold War, economic difficulties, and its political instability, Russia has had to face the fact that its future modernization and development depend on its relationship with the West. Even when that relationship is strained, as it has been since U.S. planes began bombing its traditional Serbian ally in March 1999,

A NEW ROLE FOR NATO

The North Atlantic Treaty Organization (NATO) was forced by the end of the Cold War to reassess its role in Europe. On 6 July 1990 it issued a declaration and invited Mikhail Gorbachev to speak to its council:

Europe has entered a new promising era. Central and Eastern Europe is liberating itself. The Soviet Union has embarked on the long journey toward a free society. The walls that once confined people and ideas are collapsing. Europeans are determining their own destiny. They are choosing freedom. They are choosing economic liberty. They are choosing peace. They are choosing a Europe whole and free. As a consequence, this Alliance must and will adapt. . . .

We will remain a defensive alliance and will continue to defend all the territory of all our members. We have no aggressive intentions and we commit ourselves to the peaceful resolution of all disputes. We will never in any circumstance be the first to use force.

The member states of the North Atlantic Alliance propose to the member states of the Warsaw Treaty Organization a joint declaration in which we solemnly state that we are no longer adversaries and reaffirm our intention to refrain from the threat or use of force against the territorial integrity or political independence of any state, or from acting in any other manner inconsistent with the purpose and principles of the United Nations Charter and with the C.S.C.E. [Conference on Security and Cooperation in Europe] Final Act. . . .

As Soviet troops leave Eastern Europe and a treaty limiting conventional armed forces is implemented, the Alliance's integrated force structure and its strategy will change fundamentally to include the following elements:

NATO will field smaller and restructured active forces. These forces will be highly mobile and versatile so that Allied leaders will have maximum flexibility in deciding how to respond to a crisis. It will rely increasingly on multinational corps made up of national units.

NATO will scale back the readiness of its active units reducing training requirements and the number of exercises.

NATO will rely more heavily on the ability to build up larger forces if and when they are needed.

To keep the peace, the Alliance must maintain for the foreseeable future an appropriate mix of nuclear and conventional forces, based in Europe, and kept up to date where necessary. But, as a defensive Alliance, NATO has always stressed that none of its weapons will ever be used except in self-defense and that we seek the lowest and most stable level of nuclear forces needed to secure the prevention of war.

The political and military changes in Europe, and the prospects of further changes, now allow the Alliance to go further. They will thus modify the size and adapt the tasks of their nuclear deterrent forces. They have concluded that, as a result of the new political and military conditions in Europe, there will be a significantly reduced role for sub-strategic nuclear systems of the shortest range. They have decided specifically that, once negotiations begin on short-range nuclear forces, the Alliance will propose, in return for reciprocal action by the Soviet Union, the elimination of all its nuclear artillery shells from Europe.

Source: *Current History, 89 (October 1990): 334.*

Moscow has had to swallow its pride and make concessions to the West in order to preserve the financial and commercial ties that offer the best chance to reinvigorate its economy and society. In the event, the continuing decline of Russia has impeded its ability even to keep the central authority over the country intact. The Russian military utterly failed to put down an insurrection by Chechen guerrilla fighters after several years of involvement. Remote provinces inhabited by ethnic Russians have

demonstrated increasing independence from the Federation government.

The problems of Russia at home underscore the influence it has over the other Soviet successor states. While Belarus, ruled by the dictatorship of a former communist, is politically close to Russia, the others remain jealous of their independence. The Baltic States, Ukraine, and Moldova are actively interested in close ties to the West, potentially including NATO membership. While the states of Transcaucasia and

POWER VACUUM

Central Asia have a long way to go to develop liberal democratic governments and still have ties to Russia (including, in some cases, the presence of Russian troops), they are all not under its domination.

Nor have broader international problems related to the collapse of the Soviet Union destabilized the world. Eight years after the collapse of the U.S.S.R., much-touted fears that poorly paid scientists or disgruntled military officers would sell Soviet nuclear weapons technology to "rogue" states have yet to be justified. Whatever progress countries such as Iraq or North Korea have made toward developing a nuclear device with Russian help have been thwarted by the United States and the international community. There is no evidence that the most recent emerging nuclear powers, India and Pakistan, received the necessary technology and materials from Russia.

The widespread belief that the relative stability of a bipolar world would give way to the instability in a multipolar world has not been borne out in reality. Russian reemergence as a viable economic and military power is a long way off, probably decades in the future. In addition to the fact that the movement of the EU toward economic and political integration is predicated on stability and peace within the continent, the process that many believed would cause Europe to emerge as a superpower in its own right, has generated many structural problems. Most European economies are plagued with chronic high unemployment and slowing economic growth. The overbearing presence of many European governments in national economies and the increasingly unbearable burden of their comprehensive welfare states stifles initiative, creativity, and growth. A spate of electoral victories by left-of-center political parties resulted largely from their movement away from socialism and an expressed intent to reduce the role of government in the economy and society, in some cases even to a greater extent than the parties of the right. The euro, the unified currency introduced in several EU states in January 1999, has not reversed these trends, and its value has actually declined since its introduction. Several countries, notably the United Kingdom (U.K.), have not adopted the common currency and are not likely to do so for at least another several years. Although there are now notions of a common European defense force, the EU has proven itself unable to stop the ethnic conflicts in Yugoslavia, its own backyard, without decisive American leadership and military action.

In Asia the great concerns of the 1990s over the development of the Japanese econ-omy have not been justified. Like the European economies, it too has suffered from rising unemployment, slow growth, and the burden of a social-welfare system that is becoming harder and harder to maintain. The industrialization of smaller Asian countries has meant the loss of Japanese blue-collar jobs, as has the large-scale movement of basic industries (such as textiles) overseas, the same problem faced by the United States in the 1960s and 1970s. Japanese defense and foreign policies are much more coordinated with those of the United States than any of its Asian neighbors.

The development of one of those neighbors, China, while impressive, is greatly dependent on the health of its relationship with the United States, which buys the largest single percentage of Chinese exports. Controversies over the appalling human-rights record of Beijing, recent revelations about the broad scope of Chinese nuclear espionage in the United States, past and present relations with rogue states, and its opposition to recent NATO action in Yugoslavia have made that relationship increasingly tense. Proponents of "engaging" China in broad commercial and diplomatic ties to stimulate domestic reform and geopolitical restraint, an argument stunningly similar to the one made by proponents of détente with the Soviet Union, are justifiably finding their strategic approach to China difficult to sell. Nevertheless, Chinese economic power has not yet compensated for its strategic inferiority to the United States. Even with its acquisition of what has been estimated to be nuclear parity with the United States, China remains a regional power without sufficient clout or influence even to establish control over Taiwan, which China insists is, and much of the world (including the United States) officially regards as, part of its territory. Its economic growth notwithstanding, the average national standard of living remains rather low. The political monopoly of the communist party is challenged by a large number of political, ethnic, and religious dissent movements that enjoy much notoriety and sympathy abroad. Beijing has much bark but little bite.

While information-age media technology brings various local and regional crises to the attention of the American public, and while academic studies have put forward theoretical approaches to the relative decline of the United States and the increasing turbulence in international politics, the hard facts do not bear out the conclusion that the post–Cold War world is, or will be, marred with instability. The United States stands strong as the only superpower, with an economy larger than those of the next three largest countries taken together. Despite cuts in military spending through the 1990s, the decisions of the Clinton administration to increase the defense budget (which even include the once-ridiculed idea of developing a ballistic-missile-defense system), its resolve in using military power to defend U.S. interests abroad, and the general good health and steady growth of the economy for more than two decades prove that the United States will not retreat from the global stage. Pessimists who believe that America would become, or is becoming, just another player among four or five "emerging centers of power," and that its tenure as the major world power has ended or will soon end, are wrong to believe in what Henry R. Nau, in *The Myth of America's Decline: Leading the World Economy into the 1990s* (1990), has called a myth. The United States has the preponderant influence and has every chance of keeping it for a long time.

–PAUL DU QUENOY,
GEORGETOWN UNIVERSITY

References

R. J. Crampton, *Eastern Europe in the Twentieth Century* (London & New York: Routledge, 1994);

Francis Fukuyama, *The End of History and the Last Man* (New York: Free Press, 1992);

Norman Graebner, "The Limits of Meliorism in Foreign Affairs," *Virginia Quarterly Review,* 76 (Winter 2000): 20–37;

Samuel P. Huntington, *The Clash of Civilizations and the Remaking of World Order* (New York: Simon & Schuster, 1996);

Paul Kennedy, *The Rise and Fall of the Great Powers: Economic Change and Military Conflict From 1500 to 2000* (New York: Random House, 1987);

Henry R. Nau, *The Myth of America's Decline: Leading the World Economy into the 1990s* (New York: Oxford University Press, 1990);

Kenneth Walz, "Globalization and American Power," *National Interest,* 59 (Spring 2000): 46–56.

POWER VACUUM

REAGAN DOCTRINE

Was the Reagan Doctrine prudent?

Viewpoint: Yes. Ronald Reagan's policy helped cause the destruction of the U.S.S.R., and restored confidence in the U.S. military, positioning the United States as the leading world power.

Viewpoint: No. The Reagan Doctrine contributed to European instability and damaged the American economy.

The Reagan Doctrine—named after U.S. president Ronald Reagan—was the term given to the adaptation by his administration of John Foster Dulles's "rollback" strategy of the 1950s to conditions of the 1980s. There were two differences between the versions. First, the Eisenhower administration had Central and Eastern European nations in mind—countries that came under Soviet domination as a result of the westward drive of the Red Army—while the Reagan administration concentrated on the Third World; second, there is no indication that the Eisenhower administration intended to go beyond rhetorical expressions of support, whereas the Reagan administration energetically and actively pursued their policy.

During Reagan's eight years in office (1981–1989), his administration provided financial support, weapons, and training to anticommunist insurgencies in Nicaragua, Angola, Mozambique, Cambodia (then known as Kampuchea), and Afghanistan. The administration also supported governments (for example, El Salvador) faced with communist insurgencies. In 1983 Reagan sent U.S. troops to invade the island of Grenada to topple the pro-Castro government when it began to ready airstrips and military bases for possible stationing of Cuban, and perhaps even Soviet, troops.

Some analysts see "rollback" as only one element of a broader national-security doctrine pursued by the Reagan administration. They point to three, more specifically military, elements of the doctrine: the notions that a nuclear war could be fought and "won" (Reagan's secretary of defense, Caspar W. Weinberger, preferred using the term "prevailing"), and that there would be a meaningful difference between winning and losing such a war; the idea of "horizontal escalation," the plan to expand a war against the Soviet Union to additional theaters (for example, an invasion of Cuba in case the Soviets attacked in Europe); and the decision to build a ballistic-missile defense system ("star wars" or "astrodome" defense), which would substitute deterrence-by-denial (of success in a nuclear attack) for deterrence-by-mutual-vulnerability, which had characterized the nuclear postures of the two superpowers since the early 1960s.

Viewpoint:
Yes. Ronald Reagan's policy helped cause the destruction of the U.S.S.R., and restored confidence in the U.S. military, positioning the United States as the leading world power.

While he was running for president in 1980, Ronald Reagan advocated a forceful approach to foreign policy based on military strength. During his two terms in office (1981–1989), Reagan pursued controversial spending policies that focused heavily on building American military power to an extent so great that by the time he left office it was widely believed that the United States was the only superpower. For a variety of reasons his emphasis on developing American military power was both justified and wise.

Despite significant increases in military spending toward the end of the Carter administration (1977–1981), the state of the military when Reagan entered office was deplorable. Military policy throughout the 1970s seriously impacted the efficacy and morale of American armed forces. Stung by the loss of the Vietnam War, its heavy price in men and matériel, and its serious domestic consequences, American politicians and strategic planners avoided active use of the military. Conflict situations that had even the potential to involve American troops were avoided, often at the expense of strategic interests. When the North Vietnamese communist regime violated the Paris peace accords of January 1973 and completed its conquest of South Vietnam in 1975, Congress refused to sanction any, even nonmilitary, aid to Saigon. On 7 November 1973 the War Powers Resolution curtailed executive power to make long-term military deployments without formal Congressional approval. In 1976 Congress cut all aid to anti-communist resistance fighters in Angola. Existing American conventional forces in Europe were reduced over the course of the decade, and in 1976 presidential candidate Jimmy Carter pledged to withdraw U.S. troops from South Korea. Even as several Third World nations came under the control of communist movements, directly assisted by the Soviet Union and its allies, American military policy was captured by a desire to avoid any commitment that could result in another Vietnam.

In addition to a more passive military policy, the pursuit of détente with the communist world led many to believe that more peaceful relations between the superpowers could, and should, be complemented by a demilitarization of the Cold War. Although there was little sign

of reciprocity from the Soviets, who continued to devote a large portion of their economy to the military and took advantage of opportunities to expand their influence throughout the world, the conviction that the Cold War could be stabilized through negotiation and mutual disarmament remained the guiding principle in American foreign policy until the end of the Carter administration.

Furthermore, public mood following the Vietnam War was poorly disposed toward the military as an institution. Many Americans who had opposed the war unfairly held servicemen personally responsible for belligerent, controversial, or simply bad decisions made by political elites. Popular antiwar movies such as Francis Ford Coppola's *Apocalypse Now* (1979) portrayed American soldiers at, and beyond, the brink of insanity. Many veterans returned only to be treated as pariahs in the land they had risked their lives to defend and suffered from discrimination, ostracism, and social problems. The image of the young radical, who had managed not to go to Vietnam, spitting on the less fortunate youth who had served, was a powerful cultural metaphor.

All of these factors came together and led to sharp reductions in military spending. As the defense budget declined, the size and quality of the U.S. armed forces dropped as well. By the time Reagan entered office, many enlisted servicemen were so poorly paid that they had to rely on government social-welfare programs to support their families. Many talented and able Americans either avoided military service altogether or left it prematurely because it seemed to offer poor career prospects.

Even before Reagan's election, however, the evisceration of American armed forces in the face of truculent arms-control negotiations and the Soviet invasion of Afghanistan (1979) led the Carter administration to reverse course and increase military investment. Reagan's call for increased defense spending expanded these endeavors to restore the morale, prestige, and efficiency of the U.S. military.

The condition of the military was indeed so weak in the first years of the Reagan administration that even many of those who agreed with his general goals of pursuing an activist foreign policy and rolling back communism were reluctant to make substantial use of the armed forces. Secretary of Defense Caspar W. Weinberger, charged with reinvigorating American military power, concurred with senior officers who argued against large-scale troop deployments. With the exception of minor military operations such as the deployment of marines to Lebanon (1982), the invasion of Grenada (1983), and air strikes against Libya (1986), the

administration conducted its foreign policy largely through financial and material support for anticommunist governments and resistance movements, as well as with trade policies that had strategic objectives.

As the military buildup gained momentum, however, Reagan's willingness to carry what President Theodore Roosevelt described as "a big stick" became an important component of his approach to foreign affairs. Realizing that the philosophical opposition of the Soviet government to free thought, entrepreneurial initiative, and economic liberty was a growing albatross for Moscow, Reagan's defense policies presented the Soviets with qualitative challenges they could not hope to meet. The use of emerging laser and computer technologies in such sophisticated weapons as the F-16 fighter, the Abrams tank, and the *Trident*-class submarine improved the American arsenal in ways the Soviets found difficult even to imagine. Reagan's March 1983 announcement that his administration would begin to research an orbital ballistic-missile

defense system (the Strategic Defense Initiative, or SDI) caused a great deal of agitation in the Soviet leadership; many former Soviet officials candidly admitted that SDI, along with broader military development, was the definitive factor that convinced them they could never best the United States in an arms race. Alexander A. Bessmertnykh, the U.S.S.R.'s last foreign minister, said in a 1993 speech at Princeton University that SDI was an important factor in the political collapse of his former country.

The American military buildup and Reagan's steadfast refusal to negotiate with the Soviets on arms-control issues before late 1985 left the Soviets in an intractable position. It seemed that no amount of effort on their part would allow them to recover the initiative in the Cold War. As a result, the Soviet elite began to favor a reformist course in domestic and international politics. After the succession of Mikhail Gorbachev to leadership in March 1985, perceptible signs of change in Soviet attitudes became readily apparent. Aware that the U.S.S.R. could only modern-

REAGAN DOCTRINE

ize and continue to function as a great power if it devoted more resources to domestic economic development, Gorbachev pursued foreign policies that were designed to reduce military investment and the international tension that had necessitated it. Indeed, like his predecessors in the détente era, Gorbachev hoped that a transformation of Cold War politics would even lead to commercial agreements with the West that would help facilitate the modernization and development of the Soviet Union.

Conscious of the fact that American military superiority would only increase over time, Gorbachev initially made peace overtures that were often predicated on reductions in American military power. At the first two summit meetings between Gorbachev and Reagan, in Geneva in November 1985 and Reykjavik, Iceland, in October 1986, the Soviet leader made any nuclear arms-control agreement contingent upon the elimination of SDI. Although Reagan refused to abandon the program, Gorbachev's desperation to end an arms race he could only lose eventually led him to agree to nonconditional agreements providing for the removal of intermediate range nuclear forces (INF) from central Europe and mutual reduction in conventional forces in Europe (CFE). Over the next few years Gorbachev progressively renounced the use of Soviet military power as policy, withdrew troops from Afghanistan, consented to free or partially free elections in Eastern Europe, and gave way on German reunification. It strains credulity to suggest that either the Soviet Union as a system, or a committed communist leader such as Gorbachev, would have naturally and voluntarily dismantled strong strategic positions and suddenly become more cooperative with the West were it not for the great pressure placed on the Soviet economy by the specter of unmatchable American military power.

While the Reagan military buildup compelled the Soviet Union to adopt policies that reduced its threat to international security and actually hastened the U.S.S.R.'s demise, it had no negative impact on the United States. Contrary to the arguments of Reagan's critics, military spending did not cause the growing deficits in the federal budget that began to plague government finance in the 1980s. While defense spending did increase, it never amounted to more than 8 percent of the Gross National Product (GNP) at the height of its expansion. Over the course of the administration, moreover, increases in military spending had to be authorized by congressional Democrats, who held a majority in the House of Representatives throughout the decade (and in fact from 1955 to 1995), and in the Senate before 1983 and after 1986. While many Democrats supported Reagan's military policy, just as they had Carter's, administration requests for spending increases were relatively modest and only partly fulfilled. Partially at

the insistence of Reagan's own Office of Management and Budget, defense spending rose by an average of less than 8 percent per year in the first four fiscal years of his administration, compared with Carter's 13.5 percent increase in fiscal year 1981. It was nowhere near the 20 percent increase the Truman administration had recommended for 1953. Carter's 1981 increase was merely the first year of a projected five-year buildup that would presumably have continued had Carter won reelection. In each of the five fiscal years after 1985, furthermore, the Defense Department budget was actually cut. Although economic development and tax reform caused government revenue roughly to double between 1981 and 1989, significant growth in Democrat-sponsored social and entitlement spending eclipsed these increases, led to perennial federal deficits, and was the single largest contribution to the growing national debt.

The recovery of the American domestic economy from the high unemployment and inflation of the Carter years was coincidental with, rather than inhibited by, the growth of government investment in the military. After preliminary tax reform in 1982 and the substantial increase in military spending begun under Carter, the U.S. economy grew dramatically, especially in the industrial and manufacturing sectors. Congressional and Bush administration decisions to reduce military spending in the years after 1985, which included base closings and the cancellation of many government contracts, were partially responsible for the economic downturn that cost George Bush's reelection in 1992. Additionally, many new technologies originally developed for military purposes in the 1980s or earlier (for example, the Internet, microchips, personal computers, and microwaves) have been swiftly and successfully adapted to productive civilian use on a scale so large that the national and global economy have been transformed in a manner unparalleled since the Industrial Revolution.

Critics of Reagan's military policy have argued further that the demise of the Soviet Union, which many academics now claim to have been an inevitability regardless of what Reagan did or failed to do, ultimately made costly defense expenditures unnecessary and wasteful. This argument, however, is at best a hindsight judgment. To the embarrassment of virtually the entire Western scholarly community, few students of foreign affairs and even fewer critics of Reagan's military policy at the time predicted either the fall of communism or dissolution of the U.S.S.R. Many even commented on its remarkable "success" and "stability" when its complete ruin was looming.

Even if American military pressure did not have the effect it had on the Soviet leadership and its strategic decisions in the late 1980s, such criticism would still be inaccurate. In a transitional world the effective use of American military power

REAGAN DOCTRINE

as it developed during Reagan's presidency proved its importance and refuted the notion that the United States was in decline as a world power. Shortly after Reagan left office, American military intervention deposed Panamanian dictator Manuel Noriega (December 1989), continuing the U.S. tradition of maintaining stability in the Western Hemisphere. In 1990–1991 the size, training, and quality of the military led to the swift and efficient victory of an American-led coalition over Saddam Hussein's Iraq after it occupied the strategically significant and oil-rich nation of Kuwait. The use of military power to impose seemingly successful peace settlements in Bosnia-Herzegovina in 1995 and in the Yugoslavian province of Kosovo in 1999, settlements that eluded the United Nations and European Union for years before American-led intervention, would not have been possible if the evisceration of the military in the 1970s had been allowed to continue. One can only guess how many potential aggressors have been deterred by Washington's readiness to use military force.

Reagan's decision to restore and expand the armed forces was prescient and wise. First and foremost, the quality and morale of the military was brought back from a dangerously low level. As a result the United States has remained the preeminent power in the world. Implicit in that achievement was Reagan's role in using competitive U.S. military advantages to present Soviet leaders with no alternative but to begin a process of reform that legitimately reduced superpower tension, and in the end undermined the domestic stability of most communist regimes. At home, the American economy actually benefited from military investment, which sparked the economic recovery of the 1980s and made possible more-or-less-steady economic growth. The Reagan military buildup had many benefits and hardly any consequences.

–PAUL DU QUENOY, GEORGE
WASHINGTON UNIVERSITY

Viewpoint:
No. The Reagan Doctrine contributed to European instability and damaged the American economy.

The Reagan Doctrine, and the accompanying military buildup, was hardly justified and definitely not wise. Increased military spending started under the Carter administration, following the fall of the Shah of Iran (January 1979) and Soviet invasion of Afghanistan (December 1979). The Reagan administration simply carried it out to an extreme that at best simply furthered the

REAGAN'S FOREIGN POLICY

On 24 April 1981, Secretary of State Alexander Haig spoke before the American Society of Newspaper Editors. His speech detailed the foreign-policy position of the Reagan administration. An excerpt from his remarks is presented below.

We are acting to restore confidence in American leadership through a more robust defense of U.S. ideals and interests and a more realistic approach to the dangers and opportunities of the international situation. It is my purpose today to outline briefly the philosophy behind the new direction: the Administration's view of the realities of the world and the tasks before us. . . .

First, to enlarge our capacity to influence events and to make more effective use of the full range of our moral, political, scientific, and military resources in the pursuits of our interests;

Second, to convince our allies, friends, and adversaries—above all the Soviet Union—that America will act in a manner befitting our responsibilities as a trustee of freedom and peace; and

Third, to offer hope and aid to the developing countries in their aspirations for a peaceful and prosperous future.

The President has established clear priorities in the pursuit of these projects. Understanding that American economic weakness could cripple our efforts abroad, he has proposed a revolutionary program to restore inflation-free growth. This program recognizes that America's strength is measured not only in arms but also in the spirit of individual enterprise, the soundness of the dollar, and the proper role of government in a free society.

Fundamental to this approach is also the belief that economic recovery must be accompanied by a prompt correction of defects in our military posture. For too long, we have ignored this fact: The military strength required by the United States can be achieved only through sacrifice and consistent purpose. We have proposed a heavy investment in our Armed Forces to assure safety for ourselves and the generations to come. . . .

Only the United States has the pivotal strength to convince the Soviets—and their proxies—that violence will not advance their cause. Only the United States has the power to persuade the Soviet leaders that improved relations with us serve Soviet as well as American interests. We have a right, indeed a duty, to insist that the Soviets support a peaceful international order, that they abide by treaties, and that they respect reciprocity. A more constructive Soviet behavior in these areas will surely provide the basis for a more productive East-West dialogue.

Source: *Department of State,* American Foreign Policy: Current Documents, 1981 *(Washington: 1982), 35–37.*

already accelerating demise of the Soviet Union and at worst heightened tensions between the two superpowers. This situation could have led to even worse problems had not Mikhail Gorbachev's cooler head prevailed after he ascended to the position of General Secretary in March 1985. Furthermore, military spending and the accompanying policy of "Reaganomics" tripled the U.S. national debt in eight years and caused long-lasting fiscal problems. Lastly, although few people wish that the Soviet Union was still around, if Reagan's policy accelerated the demise of the Soviet Union, then it also helped create a power vacuum, thereby destabilizing international affairs not just in Eastern Europe (especially in the former Yugoslavia), but around the world.

The fall of the Shah and the Soviet invasion of Afghanistan, as well as the general "malaise" in the United States, however, spelled doom for Jimmy Carter's chances for reelection. Both the taking of hostages in the American embassy in Tehran (4 November 1979) and the botched rescue attempt (25 April 1980) seemed, to the American public, evidence that the Carter administration was inept. Thus, they elected Ronald Reagan as president, based in part on his pledge to get tough with opponents abroad.

Indeed, it seemed that the Afghanistan policy marked a new phase of Soviet aggression. If one looked beneath the surface of this new roar, however, one could easily see that the Soviet Union was naught but a paper tiger. Although its armed forces and nuclear arsenal were definitely something to hold in awe, the rest of the country suffered from growing uneasiness. Leonid Brezhnev, who took over the Soviet Union in 1964 following Nikita S. Khrushchev's ouster, was increasingly senile. Members of the Politburo and Central Committee were so old and out of touch with what was going on in the country that their status created a new term, "gerantocracy." Furthermore, the Soviet economy, which as late as 1970 seemed to be on track to catch up with the West and the United States, had stagnated. Budgetary problems were also huge. The Soviet Union was spending up to 25 percent of its Gross Domestic Product (GDP) on the military just to try to keep up with the West. In short, the Soviet Union was already starting the long decline that would culminate with its breakup in 1991.

Even if no one pushed, it was likely that the Soviet Union was going to have to undergo massive reforms or change the way it did business. When Reagan came along, however, and started to pour billions of dollars into defense, including the development of the Strategic Defense Initiative (SDI), the Soviet Union was forced to accelerate its already absurd spending on its military, rather than using these funds for reform. When the Soviet government finally concentrated on

instituting reforms, it was too little too late. Therefore, while Reagan's policy increased Soviet military spending, it merely crippled the already badly damaged economy of the U.S.S.R.

Reagan's military policy helped bring U.S.-Soviet relations to their lowest level since the mid 1960s, as well as push Soviet military leaders closer to the forefront of Soviet politics. The saving grace was that Soviet leadership was in a period of major transition. If a stronger General Secretary than Brezhnev, Yuri Andropov, or Konstantin Chernenko had been at the helm, the situation could have been brought to a head immediately. By the time a stronger leader came to the fore with Gorbachev's ascension in 1985, the United States had obtained such a lead on the Soviet Union that there was no hope that it could catch up. Thus, it was only the result of an already declining economy, and the moderate Gorbachev assuming power, that Reagan's buildup did not create overly antagonistic relations with the Soviet Union. Had a more militaristic individual been chosen Secretary General, the Cold War could have regressed to a point as bad as the early 1950s.

The only thing that Reagan's military buildup can be said to have done with any certainty was help to triple the national debt. Just as it might have driven the Soviet economy to ruin, it almost did the same thing to the American economy. Increased military spending definitely was one of the leading causes of the recession of the early 1990s. Had the economy not been managed better, thanks in large part to the Federal Reserve, Reagan's spending spree might have sent the United States into a full-blown depression. In addition, Reagan's policy was partially responsible for ruining the presidency of his protégé, George Bush. Thus, Reagan's policy was not only destructive to the Soviet economy and political system, but also disruptive to America's economy and politics.

The Reagan Doctrine accelerated the already imminent demise of the Soviet economy, and forced the Soviet Union to divert resources that might have been used for reforming the economic and political system. Furthermore, the traditional massive-attack strategy of the Soviet military was not effective in the mountainous terrain of Afghanistan. This failure was compounded by the guerrilla nature of the Afghan resistance. Thus, not only was the economy in decline, but the military, the shining beacon of supposed Soviet success, was faltering as well. It was evident to all of those in the government who were not obsessed with keeping their perks that it would become necessary to reform all facets of the Soviet Union. Indeed, following Brezhnev's death, Andropov attempted to begin some reforms. His protégé was Gorbachev.

The Soviet Union was bound to institute reforms; Reagan, however, not only forced it to divert resources from reform, but also kept those people who advocated spending even more money on the military in positions of power. Thus, by the time the Soviet leadership became serious about reforms, the economy had been so shattered by this huge abuse of resources, that it accelerated the unavoidable demise of the Soviet Union. The speed of downfall did not leave enough time for a transition of any sort—it resembled something like a supernova. It freed all the countries around it as if they were clouds of gas, behind which a much smaller core (Russia) remained. While the initial explosion was bright and seemed to be the beginning of something spectacular, the nebula it left behind was little more than chaos. Small countries such as Czechoslovakia and Yugoslavia split into smaller entities (either peacefully or through horrific violence); and all sorts of heretofore low-level apparatchiks became the undisputed rulers of former Soviet republics. In short, what was once a stable, if rather undesirable, entity had dissolved into anarchy. Thus, Reagan can be said to have contributed to this new instability in international politics.

Since the Soviet Union was already in imminent demise, Reagan's military policy was hardly justified and was unwise. An already weak nation was forced into a situation beyond its control, and thereby became extremely weak, to the point where it was unable to sustain itself. Repercussions in international affairs can be seen most evidently in the chaos that erupted in the Balkans once the controlling factor of the Soviet Union was no longer there. Thus, the Reagan buildup was responsible not only for the economic and political ruin of the U.S.S.R., but also for economic and political instability in the United States, as well as the turmoil currently fomented in a newly unstable international environment.

–JONATHAN HUTZLEY, GEORGE WASHINGTON UNIVERSITY

References

Walter LaFeber, *America, Russia, and the Cold War, 1945–1992,* seventh edition (New York: McGraw-Hill, 1993);

Kenneth Oye, Robert Lieber, and Donald Rothchild, eds., *Eagle Resurgent?: The Reagan Era in American Foreign Policy* (Boston: Little, Brown, 1987);

Peter Schweizer, *Victory: The Reagan Administration's Secret Strategy That Hastened the Collapse of the Soviet Union* (New York: Atlantic Monthly Press, 1994);

James M. Scott, *Deciding to Intervene: The Reagan Doctrine and American Foreign Policy* (Durham, N.C.: Duke University Press, 1996);

Caspar W. Weinberger, *Fighting for Peace: Seven Critical Years in the Pentagon* (New York: Warner, 1990).

REAGAN DOCTRINE

REAGAN'S TRANSFORMATION

Did Ronald Reagan change his attitude toward military confrontation during his presidency?

Viewpoint: Yes. Ronald Reagan adopted a confrontational stance toward the Soviet Union during the first years of his presidency, but a détente-oriented policy came to the fore in his second term.

Viewpoint: No. Ronald Reagan consistently relied on military strength as the foundation of his foreign policy.

In January 1981 Ronald Reagan entered office on a platform of bullish anticommunism. Deeply convinced that the Soviet Union was the greatest threat to freedom and liberty, he publicly denounced it as an evil empire and frequently predicted its ruin. For the first several years of his administration, Reagan pursued policies that were intended to confront the Soviet Union diplomatically, overwhelm it militarily, break it economically, roll it back strategically, and leave it and its Marxist-Leninist system of rule "on the ash heap of history."

After a prolonged period of heightened Cold War tension characterized by Reagan's early confrontational approach, American strategy began to change. In November 1985 and October 1986 Reagan consented to hold summit meetings with his Soviet counterpart, Mikhail Gorbachev, something he had been unwilling to do for almost the first five years of his administration and the initial eighteen months of Gorbachev's tenure. Although little of practical value was produced in these summits, high-level talks between the superpowers resulted in breakthrough agreements over a wide array of issues in the last two years of the Reagan administration. By 1988 Reagan said that his earlier words about the Soviet Union being an evil empire referred to "a different time, a different era." The rationale behind the change is a subject of scholarly debate.

Viewpoint:
Yes. Ronald Reagan adopted a confrontational stance toward the Soviet Union during the first years of his presidency, but a détente-oriented policy came to the fore in his second term.

President Ronald Reagan and many of his political associates lived their entire adult lives with a deep philosophical opposition to com-

munism. When Reagan entered office in January 1981 there was utterly no doubt, either to his supporters or critics, that he sincerely believed the Soviet Union to be an evil empire worthy only of scorn and that socialism was a bankrupt ideology destined to fall. Face-tiously using Marxist jargon in an address to the British Parliament in 1982, Reagan said that "Marx-ism-Leninism" would shortly be left on "the ash heap of history." By the time he left office eight years later, however, there had been a dramatic shift in the attitudes of his administration. After late 1986 the Reagan administration and the Soviet government of Mikhail Gorbachev worked together on several issues. When asked during a visit to Moscow in 1988 whether he believed he was in an evil empire, he said "no." What changed and why?

Much of the answer can be found in the chronology of the foreign policy of the Reagan administration. Reagan's bullish anticommunism was already well established. His candidacy for the Republican presidential nomination in 1976, in opposition to sitting president Gerald R. Ford, had clearly established that there were crucial strategic differences in the approach to foreign affairs within the Republican Party. The collapse of détente in the late 1970s, caused largely by the failure of the Soviet Union to moderate its aggressive geopolitical strategy, and the justifiably hostile reaction of the Carter administration to that failure, seemed to vindicate Reagan and his ideas.

Despite his increasing appeal and national renown, Reagan still confronted a political system dominated by large "umbrella" parties that relied on the cohesion of disparate bodies of thought and philosophy to remain an effective force. Although Reagan had by far the best chance of winning the 1980 nomination, he nevertheless had to accommodate elements of the Republican Party that differed from him on many issues, especially foreign affairs. The nominee's outspoken identification with the right wing of the party meant that Republicans who were more closely associated with Henry Kissinger's ideas of promoting détente with the Soviet Union and a balanced multipolarity in international affairs were on the losing end, but they still had sufficient clout to demand representation of their views. Accordingly, Reagan's de facto choice for a vice-presidential nominee was between the détente-oriented former president Ford or détente-oriented moderate George Bush, who in his own candidacy for the nomination had criticized Reagan's economic policies as "voodoo economics" and had held important positions in the Ford administration. Although there was a grassroots movement to nominate conservative Representative Jack Kemp (R-New York), for reasons of political balance the ultimate choice was between Ford and Bush, the latter of whom was on the ticket.

After Reagan won the presidency, the same principle had to be applied throughout the new administration. The strategic divergence between proponents of détente and confrontation was reflected in almost every organ of government responsible for crafting foreign policy. The State Department, for instance, was to be led by Kissinger's past associate General Alexander M. Haig Jr., a proponent of what he

called "hard-headed détente," while his deputies, especially Philip Charles Habib, were close to Reagan and almost openly hostile to Haig. In the office of the National Security Adviser, the principal counterpart to the Secretary of State in foreign-policy making, the process was reversed. While the pro-Reagan Richard Allen held the office, his main deputies were generals associated with Haig.

The U.S. strategic position in the early Reagan presidency, together with the presence of proponents of détente in the ranks of the administration, for a time restrained Reagan from an activist foreign policy. Since the end of the war in Vietnam (1975), unwillingness to fight another distant conflict combined with the anticipated successes of détente, as well as intelligence reports that the Union of Soviet Socialist Republics (U.S.S.R.) was becoming less of a threat, had generated a pronounced decline in military spending. Building on President Jimmy Carter's abrupt turn toward increased military spending, put into effect after détente collapsed and the Soviets started to seem like more of an aggressor than the intelligence community had thought possible, Reagan also believed that he needed time to restore the U.S. military to great strength. Under the direction of Defense Secretary Caspar W. Weinberger, a Reaganite who had a reputation for great administrative efficiency (he was known as "Cap the Knife," alluding to Bertolt Brecht's character Mac the Knife in *The Threepenny Opera*, 1928, music by Kurt Weill), the conventional element of the military began to revive by 1983. By that same year American superiority in strategic weapons became manifest with the deployment of Pershing II cruise missiles to Western Europe and the announcement of plans to develop a ballistic-missile-defense system (the Strategic Defense Initiative, or SDI), both of which rubbed the noses of the Soviets in their own technological inferiority.

Even earlier the administration had championed "low-intensity conflicts" (LICs), which challenged Soviet-supported communist expansion around the world through technical support and covert operations. By the mid 1980s recently established communist regimes the world over were in trouble because American aid was flowing to anticommunist forces that had adopted guerrilla tactics to fight these governments. The Soviet Union itself was tied down in a bloody and costly war against the U.S.-supported mujahideen in Afghanistan. It also had to deal with dissident movements within Eastern Europe that were receiving direct U.S. aid for the first time. The emergence of Gorbachev in 1985, promoted by a faction of the Soviet leadership favoring renewed relaxation with the West in order to reduce external

REAGAN'S
TRANSFORMATION

security requirements of the U.S.S.R., was largely the result of that pressure.

Within the administration, Reagan also enjoyed great success. Despite Haig's attempts to establish proportionally greater influence over foreign policy, Reagan had learned to rely dramatically less on the State Department as a vehicle for diplomacy than some of his predecessors. Its cabinet-level status notwithstanding, the State Department had always fluctuated in its relevance depending on the administration. For Richard M. Nixon it had not been terribly important, but for Harry S Truman and Dwight D. Eisenhower it had. Cleverly, Reagan bypassed the détente-oriented Haig by running foreign policy through other organs of the executive branch. The National Security Council (NSC), first under Allen and then under Reagan's old friend Judge William P. Clark; Weinberger's Defense Department; and the Central Intelligence Agency (CIA) of William J. Casey (another close friend of the president) all played prominent roles while Haig was undermined and ignored. Despite the secretary of state's attempts to highlight his relevance and dominate foreign policy (he even proposed a full-scale invasion of Cuba in 1981), his departure from the administration, the inevitability of which he himself realized and publicly lamented, was rather swift. Since Reagan still had to win a second term in office, however, continued balance in the administration was needed. The replacement of Haig by George P. Shultz, a member of Kissinger's Trilateral Commission, served that end although the position continued to have a relatively low profile in foreign-policy making.

The year 1985 was in many ways the zenith of Reagan's confrontational approach to the Soviet Union. Strategic planners in Moscow were terrified that SDI might well become a reality and render their nuclear-weapons systems obsolete. All of their approaches to arms control, up to and including those at the Geneva (19–21 November 1985) and the Reykjavik (11–12 October 1986) summits, were predicated on the elimination of U.S. ballistic-missile defense before anything else would be discussed. More and more, the Soviets were becoming aware of their general technological inferiority. Reagan's policies of rolling back Soviet influence around the world and using economic means to sabotage Soviet attempts to modernize the economy of the U.S.S.R. were having a devastating impact on its continued viability. It was in this year that Reagan made a famous gaffe, saying, "My fellow Americans, I'm pleased to tell you today that I've signed legislation that will outlaw Russia forever. We begin bombing in five minutes," during a radio test that was accidentally broadcast nationally.

Beginning in the fall of 1986, however, the structures of Reagan administration foreign-policy-making apparatus changed dramatically. In November it was revealed in a Lebanese newspaper that officials of the U.S. government had sold weapons to Iran in order to generate revenue to finance the anticommunist contra guerrillas in Nicaragua. Apart from having dealt with an enemy of the United States, those responsible had broken laws (the Boland Amendments, 1983 and 1984) that restricted, and at times banned outright, American aid to the contra forces. Although the restrictions were lifted altogether by the time of the investigation that followed, the contras were fighting against a brutal communist regime for the freedom of their country, and the convictions that resulted were small in number and not for terribly significant crimes. The leading defendant—NSC aide Lieutenant Colonel Oliver North—was initially punished with only a suspended sentence, and the conviction was later quashed on appeal. The appearance of impropriety touched many high-ranking administration officials, including the president himself.

The nationally televised drama of the congressional hearings launched in the summer of 1987 was a pale reflection of the paralysis that the White House, NSC, Defense Department, and CIA—all of the institutions through which Reagan's foreign policy moved—now had to contend. The president became deeply depressed and increasingly lethargic as time went on. Like Nixon at the height of Watergate (1973–1974) and Bill Clinton at the height of the Monica Lewinsky scandal (1999), little else commanded Reagan's attention.

Nowhere was this preoccupation more damaging than in foreign affairs. In the year following the breaking of the scandal, most of Reagan's trusted advisers disappeared. Casey died in May 1987, to be replaced by a series of caretaker CIA directors on whose watches the profile of the agency in foreign-policy making markedly declined. Even its efficacy as an intelligence-gathering service has been called into question since the late 1980s. Under pressure relating to Iran-Contra, Weinberger resigned as Secretary of Defense in November 1987. The role of the NSC had been deteriorating since Clark's departure in October 1983, and it was now the very center of the scandal.

Proponents of détente reaped the benefits of the collapse of Reagan's foreign-affairs apparatus. Under Shultz, the State Department emerged as the leading vehicle of U.S. foreign policy. Between the fall of 1986 and the departure of the administration from office in January 1989, U.S. foreign policy changed fundamentally. Issues on which Reagan had never previously shown any meaningful sign of giving ground began to blossom into an optimistic engagement of Gorbachev's Soviet Union. The election of a Democratic majority in the Senate in November 1986 and the general inertia of executive initiative in foreign affairs caused the famous (or infamous) Reagan defense budgets to become more-or-less frozen at the same level for the last several years of his administration. In May 1987 the two countries signed an arms control agreement regulating the withdrawal of intermediate-ranged nuclear forces (INF), meaning that the American strategic advantage implicit in the presence of the Pershing II in Western Europe was surrendered. Later the two countries also agreed to mutual reductions in conventional forces in Europe (CFE). Although SDI, the old bugbear of the Soviets, remained on the books, the leveling off of U.S. military spending eliminated it as a credible threat. Diplomatic means were also employed to give Gorbachev a more graceful way out of Afghanistan than the United States enjoyed in Vietnam.

By the end of the administration it was clear that détente with the Soviet Union was again the dominant trend in American foreign policy. A superficial look at the administration might lead one to believe that Reagan went through some sort of metamorphosis that transformed him from a hawk into a dove. A much more plausible explanation, however, is that he really had no choice. The simultaneous and interrelated Iran-Contra scandal, as well as the departure of his close associates at the highest levels, ended his primacy in the crafting of U.S. foreign policy. He had no choice but to go along with détente and look like a dove. Reagan's response in 1988 to the question of the journalist in Moscow who asked him if he thought the Soviet Union was still an evil empire, seems wistful and hollow.

–PAUL DU QUENOY,
GEORGETOWN UNIVERSITY

Viewpoint:
No. Ronald Reagan consistently relied on military strength as the foundation of his foreign policy.

The U.S. military reached a low point during the Carter administration and was incapable of executing its fundamental mission of defending the country from a foreign attack. Fortunately for the United States, there seemed to be little foreign aggression to be concerned about at first. In 1979, however, the inability of U.S. forces to act effectively became all too obvious when the U.S. embassy in Tehran, Iran, was taken over by radicals. Just a decade earlier, when the United States was a "real" military power, no one would have even considered such a suicidal move.

The internal situation of the U.S. military was horrendous in the 1970s. Recruiting reached an all-time low as the military changed from conscription to an "all volunteer force." Two types of people often enlisted: those who truly wanted to be there and those who could not find other work at a time when jobs were plentiful. To the detriment of the armed services there seemed to be more enlistees who did not want to be there than dedicated volunteers. The quality of personnel was pitiful—on some installations, officers could not walk across the post for fear of being robbed by their troops! Drug use was rampant, and commanders seemed unable or unwilling to correct the problem. There simply was not enough money to enable a quality military force.

With President Jimmy Carter, an unconcerned Congress, and the dismal state of the armed forces, the United States was militarily vulnerable. Many conflicts around the world, including the invasion of Afghanistan (December 1979), demonstrated that Soviet aggression was increasing. Something was bound to happen to bring the issues of military weakness to the fore.

This situation became painfully evident when special-operations forces attempted a rescue of the embassy hostages (24 April 1980), but failed, losing eight men in the process. When details of the aborted mission became known, they sparked a debate that began a change within the U.S. military. Marine pilots had flown Navy helicopters, carrying Army troops, that were refueled by Air Force planes when disaster struck—a helicopter crashed into a fixed-wing refueling aircraft on the ground. This setback typified one general problem with the military— too many people, and all branches, had to be involved but few of the participants were actually qualified. Clearly, something had to be done, and the Carter administration was not up to the task of solving the problem.

Ronald Reagan entered office on 20 January 1981, not so much as a hawk, but with loud rhetoric and a military-recovery plan designed to reassert the military dominance of the United States. The "Great Communicator" set about convincing Americans that there was nothing wrong with the United States being a military superpower and that this capability had to be focused on fighting the Soviet Union, or at least checking and containing its actions around the globe. The new president pumped money into the long-neglected armed forces. He doubled defense spending during his first term, approving the

REAGAN AND GORBACHEV IN MOSCOW

Between 29 May and 2 June 1988, Ronald Reagan and Mikhail Gorbachev met for a summit in Moscow. Below is a portion of Gorbachev's account of these meetings.

The ensuing discussion focused on the logic of SDI. Since we were talking about Ronald Reagan's "pet project," the exchange quickly became rather heated. "What is SDI for" I asked. "What missiles is it supposed to bring down if we eliminate all nuclear weapons?"

"It will be there just in case," Reagan replied. "The know-how for developing nuclear weapons won't evaporate from people's minds. No-one will be able to take it away from them. And there will be the technology for building missiles. A madman might appear who will appropriate these secrets. There have been examples before, like Hitler—they occasionally appear in history . . ."

The American President made an unfortunate gesture, knocking over a glass of water, and apologized.

"Never mind, Mr. President," I commented jokingly. "A careless move with a glass of water is no big deal. If it had happened with missiles . . ."

We all laughed at the joke and the tension eased.

Returning to the subject, I argued that the Strategic Defense Initiative was not a purely defensive programme: it opened the way to the development of space-based weapons that could hit targets on the earth. Reagan repeated his suggestion made in Geneva that we could observe the Americans' SDI research and be present during testing.

"I am afraid I have some doubts about this," I replied. "Before making such a proposal, you should maybe first try to convince Mr. Carlucci, Mr. Shultz and the US Navy to open just two types of your warships for inspection of sea-launched cruise missiles. But as far as we know, your Navy people balk at consenting to the inspection of their warships, and Mr. Carlucci supports them. How do you intend to open sensitive SDI research for inspection if you cannot even grant our inspectors access to two types of warships? It seems to me unrealistic." . . .

After the morning talks, Mr. Reagan and I went on a walk around the Kremlin. The American President was greeted by groups of tourists. He answered their greetings good-humouredly, occasionally stopped for a chat. During one of these spontaneous "press conferences," which incidently happened next to the famous *Tsar-Pushka* ("The Tsar of Cannons"), someone from the crowd asked "Mr President, do you still see the Soviet Union as the evil empire?" Ronald Reagan's reply was short: "No." I was standing next to him and thought to myself: "Right." I recounted this incident the next day at my press conference, and the journalists reminded President Reagan of it during the press conference he gave a few hours later. A reporter insisted on learning the reasons which had prompted the American President to change his view: "Mr President, did you discover something that made you change your mind?" he asked. "Did you have the opportunity to get a better look at this country? And who deserves credit for it—you or Gorbachev?"

"Mr Gorbachev deserves most of the credit as the leader of this country," President Reagan replied. "And it seems to me that with perestroika things have changed in the Soviet Union. Judging from what I read about perestroika, I could agree with a lot of it."

For me, Ronald Reagan's acknowledgment was one of the genuine achievements of his Moscow visit. It meant that he had finally convinced himself that he had been right to believe, back in Reykjavik, that you could "do business" with the changing Soviet Union—the hopeful business of preventing a nuclear war. He could congratulate himself on having made the right choice—and I now realized why he had told me the other day he prayed to God that the next President would be a man who would support his choice. In my view, the 40th President of the United States will go down in history for his rare perception.

Source: *Mikhail Gorbachev, Memoirs (New York: Doubleday, 1996), pp. 454–457.*

largest military pay raise in the history of the United States. This spending went a long way toward improving recruiting and retention, but he also increased the overall size of the armed forces. For the first time in almost a decade, the U.S. military began to think of itself in a respectable light. Morale, which was nonexistent during the "hollow force" years of the 1970s, began to rise. Members of the armed forces started to take pride in their service and this transformation began to show in their duty performance.

At the same time, there was a profound change in the attitude of the nation toward its defenders. People no longer looked at the U.S. military as a shameful necessity. Troops were no longer considered "baby killers" or "worthless bums who only joined because they couldn't hold a real job." The military, after a fifteen-year lull, was becoming "respectable" again.

Reagan also spent money on military research, development, upgrades, and modernization. Under his watchful eye, the U.S. Navy moved close to a six-hundred-ship fleet, fully modern and capable of projecting U.S. power overseas. Some of the programs that Reagan stressed were the Aegis-class destroyers and cruisers, Strategic Defense Initiative (SDI or "Star Wars") anti-ballistic-missile defense system, B-1B "Lancer" supersonic nuclear bomber, and stealth aircraft. All of these programs came to fruition in one form or another. Although SDI was never actually implemented, the growth in technological research and development that it spurred produced benefits well into the next century.

Probably one of the greatest weapons that Reagan brought to the table was his ability to convince people of his intentions. No one can ever doubt that he was a true anticommunist, and he used his position to pursue an aggressive policy against the Union of Soviet Socialist Republics (U.S.S.R.) His increased rhetoric against the Soviets caught them completely by surprise and caused them to take his buildup seriously, as well as respond in kind. So surprised by his posturing were the Soviets that during his first term they seriously believed he might launch an offensive nuclear first strike. The Soviet leadership decided against a preemptive first strike, instead deciding to match Reagan's budgetary increases and try to win this contest of military and economic maneuver. This decision helped end the Cold War and bring down the Soviet Union. In this instance, Reagan's policies helped bring the U.S.S.R. to its knees.

The Reagan administration had quite a few military successes. The first real test of the post-Carter military came in 1983 with the invasion of the small, Cuban-held, Caribbean island of Grenada—Operation Urgent Fury. While planning for the operation was seriously flawed and

the execution was even worse, the mission was a success—the American students were freed and the communist takeover abated.

Problems experienced during the invasion took on added importance because they demonstrated the seriousness of several military issues that needed to be remedied. Corrective actions, beginning with the Goldwater-Nichols Department of Defense Reorganization Act (1986), went a long way toward fixing many of the systemic problems the military experienced during the 1970s. These reforms also broke through some of the service parochialism, forcing the independent branches to work together in a new era of "jointness."

More outstanding success came with Operation El Dorado Canyon in 1986. Repeatedly engaged by Libyan military rhetoric promising to attack U.S. naval vessels if they entered the Gulf of Sidra (which is actually in international waters), and after incidents of Libyan-sponsored terrorism, Reagan decided to take decisive action. He ordered that Libya be taught a lesson. Without the assistance of our allies France and Spain, U.S. Air Force F-111 fighter-bombers flew from the United Kingdom—around Spain and along the coast of northern Africa—and, along with U.S. Navy carrier-based aircraft, bombed Libyan targets in Tripoli and other cities. While the attacks were not militarily significant in and of themselves, they demonstrated that the United States had the competence and will to act unilaterally if necessary. This air strike sent an important message around the world that the United States was not going to tolerate aggression any more.

As in any period, there were military actions that proved unsuccessful. On 23 October 1983, just after Operation Urgent Fury, a car bomb driven by a Hezbollah terrorist broke through the gate at the Beirut, Lebanon, airport and slammed into the building housing U.S. servicemen on United Nations (UN) peacekeeping duty, killing 241 U.S. Marines and Navy personnel. This attack was the most devastating loss of life in the American military since the Vietnam War, and it ended U.S. involvement in Lebanon for more than a generation. Why the Marines were placed in the virtually unprotected position, unable to defend themselves, became a sore-point in the United States. Peacekeeping and other untraditional missions were hotly debated into the next century.

Another area of military concern was one of Reagan's top domestic priorities as well: the war on drugs. The Reagan administration, unlike previous efforts, made sure that U.S. troops became involved domestically and overseas in fighting drug trafficking. In fact, the *Posse Comitatus Act* (1878), which prohibits military personnel from engaging in civilian law enforcement, was amended by Congress in 1981 to allow for the involvement of U.S. armed forces in the antidrug campaign. While this program was not a military defeat, it was a failure nonetheless. There was no appreciable decrease in drug smuggling into the United States as a result of military operations. What did come from this program was a loss in funding to the military and a perception by the American public, when combined with a general mistrust of government, that there was something shadowy going on, a sentiment that tarnished some of the hard-earned image the military had created during the early Reagan years. The net result was an "opening of Pandora's box" with regard to use of troops for non-military purposes. Later presidents, such as Bill Clinton in the 1990s, turned to the military more frequently for policing with a net result that preparedness decreased dramatically and began to mirror that of the 1970s.

Despite his reputation, Reagan only used military force when necessary and rhetoric when appropriate. It was a combination of strident speech making and increased defense spending that enabled the United States and its allies to win the Cold War. The results of this policy were easy to see—the end of the fifty-year struggle, collapse of the Berlin Wall, ruin of the Warsaw Pact, and eventual disintegration of the Soviet Union. The United States and its allies emerged victorious.

Militarily, Reagan's programs were a resounding success, as proven in the Persian Gulf War (1991), when U.S. troops engaged an enemy halfway around the world and soundly defeated it with ease and finesse to the surprise of the American people and the world. Reagan did not have to remain "hawkish" toward the end of his presidency because it was clear to most observers that the U.S.S.R. and its sphere was in serious trouble. Who needs to fight an enemy that is no longer there?

–WILLIAM H. KAUTT, SAN ANTONIO, TEXAS

References

Raymond L. Garthoff, *The Great Transition: American-Soviet Relations and the End of the Cold War* (Washington, D.C.: Brookings Institution, 1994);

Mikhail Gorbachev, *Memoirs* (New York: Doubleday, 1996);

Alexander M. Haig Jr., *Caveat: Realism, Reagan, and Foreign Policy* (New York: Macmillan, 1984);

Peter Schweizer, *Victory: The Reagan Administration's Secret Strategy That Hastened the Collapse of the Soviet Union* (New York: Atlantic Monthly Press, 1994);

George Shultz, *Turmoil and Triumph: My Years As Secretary of State* (New York: Scribners, 1993);

Caspar Weinberger, *Fighting For Peace: Seven Critical Years in the Pentagon* (New York: Warner, 1990);

Bob Woodward, *Veil: The Secret Wars of the CIA, 1981–1987* (New York: Simon & Schuster, 1987).

REAGAN'S TRANSFORMATION

REAGAN'S VICTORY

Did Ronald Reagan and his policies win the Cold War?

Viewpoint: Yes. Ronald Reagan won the Cold War through a combination of aggressive containment and economic warfare.

Viewpoint: No. The fall of the U.S.S.R. resulted more from internal economic and social problems than the initiatives of the Reagan administration.

By the time Ronald Reagan became president in January 1981, the Cold War had entered one of its most confrontational periods. Despite some initial signs of promise, the movement toward relaxed relations between the superpowers in the 1970s had collapsed in the wake of Soviet aggression and Western responses to it. Even though President Jimmy Carter had begun to devote substantial U.S. resources to a military buildup, the American people elected Reagan on a vociferously anticommunist platform. Believing communism to be an evil and morally bankrupt ideology, Reagan, during his tenure as president, repeatedly criticized the Soviet Union and predicted its demise.

Throughout his administration Reagan oversaw a wide variety of diplomatic and military challenges to the power of the Soviet Union. Anticommunist governments and guerrilla movements in the Third World, especially in Nicaragua and Afghanistan, received large amounts of U.S. military and economic support. The American defense buildup continued with the growth of the armed forces and introduction of substantial technological innovations. The nuclear deterrent of the United States was enhanced by the deployment of Pershing II cruise missiles in Western Europe in 1983 and the declared intention of the administration to develop a ballistic-missile-defense system based in orbit. Economically, the Reagan administration annulled many commercial agreements with the Union of Soviet Socialist Republics (U.S.S.R.) and adopted policies intended to deny the Soviets the ability to develop or even stabilize their economy through trade with the West and exports of their natural resources. Until the last two years of the administration, Soviet attempts to ameliorate tensions were by and large ignored.

By the time Reagan left office in 1989, the Soviet Union was in serious trouble. Almost every communist regime in the Third World was on the verge of being toppled; the communist governments of Eastern Europe, under Soviet control for more than forty years, had all fallen. Soviet military power and diplomatic influence were incapable of stopping these events. Within the Soviet Union itself, government-sponsored programs of reform produced little, while proponents of radical reform and democratization demanded and gained concessions from Moscow. Over the next two years the U.S.S.R. faced serious domestic crises that resulted in the collapse of its communist system and in the actual disintegration of the union. Many people believed the Cold War was over, but how significant were Reagan's policies in bringing that about?

Viewpoint:
Yes. Ronald Reagan won the Cold War through a combination of aggressive containment and economic warfare.

The policies of the Reagan administration won the Cold War. Under diplomatic, military, and economic pressure from the United States, the Soviet Union found itself increasingly unable to function. Within three years of Ronald Reagan's departure from office, the tumultuous decline of the Soviet Union led to its physical disappearance. Although many scholars suggest that the Union of Soviet Socialist Republics (U.S.S.R.) was faced with inevitable collapse and that Reagan's policies did nothing to help that process along, the fact of the matter is that his administration played a decisive role in precipitating the decline and fall of the Soviet Union.

Reagan entered office in 1981, with strong personal notions of good and evil. For a long time he had seriously believed that communism was the greatest threat to liberty and that it had to be destroyed. The Soviet Union, in his eyes, was quite literally an evil empire. Like many other critics of détente, Reagan fundamentally rejected the notion that a proven aggressor could be bargained with or bribed into becoming a guarantor of international peace, to transpose into plainer language former secretary of state Henry Kissinger's doctrine of granting closer commercial and diplomatic ties in exchange for Soviet geopolitical restraint.

Reagan applied his ideas assiduously in the international arena. The rival strategy of containment, the historical counterpart to détente, did not go far enough in the minds of leading personnel in the administration. While the reactive qualities of containment were intended to resist further expansion, they nevertheless confirmed indefinite Soviet influence in the regions in which Moscow was established. The Reagan administration adopted a relatively simple threefold approach in its relationship with the Soviet Union. First, it determined to "roll back" Soviet influence the world over, including its previously secure (with respect to its confrontation with the West) position around its periphery. Secondly, the Reagan administration undertook an aggressive program of economic warfare to spoil Soviet attempts at modernization and development. Finally, it adopted as its formal goal the fundamental restructuring of the Soviet regime through the accumulation of political, economic, and military pressure.

All three of these policy approaches were successful. Attempts to roll back what the Soviet Union had gained since World War II began soon after Reagan entered office. In its first year the administration identified points where the Soviet foreign presence was most vulnerable. In Nicaragua the revolutionary Marxist regime of the Sandinistas had recently come to power and begun facilitating the supply of Marxist guerrillas in neighboring Latin American countries. Reagan authorized support for the pro-American governments under assault and, beginning in 1981, authorized Central Intelligence Agency (CIA) support for the anticommunist resistance (the contras) within Nicaragua. No Latin American countries fell into the Soviet orbit in the years that followed, and the recently established Marxist government in Grenada was deposed by a U.S. invasion in October 1983. Although fluctuating Congressional restrictions on aid to the contras hindered their progress, the Sandinistas lost control of the country and were ousted democratically in 1990.

Within the Eastern bloc the Reagan administration saw anti-Soviet resistance in Poland and Czechoslovakia as an opportunity to destabilize Soviet power in those countries. Although the Polish government had resorted to martial law, mass arrests, and military rule to prevent the spread of the dissenting Solidarity movement in 1980–1981, the Reagan administration provided crucial financial, material, and moral support to the movement. Enlisting the support of the Vatican—and even the American Federation of Labor–Congress of Industrial Organizations (AFL-CIO), no friend of the administration to be sure, but consistent in its commitment to workers' rights—to help supply both Solidarity and the Czechoslovak Charter 77 movement, Reagan kept both groups alive and operating. They blossomed into leading democratic parties when free elections were allowed in those countries later in the decade.

Further afield, the Soviet invasion of Afghanistan in December 1979 had dangerously exposed Moscow to a potential Vietnam scenario of its own. While the Carter administration and most of the rest of the world had denounced the Soviets and reflected their disapproval in largely passive-policy decisions, such as boycotting the 1980 Moscow Olympics, Reagan implemented an active policy to drive the Soviets out and inflict substantial losses on them. Throughout the 1980s consistent support to the mujahideen, the anticommunist Afghan resistance, flowed from the United States. As it had done in its efforts to support East European dissent, the Reagan

A political cartoon depicting Ronald Reagan brandishing a "peace cross" against a vampirish Leonid Brezhnev

(John Trever)

administration enlisted the help of other interested parties. Saudi Arabia matched American financial assistance to the mujahideen dollar for dollar. Pakistan allowed the transit of supplies across its territory and the training of Afghan guerrillas on its soil.

The results for the Soviet Union were catastrophic. It soon became apparent that the regime of Babrak Karmal, the pro-Soviet puppet leader of the country, could not sustain itself without a constant Soviet military presence. More than thirteen thousand Soviet soldiers died in the fighting, and the number of wounded and diseased ran into the hundreds of thousands. From the mid 1980s the mujahideen was strong enough to attack targets inside Soviet territory. It even broadened its operations to include the massive dissemination of illegal Islamic literature into the Central Asian republics, which destabilized Soviet power there, too. Until the Soviets finally withdrew in February 1989, Afghanistan was an open wound into which Reagan ground salt.

The cost of the conventional war in Afghanistan was only the beginning of economic troubles for the Soviet Union. Perceiving a general stagnation in the Soviet economy, Reagan used American technological advantages and ability to sustain higher defense spending to challenge Moscow to an arms race it could never hope to win. Indeed, even though U.S. defense spending reached a relatively high level, it never exceeded 8 per-

cent of its Gross Domestic Product (GDP), while the Soviets invested anywhere between 15 and 40 percent of their significantly smaller GDP in military expenditures. Even as the United States embarked on an unprecedented military buildup, its increase in defense spending (starting in earnest in 1983) was complemented by an economic boom that ended the chronic stagflation of the Carter years, caused federal tax revenue to double by 1989, and laid the groundwork for the impressive economic growth of the 1990s.

Thanks to the prudent fiscal policies of the Eisenhower and Kennedy administrations, Reagan was able to take advantage of a broad domestic base. The consistent Soviet reliance on high expenditures for the military and heavy industry, together with a crushing political system that destroyed initiative and efficiency, had simultaneously weakened its domestic economy and left long-term modernization in any area extremely vulnerable. The United States could afford a major defense buildup; the Soviet Union could not. Despite assertions to the contrary from proponents of détente, intelligence assessments in the early 1980s made this fact abundantly clear to the administration. Committed as he was to the destruction of communism, Reagan implemented policies designed to disrupt attempts to modernize the economy of the U.S.S.R. and exacerbate its existing economic difficulties. Early in his administration, Reagan determined to halt commercial trade that had allowed Moscow to acquire high technology for both military and industrial purposes. Détente-era commercial relationships between the United States and the Soviet Union, with the notable exception of American grain exports, largely came to a halt. The administration outlawed high-technology sales and enforced newly revived legislation that compelled foreign subsidiaries of U.S. corporations to obey American statute law in their trade practices. Diplomatic efforts were made, albeit with mixed success, to prevent West European countries from selling indigenous high-tech products, or those based on American know-how, to the Soviet Union. Subtle attempts to sabotage Soviet modernization plans were also adopted. Taking advantage of Soviet desperation to buy or steal Western technology, for industrial espionage had become an important *Komitet gosudarstvennoy bezopasnosti* (KGB, or Committee for State Security) activity, William J. Casey's CIA found out what Moscow wanted and arranged for products with defective components or faulty blueprints to fall into Soviet hands.

The international petroleum market was another arena in which Reagan tried aggressively to best the Soviets. Moscow had a history of trying to enrich itself by exporting oil. Even as early as the Eisenhower administration this policy had been cause for concern. By the 1980s the Soviet Union relied on oil sales to produce between 60 and 80 percent of its hard-currency earnings. The degree of its reliance on oil exports was a major vulnerability. Part of the assault on Soviet attempts to acquire high technology involved a series of measures that caused the failure of the Urengoi pipeline, which was designed to move large quantities of Siberian oil to West European markets. The deregulation of oil, and successful negotiations with Saudi Arabia and other Arab nations to reduce international oil prices, both helped to reenergize the U.S. economy and caused tremendous harm to Soviet purchasing power in international trade. It has been calculated that every one dollar decrease in the price of oil per barrel caused the U.S.S.R. to lose as much as $500 million in hard-currency earnings. By 1986 prices had fallen about 75 percent, or $28 per barrel. American intelligence noted increasing, yet unsuccessful, Soviet attempts to compensate by exporting weapons and precious metals. Soviet attempts to modernize went nowhere.

As if that was not enough, once the rise in defense spending began to take form in 1983, Reagan announced his intention to develop the Strategic Defense Initiative (SDI), a ballistic-missile-defense system based in outer space. Although many critics believed it would destabilize relations or be technologically unfeasible, the prospect of an antinuclear shield sent the Soviet leadership, already conscious of its growing technological inferiority, into paroxysms. Some estimates suggest that the Soviets spent as much $50 billion in research and development to find a way to counter the American system.

Just as a large part of the Soviet leadership, led at first by Yuri Andropov and then by his protégé Mikhail Gorbachev, began to believe that improved relations with the West would relieve pressure on Soviet economic development and allow Moscow to devote more resources to domestic spending, social improvements, and economic restructuring, they were faced with an insuperable challenge. It is important to remember that Reagan saw no place for communism in the future, and was personally and politically committed to its destruction. For years he refused to hold summits with Soviet leaders. When the superpowers did discuss arms control, the Soviet conditional predication of any deal on the elimination of SDI, a prerequisite abandoned only in 1987, betrayed its obsession with defusing U.S. military superiority.

The combined effect of these policies on the Soviet Union was tremendous. Reagan's resolve in checking and reversing Soviet expansion around the world forced the Soviets to choose between maintaining a high level of military spending and losing their international prestige. Domestic political stability was thereby threatened because of Leonid Brezhnev's heavy reliance on pretensions to Soviet great-power status and the ideological superiority of socialism. The collapse of communist regimes in the Third World and the draining mire of the Afghan war, events that would almost certainly not have occurred without the firm commitment of the Reagan administration, allowed the Soviets neither to achieve the modernization of their economy and society nor to save geopolitical face. Rather than expanding commercial and diplomatic relationships to help the U.S.S.R. modernize, just as advocates of "engaging" China have successfully done in more recent times, restricting those ties and adopting policies that amounted to economic warfare condemned Moscow to financial disaster. The pursuit of an arms race based on high technology that the Soviet Union simply did not possess, particularly with regard to the Strategic Defense Initiative, in addition to the less overtly belligerent policies, condemned the U.S.S.R. to oblivion. Reagan won.

–PAUL DU QUENOY,
GEORGETOWN UNIVERSITY

REAGAN ON THE SOVIET UNION

On 8 June 1982 President Ronald Reagan outlined his views on the Soviet Union to the British House of Commons.

In an ironic sense Karl Marx was right. We are witnessing today a great revolutionary crisis, a crisis where the demands of the economic order are conflicting directly with those of the political order. But the crisis is happening not in the free, non-Marxist West but in the home of Marxism-Leninism, the Soviet Union. It is the Soviet Union that runs against the tide of history by denying human freedom and human dignity to its citizens. It also is in deep economic difficulty. The rate of growth in the national product has been steadily declining since the fifties and is less than half of what it was then.

The dimensions of this failure are astounding: a country which employs one-fifth of its population in agriculture is unable to feed its own people. Were it not for the private sector, the tiny private sector tolerated in Soviet agriculture, the country might be on the brink of famine. These private plots occupy a bare 3 percent of the arable land but account for nearly one-quarter of Soviet farm output and nearly one-third of meat products and vegetables. Overcentralized, with little or no incentives, year after year the Soviet system pours its best resources into the making of instruments of destruction. The constant shrinkage of economic growth combined with the growth of military production is putting a heavy strain on the Soviet people. What we see here is a political structure that no longer corresponds to its economic base, a society where productive forces are hampered by political ones.

The decay of the Soviet experiment should come as no surprise to us. Wherever the comparisons have been made between free and closed societies—West Germany and East Germany, Austria and Czechoslovakia, Malaysia and Vietnam—it is the democratic countries that are prosperous and responsive to the needs of their people. And one of the simple but overwhelming facts of our time is this: of all the millions of refugees we've seen in the modern world, their flight is always away from, not toward the Communist world. Today on the NATO line, our military forces face east to prevent a possible invasion. On the other side of the line, the Soviet forces also face east to prevent their people from leaving.

The hard evidence of totalitarian rule has caused in mankind an uprising of the intellect and will. Whether it is the growth of the new schools of economics in America or England or the appearance of the so-called new philosophers in France, there is one unifying thread running through the intellectual work of these groups—rejection of the arbitrary power of the state, the refusal to subordinate the rights of the individual to the superstate, the realization that collectivism stifles all the best human impulses. . . .

Chairman Brezhnev repeatedly has stressed that the competition of ideas and systems must continue and that this is entirely consistent with relaxation of tensions and peace.

Well, we ask only that these systems begin by living up to their own constitutions, abiding by their own laws, and complying with the international obligations they have undertaken. We ask only for a process, a direction, a basic code of decency, not for an instant transformation.

We cannot ignore the fact that even without our encouragement there has been and will continue to be repeated explosion against repression and dictatorships. The Soviet Union itself is not immune to this reality. Any system is inherently unstable that has no peaceful means to legitimize its leaders. In such cases, the very repressiveness of the state ultimately drives people to resist it, if necessary, by force.

While we must be cautious about forcing the pace of change, we must not hesitate to declare our ultimate objectives and to take concrete actions to move toward them. We must be staunch in our conviction that freedom is not the sole prerogative of a lucky few but the inalienable and universal right of all human beings. So states the United Nations Universal Declaration of Human Rights, which, among other things, guarantees free elections.

The objective I propose is quite simple to state: to foster the infrastructure of democracy, the system of a free press, unions, political parties, universities, which allows a people to choose their own way to develop their own culture, to reconcile their own differences through peaceful means.

Source: A Hypertext on American History: From the Colonial Period to Modern Times, *Internet Web Site.*

Viewpoint:
No. The fall of the U.S.S.R. resulted more from internal economic and social problems than the initiatives of the Reagan administration.

That Ronald Reagan and his policies "won" the Cold War can be denied from three perspectives. The first asserts that the Cold War had no victors—only the victims of four decades of wasted material and psychological energy. The best example of this argument came before the end of the Cold War, when Paul Kennedy's *The Rise and Fall of the Great Powers: Economic Change and Military Conflict from 1500 to 2000* (1987) established the concept of "imperial overstretch." Kennedy's image of both superpowers standing at the limits of their endurance, like fighters in a last round, was widely developed in the early 1990s. The Union of Soviet Socialist Republics (U.S.S.R.) might have collapsed first, its argument implied, but the United States could boast of no more than standing for the proverbial five minutes longer.

Subsequent developments, with the United States riding an economic boom unprecedented in history and the former Soviet Union dissolving into an assortment of failed and near-failed states, made the "mutual overstretch" argument impossible to sustain even in academic seminars. In its place arose an argument for eschewing "triumphalism." Its adherents, regularly published in journals such as *Foreign Affairs* and *Foreign Policy*, admit more or less grudgingly that the United States might indeed have emerged as victor in the long twilight conflict of the superpowers. It is, however, bad manners and bad policy to assert that fact—to rub it in like an athlete celebrating a touchdown or home run.

It is a bit cynical, but not entirely inaccurate, to say that critics of "cold war triumphalism" include a disproportionate number of scholars and pundits who built earlier reputations on prognosticating an indefinite endurance of superpower rivalry. Their ranks are swelled by adherents to the "convergence theory," developed in the 1960s, which argued America and Russia were becoming more alike as time passed. They are reinforced as well by critics of the free market capitalism that at the turn of the present century continued to stand triumphantly on the ruins of a thoroughly discredited Marxism.

Nostalgia seldom produces good history. Examination of the patterns of the final decade of the Cold War does provide significant evidence that Reagan and his policies did not "win" that mortal conflict for the United States and the West. From the beginning, Reagan administration policies toward the Soviet Union were in practice ambivalent. On one hand Reagan sought to build up U.S. military capacities, increasing the arms budget significantly. Simultaneously Reagan intensified confrontation with what he regarded as a developing Soviet threat outside of Europe. After 1980 American support for anti-Soviet regimes took limited account of their domestic policies. The United States sponsored insurgencies against perceived Soviet clients: Nicaragua, Angola, and Afghanistan. At the same time, however, Reagan kept to the terms of a second Strategic Arms Limitation Talks treaty negotiated by the previous administration of Jimmy Carter but unratified by the Senate. Reagan continued to discuss other arms-control issues as well, such as removing intermediate-range nuclear missiles from Europe. Reagan abandoned Carter's grain embargo against Russia, implemented in response to the invasion of Afghanistan (December 1979). He also sought dialogue with Soviet leaders on levels foreign to the earlier years of the Cold War.

As much to the point, neither Reagan's arms buildup nor his Third World confrontations bore especially striking results. The war in Afghanistan continued; the Angolan conflict degenerated into multilateral low-level massacre. The Sandinista government of Nicaragua endured and seemed to flourish against the challenge of the Reagan-supported contras, while U.S.-backed counterinsurgencies in Guatemala and El Salvador suffered from efflorescent human-rights violations—described in detail by a world media that despised Reagan when it did not find him ridiculous. The American arms buildup was widely described as wasting money on weapons systems and technologies too complex to be useful. Stealth aircraft, the Abrams tank, and the Bradley armored personnel carrier were all denounced as squandering resources better applied to domestic problems. Administration support for developing and deploying a ballistic-missile-defense system evoked special concern among critics who denounced it as the kind of arms-race escalation that might well spark the war it was intended to avert. Reagan's repeated offer to share the technology with the U.S.S.R. as it was developed made no difference to his critics—particularly in the light of repeated Soviet denunciations of the president as a Cold War hawk ready to plunge the world into nuclear winter to fulfill scenarios from B-grade movie scripts.

Arguably a certain disconnectedness lay at the heart of Reagan administration policies. The president and his advisers sought to portray the Soviet Union as a mortally dangerous colossus. At the same time they took optimistic views of the prospects of the Soviet system competing with the West, as well as its long-term potential for survival. The position reflected a mixture of moral conviction of evils of communism with rational calculation of its achievements. Supporters of Reagan and his legacy frequently assert that it inspired an overall strategy of accelerating competition across the board—military, economic, and ideological—thereby forcing the U.S.S.R. into a stern chase it had no possibility of winning. If such a strategy existed, except as a tissue of hopes, final judgment of its effect must await further disclosures from Soviet archives.

Based on existing evidence, there is no clear indication that any Reagan administration initiatives, separately or together, significantly disrupted the equilibrium of the Soviet Union or inspired it to reconsider its approach to international relations. If anything, the U.S.S.R. responded by taking a hard-line approach. The Soviets refused to send athletes to the 1984 Olympics in Los Angeles, made an international incident of Reagan's lapse of taste and judgment in testing a presumably dead microphone by announcing that the bombing of Russia would begin in five minutes, and refused to consider negotiations on European missiles until the United States removed its arsenal first.

None of these behaviors prefigured nuclear war, but neither did they indicate a Soviet Union ready to abandon confrontation. That decision was initiated by the man who lost the Cold War. Mikhail Gorbachev became general secretary of the Communist Party and premier of the Soviet Union in 1985. He recognized from the beginning that he was taking over a system in deep crisis. The rate of economic growth in the U.S.S.R. was declining at the same time every indicator of human misery was accelerating. Infant mortality was rising; life spans, especially for males, were shrinking; and drunkenness, on the job and after hours, was symptomatic of a wider, deeper alienation. A military budget that since the days of Joseph Stalin had been sacrosanct was consuming a disproportionate share of a public income whose amount was increasingly impossible to calculate in a world of forged statistics. The U.S.S.R. was importing basic foodstuffs while simultaneously falling behind in the electronics technology that was clearly shaping the nature of power in the coming decades.

Superpower confrontation, in short, was a luxury the Soviet Union could no longer afford, independently of any U.S. initiatives. Gorbachev, like his nineteenth-century Hapsburg predecessor Klemens Metternich, sought to make a strength of weakness by initiating arms-control talks with a U.S. president he regarded as several cuts beneath his own capacities. What Gorbachev overlooked was Reagan's own principled commitment to ending the nuclear threat. In a series of meetings the Soviet premier made optimal use of his personal, political, and public-rela-

tions skills to move the United States toward a massive reduction of strategic nuclear weapons—perhaps even their abolition. Reagan, feeling he had stronger cards to play, was more cautious. The Intermediate Range Nuclear Forces Treaty (December 1987) actually reduced nuclear arsenals by about 5 percent. More to the point, it provided for mutual verification. Its potential as a beginning was, however, rendered moot by the dissolution of the Soviet Union.

Gorbachev's superpower strategy depended heavily on at least domestic stability, if not domestic reform. He achieved neither. His policies of "openness" and "restructuring" acted as solvents on a system and society more ramshackle and vulnerable than Gorbachev and other insiders had been able to imagine. The premier's foreign policy, sharply criticized by dissidents across the spectrum of an emerging political system, acquired a correspondingly desperate edge. What Gorbachev won in the American media, he was losing at home. The erosion of the Soviet Union was by no means fully grasped in the United States. Nevertheless Reagan and his successor, George Bush, understood enough to act on the gambler's aphorism: "bet against the one who has to win." By 1988 all that was necessary was to play out the hand. Reagan had not won the Cold War. The Soviet Union had lost it—not because of Gorbachev's shortcomings as a statesman, but because at the end he held no more than deuces and threes against his opponent's face cards.

—DENNIS SHOWALTER,
COLORADO COLLEGE

References

Raymond L. Garthoff, *The Great Transition: American-Soviet Relations at the End of the Cold War* (Washington, D.C.: Brookings Institution, 1994);

Paul Kennedy, *The Rise and Fall of the Great Powers: Economic Change and Military Conflict from 1500 to 2000* (New York: Random House, 1987);

William E. Odom, *The Collapse of the Soviet Military* (New Haven, Conn.: Yale University Press, 1998);

Peter Schweizer, *Victory: The Reagan Administration's Secret Strategy That Hastened The Collapse of the Soviet Union* (New York: Atlantic Monthly Press, 1994);

Caspar W. Weinberger, *Fighting For Peace: Seven Critical Years in the Pentagon* (New York: Warner, 1990).

REAGAN'S VICTORY

SOVIET EMPIRE

Was the Soviet Union an empire?

Viewpoint: The Soviet Union was dedicated to establishing control over the former Russian empire, as well as imposing its political system on the rest of the world.

Viewpoint: Although the Soviet Union had many imperial trappings, it differed fundamentally from traditional empires because of its ideological commitment to spreading communism rather than obtaining capitalist profit.

At the end of World War II the Soviet Union controlled a larger portion of the surface of the earth than any Russian state ever had. Its influence was beginning to be felt even in places far beyond the reach of its armies. Many observers began to feel that the Soviet Union had taken on the characteristics of an empire.

From its inception, Lenin's Soviet regime tried hard to establish control over as much of the Russian empire as possible. Promises about freeing its subject peoples from what the Bolsheviks called "the prison of nations" and treaties conceding their independence were frequently ignored. Internationally, directives from Moscow dominated foreign communist parties and subordinated them to its policies. The situation at the end of World War II left the Union of Soviet Socialist Republics (U.S.S.R.) in direct control of significant portions of Europe and Asia. Its military presence gave it great influence in determining the future political complexion of those regions; whenever possible, economic and diplomatic relationships were oriented to the advantage of the Soviet Union.

Expansion of its influence, however, created some serious problems. Even as the U.S.S.R. continued to be a major factor in international relations, it faced challenges and encountered reverses that called its "imperial" nature into serious question. In addition to the direct challenge of American containment, other communist states created difficulties for Moscow. China championed its ideological leadership of the communist world; Yugoslavia became estranged from the Soviet Union as an assertion of its sovereignty. As time went on, moreover, Soviet control over foreign communist parties waned. Although the Soviet Union enjoyed successes in the Third World, its attempts to expand its influence fell far short of the desired goals and were eventually turned back.

**Viewpoint:
The Soviet Union was
dedicated to establishing control
over the former Russian empire, as
well as imposing its political
system on the rest of the world.**

By the end of World War II, Joseph Stalin ruled a political entity that was the historical apogee of Russian power. The borders of the Soviet Union in 1945 included almost all of the territory once ruled by the tsars (with the exception of Finland and parts of Poland and Turkey) and even regions (such as the area around Königsberg and Carpathian Ruthenia) that had never been ruled by any Russian state. Wartime agreements with the West and the military success of the Red Army had confirmed these acquisitions and given Moscow a great deal more power outside its borders than any tsar ever had. The Soviets had under their immediate influence all of Eastern Europe, with the exception of Greece and Yugoslavia, and direct military control over significant territory elsewhere in Europe and Asia. Even further afield, Moscow used its role as the leading communist power to guide foreign communist parties and play a part in the domestic politics of many countries its armies never reached. While the political situation inevitably changed over time, the Soviet Union attained and never lost the characteristics of an empire.

Regardless of its international position, Soviet domestic policy alone qualified it as something imperial. Although traditional Marxist doctrine held that the oppression of less developed nations was the most decadent characteristic of the last phase of capitalist imperialism, the oppression of non-Russian ethnic groups was, ironically, a defining feature of Soviet history. The consolidation of Bolshevik rule and the Russian Civil War (1917–1921) gave the minority nationalities of the Russian empire opportunities to establish or reestablish their independence and also enabled anti-Bolshevik Russians to form rival governments. In the course of the conflict that ended with the creation of the Soviet Union in December 1922, Lenin's regime relied upon military conquest to eliminate both ethnic Russian resistance to Bolshevism and fledgling national successor states to the Russian empire. Military takeovers often occurred in violation of treaties with these new states that the Soviet Russian government had signed and in violation of the Soviet's own ideological pronouncements about opening the gates of what Lenin had called "the prison house of

nations." In effect, one multinational state patched together through conquest was replaced by another. The legal creation of the Soviet Union itself illustrated the coercive quality of the domestic policies of Moscow as the Soviet constitution provided only de jure political rights for ethnically defined Union Republics; in practice they were subordinate in every way to the state apparatus that was, in turn, subordinate to the ethnic Russian-dominated Communist Party.

Although there was a brief departure from tsarist nationality policies in the 1920s, which resulted in so-called national renaissances, domestic policies toward minority nationalities over the course of Soviet history became at least as harsh, and often harsher, than they had been under the tsars. Under Stalin, himself a Georgian by ethnicity, Great Russian chauvinism was a major factor in Soviet life. Many proponents of greater political autonomy and rights of cultural development for minority nationalities were killed during Stalin's purges in the 1930s. The use of languages other than Russian in public life was sharply curtailed, as were elements of non-Russian cultural traditions. In the aftermath of World War II, minority nationalities (for example, Chechens, Volga Germans, and Crimean Tatars) that were believed to have had members who cooperated with the German army were subject to collective punishment and deported en masse to Siberia or Central Asia. Toward the end of Stalin's rule, Jews were persecuted because of his personal prejudices and the fear that they might sympathize with pro-Western Israel. Non-Russian Union Republics were subjected to massive colonization by ethnic Russians that were so thorough that as many as thirty million ethnic Russians now live outside Russian borders.

The statistical demography of the Union of Soviet Socialist Republics (U.S.S.R.) illustrates the imperial nature of the country. While ethnic Russians made up only slightly more than one-half of the population of the U.S.S.R. at any given time in its history, and Eastern Slavs (Russians, Ukrainians, and Byelorussians taken together) never made up more than 75 percent, Soviet society was highly structured in favor of ethnic Russians. Even though Stalin's successors made concerted attempts to include more minorities in the Communist Party (practically the only route for advancement within Soviet society), its membership never reflected the ethnic composition of the country. While the dominance of ethnic Russians and other Slavs became less pronounced over time, they were much more highly concentrated in the Party than in the general population. Positions of state adminis-

trated and high responsibility, especially in the professions, the elite Moscow bureaucracy, and officer corps of the Soviet military, were even less representative.

Restrictions on the cultural development and political autonomy of minorities remained well into glasnost and perestroika, and are still a problem in the former Soviet Union, although they were eased somewhat in the later years of Mikhail Gorbachev's rule. National autonomy and the freedom of cultural development were themselves significant themes in the dissent movement that Soviet authorities vigorously persecuted from the 1960s until the late 1980s. Under the liberalizing regime of Gorbachev, people who publicly advocated national independence or even increased autonomy were still subject to arrest and imprisonment, and there were several instances in the late 1980s and early 1990s in which peaceful protestors were fired upon and killed by the secret police and the Soviet army.

Apart from the facts that the foundation of the Soviet Union rested on the reassertion of control over the Great Russian periphery through military conquest and that its domestic political system was built in part on coercive and discriminatory policies toward the non-Russian segments of its population, the U.S.S.R. certainly qualified as an empire from an international perspective. In terms of raw power, the Soviet Union after World War II maintained a direct military presence far beyond its own borders. Internationally, it was recognized as a world power.

First and foremost, the consolidation of former Imperial Russian territory continued with the reincorporation of eastern Poland, parts of Romania, and the Baltic States under the terms of the Nazi-Soviet Pact of 1939. Beyond these extended frontiers it was clear, to paraphrase Stalin, that the reach of the respective Allied armies would determine the future political system of the territories they occupied. This was especially true with regard to the Soviets because they instantly used their military presence to influence postwar political realities in a way that the Western allies did not. Throughout Eastern Europe, the Soviets decided which political parties would function legally, what the ratio of pro-Western politicians in national provisional governments would be, and often which party would control key ministries, such as Information and Interior (police). The Soviets also made no secret of their preference for national communist parties over noncommunists when Red Army administrators made decisions about allocating resources for political purposes. In Western Europe, by contrast, liberated countries were ruled by broadly representative provisional governments that quickly established relatively stable and freely elected democracies. The systems in Western Europe were so open, in fact, that the Soviets used the substantial electoral support freely enjoyed by the French and Italian Commu-

Troops and tanks representing seven Warsaw Pact nations at a military review in East Germany in 1980

SOVIET EMPIRE

nist Parties to manipulate the domestic politics of those countries.

The political influence of the Soviets enabled them to establish monolithically communist regimes in Eastern Europe after a relatively short period of time. Although scholars debate whether these regimes were created in response to Western antagonism or as a solution for Stalin's concept (rational or not) of Soviet security, the artificially strong position of the national communist parties facilitated an easy transition from fragile democracy to communist dictatorship in every case. Once the communists were firmly in power, loyal party members who did not support Moscow unequivocally were themselves arrested, and often tried and executed, as "foreign agents" or "traitors." So pervasive was the Soviet influence in determining the shape of postwar East European governments that a Soviet marshal was given pro forma Polish citizenship to become the defense minister of that country.

Moscow proceeded to organize its East European sphere of influence into what came to resemble a colonial system. By September 1947 the communist parties in these countries that had fallen into Soviet hands, together with those of France and Italy, were coordinated under the Communist Information Bureau (Cominform) into a political bloc that took orders from Moscow on questions of ideology and politics. Relationships between Moscow and the East European states were strongly biased in favor of the Soviet Union in order to facilitate its economic recovery. Soviet policy in its occupation zone in East Germany, where large parts of the population were used as slave labor and much of the industrial base was simply seized and taken to the Soviet Union, was analogous in many ways to the most abusive treatment of a colony by an imperialist power. At times when the internal political situation of a satellite country was perceived as a threat to Soviet security, as was the case in East Germany in 1953, Hungary in 1956, and Czechoslovakia in 1968, Soviet troops marched in to restore the status quo. Conversely, when the empire was too weak to intervene militarily in the domestic crises of its allies, as was the case in Poland in 1980–1981 and 1989, alternative attempts to retain control ultimately proved unable to match force and coercion as tools of domination.

Outside of its most direct and obvious region of influence, the Soviet Union profited from the collapse of other empires in its gambit for imperial power of its own. As Western powers began to lose their colonies in the Third World, Moscow aggressively moved to gain strategic advantages by replacing the lost influence of the West. Nikita S. Khrushchev's threat to use nuclear weapons against France, Britain, and Israel if those countries did not desist in their attack on Gamal Abdel Nasser's Egypt in 1956, and his subsequent program of mil-

itary and civilian aid to that country, is a prominent early example. Soviet aid to the originally noncommunist revolutionary government of Cuba in the early 1960s offered it the prospect of a strategic-missile base close to the shores of the United States. Support for the North Vietnamese communists helped tie the United States down in a long, costly war in Southeast Asia. Soviet aid to communist movements in east Africa and attempts by Moscow to court the governments of anti-Western Arab states in the Middle East, together with its invasion of Afghanistan in 1979, gave the U.S.S.R. the chance to threaten strategic oil reserves in that part of the world. Although its role as the leading communist power was challenged for both ideological and strategic reasons by communist China, Moscow was a beacon for communist and anti-Western political movements the world over.

The historical record unambiguously supports the conclusion that the Soviet Union was founded on the military restoration of the Russian empire and sustained through domestic policies that continued ethnic Russian predominance within the new state. Internationally, its participation in World War II won for it undisputed status as a world power and supplied it with the means of imposing its political system and security requirements over a large part of the world. As the Cold War set in and the dynamics of global politics changed, the Soviets perceived and took advantage of many opportunities to try to expand that influence to lands that their Imperial Russian predecessors never dreamed of controlling. Economic and military problems caused by that reach and unanswerable strategic and technological challenges from the West ultimately caused its collapse. So much was the Soviet Union an empire that, in the end, its assertions of power and aspirations to imperial hegemony precipitated its fall.

–PAUL DU QUENOY,
GEORGETOWN UNIVERSITY

**Viewpoint:
Although the Soviet Union had many imperial trappings, it differed fundamentally from traditional empires because of its ideological commitment to spreading communism rather than obtaining capitalist profit.**

To understand why the Soviet Union was not an empire, one must first comprehend the most fundamental difference between it and other empires—that of goals. Imperialism is driven by economics and stimulated by greed; the Soviet Union, on the other hand, was motivated by communist ideology. Communism, in its pure form, gives all to the people (the workers). Power, land, industry, business, resources, and wealth all theoretically belong to, and are held by, the people. Like a virus, communism has no life of its own, but seeks to replicate itself and spread to other, living organisms with the stated goal of converting the entire world to its banner. Once this happens, according to theory, there will be a "workers' paradise." Until then, no challenge is too large, no sacrifice too great, to be made for the revolution.

Unfortunately for the world, the Soviets seemed actually to believe this theory. In the process of its seventy-odd years of existence, the Soviet Union devastated its natural resources, destroyed its ecology, crushed its economy, and murdered millions of its citizens. All this upheaval was made in the name of progress. All decisions and actions of the Soviets were influenced by this ideology and supported it.

Probably the second most important difference between the U.S.S.R. and imperialist countries was that of economics. Imperialism employs many profit-making methods during its life span: collecting tribute, mercantilism, capitalism, colonies, and exploitation. All of these methods are used to support the empire. The Soviets had none of these concepts in any imperialist form, as they were not out to make a profit. That its government and all its industries always ran in a deficit amply demonstrates this point. The Soviet system existed to support the ongoing revolution around the world. It sent out whatever it created for this purpose and established no markets, nor created real trade with any of its satellites.

There were further differences between the U.S.S.R. and empires in terms of the methods of governance. Empires are monarchical and authoritarian, while the Soviet system was, at least on paper rather than in actual function, democratic, while also being authoritarian. Empires are almost always hereditarily structured, in both their leadership and any advisory councils or parliaments. While one could argue that the Communist Party and perhaps the politburo were de facto hereditary, an obvious counter would be that this appearance does not change the fact that there was no single family that controlled the destiny of the U.S.S.R. during its short existence.

One similarity between the Soviet system and empires, or monarchies, was their system of rewards. The Soviets realized the importance of some of the trappings of empire, especially in this regard. They had dozens of orders to recognize merit in various fields, which mirrored the orders of knighthood of many Western countries. While these honors also might have been a holdover from the ancient regime, one should remember that most republics including France and Italy had similar orders.

Another important difference was the official lack of religion in the Soviet Union, or more accurately, its state-sponsored atheism. Most empires were highly religious, usually promoting their particular creed to the extreme. The Soviets, while officially atheist and, in most cases, downright hostile to religion, still allowed different faiths to exist in a far more tolerant manner than many Western democracies or empires, and treated religious groups equally.

One exception to this pattern was the Russian Orthodox Church, which had been the most widely accepted religion in the former Russian empire and held the most sway in terms of the hearts of the people. It is therefore not surprising that the communists used the church to further their secular ends. Some will argue that the Russian Orthodox Church was a pawn of the Soviets, but this is unfair in that it really had no choice and did what it could to survive. One might counter that communist ideology took the place of religion and therefore the U.S.S.R. was de facto a religious state. This argument is flawed as communism lacks the mystical theology and inherent morality of any modern world religion.

Of course, there were imperial similarities in that the U.S.S.R. existed in the same land area as the former Russian empire, with the same people, languages, and cultures. All of these elements, however, are to be expected in a successor state. Assisting in its death, the Bolsheviks dismantled the imperial Russian structures and replaced them with their own.

Where the Soviet Union most closely resembled an empire was with its massive military force, which seemed capable of, and geared for, external conquest. This expansionist policy, however, simply did not exist in the classic imperial sense, for the Soviet Union was concerned with advancing the revolution, not conquest. This lack of expansionist mentality was an important factor, which is often overlooked. While few would deny that the stated goal of communism was to convert the world, this endeavor was dissimilar to imperialism, which conquers for material gain and profit. The Soviets wanted none of this.

At the same time, there were nations that were subservient to the Soviet Union; in fact, many of these countries were almost colonies in most cases. Yet, this again differs from imperialism in that while it was exploitative, the subservient states were not exploited for material gain, but rather in order to fuel the spread of the rev-

KHRUSHCHEV DEFENDS A SOCIALIST WORLD

At the 1961 meeting of the Congress of the Communist Party of the Soviet Union (CPSU), Nikita S. Khrushchev gave a report to the Central Committee. Part of his speech focused on the role of the U.S.S.R. in the socialist world and the efforts by the West to oppose it.

The combination of the effort to develop the economy of each socialist country on the one hand, and the common effort to strengthen and expand economic co-operation and mutual assistance on the other, is the main road to further progress in the world socialist economy.

Comrades, Lenin's statement to the effect that socialism exercises its influence on world development mainly by its economic achievements is today more valid than ever. The all-around and growing influence of the building of socialism and communism on the peoples of the non-socialist countries is a revolutionizing factor that accelerates the progress of all mankind. . . .

The peoples of Asia and Africa who have liberated themselves from the foreign colonial yoke are looking more and more frequently to the socialist countries, and borrowing from them experience in the organization of economic and social life. In the world socialist system they seek protection and support in their struggle against colonialist encroachments on their liberty and independence. . . .

As socialism wins new victories, the unity of the peoples, both within each socialist country and in the world socialist system as a whole, grows stronger.

In the same way as a mighty tree with deep roots does not fear any storm, so the new, socialist world does not fear upheavals. The counter-revolutionary insurrection in Hungary, organized by internal reaction with the support of the imperialist forces, and the intrigues of enemies in Poland and the German Democratic Republic showed that in the period of socialist construction the class struggle may, from time to time, grow stronger and take on sharp forms. In the future, too, the remnants of internal reaction may, with imperialist backing, attempt to sever one country or another from the socialist system and to restore the old bourgeois regime. The reactionary forces gamble on the difficulties that are inevitable in an undertaking as new as the revolutionary transformation of society, and continue sending their agents into the socialist countries.

The ruling circles of certain imperialist powers have elevated subversive activity against the socialist countries to the level of state policy. The United States of America expends, with frank cynicism, hundreds of millions of dollars on espionage and sabotage against the socialist countries, and organizes so-called "guerilla units" made up of criminal elements, cut-throats who are prepared to undertake the vilest of crimes for money. For several years in succession provocative "captive nations weeks" have been held in the United States. The paid agents of the monopolists call "captive" all those peoples that have liberated themselves from imperialist bondage and have taken the path of free development. Truly, imperialist demagogy and hypocrisy know no bounds! Monopolists who howl about "captive nations" are like the crook who has hands in somebody's pockets and shouts "Stop thief!"

Source: Documents of the 22nd Congress of the CPSU, volume one, Report of the Central Committee of the CPSU to the 22nd Congress of the Communist Party of the Soviet Union *(New York: Crosscurrents Press, 1961), pp. 18–19.*

olution. In the early days of the Soviet Union, some questioned whether the Bolsheviks would allow the different regions of the former empire to retain their autonomy from the Russian-dominated communist state. Lenin quickly decided that they would remain, and he took active and violent measures to ensure they did. This war within the revolution raged until 1923 when most of the opposition crumbled or was killed off. From the Transcaucasus to Central Asia, the Bolsheviks enforced their edict, not so much in keeping with an imperialist attitude of maintaining control over the largest land area, but in a two-fold effort to retain the resources of these regions and ensure that they remained communist (and therefore under the control of Moscow). With the Soviets determined to spread revolution to the entire world, it would have been unseemly if they allowed the perfect opportunity to retain control of these territories to slip out of their hands. This policy also allowed them to retain these oil and resource-rich regions. That they also had large populations did not hurt.

As for the external "colonies" of the U.S.S.R., especially those such as Poland, East Germany, Hungary, Romania, and Czechoslovakia, they were not taken for material gain either, but rather as a buffer zone to protect this "perfect" communist state, to add to its "perfection," and later to assist in the exportation of the revolution. Other "colonies," especially Cuba, were instrumental to Soviet strategy. Cuba exported raw materials to the U.S.S.R., as well as provided a base that was critical to their military and intelligence-collection effort. Cuba also sent tens of thousands of soldiers to fight for the Soviets, especially in Africa. In return, however, the Soviets gave much more to Cuba, in the form of subsidies, military hardware, and civilian machinery—hardly an exploitative relationship.

The Soviets, however, used their military might to maintain its influence, and on the periphery, this policy appears imperialistic. During the Cold War Soviet troops invaded several countries to keep them compliant. The reasons for these invasions may not have impressed those on the receiving end, but there was a fundamental difference between the Soviet invasions and those of the capitalist/imperialists. Two examples come immediately to mind: the U.S. interventions in Guatemala in 1954 and the Soviet invasion of Czechoslovakia in 1968. While the United States justified its actions in Guatemala by stating that it was fighting communism, this justification does not change the fact that the "communist" government was freely elected and that the main instigator of the U.S. incursion was the United Fruit Company, an American corporation that stood to lose money if the socialist government remained in power. Compared to the threat of a pro-Western Czechoslovakia in 1968, leaving a huge gap in Warsaw Pact defenses, the American "intervention" seems rather silly and totally unjustifiable.

The Soviet Union, in some ways, resembled an empire, but after one scratches the surface and sees a myriad of differences, especially in motivation, one discovers that similarities can exist for many reasons and that it was the ideology of the Soviets that separated their policies from those of traditional imperialism.

–WILLIAM H. KAUTT, SAN ANTONIO, TEXAS

References

John Lewis Gaddis, *We Now Know: Rethinking Cold War History* (Oxford: Clarendon Press, 1997; New York: Oxford University Press, 1997);

Geoffrey Hosking, *The First Socialist Society: A History of the Soviet Union From Within* (Cambridge, Mass.: Harvard University Press, 1990);

Walter LaFeber, *America, Russia, and the Cold War, 1945–1996*, eighth edition (New York: McGraw-Hill, 1997).

SOVIET EMPIRE

STALIN

Did Joseph Stalin want the Cold War?

Viewpoint: Yes. Joseph Stalin needed the Cold War in order to justify repression in the U.S.S.R. and Soviet control of Eastern Europe.

Viewpoint: No. Joseph Stalin did not want the Cold War, but his paranoia and desire for territorial expansion made it possible.

In principle, Joseph Stalin was probably as much in favor of keeping the wartime Grand Alliance of Britain, Russia, and the United States in place as were his postwar counterparts Clement Attlee and Harry S Truman. Four years as a battleground had left the Soviet Union devastated economically, disrupted administratively, and unsettled ideologically. Stalin had mobilized domestic support for the war in part by turning to nationalism and religion. Some of the more successful Red Army generals had begun the war in the gulag archipelago, victims of the purges of the 1930s.

Would the Soviet dictator continue the process of opening his society and loosening its restraints? That question was answered almost immediately in domestic contexts, as returned prisoners of war (POWs) were shipped en masse to labor camps and "enemies of the people" once again faced sham trials or administrative punishment. Thoughts of an economy reconfigured to meet civilian needs vanished as the arms factories ran overtime and rationing of all sorts continued. This tightening of domestic belts did not inevitably prefigure increased international tension. Stalin, however, made no secret even during World War II of his conviction that once common enemies were removed, the hostility between communism and capitalism would equally shape policies and behaviors.

East-West relations deteriorated slowly and uncertainly after 1945. Public opinion in the West was strongly in favor of maintaining good relations with the Union of Soviet Socialist Republics (U.S.S.R.). Winston Churchill's 1946 "Iron Curtain" speech was widely interpreted as atavistic and provocative in both Britain and the United States. Stalin's success in excluding the West from any authority in the sphere of influence Russia had acquired in Eastern Europe was, however, not matched by gestures of conciliation elsewhere. Instead, the Soviet Union began asserting an increased interest in the Near and Middle East, from Greece and Turkey to the Persian Gulf. A Britain unable to sustain its immediate postwar role as counterweight turned to a United States increasingly ready to believe that Soviet aggrandizement in those regions represented an unacceptable alteration in the balance of power—particularly when considered in the context of Russia's postwar gains in the Far East. The March 1947 enunciation of the Truman Doctrine, with its guarantee of support for "free institutions and national integrity" against external aggression, marked the end of the postwar era and the beginning of a Cold War that Stalin may not have sought, but certainly expected.

Viewpoint:
Yes. Joseph Stalin needed the Cold War in order to justify repression in the U.S.S.R. and Soviet control of Eastern Europe.

In the summer of 1945 Soviet military power was dominant from the Baltic Sea to the Pacific Ocean. An army, which only five years earlier had been humiliated by Finland, had come back to crush Nazi Germany and within ninety days of that great victory pulled off a logistical miracle, transferring significant assets to the Pacific across a single rail line of seven thousand miles for a war against Japan. As a result, there was justifiable pride in the accomplishments of the Red Army, which had saved the Union of Soviet Socialist Republics (U.S.S.R.) from a brutal Nazi occupation. Without its heroic efforts Allied casualties at Normandy, France (6 June 1944), would have been heavier. Indeed, in its final three-week offensive to take Berlin, the Red Army sustained more casualties than the combined British and American forces in their yearlong drive from Normandy to the Elbe River in Germany.

The forces that met along the Elbe River in the spring of 1945 were part of the greatest alliance in history, joined together to crush the greatest threat to civilization in the twentieth century. The reasons for fighting, how they fought, and the postwar goals of the United States and the U.S.S.R., however, were at complete opposites. The Americans had fought primarily for idealistic reasons, to stop a threat to the freedom of democracies and to liberate those neighbors crushed under Nazi tyranny. The Soviets had actually been allied with the Nazis at the start of the war and Joseph Stalin had engaged in the dividing up of Eastern Europe with Adolf Hitler until his supposed ally turned against him.

The people of the Soviet Union made a heroic defense in a battle for survival, but the goals of the valiant Red Army and their leader were not necessarily the same. Stalin saw the situation in 1945 as a platform for the expansion of his power, even while many of his countrymen assumed that they had fought to free Russia from occupation and that the conflict was now over. Stalin apologists argue that he was driven to a Cold War confrontation because the United States clearly intended to contain communism and eventually destroy it. These historians are the same ones who argue that the purges of the 1930s were justified and that there was never a deliberately created famine in

the Ukraine. If American intent had been to push back communism, or to destroy it, then the nearly complete demobilization of U.S. ground forces by the end of 1945 was a poor way to start the campaign. In May 1945 the United States had over fifty combat-ready divisions in Europe; by the end of the year barely one division could fit the definition of being prepared for war. At the same time the Soviets had well over three hundred divisions in the field and would continue to maintain their forces at nearly that level for years to come.

In the communist view, war is simply acceptable politics through the use of violence. Under the thin veil of having to maintain social order in a devastated Eastern Europe, Stalin systematically suppressed any attempt at a democratic process inside his area of control. The betrayal of the Polish Resistance fighters in Warsaw during the Soviet summer offensive of 1944 was but a foreshadowing of what was to come. In the final days of World War II many Eastern European refugees returning to their countries who posed a threat to communist control were either killed or deported to Siberia. The purges, mass executions, and deportations that occurred in the Ukraine and the Baltic states in 1944 expanded into Poland, Hungary, Romania, Bulgaria, Czechoslovakia, and Soviet-occupied Germany. Tens of millions who had expected liberation quickly found that the heel of one boot had been lifted off their backs simply to be replaced with another.

At the same time Stalin moved to aggressively export his personal brand of communism to areas outside immediate Soviet control, and he was soon engaged in the covert support of communist efforts in Greece, Turkey, and Italy. The only counterforce to full military hegemony was the American monopoly on atomic weapons. This factor alone is perhaps the sole reason that there was a Cold War rather than a World War III in the late 1940s. The United States adroitly bluffed Stalin, leading him to believe that it might be in possession of several hundred atomic weapons when in fact it had less than one hundred until 1948.

Deeply paranoid, Stalin was convinced that given an opportunity the Americans would launch a strike on the Kremlin with the sole intent of killing him, and for years highly trained troops manned antiaircraft positions around Moscow twenty-four hours a day.

The nuclear monopoly, maintained until 1949, gave the United States some semblance of a counterforce that blocked any major aggressive effort on the part of the Soviet Union. The only alternative then for maintenance of control in the occupied territories, the continuance of an Orwellian warlike mentality in the home-

STALIN

land, and the expansion of power was a war of nerves: the Cold War. It served all three purposes well. By 1948 any semblance of freedom in occupied Europe was dead. Communist governments were installed, which immediately received the backing of Soviet troops in the name of communist solidarity.

An aspect of the Cold War that is often overlooked in the West is its use as a means of maintaining an iron grip inside the Soviet Union. After four bitter years of war and sacrifice, many people within the U.S.S.R. believed that they had earned a taste of freedom and this sentiment existed even within the Red Army, which had fought such a heroic battle. The paranoia and war scares created by the Cold War enabled Stalin to continue the repression of the prewar years, covered over with the excuse that at any minute all of them might fall victim to the bombs of the capitalistic imperialists.

Thus, in an instant, the old Western allies were now the new Hitlers, who were far more dangerous, for they could strike and annihilate the entire Soviet Union without warning. Under this guise any potential threat from within was neutralized. It could not have been any other way, for without a new enemy to fear, the nightmare of postwar repression and the deportation of millions to Siberia would have been seen for what it was: the outright insanity of the Soviet leader.

Finally, there is a third driving factor, the desire to continue expansion. With direct military confrontation ruled out, the only alternative was secret support of communist movements, such as the effort in Greece and Turkey, and the support of proxy armies in such areas as North Korea.

Stalin clearly favored an evolutionary war by other means in order to avoid a conflict that was so direct that the United States would be provoked into the use of nuclear weapons. Yet, at the same time, he had to maintain a constant level of pressure that would eventually wear down the will to resist and trigger a cave-in of resolve similar to what happened to the Allies after World War I. Fortunately the generation that fought and won World War II was made of sterner stuff. When confronted by the Berlin Crisis of 1948, rather than surrender, the Western powers demonstrated moral strength and finally forced Stalin to back down. The Truman Doctrine (1947) was a clear statement of American resolve, which was finally demonstrated by direct intervention in Korea and the U.S. decision to make more thermonuclear weapons. Stalin wanted the Cold War, if for no other reason than the fact that he needed it in order to survive.

—WILLIAM R. FORSTCHEN,
MONTREAT COLLEGE

Viewpoint:
No. Joseph Stalin did not want the Cold War, but his paranoia and desire for territorial expansion made it possible.

In 1945 the Soviet Union stood at the height of its power. Nazi Germany had been crushed and Soviet troops occupied Berlin. The dominant feature in international politics for the half century that followed World War II, however, was a fierce geopolitical competition between the Union of Soviet Socialist Republics (U.S.S.R.) and its erstwhile Western allies. Was this competition something Soviet premier Joseph Stalin wanted? There is a compelling case that the Cold War resulted directly from aggressive Soviet actions. Yet, there are many convincing reasons to believe that Stalin believed his actions after the war were subtle enough, and his credibility sufficiently strong, to maintain the cordiality of his wartime relationship with the West. Hoping to have his cake and eat it, too, he worked simultaneously for Soviet aggrandizement around the world and a peaceful international environment in which the Soviet Union could recover and develop a position of competitive strength.

Stalin's activities in the months immediately after the surrender of Germany in May 1945 did not seem especially provocative. Despite attempts to distribute political resources in favor of the national communist parties in Eastern Europe and create a political culture that diminished the appeal and effectiveness of their noncommunist opponents, the ultimate effect of these activities was not clearly seen for a while to come. Promised free elections were held and none of the communist parties in Eastern Europe won a clear majority. Stalin tolerated "bourgeois" politicians in positions of authority, including many, such as Stanislaw Mikolajczyk in Poland and Jan Garrigue Masaryk in Czechoslovakia, who advocated a pro-Western orientation for their countries. In a surprising move for a Bolshevik, Stalin did nothing at all, even about monarchism, in the region. Tsar Simeon II of Bulgaria was deposed in a democratically held referendum in September 1946, one year after the conquest by the Red Army, while King Michael of Romania continued to sit on his throne as late as December 1947, more than three years after Soviet troops overran his country.

Strategically, Stalin held to his promises made during the war. Although Western forces that had marched into the demarcated Soviet occupation zones of Germany were obliged to

STALIN'S DEATH AND U.S. POLICY

On 5 March 1953, Joseph Stalin died and American diplomats scrambled to interpret the possible changes his demise might bring. The following passage is from a secret U.S. State Department memorandum dated 10 March 1953.

The death of Stalin may offer, with the progress of time, opportunities to weaken and disrupt the cohesiveness of this bloc and in particular the direct control of the Kremlin over the Eastern European satellites and its influence over Communist China. The impulses of nationalism would seem to be the chief element working against the continuation of Soviet control over the non-Soviet countries in this bloc.

The mystique and symbolism of Stalin's name assiduously cultivated by the Soviet propaganda machine was a very important factor in the Soviet system of control. His connection with the original revolution and association with Lenin, and the continuous buildup as an individual enjoying superhuman qualities, not only facilitated the original imposition of Soviet control in Eastern Europe and in the establishment of primary influence in Communist China but was also a vital factor in its perpetuation. The manner in which the name Stalin facilitated Soviet control was subtle but nonetheless real. . . .

In short, it may be stated that the death of Stalin will remove one of the elements which was able to confuse and disguise to some extent the reality of naked Soviet imperialism in the Eastern European countries. It must be recognized, however, that the element of straight Soviet control is so powerful within these Eastern European countries that the process of increased nationalism may be a very long-term process. . . .

The long-term implications of Stalin's death will undoubtedly be extremely important in their effect upon Soviet foreign policy. At the moment, however, the following facts may be noted:

1. We have no indications that the situation is not well in the hands of the new rulers. It is true that the instructions of the Central Committee and the Council of Ministers refer to the difficult situation and 'the prevention of any kind of disarray and panic'. These would appear to be less expressions of concern at possible disturbances or troubles in the country as a whole than a call for unity and possibly a discreet note of warning to certain party organizations.

2. At this stage, at any rate, the Russian people are not directly involved in that they are playing no part in the transfer of power.

3. It is to be expected that the first preoccupation of the new leadership will be to close ranks and present a united front, both to the country and particularly to the outside world. There will be an increase of the normal tendency of dictators to avoid any sign of weakness vis-à-vis their external enemies, in this case primarily the United States.

4. This preoccupation against any show of weakness will probably be accompanied by great prudence and caution in regard to any new Soviet adventures or aggressive actions. Any measures on Soviet initiative which would run the serious risk of war would obviously be dangerous for the new regime. However, by the same token the new leadership will almost certainly be prepared to take great risks to avoid the physical loss of any territories or areas they have inherited from Stalin. Thus, Soviet foreign policy for a considerable time would appear to remain virtually unchanged from the last phase in which Stalin was alive. It may become even more truculent in speech but in all probability, unless the defense of a previous position is involved, cautious in initiating new or risky adventures.

Source: Foreign Relations of the United States, 1952–1954, *volume VIII,* Eastern Europe, Soviet Union, Eastern Mediterranean *(Washington, D.C.: U.S. Government Printing Office, 1955), pp. 1108–1111.*

STALIN

Soviet leader Joseph
Stalin at the October
1952 meeting of the
Nineteenth Congress of
the Communist Party

(Russian State Archive of Film and
Photodocuments)

that he did not move against Japan earlier was no sinister plot to allow American resolve and technology to win a role in Asia for him while he sat back and did nothing. President Franklin D. Roosevelt, furthermore, had encouraged Chinese nationalist leader Chiang Kai-shek to make small territorial, mineral, and military-base concessions to the U.S.S.R. and had promised Stalin a role in postwar China. Stalin had no reason not to expect those promises to be honored. Nothing overt in Stalin's immediate postwar foreign policy in Asia indicated a desire for confrontation either.

Indeed, considering the domestic situation of the Soviet Union, Stalin had no reason to look forward to conflict with any optimism. Twenty-seven million Soviet citizens had died, at least as many (and possibly more) than all of the other combatant powers put together, including Germany and Japan. The main industrial and agricultural areas of the Soviet Union had been conquered by Germany and fully mobilized for Adolf Hitler's war effort. Somewhere between five and seven million Soviet citizens were abducted and used as forced laborers in German industrial enterprises. So thorough was the dislocation of the Soviet economy that the success of its armies depended on massive support from the United States in almost every conceivable military and industrial category. Moscow received more than $6 billion in assistance during the war, a figure almost one-half the entire U.S. defense budget of 1950.

It is fallacious, however, to assume that since a man as ruthless as Stalin tried to preserve his strategic partnership with the West after World War II, he was either only partially responsible for the Cold War or completely innocent. Even though Stalin did not want to enter into a confrontational relationship, he nevertheless did nothing to neglect the global position of the U.S.S.R. Indeed, many of his activities represented acute threats to Western security and exceeded what the West had promised him during the war.

The "adjustment" of the political cultures of Eastern Europe to favor parliamentary communism was supported by the Soviets. Gradually communists began to take full advantage of their artificially strong positions and, with indirect Soviet support and approval, to use tactics of intimidation against noncommunist political parties. Although the full consolidation of communist regimes in the region was achieved only after Stalin's definitive break with the West, the stage was set much earlier.

On the comparative strategic level, Stalin lost no time in trying to reach parity with the West, especially in jet-engine technology and atomic energy. Even as early as 1943, Soviet intelligence had developed an espionage network in the United

withdraw, the Soviets allowed British, French, and American troops into their respective sectors of Berlin and Vienna, with full transit rights across other Soviet zones. Stalin also refrained from the overt mobilization of foreign communists, in Western or Eastern Europe, under the banner of international communism. The Third, or Communist, International (Comintern), the main agency for the coordination of foreign communists by Moscow, before its abolition as a goodwill gesture for the West in May 1943, was not revived in any form for more than two years after the end of the war. The only guidance from Moscow to communists across the continent was for them to participate in their provisional governments and, after parliamentary and constitutional forms of government had been reestablished, to compete in free elections and the democratic process. Although Greece was plagued by a communist-guerrilla movement and bloody civil war, it is now known conclusively that support came from Josip Broz Tito in blatant contravention of Stalin's wishes. Put simply, nothing overt in Stalin's immediate postwar foreign policy in Europe indicated a desire for confrontation with the West.

Although many scholars have called Stalin's entry into the war against Japan shameless because he only did so two days after the United States dropped the atomic bomb on Hiroshima (6 August 1945), he was actually keeping the letter of his agreement with the West to enter the Pacific theater precisely three months after the defeat of Germany. In other words, he was to enter the war in the Pacific, and break the Soviet-Japanese nonaggression pact of 1941, on 8 August 1945—and he did exactly that. The fact

STALIN

States and Great Britain aimed at acquiring atomic-weapons technology. It is now known that immediately after the United States dropped its atomic bombs on Japan, Stalin ordered his security chief, Lavrenty Beria, to begin a crash program to develop the Soviet bomb. The espionage network in the West was expanded.

Along the Soviet periphery, Stalin attempted to insinuate his power into a variety of places. In the summer of 1946 Soviet foreign minister Vyacheslav Molotov demanded that the Allies accommodate Moscow's demands for a share in the occupation of the industrial Ruhr region, located deep inside of the western zones of Germany. He made this request even though the U.S.S.R. had absolutely no pretension to such rights in the wartime agreements and even though the Soviets did not extract massive amounts of forced labor or natural resources from their occupation zone. The Allies not only rejected the demand, but even viewed it as undermining joint control of Germany. Immediately after Molotov's demands were rejected, the Western allies began to think about the economic and political integration of their zones of occupation to the exclusion of the Soviets.

Further afield, Moscow attempted to establish a Soviet presence in entire countries in which it had been promised no postwar role. This situation occurred in 1946 in Turkey, where the Soviets demanded from Ankara the rights to maintain a naval base in the Bosporus Straits. As a result, the West grew suspicious of Soviet intentions. A similar situation occurred in Iran, where the British-owned Anglo-Iranian Oil Company held a monopoly on the petroleum fields and where the United States wanted to expand its own interests. The Soviets attempted to use a legally fictitious approach to the national self-determination rights of the Azerbaijani population to absorb strategic Iranian territory. Both of these incidents prompted immediate demands from the West for Moscow to desist. In the case of Turkey and Greece (the communist insurrection in the latter was incorrectly thought to have been Soviet-inspired), the United States and Britain gave generous financial support to noncommunist governments.

Whenever he overstepped his bounds and was called on it by the West, Stalin did indeed back down. Soviet demands on Turkey ceased and the Soviet troops who had entered Iran for temporary occupation during the war left the country without annexing any territory. Although Stalin demurred from provocations that would have elicited a Western military response, his actions on a variety of fronts showed bad faith.

The decisive break came in June 1947 when Secretary of State George C. Marshall announced that the United States would sponsor a broad pro-gram of financial assistance to promote the recovery and stability of all Europe, the Soviet Union included. Initially, it has been revealed, Stalin was keenly interested in the prospect of receiving post-war financial assistance from the United States in addition to the Lend-Lease aid he had obtained during the war. The perception that aid under the Marshall Plan would be attached to political conditions, however, gave Stalin some pause. Rather than allow Eastern Europe and his own country the chance to recover with the benefit of American finance, Stalin chose to consolidate what he already had under monolithic communist domination. The weak constitutional governments of Eastern Europe were compelled to reject Marshall Plan aid and other close ties to the West (Czechoslovakia, for instance, had come close to forming a defensive military alliance with France in 1947). By the following February every state in the region had a monolithically communist government. In later years communists who favored a more nationalist orientation for their governments were removed from power, expelled from their communist parties, and often arrested and executed. All independent political parties and social institutions were either eliminated or placed on communist "guidance."

By June 1948 the continuing economic integration of the Western sectors of Germany, caused initially by Molotov's demand that the U.S.S.R. be included in the occupation of Ruhr, gave Stalin the pretext to blockade West Berlin. By cutting off the access of the Western Allies to their legitimate presence in the western parts of the city, an arrangement sanctified by wartime agreements, Stalin had maneuvered his country and the world into a prolonged conflict of dangerous dimensions. Although he had not wanted it, the Soviet leader's obsession with security and the aggrandizement of his country made the Cold War possible.

–PAUL DU QUENOY,
GEORGETOWN UNIVERSITY

References

John Lewis Gaddis, *We Now Know: Rethinking Cold War History* (Oxford: Clarendon Press, 1997; New York: Oxford University Press, 1997);

Vojtech Mastny, *The Cold War and Soviet Insecurity: The Stalin Years* (New York: Oxford University Press, 1996);

Adam B. Ulam, *Stalin: The Man and His Era* (Boston: Beacon, 1989);

Vladislav Zubok and Constantine Pleshakov, *Inside the Kremlin's Cold War: From Stalin to Khrushchev* (Cambridge, Mass.: Harvard University Press, 1996).

STALIN

TEAM B

Did the intelligence community assess Soviet military capabilities in the mid 1970s more accurately than President Gerald R. Ford's Team B?

Viewpoint: Yes. The intelligence community provided an accurate picture of Soviet strategic forces and defenses through a series of detailed reports known as National Intelligence Estimates.

Viewpoint: No. Team B determined that Soviet missile accuracy, air defense, and strategic objectives posed a serious threat to the United States, correcting the National Intelligence Estimates.

In the mid 1970s the growing unease among conservatives with the policy of détente with the Soviets, supported by presidents Richard M. Nixon and Gerald R. Ford, became more pronounced. Conservative members on the President's Foreign Intelligence Advisory Board (PFIAB), led by the physicist Edward Teller, began to question the quality and accuracy of intelligence-community assessments of Soviet military strength. Albert J. Wohlstetter, the influential defense consultant, charged in articles and public talks that National Intelligence Estimates (NIEs), the annual reports prepared for the president by all branches of the intelligence community, understated Soviet military capabilities and gave an unjustified benign view of their intentions. PFIAB members pressured President Ford to appoint an independent committee of experts from outside the intelligence community to examine the materials on which the 1976 NIE was based, to see whether or not different conclusions could be drawn from them.

Overruling the objections of the intelligence services, Ford created an ad hoc body, known as Team B, which began its work in August 1976. It was assigned the task of examining NIE accuracy in three specific areas and, accordingly, comprised three committees: Air Defense, Missile Accuracy, and Strategic Objectives. The Strategic Objectives panel received the most publicity. Team B submitted its report in December 1976, but leaks concerning its activities began to appear in October. The fifty-page Strategic Objectives report was especially critical of the methodology, assumptions, and conclusions of past NIEs. In 1977 both the existence of competing intelligence assessments and the conclusions of Team B became part of the political give-and-take in Congress. The Carter administration, which came to power in January 1977, was initially cool to the report. However, several factors helped gain Team B recommendations a larger hearing. There was growing skepticism about the success of détente: Zbigniew K. Brzezinski, Jimmy Carter's national security adviser, agitated for a more confrontational approach to the Soviets because of their increased involvement in Africa (Angola, Mozambique, and the Horn of Africa), and their continued buildup of more accurate missiles. Members and supporters of Team B formed the Committee on the Present Danger, which painted an alarming picture of relentlessly growing Soviet military capabilities. The election of Ronald W. Reagan in 1980 was seen as a validation of this more alarmist view.

Viewpoint:
Yes. The intelligence community provided an accurate picture of Soviet strategic forces and defenses through a series of detailed reports known as National Intelligence Estimates.

In a nutshell, both the intelligence community and Team B overestimated Soviet capabilities in the mid 1970s. The politically motivated, ideologically driven Team B, however, was much farther off the mark than the intelligence community. There were actually three Team Bs, each reviewing separate areas—Soviet missile accuracy, air defenses, and strategic objectives. Only this latter team became known to the public, when at least one of its members leaked their report to the press. Each team consisted of people outside the administration who were given access to all of the information in its area of concern available to the U.S. government. Each team was to work in parallel with the intelligence analysts who were preparing the yearly National Intelligence Estimates (NIEs).

Throughout the Cold War, the most influential analyses produced by the intelligence community were the NIEs that dealt with Soviet strategic forces and defenses. These estimates, known as NIE 11-3/8 (followed by the year for which they were issued, such as 11-3/8-75), not only provided guidance for the size and shape of the defense budget, but also helped to determine the strategic stance the military would assume, as well as the overall U.S. approach to East-West relations, including arms negotiations. Such estimates present current knowledge and predict what is expected to happen within a given future period, usually five or ten years. NIEs take months to prepare and involve dozens of analysts from the Central Intelligence Agency (CIA); the Defense Intelligence Agency (DIA), the army, navy, and air force intelligence branches; the State Department; the Federal Bureau of Investigation (FBI); the Department of Energy; and the National Security Agency (NSA). Conservatives chose to challenge these estimates in their attempt to accuse the CIA of underestimating the threat from the Soviet Union.

The idea of having outsiders prepare alternative threat assessments came about because conservatives became increasingly unhappy with the Richard M. Nixon—and, later, Gerald R. Ford—Henry Kissinger doctrine of détente with the Soviet Union. Opponents of détente included organized labor, neoconservatives, eastern European immigrants and their elected representatives, human-rights activists, and champions of Jewish emigration from the Soviet Union—all of whom were certain that the Cold War was far from over and were determined that American hegemony should not disappear. They believed the world still needed a paramount policeman and that he should wear an American uniform. American military might, they felt, could contain the expansion of Russia's "evil empire," which they viewed as the fountainhead of revolution and terrorism. They expressed these views through articles, op-ed pieces, speeches, letters to editors, and lobbying. These hard-liners, who viewed themselves as modern Paul Reveres attempting to awaken a sleeping nation, kept up a steady onslaught on the policy of détente.

The official watchdog of the intelligence community is the President's Foreign Intelligence Advisory Board, known as PFIAB. During the 1970s PFIAB was composed of many hard-liners vis-à-vis the Soviet Union, such as physicist Edward Teller, editor and politician Clare Booth Luce, former director of Livermore Laboratory John Foster, Motorola CEO Robert Galvin, and former Texas governor John Connally. In 1975 PFIAB suggested that a small group of outside experts perform an alternative threat assessment. CIA director William E. Colby turned aside this suggestion, but when George Bush became the director of the CIA, PFIAB renewed the request. Bush asked the White House for advice. The administration, fearing that California governor Ronald W. Reagan, who had told President Ford that he was going to oppose him in Republican primaries, would learn if such a request was turned down, told Bush to let the experiment take place.

The analysts preparing the regular NIE (11-3/7-76) were referred to as Team A; the outsiders became known as Team B. The missile-accuracy and air-defense panels consisted mostly of scientists and engineers. The missile-accuracy panels focused on the accuracy of the Soviet SS-18 and SS-19 missiles and, interestingly, Team B used mirror-imaging reasoning in arriving at their estimates of much greater accuracy for the Soviet missiles. Team A pointed out that applying any U.S. technological trend to the Union of Soviet Socialist Republics (U.S.S.R.) was immediately suspect and that for the Team B analogy to be valid, the Soviets would have to be on a par with U.S. 1970 technology, not only in basic theory and laboratory-instrument quality, but in mass production of precision instruments as well. In 1985 the intelligence community lowered

Soviet Tu-22M Backfire bomber

(Official U.S. Navy Photo, 1990)

its estimates of the SS-19 by over 33 percent, so that it was no longer deemed a hard-target or silo killer.

The main differences between the two panels looking at Soviet air defenses centered on the differences between the Soviets' equipment, their command and control capabilities, their detection and tracking capabilities, and their tactics and operational practices. With hindsight, we now know that both Teams A and B overestimated the Soviet air defenses. The authoritative General Accounting Office (GAO) report of 1993 stated that "we found that the Soviet air defense threat had been overestimated. Evaluation of the data over the period of 1972 to 1991 showed this clearly with regard to both the number and the effectiveness of Soviet air defenses against existing US bombers and their weapons."

Team B on Soviet strategic objectives was chaired by Richard Pipes, a professor of Russian history at Harvard University who had consistently labeled the Soviets an aggressive, imperialistic power bent on world domination. Pipes's panel consisted of ten hard-liners who shared an almost apoplectic animosity toward the Soviet Union. The final report of the Pipes Team B was fifty-five pages long, and consisted of three parts and an annex. The first section, written mostly by Pipes, addressed and critiqued the methodol-

ogy of past NIEs. It accused the CIA of consistently underestimating the "intensity, scope, and implicit threat" posed by the Soviet Union, because "the hard evidence on which the NIEs are based relates primarily to the adversary's capabilities rather than his intentions, his weapons rather than his ideas, motives and aspirations." Team B stated, "the evidence suggests that the Soviet leaders are first and foremost offensively rather than defensively minded." The Team B analysts, however, slanted their evidence. In asserting that "Russian, and especially Soviet political and military theories are distinctly *offensive* in character," Team B claimed "their ideal is the 'science of conquest' (*nauka pobezhdat*) formulated by the eighteenth-century Russian general, Field Marshal A.V. Suvorov in a treatise of the same name, which has been a standard text of imperial as well as Soviet military science." The correct translation of *nauka pobezhdat*, however, is "the science of winning" or the "science of victory." All military strategists strive to achieve a winning strategy. Our own military writings are devoted to winning victories, but this policy is not commonly viewed as one of conquest. With the opening of Russian archives, no new evidence has surfaced that the Soviets ever considered deliberately launching a premeditated large-scale strike against Western Europe or the United States at any time since 1945.

TEAM B

About one-third of the Pipes's Team B report looked briefly at ten specific aspects of Soviet strategic-force developments, including economic restraints, Soviet antisatellite capabilities and Soviet antisubmarine-warfare capabilities. For each, Team B gave a brief history and their own conclusions. In all instances Team B saw the worst possible case. Anti-ballistic missiles (ABMs) and directed-energy weapons were examined together. Team B asserted that "Mobile ABM system components combined with the deployed SAM (surface-to-air missile) systems could produce a significant ABM capability." That never occurred, however. Team B wrote, "Understanding that there are differing evaluations of the potentialities of laser and charged-particle beam for ABM, it is still clear that the Soviets have mounted ABM efforts in both areas of a magnitude that it is difficult to overestimate." That, however, is precisely what the Pipes panel did. A facility at the Soviet Union's nuclear-test range in Semipalatinsk was touted as a site for tests of Soviet nuclear-powered beam weapons. In fact, it was used to test nuclear-powered rocket engines and was totally unrelated to so-called nuclear directed-energy weapons.

About Soviet antisubmarine-warfare capabilities, the Pipes panel wrote "the absence of a deployed system by this time is difficult to understand. The implication could be that the Soviets have, in fact, deployed some operational non-acoustic systems and will deploy more in the next few years." Our submarine force, however, was never vulnerable. The GAO report of 1993 stated that "we found that the Soviet threat to the weapon systems of the land and sea legs had also been overstated. For the sea leg, this capability was reflected in unsubstantiated allegations about likely future breakthroughs in Soviet submarine detection technologies, along with underestimation of the performance and capabilities of our own nuclear-powered ballistic missile submarines. Our specific finding, based on operational test results, was that submerged SSBNs [submarines carrying nuclear missiles] are even less detectable than is generally understood and that there appear to be no current or long-term technologies that would change this."

When they looked at the Soviet Backfire bomber, not only did the Pipes Team write, "we have good evidence that it probably will be produced in substantial numbers, with perhaps 500 aircraft off the line by early 1984," when, in fact, the Soviets had less than half that number, 235 by 1984; they also engaged in mirror-imaging, that is, attributing to Soviet decision makers forms of behavior that might be expected from their U.S. counterparts under analogous circumstances. They wrote, "this conceptual flaw is perhaps the single gravest cause of the misunderstanding of Soviet strategic objectives found in past and current NIEs." Yet, when they discussed the Soviet Tu-22M Backfire bomber, they wrote, "We consider our FB 111 a strategic bomber and plan its use against Soviet targets even though its unrefueled radius falls short of even the lowest estimates of Backfire performance. Our strategic air command plans multiple refueling of the aircraft which gives it on a typical mission a range (with two refuelings) of about 6400 nautical miles." Team B went on to claim that, for the Soviet bomber, "there is no question that the aircraft has the inherent capability for strategic missions, should the Soviets choose to use it this way." In later years the DIA lowered its estimate of the range of a fully loaded Backfire by about 20 percent. This meant that the Backfire could not have carried out round-trip missions against the United States without midair refueling, The bomber lacked a probe for aerial refueling and the Soviets never developed a large tanker capability, both of which would have been necessary to use the bomber for missions against the United States.

The Pipes panel also claimed that consistently low intelligence estimates of the Soviet military defense burden had serious broad warping effects on the estimating process and on the perceptions of users. In 1976, in spite of rising mortality rates for the entire Soviet population, declining life expectancy, declining numbers of new entrants into the labor force, and declining agricultural output, they wrote confidently, "Within what is after all a large and expanding GNP. . . . Soviet strategic forces have yet to reflect any constraining effect of civil economy competition and are unlikely to do so in the foreseeable future." Now we know better. In 1983 then deputy director of CIA Robert Gates testified, "The rate of growth of overall defense costs is lower because procurement of military hardware, the largest category of defense spending was almost flat in 1976–1981. Practically all major categories of Soviet weapons were affected—missiles, aircraft and ships." In January 1984 a North Atlantic Treaty Organization (NATO) study agreed with and substantiated Gates's findings. Three years later the CIA and DIA agreed that "the slowdown in procurement growth began in the year 1975." So even as Team B was writing its report, the intelligence community was overestimating, not underestimating, Soviet military expenditures.

What about the intelligence community? How accurate were their assessments and predictions about the Soviets? In a special intelligence estimate dated 10 September 1973, the intelligence community warned of "the vigorous pursuit of weapons development programs

TEAM B

that portend substantial improvements in Soviet strategic capability." Four months later, in the regular NIE, it was stated that, "The Soviets are now well into a broad range of programs to augment, modernize and improve their forces for intercontinental attack. This new round of programs follows hard on a large-scale sustained deployment effort which left the U.S.S.R. considerably ahead of the United States in numbers of ICBM [intercontinental ballistic missiles] launchers and in process of taking the lead in SLBM launchers. At least in the field of ICBM development they represent a breadth and concurrency of effort which is virtually unprecedented." In 1975 the NIE warned "the capability of the Soviet ICBM force to destroy US Minuteman silos is growing. It will probably pose a major threat in the early 1980s. A more rapid increase in this threat is possible but unlikely."

Team B accused the intelligence community of neglecting such "soft" factors as historical, political, and institutional factors. Yet, a special NIE for 1973 stated, "Since the early 1960s the Soviet military has articulated a view of strategic requirements that links deterrence with the ability actually to wage strategic war to the point of some form of victory." The regular NIE for that year also discussed Soviet objectives as "probably including an opportunistic desire to press ahead and achieve a margin of superiority if they can." In 1975 the NIE stated, "Deeply held ideological and doctrinal convictions impel the Soviet leaders to pose as an ultimate goal the attainment of a dominant position over the West, particularly the United States, in terms of political, economic, social, and military strength. We do not doubt that if they thought they could achieve it, the Soviets would try to attain the capability to launch a nuclear attack so effective that the U.S. could not cause devastating damage to the U.S.S.R. in retaliation." These were hardly "soothing" assessments as Pipes had claimed.

With perfect 20/20 hindsight, we now know that neither the intelligence community nor Team B were correct in their forecasts about Soviet strategic forces, but unquestionably the professional analysts were less wrong than the outsiders. Would the intelligence community have been more likely to predict the demise of the Soviet Union if they had not been seared by the Team B experiment? That intriguing question cannot be answered even with 20/20 hindsight.

–ANNE HESSING CAHN, AMERICAN UNIVERSITY

Viewpoint:
No. Team B determined that Soviet missile accuracy, air defense, and strategic objectives posed a serious threat to the United States, correcting the National Intelligence Estimates.

During the 1970s the American foreign policy making establishment was beset with controversy over the accuracy of the intelligence community's assessments of Soviet power. Hawkish members of the Ford administration suggested that an independent evaluation of Soviet capabilities be made and compared with the evaluations of the intelligence community. After some initial resistance, this "Team B" approach was eventually approved and put into effect in 1976. Evaluating such critical categories of comparative strategic analysis as missile accuracy, air defense, and strategic objectives, Team B reached the conclusion that the intelligence community had underestimated Soviet capabilities in its insistence that the Union of Soviet Socialist Republics (U.S.S.R.) posed less of a military and strategic threat to the United States than had commonly been thought. The historical facts illustrate that the Team B assessment was correct.

One criticism of Team B is that it rejected the intelligence community's finding because intelligence failed to consider the intentions and ideology governing Soviet conduct. While it is true that evaluations like the National Intelligence Estimates (NIEs) of the Central Intelligence Agency (CIA) were intended to calculate Soviet military capabilities alone, Team B's criticism was more than valid in that the intelligence community's approach ignored fundamental features of Soviet foreign policy.

Even a cursory understanding of Soviet history reveals that its viability as a state or as a world power, like any authoritarian police state, does not rise and fall on domestic social and economic factors. Scholars who assert that the collapse of the Soviet Union was inevitable ignore the fact that the Soviet regime survived a bloody civil war and "Red terror" followed by famine, collectivization, more famine (this one created by state policies), the state-directed "purge" murders of millions of innocent people, the tremendous suffering of World War II (twenty-seven million Soviet citizens died), more purges in the postwar period, and the continued harsh repression of political dissidents and ethnic minorities. Not only did the Soviet regime survive all of these traumatic events, but it actually saw its status as a world power increase despite them.

Why this should all suddenly have changed, making a decline of the U.S.S.R. in power-political terms "obvious" to the intelligence community in the 1970s, a time of stagnation but certainly not collapse, has not been satisfactorily explained. Even as late as November 1991 leading Soviet specialists said publicly that Mikhail Gorbachev had things well under control and that the Soviet Union would remain a factor for the foreseeable future. Respected works on international relations published throughout the 1980s contained what passed for serious and thoughtful discussions of what the output and strength of the U.S.S.R. would be in year 2000 and beyond. One unfortunate graduate student was flunked out of his political science doctoral program in 1985 because his dissertation suggested that the Soviet Union was about to collapse.

The Soviet regime was paradoxical in that even with slowing economic growth and eventual stagnation, it continued to assert itself geopolitically and did undertake actions that were justifiably seen as strategic challenges to the United States. In the five years following the presentation of the Team B reports in December 1976, the Soviet Union was providing direct military and economic support to at least the following nineteen countries—Poland, East Germany, Czechoslovakia, Hungary, Romania, Bulgaria, Albania, Iraq, Syria, Yemen, Ethiopia, Mozambique, Angola, Cuba, Grenada, Nicaragua, Vietnam, North Korea, and Afghanistan—hardly an unambitious or nonthreatening gambit from a declining power. While some of this support went to maintain hegemonic Soviet influence, much of it, especially in the Carribean and Middle East, posed a direct threat to American interests in those regions. Jeanne Kirkpatrick, a Carter administration Democrat who vehemently opposed détente with the U.S.S.R. and served as Ronald Reagan's ambassador to the United Nations (U.N.), recently remarked that while ten countries went communist under the Carter administration, none did so on her watch. Even as the intelligence community predicted Soviet decline, Moscow showed no compunction about using its military capabilities when it sent one hundred thousand troops into Afghanistan in 1979–1980. Nor did it show any sensitivity to keeping good relations with the United States, something a power at a clear disadvantage would have every reason to do, when it rejected President Reagan's comprehensive "zero-zero" arms control proposal of 1981, sent advisers to Syria to fight against Israel in 1982, shot down a Korean airliner carrying American civilians in 1983, and boycotted the Los Angeles Olympic Games in 1984.

The Soviet Union was on the march, and the intelligence community's estimates of what Moscow was capable of were not reflected in reality. What the intelligence community failed to realize was that even if the Soviet economy looked stagnant, the fundamentally undemocratic nature of Soviet society placed no pressure on the ruling elite to increase domestic investment and cut military spending in the way that grass-roots pressure, periodic elections, and civil society interest groups would do in democratic societies. They answered to no one and that was reflected in their conduct. Seeing the legitimacy of its rule inseparable from what Vladislav Zubok and Constantine Pleshakov have called the "revolutionary-imperial paradigm," a combination of what they believed to be the inevitability of socialism's triumph with traditional Great Russian imperial aspirations, the Soviet government had no choice but to make its pretensions to world power status felt and to advance the socialist cause. Recently released documentary evidence about the Soviet invasion of Afghanistan reveals that both of these concepts were factors in carrying out what many in the leadership, including senior Soviet generals, rightly believed to be a bad decision.

While it is true that Moscow was in the middle of launching a global offensive, the intelligence community nevertheless believed that its stagnant economic growth would impact military spending, and it produced figures to prove it. Analyses of their quantitative and qualitative computational methods at work, however, illustrate that these assessments failed to take into account features of a command economy in which workers were definitely not remunerated in salary or government services on par with their Western counterparts and in which pervasive state involvement determined prices and economic values, in addition to wages.

It is also clear that the Soviets, not having any domestic pressure to reduce military spending, invested enormously in it. Recently declassified CIA figures, presumably ones that Team B disputed and ones calculated under a faulty methodology, put it at approximately 15 percent of the Gross National Product (GNP). Other figures range as high as 25 percent, though Gorbachev himself estimated that military spending consumed as much as one-half when he came to power in 1985. While the United States reduced its military spending almost to prewar levels before the Korean War ($13 billion in 1950 compared with $10 billion ten years earlier), the Soviets maintained a standing army of three million men, even though that country had suffered much more than the United States. Even during the Reagan defense buildup, the United States never spent more than 8 percent of its GNP on

THE COMMITTEE ON THE PRESENT DANGER

The Committee on the Present Danger was a group of politicians, diplomats, scientists, and businessmen that took an alarmist view of the military capabilities of the Soviet Union and supported the conclusions of Team B. The following is a portion of a report released by the committee on 4 April 1977.

The Soviet military buildup of all its armed forces over the past quarter century is, in part, reminiscent of Nazi Germany's rearmament in the 1930s. The Soviet buildup affects all branches of the military: the army, the air force and the navy. In addition Soviet nuclear offensive and defensive forces are designed to enable the USSR to fight, survive and win an all-out nuclear war should it occur.

The Salt I arms limitation agreements have had no visible effect on the Soviet buildup. Indeed, their principal effect so far has been to restrain the United States in the development of those weapons in which it enjoys an advantage. Nor has the self-imposed restraint by the United States in the past decade in the development and deployment of its strategic nuclear forces evoked similar restraint on the part of the USSR. On the contrary: the Soviet Union has shown a determination to forge ahead with the development and deployment of all weapons which promise to enhance its global military posture. Neither Soviet military power nor its rate of growth can be explained or justified on grounds of self-defense.

By its continuing strategic nuclear buildup, the Soviet Union demonstrates that it does not subscribe to American notions of nuclear sufficiency and mutually assured deterrence, which postulate that once a certain quantity and quality of strategic nuclear weapons is attained, both sides will understand that further accumulation or improvement becomes pointless, and act accordingly. Soviet strategists regard the possession of more and better strategic weapons as a definite military and political asset, and potentially the ultimate instrument of coercion. The intensive programs of civil defense and hardening of command and control posts against nuclear attack undertaken in the Soviet Union in recent years suggest that they take seriously the possibility of nuclear war and believe that, were it to occur, they will be more likely to survive and to recover more rapidly than we.

STRATEGIC SUPERIORITY

In recent years, the Soviet Union has been increasing its military expenditures at an annual rate of at least 3 to 4% while the United States has until recently been decreasing its military expenditures at a rate of 3%, taking inflation into account in both cases. The experts disagree as to whether the Soviet Union is already ahead of the United States in military strength, either overall or in particular theaters. However, we are convinced, and there is widespread agreement among knowledgeable experts, that *if past trends continue, the USSR will within several years achieve strategic superiority over the United States.* The USSR already enjoys conventional superiority in several important theaters.

Superiority in both strategic and conventional weapons could enable the Soviet Union to apply decisive pressure on the United States in conflict situations. The USSR might then compel the United States to retreat, much as the USSR itself was forced to retreat in 1962 during the Cuban missile crisis. As an example, one could conceive of another war in the Middle East in which the USSR, having acquired local conventional superiority and overall nuclear superiority, could compel the United States to withdraw its influence from that area.

Soviet pressure, when supported by strategic and conventional military superiority, would be aimed at forcing our general withdrawal from a leading role in world affairs, and isolating us from other democratic societies, which could not then long survive.

Thus conceived, Soviet superiority would serve basically offensive aims, enabling the USSR to project its power in various parts of the globe without necessarily establishing a major physical presence in any single country. Soviet strategic superiority could lead the USSR to believe that should it eventually succeed in isolating the United States from its allies and the Third World, the United States would be less likely, in a major crisis, to lash out with strategic nuclear weapons, in a desperate attempt to escape subjugation.

Source: *Charles Tyroler II, ed.,* Alerting America: The Papers of the Committee on the Present Danger *(Washington, D.C.: Pergamon-Brassey's, 1984), pp. 13–14.*

TEAM B

defense, and at this writing it is now in the sixteenth year of an almost unbroken trend of unprecedented economic growth; while the United States could govern its military spending judiciously, the U.S.S.R. could not.

Intelligence assertions that high military spending endangered the Soviet Union were correct only in that it was Moscow's Achilles' heel should it be properly exploited, not in that it represented a recent weakening of the Soviet economy. Exploiting the inability of the U.S.S.R. to adapt its domestic economy in a changing world because of its military commitments was a major component of the Reagan administration's strategy of "rolling back" Soviet influence. Team B had the superior analysis when it came to strategic considerations.

In addition to Team B's insistence that the ultimate intentions of the Soviet Union, based on "imperial" and ideological grounds, posed a major threat to the United States, its findings in technological areas also vindicated its approach to assessing Soviet strength. Its report on Soviet aerial capabilities differed relatively little from that of the intelligence community. Both agreed that Soviet aerial defense could be coordinated; Team B said that it was, and the intelligence community said that it was not but should be. Why the Soviets would ignore the tactical advantage of developing something structurally similar to the Strategic Air Command (SAC) was not explained.

In missile technology Team B's assessment that the U.S.S.R. would develop a first-strike capability was discovered, to its own embarrassment, by the intelligence community within weeks of the alternate Team's December 1976 report. In its first week the Carter administration learned that the Soviets were planning to begin tests on a perfected guidance system for the SS-18 missile in the fall of 1977 with the aim of having that system operational by 1980. The intelligence community had reported that the Soviets were unlikely to challenge American strategic weapons superiority into the foreseeable future. The discovery that this was not entirely the case fundamentally altered the new administration's approach to strategic policy. A pronounced split between Secretary of State Cyrus Vance and National Security Adviser Zbigniew Brzezinski over related strategic issues damaged the cohesion of the administration's foreign policy, culminating in Vance's eventual resignation. In his first year Carter reinforced American conventional forces in Europe and abandoned his campaign promise to withdraw from South Korea. The prospect of Soviet strategic weapons superiority led him to accelerate the development of the neutron bomb and the Pershing II cruise missile, both of which would restore American nuclear preeminence, and to negotiate with West European nations to deploy these new weapons there. From these developments it can only be concluded that Team B's analysis was more accurate in technical matters, too.

–PAUL DU QUENOY, GEORGETOWN
UNIVERSITY

References

Seweryn Bialer, *The Soviet Paradox: External Expansion, Internal Decline* (New York: Knopf, 1986);

Zbigniew K. Brzezinski, *Power and Principle: Memoirs of the National Security Adviser, 1977–1981* (New York: Farrar, Straus & Giroux, 1985);

Anne Hessing Cahn, *Killing Détente: The Right Attacks the CIA* (University Park: Pennsylvania State University Press, 1998);

John Ehrman, *The Rise of Neoconservatism: Intellectuals and Foreign Affairs, 1945–1994* (New Haven: Yale University Press, 1995);

John Prados, *The Soviet Estimate: U.S. Intelligence Analysis and Soviet Strategic Forces* (Princeton: Princeton University Press, 1982);

Jerry W. Sanders, *Peddlers of Crisis: The Committee on the Present Danger and the Politics of Containment* (Boston: South End Press, 1983);

Richard C. Thornton, *The Carter Years: Toward a New Global Order* (New York: Paragon House, 1991);

Cyrus Vance, *Hard Choices: Critical Years in America's Foreign Policy* (New York: Simon & Schuster, 1983).

TEAM B

THIRD WORLD

Did the Third World play an important role in the Cold War?

Viewpoint: Yes. The Third World played too great a role in U.S. Cold War policy, often leading the United States to support repressive regimes and commit precious resources.

Viewpoint: No. The Third World was of little importance to either the U.S.S.R. or the United States, and the Non-aligned Movement never achieved sufficient economic, political, or military power to influence the Cold War struggle.

President John F. Kennedy, in his 1961 inaugural address, spoke of the "long twilight struggle" between communism and the free world. This struggle, he suggested, would be most intense—and, perhaps, even decided—in the "huts and hamlets" of the new nations of the Third World. Kennedy found support for his belief that the decisive contest between communism and the free world had moved from Europe and America to Asia, Africa, and Latin America in a secret speech that Premier Nikita S. Khrushchev delivered in January 1961 in which he promised Soviet support for "wars of national liberation."

The process of decolonization brought independence to many countries in Asia and Africa, in some cases following bitter and bloody wars against the colonial powers. U.S. policy makers were afraid that the immediate postcolonial period presented the Soviet Union with opportunities to enhance its influence and strengthen its global position. There were three reasons for that fear. First, because the colonial powers—mainly Britain and France, but also Belgium, the Netherlands, and Portugal—were members of the Western camp, the leaders of many independence movements sought, and received, assistance from the Soviet Union. Many of these leaders remained suspicious of Western intentions and sympathetic to the Soviet Union. Second, in the 1950s and 1960s the notions of centralized control of the economy and planning by government were still adhered to in many parts of the world as the best means to effectively and rapidly bring about economic development. The Soviet Union appeared to some of the newly independent countries as a more appropriate economic model to emulate than the free market system of the West. Third, the populations of many newly independent countries were mired in dire poverty, making them susceptible to a revolutionary appeal.

The U.S. government thus began a massive campaign to prevent countries in the Third World from adopting a communist system and supporting the policies of the Soviet Union. This campaign took many forms: economic aid; political support of authoritarian, anticommunist rulers; covert action; and military intervention.

Viewpoint:
Yes. The Third World played too great a role in U.S. Cold War policy, often leading the United States to support repressive regimes and commit precious resources.

By any reasonable measure, the preoccupation of Cold War American policy makers with the Third World was unjustified and, in hindsight, perplexing. A policy, to be judged wise, must relate power to interests in a prudent and effective manner. It is unwise if it pursues goals that cannot be attained or should not be pursued in the first place. On this criterion, much of U.S. policy in the Third World during the Cold War was a waste of effort—vast resources were invested, and large risks taken, in the pursuit of goals that either could not be attained or should not have been pursued.

Four arguments have commonly been offered in support of an activist U.S. policy in the Third World. The first contends that the Third World was intrinsically important to the United States, especially during the Cold War: countries grouped under this title contained resources important to the economy of the West, and some of these nations were strategically located near important sea lanes. The United States could thus ignore the Third World only at its own peril. If it did not vigorously engage in a campaign to ensure that friendly regimes controlled these countries and their resources, these important assets would come under the control of the Soviet Union, enhancing its position in its competition with the United States.

The second argument pointed to the political and psychological importance of the superpower competition in the Third World. There are more than material aspects to such a rivalry, it is argued. Even if not all parts of the Third World were of equal material importance to the United States—and, thus, would not enhance the power of the Union of Soviet Socialist Republics (U.S.S.R.) even if they came under Soviet control—the United States still had every political and psychological reason to compete for influence and control over these countries. All Western countries were democracies, with government and policies influenced by an impressionable, and not always informed, public. If country after country in the Third World were to fall under Soviet sway, then, even if materially the West would not be weakened, Western public opinion could not but begin to suspect that the Soviet Union was on the march and that there was little the West could do about it. The self-doubt and defeatism that would follow might push public

opinion in Western countries to support accommodationist policies vis-à-vis the Soviet Union, in the process weakening the ability of the West to protect truly vital interests.

There was another psychological argument for the West to make a stand in the Third World—one based on the need for a party to fight to develop a reputation for resolve. Perhaps the West did not have vital interests in many developing countries, but its unwillingness to stand and fight might persuade Soviet leaders that the West was losing its resolve, pushing them to take more risks and probe into areas closer to important interests of the West. A failure to make a stand in the Third World thus could have misled Soviet leaders into believing that Western countries would be unwilling to defend even more vital interests, causing the Soviet Union to embark on a more adventurous and risky policy that, in a nuclear world, was in the interest of the West to avoid.

The fourth argument for an active U.S. policy of intervention advanced the proposition that even if many Third World countries were not of vital interest—even if there was no need to make a stand in the Third World to make sure domestic public opinion did not weaken and the Soviets would not be led to doubt Western resolve—it was still justified for the United States to intervene because, in doing so, it advanced U.S. values around the world by spreading the blessings of liberalism and democracy. These arguments may look impressive, but they do not stand up to a close scrutiny. Would that these contentions were more carefully examined during the Cold War—the United States would have saved much blood and treasure that it spent on unnecessary, even damaging, ventures.

The two areas of the Third World in which the United States had invested most of its efforts were Central America and Southeast Asia. There is some oil in Mexico, but otherwise the countries of these two regions were of no more than marginal economic interest to the United States. Moreover, even if these regions possessed resources vital to the United States, it is not clear why the Third World would have imposed economic punishment on themselves by denying the West access to them. Indeed, the history of communist and communist-leaning regimes—for example, the Soviet Union, China, Yugoslavia under Marshall Josip Broz Tito, Romania under Nicolae Ceausescu, Chile under Salvador Allende Gossens, Nicaragua under the Sandinistas, and Angola under Antonio Agostinho Neto—shows that they actively sought economic relations with Western countries. It was the United States that tried to impose economic sanctions and embargoes on communist regimes once they came to power. The one area of the

THIRD WORLD

Jawaharlal Nehru, Josip Broz Tito, and Gamal Abdel Nasser meeting at the July 1956 conference of nonaligned nations in the Brioni islands in the Adriatic Sea

(Foto-Tanjug, Belgrade)

Third World where the United States clearly had economic interests—the Persian Gulf—was ringed by countries friendly to the United States, until 1979 when Shah Mohammad Reza Pahlavi was replaced by the mullahs in Iran and conservative regimes that naturally looked to the West.

It is also not clear that the effects on public opinion, or on the Soviet image of the United States, would be negative if the United States abstained from getting involved in Third World affairs. American public opinion is notoriously indifferent to foreign policy (short of war) and uncomfortable with large foreign-aid programs. There is an acceptance of the fact that the United States would not want to see a foreign power establish bases in the Western Hemisphere, but beyond that it has proven difficult to persuade the public that the United States should extend its efforts much beyond areas of strategic importance, such as Western Europe, Japan, and the Middle East. It is also uncertain why the Soviet Union would have concluded that if the United States refused to waste its efforts in defending unimportant areas of the world, it would also be unwilling to defend what it considered truly vital. The opposite may well be the case: nothing

would have suited Soviet designs better than to see its major competitor waste blood and treasure on marginal issues, weakening its ability to defend essential interests. The Vietnam Syndrome is an example of this: tired of the bloodshed and waste in the Vietnam War (ended 1975) and disenchanted with foreign involvement, American public opinion made it difficult for decision makers to send U.S. troops overseas even when there was a good cause to do so.

The last argument is that U.S. interventionism has helped spread American values and principles and that this policy was a good thing in and of itself. Yet, while the United States supported some moderate regimes in the Third World, anticommunism was more important to U.S. policy. When moderation and tolerance seemed to be standing in the way of the fight against communism, the United States did not hesitate to support despotic governments. Such was the case in such places as the Dominican Republic under Rafael Trujillo Molina; in Guatemala since the 1950s; in Nicaragua under the Somozas; in Chile, Brazil, Argentina, and Uruguay under different military juntas; and in El Salvador in the 1980s. An argument can be made that, at least in Latin America, most U.S. interventionism was done in support of repressive regimes, not of democratic values.

The role of the Third World during the Cold War was thus contradictory. On the one hand, by any measure most Third World countries were of no strategic or economic importance to the United States. They were poor and without resources, markets, or the industrial might that would have made them valuable as allies and dangerous as enemies. Those few countries that were of value—for example, the oil-producing nations around the Persian Gulf—were firmly pro-West. The United States, however, paid attention to developments in the Third World that were disproportional to its value. Misled into believing that if it did not make a stand in remote places its resolve to defend vital interests would be questioned, the United States invested a large effort to shore up regimes and support countries that did not truly matter to it. The belief that it needed the support of these countries in its struggle with the Soviet Union, furthermore, led the United States, especially in the Western Hemisphere, to support repressive, brutal regimes that opposed reform and liberalization.

The Americans did much good in these countries, but, upon reflection, one may conclude that were the United States to weigh the Third World and events in it by objective measures, it would have realized that developments there really had little or no consequence for the conduct of the U.S.-U.S.S.R. competition. With this more accurate assessment, the United States would probably have continued to support reformist regimes but would have abstained from lending a hand to brutal dictators whom it had supported in the name of fighting communism.

—BENJAMIN FRANKEL, SECURITY STUDIES

Viewpoint:
No. The Third World was of little importance to either the U.S.S.R. or the United States, and the Non-aligned Movement never achieved sufficient economic, political, or military power to influence the Cold War struggle.

German chancellor Otto von Bismarck convened the Berlin West Africa Conference (15 November 1884–26 February 1885) in order to alleviate tension that had arisen among the European powers during their undignified scramble for colonies in Africa in the 1880s.

The Germans, French, Belgians, Portuguese, and British agreed upon their spheres of influence on the African continent. Not six decades later, President Franklin D. Roosevelt, Prime Minister Winston Churchill, and Premier Joseph Stalin met in Yalta (4–11 February 1945), and again in Potsdam (July–August 1945), to settle the question of spheres of influence—but this time more than Africa was at stake. The international order after World War II, according to Henry Kissinger in *Diplomacy* (1994), meant that "two rigid alliances with very little diplomatic maneuvering room between them faced each other." Though reminiscent of the situation prior to World War I, this time the theater was not merely Europe, but the world, and each alliance was dominated by one power, the United States or the Union of Soviet Socialist Republics (U.S.S.R.).

The de facto result of the Potsdam conference was the beginning of the division of Europe into two spheres of influence, American and Soviet. The United States consolidated the Western occupation zones in Germany, while the U.S.S.R. transformed Eastern Europe into an extension of itself. Italy and Japan, as well as the Federal Republic of Germany, gravitated toward the West. The United States used such devices as the Truman Doctrine (1947) and the Marshall Plan (1948) to reconstruct Western Europe, the Greek-Turkish aid program to secure the eastern Mediterranean, and the North Atlantic Treaty Organization (NATO, April 1949) to protect Western European states in a united military-defense alliance. The U.S.S.R. solidified its control of Eastern Europe by supporting communist parties, and ultimately through the Warsaw Pact (1955). The superpowers had settled the question of the European continent, and the Cold War was in full force. Where did that leave the rest of the world?

The global order was also divided into two camps, yet, ironically, with no regard to the Third World, which comprised more than half the total population of the earth. These states, driven by a quest for autonomy, attempted to present an alternative to the bipolar global system—a nonaligned front. Their struggle would be in vain. The Third World during the Cold War was a pawn in a chess game because it lacked power, both military and economic; had no unified leadership; was plagued by regional and internal conflicts; and was susceptible to the incessant manipulation and exploitation by the superpowers for their own benefit.

Richard Wright, an American journalist covering the Bandung Conference (18–24 April 1955), which took place in Indonesia, later wrote in *The Color Curtain: A Report on the Bandung Conference* (1956), "This meeting of the rejected was in itself a kind of judgment upon the Western world!" The reasons that the Non-aligned Movement (NAM) was created were idealistic and even noble. Given the inherent dangers in a policy of alignment, independence was a means of survival. The purpose was to loosen the inflexible international framework resulting from two antagonistic blocs, as well as to establish freedom devoid of colonialism for the Third World. Bung Sukarno stated at the Bandung conference, "We lived in poverty and humiliation" while being controlled by others for their own interest for too long. Jawaharlal Nehru of India echoed Sukarno's sentiments, expressing that the NAM philosophy was not to be subservient to the dictates of others but to be culturally, economically, and politically independent, siding with no one. Josip Broz Tito went so far as to declare at the Belgrade Conference for Foreign Ministers (July 1978) that the NAM would "devise effective means of settling current disputes peacefully and democratically." Thus Nehru, Sukarno, and Tito would be joined by others, such as Gamal Abdel Nasser of Egypt, Mu'ammar Gadhafi of Libya, and Ayatollah Ruhollah Khomeini of Iran, in the effort to create an international movement, bowing neither to the Soviet Union nor the United States.

Neither superpower was particularly impressed or amused by the antics of this seemingly ramshackle movement. The neutrality of the movement was also misunderstood as passivity and nonparticipation. Regarding the movement, Secretary of State John Foster Dulles commented, "Neutrality is an absolute concept and except under very exceptional circumstances, it is an immoral and short-sighted concept." Apparently, Cold War circumstances were not deemed exceptional. Within the structure of the Cold War anything that was not anti-Soviet was pro-American, and vice versa. The United States and the U.S.S.R. shared interests during the early stages of the Cold War: to develop or sustain superiority and avoid a major conflict. Nothing was as vital to the United States as maintaining a free Western Europe. The U.S.S.R., on the other hand, was obsessed with controlling what it identified as its buffer zone of security, Eastern Europe. In addition, the United States and the U.S.S.R. engaged in a costly conventional and thermonuclear military competition. The Third World did not figure into that equation.

For the most part the United States ignored the movement, focusing rather on U.S.-Soviet relations and examining the actions and behavior of all other states only in respect of their effects on the superpower competition, but would later use them in the context of U.S.

interests. For example, the United States attempted to separate the U.S.S.R. from its Muslim clients by stressing the ideological incompatibility between communism and Islam and by supplying arms to Syria and Iraq. Dealings with these Middle Eastern states were a function of U.S.-Soviet rivalry rather than the importance of the role of the NAM. American policies were quite contrary to anticolonialism, and the U.S. dismissal of the Third World was evident given that American "objectional" policies were neither altered nor restrained.

The Soviet Union was somewhat more practical, in an opportunistic manner, with its approach to the Third World, though, like the United States, it also did not regard nonalignment as a key movement. Any gain of influence that the Soviet Union could make in the Third World was considered a step toward weakening the West, while setbacks were acceptable as long as the Soviet security position was not threatened. Soviet ideology of "national liberation" and "revolutionary movements" was congruent with the anticolonial sentiments and aspirations of the Third World. Declarations of "peaceful coexistence," goodwill, understanding, and cooperation were issued by the U.S.S.R. at the Twentieth All Party Congress (14–25 February 1956), Algiers Conference (5–9 September 1973), and New Delhi Summit (7–12 March 1983). The Soviets were unconcerned with the Third World so far as it stood equidistant between the United States and U.S.S.R. Basically, the Cold War "spilled over" into the Third World, and yet, Third World conflicts were often muted because of the competition between the superpowers. Regional issues were restrained in order to create a balance to prevent dominance of one superpower or the other.

Throughout history the power of a state has been defined by military strength. Through military prowess a state was able to ensure security vis-à-vis other states, achieve political influence, and assure its ability to affect the behavior of others. That interpretation of power did not alter during the Cold War. The United States and the U.S.S.R. were at times hindered or even defeated in certain efforts by nations significantly weaker than themselves, as was evidenced in the 1970s when the Organization of Petroleum Exporting Countries (OPEC) established an oil embargo following the Yom Kippur War (1973) that resulted in a 400 percent rise in prices in less than three months; by the fiascos in Vietnam or Afghanistan; and by the embarrassing seizure of the American embassy in Tehran, Iran (4 November 1979).

Both the United States and the U.S.S.R., however, dominated the globe through power politics. Their military strength, or "war-making

THIRD WORLD DECLARATIONS

Delegates from twenty-nine Asian and African countries met at Bandung, Indonesia, from 18 to 24 April 1955. They sought a unified stance against dependency and ways to achieve cooperation on economic, cultural, and political fronts. The following selection from a conference declaration emphasized ways to seek world peace.

The Asian-African conference, taking note of the fact that several states have still not been admitted to the United Nations, considered that for effective cooperation for world peace, membership in the United Nations should be universal, called on the Security Council to support the admission of all states which are qualified for membership in terms of the Charter. . . .

It expressed the view that as regards the distribution of the non-permanent seats, the Asian-African countries which, under the arrangement arrived at in London in 1946, are precluded from being elected, should be enabled to serve on the Security Council so that they might make a more effective contribution to the maintenance of international peace and security.

2. The Asian-African conference having considered the dangerous situation of international tension existing and the risks confronting the whole human race from the outbreak of global war in which the destructive power of all types of armaments including nuclear and thermonuclear weapons would be employed, invited the attention of all nations to the terrible consequences that would follow if such a war were to break out.

The conference considered that disarmament and the prohibition of production,

experimentation and the use of nuclear and thermonuclear weapons of war are imperative to save mankind and civilization from the fear and prospect of wholesale destruction.

It considered that the nations of Asia and Africa assembled here have a duty toward humanity and civilization to proclaim their support for the prohibition of these weapons and to appeal to nations principally concerned and to world opinion to bring about such disarmament and prohibition.

The conference considered that effective international control should be established and maintained to implement such prohibition and that speedy and determined efforts should be made to this end. Pending the total prohibition of the manufacture of nuclear and thermonuclear weapons, this conference appealed to all the powers concerned to reach agreement to suspend experiments with such weapons.

The conference declared that universal disarmament is an absolute necessity for the preservation of peace and requested the United Nations to continue its efforts and appealed to all concerned speedily to bring about the regulation, limitation, control and reduction of all armed forces and armaments including the prohibition, experimentation and use of all weapons of mass destruction and to establish effective international control to this end.

Source: Current History, 28 (June 1955): 372.

---

capability," designated the superpowers as the ultimate arbiters. Factors such as population, political organization, geographic position, topography, endowment of natural resources, and economic capability were relevant only in their contribution to the ability to wage war successfully. Military power, as well as the perception that it would be used, is what classified the United States and U.S.S.R. as superpowers; the lack of those qualities is what designated the Third World to its nominal role in the Cold War. Power is utilized to accomplish and maintain military and territorial security, as well as implement foreign policy, control physical and politi-

cal resources, and manipulate outcomes within one's environment—the Third World was incapable of achieving these objectives.

In a bipolar world it is difficult to differentiate defense from offense. The nuclear arsenal amassed by both superpowers rendered these weapons unusable; nuclear parity preserved global peace but also resulted in a stalemate. The United States and the U.S.S.R. were faced with the age-old security dilemma of states: expansion. The Cold War was a series of actions and reactions between the superpowers, and the Third World was merely a battleground on which such engagements took place. The Third

World did not possess power through a nuclear or conventional arsenal nor through economic strength, nor did it enjoy the perception that its limited power would be vital in the international system. As a result, when an opportunity presented itself for one superpower to better the other, the Third World was important; however, when no benefit was discerned, the United States and the U.S.S.R. took an approach similar to the old adage "children should be seen not heard" and ignored or even repressed the Third World. A perfect example was the Suez Crisis of 1956. When Great Britain, France, and Israel attacked Egypt because of Nasser's nationalization of the Suez Canal, the United States and the Soviet Union either acted against their allies or failed to provide serious support, as their interests lay elsewhere. The Soviets seized the opportunity to crush the Hungarian uprising, and the Americans took a vocal position against Great Britain and France. The Third World criticized the French and British for their behavior and were mostly silent concerning Soviet action in Hungary. On 4 November a resolution to deploy a United Nations (U.N.) emergency force to the Middle East was unanimously passed in the General Assembly, whereas a resolution requiring the Soviets to withdraw from Hungary was passed with abstention from NAM and was utterly ignored. In both cases the United States and the U.S.S.R. determined the outcome. The Americans pressured their allies to end the Middle Eastern debacle, and the Soviets strong-armed their Eastern European satellite into submission. The wishes of Nasser or Imre Nagy and their people, along with the rest of the world, were irrelevant.

Afghanistan was another example of the superpowers maximizing the Third World for their own benefit. On 9 December 1979 Soviet forces assembled along the Soviet-Afghan border and by late December launched a full-scale invasion. This direct military involvement was rooted in the historical Russian need to dominate what it considered an adjacent national security zone. The U.S.S.R. acted from the point of view of a "protective situation," much like U.S. intervention in Korea or Vietnam. The United States covertly supported the mujahideen with arms, training, and indirect assistance. More importantly, the United States took advantage of the invasion and used it as an excuse for a rapid military buildup, concentrating on the enhancement and substantial increase of conventional and military capabilities. The Soviets had supplied the Americans with the justification for abandoning the policy of détente.

The role of the Third World dwindled further after détente was discontinued. Launched by President Jimmy Carter and intensified by President Ronald Reagan, the United States pursued a drive for superiority over the Soviet Union. In addition to the aforementioned military buildup, the United States abandoned arms control and modified its military doctrine as evidenced in Presidential Directive (PD) 59 (1980) and the Carter Doctrine (1980), as well as Reagan's Defense Guidance (Strategic Defense Initiative, 1983) and National Security Decision Directives 13, 32, and 82. The United States was determined to force the Soviet Union to overextend itself in every manner. America adopted a form of "gunboat diplomacy" and became active in many areas in the world, even where American interests were minimal, in order to undercut the Soviet Union. This time the Third World was not even to play the active role of pawn in this global game of chess, but to serve as a mere chessboard. No longer was the concept that the U.S.S.R. was exploiting indigenous conflicts in the Third World for its own benefit considered. Ranging from El Salvador, Nicaragua, and Grenada to Lebanon, Reagan viewed regional interests and national liberation movements only as a device serving "Soviet geopolitical and strategic expansion." When the crisis in the Third World in no manner involved nor benefited the Soviet Union, no direct intervention occurred. For example, in December 1975 Indonesia, a founding member of the NAM, invaded and annexed the Democratic Republic of East Timor. The war raged for four years. The U.S.S.R. played no role in the Indonesian affair, and the United States, though it provided some semblance of military assistance, abstained from U.N. condemnation. In the end the United States outmaneuvered the Soviet Union, which was economically and militarily spent and thus finally collapsed, bringing about an end to the bipolar reign of the two superpowers and the Cold War.

Gadhafi, in a 1973 speech, noted that "non-alignment has been defeated, both by our own volition and by the greater forces which compel us." He admitted what both the U.S.S.R. and the United States believed and knew: "I wish to say openly that there are two important powers in the world. They are the United States, behind which stands the Capitalist world, and the U.S.S.R., behind which stands the Communist world." There was no third power in the world. The nonaligned states were far from nonaligned. Khomeini condemned the West, specifically the United States, as the origin of all problems of the world. Egyptian president Anwar as-Sadat saw the United States as an arbiter and economic redeemer that made all "run and work" in the world. The Third World had almost acquired a Soviet tilt. One member even referred to the U.S.S.R. as a "natural ally" during the Havana Summit Conference (3–9 September

1979), though other members, such as Yugoslavia and India, provided balance. The Third World allowed itself to be abused. In all fairness, however, it had little choice. States aligned themselves to one superpower or another depending upon their needs or fears. Though Nehru would be the spokesman for nonalignment for India and in many respects Asia, his country leaned toward the Soviet Union. Though India shared some similar interests and goals with the Soviet Union, a much greater concern was that of China and its threat to Indian security.

Soviet proxies would later become American clients, and vice versa. In the 1970s the U.S.S.R. supported Pol Pot's Khmer Rouge in Cambodia, while the United States aided the Vietnamese forces. By the 1980s the United States declared in the U.N. that the genocidal Pol Pot was the legitimate leader, while his forces fought with Western and Chinese arms against the Soviet-armed Vietnamese. Ethiopia, Iraq, Libya, India, Vietnam, Cuba, Yugoslavia, Morocco, Egypt, Sudan, and Somalia are among the many countries that shifted from one camp to another, depending upon which superpower, motivated by its own self-interest, was willing to assist at the time. Therefore, the Third World violated the first and foremost principle of their own movement: nonalignment.

Indira Gandhi's plea at the Summit Conference in Colombo (16–19 August 1976) that "Unity among ourselves is essential for our movement to retain its utility" seemed to go unheeded. The international movement was riddled with regional issues and squabbles, including economic rivalry such as the South-North disharmony that existed between those states that possessed oil versus those that did not; violent conflicts such as the Iran-Iraq War (1980–1988); and disagreement concerning diplomacy, as evidenced by the contest between the Association of South-East Asian Nations (ASEAN) and India, as well as other Asian countries, regarding recognition of the Kampuchean government, the military presence of the Soviets in Afghanistan, apprehensions about the Palestinians, and controversy among the Arabs concerning Egypt's relationship with Israel.

The division and impotence of the Third World was exemplified in the Iran-Iraq War. Not only were two nonaligned states engaged in a serious conflict, but other nonaligned countries were incapable of influencing and resolving the situation. Both Iran and Iraq refused to participate in the NAM meeting in Belgrade (November 1980) as they objected to the composition of the "Goodwill Committee." For the New Delhi Ministerial Meeting (9–13 January 1981), new members were appointed in a futile effort to lure Iranian and Iraqi participation. The superpowers

escalated and prolonged the conflict with moral support and, of course, a supply of arms. Despite all of the economic wealth from Arab oil, nothing was devoted to reconstruction after the end of the Iran-Iraq War. The crisis was an utter failure for the Third World in every respect: politically, militarily, and diplomatically. The Third World and the NAM was incapable of controlling or influencing outcomes within its own region and acting independently, devoid of the meddling of the U.S.S.R. and the United States.

Politically and diplomatically, the Third World practically did not exist as a force. It lacked leadership. Those who had conceived and invigorated the concept, such as Nasser and Nehru, died early in the life of the movement or, like Tito, became obsessed with domestic problems. The waning charisma of the leaders who followed was insufficient to unify and sustain the "Bandung spirit." There was no North Atlantic Treaty Organization (NATO) or Warsaw Pact. The Third World was represented by a few individual leaders at times but never managed to gain enough momentum to present a unified, strong front and thus create an impact of its own during the Cold War. Economically, the Third World was also weak. Select states such as those in the Middle East—with their tremendous petroleum resources—possessed great wealth that was not shared with poorer members of the Third World. The Group of 77 (G-77, a group of less-developed countries within the U.N.) could not remedy the economic failure that has troubled the Third World.

The Third World could not ensure its security, achieve political influence, or affect the behavior of others—it lacked power. Beleaguered by economic and military frailty, internal discord, and perpetual interference from the Soviet Union and United States, the Third World was unable to play an important role during the Cold War. The superpowers regarded the role of the Third World as had the Great Powers in Africa or Asia in the nineteenth century: to be exploited and manipulated, to serve for the benefit and interest of others, and to provide the means for competition, as well as to create balance between the powers.

There is much discussion among political scientists, policy analysts, journalists, and politicians regarding the many enlightened accomplishments that attest to the tremendous progress of mankind and that inspire great hopes for the new millennium. Yet, on 24 March 1999 nineteen members of a military-defense alliance, NATO, sidestepped both the United Nations and international law, along with their respective national parliaments and congresses, to bomb Yugoslavia, a sovereign state that was experiencing severe civil strife, in

THIRD WORLD

order to coerce the acceptance of an ultimatum, the Rambouillet Agreement, granting foreign troops access to all its territories. This ultimatum was conducted in the name of humanitarian interests. After months of bombing, an agreement (capitulation or peace, depending upon the viewpoint) was established. On 12 June 1999, in a display reminiscent of the scramble for Berlin at the close of World War II, Russian Kosovo Peacekeeping Force (KFOR) troops raced through Serbia to reach Kosovo, preempting NATO control and dominance of Pristina. NATO had carved out zones of occupation in Kosovo, all of which were to be under total NATO command. Apparently, the Russians disagreed with such an arrangement. Most obvious of all is that no one, neither the Americans nor Russians, seemed to think that the peoples who inhabit the pathetic remnants of Yugoslavia had any right to determine their own future. Whether the question is the continent of Africa in the eighteenth century, Third World states such as Korea, Vietnam, Afghanistan, or Egypt during the Cold War, or Serbia and the Balkans on the eve of the millennium, the answer was always the same: the elite, whether it be the European powers, the United States and the U.S.S.R., or NATO, possess the power, both military and economic, and the motivation, their own self interests, to dominate and dictate to others. The chess game begins anew.

–JULIJANA BUDJEVAC,
GEORGE WASHINGTON UNIVERSITY

References

Philippe Braillard and Mohammad-Reza Djalili, eds., *Tiers Monde et relations internationales,* translated as *The Third World and International Relations* (London: Pinter, 1986; Boulder, Colo.: Lynne Rienner, 1986);

Michael C. Desch, *When the Third World Matters: Latin America and United States Grand Strategy* (Baltimore: Johns Hopkins University Press, 1993);

Frederic J. Fleron Jr. and others, eds., *Contemporary Issues in Soviet Foreign Policy: From Brezhnev to Gorbachev* (New York: Aldine de Gruyter, 1991);

Raymond L. Gartoff, *Détente and Confrontation: American-Soviet Relations From Nixon to Reagan* (Washington, D.C.: Brookings Institution, 1985);

Ted Hopf, *Peripheral Visions: Deterrence Theory and American Foreign Policy in the Third World, 1965–1990* (Ann Arbor: University of Michigan Press, 1994);

Henry Kissinger, *Diplomacy* (New York: Simon & Schuster, 1994);

Manorama Kohli, "The Non-Aligned Movement and the Super Powers in Historical Perspective," *Quarterly Review of Historical Studies,* 25 (1985): 8–22;

Andrzej Korbonski and Francis Fukuyama, eds., *The Soviet Union and the Third World: The Last Three Decades* (Ithaca, N.Y.: Cornell University Press, 1987);

Douglas J. MacDonald, *Adventures in Chaos: American Intervention for Reform in the Third World* (Cambridge, Mass.: Harvard University Press, 1992);

P. A. N. Murthy and B. K. Shrivastava, *Neutrality and Non-Alignment in the 1990s* (New Delhi: Radiant Publishers, 1991);

Joseph S. Nye Jr., *Understanding International Conflicts: An Introduction to Theory and History* (New York: HarperCollins, 1993);

Alvin Z. Rubinstein, *Soviet Foreign Policy Since World War II: Imperial and Global* (Cambridge, Mass.: Winthrop Publishers, 1981);

Tony Smith, *America's Mission: The United States and the Worldwide Struggle for Democracy in the Twentieth Century* (Princeton: Princeton University Press, 1994);

Donald M. Snow, *Distant Thunder: Third World Conflict and the New International Order* (New York: St. Martin's Press, 1993);

Joseph Weatherby Jr. and others, *The Other World: Issues and Politics of the Developing World* (New York: Macmillan, 1987);

Richard Wright, *The Color Curtain: A Report on the Bandung Conference,* foreword by Gunnar Myrdal (Cleveland: World Publishing, 1956);

Zhang Yan, "I Wish I Had Met Richard Wright at Bandung in 1955: Reflections on a Conference Attended by Both Wright and the Author," *Mississippi Quarterly,* 50 (Spring 1997): 277–287.

THIRD WORLD

Was the 1948 split between Joseph Stalin and Josip Broz Tito ideological in nature?

gViewpoint: Yes. Ideological factors played a major part in the split between Joseph Stalin, who was a pragmatist in search of power, and Josip Broz Tito, who was much more a communist ideologue.

Viewpoint: No. Ideology was a rationalization for the rift between Joseph Stalin and Josip Broz Tito, whose quarrels started during World War II and included a host of domestic and foreign policy disagreements.

At the end of World War II Soviet armies had reached the center of Europe, and Moscow had a strong international communist movement under its leadership. Within a short time, however, certain fractures in the solidarity of this movement became apparent. Even as the Soviet Union successfully imposed monolithic communist governments on Eastern Europe, its relationship with communist Yugoslavia was imperiled.

Having played an important role in liberating his own country from German occupation in the closing days of World War II, Marshal Josip Broz Tito did not owe much to the arms of the Red Army and did not have to tolerate the large-scale presence of Soviet troops. Over time tensions between Belgrade and Moscow grew, leading to a firm break in the spring of 1948. Many possible explanations have been offered, including the assertion that the split between Joseph Stalin and Tito was caused primarily in different interpretations of Marxist ideology. Was this truly the case? Some evidence points to different conclusions and suggests that the split was perhaps a battle of egos or founded more in realpolitik considerations. Whatever the source, the division remained a constant feature of the politics of the communist world until both the Soviet Union and Yugoslavia fell apart in the early 1990s.

Viewpoint:
Yes. Ideological factors played a major part in the split between Joseph Stalin, who was a pragmatist in search of power, and Josip Broz Tito, who was much more a communist ideologue.

The world saw the split between Yugoslavia and the Soviet Union as a sudden event, made public in 1948 by Joseph Stalin's denunciation of the Yugoslav Communist Party

(CPY) and Yugoslavia's expulsion from the Cominform. Many analysts were surprised by the move, having perceived Josip Broz Tito as an heir apparent in the communist world to Stalin himself. It is not surprising that they did so, as Tito was following a path close to the one Stalin had trod in his own rise to power. Tito, however, was a young man at the beginning of his career; Stalin was older, nearing the end of his. Their views on socialism and its implementation grew increasingly divergent, until an ideological rift was unavoidable. What the world saw for the first time in June of 1948 had actually been brewing for several years and was the result of ideological divergences between these two men. Put simply, Tito had a vision of the Yugoslav road to socialism and did not feel obligated either to conform to the Soviet path or to seek approval of all his actions from Stalin. Occasionally referred to as "Titoism," it represented not so much a political break with the Soviet Union as an expression of ideologically divergent paths toward the same goal.

Perhaps the most basic difference between Tito and Stalin was their relative flexibility. Stalin was extremely flexible, and he played fast and loose with communist ideology. He had an excellent teacher: Lenin's seizure of power was predicated on seeming to accommodate a wide variety of factions and appearing to champion an equally vast array of viewpoints within leftist Russian circles. Just as Lenin agreed to anything in order to stay in power, and thus keep the revolution alive, so too did Stalin veer from "pure" communist ideology as necessity dictated. One could say Stalin used ideology as a tool or weapon, rather than a guiding voice; even were this not the case, however, Stalin saw as Lenin had before him that expediency outweighed dogma. Tito seems to have been a more rigid implementer of ideology, though he, too, was tempered by practical restraint. Neither man was blind to political feasibility, but in many cases Stalin was more willing to compromise on ideology in order to meet his goals. In one instance, Stalin scolded Tito during World War II for insisting his partisans wear red stars on their caps, symbolizing their ideological allegiance to communism and, by association, the Soviet Union. Stalin thought this demonstration of loyalty was absurd, given that fascists occupied Yugoslavia and only the capitalist Allies were capable of providing military support at the time.

Stalin gave an ideological nod to the notion of "continuing revolution," the inevitability, according to Karl Marx and Lenin, of a world revolution. In the 1920s and early 1930s, Stalin's Soviet Russia leant great support to the Chinese communist movement and sponsored (at least in theory, if not always in terms of tangible assistance) several other international communist organizations. When it came time to secure the Soviet Union's western flank, however, Stalin was prepared to drop all assistance to the German Communist Party, even going so far as to condemn them as harmful to a lasting peace between the two states. Similarly, during World War II Stalin urged global socialist cooperation with the allies of the Soviet Union: the need was to defeat Nazi Germany and Fascist Italy at first, then the capitalist powers. After the war, Stalin provided massive assistance to "native" communist movements in Poland, Czechoslovakia, Bulgaria, Hungary, and Romania. Regimes sprang up with a direct ideological and political link to Moscow. However, when Tito attempted to foster the same relationship with Yugoslavia's neighbors, Stalin objected. The civil war in Greece was largely fueled by Yugoslavian support of the Greek Communist Party; but Greece lay well outside the "sphere of influence" allotted to the Soviet Union, and both Britain and the United States dispatched ships and troops to support the nationalists against the communists. Stalin saw Tito's actions as risking war with the United States, and by that risking the entire socialist world (not to mention endangering Stalin's own power). This difference in views was a sticking point in Yugoslav-Soviet relations for several years. As Stalin demonstrated earlier in his conflict with Leon Trotsky, he was not a true internationalist. Instead, he had proclaimed the desirability of "socialism in one country." Tito, however, was a true internationalist, and even after the split with Stalin (and with more limited resources) he continued to support the idea of continuing revolution and was extremely active abroad.

Domestic issues led to ideological friction almost as much as issues of foreign policy. One of Stalin's grandest undertakings was the destruction of the kulaks, the peasant landowners who formed a sort of rural middle class in Russia prior to World War I. Stalin perceived them as inherently conservative and therefore a threat to communism and his power: anyone not directly dependent on the new system for his position in society was unlikely to contribute much to that system and hence was a potential threat to it. Forced collectivization, the amalgamation of kulak and other peasant holdings into massive state-run agricultural entities, left millions dead or homeless in the 1920s and 1930s. During World War II, Stalin eased up on his collectivization efforts in order to foster nationalist unity in the face of German invasion; again expediency won out over ideology. True to his pattern, one of the first things Tito did upon assuming power in Yugoslavia was to launch a brutal collectivization campaign in the Serbian and Croatian countrysides. Tito was acting on the Stalinist model, lionizing Stalin's achievements and making every attempt to emulate him. The pace of collectivization in Yugoslavia was brisk, given the extreme destruction that Yugoslavia had suffered during the war. Yet, when tension between Tito and Stalin grew, this policy was one of the areas cited in criticism of the CPY. Though presented as an ideological issue, collectivization in this case was used as a weapon against Tito by Stalin, regardless of the facts; it was more important to make Tito look bad than to praise socialist achievement in Yugoslavia.

Related to the issue of expediency versus ideological purity is the matter of internal relations in the communist world, what could be termed "Socialist unity." In the theory put forth by Marx and later expounded upon by Lenin and Trotsky, war and other social ills would be cured by a brotherhood of socialist states working in harmony toward mutual goals. Eventually the differences between states and nations (since they were artificial) would fade, and the state itself would "wither away." Stalin professed to follow these teachings, and many Red Army actions at the end of World War II were done in the name of socialist unity. "Spontaneous" uprisings against "Czech imperialism" in the province of Ruthenia in 1944–1945 were immediately backed by the Red Army, and *Narodnyi komissariat vnutrennikh del* (People's Commissariat of Internal Affairs or NKVD) units "advised" Ruthenian workers' councils on how best to govern themselves and align their "nation" toward socialism. Certainly the presence of the Red Army in Yugoslavia in 1945 went a long way toward consolidating Tito's hold on power. However, even by this point there had been friction between Tito and Stalin. Moscow at one point openly backed the nationalist Chetniks under Draža Mihajlović, whom Tito's Communists were battling as well as the Germans. The CPY complained bitterly of this, essentially accusing the Soviets of betraying their revolution. For his part, Stalin was merely hedging his bets: Mihajlović was making a greater impact in the war against Adolf Hitler than was Tito; in addition, early in the war the Western Allies backed Mihajlović (he was named one of the "Men of the Year" by *Time* in 1942), and if public declarations of support for the valiant Chetniks would bring American trucks to Russia faster, then that was what Stalin did.

Similarly, Red Army troops were accused of a variety of crimes on Yugoslav territory: theft, arson, rape, and murder. Tito and other CPY members were astonished that Yugoslavia was being treated no better than an Axis power, even though they had been allied with the Soviet Union and were now a sister socialist state. Stalin was offended at one point, when senior CPY official Milovan Djilas compared the actions of Soviet officers unfavorably with British officers. Stalin had this statement resurrected repeatedly in the coming conflict as evidence of Tito's "betrayal" of socialism, when in fact the comment was made in reaction to Stalin's own breach of "socialist unity." When Stalin berated Yugoslavia for supporting communist rebels in Albania and Greece, it could only be seen as continuing the pattern established in Yugoslavia itself during the war: when it was convenient, Stalin was a communist, when it was not he shrugged off ideology without a second thought.

Marshal Josip Broz Tito and his dog Tiger in 1950

Tito seemed to perceive a unity of purpose in world socialist movements. Certainly in later life his advocacy of, and leadership in, the nonaligned movement saw a similar unity of purpose in all noncolonial powers, for by then the Union of Soviet Socialist Republics (U.S.S.R.) was being characterized by the CPY as no better than the British with their spheres of interest and commonwealth of dependent states. Perhaps it was to this end that Tito so readily ignored the potential political dangers of intervention in Greece. Moreover, it might also explain his seeking closer ties with neighboring socialist states. No other Soviet bloc country sought bilateral agreements with its neighbors independently of Moscow. One of Tito's proposals to Georgi Mikhailovich Dimitrov of Bulgaria dealt with Danube River trade and other economic issues; the two countries even went so far as to discuss a sort of customs union like the Benelux countries enjoyed in western Europe. When the two leaders started to discuss a federation between the states (to be the core of a pan-Balkan supra-state), this was going too far

TITO

for Stalin. The leaders of the Balkan communist states were summoned to Moscow to explain themselves and were forced to sign a variety of treaties at first condemning any sort of union, and then later they were induced to sign an opposing agreement, promising various levels of cooperation. None of this mattered much, as the chief byproduct of the Moscow talks was fear—it was clear that socialist unity was all well and good as long as it was either meaningless or, most importantly, sponsored by Moscow. Given the stated communist goals of the dissolution of borders, Stalin's behavior represents a significant deviation.

Another facet of this issue of unity is that of equality. One communist organization was ideologically equivalent to any other, regardless of size or number of armored divisions it commanded in the field. These were the "rules" on paper, and as they were exercised in the Comintern; but much like the United Nations, or the League of Nations before it, smaller countries and smaller Parties were less important than larger ones and were just as subject to the whims of the larger under Socialism as under the realpolitik capitalist world system. Tito saw himself as a major player in the communist world, and this belief led him to conclude that he could negotiate with his brother communist leaders on an equal footing but also without the prior consent of the Communist Party of the Soviet Union (CPSU). Tito probably perceived both he and all the other Socialist leaders, including Stalin, were working toward the same goals, using the same ideological handbook, but this was not the case. Stalin was clearly in charge of the communist world, at least in Europe in 1945–1948, and he looked unfavorably on any independent actions on the part of communist leaders.

To this end, the NKVD had operatives in all the East European communist parties. In some cases, such as Mátyás Rákosi of Hungary, the local communist elite had spent the entire war in the Soviet Union and had even lived there in exile for many years before the war as well. Poland, Romania, Bulgaria, Czechoslovakia, and even East Germany had similar situations: domestic parties had been liquidated either before or during the war, and its postwar communist leadership was trained in, and loyal to, the Soviet Union. These men had not participated in the communist underground or resistance movements, appearing on the scene in the wake of the Red Army and assuming control of a chaotic situation with the aid of the NKVD. Yugoslavia was an exception to this pattern in several ways. Tito had stayed in Yugoslavia throughout World War II and had led the communist partisan movement personally—he had a loyal cadre of supporters in his native Croatia

and did not rely on the Soviets for his power base. Furthermore, the Soviets had not supported the partisans to the extent promised or expected, which made them even less dependent on Moscow. From Tito's perspective, one might indeed wonder why Stalin felt the need for a "Man in Belgrade," either to advise the CPY on how to be better communists or to control the Yugoslav government. The CPY came to resent the NKVD presence, not so much because it was foreign, but because it was unnecessary: had not the Partisans and Tito himself proven to be true communists, as well as staunch supporters and allies of the Soviet Union?

This last query perhaps summarizes Tito's issues with Stalin. In everything he had set out to do, Tito looked to the Soviet Union, and Stalin in particular, as his role model. In much of his writing Tito echoed Stalin's words, and his actions oftentimes mirrored many of Stalin's—they certainly shared much of the same ruthlessness and disregard for human life. Perhaps Tito's attempt to shadow Stalin made the latter nervous, or resentful: Stalin had left no provision for his succession, even five years after the split with Yugoslavia. Like a nervous medieval sultan, whose greatest threat was from his own sons, Stalin was jealous of his power and realized that even to support the actions of someone like Tito was to take away from his own prestige. Thus, the more Tito sought to ingratiate himself with Stalin, perhaps with an eye toward becoming his successor (since all Communist Parties were coequal, this was a reasonable assumption, according to Tito), the more Stalin saw a reason to criticize Tito and the CPY, regardless of any ideological "progress" they had made in furthering world socialism.

The ideological divergence between Tito and Stalin grew increasingly obvious after the split between the two countries. Tito developed and espoused the concept that not all nations had to follow an identical path to communism. While the goal was the same, the means could, and indeed should, vary. By the late 1950s a different economic system was evolving in Yugoslavia, one for which it became famous: the system known as "self-management." The overarching feature of this system was decentralization, which was at antipodes with all of Stalin's machinations. For Stalin, centralization was the goal, both at home within the political and economic spheres, and abroad within the communist movement.

Stalin characterized the break between the two men as one of ideology—and while he was correct, it was Stalin and his flexible conception of communist ideology who broke with traditional Marxist/Leninist principles. Indeed, much of the literature on the Yugoslav-Soviet split paints Tito as baffled by Stalin's reactions. Tito was trying to emulate the man he saw as the successful embodiment of the communist movement, the man who had pulled the workers' paradise through civil war and world-wide depression, and finally had led it through its great struggle with that ultimate outgrowth of capitalism, Nazi Germany. In his attempt to out-Stalin Stalin and win the latter's approval for his actions, Tito grew ever more conservative in his adherence to the "letter of the law." The CPY was purged of all "counter-revolutionary" elements; collectivization and other anti-bourgeoisie efforts were stepped up; Yugoslavia supported the international socialist movement by sponsoring revolution abroad; and Tito even adopted Stalin's practices in negotiating between socialist countries. He missed one important point, however: Stalin was not interested in that "law." Communist ideology, which Tito attempted to implement with such fervor, was only a means to the end of the maintenance and expansion of Stalin's personal power. Stalin easily could have become a robber baron or a fascist, or an adherent to any other system, so long as it furthered his own ambitions to power. Tito did not see this, nor the fact that he was seen by Stalin not as a friend and ally, but as a threat. It was this ideological difference that led to the split between the two leaders; or, more precisely, the split was caused by Tito's ideology and Stalin's lack of one.

–LAWRENCE A. HELM,
GEORGE WASHINGTON UNIVERSITY

Viewpoint:
No. Ideology was a rationalization for the rift between Joseph Stalin and Josip Broz Tito, whose quarrels started during World War II and included a host of domestic and foreign policy disagreements.

Part of the common image of the Soviet-Yugoslav break is that Josip Broz Tito broke from Joseph Stalin and that the conflict was of an ideological nature. The corollary to this is that "Titoism," a deviation from Stalinism, calling for indirect communist control and self-management, was one of the reasons for the break with Moscow. Yet, if one looks back to World War II and the Partisan resistance movement in Yugoslavia, one can see that from the start of the war there were problems between the two communist parties, many of which would develop slowly into deep resentments.

At the onset of the war the communists of Yugoslavia were able to maintain communications with Moscow. However, as they became directly involved in resistance and formed what became known as the Partisans, they lost direct contact with Moscow and its mandate. They grew accustomed to making their own decisions based on the information and needs of the moment. Later, when contact with the Soviets was reestablished, this pattern continued. During the war Stalin's primary concern was defeating Adolf Hitler; thus, he was more inclined to let each country's communists go their own way, as long as their methods were effective and did not endanger Stalin's own plans or position with the other Allies. From Stalin's perspective, the way to defeat German forces in Yugoslavia was to support the winning resistance movement and maintain good relations with the Western Allies. These two aims led Stalin to take many actions that were deeply resented by the Partisans.

One of the initial difficulties that arose concerned the favorable Soviet attitudes toward Draža Mihajlović and his Chetniks, the Royalist resistance movement. The Partisans repeatedly implored Moscow to stop supporting Mihajlović. Another aspect of this issue was that while Soviet observers mentioned the Chetniks in glowing terms, they made no mention of the Partisans and their efforts.

The Partisans continued to perceive themselves as abandoned by Moscow. On 29 December 1941, Tito appealed for the first time to the Union of Soviet Socialist Republics (U.S.S.R.) for assistance. The Comintern informed him in February of 1942 that they might be able to fly men in to him; nothing happened. After another three requests a reply finally arrived, stating that the difficulties were too great, that the Partisans should not count on the Soviets, and that they should "get arms from the enemy and make the most economical use of what armament [they had]." Throughout the war Tito continued to request aid from Moscow but received little. In fact, Moscow would not even decide to send a military mission to the Partisans until more than seven months after the British mission had already arrived!

Stalin frequently cautioned the Partisans not to be overzealous, fearing their communist ideology and ties to Moscow would make the Allies nervous. Once again Stalin's concerns were pragmatic: expediency over ideology. In 1944, when the new provisional communist government prohibited King Peter II of Yugoslavia from returning, Stalin was furious at first, then surprised when he discovered his Western Allies apparently did not care. Stalin's concern for Western opinion and Yugoslavia's ability to adversely affect it, and thus Soviet policy concerns, was to continue into the postwar period.

In 1944 Tito traveled to Moscow, where he met Stalin for the first time. He stated of this encounter, "Tension arose at this first meeting with Stalin. We were more or less at cross-purposes on all the matters we discussed. I noticed then that Stalin could not bear being contradicted." Yugoslav leader and writer Milovan Djilas's accounts bear witness to this fact. It became increasingly apparent that a personality conflict was developing between Stalin and Tito.

By the end of the war, "diversity" had outlived its usefulness. On the one hand, the Soviets had advisers stationed in Belgrade; they expected to be informed of each move the new government made and to have their instructions obeyed. On the other hand, the Communist Party of Yugoslavia (CPY) continued to conduct business as usual; they governed and did not concern themselves much about notifying the Soviets of their every action, or about constantly asking for "advice." One of the first instances where this situation became a problem involved the capture of Mihajlović. Stalin was informed of this event by the *Narodnyi komissariat vnutrennikh del* (People's Commissariat of Internal Affairs or NKVD), which had obtained its information from the Yugoslav newspapers! Stalin was furious, and the NKVD complained that they ought to have been notified by the CPY of its plans to capture Mihajlović. There was no question that both Stalin and Tito found Mihajlović an ideological and practical threat who had to be eliminated. The capture, trial, conviction, and eventual execution of Mihajlović were all conducted according to standard communist operating procedures. The real issue was that something of importance had occurred, and not by Stalin's command.

While Moscow was not pleased by its protégé, the Yugoslavs would soon have a myriad of Soviet actions about which to complain. The CPY was uncomfortable to discover that the NKVD was attempting to recruit agents from among its own members—members who held a variety of government positions. The process of cultural exchange became an additional irritant to the CPY. The Soviets expected the Yugoslavs to print enormous amounts of Russian literature and publish as many Soviet articles as they were sent, yet the Soviets themselves were unwilling to reciprocate.

By far the greatest clash with the Soviets on a domestic issue occurred over economic factors. The CPY expected a certain amount of assistance from the Soviets, as they were looked upon as the older brother in the relationship. This support was envisioned to take the form of favorable prices for any products traded and the creation of joint-stock companies, with perhaps slightly more favorable terms for Yugoslavia as the weaker partner. The CPY also hoped the Soviets would assist them in the fulfillment of their five-year plan and in their process of industrialization. At this time Tito and the CPY were attempting to proceed with their economic plans in accordance with Stalinist models: rapid collectivization and five-year plans calling for increased industrialization with emphasis on heavy industry. The Soviets were willing to trade with the Yugoslavs but charged world prices for the goods they sold, and they often paid Yugoslav prices for the goods they purchased in return. Further, they strongly disapproved of the first five-year plan the CPY developed, especially its call for the development of heavy industry. The Soviets suggested this was unnecessary for Yugoslavia, which could obtain whatever it needed from the U.S.S.R.. They preferred that the Yugoslavs concentrate on agriculture and the extraction of raw materials, which was seen as a form of socialist colonialism by the Yugoslavs. Be that as it may, the most acute conflict occurred over the establishment of the joint-stock companies. The terms were more than unfavorable toward Yugoslavia—they were exploitative. After Yugoslav peevishness, Stalin decided unilaterally that joint-stock companies would not properly suit Yugoslavia's economy and that more direct aid, loans, or subsidies would be preferable and should be instituted immediately. Most of this promised relief was never received, continuing a well-recognized pattern set during the war.

As much friction as occurred between the two nations over Yugoslav domestic-policy issues, it was minor compared to the foreign-policy questions. Though Western perception was that the Yugoslavs always followed the Soviet line, in reality, the two states seemed rarely to agree. The Yugoslavs therefore proceeded to develop a foreign policy, especially in the Balkan region, which they saw as serving Yugoslav interests. As a result, the Soviets had much to criticize, and they then acted in their own best interest, which in turn caused concern among the Yugoslavs. Neither side was motivated by, or overly interested in, ideological concerns.

At the end of the war, Yugoslavia was faced with two main border issues, and in both cases expected Soviet support. The areas in question were the provinces of Carinthia (on the border with Austria) and Trieste (on the border with Italy). Yugoslav interest in Carinthia was partially economic and partially ethnic. When the war had ended, Yugoslavia discovered Stalin's main interest in this region had been a certain amount of former German property that he wanted for the Soviet Union. In the end, the

A TIME FOR CHANGE

Yugoslavian leader Josip Broz Tito often failed to follow directions from the Soviet Union and questioned its policies. On 22 April 1958, Tito gave a speech to the Yugoslav Communist Party Congress, a portion of which follows.

Certain comrades in the Soviet bloc countries still manifest tendencies of distrust, as well as evidence of wrong estimates of the internal development in our country. Suspicion is expressed with regard to the socialist character of Yugoslavia. There is talk of her anarchist trade union development.

Inside the party it stressed, and then further spread, that a tactical attitude should be taken in connection with Yugoslavia, that she should be re-educated and again brought into the camp, and so forth.

It would be very useful if these comrades would finally abandon such absurd tendencies, which are only harmful and prevent the proper development of our relations.

We are often accused of not being internationalists, because we are not in the camp. These comrades seem to think that internationalism is conditioned by adherence to the camp and not to the socialist world, in the broader sense. They do not start out from what sort of policy you are conducting, whether you are loyal to the principles of internationalism, which means solidarity with workers and progressive movements in a universal sense, whether you are building socialism in a way that strengthens socialist ideas, not only inside the country but generally speaking.

Internationalism, first and foremost, obligates the working class to develop steadfastly in its own country . . . the forms of revolutionary work while it does not possess power in its hands, and to develop all the forms of creative work in the building-up of socialism when it already possesses that power.

Internationalism means respect for equal relations and a comradely attitude towards those countries that are building socialism and toward all Communist and progressive parties outside Socialist countries.

Internationalism cannot be divided into narrow and broad areas, into the camp and the non-camp groups, because it is universal in the sense that it develops the science of Marxism and Leninism and increases its practical applications.

Internationalism, then, is practice—not words and propaganda. This should be borne in mind by those who would like to make the classifications internationalists and noninternationalists. . . .

Present world developments require the workers' movements to engage more actively in resolving international problems, such as the struggle for peace, for disarmament, for the prohibition of nuclear weapons experiments for the purposes of war, and the use of atomic weapons, for the rejection of war as a means for settling international problems, for the cessation of aggressive pressures and belligerent adventure against certain Asian and African countries and colonial liberation movements, and so forth. . . .

It is especially important that the old forms of cooperation are being gradually abandoned and that bilateral relations are being adopted. This does not in any way mean that there is a weakening of the Socialist world, or of its unity and effectiveness, but precisely the opposite—this makes possible the mobilization of all the forces of socialism.

In this way there ensues a wealth of new forms and experiences that are placed in the service of socialism because there is a liberation of creative thought that, obstructed by former forms of cooperation, was completely dormant in the present phase of development. Because of this attitude of ours regarding cooperation between Communist parties and progressive movements in the world in general, we could not sign the declaration of the twelve Communist and workers' parties of the Socialist countries, in Moscow.

Source: Current History, 35 (July 1958): 40–42.

Soviets were willing to concede the border matter in return for an agreement on the German property issue. The question of Trieste was settled by Soviet foreign minister Vyacheslav Mikhailovich Molotov without even informing the Yugoslavs. In return, the Soviets were paid reparations by Italy.

The main source of conflict between Yugoslavia and the Soviet Union was the policy of the former toward its immediate neighbors; specifically, its dealings with Bulgaria, Greece, and Albania. Yugoslav-Bulgarian relations in particular provoked the most heated and often contradictory reactions from Stalin. The two countries were both nations of South Slavs, and their leaders, Tito and Georgi Mikhailovich Dimitrov, had a long-standing amicable relationship. Relations between the two states were growing constantly closer and eventually led to discussions of the possibility of a federation. This union was Tito's grand plan for increasing power in the region. Naturally, Yugoslavia, with the largest military and a Communist Party with the strongest base at home, would lead this federation (with Tito at the helm, of course). It was also important for guaranteeing Yugoslavia's preeminent position that it had fought on the winning side of World War II, unlike the other potential federation members. Once again, Yugoslavia was the obvious leader. Its only real competition was a noncommunist Greece. Tito, however, figured he could change this situation and eventually pull a communist Greece into the federation, neutralizing it.

The situation in Greece after 1945 was volatile. There was a civil war being fought, and the local communists were receiving support from Yugoslavia. According to the agreement made between British prime minister Winston Churchill and Stalin, Greece was to remain under the Western sphere of influence. It appears, at least at this point, that Stalin intended to honor this agreement. Again, as during the war, Stalin was concerned that Yugoslav actions would have an adverse effect on Soviet-Western relations. Stalin hoped to maintain the Anglo-Soviet-American coalition forged during the war. Yugoslavia's actions endangered this plan with its overzealous anti-Western posturing.

Albania caused further contention between the socialist states. Yugoslavia had adopted a stance in regard to Albania that was similar to the Soviet position toward the Eastern European nations. During the war the Partisans had helped found the Albanian Communist Party, and the Albanian resistance movement was also largely under Yugoslav control. After the war Yugoslavia continued its close involvement in Albanian affairs, providing technical assistance, advisers, and economic aid. The two countries also estab-

lished joint-stock companies, and there was even some talk of unification.

In *Tito: The Story from Inside* (1980), Djilas describes Yugoslav-Albanian relations with respect to Yugoslav-Soviet relations as follows:

> In that struggle with Moscow, in those reverberations of thought and emotion, there were blunders and excesses, particularly the persistent attempt, for which Tito was largely responsible, to extricate Albania from Soviet influence and subjugate it to Yugoslavia. Stalin and the Soviet government took these unbalanced and hegemonic Yugoslav designs on Albania as a pretext to launch attacks on Yugoslavia, and to subjugate further the Eastern European countries. Tito's aggression toward Albania was both an imitation of Soviet methods and one of protecting himself against them.

While imitation is frequently said to be the sincerest form of flattery, Stalin was not flattered. In fact, it would not be going too far to say that he was irate and felt threatened. The communist world was simply not large enough for them both.

As a result of the increased discussions between Bulgaria and Yugoslavia, Stalin called for delegations to be sent from both countries to Moscow for consultation. At this "consultation," Moscow voiced complaints over Yugoslavia's dealings with all three of its neighbors. It quickly became clear that its main thrust was that decisions had been reached without seeking Moscow's guidance. Stalin repeatedly shouted, "Yes but you didn't consult with us!" It was for Stalin to suggest a course of action and approve any decisions made; independent actions between two socialist nations were unacceptable.

Indirectly, the whole affair made clear to the leadership of Bulgaria and Yugoslavia exactly what their position was to be in the Soviet-dominated socialist world. Shortly thereafter, Moscow began to send communiques directly attacking the Yugoslav leadership. There was a series of exchanges between Stalin and Tito, where Stalin attacked the CPY, claiming it was committing ideological errors, and Tito attempted to defend himself. By 19 June 1948 the division between the two states became evident to the rest of the world. Eventually Tito realized that arguing with Stalin was useless, and he sent a firm response that declared that, since he could not defend Yugoslavia with words, he would show by deeds that it remained true to the Soviet Union and "the doctrine of Marx, Engels, Lenin, and Stalin."

Initially, Tito did try to prove through action that he was still a "Stalinist." For example, on 21 December 1948 *Borba* published a long editorial, complete with picture, in honor of Stalin's birthday. Tito and the Party also took more

TITO

concrete actions: it was during this early period of conflict with the Soviet Union that the most stringent measures were taken in the countryside toward the goal of total collectivization. The stronger the attacks from Moscow, the more "Stalinist" was the behavior of the CPY. On the whole, the Yugoslavs were slow to move to an anti-Soviet, or anti-Stalinist, position.

The problems between the two states, and thus between the two men, were problems of power and control: questions of Tito's power within his own country and within the communist world, and Stalin's ability to control Tito and his party. During the war Stalin had two goals: first to defeat Hitler, and second to do this with the assistance of the Allies. Everything, ideology included, was subordinate to these two aims. At the time, Tito and his resistance movement was allowed latitude to do anything that would expedite Stalin's interests. To be sure, the Partisans were often criticized and scolded, but only if Stalin believed they were threatening his relations with the Allies. After the war, diversity became no longer acceptable as Stalin began to consolidate his hold over eastern Europe. Tito and the Yugoslav communists were slow to realize that independence from Moscow, even over the most trivial issues, would no longer be tolerated. Nor did they seem to realize that Stalin was playing a careful balancing game with the West, with whom he was not yet ready to sever relations. Yugoslavia seemed to be putting this strategy in jeopardy constantly with its zealous communist actions. In addition, Tito had begun to see himself as Stalin's successor in the communist world. Tito was emulating Stalin, perceiving himself as the heir apparent—who better to take up the reigns of the socialist development in Eastern Europe and the international communist struggle? However, Tito did not recognize that being a communist, even a proclaimed Stalinist, by no means convinced Stalin of one's loyalty. Stalin's only interest was in control and power through the use of coercion and absolute submission. He had no use for loyalty if it came with any semblance of independent thought. According to historian Ivo Banac, "The dramatic denouement of 1948 was related most directly to Stalin's fear that Yugoslavia was beginning to see itself as a regional communist center with all the possibilities for mischief in relations with the West that such a role implied."

A few words should also be mentioned about what this conflict was not. Stalin attempted to claim in his early letters to Tito and the CPY that the rift was of an ideological nature. Yet, Tito himself refuted this at the Central Committee session of 12 April 1948, when he stated:

Comrades, remember that it is not a matter here of any theoretical discussions, it is not a

question of errors committed by the Communist Party of Yugoslavia . . . the issue here, first and foremost, is the relationship between one state and another. It seems to me that they are using the ideological question in order to justify their pressure on us, on our state.

Ideology was not an inherent cause of the conflict. It was used by Stalin to discredit the Yugoslav communists as he had often discredited other opponents in the past. Later, Tito was also to use ideology as the excuse for the split with Moscow, only in a different fashion.

Tito had to justify the enormous change in relations with the Soviets to his people; for years the CPY had held Stalin up as the glorious father of communism, as a prophet in the same league with Lenin, Marx, and Engels. How was the CPY to justify the new policy that was anti-Soviet and anti-Stalin? To do this, the Party, specifically Edvard Kardelj, developed the concept of self-management. He argued that each nation was unique and must follow its own way to communism, and Yugoslavia's path was that of self-management. This change in "ideology," which was to become labeled by both East and West as Titoism, came after the schism with Stalin and was the rationalization, not the reason for the rift.

Djilas describes Tito in the following manner: "Josip Broz Tito was conspicuously without a particular talent except one—political. He had an exceptional sharp and quick intelligence and a powerful and selective concentration. I observed similar characteristics in Stalin." The two men were similar in many ways, and there was little to choose between them. The recriminations that flew back and forth during the conflict were truly a case of the pot calling the kettle black. Stalin criticized the Yugoslavs for not collectivizing quickly enough, yet during the immediate post-revolutionary period in Russia, collectivization had been put on hold. Tito disliked Moscow's treatment of Yugoslavia, which practically relegated it to the status of a colony, but he then attempted to establish the same relationship with Albania. Stalin criticized the Yugoslavs' overly ambitious five-year plan, with its calls for rapid industrialization, yet the Yugoslavs were only emulating their Soviet brother to the northeast. In the end, while Tito may have been content to await Stalin's demise before assuming the role of leader of the international socialist world, Stalin preferred not to take that chance. He had not retained power by allowing the strong to survive. He saw little difference between an actual and potential threat: both had to be eliminated. It was not a question of ideological differences but of personal similarities. Could one truly expect Stalin to trust a copy of himself for long?

–JULIJANA BUDJEVAC,
GEORGE WASHINGTON UNIVERSITY

References

Ivo Banac, *With Stalin Against Tito: Cominformist Splits in Yugoslav Communism* (Ithaca, N.Y.: Cornell University Press, 1988);

Robert Bass and Elizabeth Marbury, eds., *The Soviet-Yugoslav Controversy, 1948–58: A Documentary Record* (New York: Prospect Books, 1959);

Ivo Bicanic, "Fractured Economy," in *Yugoslavia: A Fractured Federalism,* edited by Dennison Rusinow (Washington, D.C.: Wilson Center Press, 1988), pp. 120–141;

J. F. Brown, *Eastern Europe and Communist Rule* (Durham, N.C.: Duke University Press, 1988);

Zbigniew K. Brzezinsky, *The Soviet Bloc: Unity and Conflict* (Cambridge, Mass.: Harvard University Press, 1960);

John C. Campbell, "Soviet Policy in Eastern Europe: An Overview," *Soviet Policy in Eastern Europe,* edited by Sarah Meiklejohn Terry (New Haven, Conn.: Yale University Press, 1984), pp. 1–31;

Stephen Clissold, *Yugoslavia and the Soviet Union, 1939–1973: A Documentary Survey* (London & New York: Oxford University Press, 1975);

Vladimir Dedjer, *The Battle Stalin Lost: Memoirs of Yugoslavia, 1948–1953* (New York: Viking Press, 1971);

Dedjer, *Tito Speaks: His Self Portrait and Struggle with Stalin* (London: Weidenfeld & Nicholson, 1953);

Milovan Djilas, *Conversations with Stalin,* translated by Michael B. Petrovich (New York: Harcourt, Brace & World, 1962);

Djilas, "Tito and Stalin," *Survey,* 28 (Autumn 1984): 73–83;

Djilas, *Tito: The Story from Inside,* translated by Vasilije Kojic and Richard Hayes (New York: Harcourt Brace Jovanovich, 1980);

Slobodan M. Draskovich, *Tito, Moscow's Trojan Horse* (Chicago: Regnery, 1957);

John Lewis Gaddis, *We Now Know: Rethinking Cold War History* (Oxford: Clarendon Press; New York: Oxford University Press, 1997);

Thomas T. Hammond, "Foreign Relations Since 1945," *Yugoslavia,* edited by Robert Francis Byrnes (New York: Praeger, 1957);

Beatrice Heuser, *Western "Containment" Policies in the Cold War: The Yugoslav Case, 1948–1953* (London: Routledge, 1988);

Barbara Jelavich, *History of the Balkans* (Cambridge & New York: Cambridge University Press, 1983);

Andrzej Korbonski, "The Impact of the Soviet Yugoslav Rift on World Communism," *At the Brink of War and Peace: The Tito-Stalin Split in a Historic Perspective,* edited by Wayne S. Vucinich (New York: Brooklyn College Press, 1982);

Vojtech Mastny, *The Cold War and Soviet Insecurity: The Stalin Years* (New York: Oxford University Press, 1996);

Daniel N. Nelson, ed., *Communism and the Politics of Inequalities* (Lexington, Mass.: Lexington Books, 1983);

Michael B. Petrovich, "The View from Yugoslavia," *Witnesses to the Origins of the Cold War,* edited by Thomas T. Hammond (Seattle: University of Washington Press, 1982), pp. 34–59;

Joseph Rothschild, *Return to Diversity: A Political History of East Central Europe Since World War II* (New York: Oxford University Press, 1989);

The Soviet-Yugoslav Dispute: Text of the Published Correspondence (London & New York: Royal Institute of International Affairs, 1948);

Charles Zalar, *Yugoslav Communism: A Critical Study,* prepared for the Subcommittee to Investigate the Administration of the Internal Security Act and other Internal Security Laws of the Committee on the Judiciary, United States Senate, Eighty-Seventh Congress, First Session (Washington, D.C.: U.S. Government Printing Office, 1961);

William Zimmerman, "Soviet Relations with Yugoslavia and Romania," in *Soviet Policy in Eastern Europe,* edited by Terry (New Haven: Yale University Press, 1984), pp. 125–154;

Vladislav Zubok and Constantine Pleshakov, *Inside the Kremlin's Cold War: From Stalin to Khrushchev* (Cambridge, Mass.: Harvard University Press, 1996).

WAR POWERS RESOLUTION

Was the War Powers Resolution an appropriate curb on presidential authority to commit U.S. troops to combat?

Viewpoint: Yes. The War Powers Act controlled the president's power to commit U.S. troops to undeclared wars without congressional oversight.

Viewpoint: No. The War Powers Act was a misguided congressional reaction because it improperly limited the power of the presidency in handling foreign affairs.

Reacting to the long U.S. involvement in the Vietnam War (ended 1975), in November 1973 the Congress of the United States passed the War Powers Resolution, a bill that prohibits the president from committing American military forces to a conflict situation for more than sixty days without expressed congressional approval. Building on acts that progressively limited U.S. military support to South Vietnam and outlawed American military activities in Indochina, this measure was undertaken largely in response to the costly and unpopular war. Since that time, however, the resolution has found additional political relevance as U.S. presidents relied on the military to advance military and political objectives. American military activities in Central America in the 1980s, the Persian Gulf War (1990–1991), in Haiti in the mid 1990s, and during the Kosovo Crisis (1999) were dogged by discussions—and legal appeals to the highest court in the land—concerning the degree to which the president must secure congressional approval before committing U.S. troops. The War Powers Resolution also opened the door for related limitations on American military aid to anticommunist forces in the Third World, especially Angola and Nicaragua, and placed constraints on covert activity in general.

An important feature of the U.S. Constitution is its division of powers among three branches of government. Although the president is always the commander in chief of the armed forces, many scholars argue that the War Powers Resolution was a wise measure, for it limited the executive's ability to indulge in conflicts, such as Vietnam, that did not enjoy popular support and harmed the national interest. Critics argue, on the other hand, that the assertion of congressional authority over military and defense policy constrains the ability of the president to react efficiently to international conflicts as they develop, inhibits his ability to address the strategic interests of the country without partisan political interference, and intrudes on constitutional prerogatives of the executive.

Viewpoint:
Yes. The War Powers Act controlled the president's power to commit U.S. troops to undeclared wars without congressional oversight.

The framers of the Constitution developed the doctrine of the separation of powers with respect to the power to make war in order to avoid a situation in which this power would be in the hands of too few people. That is, they sought to ensure democratic accountability in this most sensitive of government powers. During the American struggle against Soviet communism, the executive branch took too much power from Congress. The War Powers Resolution created a process or mechanism for constraining the tendency of the executive to arrogate excessive power in a manner inconsistent with the framers' scheme to separate the power to make war. Thus, the War Powers Resolution is not a redistribution of power in itself. Rather, it was constitutionally necessary in light of the increasing autonomy of the president on military affairs during the undeclared wars in Korea and Vietnam.

Textually, the constitutional roles of Congress and the president with regard to the power to make war are shared and overlapping, both in formulation and implementation. The font of congressional power is Article I, Section 8, which grants Congress the power to declare war. The Constitution also invests Congress with the powers to raise and support armies, to provide and maintain a navy, to lay taxes and provide for the common defense, and to make all laws necessary and proper to execute these powers. Conversely, the president "shall be the Commander in Chief of the Army and Navy of the United States." Thus, the separation of powers has a degree of ambiguity, as the Constitution does not designate with any greater specificity the more-technocratic duties and privileges of each branch. The political arena thereby obtains a heightened sense of importance such that effective cooperation between Congress and the president is a matter of constitutional necessity. Without effective cooperation, the constitutional doctrine of the separation of powers is violated.

Within the framework of the separation of powers, the framers intended to limit presidential authority. In *War, Foreign Affairs and Constitutional Power* (1976, 1984), Abraham D. Sofaer, citing various discussions during debates over the Constitution and in *The Federalist,* argues that the authors of the Constitution planned to limit presidential power as

commander in chief to managing "military engagements and other objectives authorized by Congress." Sofaer additionally contends that the framers, by granting Congress the power to declare war, intended the president only to respond to sudden attacks without a declaration of war and not to permit the executive to make war in the absence of a declaration. A somewhat stronger view, argued by Alexander Bickel in an article in the *Chicago-Kent Law Review* (1971), is that Congress, at its discretion and despite contrary historical practice, could "prescribe the mission of our troops in the field in accordance with a foreign and war policy of the United States which it is for Congress to set."

As the Cold War progressed, the wielding of the power by the president to make war increased at the expense of the legislative branch and reached an apex during the latter stages of the Vietnam War (ended 1975). The Korean War (1950–1953), not only undeclared but to which the United States was committed solely by virtue of the recommendation of the United Nations Security Council, has been frequently cited as precedent for presidential autonomy on the deployment of troops without congressional authorization. In 1966 the State Department legal adviser cited the Korean War as precedent for the exercise of intrinsic Article II power by the president to send the U.S. military into battle without consulting Congress. President Lyndon B. Johnson affirmed this interpretation of Article II when he claimed that the Gulf of Tonkin Resolution (5 August 1964) was unnecessary and that his orders to bomb North Vietnam and send troops to South Vietnam were based on his authority alone. Finally, President Richard M. Nixon asserted that with respect to the invasion of Cambodia (April 1970), his constitutional role as commander in chief permitted him almost unlimited discretion over the deployment of troops.

From Harry S Truman to Nixon, the effective cooperation that the Constitution demands on the matter of deploying the U.S. military abroad was ignored by a succession of presidents in their noble, if misguided, attempt to contain communism. In order to restore the congressional role, the enactment of the War Powers Resolution over the veto of a politically weakened Nixon was a constitutionally necessary measure to ensure compliance with the doctrine of the separation of powers. The separation of the power to make war, shared and ambiguous as it is, permits flexibility in relations between the president and Congress and thus some shifting of constitutional power. Yet, this system of effective cooperation and flexibility was effectively ignored when Johnson and Nixon deliberated alone in determining whether to invade Cambodia or bomb North Vietnam. Thus the basic requirement of the War Powers Resolution that the president cooperate with Congress is a constitutionally essential constraint that restores the flexibility that the Constitution demands and forecloses the possibility of a president acting unchecked.

—JUSTIN WYATT

Viewpoint:
No. The War Powers Act was a misguided congressional reaction because it improperly limited the power of the presidency in handling foreign affairs.

The constitutional doctrine of the separation of powers extends to the power to make war. While the precise contours of this power have never been conclusively defined, Congress perceived an excess of executive-branch strength with respect to military affairs during the undeclared wars in Korea and Vietnam, and subsequently enacted the War Powers Resolution in 1973. In doing so, Congress believed that it was reasserting its authority, consistent with the doctrine of separation of powers, by attempting to grant itself greater oversight over the wielding of military power by the president. In actuality, the constitutional crisis was nonexistent and the enactment of the War Powers Resolution was merely an overreaction to poor American foreign policy decisions during the Korean War (1950–1953) and Vietnam War (ended 1975).

The unambiguous legislative purpose of the War Powers Resolution was "to insure that the collective judgment of both the Congress and the President will apply to the introduction of the United States Armed Forces into hostilities, or in situations where imminent involvement is clearly indicated by the circumstances, and to the continued use of such forces in hostilities or in such situations." The resolution requires the president, absent a declaration of war, to report to Congress on the status of a deployment of troops into foreign territories within forty-eight hours of such action, and, after sixty days, to terminate the use of the U.S. military if Congress has not specifically authorized the continued presence of American troops. The resolution also requires the president to remove troops from deployment outside the United States if Congress, by a concurrent resolution, directs the executive to do so—in essence, a legislative veto

JAVITS DEFENDS THE WAR POWERS BILL

On 29 March 1972, Senator Jacob K. Javits (R-New York) defended the War Powers Resolution before the Senate. Three lengthy exhibits were later entered into the official record, a portion of which, Exhibit 3, appears below.

The purpose of the war powers bill, as set forth in its statement of "purpose and policy," is to fulfill—not to alter, amend, or adjust—the intent of the framers of the United States Constitution in order to insure that the collective judgment of both the Congress and the President will be brought to bear in decisions involving the introduction of the Armed Forces of the United States in hostilities or in situations where imminent involvements in hostilities is indicated by circumstances. The constitutional basis for this bill is found in Article 1, Section 8, of the Constitution, which enumerates the war powers of Congress, including the power to declare war and to make rules for the Government and regulation of the Armed Forces, and further specifies that Congress shall have the power "to make all laws necessary and proper for carrying into execution" not only its own powers but also "all other powers vested by the Constitution in the Government of the United States, or in any Department or Officer thereof."

The essential purpose of this bill, therefore, is to reconfirm and to define with precision the constitutional authority of Congress to exercise its constitutional war powers with respect to "undeclared" wars and the way in which this authority relates to the constitutional responsibilities of the President as Commander-in-Chief. The bill is in no way intended to encroach upon, alter or detract from the constitutional powers of the President, in his capacity as Commander-in-Chief, to conduct hostilities authorized by Congress, to repel attacks upon the United States or its armed forces, and to rescue endangered American citizens and nationals in foreign countries. . . .

. . . It is legislation essential to our security and well being. It is legislation in the interest of the President as well as of Congress. . . . We live in an age of undeclared war, which has meant Presidential war. Prolonged engagement in undeclared, Presidential war has created a most dangerous imbalance in our Constitutional system of checks and balances. . . . [The bill] is rooted in the words and the spirit of the Constitution. It uses the clauses of Article I, Section 8 to restore the balance which has been upset by the historical disenthronement of that power over war which the framers of the Constitution regarded as the keystone of the whole article of Congressional power—the exclusive authority of Congress to "Declare war"; the power to change the nation from a state of peace to a state of war.

Source: Congressional Record, 93rd Congress, 1st Session, volume 119, part 2 (18 January 1973–30 January 1973), pp. 1402–1403.

A protester preparing to throw a tear gas canister at police during demonstrations in Berkeley, California, against the 1970 invasion of Cambodia

(Stephen Shames—Visions)

over any presidential use of the military. The constitutionality of the legislative veto will not be addressed, but appears dubious in light of its being proscribed by *INS* v. *Chadha* (1983).

In enacting the War Powers Resolution, Congress believed that the modern presidency had usurped too much power with respect to military affairs and regarded this perceived aggrandizement as inconsistent with the constitutional scheme that the founders had devised.

This perception of constitutional imbalance in the power to make war stemmed from confusion in Congress over the notion of smaller-scale presidential wars, which historically were not subject to congressional oversight, and declared wars. Textually, the Founders only conferred upon Congress the power to declare a state of war and did not invest it with much of a supervisory role, if any, with respect to smaller-scale hostilities when the United States was not formally at war. Eugene V. Rostow argued in a *Texas Law Review* (1972) article that the president possessed inherent power to commit troops without first seeking congressional approval and that Congress could prevent any combat that it disapproved of through its power over appropriations

and power to raise armies. Congress has rarely issued formal declarations of war, but the United States has historically engaged in many military conflicts on foreign soil that were not accompanied with these formal declarations. Between 1798 and 1972, the United States participated in 199 undeclared conflicts, while declaring war only five times.

In enacting the War Powers Resolution, Congress failed to consider this history and thereby misinterpreted its power to control all smaller-scale activities, traditionally and constitutionally a presidential prerogative. Despite congressional belief to the contrary, the balance concerning constitutional authority over American military incursions was no different after 1945 than it was before. In the case of the Vietnam War, no constitutional imbalance existed. Despite enacting the War Powers Resolution in order to end this perceived constitutional aggrandizement, Congress displayed consistent support for the war in Vietnam and participated in the decision-making process. In addition, Congress could have denied financing to the war effort, which it chose not to do, thus acquiescing to the war. Moreover, even if the War Powers

Resolution had been enacted prior to hostilities in Indochina, it would not have prevented the war, because Congress authorized the use of military force by ratifying the Southeast Asia Treaty Organization (SEATO) treaty and passing the Gulf of Tonkin Resolution (5 August 1964). In short, the enactment of the Resolution was premised on a poor understanding by Congress of its own role in the Cold War era and of American military and constitutional history.

In reality, Congress was reacting to an American foreign policy in shambles, and not to a perceived constitutional crisis. The lessons of World War II provided the basis for American foreign policy for twenty-five years, but their usefulness had expired in the bipolar world of the Cold War. Specifically, the United States assumed that if it had acted early and decisively against German and Japanese aggression, World War II could have been avoided, and so it sought to apply this rule to containing the communists. The idea that fighting "small" wars to prevent larger ones, however, an idea that had appeared so enticing, lost its attractiveness in the fiascos of Vietnam and Korea. Moreover, the American public did not agree with the foreign policymakers and their support for "small" wars. A change in policy was therefore needed, not the War Powers Resolution.

—STEVE GRAINES

References

Alexander Bickel, "Congress, the President and the Power to Wage War," *Chicago-Kent Law Review,* 48 (Fall–Winter 1971): 131–147;

Stephen Dycus and others, *National Security Law,* 2 volumes (Boston: Little, Brown, 1990, 1997);

Terry Emerson, "War Powers Legislation," *West Virginia Law Review,* 74 (August–November 1971): 53–119;

Alton Frye, *A Responsible Congress: The Politics of National Security* (New York: McGraw-Hill, 1975);

Louis Henkin, *Foreign Affairs and the Constitution* (Mineola, New York: Foundation Press, 1972);

Eugene V. Rostow, "Great Cases Make Bad Law: The War Powers Act," *Texas Law Review,* 50 (May 1972): 833–900;

Abraham D. Sofaer, *War, Foreign Affairs and Constitutional Power,* 2 volumes (Cambridge, Mass.: Ballinger, 1976, 1984);

Cyrus R. Vance, "Striking The Balance: Congress and the President Under The War Powers Resolution," *University of Pennsylvania Law Review,* 133 (December 1984): 79–95.

REFERENCES

1. Memoirs, Biographies, and Evaluations of Major Participants in the Cold War

Acheson, Dean. *Present at the Creation: My Years in the State Department.* New York: Norton, 1969.

Beschloss, Michael R., ed. *Taking Charge: The Johnson White House Tapes, 1963–1964.* New York: Simon & Schuster, 1997.

Brandt, Willy. *My Life in Politics.* London & New York: Hamish Hamilton, 1992.

Brzezinski, Zbigniew K. *Power and Principle: Memoirs of the National Security Adviser, 1977–1981.* New York: Farrar, Straus & Giroux, 1985.

Burns, James MacGregor. *Roosevelt: The Soldier of Freedom.* New York: Harcourt Brace Jovanovich, 1970.

Carter, Jimmy. *Keeping Faith: Memoirs of a President.* New York: Bantam, 1982.

Chambers, Whittaker. *Witness.* New York: Random House, 1952.

Churchill, Winston S. *The Sinews of Peace: Post-war Speeches,* edited by Randolph S. Churchill. London: Cassell, 1948.

Dallek, Robert. *Flawed Giant: Lyndon Johnson and His Times, 1961–1973.* New York: Oxford University Press, 1998.

Dedjer, Vladimir. *Tito Speaks: His Self Portrait and Struggle with Stalin.* London: Weidenfeld & Nicolson, 1953.

Djilas, Milovan. *Conversations with Stalin,* translated by Michael B. Petrovich. New York: Harcourt, Brace & World, 1962.

Djilas. *Tito: The Story from Inside,* translated by Vasilije Kojic and Richard Hayes. New York: Harcourt Brace Jovanovich, 1980.

Draskovich, Slobodan M. *Tito, Moscow's Trojan Horse.* Chicago: Regnery, 1957.

Gorbachev, Mikhail. *Memoirs.* New York: Doubleday, 1996.

Hiss, Alger. *In the Court of Public Opinion.* New York: Knopf, 1957.

Hiss. *Recollections of a Life.* New York: Seaver Books/ Holt, 1988.

Hiss, Tony. *The View From Alger's Window: A Son's Memoir.* New York: Knopf, 1999.

Hoopes, Townsend. *The Devil and John Foster Dulles.* Boston: Little, Brown, 1973.

Khrushchev, Nikita. *Khrushchev Remembers,* translated by Strobe Talbot. New York: Little, Brown, 1970.

Kissinger, Henry. *Diplomacy.* New York: Simon & Schuster, 1994.

Kissinger. *White House Years.* Boston: Little, Brown, 1979.

Kissinger. *Years Of Renewal.* New York: Simon & Schuster, 1999.

Kissinger. *Years Of Upheaval.* Boston: Little, Brown, 1982.

Lacouture, Jean. *Charles de Gaulle,* 3 volumes. Paris: Seuil, 1984–1986.

McCullough, David. *Truman.* New York: Simon & Schuster, 1992.

Nixon, Richard. *RN: The Memoirs of Richard Nixon.* Boston: Grosset & Dunlap, 1978.

Rovere, Richard. *Senator Joe McCarthy.* New York: Harcourt, Brace, 1959.

el-Sadat, Anwar. *In Search of Identity: An Autobiography.* New York: Harper & Row, 1978.

Schlesinger, Arthur M., Jr. *A Thousand Days: John F. Kennedy in the White House.* Boston: Houghton Mifflin, 1965.

Shultz, George P. *Turmoil and Triumph: My Years As Secretary of State.* New York: Scribners, 1993.

Stoessinger, John G. *Henry Kissinger: The Anguish of Power.* New York: Norton, 1976.

Tanenhaus, Sam. *Whittaker Chambers: A Biography.* New York: Random House, 1997.

Thornton, Richard C. *The Carter Years: Toward a New Global Order.* New York: Paragon House, 1991.

Ulam, Adam B. *Stalin: The Man and His Era.* Boston: Beacon, 1989.

Vance, Cyrus. *Hard Choices: Critical Years in America's Foreign Policy.* New York: Simon & Schuster, 1983.

Weinberger, Caspar W. *Fighting for Peace: Seven Critical Years in the Pentagon.* New York: Warner, 1991.

2. Histories of the Cold War

Blacker, Coit D. *Reluctant Warriors: The United States, the Soviet Union, and Arms Control.* New York: Freeman, 1987.

Evangelista, Matthew. *Unarmed Forces: The Transnational Movement to End the Cold War.* Ithaca, N.Y.: Cornell University Press, 1999.

Fukuyama, Francis. *The End of History and the Last Man.* New York: Free Press, 1992.

Furet, François. *The Passing of an Illusion: The Idea of Communism in the Twentieth Century,* translated by Deborah Furet. Chicago: University of Chicago Press, 1999.

Garthoff, Raymond L. *Détente and Confrontation: American-Soviet Relations From Nixon to Reagan.* Washington, D. C.: Brookings Institution, 1985.

Garthoff. *The Great Transition: American-Soviet Relations and the End of the Cold War.* Washington, D.C.: Brookings Institution, 1994.

Hammond, Thomas T., ed. *Witnesses to the Origins of the Cold War.* Seattle: University of Washington Press, 1982.

Huntington, Samuel P. *The Clash of Civilizations and the Remaking of World Order.* New York: Simon & Schuster, 1996.

LaFeber, Walter. *America, Russia, and the Cold War, 1945–1996,* eighth edition. New York: McGraw-Hill, 1997.

Lebow, Richard Ned, and Janice Gross Stein. *We All Lost the Cold War.* Princeton: Princeton University Press, 1994.

McMaster, H. R. *Dereliction of Duty: Lyndon Johnson, Robert McNamara, the Joint Chiefs of Staff, and the Lies That Led to Vietnam.* New York: HarperCollins, 1997.

Menges, Constantine C. *The Twilight Struggle: The Soviet Union v. The United States Today.* Washington, D. C.: AEI Press, 1990.

Nelson, Daniel N., ed. *Communism and the Politics of Inequalities.* Lexington, Mass.: Lexington Books, 1983.

Schlesinger, Arthur M., Jr. *The Imperial Presidency.* Boston: Houghton Mifflin, 1973.

3. The Cold War in Europe

Banac, Ivo. *With Stalin Against Tito: Cominformist Splits in Yugoslav Communism.* Ithaca, N.Y.: Cornell University Press, 1988.

Barnett, Correlli. *The Collapse of British Power.* London: Eyre Methuen, 1972; New York: Morrow, 1972.

Bass, Robert, and Elizabeth Marbury, eds. *The Soviet-Yugoslav Controversy, 1948–58: A Documentary Record.* New York: Prospect Books, 1959.

Black, C. E., and E. C. Helmreich. *Twentieth Century Europe: A History,* fourth edition. New York: Knopf, 1972.

Brown, J. F. *Eastern Europe and Communist Rule.* Durham, N.C.: Duke University Press, 1988.

Brzezinsky, Zbigniew K. *The Soviet Bloc: Unity and Conflict.* Cambridge, Mass.: Harvard University Press, 1960.

Byrnes, Robert Francis, ed. *Yugoslavia.* New York: Praeger, 1957.

Clissold, Stephen. *Yugoslavia and the Soviet Union, 1939–1973: A Documentary Survey.* London & New York: Oxford University Press, 1975.

Cogan, Charles G. *Oldest Allies, Guarded Friends: The United States and France since 1940.* Westport, Conn.: Praeger, 1994.

Costigliola, Frank. *France and the United States: The Cold Alliance since World War II.* New York: Twayne Publishers; Toronto: Maxwell Macmillan Canada; New York: Maxwell Macmillan International, 1992.

Cradock, Percy. *In Pursuit of British Interests: Reflections on Foreign Policy under Margaret Thatcher and John Major.* London: Murray, 1997.

Crampton, R. J. *Eastern Europe in the Twentieth Century.* London & New York: Routledge, 1994.

Dedjer, Vladimir. *The Battle Stalin Lost: Memoirs of Yugoslavia, 1948–1953.* New York: Viking, 1971.

Duroselle, Jean-Baptiste. *France and the United States: From the Beginnings to the Present,* translated by Derek Coltman. Chicago: University of Chicago Press, 1978.

Gardner, Lloyd C. *Sterling-Dollar Diplomacy: Anglo-American Collaboration in the Reconstruction of Multilateral Trade.* Oxford: Clarendon Press, 1956.

Gati, Charles. *The Bloc That Failed: Soviet-East European Relations in Transition.* Bloomington: Indiana University Press, 1990.

Gati. *Hungary and the Soviet Bloc.* Durham, N.C.: Duke University Press, 1986.

Gedmin, Jeffrey. *The Hidden Hand: Gorbachev and the Collapse of East Germany.* Washington, D.C.: American Enterprise Institute Press, 1992.

Gordon, Philip H. *A Certain Idea of France: French Security Policy and the Gaullist Legacy.* Princeton: Princeton University Press, 1993.

Gordon. *France, Germany, and the Western Alliance.* Boulder, Colo.: Westview Press, 1995.

Harrison, Michael M. *The Reluctant Ally: France and Atlantic Security.* Baltimore: Johns Hopkins University Press, 1981.

Heinrich, Hans-Georg. *Hungary: Politics, Economics and Society.* London: Pinter, 1986.

Heuser, Beatrice. *Western "Containment" Policies in the Cold War: The Yugoslav Case, 1948–1953.* London: Routledge, 1988.

Jelavich, Barbara. *History of the Balkans.* Cambridge & New York: Cambridge University Press, 1983.

Jenkins, Peter. *Mrs. Thatcher's Revolution: The Ending of the Socialist Era.* London: Cape, 1987.

Kiernan, V. G. *European Empires From Conquest to Collapse, 1815–1960.* Leicester, U.K.: Leicester University Press, 1982.

Laqueur, Walter. *Europe in Our Time: A History, 1945–1992.* New York: Viking, 1992.

Litván, György, ed. *The Hungarian Revolution of 1956: Reform, Revolt and Repression 1953–1963,* translated by János M. Bak and Lyman H. Legters. New York: Longman, 1996.

Newhouse, John. *De Gaulle and the Anglosaxons.* New York: Viking, 1970.

Rothschild, Joseph. *Return to Diversity: A Political History of East Central Europe Since World War II.* New York: Oxford University Press, 1989.

Rusinow, Dennison, ed. *Yugoslavia: A Fractured Federalism.* Washington, D.C.: Wilson Center Press, 1988.

Shumaker, David H. *Gorbachev and the German Question: Soviet–West German Relations, 1985–1990.* Westport, Conn.: Praeger, 1995.

Simons, Thomas W., Jr. *Eastern Europe In the Postwar World.* New York: St. Martin's Press, 1991.

Sked, Alan, and Chris Cook. *Post-War Britain: A Political History.* Sussex, U.K.: Harvester Press, 1979; New York: Barnes & Noble, 1979.

Snowman, Daniel. *Britain and America: An Interpretation of Their Culture, 1945–1975.* New York: New York University Press, 1977.

Sodaro, Michael J. *Moscow, Germany, and the West: from Khrushchev to Gorbachev.* Ithaca: Cornell University Press, 1990.

The Soviet-Yugoslav Dispute: Text of the Published Correspondence. London & New York: Royal Institute of International Affairs, 1948.

Vucinich, Wayne S., ed. *At the Brink of War and Peace: The Tito-Stalin Split in a Historic Perspective.* New York: Brooklyn College Press, 1982.

Walmsley, Jane. *Brit-think, Ameri-think: A Transatlantic Survival Guide,* with cartoons by Gray Jolliffe. London: Harrap, 1986.

Zalar, Charles. *Yugoslav Communism: A Critical Study.* Prepared for the Subcommittee to Investigate the Administration of the Internal Security Act and other Internal Security Laws of the Committee on the Judiciary, United States Senate, Eighty-Seventh Congress, First Session. Washington, D.C.: U.S. Government Printing Office, 1961.

4. The Cold War in the Middle East, Asia, and Africa

Bauer, P. T. *United States Aid and Indian Economic Development.* Washington, D.C.: American Enterprise Association, 1959.

Blair, Clay. *The Forgotten War: America in Korea, 1950–1953.* New York: Times Books, 1987.

Bradsher, Henry S. *Afghanistan and the Soviet Union.* Durham, N.C.: Duke University Press, 1983.

Breslauer, George W., ed. *Soviet Strategy in the Middle East.* Boston: Unwin Hyman, 1990.

Cain, P. J., and A. G. Hopkins. *British Imperialism: Crisis and Deconstruction, 1914–1990.* London & New York: Longman, 1993.

Chen, Frederick Tse-shyang, ed. *China Policy and National Security.* Dobbs Ferry, N.Y.: Transnational Publishers, 1984.

Collins, Joseph J. *The Soviet Invasion of Afghanistan: A Study in the Use of Force in Soviet Foreign Policy.* Lexington, Mass.: Lexington Books, 1986.

Crocker, Chester A. *High Noon in Southern Africa: Making Peace in a Rough Neighborhood.* New York: Norton, 1992.

Cumings, Bruce. *The Origins of the Korean War,* 2 volumes. Princeton: Princeton University Press, 1981, 1990.

Fairbank, John King. *The Great Chinese Revolution, 1800–1985.* New York: Harper & Row, 1986.

Foot, Rosemary. *The Wrong War: American Policy and the Dimensions of the Korean Conflict, 1950–1953.* Ithaca, N.Y.: Cornell University Press, 1985.

Freedman, Robert O. *Moscow and the Middle East: Soviet Policy Since the Invasion of Afghanistan.* Cambridge & New York: Cambridge University Press, 1991.

Halberstam, David. *The Making of a Quagmire: America and Vietnam During the Kennedy Era,* revised edition, edited by Daniel J. Singal. New York: McGraw-Hill, 1988.

Hammond, Thomas T. *Red Flag Over Afghanistan: The Communist Coup, the Soviet Invasion, and the Consequences.* Boulder, Colo.: Westview Press, 1984.

Jian, Chen. *China's Road to the Korean War: The Making of the Sino-American Confrontation.* New York: Columbia University Press, 1994.

Laïdi, Zaki. *The Superpowers and Africa: The Constraints of a Rivalry, 1960–1990,* translated by Patricia Baudoin. Chicago: University of Chicago Press, 1990.

Legum, Colin, ed. *Crisis and Conflicts in the Middle East: The Changing Strategy: From Iran to Afghanistan.* New York: Holmes & Meier, 1981.

Monks, Altred L. *The Soviet Intervention in Afghanistan.* Washington, D.C.: American Enterprise Institute for Public Policy Research, 1981.

Newman, John M. *JFK and Vietnam: Deception, Intrigue, and the Struggle for Power.* New York: Warner, 1992.

Organski, A. F. K. *The $36 Billion Bargain: Strategy and Politics in U.S. Assistance to Israel.* New York: Columbia University Press, 1990.

The Pentagon Papers: As Published by the New York Times. New York: Quadrangle, 1971.

Quandt, William B. *Decade of Decisions: American Policy Toward the Arab-Israeli Conflict, 1967–1976.* Berkeley: University of California Press, 1977.

Quandt. *Peace Process: American Diplomacy and the Arab-Israeli Conflict Since 1967.* Washington, D.C.: Brookings Institution; Berkeley: University of California Press, 1993.

Rubinstein, Alvin Z. *Red Star on the Nile: The Soviet-Egyptian Influence Relationship Since the June War.* Princeton: Princeton University Press, 1977.

Smolansky, Oles M. *The Soviet Union and the Arab East Under Khrushchev.* Lewisburg, Pa.: Bucknell University Press, 1974.

Stuart, Douglas T., and William T. Tow, eds. *China, the Soviet Union and the West: Strategic and Political Dimensions in the 1980s.* Boulder, Colo.: Westview Press, 1982.

Stueck, William. *The Korean War: An International History.* Princeton: Princeton University Press, 1995.

Thornton, Richard C. *China, a Political History, 1917–1980.* Boulder, Colo.: Westview Press, 1982.

Zhang, Ming. *Major Powers at a Crossroads: Economic Interdependence and an Asia Pacific Security Community.* Boulder, Colo.: Lynne Rienner, 1995.

5. The Cold War in Latin America

Blight, James, and David Welch. *On the Brink: Americans and Soviets Reexamine the Cuban Missile Crisis.* New York: Hill & Wang, 1989.

Brugioni, Dino. *Eyeball to Eyeball: The Inside Story of the Cuban Missile Crisis,* edited by Robert F. McCort. New York: Random House, 1991.

Burns, E. Bradford. *At War in Nicaragua: The Reagan Doctrine and the Politics of Nostalgia.* New York: Harper & Row, 1987.

Carothers, Thomas. *In the Name of Democracy: U.S. Policy Toward Latin America in the Reagan Years.* Berkeley: University of California Press, 1991.

Desch, Michael C. *When the Third World Matters: Latin America and United States Grand Strategy.* Baltimore: Johns Hopkins University Press, 1993.

Fursenko, Aleksandr, and Timothy Naftali. *One Hell of a Gamble: Khrushchev, Castro, and Kennedy, 1958–1964.* New York: Norton, 1997.

Garthoff, Raymond L. *Reflections on the Cuban Missile Crisis.* Washington, D.C.: Brookings Institution, 1989.

Gutman, Roy. *Banana Diplomacy: The Making of American Policy in Nicaragua, 1981–1987.* New York: Simon & Schuster, 1988.

Kagan, Robert. *A Twilight Struggle: American Power and Nicaragua, 1977–1990.* New York: Free Press, 1996.

Kiewe, Amos, and Davis W. Houck. *A Shining City on a Hill: Ronald Reagan's Economic Rhetoric, 1951–1989.* New York: Praeger, 1991.

Kornbluh, Peter, ed. *Nicaragua: The Making of U.S. Policy, 1978–1990.* Alexandria, Va.: Chadwyck-Healey, 1991 [microform].

Kornbluh. *Nicaragua, the Price of Intervention: Reagan's Wars Against the Sandinistas.* Washington, D.C.: Institute for Policy Studies, 1987.

References

REFERENCES

Lake, Anthony. *Somoza Falling*. Boston: Houghton Mifflin, 1989.

Pastor, Robert A. *Condemned to Repetition: The United States and Nicaragua*. Princeton: Princeton University Press, 1987.

Smith, Peter H. *Talons of the Eagle: Dynamics of U.S.-Latin American Relations*. New York: Oxford University Press, 1996.

Walsh, Lawrence E. *Final Report of the Independent Counsel for Iran/Contra Matters*. Washington, D.C.: U.S. Court of Appeals for the District of Columbia Circuit, 1993.

6. The Third World

Bauer, P. T. *Equality, the Third World, and Economic Delusion*. Cambridge, Mass.: Harvard University Press, 1981.

Braillard, Philippe, and Mohammad-Reza Djalili, eds. *Tiers Monde et relations internationales,* translated as *The Third World and International Relations*. London: Pinter, 1986; Boulder, Colo.: Lynne Rienner, 1986.

Hopf, Ted. *Peripheral Visions: Deterrence Theory and American Foreign Policy in the Third World, 1965–1990*. Ann Arbor: University of Michigan Press, 1994.

Korbonski, Andrzej, and Francis Fukuyama, eds. *The Soviet Union and the Third World: The Last Three Decades*. Ithaca, N.Y.: Cornell University Press, 1987.

MacDonald, Douglas J. *Adventures in Chaos: American Intervention for Reform in the Third World*. Cambridge, Mass.: Harvard University Press, 1992.

Matheson, Neil. *The "Rules of the Game" of Superpower Military Intervention in the Third World, 1975–1980*. Washington, D.C.: University Press of America, 1982.

Murthy, P. A. N., and B. K. Shrivastava. *Neutrality and Non-Alignment in the 1990s*. New Delhi: Radiant Publishers, 1991.

Rodman, Peter W. *More Precious Than Peace: The Cold War and the Struggle for the Third World*. New York: Scribners, 1994.

Snow, Donald M. *Distant Thunder: Third World Conflict and the New International Order*. New York: St. Martin's Press, 1993.

Weatherby, Joseph, Jr., and others. *The Other World: Issues and Politics of the Developing World*. New York: Macmillan, 1987.

Wright, Richard. *The Color Curtain: A Report on the Bandung Conference,* foreword by Gunnar Myrdal. Cleveland: World Publishing, 1956.

7. U.S. Foreign and National-Security Policy

Beschloss, Michael R. *The Crisis Years: Kennedy and Khrushchev, 1960–1963*. New York: Edward Burlingame, 1991.

Cohen, Warren I. *The Cambridge History of American Foreign Relations,* volume 4: *America in the Age of Soviet Power, 1945–1991*. Cambridge & New York: Cambridge University Press, 1993.

Craig, Gordon A., and Alexander L. George. *Force and Statecraft: Diplomatic Problems of Our Time*. New York: Oxford University Press, 1983.

Dougherty, James J. *The Politics of Wartime Aid: American Economic Assistance to France and French Northwest Africa, 1940–1946*. Westport, Conn.: Greenwood Press, 1978.

Dycus, Stephen, and others. *National Security Law*. Boston: Little, Brown, 1990, 1997.

Ehrman, John. *The Rise of Neoconservatism: Intellectuals and Foreign Affairs, 1945–1994*. New Haven, Conn.: Yale University Press, 1995.

Ferrell, Robert H. *American Diplomacy: A History*. New York: Norton, 1959.

Frye, Alton. *A Responsible Congress: The Politics of National Security*. New York: McGraw-Hill, 1975.

Gaddis, John Lewis. *Strategies of Containment: A Critical Appraisal of Postwar American National Security Policy*. New York: Columbia University Press, 1972.

Gardner, Lloyd C., Walter F. LaFeber, Thomas J. McCormick. *Creation of the American Empire: U.S. Diplomatic History*. Chicago: Rand McNally, 1973.

Gartoff, Raymond L. *Détente and Confrontation: American-Soviet Relations From Nixon to Reagan*. Washington, D.C.: Brookings Institution, 1985.

Goldstein, Joshua S., and John R. Freeman, *Three-Way Street: Strategic Reciprocity in World Politics*. Chicago: University of Chicago Press, 1990.

Haig, Alexander M., Jr. *Caveat: Realism, Reagan, and Foreign Policy*. New York: Macmillan, 1984.

Henkin, Louis. *Foreign Affairs and the Constitution*. Mineola, New York: Foundation Press, 1972.

Kimball, Warren F. *The Most Unsordid Act: Lend-Lease, 1939–1941*. Baltimore: Johns Hopkins Press, 1969.

Kirkpatrick, Jeane J. *Dictatorships and Double Standards: Rationalism and Reason in Politics*. New York: Simon & Schuster, 1982.

LaFeber, Walter. *The American Age: United States Foreign Policy at Home and Abroad Since 1750*. New York: Norton, 1989.

MacDonald, Douglas J. *Adventures in Chaos: American Intervention for Reform in the Third World*. Cambridge, Mass.: Harvard University Press, 1992.

Nau, Henry R. *The Myth of America's Decline: Leading the World Economy into the 1990s*. New York: Oxford University Press, 1990.

Oye, Kenneth, Robert Lieber, and Donald Rothchild, eds. *Eagle Resurgent?: The Reagan Era in American Foreign Policy*. Boston: Little, Brown, 1987.

Sanders, Jerry W. *Peddlers of Crisis: The Committee on the Present Danger and the Politics of Containment*. Boston: South End Press, 1983.

Schweizer, Peter. *Victory: The Reagan Administration's Secret Strategy That Hastened the Collapse of the Soviet Union*. New York: Atlantic Monthly Press, 1994.

Scott, James M. *Deciding to Intervene: The Reagan Doctrine and American Foreign Policy*. Durham, N.C.: Duke University Press, 1996.

Smith, Tony. *America's Mission: The United States and the Worldwide Struggle for Democracy in the Twentieth Century*. Princeton: Princeton University Press, 1994.

Snyder, Glenn H., and Paul Diesing. *Conflict Among Nations: Bargaining, Decision Making, and System Structure in International Crises*. Princeton: Princeton University Press, 1977.

Sofaer, Abraham D. *War, Foreign Affairs and Constitutional Power,* 2 volumes. Cambridge, Mass.: Ballinger, 1976, 1984.

Tetlock, Philip E., and others, eds. *Behavior, Society, and International Conflict,* volume 3. New York: Oxford University Press, 1993.

Thornton, Richard C. *The Nixon-Kissinger Years: Reshaping American Foreign Policy.* New York: Paragon House, 1989.

Walton, Richard J. *Cold War and Counterrevolution: The Foreign Policy of John F. Kennedy.* New York: Viking, 1972.

Williams, William Appleman. *The Tragedy of American Diplomacy.* Cleveland: World, 1959.

Zakaria, Fareed. *From Wealth to Power: The Unusual Origins of American's World Role.* Princeton: Princeton University Press, 1998.

8. U.S. Domestic Aspects of the Cold War

Anderson, Terry H. *The Movement and the Sixties.* New York: Oxford University Press, 1996.

Anderson. *The Sixties.* New York: Longman, 1999.

Cortright, David. *Peace Works: The Citizen's Role in Ending the Cold War.* Boulder, Colo.: Westview Press, 1993.

DeGroot, Gerard J., ed. *Student Protest: The Sixties and After.* New York: Addison Wesley Longman, 1998.

Fried, Albert, ed. *McCarthyism: The Great American Red Scare: A Documentary History.* New York: Oxford University Press, 1997.

Fried, Richard M. *Nightmare in Red: The McCarthy Era in Perspective.* New York: Oxford University Press, 1990.

Gitlin, Todd. *The Sixties: Years of Hope, Days of Rage.* Toronto & New York: Bantam, 1987.

Graham, Thomas W. "The Politics of Failure: Strategic Nuclear Arms Control, Public Opinion, and Domestic Politics in the United States, 1945–1980." Dissertation. Massachusetts Institute of Technology, 1989.

Kaiser, Charles. *1968 In America: Music, Politics, Chaos, Counterculture, and the Shaping of a Generation.* New York: Weidenfeld & Nicolson, 1988.

Knopf, Jeffrey W. "Domestic Politics, Citizen Activism, and U.S. Nuclear Arms Control Policy." Dissertation. Stanford University, 1991.

Knopf. *Domestic Society and International Cooperation: The Impact of Protest on US Arms Control Policy.* Cambridge & New York: Cambridge University Press, 1998.

Nye, Joseph S., Jr. *Understanding International Conflicts: An Introduction to Theory and History.* New York: HarperCollins, 1993.

Oshinsky, David M. *A Conspiracy So Immense: The World of Joe McCarthy.* New York: Free Press, 1983. London: Macmillan, 1983.

Schrecker, Ellen. *Many Are the Crimes: McCarthyism in America.* New York: Little, Brown, 1998.

Theoharis, Athan G. *Seeds of Repression: Harry S Truman and the Origins of McCarthyism.* Chicago: Quadrangle Books, 1971.

Wittner, Lawrence S. *The Struggle Against the Bomb,* volume 1: *One World or None: A History of the World Nuclear Disarmament Movement Through 1953.* Stanford, Cal.: Stanford University Press, 1993.

Wittner. *The Struggle Against the Bomb,* volume 2: *Resisting the Bomb: A History of the World Nuclear Disarmament Movement, 1954–1970.* Stanford, Cal.: Stanford University Press, 1997.

9. The Soviet Union

Adelman, Jonathan R. *Torrents of Spring: Soviet and Post-Soviet Politics.* New York: McGraw-Hill, 1995.

Bialer, Seweryn. *The Soviet Paradox: External Expansion, Internal Decline.* New York: Knopf, 1986.

Dawisha, Karen. *Soviet Foreign Policy Toward Egypt.* London: Macmillan, 1979; New York: St. Martin's Press, 1979.

Fleron, Frederic J., Jr., and others, eds. *Contemporary Issues in Soviet Foreign Policy: From Brezhnev to Gorbachev.* New York: Aldine de Gruyter, 1991.

Gorbachev, Mikhail. *Perestroika: New Thinking For Our Country and the World.* Cambridge & New York: Harper & Row, 1987.

Hosking, Geoffrey. *The First Socialist Society: A History of the Soviet Union From Within.* Cambridge, Mass.: Harvard University Press, 1990.

Hough, Jerry F. *Democratization and Revolution in the USSR, 1985–1991.* Washington, D.C.: Brookings Institution, 1997.

Lazitch, Branko, and Milorad M. Drachkovitch. *Lenin and the Comintern.* volume 1, Stanford, Cal.: Hoover Institution Press, Stanford University, 1972.

Mastny, Vojtech. *The Cold War and Soviet Insecurity: The Stalin Years.* New York: Oxford University Press, 1996.

Nation, R. Craig. *Black Earth, Red Star: A History of Soviet Security Policy, 1917–1991.* Ithaca, N.Y.: Cornell University Press, 1992.

Porter, Bruce D. *The USSR in Third World Conflicts: Soviet Arms and Diplomacy in Local Wars, 1945–1980.* Cambridge & New York: Cambridge University Press, 1984.

Rubinstein, Alvin Z. *Soviet Foreign Policy Since World War II: Imperial and Global.* Cambridge, Mass.: Winthrop Publishers, 1981.

Terry, Sarah Meiklejohn, ed. *Soviet Policy in Eastern Europe.* New Haven: Yale University Press, 1984.

Ulam, Adam B. *Expansion and Coexistence: Soviet Foreign Policy, 1917–73.* New York: Praeger, 1974.

Zubok, Vladislav, and Constantine Pleshakov. *Inside the Kremlin's Cold War: From Stalin to Khrushchev.* Cambridge, Mass.: Harvard University Press, 1996.

10. Military Aspects of the Cold War

Blainey, Geoffrey. *The Causes of War.* New York: Free Press, 1973.

Doughty, Robert A. *The Evolution of US Army Tactical Doctrine, 1946–76.* Fort Leavenworth, Kans.: Combat Studies Institute, U.S. Army Command and General Staff College, 1979.

DuPuy, R. Ernest, and Trevor N. DuPuy. *The Encyclopedia of Military History: From 3500 B.C. to the Present.* New York: Harper & Row, 1970.

Herbert, Paul H. *Deciding What Has to Be Done: General William E. DePuy and the 1976 Edition of FM 100–5, Operations.* Fort Leavenworth, Kans.: Combat Studies Institute, U.S. Army Command and General Staff College, 1988.

Kennedy, Paul M. *The Rise and Fall of the Great Powers: Economic Change and Military Conflict from 1500 to 2000.* New York: Random House, 1987.

Millett, Allan R., and Peter Maslowski. *For the Common Defense: A Military History of the United States of America.* New York: Free Press, 1984; London: Macmillan, 1984.

Odom, William E. *The Collapse of the Soviet Military.* New Haven, Conn.: Yale University Press, 1998.

Rhodes, Richard. *Dark Sun: The Making of the Hydrogen Bomb.* New York: Simon & Schuster, 1995.

11. Intelligence, Spying, and Covert Action

Andrew, Christopher M. *For the President's Eyes Only: Secret Intelligence and the American Presidency from Washington to Bush.* New York: HarperCollins, 1995.

Andrew, and Oleg Gordievsky. *KGB: The Inside Story of Its Foreign Operations From Lenin to Gorbachev.* New York: HarperCollins, 1990.

Cahn, Anne Hessing. *Killing Détente: The Right Attacks the CIA.* University Park: Pennsylvania State University Press, 1998.

Cook, Fred J. *The Unfinished Story of Alger Hiss.* New York: Morrow, 1958.

Haynes, John Earl, and Harvey Klehr. *Venona: Decoding Soviet Espionage in America.* New Haven, Conn.: Yale University Press, 1999.

Klehr, and Fridrikh Igorevich Firsov. *The Secret World of American Communism.* New Haven, Conn.: Yale University Press, 1995.

Prados, John. *The Soviet Estimate: U.S. Intelligence Analysis and Soviet Strategic Forces.* Princeton: Princeton University Press, 1982.

Sudoplatov, Pavel, and Anatoli Sudoplatov, with Jerrold L. and Leona P. Schecter. *Special Tasks: The Memoirs of an Unwanted Witness, A Soviet Spymaster.* Boston: Little, Brown, 1994.

Weinstein, Allen. *Perjury: The Hiss-Chambers Case.* New York: Knopf, 1978.

Weinstein, and Alexander Vassiliev. *The Haunted Wood: Soviet Espionage in America—The Stalin Era.* New York: Random House, 1999.

Woodward, Bob. *Veil: The Secret Wars of the CIA, 1981–1987.* New York: Simon & Schuster, 1987.

CONTRIBUTOR NOTES

BALL, Simon J.: Senior lecturer in Modern History at the University of Glasgow, Scotland; author of *The Cold War: An International History, 1947–1991* (1998).

BATEMAN, Major Robert L., III: Professor of history at the U.S. Military Academy, West Point; author of more than forty articles on the tactical application of technology in U.S. military history and U.S. civil-military relations; editor of *Digital War: A View from the Front Lines* (1999).

BUDJEVAC, Jelena: Studied history and international affairs in Washington, D.C., and Prague; worked for international humanitarian organizations in both cities; currently a consultant at Ernst and Young.

BUDJEVAC, Julijana: Doctoral fellow in Eastern European history at George Washington University.

CAHN, Anne H.: Scholar-in-residence in national security, intelligence, and arms control at American University; former president and executive director of the Committee for National Security; former special assistant to the deputy assistant secretary of defense and chief of the Social Impact Staff at the U.S. Arms Control and Disarmament Agency; author of *Killing Détente: The Right Attacks the CIA* (1998).

CUMMINS, Emily: M.A. in political science from George Washington University; currently a consultant at Ernst and Young.

FORSTCHEN, William R.: Assistant professor of history at Montreat College; author of *The Last Regiment* series.

FRANKEL, Benjamin: Founder and editor of *Security Studies;* editor of *Roots of Realism* (1998) and *Realism: Restatements and Renewal* (1996); and co-editor of *The Origins of National Interests: Identity and State's Foreign Policies.*

GOLDSTEIN, Lyle J.: Doctoral candidate in political science at Princeton University; author of "The Civil-Military Relations of Aerial Terror Weapons," *Security Studies,* 8 (Autumn 1998) and "General John Shalikashvili and the Civil-Military Relations of Peacekeeping," *Armed Forces and Society,* 26 (Spring 2000).

GRAINES, Steve.

HELM, Lawrence A.: Director of Internet Research and Development, Office of Earth Science, NASA Headquarters; M.A. in Eastern European history at George Washington University.

HIXSON, Walter L.: Professor of history and chair of the Department of History, University of Akron; author of *Parting the Curtain: Propaganda, Culture, and the Cold War* (1996) and *George F. Kennan, Cold War Iconoclast* (1989).

HUTZLEY, Jonathan: George Washington University.

KAUTT, Captain William H.: U.S. Air Force, San Antonio, Texas; former assistant professor of history at U.S. Air Force Academy, Colorado; author of *The Anglo-Irish War, 1916–1921: A People's War* (1999).

KNOPF, Jeffrey W.: Senior research associate at the Center for Nonproliferation Studies, Monterey Institute of International Studies; author of *Domestic Society and International Cooperation: The Impact of Protest on U.S. Arms Control Policy* (1998).

KRAMER, Mark: Director, Harvard Project on Cold War Studies; Senior Associate, Davis Center for Russian Studies, Harvard University; and editor of the *Journal of Cold War Studies.*

LOBELL, Steven E.: Assistant professor of political science at the University of Northern Iowa; author of "Second Image Reversed Politics: Britain's Choice of Freer Trade or Imperial Preferences, 1903–1906, 1917–1923, 1930–1932," *International Studies Quarterly,* 43 (December 1999) and "Britain's Paradox: Cooperation or Punishment Prior to World War I," *Review of International Studies* (forthcoming); co-author, with Arthur A. Stein, of "Geostructuralism and International Politics: The End of the Cold War and the Regionalization of International Security," in *Regional Orders: Building Security in a New World* (1997), edited by David A. Lake and Patrick M. Morgan.

MCJIMSEY, Robert: Professor of history at Colorado College; author of "A Country Divided: English Politics and the Nine Years' War," *Albion,* 23 (Spring 1991) and "Crisis Management: Parliament and Political Stability, 1692–1719," *Albion* (forthcoming).

PERLMUTTER, Amos: Professor of government at American University, Washington, D.C.; his books include *Making the World Safe for Democracy: A Century of Wilsonianism and Its Totalitarian Challengers* (1997); *FDR & Stalin: A Not So Grand Alliance, 1943–1945* (1993); and *Egypt: The Praetorian State* (1974).

QUENOY, Paul du: Doctoral candidate in history at Georgetown University.

ROMMEL-RUIZ, Bryan: Graduate student in political science at Colorado College.

SHOWALTER, Dennis: Professor of history at Colorado College; president of the Society for Military History; visiting professor at the U.S. Military Academy and U.S. Air Force Academy; author and editor of many books; joint editor of *War in History*.

SOARES, John A., Jr.: Doctoral candidate in history at George Washington University.

STEELE, Brent: Graduate student in political science at the University of Northern Iowa.

WELLER, Captain Grant T.: Assistant professor of history at the U.S. Air Force Academy, Colorado.

WHEATLEY, John: Independent scholar, Brooklyn Center, Minnesota.

WYATT, Justin.

ZHANG, Ming: Director of the Asia Research Institute (ARI) in Virginia; author of *Major Powers at a Crossroads* (1995) and *China's Changing Nuclear Posture* (1999); co-author of *A Triad of Another Kind: The United States, China, and Japan* (1999).

INDEX

INDEX

INDEX

INDEX

Indian Reorganization Act (IRA, 1934) III 139–146, 151, 162
Indochina I 44–46, 86, 290; VI 59, 81, 103, 106, 141, 188, 203, 209, 283
Indonesia I 269, 273, 277, 295; II 40, 117; VI 81, 188
  invasion of East Timor VI 270
in loco parentis VI 25
integration II 24, 90, 92, 136, 292
Intercontinental Ballistic Missile (ICBM) I 49, 189, 192, 230; II 118
Intermediate Range Ballistic Missile (IRBM) I 193
Intermediate Range Nuclear Forces (INF) Treaty VI 17–18, 44, 224, 232, 242
  Soviets walk out of VI 44
INS v. Chadha VI 286
Intercontinental Ballistic Missile (ICBM) VI 50, 110, 144, 202, 260
Internal Security Act (1950) I 74–77; II 131
International Bank for Reconstruction and Development (IBRD, or World Bank) VI 78
International Labor Defense (ILD) III 186, 236
International Ladies Garment Workers Union (ILGWU) III 191
International Military Tribunal (IMT) V 221, 224
International Monetary Fund (IMF) I 22; VI 53, 78, 120
International Workers of the World (IWW) III 223
International Working Men's Association (First International, 1864) VI 178
Interstate Commerce Commission (1887) III 10
Interstate Highway Act (1956) II 105–113
interwar naval treaties V 201–209
Iran I 15, 82, 87–89, 110, 113, 141, 145, 263, 294; II 34, 103, 144, 153; VI 21, 54, 113, 131, 162, 165–166, 195, 201, 215–217, 231–232, 266
  arms sales I 51
  CIA involvement I 211
  crucial to U.S. security I 85
  hostage crisis in VI 107, 166, 226, 232, 268
  sale of U.S. missiles to VI 196
  Soviet interests in VI 255
  Soviet occupation of VI 165
  Soviet withdrawal from VI 161
  tensions with Afghanistan I 15
  territorial concessions I 288
  war with Iraq I 54
  Western interest in VI 255
Iran-Contra Affair VI 3, 57–58, 191–196, 231–232
Iran-Iraq War (1980-1988) VI 162, 271
Iraq I 202; II 144, 153; 54, 58, 107, 162–163, 213, 215, 217, 219, 261, 268, 271
  Gulf War I 163; VI 225
  invasion of Kuwait I 289
  Kurds in VI 54, 61, 217
  nuclear reactor at Osiraq VI 106
  overthrow of Faisal II (1958) I 282
  Pan-Arab campaign I 281
  Shiites in VI 61, 217
Iron Curtain VI 49, 118, 173, 206
Iron Curtain speech (1946) VI 250
Isma'il, Hafiz I 309–312
Israel I 56, 162–164, 278, 283, 309, 316–317; VI 43, 83, 164, 172, 188, 200–201, 215, 246, 261, 271
  Arab opposition to VI 160
  attacked by Egypt and Syria VI 163
  founding of IV 160
  invasion of Lebanon I 196
  Iraqi bombing of I 195
  military I 163, 278, 308
  nuclear weapons development I 218, 222
  preemptive strikes against Egypt and Iraq I 239
  Suez Crisis I 192, 277, 280, 289; VI 11, 106, 135, 270
Israeli Air Force (IAF) VI 172
Israeli Defense Forces (IDF) VI 161
Italian Communist Party VI 179, 245

Italy I 293; II 39; VI 178, 246–247, 251, 267, 274
  aftermath of World War II I 173
  antinuclear protest in VI 16
  hindering the Axis effort V 175–182
  postwar influence of Communist parties I 174, 176
  Yalta Agreement (1945) I 301, 306

J

Jackson, Justice Robert H. III 27; V 188, 222–224
Jackson State College VI 23
Jackson-Vanik Amendment I 140, 142
Japan I 30, 85, 88, 259, 285, 288; II 35, 39–40, 264; III 10, 12, 108; VI 53, 113, 147, 149, 151, 204, 217, 254, 266–267
  atomic bombing of I 4, 183, 239, 263; VI 71, 255
  domino theory I 266
  economic problems in VI 219
  Greater East Asia Co-Prosperity Sphere IV 258
  industrialization of IV 254
  interest in Arab oil I 162
  invasion of China IV 254
  Manchurian occupation I 59
  military conduct IV 151–156
  military tradition in VI 27
  mutual defense relationship with United States VI 54
  occupation of Korea VI 146
  postwar recovery of I 263, VI 59
  postwar occupation I 3
  Soviet war against VI 251
  surrender III 11, 15; VI 49
  treatment of prisoners of war IV 152
  wars with Russia I 263
  women in World War II V 305
  WWII peace terms VI 146
Japanese Americans
  internment of III 102–109; V 183–190; VI 57
Japanese death marches
  Bataan (1942) IV 152
  Sandakan (1945) IV 152
Javits, Jacob K. VI 285
JFK (1991) VI 138
Jim Crow II 23–28, 43–45, 90, 140–142, 163
Jodl, Alfred V 3, 22, 127, 224
Johnson, Andrew VI 57
Johnson, Louis A. I 3–8
Johnson, Lyndon B. I 8, 64, 66, 89, 119, 130, 159, 291; II 5–7, 45, 93, 114–115, 141, 161; III 31; VI 23, 28, 66, 86, 95, 138–145, 185, 201, 284
  criticism of Eisenhower administration I 193
  decides not to run for reelection VI 145
  defense spending VI 144
  Great Society I 292; II 162, 175, 181, 270–271, 276
  Gulf of Tonkin incident I 291
  opinion of space program II 247, 260
  opposition to VI 24
  Philadelphia Plan II 182
  Vietnam War I 292, 296; II 4, 266; VI 59
  views on Latin America I 18
  War on Poverty II 166, 270–279
Johnson administration I 68; II 4, 163; VI 26, 28, 59, 103, 138–145, 199, 204
  arms control VI 33
  arms race I 190
  atmospheric-testing bans VI 20
  Central Intelligence Agency I 64
  policies on Latin America I 18, 24
  responsibility for Vietnam War VI 99
  tension with Great Britain VI 10
  Vietnam policy I 41, 293; VI 103, 202
Johnson v. Virginia (1963) II 138
Joint Chiefs of Staff I 201; VI 151
Jordan VI 201
  fundamentalist movements in I 163

INDEX

view of Khrushchev I 294
Mapp v. *Ohio* (1961) II 281, 286
Marbury v. *Madison* (1803) II 286
March on Washington (1941) III 218
March on Washington (1963) I 192
Marshall, George C. I 34, 60, 159, 304; II 36; III 15, 218; IV 65, 176, 213, 221; V 25, 39, 42–43, 46, 51, 126–127, 136, 188, 196, 258, 279, 314; VI 90, 153, 255
    Balkans campaign V 72
    Marshall Plan I 173
    purpose of Marshall Plan I 177
    Soviet participation in Marshall Plan I 176
Marshall, Justice Thurgood II 19–20, 22, 42, 91, 137–138, 141, 289
Marshall Plan I 18, 22, 36, 75, 86, 88, 107–109, 112–113, 151, 173–179, 181–182, 208, 258, 288; II 36, 40, 42, 100, 132, 209, 264; III 53; VI 9, 101, 104, 148, 211, 255, 267
    list of countries recieving monatery aid I 174
    opposition I 80
Marx, Karl I 139, 149; II 56–57, 74; VI 122, 176, 178, 187, 274–275, 281
Marxist Popular Movement for the Liberation of Angola (*Movimento Popular de Libertação de Angola* or MPLA) VI 1, 6, 87, 165
mass media II 121–128, 166
    ability to segment American society II 125
    impact on American society II 122
    and politics II 127
    populist strain, 1990s II 124
    revolution of print culture II 122
    studies of II 124
massive retaliation policy I 115–117; II 30–31, 51, 118
Matsu I 211, 275; II 52
    Chinese attack I 265–270
    Eisenhower administration I 213
McCarran Act (1950) I 77, 79–81
McCarthy, Eugene II 162, 198
McCarthy, Joseph R. I 58, 62, 75, 77–80, 87, 197, 272, 274, 295; II 129–135, 207, 211, 229; V 197; VI 139, 150, 153–159, 178
    anticommunism as ideological war II 131
    anticommunist hysteria I 236
    attacks George C. Marshall II 134
    censure of II 132; VI 153, 156
    death VI 153
    supporters VI 154
    Wheeling speech (1950) VI 153–154
McCarthyism I 75, 304, 306; II 47–48; 129–135, 160
    and the Cold War II 132
    and the New Deal II 132
    beginnings of II 30
    "red baiting" I 75
    Red Scare II 133
McCormack Act (1938) III 11
McGovern, George VI 26, 88
McKinley, William III 241, 272
McMahon Act (1946) VI 10
McNair, Lesley J. IV 246, 248; V 126
McNamara, Robert S. I 41, 166, 294, 296; II 9; VI 59, 75, 95, 103, 144
McPherson, Aimee Semple III 33, 39
McReynolds, Justice James III 25–26, 28
Mein Kampf (1925–1927) IV 111, 123, 137, 186, 227; V 132
Meir, Golda VI 163
Mencken, H. L. III 32, 37, 78, 98, 128, 175
    flu epidemic III 101
Merrill's Marauders V 198
Mexican Revolution III 124–131
Mexico III 124–131
    cientificos (scientific ones) III 125
    criticism of Libertad Act I 98
    Cuban investment I 97
    departure of French army (1867) I 125
    land reform I 21
    mining industry III 125

nationalization of U.S. businesses, 1930s I 130
Middle East I 157–158, 161, 277; VI 53, 79, 90, 135–136, 162, 171, 188, 266, 268, 271
    Arab-Israeli conflict II 145
    infrastructure I 158
    peace process I 289
    relations with United States I 278
    Soviet influence VI 160–167, 261
    Suez Canal Zone II 146
    U.S. interests I 162; VI 61
Mihajlovic, Draza VI 275, 277–278
military gap between U.S. and Soviet Union I 188–194
Military Intelligence Service (MIS) III 14–15
Milliken v. *Bradley* (1974) II 293, 298
Minow, Newton II 121, 23
Miranda, Ernesto II 284
Miranda v. *Arizona* (1966) II 281, 284, 286
missile gap I 182–194; II 260; VI 21, 141
Mitchell, William A. (Billy) IV 2; V 3, 14, 126
Mitterand, François-Maurice VI 102, 104
Mobutu Sese Seko VI 81
Mohammad Reza Pahlavi (shah of Iran) I 11, 141–146; II 97
Molotov, Vyacheslav I 36, 113, 175, 177, 238, 303; II 35; VI 101, 255, 280
    Molotov Plan I 178; II 40
    Soviet nuclear spying I 245
Molotov-Ribbentrop Pact I 110
Moltke, Helmuth von V 43
Monroe Doctrine (1823) I 124–125, 132; II 98, 156, 257; III 45–46, 243, 247; VI 75
    as applied to Cuba VI 71
    Roosevelt Corollary (1904) III 46
Montgomery bus boycott II 22–24, 90, 140
Montgomery, Field Marshal Bernard Law II 50; IV 64, 66, 144, 177–184; V 16, 19–25, 28, 34, 42, 44, 122–125, 129
Morgenthau, Hans J. I 266; II 8
Morgenthau, Henry III 257
    Morgenthau Plan (1944) II 210
Morrill Act (1862) III 2
Mosaddeq, Mohammad I 66, 69, 211; II 146; VI 131
Moscow Conference (1944) V 311
Moscow Olympics (1980) VI 166, 237
    U.S. boycott VI 43
Mountbatten, Lord Louis V 42, 196
Movimiento de Izquierda Revolucionaria (MIR) I 127, 130
Movimiento Nacionalista Revolucionario (MRN) I 125–126
Moynihan, Daniel Patrick II 166, 271, 276
Mozambique VI 1–7, 188, 221, 256, 261
    aid from Soviet Union VI 2
    independence VI 2
Mozambique Liberation Front (*Frente da Libertação de Moçambique* or FRELIMO) VI 2, 6
Mozambique National Resistance Movement (*Resistência Nacional Moçambicana* or RENAMO) VI, 2, 4, 6
Mubarak, Hosni I 163, 317
mujahidin (*mujahideen*) I 10–16; VI 2, 133, 165, 238
    U.S. support VI 229
Mundt, Karl E. I 74, 306; II 131, 211
Mundt-Nixon Bill I 74
Munich Agreement (1938) I 293, 300
Munich Conference (1938) IV 127
Murphy, Charles Francis III 262
Murphy, Justice Frank V 188
music
    "folk revival" II 214
    as political force II 214
music industry
    impact of television II 218
    record companies at Monterey Music Festival II 219
    sheet music production II 217
    technological advances II 216
    youth market II 219

Mussolini, Benito I 134; IV 14, 80; V 36, 108–109,
117, 135, 169, 175–177, 226, 233
 alliance with Hitler V 179
 downfall V 2
 invasion of Ethiopia V 118, 120
 proposal of the Four Power Pact V 120
 removal from power V 178, 179
 support of Franco IV 224, 226
Muste, A. J. II 7; III 184
Mutual Assured Destruction (MAD) I 154, 169–171,
191, 198, 202, 226–227, 230–232, 251–252;
II 67; VI 31, 168, 174
Mutual Defense Assistance Act (1949) I 59
Mutual Security Act I 175
Mutual Security Program (MSP) I 175
MX missile VI 17–18

N

Nagasaki I 30, 230, 239, 242–245, 249, 268; III 12,
15; V 3, 8, 49, 52, 111, 154, 192; VI 31
Nagy, Imre VI 130–131, 134, 270
Namibia VI 1, 6
 withdrawal of South African troops VI 7
Nanking Massacre (1937) V 151
Napoleonic Wars (1803–1815) I 166, 259
narcotics III 133–137
 Boxer Rebellion III 136
 Foster Bill (1910) III 137
 Harrison Act (1914) III 137
 history of legal regulation III 133
 progressive movement III 135
Narodny Kommisariat Vnutrennikh Del (People's
Commissariat for Internal Affairs,
NKVD) IV 50; V 233; VI 275, 278
Nassau Agreement (1962) VI 11, 13
Nasser, Gamal Abdel I 110, 162, 273, 277–278, 283,
314; II 117, 146–147; VI 11, 80–81, 106, 161,
246, 268, 270
 challenges Britain I 280
 pan-Arab campaign I 281
 "positive neutrality" II 148
Nation of Islam II 93–95
National Aeronautics and Space Administration
(NASA) II 246, 258, 260
 creation of II 242
 funding of II 261
National Association for the Advancement of Colored
People (NAACP) II 19–20, 23, 25, 27, 44–
45, 90, 94, 138, 140–141; III 80, 93, 118,
121, 182, 184–186, 217, 270–274
 opposition to Model Cities housing projects II
277
 Scottsboro case III 185
National Association of Black Journalists II 96
National Association of Broadcasters II 123
National Association of Colored Women III 167
National Black Political Convention (1972) II 95, 198
National Committee of Negro Churchmen II 95
National Committee to Re-Open the Rosenberg
Case II 228
National Council of Negro Churchmen (NCNC) II 94
National Defense and Interstate Highway Act (1956) II
107
National Defense Highway Act (1956) II 249
National Education Association II 190, II 191
National Environmental Policy Act (NEPA) II 183
National Farmers Process Tax Recovery Association III
159
National Front for the Liberation of Angola (Frente
Nacional de Libertação de Angola or FNLA)
VI 1, 6, 87, 165
National Industrial Recovery Act (NIRA, 1933) III
27–28, 62, 65, 149,154
 Supreme Court ruling III 25
National Intelligence Estimates (NIEs) VI 256–258,
260

National Labor Relations Act (Wagner Act, 1935) III
149, 193
National Labor Relations Board (NLRB) II 188; III
30, 62, 149, 190–191, 193, 195
National Liberation Front (NLF) I 296; II 119, 263–
264, 266
National liberation movements VI 183–187
National Negro Congress (NNC) III 184
National Organization of Women (NOW) II 78
National Organization for Women v. Joseph Scheidler
(1994) II 223
National Prohibition Act (1919) III 200
National Reclamation Act (1902) III 243
National Recovery Administration (NRA, 1933) III
30, 154
National Security Act (1947) I 5, 7, 64, 69; VI 61
National Security Agency (NSA) I 74; II 230; VI 157
National Security Council (NSC) I 54, 64, 83, 121; VI
41, 90, 96, 196, 231
National Security Council memorandum 68 (NSC-
68) I 83–84, 89, 149, 182, 211, 274
National Security Decision Directives (NSDD) VI 13,
32, 82, 166
National Socialist German Workers' Party (Nazi
Party) I 35; IV 267; VI 49, 176, 254, 274,
277
National Union for the Total Independence of Angola
(União Nacional para a Independência Total de
Angola or UNITA) VI 1–2, 6, 87, 165
National Urban League II 94; III 80, 184
Native Americans
 relationship with U.S. government III 139–146
Naturalization Act (1952) I 74
Naval Disarmament Conference (1921) V 203
Nazi Germany I 108, 135–136, 138, 149, 152, 241,
255, 266, 274, 288, 293, 301
 administrative system IV 96
 Brownshirts (1934) I 134
 concentration camp system III 252
 Final Solution III 256
 ideology IV 86
 influence on German army IV 86
 mass extinction of Jews III 251
 nonaggression pact with Soviet Union I 306
 policy toward Jews III 250–257
 racial ideology IV 124
 support of German population V 210–217
 war aims V 210
Nazi-Soviet Non-Aggression Pact (1939) I 107, 110,
136; IV 57, 125; V 224–227; VI 179, 245
Nehru, Jawaharlal VI 268, 271
Netherlands VI 77, 183, 188, 264
 antinuclear protests VI 16
 Brussels Treaty I 208
 human rights foreign policy II 102
Neto, Antonio Agostinho VI 1, 165, 265
New Alliance Party II 198
New Deal I 241, 301, 306; III 63, 90, 147–155; VI 56,
129, 151, 158
 agricultural policies III 156–163
 Great Depression III 60
 programs III 63
New Delhi Summit (1983) VI 268
New Federalism II 183, 185
New Left I 77; II 159–160, 162, 164; VI 25
New Look I 115, 117, 210–215, 266; VI 133, 141
New Negro movement III 80, 117
New Woman
 birth control III 171
 fashion III 171
 lesbianism III 168
 physical expectations III 170
 Progressive Era (1890–1915) III 165–173
New World Order
 double-standard of II 157
 Persian Gulf crisis II 153
 purpose of II 154

INDEX

X

Y

Z

ISBN 1-55862-412-0

90000